Champions of Charity

Champions of Charity

War and the Rise of the Red Cross

John F. Hutchinson

Westview
PRESS

A Member of the Perseus Books Group

03/09
$45.00
AMZ

Copyright © 1996 by Westview Press, Inc., A Division of HarperCollins Publishers, Inc.

Published in 1996 in the United States of America by Westview Press, Inc., 5500 Central Avenue, Boulder, Colorado 80301-2877, and in the United Kingdom by Westview Press, 12 Hid's Copse Road, Cumnor Hill, Oxford OX2 9JJ

Library of Congress Cataloging-in-Publication Data
Hutchinson, John F.
  Champions of charity : war and the rise of the Red Cross / John F. Hutchinson.
    p. cm.
  Includes bibliographical references and index.
  ISBN 0-8133-2526-9; ISBN 0-8133-3116-1 (if published as a paperback) ISBN 0-8133-3367-9
    1. Red Cross—History.   2. War—Relief of sick and wounded—History.   I. Title.
HV568.H87   1996
361.7'634—dc20   95-26628
                                                                                                  CIP

The paper used in this publication meets the requirements of the American National Standard for Permanence of Paper for Printed Library Materials Z39.48-1984.

10   9   8   7   6   5   4   3   2   1

The desire to consecrate one's self to a sublime mission, the transcendent attraction that a holy cause possesses for noble hearts, and which makes the chords of religious virtue and military valor vibrate in unison to the very depths of the soul, the seductions of danger and warlike enthusiasm, will every day produce champions of charity upon the field of battle.

—C. Frégier, *Le droit du sang, ou de l'organisation d'une Société internationale d'hospitaliers volontaires pour le secours du blessés militaires,* 1864

Contents

Part Three The Pains of Rebirth

Illustrations

Pictorial Essay   following page 276

Preface and Acknowledgments

My interest in the historical role of the Red Cross began a decade ago. How it was sparked is explained in the Introduction; here I will say only that it has never flagged and that I finish this book acutely aware of how much more remains to be said. I will be delighted if this book persuades others to take up a subject that is far richer and more complex than many people would suspect. The history of philanthropy and humanitarianism, indeed of the Red Cross itself, is still in its infancy. I suspect this is because so many philanthropic institutions have conceived of writing their histories as a matter of recording their (often impressive) achievements. An uncritical approach, however, precludes serious analysis: It becomes unnecessary, if not ill-mannered, to question motives or to ask why some causes succeed in attracting support while others do not. To be sure, I am not suggesting that the critical historian of philanthropy must run to the other extreme, mean-spiritedly assuming the worst about the people and institutions involved or cynically dismissing the rhetoric of altruism as mere cant. The plain fact is, however, that all charitable and philanthropic activity takes place in a particular social, political, and cultural context and, like every other aspect of the past, cannot be properly understood outside that context. What is necessary, therefore, is to bring to this subject the same degree of healthy skepticism and curiosity that one finds in other areas of contemporary historical analysis.

Over the years my efforts to place the Red Cross in the context of late-nineteenth- and early-twentieth-century international history have been assisted by numerous individuals and institutions. Pride of place must be given to the Social Sciences and Humanities Research Council of Canada, which over many years provided the financial support necessary to undertake the research on which this book is based. My first blundering efforts drew encouraging responses from two scholars who have done much to increase our understanding of humanitarianism, Geoffrey Best and David P. Forsythe, and from two others who have themselves contributed much to our knowledge of the medical and social aspects of philanthropy, James H. Cassedy and Adele Lindenmeyr. At various stages in the project, I have benefited from the advice, comments, and criticisms of Leo van Bergen, Roger Cooter, Dan Fox, Gordon Martel, Angus McLaren, Allan Mitchell, Ellen More, John Norris, Stuart Robson, and Jim Winter. Bill McAllister willingly shared with me his work on military medicine in Germany, and Dr. Alexander Sudahl kindly took time from his own research on the history of emergency medical services to furnish me with copies of scarce items about the history of the Red Cross in Germany. Obtaining any material at all on the Ottoman Red Crescent

Society proved to be a special challenge; without the help of Inci Bowman at the University of Texas Medical Branch at Galveston and Dr. Nil Sari, head of the Departments of the History of Medicine and Medical Ethics at the University of Istanbul, I would have had an almost fruitless search.

Librarians, archivists, and curators in many different places assisted my research at every turn. I am particularly indebted to the librarians of the ICRC Library in Geneva, Madames Gonset and Meriboute; the latter's unrivaled knowledge of the contents of the *Ancien Fond du CICR* is one of the scholarly wonders of the world. All of the staff in the two Red Cross documentation centers—at the ICRC and at the International Federation of Red Cross and Red Crescent Societies (formerly the League of Red Cross Societies)—were remarkably helpful to an inquisitive outsider. Daphne Ann Reid cheerfully gave me the benefit of her special knowledge of the archives of the League of Red Cross Societies. Margaret Poulter, archivist of the British Red Cross Society, helped to make my visit to Barnett Hill both efficient and profitable. In London, Shirley Taylor of the Wellcome Tropical Institute and Pamela Willis, curator of the museum and library of the Order of St. John of Jerusalem, made it possible for me to consult the papers and letters of Sir Thomas Longmore and Sir John Furley. In Paris, Madame Simone Bellenger and the documentation staff of the French Red Cross not only permitted me to use their library but also brought several uncataloged items and some splendid illustrations to my attention. In Brussels, Luc de Munck, archivist of the Flemish Red Cross, enthusiastically shared with me his unique knowledge of the earliest days of the Red Cross movement. At the National Headquarters of the American Red Cross in Washington, D.C., the once proud Historical Division has long since fallen to the budgetary ax, but both Jackie Berry and Patrick Gilbo did their best to locate materials that a recent reorganization had apparently put out of reach: The Davison Papers, for example, had to be rescued from the attic! At the National Archives and Records Administration, Aloha South led me through the complexities of "RG 200"—the hundreds of boxes that contain the pre-1950 records of the American National Red Cross. In California, Alice Phillips Rose was a helpful guide to the materials on the League of Red Cross Societies held by the Hoover Institution. During these various trips, friends kindly helped with accommodation: Russell Maulitz in Paris, Katherine Archibald in New York City, and Janet and Bob Joy in Washington, D.C.

Several of my colleagues at Simon Fraser University have read and commented on parts of the manuscript or otherwise offered useful advice. These include William Cleveland, Michael Fellman, Don Kirschner, Mary Lynn Stewart, and Andrea Tone. Two graduate students, Sharon Hall and Alexander Freund, contributed much to the project as energetic and industrious research assistants; another, Gul Civelekoglu, translated some Turkish-language material on the Ottoman Red Crescent. Letia Richardson helped me to see Red Cross pictorial art in a broader context. A special word of thanks goes to Fred Kyba of the Instructional Media Center; his talents in the "digital darkroom" are responsible for the quality of many of the illustrations reproduced in the book. The Inter-Library Loan staff were undaunted by my many requests, despite the fact that obtaining five items on microfilm from the National Library of Medicine in Bethesda took nearly three years, surely a record though hardly an enviable one.

I must also thank my editor at Westview Press, Peter Kracht, who from the very first has been an enthusiastic supporter of the project. I am very grateful to the two "anonymous" external readers of the manuscript; their suggestions for improvements and corrections greatly improved the work, as did the careful editing of Jon Howard. All three did their best to save me from myself, but for whatever errors remain, I am of course solely responsible. During the months and years when this book was taking shape, Virginia Hayes and Julia Hutchinson provided support and companionship to a frequently preoccupied, and often itinerant, author.

A preliminary version of Chapter 1 appeared as John F. Hutchinson, "Rethinking the Origins of the Red Cross," in *Bulletin of the History of Medicine* © 1989 Johns Hopkins University Press; it is used here by permission of the editors and of the Johns Hopkins University Press. A segment of Chapter 5 appeared as "The Nagler Case: A Revealing Moment in Red Cross History," in *Canadian Bulletin of Medical History* 9 (1992):177–190. I gratefully acknowledge the editors' permission to draw upon this copyright material. Part of Chapter 6 appeared as "Custodians of the Sacred Fire: The ICRC and the Postwar Reorganisation of the Red Cross," in Paul Wendling (ed.), *International Health Organisations and Movements, 1918–1939,* © 1995 Cambridge University Press; reprinted with the permission of Cambridge University Press. Excerpts from the novels of Evelyn Waugh are reprinted by permission of Peters, Fraser, and Dunlop, Literary Agents, on behalf of the Estate of Evelyn Waugh. Permission was granted by International Creative Management, Inc., to reprint an excerpt from "Beyond the Fringe," © 1963, copyright renewed by Alan Bennett, Peter Cook, Jonathan Miller, and Dudley Moore.

* * *

Finally, I wish to pay tribute to the one person who, since the inception of this project, has always encouraged me, often challenged me, sometimes nagged me, and occasionally infuriated me; moreover, he has filled almost an entire drawer in my filing cabinet with letters, photocopies, and bibliographic references, testimony to his constant—not to say relentless—interest in this book. That person is Bob Joy, who will soon retire as head of the Section of Medical History at the Uniformed Services University of the Health Sciences in Bethesda, Maryland. His unique role as an impresario of scholarship has already been recognized by others, but I still take pleasure in dedicating this book to him as my personal festschrift for his retirement.

John F. Hutchinson

Acronyms

AARC	American Association of the Red Cross
ADF	Association des Dames Françaises
ANRC	American National Red Cross (see note 74 in Chapter 5, explaining the distinction between the ANRC and the ARC)
ARA	American Relief Administration
ARC	American Red Cross
BRCS	British Red Cross Society
CBRCC	Central British Red Cross Committee
ICRC	International Committee of the Red Cross
JRCS	Japanese Red Cross Society
LRCS	League of Red Cross Societies
ORCS	Ottoman Red Crescent Society
POWs	prisoners of war
RAMC	Royal Army Medical Corps
SEC	Supreme Economic Council
SGUP	Geneva Society for Public Utility, the Society
SSBM	Société de Secours aux Blessés Militaires des Armées de Terre et de Mer
UFF	Union des Femmes de France
VADs	voluntary aid detachments

Credits for Illustrations

1.1 Reproduced from *The International Red Cross Committee in Geneva, 1863–1943* (Geneva: ICRC, 1943).

1.2 Reproduced from *The International Red Cross Committee in Geneva, 1863–1943* (Geneva: ICRC, 1943).

1.3 Courtesy of the Bibliothèque Publique et Universitaire, Cabinet des Estampes, Geneva. Photo by François Martin, Geneva.

1.4 Reproduced from *The International Red Cross Committee in Geneva, 1863–1943* (Geneva: ICRC, 1943).

1.5 Reproduced from *The International Red Cross Committee in Geneva, 1863–1943* (Geneva: ICRC, 1943).

1.6 Courtesy of the ICRC Library.

2.1 Reproduced from *The International Red Cross Committee in Geneva, 1863–1943* (Geneva: ICRC, 1943).

2.2 Courtesy of the ICRC Library.

2.3 From *Secours aux blessés* (Geneva: Fick, 1864). Reproduction courtesy of the Museum and Library of the Order of St. John.

2.4 Courtesy of the ICRC Library.

3.1 Courtesy of the French Red Cross.

3.2 Courtesy of the French Red Cross.

3.3 Courtesy of the French Red Cross.

3.4 Reproduced from Ludwig Kimmle, *Das Deutsche Rote Kreuz*, vol. 1 (Berlin: 1910). Courtesy of the National Library of Medicine.

3.5 Reproduced from Ludwig Kimmle, *Das Deutsche Rote Kreuz*, vol. 1 (Berlin: 1910). Courtesy of the National Library of Medicine.

3.6 Reproduced from Ludwig Kimmle, *Das Deutsche Rote Kreuz*, vol. 1 (Berlin: 1910). Courtesy of the National Library of Medicine.

3.7 Reproduced from Ludwig Kimmle, *Das Deutsche Rote Kreuz*, vol. 3 (Berlin: 1910). Courtesy of the National Library of Medicine.

3.8 Courtesy of the National Library of Medicine.

3.9 Reproduced from *Questions Philanthropiques de la Comte de Beaufort* (Paris: Imprimerie Nationale, 1875). Courtesy of the Museum and Library of the Order of St. John.

3.10 Courtesy of the ICRC Library.

3.11 Courtesy of the ICRC Library.

3.12 Courtesy of the National Library of Medicine.

3.13 Courtesy of the National Library of Medicine.

4.1 Reproduced from Clara Barton, *The Red Cross in Peace and War* (Washington, D.C.: American Historical Press, 1899). Courtesy of the Library of the Uniformed Services, University of the Health Sciences.

4.2   Courtesy of the ICRC Library.

4.3   Courtesy of the ICRC Library.

4.4   Courtesy of the ICRC Library.

4.5   Reproduced from *The Book of the Red Cross*, a commemorative album compiled by the central committee of the Spanish Red Cross. Courtesy of the Museum and Library of the Order of St. John.

4.6   Reproduced from *The Book of the Red Cross*, a commemorative album compiled by the central committee of the Spanish Red Cross. Courtesy of the Museum and Library of the Order of St. John.

4.7   Reproduced from *The Book of the Red Cross*, a commemorative album compiled by the central committee of the Spanish Red Cross, courtesy of the Museum and Library of the Order of St. John.

4.8   Reproduced from *The Book of the Red Cross*, a commemorative album compiled by the central committee of the Spanish Red Cross, courtesy of the Museum and Library of the Order of St. John.

4.9   Reproduced from Bodo von dem Knesebeck, ed., *Das Deutsche Rote Kreuz und die Tuberkulose-bekämpfung* (Berlin-Charlottenburg: 1912). Courtesy of the National Library of Medicine.

4.10   Reproduced from Bodo von dem Knesebeck, ed., *Das Deutsche Rote Kreuz und die Tuberkulose-bekämpfung* (Berlin-Charlottenburg: 1912). Courtesy of the National Library of Medicine.

4.11   Courtesy of the British Red Cross Library and Archives.

4.12   Courtesy of the British Red Cross Library and Archives.

4.13   Courtesy of the British Red Cross Library and Archives.

4.14   Courtesy of the British Red Cross Library and Archives.

4.15   Reproduced from Clara Barton, *A Story of the Red Cross: Glimpses of Field Work* (New York: D. Appleton, 1913). Courtesy of the Library of the Uniformed Services, University of the Health Sciences.

4.16   Courtesy of the ICRC Library.

5.1   Courtesy of the ICRC Library.

5.2   Reproduced from James H. Hare, ed., *A Photographic Record of the Russo-Japanese War* (New York: P. F. Collier and Son, 1905).

5.3   Courtesy of the ICRC Library.

5.4   Courtesy of the ICRC Library.

5.5   Reproduced from James H. Hare, ed., *A Photographic Record of the Russo-Japanese War* (New York: P. F. Collier and Son, 1905).

5.6 Reproduced from James H. Hare, ed., *A Photographic Record of the Russo-Japanese War* (New York: P. F. Collier and Son, 1905).

5.7 Reproduced from James H. Hare, ed., *A Photographic Record of the Russo-Japanese War* (New York: P. F. Collier and Son, 1905).

5.8 Reproduced from James H. Hare, ed., *A Photographic Record of the Russo-Japanese War* (New York: P. F. Collier and Son, 1905).

5.9 Collection of the author.

5.10 Courtesy of the National Library of Medicine.

5.11 Courtesy of the National Library of Medicine.

5.12 Courtesy of the National Archives and Records Administration.

5.13 Collection of the author.

5.14 Reproduced from *Proceedings of the Eighth International Red Cross Conference, Held in London, June 10th to 15th, 1907* (London: 1908). Courtesy of the Museum and Library of the Order of St. John.

5.15 Reproduced from John Furley, *In Peace and War: Autobiographical Sketches* (London: Smith, Elder, 1905). Courtesy of the British Red Cross Library and Archives.

5.16–5.21 Reproduced from L. Arnaud and P. Bonnette, *La Femme sur le champs de bataille* (Paris: Charles-Lavauzelle, n.d.[1912]). Courtesy of the French Red Cross.

5.22 Courtesy of the Library of Congress.

5.23 Courtesy of the Library of Congress.

5.24 Courtesy of the Library of Congress.

5.25 Courtesy of the Library of Congress.

6.1 Reproduced from *The International Red Cross Committee in Geneva, 1863–1943* (Geneva: ICRC, 1943).

6.2 Courtesy of the American Red Cross.

6.3 Reproduced from *Proceedings of the Medical Conference Held at the Invitation of the Committee of Red Cross Societies, April 1 to 11, 1919, Cannes, France* (Geneva: LRCS, 1919). Courtesy of the National Library of Medicine.

7.1 Charles-Edward Amory Winslow Papers, Manuscripts and Archives, Yale University.

7.2 Reproduced from *The League of Red Cross Societies, 1919–1929* (Paris: LRCS, 1929). Collection of the author.

Pictorial Essay

1 Courtesy of the French Red Cross.

2 Courtesy of the French Red Cross.

3 Courtesy of the French Red Cross.

4 Collection of the author.

✚ Introduction: The Sacred Cow & the Skeptical Historian

THANKS TO THE PUBLIC QUESTIONING of the role of the Red Cross in the "tainted blood" scandals in France and Canada, the AIDS-conscious generation now coming of age will never be likely to regard the Red Cross as a sacred cow. Half a century ago, however, the climate of opinion was entirely different. As World War II came to an end, the Red Cross was expected to play a beneficent role in the peacetime world by caring for veterans, teaching children about hygiene and international friendship, and providing useful community services such as first aid training and swimming lessons. As a boy in Toronto in the late 1940s, I can remember our school choir singing at the dedication of a Red Cross Lodge at Sunnybrook Hospital for veterans; the distinctive red and white flag was as familiar to us as any national flag and almost as frequently seen. In 1952, the International Red Cross held a conference in Toronto, and we schoolchildren were told what an important event this was; we may even have been told something about the Geneva Convention, but if so, we quickly forgot. I clearly remember "Junior Red Cross time" in the classroom, when the teacher distributed little cards surmounted by a Red Cross, containing the ten rules of good hygiene that we were expected to observe. At summer camp, the standards for swimming tests were set by the Red Cross, and the badges on our bathing suits bore its familiar symbol. However, like most of my generation, once I grew up I had little more contact with the organization, apart from occasional visits to blood donor clinics. One knew that the Red Cross existed and that its existence was a good thing, but one took it and its goodness entirely for granted.

The enduring legacy of this childhood experience, I discovered years later, was an implicit belief that the Red Cross was beyond criticism. It was as unthinkable to make negative comments about the Red Cross as it was to desecrate the graves of fallen soldiers. I was thus amazed and wholly unprepared when, many years later while doing research for a book on health reform in revolutionary Russia, I discovered a group of people who had little good to say for their country's Red Cross society. These were the public physicians of tsarist Russia, most of whom were employed by county councils

1

and municipalities; they were well educated and obviously knowledgeable about matters of health. Despite the fact that they were all advocates of preventive medicine, popular enlightenment, and health reform, they clearly did not regard the Russian Red Cross as their ally.[1] Indeed, there were times when they treated it almost as an enemy. For example, during the cholera epidemic in South Russia in 1910, the Red Cross was sent in by the government to make up for inadequacies that had produced the epidemic in the first place and then went quietly away without pointing a finger at those whom contemporary epidemiological knowledge might have held to be negligent: the local mine-owners and the health bureaucracy of the tsarist regime. These criticisms stuck in my mind, leading me to wonder whether the Russian Red Cross—tsarist or Bolshevik, for that matter—was atypical in being tied so closely to the interests of the regime of the day.

I could have answered my question about the Red Cross and its relations with governments elsewhere if I could have found a historical evaluation of what might be called the political economy of the Red Cross, but I soon discovered that no such book existed. Professional historians of medicine, war, and philanthropy seem to have ignored the Red Cross; one suspects that like their fellow citizens they have largely taken it for granted.[2] Consequently, the vast majority of the hundreds of books about it fall into two categories: laudatory and didactic biographies of Henry Dunant, and self-serving institutional histories written to describe and record the charitable work of the Red Cross in this or that war or disaster. The sort of book that I sought, however, was not one that asked *what the Red Cross did* but rather *what the Red Cross was*: what explained its emergence and remarkable growth in the period between the 1860s and World War I? How and why did it survive "the war to end all wars"? What light does its history shed on relations between states, philanthropy, war, and medicine? Eventually my frustration with the available literature led me to try to answer these questions myself.

As this project began to take shape, my previous training in Russian history stood me in unexpectedly good stead. It had never occurred to me that the archives of a benevolent international organization would not be open to scholars, but I soon learned otherwise when I requested access to the archives of the International Committee of the Red Cross (ICRC) in Geneva. The first ominous sign was that archival inquiries were dealt with by the ICRC's Department of Principles, Law, and Relations with the Movement—rather like the old Soviet archival administration, which was administered under the supervision of the politburo. It was explained to me that unrestricted access to the archives was out of the question but that some limited access might be possible if I was prepared to sign a document pledging to submit my manuscript to be vetted by the ICRC and promising to remove any passage that it considered not to be in the best interests of the movement. This was not an option that I chose to pursue. Failing this, a kind of indirect access was possible: If I would submit detailed questions, a research officer would endeavor to supply the answers. This route was scarcely promising because no inventories or finding aids were available and because I was told that the minutes (*procès-verbaux*) of ICRC meetings were off limits no matter how early the meeting date. (National archives usually observe thirty-year and fifty-year rules of confidentiality, so the ICRC has probably set a record here.) Most of my attempts to gain information by this route were met with what can only be described as courteous stonewalling. Although the ICRC is today a part of the International Red Cross, it is also an autonomous, self-perpetuating private organization that has the right to make its own rules, as it has done since its foundation. Courteous stonewalling, I soon discovered, has been one of its favorite tactics.

How could a history of the first half-century of the Red Cross be written without free access to the ICRC archives? If I had not been trained in Russian history—and therefore accustomed to closed archives, lack of finding aids, uncooperative officials, and the like—I might well have given up at this stage. Instead, the closed door became a challenge, one that has meant pursuing the inquiry by circuitous rather than direct routes. To be sure, the ICRC Library and its staff were both cooperative and helpful, unlike the custodians of the ICRC archives. This book literally could not have been written without access to the contents of the *Ancien Fond du CICR*, the huge collection of books, pamphlets, and press clippings initially assembled by Gustave Moynier (president of the ICRC from 1864 until his death in 1910), maintained intact after his death, and now housed in the library of the ICRC. Its riches will be apparent in almost every chapter that follows. Most of the pre-1939 archives of the League (now Federation) of Red Cross and Red Crescent Societies were lost or destroyed during World War II, but what survives is a useful supplement to materials available in other repositories. (It is a curiosity of Red Cross history that the origins of the League can now be better studied at the National Archives in Washington and at the Hoover Institution in Palo Alto than in Geneva.) The ICRC has always been in communication with the national Red Cross societies, and the latter either maintain their own archives or, in the case of the United States, have given their early records to the public archives; the interested researcher can thus observe, albeit at a distance, the priorities and concerns of the ICRC. Outside Geneva there are manuscript collections such as those of Lord Wantage and Sir John Furley in England, and of Clara Barton, Mabel Boardman, and Henry P. Davison in Washington, that have been of considerable use. An unexpected treasure-house for the student of this aspect of the history of philanthropy is the library of the Order of St. John of Jerusalem in London. Nevertheless, at certain moments I have felt keenly the lack of access to the ICRC minutes and to the papers of Gustave Moynier and Louis Appia. Where necessary, I have tried to explain ICRC behavior by using other sources, in some cases documents that I have not myself seen.[3] In a very few instances, I have been forced into speculation about motives and actions; if I have erred, I hope that the ICRC will be encouraged to review its position on archival access so that other scholars will be able to set the record straight.

It need hardly be said that because this is an unauthorized history it differs in purpose, tone, and content from the official and popular histories published by the Red Cross itself. I have, for example, found it neither helpful nor appropriate to canonize Henry Dunant; and I have treated Gustave Moynier, his successor Gustave Ador, and their ICRC colleagues as active participants in their own history, as intelligent people who pursued goals that may have shifted in response to events and who shrewdly adopted strategies and tactics that would enable them to disarm critics, outwit opponents, and generally further their aspirations. This approach will, I fear, hardly commend itself to the Red Cross, which regards itself as much more than an international charity or welfare society: It is a *movement* that has aspirations for the future of humanity. Therefore it promotes particular ideas about voluntary service, neutrality, the prevention of war, and the law of nations.[4] Like a religion, the Red Cross movement has its doctrines and dogmas, and their guardian is the ICRC's Department of Principles, Law, and Relations with the Movement. It therefore makes sense that this department also controls the archives because many of the elements of this doctrine are based upon versions of its past that might be open to interpretation and debate among historians. I am well aware that some of the arguments and conclusions advanced in this book will be seen to conflict with current Red Cross doctrine and dogma. It has never been my intention deliberately to cast doubt on what are unquestionably deeply held beliefs; it is, however, no more than realistic to expect that an outsider will ask different questions from someone who is initiated into the movement and who therefore feels compelled to put its interests first.

Historical understanding of the Red Cross has not benefited from the fact that its past has been explored either too cautiously by members of its inner circle or too enthusiastically by well-meaning but naive admirers of Henry Dunant and of the institution they conceive to be his creation. "Great Man" biographies and simplistic whig epics abound;[5] they are at best superficial, at worst full of sentimentality and legend. Many of the histories produced by the various national societies replicate these shortcomings, adding for good measure a strong dose of patriotism. Yet in a sense it is pointless to judge these books as one would judge the works of academic historians: For its own purposes, the Red Cross may have, and indeed will have, whatever history it chooses. Those involved in its day-to-day work would probably argue that an inspiring legend or two is a good thing for an organization that has so many tasks more urgent than promoting research into its history. Be that as it may, I am convinced that if one puts the legends, doctrines, and dogmas aside, the history of the Red Cross can help us to a clearer understanding of the relationship between organized charity, war, and the state. This understanding will help to provide the historical context that is usually missing in the many books that have faithfully recorded countless individual acts of charity performed by Red Cross volunteers who have assisted—often in the most difficult circumstances—sick and wounded soldiers, prisoners of war, refugees, and needy children.

It is important to establish here that this book is not a history of the Geneva Convention. From the outset, Gustave Moynier had to contend with the fact that people confounded the Red Cross societies with the Geneva Convention. As he wrote in 1883, "There is a vague notion that because they had the same origin, that they cooperate for the same object, and that they have the same flag, people are willingly led to imagine that they are one and the same thing."[6] Of course they are not, and never have been; the negotiation and revision of the Geneva Convention are part, but only part, of the story told here. There is still a need for a critical history of the Convention that would pick up where earlier authors such as C. Lueder and Louis Gillot left off.[7] If some readers are saddened by this disclaimer, I can only plead that I have no expertise in international law and so have chosen to concentrate on assistance to the sick and wounded rather than on the protection of prisoners of war. Here again, there is a substantial topic awaiting its historian. Finally, it need hardly be said that this is not a comprehensive examination of the first six decades of Red Cross history; such an enterprise would involve incorporating the history of some four dozen national societies that were in existence by 1914 and of the many more that were founded in the 1920s.

The subject matter of this book is the international Red Cross movement from the first Geneva conference in 1863 until the Tenth Conference in 1921. The 1863 conference began to organize charity in wartime; in the wake of the Great War, the 1921 conference tried to reorganize the Red Cross as a force for peace. This book is not intended as a history of the ICRC: To do full justice to the subject of war, charity, and the state, the net must be cast rather more widely. Nevertheless, my starting point was determined by the fact that the Genevan "committee of five"—the ancestor of the ICRC—and the first central committees—the ancestors of the national societies—all date from 1863–1864. The creation of the League of Red Cross Societies (LRCS, see Chapters 6 and 7) in 1919 was largely an American effort to reshape Red Cross priorities; its brief and limited success necessitated some lengthy and complex maneuvering to make room for a new arrival that was not entirely welcome, indeed not fully legitimized until 1928. In that year, and for the first time, a legal entity called the International Red Cross came into existence, composed of the national societies, the League, and the ICRC, each element of which was deemed to have its own peculiar sphere of action; since then, all three elements have continued to meet at international Red Cross conferences. However, international conferences had begun long before then, and the idea of an international Red Cross has had a much longer history than many people realize.

It may be helpful to include here a word about Red Cross terminology, in particular the many references to the *International Commitee*. From October,

1863, until the early 1880s, the group of Genevan citizens who spearheaded the entire enterprise was known as the *International Committee for the Assistance to Sick and Wounded Soldiers* (shortened titles included the Comité International, the International Committee, the Geneva committee, or simply the Genevans). The word *international* was intended to refer not to the composition of the committee itself but rather to the scope of its activities. The several *central committees* formed in various states during these years usually, but not always, adopted some variation of the name *Society for Assistance to Sick and Wounded Soldiers*. The Dutch society was the first to become known popularly by its nickname, the *Red Cross* society. In a conscious effort to give the movement greater coherence and visibility, the Geneva committee decided, at the end of the 1870s, to encourage all of the national central committees to adopt the term *Red Cross society* as part of their name; most of them soon complied. By 1884, the Geneva committee had itself become the *International Committee of the Red Cross*, and meetings of delegates from all the national societies had become known as *international Red Cross conferences*. In this work, the Geneva committee will be referred to as the Comité International prior to 1880 and as the ICRC after that date. Despite sporadic efforts to change the ICRC into an agency that is international in composition as well as mission, the ICRC remained, and remains, a body made up exclusively of Swiss citizens. Why that is so forms part of the story that is told here.

Part 1 of this book introduces the first champions of the cause of charity toward the sick and wounded: the Genevan philanthropists and physicians who banded together to capitalize on the wave of sentimentalism that swept Europe after the publication of Dunant's *Un Souvenir de Solférino*. Motivated by religious conviction joined with enlightened humanitarianism, they promoted a civilizing mission for the Red Cross, the full implications of which were elaborated in the writings of Gustave Moynier and Louis Appia. Their plans could go nowhere, however, without acceptance by governments and armies, a fact they recognized from the beginning by associating with their enterprise the Swiss war hero General Dufour. Yet their very success in 1864 created the basis not for failure but rather for a selective and distorted realization of their ideas by the national governments of the day. Hence Part 2 examines the process by which organized charity, instead of making war more civilized, became militarized and adapted to the needs of belligerent nations, who soon became champions of this different conception of wartime charity. In these chapters I have employed the definition of militarism offered by political sociologist Michael Mann: "an attitude and a set of institutions which regard war and the preparation for war as a normal and desirable social activity."[8] A bizarre consequence of this development was the flowering during the Great War of the notion of "Red Cross patriotism"; in the 1860s, the true test of philanthropy had been assisting wounded enemy soldiers, but now it had become helping your own soldiers and those of your allies. In 1919, there were fresh efforts to rekindle a conception of fraternity that had been nearly extinguished during the war, but it proved not as easy as some enthusiasts had supposed to fashion a new peacetime Red Cross with substantially different priorities. Neither the ICRC nor the national societies were unanimous in welcoming these new champions of a broader conception of charity toward civilians, and Part 3 examines the labor pains associated with this rebirth, some of which continued to be felt throughout the 1920s. I hope to treat in a future study the efforts of both the ICRC and the LRCS to promote internationalism in the fields of health and welfare during the 1920s.

Part One

The Civilizing Mission

There's nothing wrong with war except the fighting.

—Evelyn Waugh, *Unconditional Surrender* (1961)

✚ 1
A Happy Coincidence

ONE DAY IN 1862, Genevan philanthropist Gustave Moynier received in the mail a small book entitled *A Memory of Solferino*. Moynier knew nothing of its author, a young businessman named Henry Dunant, but as president of the Geneva Society for Public Utility (SGUP) he was used to being approached with requests to support various good causes. On reading this book, he discovered that Dunant's cause was that of caring for wounded soldiers. The author, it seemed, had been an involuntary witness to the human carnage caused by the battle of Solferino in 1859, when French and Sardinian armies fighting to liberate Lombardy from Austrian rule had clashed with the armies of Emperor Francis Joseph. Moynier read with growing interest and concern Dunant's harrowing descriptions of soldiers grievously wounded and then seemingly abandoned to a gruesome fate by armies that lacked sufficient doctors, nurses, dressings, and field hospitals to care for them properly. In a few paragraphs at the end of the book, Dunant appealed to his readers to take up the cause of the war wounded by promoting the formation of voluntary aid societies that could furnish supplies and trained nurses to remedy the deficiencies of the official army medical services.

Thinking this a cause worthy of support, Moynier asked Dunant to call on him to discuss what plans the young author had made to bring the proposed aid societies into being. Apart from having his book printed at his own expense and having sent it around Europe to influential persons such as Moynier himself, Dunant had done nothing; as he had written in *A Memory of Solferino*, he hoped that his book would "attract the attention of the humane and philanthropically inclined."[1] Moynier, quickly sizing up Dunant as an idealist rather than an organizer, offered to help; he would be happy, he said, to raise the subject of voluntary aid societies at the next meeting of the SGUP, in order to gauge by the reaction of its members—all of them men of affairs—whether such a proposal was feasible and worth pursuing further. Delighted by this promise of support Dunant took his leave, convinced that his cause would find immediate and unwavering sympathy among everyone

11

who heard about it. The more practical Moynier, meanwhile, began to wonder whether men who knew more about armies and medicine than himself or Dunant would be receptive to the idea.

Two more unlikely collaborators than Dunant and Moynier could scarcely have been imagined. On the face of it, they shared a good deal: Genevan upbringing, respectable bourgeois backgrounds, the Protestant religion, and a desire to improve the lot of suffering humanity. Yet they were as different in their temperaments as they were in their ideas of how to achieve this goal. The impulsive Dunant was a fervent evangelical Christian who, like an Old Testament prophet, sought to bring himself and others closer to God through acts of repentance and contrition; Moynier, on the other hand, was an austere and high-minded Calvinist who had found in utilitarian philanthropy the path to a new moral world of rationality, sobriety, and self-discipline. Their collaboration would be brief, awkward, even strained; for each soon found the other extremely difficult to work with.

However, their first meeting was one from which, "by a happy coincidence," as Moynier later put it, momentous consequences were to flow.[2] The coincidence lay in the fact that the 1860s happened to be a decade when the European powers—for their own good reasons—were prepared to give some attention, in a concerted way, to the care of wounded soldiers. In these peculiarly favorable circumstances, Moynier and Dunant were able to influence, in their very different ways, both the birth of the Red Cross and the signing of the Geneva Convention. Because of this happy coincidence—and only because of it—Moynier's interview with Dunant became a memorable event in the history of both war and charity.

Dunant and Solferino

Henry Dunant was a devotee of Christian pietist philanthropy. He was raised in a family that had been heavily involved in the religious revival that swept Geneva after the turmoil of the Revolutionary and Napoleonic Wars. An enthusiastic volunteer even as a youth, Dunant had joined a charitable society whose members visited and gave small allowances to the city's poor and sick and distributed moral tracts to prisoners.[3] He was also a promoter of the "Christian Unions" that appeared in France in the 1850s, organizations that have been regarded as the forerunners of the Young Men's Christian Association. Dunant took his religion very seriously and very personally. When he sat down to write about what had happened at Solferino, he later confessed, he believed himself to be an instrument of God: "I was as it were, lifted out of myself, compelled by some higher power and inspired by the breath of God. . . . In this state of pent-up emotion which filled my heart, I was aware of an intuition, vague and yet profound, that my work was an instrument of His Will; it seemed to me that I had to accomplish it as a sacred duty and that it

1.1   Henry Dunant, author of *A Memory of Solferino.*

1.2   Genevan philanthropist Gustave Moynier was the real architect of the Red Cross, although in the twentieth century members of the movement have, for their own reasons, preferred to accord this role to Henry Dunant.

was destined to have fruits of infinite consequence for mankind. This conviction drove me on."[4]

Dunant's notion that he had been chosen to accomplish a divine mission attracted to his cause those who wanted to believe in him; for more practical souls such as Moynier, this belief in divine inspiration was one of the things that made Dunant a difficult collaborator.

It was, however, not evangelical religion but business that had taken Dunant to Lombardy in the summer of 1859. He was, in fact, searching for Napoleon III, in the hope that an appeal to the sovereign himself could cut through the red tape that threatened to block a business deal in which Dunant was involved in French Algeria. The details of the enterprise may be passed over; what matters is that Dunant, anxious to overcome these bureaucratic obstacles, had gone to Paris to find the emperor but had been told that Napoleon III was already on his way to Piedmont.[5] Dunant was disappointed, not least because he had hoped to present the emperor with two of his writings, one a memorandum concerning his Algerian company (the Société anonyme des Moulins de Mons-Djémila) and the other a tract on the reestablishment of Charlemagne's empire by Napoleon III—an extraordinary piece of pseudoreligious nonsense in which Dunant claimed that the restoration of the Holy Roman Empire had been foretold in the Book of Daniel.[6] Swallowing his disappointment, Dunant set out for Italy in the hope of tracking down the emperor. Thus it was that he happened upon the scene of the battle of Solferino on 24 June to find the many wounded from both armies who had been brought to an improvised field hospital in the church building and churchyard of nearby Castiglione.

Appalled by the plight of so many untended wounded soldiers, Dunant forgot the purpose of his trip and spent several days doing what he could to relieve their misery. In the absence of adequate supplies, this often meant simply comforting them or saying a prayer because there was little water available to clean a wound or relieve parched lips. Only after he had done everything he could for the wounded did he proceed to the encampment of the French army to resume his search for the emperor. There were others in Castiglione as well—many local women, an Italian priest, a journalist from Paris, a couple of English tourists—but it is Dunant's perception of these terrible days that has survived in *A Memory of Solferino*. He was far too busy on the days in question to keep a diary, so the book was composed from memory two or three years after the event. Despite this, it is as vivid and immediate as if it had been written at the time; reading it, one can easily believe that Dunant was driven to write it by the nightmare visions that must have stayed with him after such an experience.

So much hagiography has been written about this man and his book that both have been seriously distorted. The reality is that Dunant was as impressed by the sight of armies in conflict as he was appalled by the human carnage that resulted. His account of the battle itself is full of examples of courageous officers who led charges, rallied their men, and inspired others to emulate their bravery. One such incident concerned Lieutenant de Guiseul, who

> carrying his regimental flag, was surrounded with his battalion by a force ten times the size of his own. He was shot down, and as he rolled on the ground he clutched his precious charge to his heart. A sergeant who seized the flag to save it from the enemy had his head blown off by a cannon-ball; a captain who next grabbed the flag-staff was wounded too, and his blood stained the torn and broken banner. Each man who held it was wounded, one after another, officers and soldiers alike, but it was guarded to the last with a wall of dead and living bodies. In the end, the glorious, tattered flag remained in the hands of a Sergeant-Major of Colonel Abattuci's regiment.[7]

Such passages could have come straight out of a regimental history, so completely do they reflect an uncritical acceptance of the glory of war. Not only men but even beasts were affected by the quest for glory: Dunant describes cavalry horses who were so "excited by the heat of battle" that they "played their part in the fray, attacking the horses of the enemy and biting them furiously, while their riders slashed and cut at one another." Even a goat, which had evidently attached itself to a regiment of sharpshooters, "pushed fearlessly forward in the attack on Solferino, braving shot and shell with the troops." Of his visit to French headquarters after the battle, he wrote, "The panoply of war which surrounded the General Headquarters of the Emperor of the French was a unique and splendid sight." In short, Dunant's romantic imagination was greatly stirred by this exposure to the battlefield.[8]

Nevertheless, it struck him forcefully that war produced enormous cruelty as well as great courage. The cruelty was most apparent in clashes between the Algerians, who fought on the French side, and the Croats, who fought with the Austrians. The Algerians, he wrote, "rushed at their enemies with African rage and Mussulman fanaticism, killing frantically and without quarter or mercy, like tigers that have tasted blood."[9] The Croats, he was told, were notorious for killing all wounded prisoners, such as the luckless Captain Pallavicini, whose skull they crushed with building stones. "We have real barbarians in our army," one Austrian officer told him.[10] Both the Algerians and the peasants of Lombardy (in whose fields the battle was fought) engaged in looting, particularly boots, which they took from the dead and dying.[11] However, despite the behavior of the Algerians, Dunant praised the French army not only for "the courage of its officers and men" but also for "the humanity of simple troopers."[12]

Dunant's description of the misery produced by the battle faithfully reflected the social outlook of a nineteenth-century bourgeois. More than half of his book is devoted to the sufferings endured on both sides of the conflict by the wellborn, who are identified by name as well as by regiment and rank. Dunant was particularly moved by the fate of the young Prince of Isenberg, who was found alive after the battle only because the return to camp of his riderless horse touched off a special search; if the Prince "had been raised sooner by compassionate hands from the wet and blood-stained earth on which he lay senseless, [he] would not be suffering still today from wounds which became serious and dangerous during the hours when he lay there helpless."[13] If the men of the aristocracy endured danger and hardship, the women of this class were equal to the challenge: "The gracious and lovely ladies of the aristocracy, made lovelier still by the exaltation of passionate enthusiasm, were no longer scattering rose-leaves from the beflagged balconies of sumptuous palaces to fall on glittering shoulder straps, on silks and ribbons, and gold and enamel crosses; from their eyes now fell burning tears, born of painful emotion and of compassion, which quickly turned to Christian devotion, patient and self-sacrificing."[14]

On a different level altogether was Dunant's discussion of the sufferings of ordinary soldiers. Although he related several examples of the dreadful tortures undergone by the horribly wounded, including the most unforgettable description of a battlefield amputation ever written, it is clear that courage, honor, and valor were for him the prerogatives of the aristocracy.[15] The common soldiers that he liked best were those who bore their fate with fortitude. He was particularly taken by the "resignation generally shown by these simple troopers. . . . Considered individually, what did any one of them represent in this great upheaval? Very little. They suffered without complaint. They died humbly and quietly."[16] He was especially moved by those who feared that their wounds might make it impossible for them to work again and that, as a consequence, they might become a burden to their families.[17] As a devout evangelical Christian, Dunant was also upset by the fact that so many common soldiers died with curses and blasphemies on their lips, with no one beside them to bring words of consolation.[18] Both virtue and industry among the lower classes threatened to become casualties of modern warfare.

If, in matters of class, Dunant expected the wellborn to display loftier emotions than the common people, in matters of nationality he found the "amiable . . . chivalrous and generous French" more admirable than the stolid and unremarkable Austrians. He quoted General von Salm's comment to the Chevalier du Rozel on being taken prisoner at the battle of Neerwinden (1793): "What a nation you are! You fight like lions, and once you have beaten your enemies you treat them as though they were your best friends."[19] To be sure, in Italy local sentiment was strongly for the French, with the result that after the battle "the French met with kindness from everyone," whereas "the Austrians had no such good fortune."[20] The Lombard peasants also found that the French were willing to pay very high prices for the supplies that they requisitioned.[21] Differences in national character were particularly evident, according to Dunant, in the response to misfortune: "For the most part . . . [the wounded Austrian prisoners] lacked the expansiveness, the cheerful willingness, the expressive and friendly vivacity which are characteristic of the Latin race."[22] By contrast, "In the French soldiers could be noted the lively Gallic character, decisive, adaptable and good-natured, firm and energetic, yet impatient and quick-tempered. Worrying little, and showing hardly any emotion, their light-heartedness made them better operation patients than the Austrians who, taking things less lightly, were much afraid of amputations and inclined to fret in their solitude."[23] In a footnote, Dunant paid a generous tribute to the French Minister of War, Marshal Randon, and to the commanders of the army in Italy for the "excellent organization of the French Army from the humanitarian point of view."[24] Indeed, he had already pointed out that it was neither "bad organization [n]or lack of foresight on the part of the administrative services" that accounted for the chaos after Solferino but rather "the unheard-of and unexpected number of the wounded," for whom there were simply not enough doctors, helpers, and orderlies.[25]

The situation of the wounded was worst at Castiglione, where Dunant himself worked, sometimes with help but often alone, to relieve their plight. Here everything was lacking: dressings, medical attention, water for drinking and for washing wounds, food and drink, transport for the wounded so that they could be sent on to improvised hospitals.[26]

> On the Monday morning I sent my coachman into Brescia for provisions. He came back a few hours later with the carriage loaded with chamomile, mallows, elder-flower, oranges, lemons, sugar, shirts, sponges, linen bandages, pins, cigars and tobacco. This made it possible to give out a refreshing drink of lemonade for which the men had been pining—to wash their wounds with mallow-water, to apply warm compresses, and change their dressings.[27]

Soldiers of the French garrison endeavored to help, but the spectacle of so much misery "told upon their morale"; in their place the French quartermaster authorized the use of able-bodied prisoners from the Austrian army, but their effectiveness was impeded by lack of training, the language barrier, and the hostility of the local population.[28]

Only a few miles away, in Brescia, the situation was quite different. There the town council had created a committee of physicians to organize medical care and hospital beds, assisted by numerous auxiliary committees that received supplies and donations of all kinds of useful items and materials. It was here that Dunant met the "noble Brescian lady, Countess Bronna"; he was enormously impressed by "the splendor of her sacrifice" in caring for amputees at the St. Clement Hospital.[29] From Brescia many of the wounded were sent on for convalescent care to Milan, where another noblewoman, Countess Verri, provided effective leadership for the central relief committee and where "many other noble ladies forgot their usual habits of elegance and comfort, and spent months at a time beside those beds of pain, becoming the Guardian Angels of the sick."[30] Ladies' auxiliary committees were also active at Bergamo and Cremona. Just as Dunant found the sufferings of aristocratic officers more poignant than those of common soldiers, so he also found the "sacrifice" of these noblewomen more remarkable than that of ordinary women.

In one of the best-known passages in the book, Dunant eulogized the women of Castiglione, who "seeing that I made no distinction between nationalities, followed my example, showing the same kindness to all these men whose origins were so different, and all of whom were foreigners to them. *Tutti fratelli*' [all are brothers], they repeated feelingly. All honor to these compassionate women, to these girls of Castiglione! Imperturbable, unwearying, unfaltering, their quiet self-sacrifice made little of fatigue and horrors, and of their own devotion."[31] On the face of it, this is a generous tribute, but in his concluding pages, Dunant suddenly cautioned the reader against thinking that "the lovely girls and kind women of Castiglione" had saved many of the wounded from death. "All they could do was to bring a little relief to a few of them. What was needed here was not only weak and ignorant women, but, with them and beside them, kindly and experienced men, capable, firm, already organized, and in sufficient numbers to get to work at once in an orderly fashion. In that case many of the complications and fevers which so terribly aggravated wounds originally slight, but very soon mortal, might have been avoided."[32]

Weak and ignorant women? No such phrase came from Dunant's pen when he wrote about the "splendid sacrifice" of the noble ladies of Milan; yet can it be that they were stronger, or knew more of medicine, than the ordinary women of Castiglione? What the latter needed, apparently, was organization:

> Oh, how valuable it would have been in those Lombardy towns to have had a hundred experienced and qualified voluntary orderlies and nurses! Such a group would have formed a nucleus around which could have been rallied the scanty help and dispersed efforts which needed competent guidance. As it was, there was no time for those who knew their business to give the needful advice and guidance, and most of those who brought their own goodwill to the task lacked the necessary knowledge and experience, so that their efforts were often inadequate and ineffective.[33]

With organization and advance planning, it would have been possible to collect the wounded more quickly, to provide immediate assistance, and to arrange transport to the nearest improvised hospital.

What Dunant proposed in the last dozen pages of *A Memory of Solferino* naturally reflected his own experience at Castiglione:

> Would it not be possible, in time of peace and quiet, to form relief societies for the purpose of having care given to the wounded in wartime by zealous, devoted and thoroughly qualified volunteers?
>
> Societies of this kind, once formed and their permanent existence assured, would naturally remain inactive in peacetime. But they would always be organized and ready for the possibility of war. They would have not only to secure the goodwill of the authorities of the countries in which they had been formed, but also, in the case of war, to solicit from the rulers of the belligerent states authorization and facilities enabling them to do effective work.
>
> The societies, therefore, should include, in each country, as members of their governing board, men enjoying the most honorable reputation and the highest esteem. The committees would appeal to everybody who, for sincere philanthropic motives, would undertake to devote himself for the time to this charitable work. The work itself would consist in bringing aid and relief (in agreement with the military commissaries, i.e. when necessary with their support and under their instructions) onto the battlefield whenever battle was joined, and subsequently to continue to care for the wounded in the hospitals until their convalescence was complete.[34]

This proposal obviously reflected his assumptions about war, class, and the role of women. In no sense did he regard these aid societies as pacifist organizations. On the contrary, he justified their existence on the pragmatic grounds that wars were unavoidable in the present state of Europe and were likely to become more bloody in future "since new and terrible methods of destruction are invented daily, with perseverance worthy of a better object, and since the inventors of these instruments of destruction are applauded and encouraged in most of the great European states, which are engaged in an armament race."[35] Dunant fully accepted the proposition that alleviating the horrors of war was a humane and civilized task in an era when it seemed impossible to avoid war entirely. This position brought him very close to the outlook of generals who appealed to their men to fight the enemy in a disciplined, sober, and exemplary fashion. Indeed, he quoted with approval General Trochu's proclamation to his men in Alexandria, 1859: "We will wage war in a manner humane and civilized."[36] Given the enthusiasm he evinced when writing about the panoply of war and the courage of aristocratic officers, his acceptance of the idea of civilized warfare should come as no surprise.

Equally clear is his assumption that the relief effort would be led by the wellborn, those "lofty souls" whose "hearts . . . can be stirred by the sufferings of their fellow-men." Dunant claimed that, provided the opportunity existed to be of real use, "plenty of people . . . would certainly be prepared to go, *even at their own expense*, and undertake for a limited time such an eminently philanthropic task."[37] In a revealing passage, he extolled the opportunity this would provide: "In this age, which is often called selfish and cold . . . for noble and compassionate hearts and for chivalrous spirits to confront the same dangers as the warrior, of their own free will, in a spirit of peace, for a purpose of comfort, from a motive of self-sacrifice!"[38] History, he claimed, was full of examples of such compassion and sacrifice: bishops and archbishops who brought relief to plague-stricken cities, nuns who tended the wounded during the Revolutionary and Napoleonic Wars; Grand Duchess Elena Pavlovna of Russia, who led the Sisters of Mercy during the Crimean conflict; and, of course, Florence Nightingale, whose "passionate devotion to suffering humanity is well known."[39] Dunant evidently believed that Europe was full of "noble and compassionate hearts and . . . chivalrous spirits" who, with some encouragement, could be relied upon to seize the opportunity provided by the frequent, bloody wars of the mid-nineteenth century to realize their spiritual mission on the battlefield.

People who were motivated by such lofty emotions would be infinitely preferable to "paid help":

> Only too often hospital orderlies working for hire grow harsh, or give up their work in disgust or become tired and lazy. . . . There is need, therefore, for voluntary orderlies and volunteer nurses, zealous, trained and experienced, whose position would be recognized by the commanders in the field, and their mission facilitated and supported. The personnel of military field hospitals is always inadequate, and would still be inadequate if the number of aid[e]s were two or three times as many, and this will always be the case. The only possible way is to turn to the public. It is inevitable, it will always be inevitable, for it is through the cooperation of the public that we can expect to attain the desired goal.[40]

At this point, Dunant's rhetoric began to take flight:

> The imploring appeal must therefore be made to men of all countries and of all classes, to the mighty ones of this world, and to the poorest workman: for all can, in one way or another, each in his own sphere and within his own limitations, do something to help the good work forward. Such an appeal is made to ladies as well as men—to the mighty princess seated on the steps of the throne—to the poor devoted orphan serving maid—to the poor widow alone in the world and anxious to devote her last strength to the welfare of her neighbor. It is an appeal that is addressed equally to the General and the Corporal; to the philanthropist and to the writer who, in the quiet of his study, can give his talents to publications relating to a question which concerns all the human race and in a more particular sense, concerns every nation, every district, and every family, since no man can say with certainty that he is forever safe from the possibility of war.[41]

Finally, in what is in retrospect the single most important passage in the book, Dunant envisioned that the activity of these volunteer aid societies might be sanctioned by an agreement among Europe's military leaders:

> On certain special occasions, as, for example, when princes of the military art belonging to different nationalities meet at Cologne or Châlons, would it not be desirable that they should take advantage of this sort of congress to formulate some international principle, sanctioned by a Convention inviolate in character, which, once agreed upon and ratified, might constitute the basis for societies for relief of the wounded in the different European countries?[42]

To his mind, opposition to such an agreement was inconceivable because "humanity and civilization call imperiously for such an organization as is here suggested . . . the cooperation of every man of influence, and the good wishes . . . of every decent person can be relied upon with assurance." To Dunant it was axiomatic that his proposal would gain the adherence of every ruler who cared about the welfare of his soldiers; every government that cared about the lives of its citizens; and every general, military commissary, or army doctor who would be "grateful for the assistance of a detachment of intelligent people, wisely and properly commanded and tactful in their work."[43] It was this conviction that no sensible person would disagree with his proposal that had led him to send copies of the book to people of influence all over Europe.

Moynier and Genevan Philanthropy

Moynier was one of the few recipients of *A Memory of Solferino* who knew little about armies and wounded soldiers. The military officers and army surgeons who knew a great deal more praised Dunant's generosity but expressed skepticism about the idea of forming aid societies in peacetime. Most of them believed that only in wartime would patriotic enthusiasm stimulate volunteer activity.[44] By contrast, Moynier's positive response to Dunant's vision was entirely the product of his interest in philanthropy. He was a typical utilitarian philanthropist of the mid-nineteenth century, concerned about alcoholism, child mortality, the morals and health of the working classes, and the "reclamation" of such potentially useful citizens as orphans and deaf-mutes. Trained in the law but disinclined to pursue a career at the bar, he enjoyed an income sufficiently large to devote himself, with relentless high seriousness, to improving the lot of the working classes. Moynier was also a devout Christian, although he lacked Dunant's evangelical fervor; as Pierre Boissier shrewdly observes, Dunant was fascinated by the Old Testament prophets, whereas Moynier was an admirer of St. Paul.[45]

The Geneva Society for Public Utility, of which Moynier became president in 1858, had been founded thirty years previously. It brought together high-minded Genevan pietists, men of affairs who sought to improve both the moral and the material lives of the common people. Beginning with rather abstract discussions of how to reduce poverty, encourage industry, and improve public education, the members of SGUP had gradually begun to engage in practical philanthropic work. By 1863, their foundations included a house of industry, a society for the improvement of worker housing, a pension for convalescent girls, and a children's playground.[46] Moynier joined the SGUP in 1855 and represented it at the international welfare congresses held in Brussels in 1856 and Frankfurt in 1857. By the time he became president of SGUP in the following year, he had already developed a rudimentary network of contacts among leading European philanthropists.

Dunant's vision of voluntary societies appealed to both the Christian and the utilitarian dimensions of Moynier's philanthropy. On the one hand, aiding the wounded was a practical way to demonstrate individual Christian commitment to the unfortunate, to play the Good Samaritan in the face of the horrors of contemporary war, thus reasserting the dignity and worth of the individual human life. On the other, organizing such aid involved precisely the sort of provident activity in which utilitarians believed; discipline, efficiency, and preparedness were all crucial to its success. Moynier was also much attracted by the prospect that such societies could be a force for spreading more civilized standards of conduct. After all, he was the scion of a patrician family that had fled Geneva after the popular disturbances of 1846. Other young men may have been on the barricades in 1848, but Moynier was in Heidelberg, imbibing Schelling and Goethe, before proceeding to Paris to study law. While in France he must have become aware of Alexis de Tocqueville's *Democracy in America* (1835–1840), regarded by some European readers as a warning of what the coming mass age might be like. If voluntary societies to aid the wounded could teach armies—and through them the common people—more civilized standards of conduct, then there was hope that the advancing tide of popular government would not destroy the achievements of European civilization.

Once Moynier the philanthropist was convinced of the worth of the idea, Moynier the organizer set about realizing it; one meeting with Dunant had convinced him that the latter had no concrete plans for making his vision a reality. Using his position as president, Moynier raised with the members of SGUP the possibility of their endorsing a plan for the formation of voluntary societies to aid the wounded, a plan that could in turn be considered at the international congress on charity and social welfare scheduled to meet in Berlin in the autumn of 1863.[47]

By involving SGUP, Moynier drew in as collaborators three of its most respected and influential members. General Guillaume Henri Dufour, hero of the Sonderbund War of 1847, enjoyed both an enviable reputation as a humane commander and a degree of influence with Emperor Napoleon III, whose tutor he had once been.[48] Dr. Théodore Maunoir, a distinguished surgeon who had been twice president of the Geneva Medical Society, possessed both a lengthy experience in medical philanthropy and an awareness of developments in the English-speaking world that the others lacked.[49] Maunoir's protegé, Louis Appia, the current president of the Geneva Medical Society,

1.3   This lithograph of General Guillaume Dufour by J. Heymann, entitled "When Father Dufour Calls," portrays the hero of the Sonderbund War as the conciliator of his nation. In a sense the founders of the Red Cross, with their plans for the civilizing of warfare, sought to become conciliators among nations.

had been brought up an evangelical Protestant; he shared both Dunant's enthusiasm for personal charity and Moynier's educational experience in Heidelberg and Paris.[50] Appia had drawn upon his experiences as a surgeon in the Italian War and his knowledge of gunshot wounds to write a textbook, *Le chirurgien à l'ambulance* (1859), and a prize-winning essay, *Aforismi sul transporto de' feriti* (1862).[51] Under Moynier's direction, these three plus Dunant himself drew up guidelines for the establishment of national societies to aid the wounded.

As he had promised Dunant, Moynier raised the matter of voluntary relief committees at a meeting of SGUP held on 9 February, 1863. Members agreed that the subject deserved to be pursued further and struck a committee of five—Moynier himself, General Dufour, Dr. Appia, Dr. Maunoir, and the hastily co-opted Dunant—to investigate the practicality of the scheme.[52] The first meetings of this group, subsequently known to the Red Cross movement as the committee of five, took place almost immediately. Several important steps were taken at the very first meeting on 17 February. In the first place, at Moynier's urging, the five boldly decided to assume an independent existence, voting to continue as a permanent International Committee to Assist the War Wounded after the mandate given them by SGUP had expired.[53] After that, they resolved to press for the formation of similar committees throughout Europe and to use their influence to persuade governments to encourage and approve the formation of such committees. Everyone agreed that the best means of achieving this goal was to make it clear from the outset that there would be no pressure or dictation from Geneva; instead, they would encourage each nation, each region (*contrée*), even each city, to create whatever sort of committee seemed appropriate in the circumstances.

It is clear from the minutes, written in Dunant's own hand, that the participants each had their special concerns.[54] For Dufour, the most important thing was to secure the unanimous agreement of the rulers and governments of the states of Europe and to make it clear that the relief committees would work to assist, not displace, the appropriate military and medical authorities. Maunoir was thinking about the need for information and education in order to ensure that the idea found favor among the populace. Dunant, far more visionary than the others, was already conceiving of an enterprise (*oeuvre*) that went far beyond forming aid committees and included improving means of transport for the wounded, encouraging innovative treatments, and promoting the creation of museums and displays. He was asked by his colleagues to prepare a memoir on the subject for the forthcoming Berlin welfare congress.[55]

A month later, members of the group met again to further clarify their plans and ideas. Eschewing for the moment Dunant's grandiose schemes, they all agreed to a more limited program: to work for the creation of committees that would be in a position to undertake practical relief measures in the event of a war involving the great powers of Europe. Maunoir advanced three propositions that won unanimous approval: that the committees must be officially recognized; that the corps of volunteer nurses must be subject to military authority and discipline when employed in the field; and that the volunteers must be employed without creating expense or inconvenience for the armies themselves. Dunant was already thinking of the formation of a central directing committee that could keep a register of trained volunteers and to which generals could apply in the event of war in order to obtain auxiliaries for their sanitary corps. The others, however, insisted on the importance of each country being allowed to realize the common goal in ways that suited its own ideas and customs.[56] Even at this early stage in the proceedings, there was already a nascent tension between Dunant's vaulting universalism and his colleagues' unquestioning acceptance of the limitations imposed by the existence of nation-states.

When the group met again on 25 August, Moynier imparted the news, recently received, that the Berlin welfare congress had been canceled. What should they do now? His opinion, shared by Dunant, was that the committee of five should proceed on its own and convene an international conference in Geneva to discuss the whole matter of assistance to the war wounded. The others "warmly applauded this idea" and agreed that it ought to take place in October. Dunant enthusiastically announced that he would promote the idea at the International Statistical Congress, which was due to meet in Berlin in early September, and that he would visit a number of German capitals in order to arouse support for the proposed Geneva conference. He had already prepared a draft "concordat" of some ten articles embodying their thinking on the proposed aid committees, and this was discussed with great care; in the end it was agreed that Moynier and Dunant would prepare a circular that included this revised draft and send it to "all those persons who could be presumed to be interested in this question."[57] The work was quickly completed, and on 1 September circulars were sent out announcing the "convocation of an International Conference at Geneva, in order to examine the means of remedying the insufficiency of sanitary service in armies in the field."[58]

"The Altered Circumstances of Our Times"

Despite the fulsome praise that has been lavished on these events by Dunant's biographers, it is useful to bear in mind that this was by no means the first time that Europeans had been urged to devote special attention to the war wounded. In early modern Europe, the idea that the sick and wounded deserve special treatment was common enough to be included in the terms of surrender of many besieged towns.[59] During the seventeenth and early eighteenth centuries, opposing armies frequently made prisoners of enemy wounded, although this practice was less common in eastern Europe.[60] After the battle of Fontenoy in 1745, often considered a milestone in the history of military medicine, the wounded received splendid treatment so long as they could survive the journey from the battlefield to the field hospitals some distance away.[61] Two years earlier, at the battle of Dettingen, Lord Stair and the Duke de Noailles, the opposing commanders, agreed that surgeons and other hospital personnel would be treated as noncombatants and that the sick and wounded would not be made prisoners but rather receive appropriate medical care and be returned to their own forces as soon as practicable.[62] At the beginning of the Revolutionary War, the Americans and the British agreed that medical personnel would be treated as neutrals.[63] Such ad hoc agreements were frequently resorted to in the eighteenth century, and soon the idea of a more permanent agreement was being canvassed.[64] In 1776, Prussian surgeon Jean Leberecht Schumucker advocated that belligerents should agree among themselves on how they would behave for the duration of a war.[65] In the 1780s, the idea of an agreement or convention among the sovereigns of Europe was advanced by the French philanthropist Piarron de Chamousset and (independently) by his compatriot Bernard Peyrilhe, professor of chemistry at the Sorbonne but better known for his *Histoire de la chirurgie*, published in 1780.[66] De Chamousset went on to propose the creation of a special order, modeled on the Knights of Malta, the members of which would be trained as "administrators, quartermasters, clerks, bursars, etc. and medical orderlies" and who would be distinguished by a special "uniform, ribbon or cross."[67] In the early nineteenth century, the formation of an order of Hospitaller or Nursing Brethren was proposed by the great Napoleonic military surgeon P. F. Percy and revived in 1845 by Marshal Marmont, Duke of Ragusa, in his *Esprit des institutions militaires*.[68] Percy also proposed in 1800 a draft convention for the neutralization of hospitals and wounded, but Austrian General Kray refused to accept its terms.[69] Thus, all of the basic ideas later embodied in the Geneva Convention and the Red Cross movement were in circulation well before 1850. Indeed, it can be argued that de Chamousset's proposal for a trained order of hospitallers was better thought out and more practical than the somewhat hazy vision propounded by Dunant in *A Memory of Solferino*.

Two matters demand investigation at this point: Why was there no concerted response from the rulers and governments of Europe to any of the proposals made before 1850, and why was there, as we now know, an overwhelming response to those that emanated from Geneva in 1863? If it had been simply a matter of adhering to the ethical maxims of Christianity, one might have expected Europeans to form aid societies long before the 1860s. If it had been the absence of concrete proposals for a convention, or for the formation of corps of trained nurses, one might have expected something substantial to have been undertaken during the Revolutionary and Napoleonic Wars. Yet because the political will was lacking, nothing of the kind was done. This inaction was, if anything, reinforced by the sheer scale and scope of Napoleonic warfare. After peace came to Europe in 1815, the efforts of diplomats and statesmen were so fully directed at keeping the peace that these officials were scarcely disposed to discuss setting the rules for the next war. Not even the supporters of Tsar Alexander I's Holy Alliance scheme, who were usually keen on occupying the moral high ground, took up the cause of neutrality for field hospitals. As the horrors of war began to recede in the peaceful decades that followed the Congress of Vienna in 1815, there was little reason for Europeans to concern themselves with proposals to reduce battlefield carnage.

Half a century later, Europe was a very different place. In most states—Great Britain excepted—the introduction of conscription both signaled and fostered a different relationship between nations and their armies. Proponents of sanitary reform, such as Edwin Chadwick in England and Louis-René Villermé in France, insisted upon the relationship between political economy and public health, a lesson that was bound to extend rapidly from civil to military affairs.[70] Above all, the face of Europe was changed during the middle decades of the nineteenth century by what historians have called "the communications revolution": the telegraph, the popular press, the railway, and the steam engine. These innovations revolutionized the way Europeans lived, the way they fought wars, and especially the way they thought about war. The effects of what English military surgeon Thomas Longmore was to call "the altered circumstances of our times"[71] could be seen clearly in the public response to the Crimean and Italian Wars, most notably in the rapid growth of public concern for the sufferings of sick and wounded soldiers.

The Crimean War, though fought far away in "the East," was literally brought to the breakfast tables of Western Europe by the telegraphed reports of journalists in their new role as war correspondents. Concern for the sick and wounded centered around the work of Grand Duchess Elena Pavlovna, who organized Sisters of Mercy in the Russian field hospitals, and Florence Nightingale, whose work in the hospitals of Scutari has become the stuff of legend as well as history.[72] Those who witnessed the soldiers' plight concluded that it was the duty of the state to reorganize its own military medical administration in order to provide soldiers with better diet, sanitation, and medical care. This became the burden of the lengthy and magisterial report written for the council of health of the French army by an eminent military surgeon, Dr. Jean-Charles Chenu, who had directed military medical operations in Turkey and the Crimea.[73] In Great Britain, Florence Nightingale took the same position; the campaign she waged to improve army hospitals and military medical administration has been described in detail elsewhere.[74] As John Keep has recently shown, the Russian army also made substantial changes in the operation of its military medical department in the wake of the Crimean War.[75]

The horrific battles of the Italian War produced a spate of pamphlets, books, and lectures, of which Dunant's *A Memory of Solferino* was only one example. In 1861, the Neapolitan professor Fernando Palasciano gave a lecture to the Accademià Pontaniana in which he advocated the neutralization of army field hospitals, and French pharmacist Henri Arrault wrote a pamphlet urging that field hospitals be supplied with better medical equipment.[76] On Palasciano's initiative, the Neapolitan academy sponsored an essay competition on the improvement of methods of treating the war wounded; the prize essays, one by Dr. Louis Appia of Geneva, were published in 1862.[77] Although lacking Dunant's grand vision of organized aid societies, each of these authors made specific and practical suggestions about improving the care of the wounded.

The Crimean and Italian Wars taught Europeans an important lesson about the changing relationship between armies, states, and peoples; namely, that information about battles and casualties could no longer be controlled or delayed as it had been in the past. The consequences of this simple fact were profound. As Thomas Longmore was to point out in a lecture to the Royal United Service Institution in 1866, "all of the machinery for the rapid diffusion of intelligence and personal observations, which exists in our epoch" had fostered such a degree of awareness "among all ranks of society" that states could no longer treat their soldiers as callously as they had done in the past.[78] He continued:

> In former days, the general results of war were made public, the knowledge of personal circumstances was exceptional, and limited to a narrow sphere; now the personal are almost as widely known as the general results. No wonder, then, on the one hand, that in former days the evils of war, being regarded as incapable of mitigation, or being unknown until all power of affording aid was passed, were left to be dealt with entirely by the governing authorities; or, on the other hand, that in our time public sympathy has sought to lessen these evils by committees of relief, by volunteer assistance . . . and by various other means too numerous to be mentioned; or even that the mitigation of the rigors and sufferings of war should be thought worthy of being made an object of international concern.[79]

When the telegraph and the press could quickly and easily arouse "the fears and hopes of thousands,"[80] states fighting wars with mass armies could no longer afford to appear indifferent to the fate of their soldiers. Russell's dispatches from the Crimea, as well as graphic descriptions of the battles in the Italian War, underlined the truth of Longmore's observation.[81]

Moynier and Appia advanced a similar argument about the impact of technology and the changing nature of war in the treatise that they published in 1867 under the title, *La guerre et la charité*.[82] This work, destined to become the blueprint for the Red Cross movement, put the argument from necessity in even stronger terms than Longmore had done. Quoting with approval the Crimean veteran Chenu, they maintained that states that choose to fight wars with conscript armies have an obligation to take the place of the families of their soldiers to ensure "prompt and efficacious assistance . . . in order to soothe the pain, save the life, or lessen the agony" of those who have been forced to take up arms.[83] This obligation, they continued, has become all the greater "at a time like the present, when means to injure the enemy are being incessantly multiplied and brought to perfection. . . . It would be a disgrace to humanity if its imagination were less fertile for good than for evil. Murderous refinements of war should have correlative refinements of mercy."[84] The prospect of more lethal weapons could not be ignored, they argued, because

> Modern armies differ very much in their composition from those of former days. These, for the greater part, were recruited from amongst the vagabonds, whose bad habits made them unfitted for a quiet laborious life, and who excited but little interest in their fellow-countrymen; whilst the custom of conscription, generally employed in these days, or that of the Landwehr in use amongst the Prussians and the Swiss, have given rise to armies which are really national, and the misfortunes of which strike home to the bosom of every family in the country. The army has struck its roots so deeply into the midst of the population, that it is impossible that people can remain passive spectators of its sufferings.[85]

Like Longmore, Moynier and Appia stressed the new urgency that the communications revolution had brought to the plight of wounded soldiers: "The increasing rapidity, the very instantaneousness of communications, has favored this awakening, for by this means we live much more in the intimacy of the army than we formerly did. Those who remain at their hearths follow, step by step, so to speak, those who are fighting against the enemy; day by day they receive intelligence of them, and when blood has been flowing, they learn the news almost before it has been stanched, or has had time to become cold."[86] Such intimate knowledge of the sufferings of relatives and friends, they concluded, produced the laudable result that citizens "could no longer remain idle spectators of the horrors of war."[87]

When the committee of five sent out their proposals and invitations to a conference, they sent them to a Europe that for the reasons just discussed was far more disposed to respond in a positive way than it had been when Percy and de Chamousset had advanced their ideas. To be sure, personal contacts were still important in ensuring that influential persons persuaded governments to send representatives to this private, unofficial conference. Wherever possible, Maunoir and Appia used their medical contacts; Moynier, of course, was already known outside Switzerland by those who had attended the international welfare conferences.

However, the most dramatic personal influence on contemporaries was exercised by Dunant himself. As he toured the courts of the German states in the late summer of 1863, Dunant found himself lionized as the author of *A Memory of Solferino*, the book that everyone in influential social circles was talking about. The cause of the wounded had evidently become the fashionable cause of the day. First at the Prussian court in Potsdam and then in

1.4   A man of action and of passion, Genevan surgeon Louis Appia was a great admirer of Garibaldi, a lifelong correspondent of Clara Barton, and a bulwark of the Comité International (later ICRC) until his death in 1898.

1.5   Former president of the Genevan Medical Society, Dr. Théodore Maunoir was for many years head of the city's hospital board. Fluent in English, he was well informed about the work of the United States Sanitary Commission.

Dresden (Saxony), Vienna, Darmstadt (Hesse), Stuttgart (Wurtemburg), and Karlsruhe (Baden), Dunant found rulers and ministers who were well disposed toward him, his book, and the forthcoming Geneva conference; only in Munich did he encounter some momentary coolness, principally because of Bavarian concern about the unofficial nature of the forthcoming conference.[88]

Dunant naturally assumed that all these people were extending their support solely because religious sentiment or humanitarian motives had made them respond in this way. It never occurred to him that proposals for the formation of relief societies might fit well with the military reforms then being undertaken by some of the countries he visited. In retrospect it is scarcely surprising that his interviews with Prussian King Wilhelm I and his war minister, Count von Roon, were so satisfactory: Both had a keen sense of how a more efficient use of medical resources would bear upon the political economy of war. One can hardly blame Dunant for treating their support as evidence that he had unleashed a torrent of humanitarian internationalism, but it is unfortunate that his biographers have accepted so uncritically this naive explanation of events. Realpolitik was every bit as important as humanitarianism and internationalism; in some circles—as will soon become apparent—it was even more important.

Dunant had gone to Berlin with the blessing of his Geneva colleagues to publicize their proposals at the International Statistical Congress, one section of which was composed largely of military surgeons who were examining comparative morbidity and mortality statistics of armies and civilian populations.[89] A resolution expressing sympathy for the Geneva scheme was indeed passed at the final plenary session of the congress. While there, however, Dunant fell completely under the spell of one of his admirers, Dr. J. H. C. Basting, a military physician who was translating *A Memory of Solferino* into his native Dutch. Like Dunant, Basting was a fervent evangelical Protestant. In the course of lengthy discussions, Basting convinced Dunant that the whole scheme would come to naught unless surgeons and volunteers were protected from enemy action while rendering assistance on the battlefield. On the spur of the moment, these two enthusiasts, convinced that their meeting was another manifestation of divine intervention, decided to distribute, in the name of the Geneva committee, an addition to the draft convention that proposed not only official protection and patronage of national committees but also international recognition of the neutrality of "military medical personnel and their assistants, including members of voluntary aid detachments."[90]

When Moynier and his colleagues in Geneva learned of the "Berlin circular," they reacted with considerable apprehension, fearing that Dunant's impetuous behavior might well have jeopardized the chances for an international agreement. In raising the neutrality issue, Dunant and Basting were "asking for the impossible," rebuked Moynier when Dunant finally returned to Geneva only three days before the conference was due to begin.[91] As it turned out, Moynier was wrong and Basting was right. The neutrality idea, coupled to the scheme for voluntary aid societies, provided exactly that additional degree of complexity and promise for the future that made the entire proposal occupy the attention of the states of Europe.

The initial proposal of the Geneva committee—that voluntary aid societies be formed in every country—did not in itself demand concerted international action. The neutrality proposal, on the other hand, could go nowhere without it. Faced with the original proposal, many states might well have concluded that such societies were unnecessary, impractical, or inconvenient. Joined with the idea of a neutrality convention, however, the scheme took on an entirely different aspect. Invoking a humanitarianism that could be justified in both pietist and utilitarian terms, states could now respond to an increasingly vocal public opinion aroused by reports of the callous treatment of soldiers, protect their investment in improved military medical services, and graciously accede to this manifestation of patriotic enthusiasm. In short, coupling the two proposals made them not only palatable but even desirable.

The Geneva Conference, 1863

When the conference delegates assembled on 26 October, the point of departure for their discussion was the draft agreement drawn up by Moynier. A model of brevity, it comprised ten articles, the last three of which were to apply only in wartime:

1. In each country signing the concordat, there shall be a national Committee charged with remedying, by every means in its power, the inadequacy of the official sanitary service provided for armies in the field. This Committee shall organize itself in whatever manner seems to it to be most useful and expedient.
2. An unlimited number of sections may be formed to assist the national Committee. They are necessarily dependent on this Committee, to which belongs the overall direction.
3. Each national Committee shall be in communication with the government of the country, and shall assure itself that its offers of service will be accepted in case of war.
4. In peacetime, the Committees and the Sections shall concern themselves with improvements to be introduced into the military sanitary service, with the installation of ambulances and hospitals, with means of transport for the wounded, etc., and will work towards their realization.
5. The Committees and Sections of the various countries shall meet in international Congresses to communicate with one another about their experience, and to agree on measures to be taken to further the enterprise.
6. In January of each year, the national Committees shall present a report on their work during the previous year, and may append to it whatever information they wish to bring to the attention of the Committees in other countries. These communications and reports should be addressed to the Geneva Committee, which will undertake to operate this exchange.
7. In the event of war, the Committees of the belligerent nations shall furnish necessary assistance to their respective armies, and in particular shall undertake to form and organize corps of volunteer nurses.[92] They may solicit the support of Committees belonging to neutral nations.
8. Volunteer nurses will undertake to serve for a limited time, and not to interfere in any way in the conduct of the war. They will be employed according to their wishes in field service or in hospitals. Of necessity, women will be assigned to the latter.
9. In all countries, volunteer nurses shall wear an identical and distinctive uniform or badge. Their persons shall be sacred, and military leaders shall owe them protection. When a campaign begins, the soldiers of both armies shall be informed of the existence of this corps, and of its exclusively charitable character.
10. The corps of volunteer nurses or helpers will march behind the armies, to which they will cause neither difficulty nor expense. They shall have

their own means of transport, their own provisions and supplies, of medications and first aid of all kinds. They shall be at the disposal of the chiefs of the army, who will use them only when they feel the need. For the duration of their active service, they shall be placed under the orders of the military authority, and subjected to the same discipline as ordinary [military] nurses.[93]

Moynier's draft was a reasonable attempt to put before the assembled delegates a practical means of realizing the vision that Dunant had articulated in the final pages of *A Memory of Solferino*. The only surprising omission was the absence of any reference to the need for training volunteer nurses in advance; Dunant had made a point of stressing the need for training. Particularly noteworthy is the fact that Moynier believed it might be possible to agree on an international uniform to be worn by all volunteer nurses corps, no matter to which national army they were attached; this suggests that he had in mind a sort of international charitable brigade, the members of which might have more in common with one another than with the soldiers whose needs they served. It remained to be seen whether such a conception of voluntary assistance would be acceptable to the civil and military leaders of the states of Europe.

The conference began with general opening statements about the feasibility of the whole enterprise. Dr. Friedrich Loeffler, one of the Prussian delegates, noted that states had been forced to turn to private charity because "it would not be in accord with the principles of a wise economy of state" for them to spend as much on medical services in peacetime as in wartime.[94] However, that did not mean that the Geneva proposals would have an easy time of it because governments, and especially military intendants, would be unlikely to promise to allow companies of volunteer nurses onto the battlefield.[95] He dismissed out of hand the idea of an international uniform "because we will never agree about it."[96] These sentiments were strongly supported by the Spanish delegate, Dr. Nicasio Landa: "Let us be happy enough to discover, in our discussion of these articles, those bases that would render effective and durable the salutary institution that we aspire to found, bases broad enough to permit variety in form and unity in purpose, bases that are simple but which carry within them the living germ of its future development."[97] Clearly the challenge facing them was to find arrangements that would be workable in the eyes of generals and politicians.

Soon a more skeptical note crept in. The British delegate, Dr. Rutherford, reported that everything was satisfactory in the British army, where trained bearers and nurses were already used and where army doctors "are, so to speak, kings in their own domain."[98] If only European armies could do as well, he managed to imply, none of this discussion would be necessary.[99] The French intendant, Seguineau de Préval, poured cold water on the whole idea of volunteer assistance. He argued that the battlefield was entirely the province of the army and that care of the wounded was entirely the province of military surgeons and nurses, *hommes du metiér* who knew their business.[100] "The militarization of the troops of the administration is one of the good results of our great wars. Let us not go back a century by permitting elements who are strangers to the army onto the battlefield."[101] In his view, there was no role whatever for volunteers either on the battlefield or in the ambulances; consequently, he concluded, the only role left for the proposed committees was to collect matériel that could be used to help the wounded and also to educate the public "that whoever brings help to the wounded ought to be regarded as sacrosanct by both sides."[102]

The other French delegate, Dr. Boudier, physician-in-chief of the French army, was even more outspoken in his remarks. He questioned whether anything useful could come out of the proposed scheme for volunteers. If only a small number of them were raised, they would be no use after a big battle, and large numbers of well-meaning but awkward duffers would simply get in the way. In his view, volunteers would be most likely to come from those groups "possessed of birth, fortune, or intelligence," but none of these qualities would make them useful substitutes "for the aptitudes of a simple *infirmier*," who possessed discipline, obedience, and esprit de corps.[103] Like Préval, he saw only a small role for the committees; they could persuade armies to use more nurses, press for the replacement of horses by mules as transport for the wounded, and publicize the idea that a wounded man is no longer an enemy.[104]

Boudier had treated the whole proposal as an implied rebuke to governments and military authorities, but given the French record in Lombardy, he was scarcely in a position to maintain such stiff-necked opposition to the idea of volunteers. Dr. Maunoir, who had taken no part in the proceedings to this point, made a particularly effective rejoinder, claiming that Boudier had vastly exaggerated the obstacles by treating difficulties as impossibilities. As Solferino itself showed, he went on, even with a well-organized military sanitary service there was still plenty that volunteers could do and indeed had done, and Dunant's book proved the point.[105] This rebuke was echoed by Loeffler, who caustically reminded Boudier that it was not the French government who had taken care of the French sick and wounded during the Italian War.[106] Boudier finally had to resort to silence, and General Dufour brought the opening session to a close.

Discussion was less heated on the remaining days of the conference; even Boudier was more restrained, claiming that he had mentioned only difficulties, not impossibilities. Three major issues were addressed: the peacetime role of the committees, their relations with governments and armies in the field, and the adoption of a distinctive sign. Although discussion began with the clauses and wordings in Moynier's draft, alternative wordings were often introduced, especially by Loeffler, who had apparently given a great deal of thought to the proposed concordat. His guiding rule was that they should avoid assigning to the committees any future task that could appear to constitute "an indirect and perpetual interference in the official mission of the authorities, because then it will not be easy to obtain the authorization of governments."[107] On the whole, this cautious view won the support of most delegates.

No one endorsed the view that Dunant had put forward in *A Memory of Solferino*, that the committees should be relatively inactive in peacetime. Loeffler believed that this was the time for them to train volunteers and to study the best means of treating and transporting the wounded.[108] Préval took the position that the volunteers ought to be trained for hospital work in the rear, so as to release the army's trained nurses for service on the battlefield.[109] Reassured by Maunoir that no one was trying to tell countries what to do or how to do it, even Boudier accepted a wording for Article 4 that simply called upon the committees to form and train volunteer nurses, leaving each country to work things out, as Maunoir observed, "according to its own laws, habits, and institutions."[110] Interestingly, several delegates expressed doubts as to whether the committees would succeed in finding, in peacetime, people who were prepared to undergo the lengthy training period required; only the kind of patriotic enthusiasm generated by actual hostilities, they supposed, would bring out volunteers in large numbers.[111]

When it came to deciding what the volunteers would actually do in wartime and under whose authority they would act, some significant differences of opinion emerged. Loeffler took a pragmatic view, arguing that to ensure the support of governments they should not specify that volunteers would serve on the battlefield itself. The old soldier Dufour took a similar position, arguing that in practice what the committees did, and what their volunteers were permitted to do, would be decided by commanders in the field, not by conferences of philanthropists or even by ministers of war. This was too much for those who had been attracted by Dunant's evocation of "zealous" volunteers whose "noble and compassionate hearts and . . . chivalrous spirits" would lead them to risk their lives in self-sacrifice. Van de Velde reminded the conference that Dunant himself had not been part of an organized corps and that the sort of people who would volunteer to help the wounded would expect to be with the army in the field, in the combat zone itself, and not relegated to some hospital in the rear where they would "carry soup to the sick and give them remedies." Predictably, Louis Appia shared this fear that everything was becoming far too organized and circumscribed; along with Landa, the Spanish delegate, he spoke out against subordinating the committees and volunteers to commanders in the field, saying that "nothing should be done that prevents enthusiasm, this moral force, from operating with a certain amount of liberty, without which it cannot long exist."[112] The enthusiasm of which Appia spoke was not, of course, patriotism and still less militarism; what he had in mind was the charitable impulse, the desire to sacrifice oneself for others, and in doing so to find meaning and worth in one's own life. Appia's dedication to this idea of voluntarism was passionate, total, and unwavering; in future years he would find less and less room in the Red Cross organization for this conception of voluntary activity.

The possibility of adopting a distinctive uniform for all volunteers was killed when General Dufour agreed with Loeffler that there was no point in trying to force it upon all the countries that might comply with the resolutions of the conference.[113] On the adoption of a distinctive sign or brassard (armband)—which eventually became the universally known Red Cross emblem—the minutes of the conference are tantalizingly brief and uninformative.[114] Louis Appia proposed that all volunteers should wear a white armband, but "after some discussion" (the nature of which is not specified in the minutes) this was modified, and a new article was approved, which read, "In all countries, they will wear, as a distinctive uniform sign, a white armband with a red cross."[115] On the basis of the meager published evidence, it is impossible to say with certainty who suggested the red cross emblem. Dufour or any of the other military men present might well have pointed out that a purely white flag or armband could be mistaken for a sign of truce; it is conceivable that he, or perhaps Prince Henry of Reuss, the delegate of the Order of St. John of Jerusalem, may have suggested that a cross was an appropriate emblem for those engaged in tending the wounded.[116] There is certainly no indication that the cross was adopted in imitation of the crusaders.[117] Nor is there any evidence in the minutes of the conference to support the allegation made later that these colors (which reversed the Swiss federal colors) were chosen as a tribute to Switzerland.[118] Indeed, the "tribute to Switzerland" interpretation was not advanced until after the Turkish sultan had raised the issue of the cross as a religious emblem in 1876.[119]

Predictably, Moynier did his best to steer clear of the neutrality issue, which had not figured in the original draft concordat. Dunant's participation in the deliberations had been effectively limited by his appointment as secretary, so he was unlikely to raise the question. However, Dr. Basting, his collaborator in issuing the Berlin circular, was determined to see it discussed. When it became clear that the conference was moving toward the adoption of resolutions, Basting asked anxiously about "the three points of Berlin." Moynier replied that the Geneva committee did not intend to raise them for separate discussion since—or so he alleged—they had all been discussed when the proposed concordat had been drawn up.[120] Basting then spoke with great emotion, claiming that the principal reason delegates had attended was because of the interest shown by the Prussian monarch and his war minister in the proposed article conferring neutrality on those engaged in helping the wounded. Taken aback by the force of Basting's words, Moynier was forced to concede that the idea of neutral status was "implicit" in the draft that was before them.[121] The difficulty, of course, was that those attending this unofficial conference had no power to bind their governments either to grant neutral status or to extend official recognition to the proposed committees. At this point Moynier devised an ingenious expedient that appeared to meet

Basting's concerns: The articles proposed in the Berlin circular, although not incorporated into the resolutions of the conference, could nevertheless be appended to those resolutions as a list of recommendations. At the urging of Dr. Maunoir, it was agreed that governments should be urged to confer neutral status not only on the official sanitary services and on the wounded themselves but also on the volunteer nurses.[122] At the same time, Dr. Unger, the Austrian surgeon-in-chief, suggested that the recommendations might also include urging the military authorities to end the confusion by adopting a uniform symbol for all their hospitals and ambulances. He thought it possible that the emblem chosen for the aid societies could also serve as the badge for official sanitary services, but the conference stopped short of urging upon governments the adoption of any particular emblem.[123]

The record of this conference also reveals that at least one member of the committee of five thought that its task was now over. When Article 6 of Moynier's draft—assigning to the Geneva committee the role of intermediary—was discussed, Dr. Maunoir moved to delete this section on the grounds that it was useless to send through Geneva "packets of papers that could go more directly from one committee to another . . . since they would all end up agreeing that there could be no question of a general report being elaborated at Geneva."[124] However, he received no support for his views from the other delegates, nor from Moynier, and so the article was approved as drafted. Before adjourning the conference, Moynier asked all of the delegates to keep the Geneva committee informed of their efforts to form central committees in their various countries, so that this information could be communicated to all the others; members of the Geneva committee, he assured them, would "keep in correspondence with the others quite voluntarily in the interests of the common work."[125]

When the final resolutions were adopted, they were on the whole close to the substance of Moynier's draft:

The International Conference, desirous of coming to the aid of the wounded should the Military Medical Services prove inadequate, adopts the following Resolutions:

Article 1.   Each country shall have a committee whose duty it shall be, in time of war and if the need arises, to assist the army medical services by every means in its power.

The committee shall organize itself in the manner which seems to it most useful and appropriate.

Article 2.   Any number of sections may be formed to assist the committee, which shall be the central directing body.

Article 3.   Each committee shall get in touch with the government of its country, so that its services may be accepted should the occasion arise.

Article 4.   In peacetime, the committee and sections shall take steps to ensure their real usefulness in time of war, especially by preparing material relief of all sorts and by seeking to train and instruct volunteer nurses.

Article 5.   In time of war, the committees of belligerent nations shall supply relief to their respective armies as far as their means permit; in particular they shall organize volunteer nurses and place them on an active footing and, in agreement with the military authorities, shall have premises made available for the care of the wounded.

They may call for assistance upon the committees of neutral countries.

Article 6.   On the request or with the consent of the military authorities, committees may send volunteer nurses to the battlefield where they shall be placed under military command.

Article 7.   Volunteer nurses attached to armies shall be supplied by the respective committees with everything necessary for their upkeep.

Article 8.   They shall wear in all countries, as a uniform, distinctive sign, a white armband with a red cross.

Article 9.   The committees and sections of different countries may meet in international assemblies to communicate the results of their experience and to agree on measures to be taken in the interests of the work.

Article 10.   The exchange of communications between the committees of the various countries shall be made for the time being through the intermediary of the Geneva committee.

Independently of the above resolutions, the Conference makes the following recommendations:

(a) that governments should extend their patronage to relief committees which may be formed, and facilitate as far as possible the accomplishment of their task;

(b) that in time of war the belligerent nations should proclaim the neutrality of ambulances and military hospitals, and that neutrality should likewise be accorded, fully and absolutely, to all official medical personnel, to volunteer nurses, to the inhabitants of the country who go to the relief of the wounded, and to the wounded themselves;

(c) that a uniform distinctive sign be recognized for the medical corps of all armies, or at least for all persons of the same army belonging to this service; and that a uniform flag also be adopted in all countries for ambulances and hospitals.[126]

Preparations for the Congress

For Moynier and Dunant, the months following the Geneva conference of 1863 were even busier than those that preceded it. There were two immediate tasks: One was to provide encouragement to those who were forming relief societies in many of the European states; the other was to arrange, in consultation with the Swiss Federal Council, for official invitations to be sent to those governments that might be expected to attend an international congress held to endorse the three recommendations of the unofficial conference.

As if this were not enough, members of the Geneva committee decided to test the practicality of their proposals by sending "neutral" delegates into an actual war zone. Hostilities had broken out in January, 1864, when Prussia, supported by Austria, had endeavored to seize the Danish border areas of Schleswig and Holstein. The Geneva committee reasoned that it was important to find out what role civilian volunteers could play on or near a real battlefield. The idea of sending delegates came from Dunant, who would have liked to go himself but decided that his time could be spent more productively in Paris. The committee discussed the matter briefly at its meetings on 13 and 17 March, 1864. Captain van de Velde, one of the Dutch representatives at the Geneva conference of 1863, had volunteered to go to the war zone and so had Louis Appia, although the latter stipulated that he wished to be sent to the German, not the Danish, army. It was agreed that van de Velde and Appia would each carry out an inquiry into the need for, and use of, voluntary ambulances; the former on the Danish side and the latter on the German side.[127] Both men took with them into the field white armbands bearing a red cross, the first to be made in conformity with the decision of the Geneva conference of 1863. The lengthy reports that they sent to Geneva—to be discussed in the following chapter—were to have a considerable influence on the committee and the way in which it conceived the development of charity on the battlefield for the remainder of the decade.

Moynier himself took on most of the work of corresponding with sympathetic individuals and societies in other countries, and he also carried on the negotiations with the Swiss Federal Council. Following the Geneva conference of 1863 he had assumed the presidency of the Comité International, General Dufour having been made honorary president. On 15 November Moynier wrote to all those who had been delegates at the Geneva conference of 1863, asking them to find out whether their government was prepared to extend recognition and patronage to a society to aid the wounded; whether it would be willing to support the principle of neutrality for hospitals, volunteers, civilian helpers, medical personnel, and the wounded themselves; whether it would approve the adoption of an identical distinctive emblem and flag for ambulances, hospitals, and medical personnel; and whether there would be any objection to the use of flags and armbands bearing a red cross on a white background.[128] At the same time, he arranged for the publication and distribution of the proceedings of the conference and also prepared shorter summaries of its work and recommendations for distribution to the press. With Maunoir's help, he also set about preparing a sort of compendium, entitled *Secours aux blessés*, that could be sent to friends and associates throughout Europe and abroad in the hope that diffusing information would both increase support for the cause and help to recruit members for incipient national committees. A follow-up to the proceedings of the Geneva conference of 1863, *Secours aux blessés* included the reports made by Appia and van de Velde of their tours of inspection in Schleswig and material on the U.S. Sanitary Commission.[129]

Six national aid societies were quickly established in the months following the Geneva conference of 1863. Dr. Ulrich Hahn organized one in Wurtem-

burg in December, 1863, and his friend Dr. Lasius did the same in Oldenburg in January, 1864. A Belgian society came into existence in February,
thanks largely to the work of Dr. André Uytterhoven.[130] Early in 1864,
thanks to the initiative of Count Ripalda and Dr. Landa, a Spanish central
committee was formed in Madrid; five provincial branches were also organized.[131] In Italy, committees were formed in Milan, Florence, and Turin; the
Milanese committee regarded itself as the Italian central committee.[132] By far
the most important development during this period, however, was the formation of a society in Prussia, the first great power to lend its full support to the
Geneva proposals. With the encouragement of King Wilhelm I, the three
Prussian representatives at the Geneva conference of 1863—Prince Henry of
Reuss, head of the Prussian branch of the Order of St. John, and the physicians Loeffler and Houselle—organized a central committee in Berlin in
February. Not surprisingly, War Minister von Roon heartily approved of the
organization and work of the Prussian committee. With such strong official
support, it was an easy matter to organize subsections at the local level; some
eighty-five of these were created in the first year of operation.[133]

The response from the other great powers was rather different. The Austrians replied to Moynier's inquiry by pointing out that they had established
just such a society in 1859, called the Austrian Patriotic Society for Aid to
Wounded Soldiers, War Widows, and Orphans. (This Society had, however,
disbanded in 1860, so Austria had no permanent aid society.) Nevertheless,
believing that they were well in advance of other European countries in this
field, the Austrians evinced no enthusiasm for the idea of neutrality protected
by a distinctive emblem and for the next couple of years remained aloof from
Geneva's organizing efforts. In St. Petersburg, the Russian commander-in-
chief, Grand Duke Konstantin Nikolaievich, was sympathetic to the work of
the Geneva conference, but a special committee of senior officers and physicians advised War Minister Dmitrii Miliutin against sanctioning volunteer
medical personnel on the battlefield. Miliutin thereupon replied to Moynier
that he could not encourage the formation of a national aid committee in
Russia.[134] (Even if Miliutin had received a favorable recommendation, it is
doubtful whether a Russian committee could have been established at this
time, given the degree of official hostility to public participation in national
affairs in the aftermath of the Polish uprising of 1863.)[135] The British response, conveyed to Moynier by Dr. Rutherford, was predictable: Since the
War Office had undertaken an extensive and successful reform of the military
medical administration following the Crimean War, there was no "insufficiency" of resources and hence no need for the formation of a relief committee.[136] Faced with such a lofty declaration, Moynier could only extend his
congratulations.

Behind the British attitude lay an important point of principle that, it soon
became apparent, had its devotees elsewhere, especially in France. The
Geneva proposals were based on Dunant's assumption, formulated at

Solferino, that the official medical services would always be inadequate to cope with the needs of war and hence would always require supplementing by a voluntary aid society. However, certain influential individuals rejected this proposition entirely. Unfortunately for the Genevan cause, two of them were well-known veterans of the Crimean War. One was Dr. Jean-Charles Chenu, formerly *médicin principal* in the French army; the other was the famous "lady with the lamp," Florence Nightingale. Both took the position that it was the duty of the state to provide adequate medical supplies and personnel for its armies and that private charity ought not to relieve the state of this awesome responsibility by providing volunteers to assist on the battlefield.

Since Dunant had invoked Florence Nightingale as one of his inspirations during the trying days at Castiglione, it may seem ironic that she should have had so little sympathy for the Geneva proposals. Dunant praised Nightingale as one of those lofty souls whose example he urged others to follow, but when he later invited her to become the standard-bearer of the Red Cross cause in England, she brusquely replied that "such a [voluntary relief] society would take upon itself duties which ought to be performed by the government of each country and so would relieve them of responsibilities which really belong to them and which they can properly discharge and being relieved of which would render war more easy."[137] In July, 1864, she wrote to Thomas Longmore, professor of military surgery at the Royal Army Medical School, Netley, and one of the British delegates to the forthcoming Geneva Congress, about her reaction to the 1863 resolutions:

> I need hardly say that I think its views most absurd—just such as would originate in a little state like Geneva, which never can see war. They tend to remove responsibility from Governments. They are *practically impracticable*. And voluntary effort is desirable, just in so far as it can be incorporated into the military system. . . . Our present system (military) is the result of voluntary additions made to the service during the Crimean War, but was prepared to obviate the necessity of future voluntary efforts as far as possible. . . . If the present Regulations are not sufficient to provide for the wounded they should be made so. But it would be an error to revert to a voluntary system, or to weaken the military character of the present system by introducing voluntary effort, unless such effort were to become military in its organization.[138]

Three years later, she had become even more resolute in her opposition, warning Longmore, "No steps should be taken with the public in any country which should lead their War Office to think that its own work . . . will be done for it by anybody else."[139]

If Nightingale's negative response seems surprising, the explanation is a simple one: It was Dunant who had misunderstood Nightingale's objectives, not the reverse. The latter had dedicated herself not to a life of volunteer philanthropy but rather to an intensely waged campaign to improve official medical and supply services. She had no sympathy whatever for the well-meaning efforts of enthusiastic volunteers; on the contrary, at every turn she preferred professionalism to amateurism. Her principal fear was that governments bent on making war might welcome the formation of such aid societies and treat it as a convenient excuse for doing less for their soldiers than she thought necessary and appropriate. In her opinion, those concerned about the fate of the war wounded would do far better to pressure armies and governments to do more for the health and welfare of their soldiers. Dunant and his Genevan colleagues were thus surprised to find that instead of leading the campaign to form a national aid society in England, Nightingale privately disparaged the entire scheme and kept herself aloof from public efforts to promote it. She was equally opposed, again on the grounds of practicality, to the Geneva Convention itself. In 1869, she wrote once more to Longmore: "I fear that the practical objections which struck me at the beginning will come up whenever the [Geneva] Convention [of 1864] is brought into active operation. But I will not anticipate evil."[140]

The other well-known opponent, Dr. Chenu, had such serious reservations about the work of the Geneva conference that he decided to publish them in a pamphlet that he entitled *Observations sur l'insuffisance du service de santé en campagne.*[141]

Although he paid a brief tribute to Dunant's "generous illusions," he made it plain that he thought the Geneva proposals absurdly unrealistic. Like Nightingale, Chenu believed that improving military medical services was the responsibility of governments and military authorities, not philanthropic societies.

> It is easy to see that I do not share the hopes that are founded upon the employment of volunteer nurses on the battlefield. . . . [Let us leave] to the military element the realization of the projects of the [1863] Conference and leave to governments the responsibility for a service which it is their duty to provide no matter what the cost. . . . States that demand sacrifices from all their citizens, high and low, must do so on the condition that the state replaces the absent family [of the soldier] and assures its defenders care and assistance which must be prompt as well as enlightened.[142]

Chenu shared Nightingale's deep concern with improving the lot of the wounded; much of his pamphlet was a plea for an improved army sanitary service that would include reserve ambulance units and trained brigades of nurses.[143]

To prove his point about the dangers of permitting civilian volunteers on the battlefield, Chenu pointed to the example of America:

> The admission of a civil volunteer element would only cause disorders of more than one kind. What happened in America? The sanitary commissions invaded most of the services; they arrogated control to themselves, they made reports, they soon functioned like an independent power; they were better informed than the government itself; newspapers have published their correspondence

1.6   A Crimean War veteran, French military surgeon Dr. Jean-Charles Chenu was, like Florence Nightingale, an early and influential critic of voluntary charity on the battlefield.

> [whether it was] true, exaggerated, or false, etc.; they [the commissions] did not hold back from any intervention that was not submitted to military discipline; only America can permit itself such eccentricities.[144]

It is worth noting, however, that Chenu's knowledge of the American situation was both skimpy and inaccurate; he was evidently unaware of the tracts already being published by the European branch of the Sanitary Commission and had relied instead on an article by Elisée Reclus published in *Revue des Deux Mondes*.[145] Nevertheless, he reiterated his view that armies cannot admit nonmilitary volunteers who are not subject to military discipline and who can withdraw when it suits them:

> If they [volunteers] were not officially authorized . . . [they] would exercise a control that the command and the administration [of the army] could not tolerate; their position would be untenable and there would be conflicts every day. [If they were] officially authorized, they would constitute a second administration, competing with the arrangements that should be made by the military authority, which is rightfully jealous of the care which it must take of its soldiers.[146]

In his view, those concerned with the fate of the wounded would do far better to insist—as did Nightingale—that army sanitary services be expanded, reorganized, and better paid.[147] The best advice for philanthropic societies, he concluded, was "to keep themselves at a distance from the armies and abstain from all superfluous intervention; to keep clearly in mind that charity always has its limits . . . [and] to avoid having its agents interfere with armies while a war is on."[148] If they kept within these bounds, he conceded, they could be useful in spreading ideas about charity, raising money in wartime, promoting improvements in the care and treatment of the wounded, and supplying volunteers to work in regular military hospitals so that trained personnel could be sent with the army into the field.

Chenu's pamphlet was a foretaste of the problems that supporters of the Geneva proposals would encounter in their dealings with senior officers of the French army and with the war minister, Marshal Randon. The French representatives at the Geneva conference of 1863, Boudier and Préval, had made it abundantly clear that they disliked the idea of volunteer auxiliaries, trained or otherwise, so it was unrealistic to expect either of them to take the initiative in organizing a national aid society.[149] Dunant himself went to Paris in November, 1863, ostensibly to help with the founding of a French society, but at first he found it much easier to gather invitations to the salons of the nobility than to gain access to government ministers. As he had done in 1859, Dunant decided to seek out the emperor himself, enclosing with his request for imperial favor a letter from the sovereign's old tutor, General Dufour. On 21 December, he was rewarded with a declaration that the emperor not only supported the objectives of the Geneva conference but had also made it clear to Marshal Randon that he wished the army to cooperate in setting up a French national aid committee.[150] Unwilling but overruled, the Marshal began to correspond with Dunant about the composition and role of such a committee.[151] This grudging compliance with the emperor's wishes needs to be kept in mind because it affected relations between the army and what was to become the French national aid society until well into the 1870s.

The Geneva conference of 1863 had recommended an international agreement about the neutrality of hospitals and medical personnel, but for such an agreement to be concluded, one of the great powers had to be willing to sponsor the holding of a congress to this purpose. Prussia, it seemed, was already prepared to act as sponsor, but both Dunant and Moynier preferred to see France take the initiative. Indeed, even before the conference delegates had replied to Moynier's November questionnaire, Dunant had written Moynier from Paris that he was already taking steps to see that the French foreign minister raised the neutrality issue with other states.[152] Moynier wrote a strongly worded reply insisting that any such action was premature.[153] However, once assured of the emperor's support, Dunant wrote to Marshal Randon, telling him of the Prussian king's willingness to sponsor such a congress and appealing to him "to take this initiative since France has always been in the vanguard with respect to noble and generous ideas and cannot be led by others."[154]

Invoking the specter of Prussian sponsorship worked like a charm, and on 6 February Dunant was informed that the emperor desired him to meet soon with the foreign minister, Drouyn de Lhuys, to discuss arrangements for the congress. These discussions produced three contentious issues. The first was whether the congress should take place in Bern as Napoleon III proposed—a gesture that recognized both the Swiss origins of the proposal and the advantageous neutral status of the country—or in Geneva, as Dunant had strenuously advocated. The second was whether, as the French proposed, only European states ought to be invited or whether, as Dunant argued, invitations ought also to be sent to the United States, Mexico, Brazil, and Japan. The third was whether one invitation should be sent to the Germanic confederation—the predictable French view—or whether, as Dunant urged, each of its member states should receive a separate invitation. Once again the personal influence of Napoleon III appears to have been decisive: Having received a flattering, not to say obsequious, letter from the Geneva committee, the emperor agreed on all points with the stand taken by Dunant and his colleagues. On 21 May, Dunant wrote to Moynier conveying the good news; the emperor had also graciously conceded that the invitations should be sent out by the Swiss Federal Council and that his interest in the project would be communicated informally, so as to let it appear that the initiative lay with the Swiss.[155] As the Geneva committee wrote on 15 June, the support of a great military power such as France removed a great many difficulties.[156] Four days later, Dunant cheerfully attended the founding meeting in Paris of the Society for Aid to Wounded Soldiers.

At this point the focus of activity shifted back to Switzerland, where Moynier took up the matter of the congress with the Swiss Federal Council. Twelve countries, including France and Prussia, had responded positively to the questions he had asked in the November questionnaire; Russia was the only great power to oppose granting neutrality to a volunteer corps.[157] For the next two weeks he traveled regularly to Bern to make the necessary arrangements, and on 6 June the council resolved that a diplomatic congress should be held in Geneva, beginning on 8 August. Invitations were sent to all European states, the United States of America, Mexico, and Brazil. (Distance alone apparently dictated the decision not to invite Japan.) The formal letters of invitation reviewed the 1863 recommendations and continued thus:

> The provisional International Committee of Geneva is of the opinion that it would be appropriate to word those recommendations as obligations and have them recognized by all States. It was for this reason, encouraged by the high degree of interest on the part of both governments and people, that it requested the Swiss Federal Council to convene a general congress for the purpose of sanctioning these principles in conformity with international law. The Federal Council believes that it has a duty to meet this request. Existing treaties assign to Switzerland a position [of neutrality] which justifies this country's interest in the wounded and the measures proposed to other States to take care of the wounded.[158]

The Geneva committee decided that Moynier and Dufour should work together to draw up a draft convention that could be discussed by the delegates, and both immediately set to work on this task. With the invitations sent, members of the committee also had to plan both the program of the congress and what would now be called the local arrangements. It is ironic that Dunant, who had first called for the signing of a diplomatic convention to protect the wounded, was on this occasion put in charge of organizing the entertainments.

The International Congress, 1864

The International Congress, held in Town Hall at Geneva in August, 1864, brought together representatives of sixteen states. France, Prussia, and Switzerland sent three-member delegations, and a few other states sent two representatives, but most were content to send only one. Of the twenty-four official representatives, half had also attended the 1863 conference, so there was a good deal of continuity in membership. Senior army physicians, who had been well represented in 1863, made up half of the delegates in 1864 (seven of them attended both); the remainder were diplomats and officials. The Swiss delegation consisted of Moynier, General Dufour, and Dr. Lehmann, chief physician of the Swiss army. Dr. Loeffler was there again for Prussia, and so was Dr. Rutherford for Great Britain; Préval and Boudier also returned as French delegates. George Fogg was an unofficial representative of the United States; Charles Bowles represented the Sanitary Commission.[159] Three of the states that had attended the 1863 conference—Austria, Bavaria, and Russia—were not represented in 1864, but three that had not attended in 1863—Belgium, Denmark, and Portugal (four if one counts the unofficial American representatives)—were now represented by delegates.

There was a flurry of concern when consultation revealed that only the French and Swiss delegates had been empowered by their governments both to negotiate and to sign whatever document emerged from the congress. The senior French delegate, Charles Jagerschmidt, a punctilious diplomat, was at first inclined to abandon the entire proceeding on these grounds and had to be prevailed upon to remain at the table as the other delegations, empowered only to negotiate, endeavored to secure from their governments full power to sign the proposed convention. As it happened, all except Great Britain, Sweden, the Kingdom of Saxony, and of course the United States—whose representatives took no official part in the proceedings—were by the end of the congress in a position to put their signatures to the document.

The Geneva committee had intended that the congress would draw up a convention embodying the three recommendations of the 1863 conference: that states extend their patronage and encouragement to the formation and activities of relief societies; that neutrality be accorded to all ambulances, hospitals, and personnel engaged in caring for the wounded; and that a uniform distinctive sign and flag be adopted for all ambulances and hospitals. All three points had been addressed in the draft convention that Moynier had discussed with members of the Swiss Federal Council, the official host of the congress, at the time that the invitations were sent out. In the course of these discussions it was pointed out that patronage and encouragement for volunteer relief societies were matters to be decided by each state individually, and hence it was decided that the convention itself ought to say nothing about them.[160] In other words, there was a tacit understanding, at least among the Swiss, that although some states might welcome and actively encourage the formation of aid societies, others might prove much less receptive to the idea, and that it was sensible not to press the issue at this stage. Thus the draft convention that Moynier circulated to the delegates at the informal evening session prior to the official opening of the congress did not contain any statement about official recognition of relief societies.

This change was bound to upset some delegates because those who had attended the 1863 conference naturally expected that such a clause would be included in the proposed convention. That is why General Dufour, who was elected president of the congress, was at such pains to explain the situation in his opening address:

> In regard to the first [recommendation] . . . there is no occasion for any international treaty, as every Government must, within the limits of its domestic policy, take such action as it shall deem best, either to facilitate the organization of Volunteer Sanitary Commissions, or to merely tolerate them. On this subject each Government must have perfect liberty of action. There can be no outside dictation or pressure exercised to compel any Government to execute any stipulation covering this ground. . . . At present, there is no question involved as to the formation of Voluntary Relief Associations, nor of any alterations in or interference with the consecrated military code of nations, which would certainly be calcu-

lated to create embitterment or distrust. Those who have entertained a contrary impression, are completely in error in regard to our purposes and aims. And if it has been these fears which have prevented several States from sending delegates to our Congress, I cannot help expressing a profound regret. They have entirely misunderstood our intentions. They will better appreciate our true aims when they shall recognize them in the Treaty which is to be evolved from our deliberations here. For this reason, it will be best to allow them the opportunity to approve this Treaty, and, therefore, to let the protocol remain open.[161]

In fact, it is doubtful whether it was this issue that prevented either Austria or its ally Bavaria from sending delegates. Officially, both states declined to be represented in Geneva for religious reasons, but other considerations were certainly operating in this situation. For one thing, the Austrians considered themselves pioneers in the field after their experience in 1859–1860. More important, however, was the fact that Austria's late enemy, Napoleon III, had associated himself with the humanitarian sentiments of the proposal; there was no reason why Austria should add to his prestige by joining the delegates in Geneva. In the case of Russia, however, it was precisely the possibility of voluntary relief committees sending personnel onto the battlefield that aroused opposition. Russian fears about volunteers on the battlefield were shared by the French, who insisted that all such personnel must be subject to military discipline at all times. Dufour's words were probably directed as much at the French and at the British (who had argued in 1863 that they had no need for such a society) who were in attendance as at the Austrian and Russian absentees.

Having put that contentious issue aside, Dufour went on to emphasize the need for a permanent agreement about the neutralization of ambulances and sanitary personnel. For the conclusion of such an agreement, he noted with satisfaction, the atmosphere had never been so favorable:

> Inasmuch as conflicts of arms are inevitable, so long as human passions and interests continue as they are, it is at least the duty of the intelligent and liberal minds of all nations to unite in endeavoring to mitigate, as far as possible, the horrors of such conflicts, and to stimulate philanthropic effort in behalf of their victims. Already a great step has been taken in the right direction. The wounded are no longer maltreated, whatever may be the animosities of the parties engaged. The victor collects the enemy's wounded, and treats them with the same care as his own. The aids of charity are not wanting, being generously extended both by the regular physicians in charge, and by the noble imitators of Florence Nightingale, a name universally cherished and venerated. But this is not enough. We must advance a step further, and seek to obtain for the wounded the benefits of neutrality, so that when we have extended the pitying hand to them in their hour of misfortune, when we have bathed their wounds and relieved their sufferings, we may guarantee their future liberty from all restrictions. On more than one occasion in the past, the neutrality of the ambulance services and of the wounded has been admitted, and commanders of opposing armies have signed cartels or special conventions, guaranteeing these points in particular cases. But

these generous efforts have not left any durable results. The moment had not yet arrived to ask for concessions from the old stereotyped usages of society. Let us then labor together to arrive at this object in a permanent practical way, sustained, as we must ever be, by the benevolent dispositions of Governments themselves. Propitious circumstances favor us. The public mind is already prepared for it. It is for this that we are united here. Such is our mission, than which none could be higher or more noble. May we succeed, and only separate with the conviction of having done something for the good of suffering humanity.[162]

Given Dufour's record as a humane commander in the field and an active member of the committee of five, there can be no doubt that his sentiments were completely genuine. Like Dunant, Palasciano, and Percy, he believed that the neutralization of ambulance and hospital services was a goal worth achieving solely because of the relief it would bring to the sufferings of wounded soldiers. At the same time, it is clear that both he and his listeners believed that wars were not only inevitable but likely to be fought with ever more fiendish and lethal weapons and that there was nothing they could do to impede or prevent these developments. The most that could be contemplated was an arrangement that made permanent the temporary, ad hoc agreements of the past concerning the neutrality of hospitals, ambulances, and field medical personnel. Despite Dufour's reference to the "benevolent dispositions of Governments," he and others around the table knew that there were limits to that benevolence: Several governments, for example, refused to commit themselves to assist and promote the activities of voluntary aid societies; none wished to see the current convention fortified with sanctions that could be taken against states that violated its provisions; most believed, as did Dufour himself, that any convention could only express general principles and that their application in wartime conditions would have to be decided by commanders in the field. One is therefore tempted to conclude that the general's rhetoric notwithstanding, this was the least, perhaps the very least, that could be done to reduce the horrors of war.

When the draft convention was put forward for discussion article by article, there was a great deal of haggling over wording, and in many cases it was necessary for General Dufour to intervene, appealing to the delegates to adopt the most general language possible in order to avoid future complications. In only a few cases were there substantial discussions of principle. Loeffler and the Prussians were unhappy to find no explicit mention of volunteer aides being granted the neutrality that was to be extended to hospital and ambulance personnel. Moynier tried to reassure them that volunteers were subsumed in this broader category, but as Loeffler pointed out, volunteers "might be acting in complete independence of any official position of service," a comment that indicated how much he was indebted to Dunant's original idea.[163] It soon emerged, however, that the French delegates were under instructions from their government not to sign any convention that embodied the principle of independent volunteer aides. Dufour ended this disagreement by stating that the volunteers need not be specially designated, since "they must stand on the same footing as other persons attached to the Sanitary Service."[164]

Having taken such a firm position on this issue, the French were nevertheless anxious to appear sympathetic to the broad objectives of the congress and therefore went out of their way to encourage spontaneous civilian assistance to the wounded. Moynier's draft of Article 5 had stated, "The inhabitants of the country, who shall be employed in the transportation of the wounded, or in affording them succor on the field of battle, shall, in like manner, be respected as neutrals, and shall be free from hindrance or molestation." To this the French proposed an amended wording that significantly extended the scope of the article:

> The inhabitants of the country occupied who shall afford succor to the wounded shall be respected as neutrals, and shall remain absolutely free. Generals in command of belligerent forces shall have instructions to advise the inhabitants of the country occupied of the appeal made to their humanity, and of the consequent neutrality guaranteed to them. Every wounded man received and cared for in a household shall serve that household as a safeguard. His presence shall exempt that house from all military occupation, and its inhabitants also from the payment of a portion of the war contributions ordinarily levied.[165]

American historian William Q. Maxwell has disparaged this clause as evidence that the Europeans preferred "primitive household charity" to organizations such as the U.S. Sanitary Commission, whose role in the Civil War he has so enthusiastically described.[166] This judgment is wide of the mark. For one thing, it neglects the fact that the French needed to counter the bad impression that their opposition to volunteer aides had created. Moreover, recent European experience suggested that there was good reason to offer civilians an incentive to care for the wounded: It might well keep them from pillaging the wounded on the battlefield or from threatening the lives of surgeons and stretcher parties. Certainly such an approach, which did not preclude the organization of volunteer aides, was in keeping with Moynier's general desire to raise the moral standards of the common people. Nothing could have been more splendidly utilitarian than to offer those who helped the wounded an exemption from billeting, requisitions, and other unpopular contributions to war traditionally expected from those unlucky enough to find themselves living near a battlefield.

The more important thing to note about this amended Article 5 is that it was "received with warm satisfaction, and . . . adopted without discussion."[167] In view of the trouble that this article was to cause during the Franco-Prussian War a few years later, it is remarkable that none of the delegates foresaw the likelihood that it would be abused. In the closing moments of the congress, when approval was being given to the final wording of the proposed convention, the Italian delegate, Baroffio, asked to have inserted in the minutes a declaration to the effect that "the last words of Article [5] should not be taken in an absolute sense: that is to say, that the presence of one or several wounded soldiers in his house could not discharge the inhabitant from his obligations of contributing, in proportion to his means, to the needs of the army."[168] General Dufour confirmed that this was indeed the sense in which all delegates understood it, and the final wording was changed: "An inhabitant who has given shelter to the wounded shall be exempted from billeting and from a portion of such war contributions as may be levied." This wording tempered the encouragement of humanity by ensuring that the requirements of war were not completely obscured, but its vagueness was to become the subject of endless controversy in later years.

When the congress assembled for its sixth session on 17 August, most delegates expected that the final document would be ready for signing. Instead, Jagerschmidt announced that the French minister of war insisted on two amendments, and the delegates of Belgium and Saxony announced that their power to sign this convention had been withdrawn. The French amendments were incorporated without too much difficulty; one provided that enemy surgeons who had finished caring for captured wounded would be *escorted* back to the outposts of their own forces, so as to control their movements; the other permitted commanders-in-chief to arrange for the exchange of enemy wounded whenever circumstances would permit it, subject to mutual agreement.[169] In the end it was decided to adjourn for five full days, so as to allow as much time as possible for delegates to communicate with their governments and secure the necessary permissions for signing the proposed convention. When the congress reconvened on 22 August, twelve delegations were able to sign immediately. Neither the Swedish nor the Saxon delegates had received the necessary permission, and the British delegates had been instructed to submit the final text for the approval of the cabinet in London before signing. Much to Bowles's disappointment, the American delegation also found itself on the sidelines at the signing ceremony.[170]

The 1864 convention itself was a model of brevity—its ten articles contained just over five hundred words—but it had taken the delegates two full weeks to put it in a form acceptable to the participating states.[171] To be sure, not all of their time was spent in meetings. Many of them stayed at the Hôtel des Bergues, with its magnificent view of Lac Leman and Mont Blanc in the distance. "The wealthy citizens of Geneva," one delegate wrote, " . . . seemed to vie with each other in magnificent entertainments in honor of the Congress and for the diversion of its members. Fêtes, regattas, illuminations, and excursions on the Lake—which is the most beautiful in the world—followed in daily and nightly succession."[172] Moynier himself began the social round with a tea party at his villa in Sécheron, but this affair was modest compared with what was to follow. No less than three *fêtes champêtres* were held for the delegates: One was given by General Dufour's aide-de-camp, Colonel Edouard Favre, at his villa on the Italian side of the lake; another by the

Genevan millionaire Théodore Vernes at his villa on the French side, to
which the delegates were conveyed on a steamer with a military band on
board; the third was given at the Villa Bartholoni in Sécheron by the Parisian
banker and philanthropist François Bartholoni. The last occasion included
not only a concert with fireworks during the intermission, but also a performance by the Choral Society of Geneva of a "Cantata for Wounded Soldiers," especially written for the occasion by Paul Privat. Ironically, its final
verse ran as follows:

> *Wounded soldiers, take courage!*
> *For your fate will be gentler:*
> *Look! look! from all sides*
> *True friends are coming to you.*
> *To put an end to your miseries*
> *They will labor night and day:*
> *Who is leading them, these noble brothers?*
> *Charity, faith, and love.*[173]

Doubtless the composer of these words was under the impression that the
delegates were in Geneva to further the work of "these noble brothers"; presumably no one told him that official reluctance and opposition had made it
impossible even to mention the existence of volunteer aid societies in the
Convention itself.

One other social event deserves mention. On the night of 17 August,
which is when it had first been expected that the Convention would be
signed, the Council of State of the City and Canton of Geneva had organized
a banquet for the delegates at the Hôtel de l'Écu. In the embarrassing absence of a signed Convention something had to be done to fill the vacuum, so
the Genevans decided to use the occasion to honor the American delegates,
hoping, no doubt, that a little extra recognition might help to persuade Secretary of State William Henry Seward to reconsider his opposition to European entanglements. The ensuing events were recorded in detail by the im-
pressionable Charles Bowles:

> Most particular attentions were paid to the U.S. delegates, as being the repre-
> sentatives of a sister Republic. They were placed in the first seats at the table,
> next to or opposite the President, a mark of preference which is held in great es-
> teem by Continental peoples. In the center of the table was a large piece of con-
> fection, representing a fortress, with its garrison and sanitary workers distin-
> guished by the red-crossed brassard, pursuing their vocations. The tower was
> surmounted by small silk flags of the Swiss Republic and Canton of Geneva,
> around a central flag with a red cross on a white field, the emblem of our neu-
> trality, just adopted by the Congress. After the first toast, this flag was taken
> from its place by the President, who, turning to me as [the] representative of the
> U.S. Sanitary Commission, presented it as a token of appreciation of its labors
> for the good of all humanity. To this kind and unexpected compliment to our

Commission, and to the accompanying speech of the President, I replied as well as I could, but the act, the sentiment, the acclamations of surrounding friends, and, withal, the proud consciousness of a deserving cause almost overwhelmed me. The full outburst of a chorus from "William Tell" given by the Geneva Musical Society, in the hall outside, though it covered my retreat, did not add to my equanimity.[174]

Moynier and the Geneva committee considered it very important to secure American adherence to the Convention, since that would be proof positive that a more civilized approach to warfare was winning support in the new world as well as the old. However, despite the tributes lavished on Bowles, Secretary of State Seward remained adamant that America should remain aloof. His attitude never failed to surprise the Genevans, who could not understand how the country that had given birth to the Sanitary Commission could refuse to sign the Convention.

The delegates finally departed for their home countries, carrying with them copies of the new Convention itself as well as a host of pleasant memories of Genevan hospitality. Only one sour note had obtruded briefly on the entire proceedings. On the very last day of the congress there was a clash in the streets of Geneva between followers of Radical Party leader James Fazy and supporters of the Independents; the latter, upset by a recent change in their political fortunes and believing the Council of State to be in session, endeavored to force their way inside Town Hall; on being told by General Dufour that the hall was being used for a different purpose, they quickly went elsewhere.[175] For Moynier the incident must have brought back unpleasant memories of the 1846 uprising, when his family had been forced to flee the city. For many of the other delegates it was a forceful reminder of the turbulence that lay just below the surface of the ordered world in which they were accustomed to move. Bowles could eulogize American philanthropy all he liked, but for the European delegates, whose sympathies lay with the patrician elite who had been their hosts, this incident represented democracy in the flesh.

Over the Threshold

The wars of the 1850s and early 1860s convinced most European states of the need to provide a constructive response to what Longmore called "the altered circumstances of our times." In the wake of the Crimean and Italian Wars, the Geneva proposals were attractive to the great powers because they gave European states the opportunity to say to their peoples, in effect, "Look, here we are agreeing that our soldiers deserve better treatment and promising to do whatever we can to remedy this notorious deficiency." Although the stated purpose of the 1864 congress was to draw up the terms of this agreement, it served another, equally important purpose: To reassure the governments involved that they would still retain control over all of the essential aspects of making war. Voluntary assistance, it was agreed, would function only with the agreement of commanders in the field, all volunteers being clearly identified by their distinctive armbands. The red cross brassard was, in this sense, a license granted to the volunteers by the competent military authorities.[176] As with all licenses, it could be revoked by the issuing body. The terms of the Geneva Convention left each state free to do as much or as little as it wished to encourage the development of a national society to aid the wounded.[177] Most important of all, the congress set up no mechanism to police the observance of the Convention. In this form, then, as an agreement that committed states to relatively little and contained no sanctions against violation, but which was of enormous potential value in allaying the anxieties of citizens in states where conscription was practiced, the Convention was approved.

Did the American Civil War have as much influence on these events as the Crimean and Italian Wars? Did the example of the U.S. Sanitary Commission help to push Europeans over the threshold? William Q. Maxwell, in his 1956 book, *Lincoln's Fifth Wheel: The Political History of the United States Sanitary Commission*, claimed that the example of America was crucial to the success of the Geneva proposals: "Without the American experiences Dunant's efforts might have been fruitless. The Sanitary Commission had solved problems of cooperation between civilian volunteers and the official medical service; it was proof that the people could be organized for relief as effectively as armies for war."[178] Although acknowledging that the 1864 International Congress stopped short of requiring states to establish and protect committees of volunteers, Maxwell nevertheless concluded that "one would like to think of the Sanitary Commission as the midwife of the Red Cross."[179] Maxwell's comments could easily lead historians of Civil War medicine to conclude that it was Charles Bowles, one of the U.S. representatives at the 1864 congress, who opened the eyes of the Europeans to the possibilities of harnessing to productive charitable work popular enthusiasm for war and who thus ensured the success of the Red Cross movement.

This picture is wide of the mark, largely because Maxwell's treatment of the issue replicates the tone of self-congratulatory exaggeration that he found in Charles Bowles's *Report to the Executive Committee of the European Branch of the United States Sanitary Commission*.[180] The Sanitary Commission had been formed in June, 1861, but Europeans knew virtually nothing about its activities until its European branch, founded in November, 1863, began to publish pamphlets of its own in French and to circulate copies of the commission's English-language publications.[181] Without knowing anything of the American experience, the Geneva conference of October, 1863, had drawn up rules for the operation of national committees to aid the wounded and had chosen the red cross insignia for voluntary medical personnel. The red cross brassard was worn for the first time on the battlefield during the Schleswig War in the summer of 1864, when Drs. Appia and van de Velde visited the field hospitals of the Prussians and Danes respectively. The extensive reports that these two sent to Geneva were regarded by the Europeans as far more germane to the main subject of the 1864 International Congress—neutrality— than was Bowles's recitation of the stupendous achievements of the Sanitary Commission.[182] Maxwell repeats Bowles's disparaging comments about the Europeans preferring "primitive household charity" to the organization of sanitary commissions and volunteer nurses, when in fact the 1863 conference had already dealt with voluntary nurse corps and organizational committees. In fact, had Bowles only realized it, another aspect of the American war experience was of considerable potential relevance: In April, 1863, the Union government had officially accorded battlefield neutrality to medical personnel and installations.[183] Yet the records of the 1864 congress indicate that Bowles (who was, after all, only an unofficial delegate) contributed nothing of substance to its discussion of neutrality.

Several of the publications of the Sanitary Commission were brought to the attention of the Geneva committee by Dr. Maunoir, who was fluent in English.[184] *L'oeuvre d'un grand peuple*, a sixty-four-page pamphlet written by a French employee of the Commission's European branch, was read with interest by the Europeans; Bowles had taken 150 copies of it to Geneva with him.[185] Maunoir also contributed an essay review of the principal publications of the Sanitary Commission to *Secours aux blessés*, the compendium that Moynier produced for the guidance of the fledgling societies that were forming in the wake of the 1863 conference.[186] An enthusiast for democracy and popular representative government, Maunoir was impressed by the sheer size of what the American people had accomplished through the Sanitary Commission. Where other Europeans may have doubted whether a noble impulse such as philanthropy could survive in a democracy or assumed that ordinary people could organize nothing on their own without the leadership of an elite, Maunoir saw in the Sanitary Commission proof that popular sovereignty and organized philanthropy were by no means incompatible.[187] Dunant probably shared Maunoir's enthusiasm for popular moral regeneration, but Moynier, convinced of the superiority of European civilization and alert to the realities of power in the European states, was not to be swept away by paeans to the virtues of popular government. Accordingly, though the Geneva committee brought the work of the Sanitary Commission to the attention of those who were forming societies to aid the wounded, it steered well short of suggesting that Europeans need only follow where the Americans had already led. Like so many of his countrymen, Bowles mistakenly assumed that Europeans were only waiting to be taught about democracy by the Americans; ironically, the Europeans who learned best that "the people could be organized as effectively for relief as armies for war" were the Prussians.

The Signing of the Geneva Convention, a huge, formal painting by Charles-Edouard Armand-Dumaresq still hangs in Geneva's Town Hall; it depicts the twenty-six delegates to the 1864 International Congress. Gustave Moynier and General Dufour are in the center presiding over the proceedings, but by far the most imposing figure in this group portrait is Loeffler, the senior Prussian delegate. No doubt unintentionally, the artist's work cannot fail to underline the dominant role that Prussia was to play in the Red Cross movement from the moment of its inception. During his visit to Berlin in September, 1863, Dunant discovered that there had been no more fervent readers of *A Memory of Solferino* than Queen Augusta, Prince Charles, and Prince Henry of Reuss; both princes were leading figures in the recently revived Order of St. John of Jerusalem. More important, Dunant found that both King William and his war minister were well disposed toward both the formation of voluntary corps of nurses and the neutralization of medical personnel on the battlefield.[188] At both the 1863 Geneva conference and the 1864 International Congress, Loeffler and the other Prussian delegates had strongly supported all aspects of the Geneva proposals.

Unlike the French, whose generals refused to admit that there was anything the matter with their military medical service or to concede that volunteer nurses might be a useful addition to their army, the Prussians from the outset appreciated not only the potential benefits of additional help, but also the protection that neutrality would confer on their army surgeons and the wounded, as well as on the auxiliary nurses that they planned to organize. Whereas the would-be organizers of a French society spent the rest of the 1860s alternately wrestling with the intransigence of senior military officers and trying to make Paris rather than Geneva the home of the international movement, the Prussians simply got to work.[189] The Prussian society, unlike the French, enjoyed the full support of the army's general staff and soon became an integral part of what William H. McNeill has called "the Prussian way of war."[190] Devout Protestants such as Queen Augusta may have believed that Dunant was a messenger from God, but in Berlin it was the provident, not the providential, aspects of the Geneva proposals that ensured their warm welcome.

In *War and Charity*, Moynier and Appia enunciated the proposition that the provision of better treatment for sick and wounded soldiers "is a duty of conscience and humanity, which, by a happy coincidence, harmonizes with the acknowledged interest of the belligerents."[191] In these few words they summarized precisely what this chapter has endeavored to demonstrate: Although philanthropists may have been moved by pietist appeals to Christian conscience or by the utilitarian aspiration to create a more civilized world, the agreements of 1863–1864 could not have taken place unless those states most likely to go to war calculated that the provisions contained therein were in their own best interests. The revolution in communications helped both to provoke and to influence the result of this calculation, and thus it played an important role in the origins of the Red Cross. It is, of course, because this "happy coincidence" was only a coincidence, unique to the early 1860s, that these events set the stage for the great paradox of later Red Cross history: The continuing tension, verging at times on a tug-of-war, between those who saw the Geneva Convention as a first step on the road to building a higher civilization and those who perceived what useful services these volunteer organizations could render to the militaristic nationalism of late-nineteenth-century Europe.

✚ 2
The Delegates
of Humanity

AS DELEGATES RETURNED HOME to report to their governments on the outcome of the International Congress, Moynier and his colleagues remained in Geneva. No one could blame them for basking, however briefly, in the glow of success. After all, they had accomplished what many might have considered an impossible task: They had managed to secure a broad measure of international agreement for proposals that had originated with a mere subcommittee of a civic philanthropic society. A century later, after this agreement had been recognized as the first multilateral humanitarian convention, the Red Cross movement proudly hailed these events as a glorious triumph for the private and unofficial over the public and official elements in European society. This is, of course, an exaggeration: There was nothing private about General Dufour's reputation in European military circles, just as there was nothing unofficial about the support that came from the king and queen of Prussia or from the French emperor and empress. The invitations that went to governments were sent not by the committee of five, nor by the SGUP, but by the Swiss Federal Council. True, the Geneva committee had played an important role in promoting both the formation of aid societies and official recognition of the principle of neutrality, but its efforts might have been fruitless if they had not been directed to an audience that was ready to treat these proposals sympathetically.

If there was cause for satisfaction, there was also some reason to be apprehensive about the future. It remained to be seen how many governments would actually ratify the Convention and, more important, how many of those would observe its provisions on the battlefield. Not until another war broke out would the Geneva committee know the answer to this question. Equally uncertain at this point was the degree of success that their friends and associates would have in creating aid societies in their own countries or in securing official recognition for their activities. There was always a danger that the strongly emotional response to Dunant's book would prove transitory, in which case the cause of the wounded would have been no more than a fad among the social elite of Europe. *A Memory of Solferino* provided little enough in the way of direction to those who were engaged in setting up aid societies; it might persuade individuals that the wounded deserved better treatment, but there its usefulness stopped.

Moynier had already foreseen this deficiency and had attempted to remedy it. He decided to provide all those interested in the 1863 resolutions with additional written materials to explain the role that volunteer philanthropy could play in wartime. Thus the compendium that he had sent out prior to the International Congress, entitled *Secours aux blessés*, contained the reports that Appia and van de Velde had sent back to Geneva from the Schleswig War as well as a brief introduction to the publications and activities of the U.S. Sanitary Commission written by Dr. Maunoir. On the strength of these materials, Moynier had hoped that two parallel meetings would take place in August: While the diplomats were settling the text of the Convention at Town Hall, those interested in the formation and work of the aid societies would convene at the Athénée. The latter meeting, Moynier hoped, would discuss the relations that should obtain between a national aid society, the government of a country, and those responsible for organizing the army medical service. In addition, he hoped that it would address the question of the role of religious orders and of orders of chivalry (such as the Order of St. John and the Knights of Malta), in the work that the aid societies were planning to undertake. However, once the delegates arrived in Geneva, the official sessions at Town Hall so dominated proceedings that the Athénée meetings were quickly abandoned. Thus the very questions that Moynier hoped would be settled by the Geneva meeting remained not only unresolved but unaddressed.

In these circumstances, Moynier understandably looked for guidance to his colleague, Louis Appia, who had learned a great deal about aid to the wounded during the summer of 1864, first in Berlin and then behind the Prussian lines in Schleswig-Holstein. The other Genevan delegate, Captain van de Velde, did not have such a profitable experience on the Danish side; he was often treated with indifference and sometimes with outright hostility by stiff-necked military surgeons who would brook no interference from meddling foreigners. In any case, because the Danes immediately evacuated their wounded by boat to existing hospitals in larger centers of population, van de Velde had no real chance to observe how aid was provided to the wounded at or near the battlefield. By contrast, Appia's welcome, both in Berlin and at the front, could scarcely have been warmer. As he recounted in more than three dozen letters sent to the Geneva committee, he was given every opportunity not only to observe the organization of care for the wounded but also to propagandize on behalf of the resolutions passed at the 1863 conference. His final report, which ran to a hundred printed pages, naturally became a useful guide for everyone involved in the creation of national aid societies.[1]

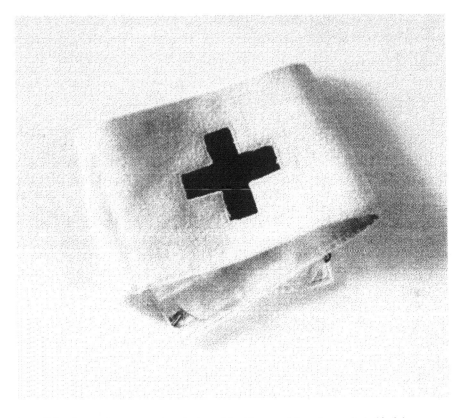

2.1   The first red cross armband, signed by Gustave Moynier on behalf of the Comité International. It was worn by Dr. Louis Appia during the Schleswig War in the summer of 1864.

Appia and the War of 1864

Appia's first stop was Berlin, where he explained his mission to the Prussian minister of war. After meeting members of the Berlin committee, he proceeded immediately to the front, where the commander, Marshal Wrangel, gave him blanket permission to go wherever he wished. Though Appia was an experienced military surgeon and had a small traveling kit with him, he made little use of it; instead, he found that several bottles of wine and a box of good cigars helped to gain him entrance to hospitals and storage depots and to promote conversations with individual officers and military physicians.[2] As a foreigner and a civilian, albeit one wearing a white armband with a red cross—the symbol established at the Geneva conference—Appia frequently needed an escort as he moved behind the Prussian lines in North Schleswig; this was sometimes provided by sympathetic officers, sometimes by high-ranking members of the aid committees. Although the Berlin committee coordinated assistance on a national basis, local committees in Hamburg and Magdeburg (the latter headed by Dr. Loeffler) also played a major role in the 1864 campaign. Appia also spent some time visiting the encampments of Prussia's ally, Austria, at nearby Kolding. Thorough, personable, and enthusiastic, Appia fulfilled his mission in an exemplary fashion and provided his colleagues in Geneva with useful information and revealing insights about the role that voluntary aid might play in wartime.

In *A Memory of Solferino*, Dunant had called for "noble and compassionate hearts . . . and chivalrous spirits" who would devote themselves to the philanthropic task of caring for the wounded; here in Schleswig-Holstein, Appia believed he had found them. The organizers of the entire voluntary endeavor, he soon discovered, were the aristocrats of the Knights of St. John of Jerusalem and the Knights of Malta; the field workers were mostly members of religious confraternities, male and female, Protestant and Catholic, loaned for the occasion, as it were, by their superiors; to their efforts were joined those of the committees of civilian volunteers, who raised money, provided supplies, and generally encouraged the civilian population to regard helping the wounded as part of their patriotic duty. Appia soon became convinced that the success of voluntary assistance in Prussia depended upon the philanthropic ideals of the elite, the religious dedication of the stretcher-bearers and nurses, and the patriotic generosity of the urban population.

The Order of St. John, revived in Brandenburg (Prussia) in 1812 as a Protestant order of chivalry, included some of the most exalted figures in the kingdom. After the grand master, Prince Henry XIII of Reuss, and several other male members of the royal family, its most prominent members were Count von Arnim Boytzenburg and Count Othon von Stolberg-Wernigorode, both of whom were also members of the Berlin central committee of the Prussian Society for the Relief of Wounded Soldiers.

Appia first met Stolberg during his visit to Berlin and subsequently observed him at the front, where he directed the relief efforts of the Order during the War of 1864. Since midcentury, the Order had founded and operated more than two dozen hospitals. In 1859, when war had threatened to involve Prussia, the Order was ready to supply a one hundred-bed mobile hospital as well as a considerable sum of money, and it had arranged with religious confraternities for a supply of male and female nurses and orderlies; as it happened, its efforts were not required. Five years later, the Order was more than ready to meet the challenge of the occasion: Count Stolberg hastened to the front to organize field hospitals at Altona, Flensburg, and near the besieged Danish fortress at Duppel; he also organized and equipped a supply depot at Flensburg and obtained the services of an extremely distinguished surgeon, Friedrich von Esmarch of Kiel, as an unofficial consultant to the hospital at Flensburg. Stolberg's duties were primarily administrative, but several other members of the Order took personal risks on the battlefield.

2.2   A prominent member of the Prussian branch of the Order of St. John, Count Othon von Stolberg-Wernigorode directed the work of the Prussian Society for the Relief of Wounded Soldiers during the Schleswig War in 1864.

According to Appia, "They were not afraid to expose themselves to enemy fire wherever their presence could prove useful, whether it was to lead some wounded man off the battlefield, or to bring refreshment to those in the advance posts."[3] The Knights of Malta were also represented in Schleswig-Holstein in 1864, although they figured less prominently than did the members of the Order of St. John.

If Appia was impressed by the organizational abilities and dedication of these philanthropic aristocrats, he was positively enraptured by the work of the volunteer nurses and orderlies from various religious foundations. Altogether there were 158 of them behind the Prussian and Austrian lines, most of them nurses in the various hospitals set up to care for the wounded. The majority of the female nurses—77 out of 110—were Catholic nuns from various orders; there were also thirty-eight Protestant deaconesses from the Bethany community in Berlin and the Kaiserwerth Institution in Rhenish

Prussia.[4] Ten of the forty male volunteers were also Catholics, most of them Alexian fathers whose novitiate included some training in practical medicine. However, it was the twenty-eight young men from Protestant charitable institutions on whom Appia lavished most of his attention and much of his praise. Twelve of these were deacons-in-training at the Duisburg philanthropic establishment near Kaiserwerth, and the remainder were from its counterpart, the Rauhehaus Institution in Hamburg. According to Appia, these young men best exemplified precisely the qualities that he and the others members of the Geneva committee had in mind when they thought of volunteers on the battlefield: practicality, courage, and modesty.

An evangelical Protestant foundation, the Duisburg Institution trained young men who wished to devote their lives to serving the poor, the sick, needy children, and prisoners. Its admission policy specified that only those powerfully motivated by the strength of their faith yet humble in manner and without any worldly ambitions whatsoever would be selected for a training that was as rigorous as it was relentless. Soon after hostilities broke out, a dozen of them were sent to various locations in North Schleswig; two happened to arrive as a battle was taking place and immediately helped to transport and care for several seriously wounded soldiers from both armies. The surgeons later told Appia that they had been of real service and praised their modesty, devotion, bravery, and inventiveness and also "their seemingly inexhaustible liberality [that] became almost proverbial in the region; there was nothing that they did not know how to find and have ready to supply whenever it was needed."[5] When he met two of the Duisburg men several days later, Appia found their silence, lack of pretension, and unassuming civilian dress inspiring. "It did not require much perspicacity to recognize [he wrote] that the sole force that sustained them, that gave them perseverance and self-sacrifice, was not enthusiasm, but *charity* drawn from the source of a profound and living faith."[6] The Duisburg students even wore a white armband with a cross on it, although their cross was black rather than red; Appia assured his Geneva colleagues that it would not be difficult to persuade them to change its color.

What Appia admired most about the sixteen brothers from the Hamburg Rauhehaus was the fact that they risked their lives by going onto the battlefield itself, even while the guns were still firing. They had decided in advance that whenever serious fighting broke out, they would place themselves at the disposal of the Knights of St. John and would work as stretcher-bearers for the field ambulances operated by the Order.[7] Appia himself sketched them at work and later turned the sketch into an illustration for his *Report*. Their courage and devotion, he argued, proved that the idea of civilian volunteers "was no chimera."[8] In *Secours aux blessés* he wrote: "No, gentlemen, we were not dreaming when we expressed the hope that men who were not incorporated in the army, without uniforms, and wearing only a simple armband, could, without compromising military discipline, go right onto the battle-

Transport des blessés par les Chevaliers de S͎ Jean et les frères du Rauhen-Haus

2.3   In 1864, Louis Appia sketched this scene, which shows several Brothers from the Hamburg Rauhehaus working as stretcher-bearers for the Prussian field ambulances operated by the Order of St. John during the Schleswig War. It was probably such a spectacle that led him to describe charitable volunteers as "delegates of humanity."

field, and there work usefully to relieve the wounded and give them first aid. This alleged dream has in fact happened, it has passed from the realm of the imagination to that of history."[9] Appia pointed out that the Geneva committee could learn much from the deacons of Duisburg and the brothers of the Rauhehaus about how to train and equip volunteers who would be truly useful on the battlefield. One of the brothers, for example, pointed out that in addition to bandages and dressings for wounds, they usually had available all kinds of small, simple items that armies never thought necessary to supply to the troops, such as needles, thread, buttons, writing paper, and envelopes.

Reflecting on the seemingly universal gratitude and respect for the work of these volunteers among soldiers and officers alike, Appia wrote:

> The utility of civilian work for the army has been indisputable; [there is also] the almost universal conviction that in a great war the State could never provide adequately the care that would be required by the victims that it would produce; this insufficiency is recognized, sometimes even proclaimed in principle, and the most military spirit is obliged to bow before the evidence of the experiment that has been carried out; even hardened veterans [*de vieilles moustaches*] acknowledge the usefulness of the work of the modest brothers of Duisburg or of the Rauhehaus; it is true that these last have above them the captain of the armies . . . the

invisible commander-in-chief of this great army always at war that we call the human race.[10]

In Appia's mind, bodies of volunteers wearing the red cross armband would constitute a kind of volunteer army of Christian charity that would parallel the official military organizations. Where soldiers owed unquestioning obedience to their commanding officer, the volunteers would acknowledge the Christian God as their supreme commander; where armies filled their storage depots with weapons and ammunition, the volunteers would fill their storehouses with blankets and bandages; where ordinary soldiers were trained to kill and wound, the volunteers would be trained to provide care and comfort. From observing the brothers of the Rauhehaus, Appia had come to realize that the most useful function that the volunteers could perform was one midway between that of almoner and that of physician, providing both material assistance and moral support to the sick, the wounded, and the dying. He believed that this role could best be performed by persons in religious orders who were, after all, trained for this sort of work; they were already accustomed to subordination; and they routinely kept everything in good order.

Finally, Appia described the organization and activity of the Hamburg committee, which he saw as a model that the Genevans ought to encourage others to follow. He found much to praise: Its spontaneity, independence, liberality, and pragmatic mode of operation all impressed him. Its great success he attributed largely to its prudence; thanks to its discretion, it enjoyed both the benevolent protection of the military authorities and free access to military hospitals.[11] Because the committee had worked directly with the military authorities and had treated them with respect, there had been no conflicts, even though this was the first time that the army had cooperated with civilian assistance.

In addition to praising the record of the Hamburg committee, Appia drew from its experience three important lessons for the future. The first and most obvious was that aid committees should collect as much money as possible in advance of any conflict, so that they could begin their work with a well-stocked treasury. The second was that they should prepare in advance a sort of "battle plan," so that they would know what goods were available and their price as well as the probable cost of transporting goods to wherever they were likely to be needed. The third lesson of the Schleswig War was that committees should appreciate that they would need to send to the front delegates, or *chargés d'affaires*, who would be responsible for organizing the distribution of supplies and for preventing abuses. If all aid committees became as well organized and prepared as the Hamburg committee, he implied, the future of voluntary assistance would be assured.

Appia concluded his *Report* with a stirring invocation of the role of charity in wartime:

What, gentlemen, is the essence of all our work? To reduce, to mitigate the sufferings of war by works of charity. Everyone understands that in our era war is not fought to make the enemy suffer, but only to put him beyond being able to inflict damage, and that consequently, the means of relieving [suffering] must be accorded a large place; but, on the other hand, no matter how much good one would wish to see philanthropy accomplish, the exigencies of politics do not permit us to interfere, for humanitarian reasons, with the success of war, once it has broken out. To humanize war—if it is not a contradiction to bring such things together—that is our mandate. Let us proclaim loudly our deep regret, our sorrow that we cannot do more; let us protest against the great collective iniquity called war, an iniquity which is only one of the forms of evil in the world; but after this unequivocal protest, taking war for what it is, let us unite our efforts to relieve its distress; let us openly and energetically demand that above the flag of victory shall be flown the white flag and red cross of charity![12]

Appia's "protest against the great collective iniquity called war" was, it must be said, largely rhetorical; as we have seen, such sentiments formed no part of the 1863 resolutions or of the Geneva Convention itself. Although feelings of revulsion against war itself were certainly held by many who participated in the enterprise, their primary purpose in forming aid societies was not to outlaw war or to promote less violent means of resolving disputes among nations but rather to relieve the distress presently associated with war. And even here there were clear priorities: The international agreements concerned only the plight of soldiers; sailors were not yet included; refugees and other civilian casualties of war were left to fend entirely for themselves. In other words, only certain victims of war were eligible to seek protection under the flag of charity.

Anyone reading Appia's report would have taken away from it three or four simple propositions about the initial aims and expectations of the organizers of the Red Cross. First, it was clear that they were opposed not to war itself but to the unnecessary suffering that wars caused to those who fought them. In accepting what Appia called "the exigencies of politics," supporters of the Red Cross were tacitly accepting that, at least for the moment, war was an unpleasant but necessary instrument of state policy. Second, it was obvious that Appia shared Dunant's belief that there was a special role for the social elite in the organization of charitable activity; his comments about the orders of chivalry make it clear that he ascribed to them a particularly keen understanding of the obligations of charity. Third, his emphasis on the personal qualities and training of the men from Duisburg and the Rauhehaus suggested that only individuals such as these, whose religious commitment was profound, would be able to fill the difficult role of the civilian volunteer. Finally, his comments about the Hamburg committee indicated that enthusiastic citizens should not direct relief efforts in wartime nor venture onto a battlefield with only an armband for protection, but rather they should provide the money and supplies necessary to sustain an enterprise best left to people like the Knights of St. John and the deacons of Duisburg.

War and Charity

In May, 1865, the Prussian society, anxious in the wake of the Schleswig campaign to make whatever improvements were appropriate, announced an essay competition. The subject was, "How private charity should organize the assistance it can provide to sick and wounded soldiers in the field," and entrants were asked to draw upon the experience of recent wars in shaping their opinions. This was precisely the subject that Moynier had hoped would be discussed in Geneva by the national societies' delegates while the diplomats were arguing over the text of the Convention. Since they had not done so, and because the subject was of such vital importance, he decided to compose such an essay himself, or rather to collaborate with Appia, whose Schleswig experience fitted him ideally to write the sections on the practical work of relief. Moynier himself would write the theoretical and historical chapters and review the work of the 1863 conference and the 1864 congress. The finished product, a treatise of some four hundred pages entitled *War and Charity* (*La guerre et la charité*), was published in Geneva early in 1867. Several copies were sent to Berlin for the judges to read; the remainder were sent to those national committees that had already been established and to those individuals who were actively engaged in trying to form them.

Moynier intended the historical chapters of *War and Charity* to establish the inadequacy of official medical services, to demonstrate the need for auxiliary assistance, and to describe the recent history of volunteer aid. Naturally he used the occasion to defend the enterprise against the critics and skeptics who had cast doubt upon various aspects of the Red Cross idea and especially to answer those who had questioned whether voluntary intervention was appropriate in an area where responsibility was generally acknowledged to lie first with the military authorities and ultimately with governments. Many of these objections had been raised in speeches, pamphlets, and articles in newspapers and journals; with his typical thoroughness, Moynier had them all before him as he wrote the first four chapters of *War and Charity*. Fortunately for him, Nightingale had chosen not to make public her criticisms, so her opposition did not require (or receive) explicit acknowledgment. Of the public critics, the most formidable was, of course, Dr. Chenu, who had urged in print that philanthropists should be kept away from military affairs and restrained from interfering in the state's business.

In his response, Moynier did not dispute that aiding sick and wounded soldiers was the state's responsibility; indeed, he even quoted Dr. Chenu's very words on this subject.[13] He acknowledged that "all civilized nations" had already done much in the field of army sanitary reform and that "the most laudable endeavors are being made to realize schemes to afford prompt and efficacious assistance."[14] He particularly noted the contribution of medical officers to this endeavor: "Let us boldly assert that, if the sanitary administration still leaves something to be desired, the fault is not due to the men in whom it is personified, for we well know that they have done all that it was possible for them to do."[15] Ignoring Chenu's proposals for the further improvement of army sanitary services—which made it clear that the agenda for army sanitary reform was still far from complete—Moynier quickly moved on to put the question, "If, notwithstanding so many energetic and generous efforts, there is still much suffering for which there is no sufficient relief, must we not admit that the medical staff has found itself in the presence of obstacles which its own powers have been quite unable to surmount, and that the very nature of human affairs imposes limits to the beneficent activity of constituted authority?" Replying immediately to his own question, he concluded that "a State, even the most vigilant, is incapable of satisfying its exigencies."[16]

Moynier went on to assert that "*several* reasons induce us to think that, in a great war, no army sanitary service can ever suffice to accomplish its most imperative duties."[17] Here he advanced only two: First, financial and practical constraints, which would inevitably limit the size of an army's medical service; second, the primary obligation of commanders to conquer the enemy, a fact that would always relegate care of the sick and wounded to a secondary consideration. Hence, he argued, a state monopoly over the care of sick and wounded soldiers cannot be justified; society derives no advantage from it because it "attains its object very imperfectly."[18] Predictably, he concluded that because the state cannot fulfill all of its obligations to soldiers, it has a duty to allow others—that is, organized volunteers—to do what it is unable to do by itself.

In these few lines Moynier provided the only significant theoretical explanation advanced during the 1860s to justify the formation of national aid (Red Cross) societies. The argument was not without its flaws. For one thing, it assumed that army sanitary reform would be unable to make substantial progress in the future because of finite administrative and financial limits. Moynier offered no evidence to show that those limits had already been reached or indeed would soon be reached if the additional improvements advocated by Chenu were pursued. Moreover, he did not explain why the same citizens that he assumed would not pay higher taxes to support an expanded army medical service would nevertheless gladly contribute to a philanthropic society that intended to pay for similar improvements. (With the benefit of hindsight one can say that he may well have been right on this score, but at the time there was no evidence to support this proposition.) Even his argument about the obligations of commanders was questionable: As Florence Nightingale was to argue, a commander who paid attention to military hygiene could make an army healthier and hence put it in a better position to conquer the enemy.

War and Charity did not refute satisfactorily the argument that looking after soldiers was the business of governments and armies, not philanthropists. Nowhere did Moynier and Appia explain *why* forming philanthropic societies would do more to aid wounded soldiers than exerting pressure on governments to improve army medical and sanitary services. Nowhere did they attempt to answer Nightingale's fear—expressed in her response to Dunant—that the existence of voluntary societies might well "render war more easy" by helping governments to cover the extraordinary costs of caring for soldiers in wartime. Indeed, the argument advanced in *War and Charity* is somewhat spurious because it assumed that the *only* choice to be made was between forming voluntary aid societies or doing nothing at all; it never addressed the position taken by Chenu and Nightingale: that forming aid societies was not necessarily the *best* way to assist the cause of the wounded.

It was much easier for Moynier to respond to a different sort of criticism—the argument that those opposed to war on moral grounds should resist all attempts to reduce its misery. A French physician called Dr. Diday had taken precisely this position in a letter to the *Gazette Médicale de Lyon*, asking, "Is it logical, is it prudent, is it truly philanthropical, to accept as a necessary evil a calamity which one ought to, and which one could, avoid? . . . We must leave to war all its horrors, if this be the only way to open the eyes of those who order it, and those who submit to it. . . . Let us not encourage the scourge by an organization, every offering to which would be a vote against the return of a general peace."[19]

Moynier had plenty of arguments in reply. In the first place, he pointed out, the same logic could be used to call for the suppression of the army medical service itself. Second, he took issue with Diday's implicit assumption that in this case the end justified the means. "We do not admit," Moynier replied loftily, "that charity can conform itself to systematic inaction."[20] Third, he turned Diday's argument about the horrors of war into an argument *for* the existence of aid societies, as he had done already at the 1863 conference:

> I am persuaded that, in organizing succor for the wounded, in addressing fervent appeals in their favor to the various nations, in exciting pity by the relation of their miseries, and in laying bare, with a view to help our cause, the lamentable spectacle of a field of battle, in unveiling the terrible realities of war, and in proclaiming, in the name of charity, that which policy has often an interest to keep concealed, we shall do more for the disarmament of nations than those who have recourse to economical arguments, or to the declamations of a sterile sentimentalism.[21]

In these words Moynier revealed the very essence of his commitment to the Red Cross idea and the real reason why he was blind to the objections of Chenu and Nightingale: For him, the object of the exercise was not only to provide additional relief to the wounded but to use charity as a weapon in the long struggle against war itself. Just as philanthropists and social investigators had aroused the nineteenth-century public against the evils of prostitution, child labor, and a host of other causes, so Moynier believed that aid committees could, in time, arouse public opinion against the waging of war.[22] Such a course would give real meaning to what Appia had called their "protest against the great collective iniquity called war." A similar conviction was also expressed by Léonce de Cazenove, one of the founders of the French national aid society, in his own reply to Diday: "[Aid committees] will have statistics, unanswerable in their exactness and their veracity; and when the partisans of war shall see those long lists of dead and wounded, of amputations, mutilations, and disfigurements, perhaps they will begin to reflect on, and to recognize, their cruel folly."[23] Far from reproaching Moynier for naiveté—an unpardonable exercise in hindsight—one should rather be impressed by the extent of his faith in the power of reason and moral conviction to change the world. Looking out on the world from Geneva in the mid-1860s, it seemed to him that, just as the SGUP had made the city a more civilized place to live in, so the Convention and the aid societies could make the larger world less violent and more humane. It need scarcely be said that the events of the next four decades would give him repeated cause to question whether the world was as ready as he had hoped to repudiate war as an instrument of state policy.

Having done their best to reply to critics of the whole scheme, Moynier and Appia devoted the remainder of *War and Charity* to discussing the role of the aid committees and the work of the volunteers themselves. Here the thorniest issue was whether committees would be able to send their volunteers onto the field of battle while fighting was taking place. Several voices had spoken out against this idea at the international meetings held in 1863 and 1864. Moynier briefly acknowledged these objections in his treatment of these events, yet it is clear that he and Appia remained adamantly committed to the idea. In chapter two of *War and Charity*, there is a lengthy description of a typical battlefield situation, written to persuade readers that volunteers will always be necessary:

The battle is raging, volleys of musketry succeed one another, and after each a fresh rank of these courageous fellows is seen to fall, strewing the ground and filling the trenches. But how can we describe the field of dead and wounded, when the furious discharges of heavy shot begin to plow broad and bloody furrows through the compact mass of friends and foes? . . . The stretcher-bearers (of the field hospital Corps) have bravely taken away wounded men from under the very guns of the enemy, and have removed them to a less exposed place; the surgeons are at their posts to apply the first dressings; but the battle continues, the bearers have to pass a distance of a quarter or even half a league, between the thickest of the fight and the first hospital station, carrying a burthen of from 150lbs. to 200lbs. weight. How many of these journeys can each bearer make? Eight to ten, at the most; his arms begin to grow weak, and perhaps the day is already declining; the night approaches, 100, it may be 200, wounded men are likely to remain during a long night, without assistance, on frozen or damp ground which will become their grave! Hospital orderlies, surgeons, everybody has performed prodigies of valor, devotion, and energy; but alas! human strength has limits; it is dangerous to remain there, and, in proportion as one labors, the work seems mercilessly to increase.

But, look! young men, strong, vigorous, and unassuming, are running forward, led on by a generous enthusiasm, and by a few noble chiefs animated by chivalrous valor. These are neither soldiers nor employees of the medical corps. They are come to relieve for a time the wearied arms of the bearers. "It is for us now to help you," they cry; "you have done what seemed impossible, let us also do something to exercise a little of the strength and courage such as you employ every day! For mercy's sake, let there be no distinction here between the official and the unofficial; nevertheless, if you demand our titles and our rights, we are the official delegates of Humanity, who regard you with eyes full of emotion and sympathy, and who wish to supply your momentary insufficiency, and afterwards we retire into the shade. We are volunteers; officers, surgeons, pray let us pass."[24]

This vision of the "delegates of humanity" as vigorous young men led on by a few noble chiefs is easily recognized as a sort of rhapsody on Appia's experience in Schleswig. (Indeed the evocative romanticism of the whole passage suggests that it came from Appia's pen; Moynier's style is much more prosaic.) That they chose to include such a passage in the face of the objections that had already been raised against the "intrusion" of volunteers into an area of military jurisdiction demonstrates their resolute, not to say defiant, attachment to the idea that the battlefield itself was the best place to dispense the kind of charity that they had in mind. It might have served their cause better had they confined themselves to recording precisely what Appia had seen in Schleswig, for the Knights of St. John and their young Protestant helpers were scarcely self-appointed "delegates of humanity" who arrived on the battlefield asking to be allowed to pass; on the contrary, they were part of a system of auxiliary aid organized by Count Stolberg, who ensured that the volunteers went where they were needed and did nothing to hinder the functioning of the army.

Inevitably, opponents of civilian interference in military affairs seized upon these ill-considered paragraphs in *War and Charity* as evidence that volunteers—these self-appointed "delegates of humanity"—could not be trusted and indeed that on the battlefield they might be more of a headache than a blessing. The French military surgeon Léon Le Fort, for example, having quoted the passage in question, observed dryly,

Doubtless this is ingeniously put, and written in a lively style, but if we come down to the level of practical common sense, I presume that no one of military experience would recommend the admission on a battlefield of a corps, not wanting in bravery certainly—that is a cheap commodity—but deficient in that coolness which characterizes the trained soldier. . . . Excited by the sound of battle, the volunteer is intoxicated with courage; but this feverish excitement is absent, and it is imperatively necessary that it should be absent, in the military surgeon, who must maintain coolness and composure in the execution of his difficult mission. Fancy the ambulances of the voluntary associations inadvertently exposed to fire by some retrograde manoeuvre! Are we quite sure that the volunteer nurses would not create a panic, a disaster common to all armies? What security would there be that the volunteer ambulances would not block the road of the batteries, and caissons, and ammunition trains?[25]

Le Fort's doubts and fears were widely shared by military officers and surgeons; the members of the Geneva committee would soon discover that not all those who cared about the wounded saw voluntary associations as the best way to ameliorate their condition.

The Austro-Prussian War of 1866

So far, fortune had smiled upon the Geneva committee; both international meetings had been successful, governments were beginning to ratify the Convention, and national aid committees were taking shape in many countries. Doubtless Moynier and Appia believed that *War and Charity* would serve as a kind of blueprint for the work of aiding the wounded. Yet even before they had finished the manuscript the pace of events began to quicken, and it became apparent that the Geneva committee was no longer in such complete control of the enterprise as it had been in 1863–1864. Other bodies, with their own agendas and issues, appeared on the scene, and the Genevans were forced to respond to these as best they could. Moynier, for example, felt compelled to defend his conception of the proper peacetime work of aid societies against new and dangerous ideas that were advanced at a meeting in Bern of the International Association for the Advancement of Social Science in August, 1865. This congress had invited reports on the extent to which such societies could, in peacetime, provide assistance to the civilian population in the event of disasters such as floods and epidemics. Clearly upset that another body was venturing into what he regarded as "his" terrain—a sacred trust, as it were, from the international community that had met in Geneva—and fearing the possible consequences for the work at hand of such a drastic change in emphasis, Moynier assembled a score of representatives of aid societies in Bern and did his best to quash this unwelcome interference from outsiders. In his view, the aid societies should limit their work entirely to relieving the evils of war and should resist any temptation to broaden their field of activity to include civilian disaster relief, lest "in time, these secondary activities could acquire a certain prejudicial preponderance. . . . Some can deal with epidemics, others with floods, yet others with storms and fires. Mankind will be better protected in this way than if a single entity undertakes to protect it from all these dangers."[26] Much more welcome than the meeting in Bern was the news from Paris, where plans were already afoot for a world exposition to be held in 1867; the French national committee had written to Geneva proposing that the aid societies put on a display of materiel used in assisting sick and wounded soldiers. Before further plans for the Paris Exposition could take shape, however, war broke out again in Europe, and the energies of several aid societies were entirely taken up with relieving wounded soldiers in the wake of real battles.

Anxious to put an end to its long rivalry with Austria for control over the future of Germany, Prussia declared war on the Habsburg monarchy in June, 1866. Writing about the Prussian "military revolution" of the 1860s, Paul Kennedy observes, "The real point about the Prussian [military] system was not that it was free of errors, but that the general staff carefully studied its past mistakes and readjusted training, organization, and weapons accordingly."[27] Part of this continuing reorganization included attending to everything that could maximize the efficient use of manpower and resources, including, of course, care for the wounded. The Schleswig War had convinced Prussia's war ministry that a voluntary aid society could indeed play a useful role in supplementing the personnel and supplies of the army medical corps, and after the war was over the government took steps to bring the Prussian aid society more closely under its control. In April, 1865, the king and queen of Prussia extended royal patronage to the society; this measure was followed, within a year, by a decree that granted the society the legal status of a corporation (meaning that it could carry out commercial and financial transactions, own property, and protect its rights at law).[28] When it became apparent that war with Austria was imminent, the government took three more important steps. First, it declared that the Berlin central committee was to be regarded as "the central organ of public charity"; all civilian assistance to the military forces was to be channeled only through the national aid society.[29] Second, in approving a new statute for the society, the government provided for the appointment to its central committee of three commissioners, high state officials who were to "give the society the benefit of their advice, ensure that its activity conformed to the needs of the military administration and operated in a manner that was useful to the state military hospitals."[30] Third, the Prussian government created the new position of commissary general and inspector of the voluntary hospital service and appointed to this position none other than Count Stolberg, who had organized the relief work of the Knights of St. John during the Schleswig War.[31] According to Thomas Evans, author of the standard work on the medical and sanitary aspects of the War of 1866, Count Stolberg became "the medium between the relief society and the medical bureau of the army, and through his solicitude and vigilance, the committee was always made acquainted with the movements of the troops, and its attention always directed in good time to the points where assistance was urgent."[32]

The cumulative result of these innovations was to accord the Prussian aid society a unique quasiofficial status that made it utterly different from any mere philanthropic or charitable society. In effect, the government had designated this one society as the only channel of communication between the people and the army, had taken considerable responsibility for the integrity of the society's charitable operations, and on this basis had decided to divulge to its leaders secret details about troop movements and the likely location of major battles. This was already some considerable way from the volunteer battlefield charity that Louis Appia had so much admired in Schleswig. To be sure, the 1863 conference resolutions had called upon aid committees to put themselves in communication with governments and had called upon governments to extend protection to the committees. The Prussians, in the throes of their military revolution, had swiftly found appropriate ways of responding to this challenge. The founders of the Red Cross set out to civilize war through organized charity, but they would soon discover that organized war on the Prussian model was much more likely to militarize charity.

The wartime operations of the Berlin central committee greatly impressed American physician Thomas Evans:

> On all sides local relief societies were organized, which attached themselves to the mother society; and gifts in money and kind were sent forward to Berlin from all parts of the monarchy. When I visited the Prussian Capital—the war was then at its height—the central depot of this institution was established in one of the most opulent quarters of the city; but the premises appeared to me a great deal too limited for the use to which they were destined. Offerings had arrived there in abundance, enormous boxes obstructed the passages, objects of every nature, mattresses, oilcloths, instruments, bandages, etc., etc., were laying about without order on the stairways. In the same room persons were busy in receiving the supplies which arrived and in shipping others to the field of war; the workmen who packed labored side by side with those who were unpacking. They were nailing and shouting, the noise of the hammers mingled with the voices of superior officials, who were replying to those coming and going; orders and demands were made on all sides, and at times even animated discussions arose.[33]

All this activity at headquarters meant that the Prussian aid society was able to send convoy after convoy to the two major theaters of war, which were in Bohemia and Bavaria. The Prussian government, anxious to further the work of the central committee, had granted it free use of the railways, the telegraph, and the postal service. Owing to congestion on the railways, not all of the supplies reached their destinations in a timely fashion, but that was scarcely the fault of the Berlin committee. Some shipments of provisions spoiled while waiting in railway stations; one hopes that this loss did not include the four tons of ice that the committee sent for use in the field hospitals![34] According to Dr. Evans, "It would have been easy to have sent the shipments of the Society to Prague, by organizing a transport service on the Elbe; but unfortunately the Saxon commander of the fortress of Koenigstein, a fortress which commanded the river, had declared that he would sink every transport that passed under the guns of the place."[35] (Saxony had not yet signed the Geneva Convention.) Saxon soldiers may well have suffered as a result of the delays; many of them were in Prussian field hospitals in Bohemia, tended by army surgeons and nurses who doubtless could have used these supplies.

No doubt it suited the larger purposes of the Prussians to ensure that the soldiers of the Habsburg army were treated with humanity. The war was being fought, it should be recalled, not to destroy Austria but rather to shrink its influence on German affairs: At its conclusion, Austria was neither occupied nor forced to pay an indemnity, but only to cede Venetia to Italy and withdraw from the North German Confederation.[36] For the Prussian government to live up to its signature on the Convention was therefore good politics as well as the fulfillment of a moral obligation. Prussian military medical personnel routinely treated enemy sick and wounded along with their own. When Evans toured the field hospitals, he found that "there were always two and even three times as many Austrians as Prussians," and he noted with satisfaction that the Berlin central committee had "sent repeatedly considerable sums of money to the Austrian relief societies, particularly that of Prague."[37] Naturally, the Knights of the Order of St. John played a big role in the society's work; they managed its supply depots and kept Berlin informed of their requirements for provisions and medical supplies.

The Prussian aid society also provided extensive catering services for troops in transit from the fronts. These usually took the form of buffets established at main railway stations. Evans visited one such at Pardubitz, a major junction on the line from Dresden to Vienna:

> From eight to ten thousand men were in garrison there, and towards the end of July the military hospitals of the place were crowded with cholera patients. At this important point the society had established a principal depot which was able to supply the hospitals with everything necessary for their sick and wounded, and with all the food suitable for convalescents. In addition it had fixed in the railway station one of these *buffets* of which I speak, in order to be better able to distribute its help to the troops that passed, or were temporarily stationed there. It gave daily to each soldier, convalescent or suffering, beef soup, meat, a large glass of wine, a small glass of cognac, with sugar or fresh water, bread, cigars, and, in the morning, a cup of coffee and sweetened bread. From the month of May to July, the number of soldiers passing through Pardubitz, and assisted by the society amounted, on the average, to three hundred daily.[38]

It would be erroneous to conclude, however, that the aid society was nothing more than an impromptu catering service for the Prussian army. In addition to sending medical supplies to the fronts, the society established temporary hospitals along the railway lines, where those too ill to continue their journey were tended; it also distributed medical supplies and provisions to the overcrowded hospitals of Berlin and other large centers throughout Prussia. Nor did it limit its definition of comfort for the sick and wounded to food and dressings; the city's booksellers and publishers were solicited to donate "such books as might enable the sick and wounded to support their sufferings more patiently, by affording them attractive and profitable reading," and a special committee of academics, booksellers, and teachers was established to sort and distribute the items donated. Here again the society, bearing in mind the polyglot nature of the Habsburg army, was careful to ensure that books sent to hospitals where there were enemy wounded included titles in languages other than German.[39]

Prussian treatment of enemy wounded is all the more impressive when it is recalled that when the war began Austria had not yet signed the Geneva Convention. In the early months of 1866, when it became clear that war between Prussia and Austria was probable, the Geneva committee tried its best—acting through the Swiss Federal Council and the good offices of a number of French diplomats—to secure the speedy adherence of Austria and Russia, but to no avail. Both these empires took the position, legally absurd but politically understandable, that ratification of the Convention was tantamount to declaring that their military medical services were inadequate. Moynier fumed at what he regarded as their ignorance and irresponsibility, but he could do nothing to change the situation.[40] On the day that hostilities began, Prince Henry of Reuss, president of the Berlin central committee, informed Moynier that Prussia intended to apply the principles of the Convention whether or not Austria had agreed to do so and that the king had given Prussian commanders orders to this effect. The prince went on to ask that the Geneva committee publish this news, "so that Europe is aware that at least Prussia is firmly decided to respect humanitarian principles even if its adversary does not believe it is in a position to do the same. Public opinion will be our judge."[41] Accordingly, all Prussian military medical personnel, as well as members of the stretcher-bearer corps attached to each regiment, wore the red cross armband, and military hospitals flew the Red Cross flag. Supply convoys organized by the aid society also bore the Red Cross emblem, and the directors of its depots and field hospitals also wore the armband. This was the first full observance in wartime conditions of the provisions of Article 7 of the Geneva Convention.

On the Austrian side, by contrast, the Red Cross flag was nowhere to be seen. The Austrian army played by the pre-1864 rules: They took prisoner a Prussian army surgeon and, whenever it was necessary to retreat, they abandoned their own wounded, assuming that the Prussians would do likewise. The Austrian Patriotic Society sprang back to life when hostilities began, but, after having been dormant since 1859, it was forced to improvise everything and had difficulty communicating with the military authorities. Its personnel did not, of course, wear the red cross armband. Three weeks after their disastrous defeat at the battle of Koeniggratz, however, with thousands of Austrian wounded in Prussian hands, the Austrians finally relented and ratified the Geneva Convention.[42]

With Austria and Prussia at war, it is scarcely surprising that the fledgling Italian kingdom attempted to wrest control of Venice and its hinterland from the Habsburg monarchy. The Italian dimension of the war is noteworthy here for three reasons. First, the terrible loss of life that ensued when the Austrian fleet sunk several Italian ships at Lissa underlined the fact that the Geneva Convention needed to be broadened to include war at sea; literally hundreds of Italian sailors drowned who might otherwise have survived. Second, the efforts of the Milan central committee to attract assistance from the aid societies of neutral nations revealed that there were different ways to interpret Article 5 of the 1863 resolutions: The Italians sought to organize additional support from neutral societies even before hostilities began, whereas Moynier took the view that such an appeal was premature and ought to wait until real need had been demonstrated. Naturally there were those who pointed out that unnecessary deaths might occur in the interval; the whole episode underlined the need to spell out more clearly the channels of communication among the societies of neutral and belligerent nations. The third interesting incident on the Italian front took place after the Italian armies had been halted by the Austrians at Custozza and Garibaldi raised a volunteer force with the intention of liberating the city of Trent from Austrian control. The exploits of this force provided Louis Appia, who was a passionate admirer of Garibaldi, with an unexpected opportunity to play the Samaritan of the battlefield, just as Dunant had done at Solferino.

Appia's brother, George, a Protestant minister in Florence, apparently decided to embark on a mission to the wounded as soon as Italy declared war.[43] When his offers of help were (for unknown reasons) turned down by the Milan committee to aid the wounded, he traveled to Geneva to persuade his brother to join him. Louis, unwell, was eventually persuaded to join this unofficial mission. Armed only with his medical bag and a letter of introduction from General Dufour—one suspects that Moynier refused to give him one from the Geneva committee—Louis Appia nevertheless decided to make their enterprise a little more official by having a local tailor make them knapsacks and armbands bearing the Red Cross emblem. (So much for his concern that Article 7 of the Convention be strictly observed!) Scarcely had he and his party, which by now had grown to four, been received by Garibaldi when news came that many wounded volunteers, defeated by the Austrians at Bezzeccia, were stranded without surgeons or medical equipment in the Tiarno valley. Appia and his squadron of volunteer assistants hastened to the Tiarno, where they cared for the wounded as best they could for more than forty-eight hours. Then they helped to evacuate them to Storo, where surgeons and supplies were available.

The episode is worth recalling only because Appia was himself a founding member of the Geneva committee and would continue as a member until his death in 1898. The Tiarno exploit, when set alongside the praise he lavished on the Protestant volunteers in Schleswig, reveals the deeply individualistic and fundamentally religious approach that he took to charity on the battlefield. According to his biographer, Roger Boppe, the religious aspect of helping the wounded was one of Appia's favorite ideas.[44] Like Dunant, he believed in the volunteer as an exemplar of Christian charity. Indeed, nothing could have been more different than the way Louis Appia on the one hand and Count Stolberg on the other approached charity in wartime: Their experiences of the War of 1866 were almost diametrically opposed. Appia continued to believe in the spontaneous, even freelance approach, but as Stolberg's emphasis on planning, system, and regimentation gradually became the model for Red Cross activity in future years, he often appeared a lonely figure whose personal, Samaritan approach to charity was less and less appreciated.

Exit Dunant

The Prussian victory celebrations, held in Berlin in September, 1866, were Dunant's finest hour. Invited by Queen Augusta herself, he attended the victory parade—where red cross armbands were much in evidence—the state victory banquet, a palace reception, a royal dinner party, and a private audience with the queen. It was a fitting culmination to the enterprise that he had almost accidentally begun with his remembrance of Solferino. Three years earlier, when he and Basting had collaborated on the Berlin circular, the whole scheme seemed problematical at best; now he rejoiced in the plaudits that he received from the Prussian monarchs and their court. It was some compensation for the fact that he had been pushed out of the limelight by Moynier and Dufour at the time of the International Congress of 1864.

While Dunant was on his travels—he went from Berlin back to Paris to encourage the work of the French society—a personal disaster was taking shape in Geneva. In the spring of 1867, rumors began to circulate that one of the city's banks, Crédit Genevois, was in difficulties; angry shareholders accused its board of directors, of whom Dunant was a member, of irresponsible and improper behavior. The directors had apparently made a number of ill-advised loans and purchases, including some stone quarries at Felfela in Algeria that were owned by Dunant himself until he sold them to his fellow directors. According to Pierre Boissier, Dunant was guilty of naiveté rather than trickery: He himself had never visited the quarries and had relied on assessments of their worth provided by a rather shady business partner called Nick.[45] Be that as it may, the fact remains that the directors of Crédit Genevois were culpable for bad judgment and conflict of interest, and it soon became apparent that a scandal of major proportions was brewing. The case went before the city's Commercial Court in May, 1867; on 17 October, the court pronounced its verdict, which was that the directors' actions were "grossly beyond the limits that a vigilant and conscientious board of directors should have permitted."[46]

Understandably, Moynier's first concern was not the fate of Dunant, whom he had always found a somewhat trying colleague, but rather the integrity of the great international enterprise that the Geneva committee had launched. In *War and Charity*, he had discoursed at length on the importance of raising a great deal of money for the cause and had enjoined national committees "to exclude all persons whose presence would injure the committee in the eyes of official administrators."[47] Yet the ill-fated Dunant, now in Paris, was still secretary of the Geneva committee; moreover the French national committee had selected Dunant a vice-chairman of the international conference of aid societies that Moynier had urged them to hold during the forthcoming Paris Exposition.

The conference was to begin in late August. Fearful of the impending scandal, Moynier wrote in June to the commissioner of the exposition and to the French central committee stating that the Comité International no longer wished to be represented by Dunant.[48] The rumors continued to grow, and on 10 August he wrote to one of the leading members of the French committee that, although Dunant could be invited to attend the conference as a private individual, he, Moynier, could not "under any circumstances consent to sit beside him as vice-chairman."[49] Five days later, he virtually ordered the hapless Dunant to resign as secretary of the Comité International; on 25 August, the day before the conference began, Dunant complied. This was almost two months before the verdict of the Commercial Court came down; Moynier had been nothing if not prudent. Of course most of those who attended the Paris Exposition knew nothing of these events. It is a delicious irony that while Moynier was doing his best to sever all official ties with Dunant the French organizers of the aid societies' exhibit had placed a bust of Dunant, crowned with laurels, in the place of honor. Those attending the conference were discreetly told why Dunant could not occupy the vice-chairmanship; they responded by designating him "promoter of the international movement" and by granting him special voting rights, perhaps the most that could be done in the circumstances.[50]

Dunant's humiliation in 1867 was only the beginning of his personal disaster. Ostracized by the respectable citizens of Geneva, he was doubly shamed when the Court of Civil Justice, which heard the appeal of the decision of the Commercial Court, found him guilty of willful deception and held him primarily responsible for the collapse of Crédit Genevois. Whether this decision was entirely fair is open to question.[51] What is clear is that it ruined Dunant, who was soon transformed into a penniless vagabond, wandering in poverty through the cities and towns of Europe.

Inevitably, biographers have treated Dunant's life as one of triumph and tragedy and have regarded it as singularly unjust that an individual who did so much good for humanity should have suffered such an abysmal fate.[52] Yet this melodramatic judgment surely exaggerates Dunant's personal role in the creation of both the Red Cross and the Geneva Convention; it also disregards the obvious fact that without the support of contemporary opinion—the same respectable opinion, it can be said, that held financial impropriety to be an unpardonable sin—the Geneva proposals would have been a dead letter. The more important question to be asked here is whether Dunant's departure at this early stage in the development of the Red Cross had a significant effect on its future. His personal contribution was obviously greatest in the months prior to the 1863 conference; at the 1864 congress, he had been relegated to the sidelines by the diplomats and medical officers, and since then he had spent a good deal of time away from Geneva, much of it in Paris. The everyday work of the Comité International was increasingly in the hands of the cautious and methodical Moynier; one cannot imagine Dunant as any kind of successful administrator. True, the latter enjoyed the favor of the king and queen of Prussia, but the success of the Red Cross idea in Berlin was as much a consequence of the Prussian military revolution of the 1860s as it was the product of royal favor. Dunant's connections in Paris had helped in setting up the French society, but that society continued to be treated with barely concealed disdain by the war minister, Marshal Randon, who continued to regard him as the author of a scurrilous anti-French tract. In short, it is difficult to avoid the conclusion that Dunant's most useful contribution to the development of the Red Cross was already behind him when he resigned in 1867.

The Paris Conference of 1867

In these somewhat strained circumstances, the Paris conference—officially the "International Conference of Societies for the Relief of the War Wounded"—took place. The Dunant scandal was not the only source of tension, however; another stemmed from the fact that the aristocratic leaders of the French national committee wanted to transfer the international direction of the enterprise from Geneva to Paris. Luckily for Moynier, he was forewarned by a friend, Théodore Vernes, the banker who was treasurer of the French national committee, and was able to prepare his defense. He was in any case irritated with the members of French central committee who, instead of planning the conference themselves, had entrusted it to a "General Commission" composed of whichever delegates national societies sent to Paris to organize their displays at the exposition. Count Sérurier, who organized the General Commission, had deliberately tried to reach beyond the existing membership of national committees in order to attract physicians, philanthropists, and members of the orders of chivalry; his list of invitees was almost as broad as that used by the Geneva committee in 1863. Moynier disapproved and thought Sérurier's behavior irresponsible; he believed that the conference should have been planned only by members of the existing central committees. The General Commission, he wrote stuffily, was "a mixed body in which an important role was played by an unstable and exotic element."[53] Despite his reservations, he was unable to change what had already happened, so he went to Paris and himself joined in the planning.

In any event, Moynier's fear that strangers would dominate the Paris conference proved unfounded. Only fifty-seven delegates attended, many of whom were familiar faces: van de Velde from Belgium, Longmore from Great Britain, Basting from the Netherlands, Loeffler and von Langenbeck from Prussia, Adolf Steiner from Baden, and Hahn from Wurtemberg. Three Americans attended: Charles Bowles; Dr. Thomas Evans, whose analysis of the medical-sanitary aspects of the recent war had just been published; and Dr. Charles Crane.[54] The governments and/or ministers of war of nine states were represented: Austria, Baden, Bavaria, Great Britain, Netherlands, Prussia, Russia, Sweden and Norway, and Switzerland. Both the Spanish and the Prussian Orders of St. John sent delegates, and there was even a representative of the Imperial Ottoman Commission for the Paris Exposition, in the person of Dr. Abdullah Bey of the Hospital of the Imperial Guard in Constantinople. (The sultan had ratified the Geneva Convention in May, 1865, but there was as yet no sign of the formation of an aid committee in Constantinople.)

Suggestions for improving the Geneva Convention abounded. One draft text came from a subcommittee of the General Commission;[55] other suggestions came from those who had experience of its workings in the recent war. During the spring of 1867, the Prussian war ministry had held a postmortem on the war, from which emerged a number of proposed modifications to the Convention. Just before the Paris conference began, representatives of the German and Austrian aid societies that had participated in the war met in Wurzburg, and they too had ideas about changing the Convention; in particular, they wanted the existence of the aid societies to be officially recognized in the text of the document.[56]

In the end the Paris conference agreed on four major modifications to the Convention.[57] First, it was decided to extend its scope by adopting specific clauses relating to war at sea. Second, it was agreed that wounded soldiers needed protection against robbery and gratuitous injury (for example, by looters); accordingly, the conference decided that belligerents should themselves take responsibility for policing battlefields in the wake of combat. Third, delegates agreed that much confusion about who had been killed, injured, or taken prisoner could be eliminated if all soldiers were required to wear identity tags; this information, which was of immediate use to both military and civil authorities, could also be made available to soldiers' families by the aid societies. Finally, the delegates resolved that at the conclusion of hostilities all belligerents should provide the enemy with a list of all known dead, sick and wounded, and ordinary prisoners of war in the hands of the enemy. A revised Geneva Convention containing these four changes would, the delegates hoped, be approved by all of the states that were signatories to the 1864 document; naturally, a new international congress would be necessary to seek their approval.[58]

No similar consensus emerged from their discussions about the composition and role of aid societies. The General Commission had urged the conference to decide whether societies ought to include—on a virtually ex officio basis—members of the clergy, members of religious corporations and orders of chivalry, physicians, pharmacists, and administrative officials; it also raised the question of whether membership in one national aid committee automatically conferred membership in the committees of all countries. Behind these questions lay obvious uncertainties about how far the principles of voluntarism and internationalism ought to be carried. Contemporary prejudice was never far below the surface of the discussion; for example, when it was asked whether the Knights of Malta and the Teutonic Order could be considered religious corporations, Baron Mundy of the Austrian society replied firmly, "Those which follow the Catholic rite, yes; those which are Protestant, no."[59] In the end those attending the session limited themselves to vague but positive responses to both of the questions raised about membership.

The role of women also proved to be a controversial subject. The American Bowles, drawing on the experience of the Sanitary Commission, proposed that numerous small local committees of ladies [*dames*] should form the basis of organization in every country. This he justified on the grounds that men were too busy to give much time to it; that the work done in peacetime would be principally women's work; that the American experience proved its success; and that women were predestined by God for works of charity requiring long and patient devotion.[60] These committees of ladies would prepare stocks of sheets and towels, locate suitable women [*femmes*, not *dames*] to act as nurses in wartime, and make collections of money, books, and other useful items. Above them would be the executive committees, composed of men trained in medicine who would ensure the availability of surgical instruments, find means of transporting the wounded, and deal with "all of the specialized questions that are beyond the competence of women."[61] At the top there would be a "higher council" (*conseil superieur*) that would coordinate the work of the executive committees and deal with questions of national interest.

Bowles's assumption that women rather than men would constitute the front line of charitable work did not find unanimous support among the Europeans. Several delegates were willing to concede them a useful subordinate role—such as they already played in Italy, Prussia, and Austria—but the senior member of the French delegation, Count Bréda, expressed grave doubts about whether it was either feasible or desirable to organize committees of ladies in France. Behind his doubts lay a thinly concealed contempt for the ability of women to organize and sustain serious activity. The count's skepticism was unjustified; not only was it disproved by the American experience, but just across the French border in Baden a flourishing national aid society organized by Grand Duchess Louise was entirely the creation of women. Once again the delegates limited themselves to a vague endorsement of Bowles's proposal, qualifying their approval with references to the necessity of taking national peculiarities into account.

Unable to arrive at firm conclusions about the shape and direction of the national committees, the delegates finally decided to postpone further discussion to another conference, which they expected would take place the following year in Berlin. Before adjourning, however, they dealt with one last issue, which proved to be the most controversial of all: The nature and role of the Comité International. According to Théodore Vernes, who had written to Moynier in mid-June, several members of the French aid society hoped that the conference would decide to move the international administrative center of their work from Geneva to Paris.[62] The leading force in this group was Count Bréda, himself the author of a proposal for the formation of an international brigade of hospitaller nurses.[63] His ally was Count Sérurier, who had organized the aid societies' exhibit at the exposition; he was still smarting from the fact that the jury, impressed by the quality of the exhibit, had decided to award its grand prize and gold medal to Moynier, representing the Comité International, rather than to him. Well before the contretemps over the prize, Moynier had submitted a proposal that the conference create a "supreme council" to act as a permanent link between the national committees. In his scheme, the supreme council was not intended to replace but rather to supplement the current Comité International, whose members would constitute the council's standing administrative body; the supreme council would be composed of one representative from each national committee and would meet whenever necessary "in a place where no committee could exercise a preponderant influence,"[64] by which phrase Moynier undoubtedly meant Geneva.

When the conference sent Moynier's proposal to be reviewed by a committee, Count Bréda launched his offensive, arguing that Geneva had none of the advantages necessary for the functioning of a truly international body, whereas Paris, the acknowledged center of European diplomacy and culture, had all of them. Moreover, he continued, no sensible person would place his faith in the inviolability of Swiss neutrality; in the event of a major European conflict, Switzerland was just as likely as Belgium to be overrun by belligerents.[65] Members of the subcommittee were not persuaded by this argument, however, and agreed to maintain Geneva as the international center. Nevertheless, in an attempt to placate the French, they went on to suggest that there could be a second international center in Paris, "a sort of university or museum," which would be run by an international subcommittee subordinated to the Geneva committee but which would "profit from the advantages of every kind that this great and beautiful metropolis offers."[66] Outraged by this feeble attempt at conciliation, Count Bréda resigned and stalked out of the conference. When the subject was discussed at the plenary session, Baron Mundy of Austria tried to have Bréda's report put before the assembly, but suddenly no one seemed to have a copy of it—Moynier had left his at home, he confessed—and so the arguments for Paris were quietly ignored.[67] Moynier had successfully warded off this challenge to the primacy of Geneva.

However, as Moynier acknowledged, this unambiguous endorsement of the Geneva committee, though certainly welcome, did nothing to clarify precisely what the national committees expected of it. This he sought to obtain from the conference before it adjourned. Since, as he pointed out, the national committees were perfectly capable of communicating with one another in peacetime, the Comité International would presumably serve as a the communications link in wartime between the societies of belligerent states. He assumed from what had been said at the conference that everyone expected the Comité International to play a leading role in wartime, organizing assistance for the armies of the belligerents according to their needs and the resources available. He speculated that in a particular war the committee might well establish a bureau outside Geneva at some location closer to the actual fighting. Mention had also been made of the possibility that the Comité International might publish a journal for the entire movement; the success of such a venture, he noted, would require considerable assistance from the national committees. Five or six people in Geneva, he observed, could scarcely undertake the production and distribution of a regularly published journal without editorial assistance and financial support from elsewhere. The same thing was true of the idea of a museum or permanent display of ambulance technology; if it were located in Paris, then the French national committee would be expected to carry a major share of the cost.

Moynier also used the occasion to raise once again his idea of widening the composition of the Comité International to include representatives chosen by the national committees:

> Individuals could be chosen who have done the most for the cause in their country; it would be an honorary reward given by each Society to its most eminent members; these representatives, who would form part of the bureau in Geneva, would be drawn from the whole surface of the globe, Europe and America, wherever Committees can be found. Now, how would this Committee function? When it meets as an international Committee, as we are doing at the moment, I believe that the role of these representatives would be to inform those who have sent them. When this Committee is convened in an emergency, in the case of war, for example, to decide on the best course of action or to take a grave decision, then the bureau on its own initiative or on the request of some member,

could convoke the international committees abroad to invite them to meet to examine the delicate, important questions which can arise when war breaks out. But in ordinary times I see no reason or necessity to bring together the members of the international committee; their tasks would be few; the Geneva bureau would see to ordinary business.[68]

What Moynier proposed was really no more than a modest alteration in the workings of the Comité International. Its Genevan members would constitute the bureau, who would carry on running the day-to-day business and international correspondence. Only in times of crisis would it convene with an extended membership, presumably immediately after war had been declared, and the decisions taken at that time would be communicated back to the various national societies by their representatives. Whether such a scheme was feasible, given the speed with which wars could be declared and the consequent interruption of the normal means of travel, was not discussed.

It soon became apparent that the organizers of the Paris conference had grossly underestimated how much time would be needed to consider both the proposed revisions to the Geneva Convention and the many unanswered questions about the composition and workings of the aid societies. Another conference was clearly called for. With more issues raised than answered, the conference came to an end and the delegates went home. Moynier returned to Geneva with a mandate to continue the work of the Comité International, but with few of the really important matters settled and no sign of financial support from any of the national committees. After the triumphs of previous years, it was something of a letdown. However, at least there had been general agreement about revising the 1864 Convention, so Moynier and his colleagues decided to approach the Swiss Federal Council with a request that it once again invite signatory states to send delegates to a new Geneva conference, to be held in 1868, to consider proposed revisions to the original Convention.[69] Not to overload already busy schedules, they also suggested to the Prussian society that the proposed international conference of aid societies be postponed until 1869.

Two Steps Forward

While the idea of another diplomatic congress was being canvassed among governments, Moynier and his colleagues decided to take up some of the other proposals that had been made at the Paris conference. Before it adjourned, the conference had agreed that the Comité International could conduct an inquiry (*enquête*) to find out how far the various national committees were prepared to support the proposed museum and international journal and what their views were on the composition of the Comité International and its wartime role.[70] The inquiry had been sent to all national committees in a circular letter dated 21 September, 1867; in order to give everyone time to consider its findings well before the upcoming Berlin conference, Moynier circulated a commentary on its results in June, 1868.

The commentary was signed by the five members of the Comité International; General Dufour, who now attended irregularly due to his advanced age, had been designated honorary president, while in Dunant's place the others had selected yet another Genevan Protestant, Colonel Edmond Favre of the Swiss army. It is noteworthy that the Genevans made this choice on their own, without any reference to the Paris conference. To be sure, the original Geneva committee had been self-selecting, and its rules of operation had never been codified; nor was it a creature of the international conference. On the other hand, given Moynier's expressed intention to involve representatives of the national committees more closely in the workings of the Comité International, it might have been politic to consult them about imminent changes in its composition. According to Boissier, Moynier was certainly aware that there was some feeling in the French society that it was high time a Catholic member was selected.[71] If the Genevans had wished to smooth ruffled feathers in Paris in the wake of Count Bréda's resignation, they could have sought out a Swiss Catholic member. That they instead selected Favre, who was an expert on the organization of the Prussian and Austrian armies, suggests that they were far more concerned with developing voluntary assistance in those states where armies were receptive to the idea than they were with placating offended French aristocrats.

Written in the form of a memorandum addressed to the presidents and members of the various central committees, Moynier's analysis both reported and commented on their responses to the questions that they had been asked. With regard to the creation of an international museum in Paris, ten of the committees had responded positively; three others stated plainly that they would contribute nothing toward its cost; one (Berlin) replied that it wished to create its own museum; another (Oldenburg) proposed the creation of museums in *several* important cities; and five refused to commit themselves one way or the other.[72] There was at least a nucleus of support for creating a museum in Paris that would preserve and build upon the displays already mounted there, but the Comité International expressed its strong preference for creating several such institutions, as the Oldenburg committee had suggested. In putting aside the apparent support for Paris, the Comité International used an ingenious logic: Instead of counting the committees for and against, it counted the total population of the countries involved, and thus arrived at the conclusion that out of the nearly 200 million people in Europe, less than one quarter lived in countries whose committees had supported the Paris proposal.[73] Moreover, the Genevans noted, the vitality of the movement as a whole would profit from the healthy competition that would accompany the creation of several museums, "four or five, for example, in the most important centres."[74] Nevertheless, they were careful to pay tribute to the "zeal and initiative" that Count Sérurier had shown in organizing the

Paris display and suggested that it could well form the basis of a future French museum of sanitary equipment.[75] The idea of creating several museums also neatly disposed of the suggestion that there should be a second, albeit subordinate, Comité International in Paris; if there were simply a French museum in that city, then clearly it could be run by the Paris central committee, and additional arrangements would be unnecessary.

A closely related issue was the founding of an international journal. Here, the *Mémoire* reported, fifteen of the twenty committees responding were in favor of the idea; none was opposed, but five expressed doubts (the same five, by the way, that had no opinion about the museum question: Copenhagen, Madrid, Milan, Schwerin, and New York).[76] This time the authors did not count aggregate population; instead they noted with satisfaction that the three national committees that were already producing periodical publications—in Paris, Brussels, and Berlin—were among those who responded positively:[77]

> All those who supported the idea seemed to want a collection which would bring together all important information, historical, administrative, technical, bibliographic, etc., and which would be sufficiently complete to keep its readers abreast of everything that would be of interest to the members of our associations. There is also a desire that it be used as a means of correspondence among the various Committees, in ways that would stimulate their zeal and strengthen their network by the frequent exchange of news and ideas.[78]

Finally, there was agreement that the journal should appear regularly, that it should be published in the French language, and that its editorial policy should avoid giving preference to any nationality. The only matter that seemed still to be at issue was where it would be published, in Paris or Geneva. The Paris conference had discussed entrusting the publication of a journal to the Comité International in Geneva, but both the Paris and Brussels committees replied that in their view it should be published in Paris, because the museum and the journal would support each other; indeed their administration could be placed in the same hands.[79]

Before entering into this controversy, the Genevans did their best to make it appear that they had no particular ax to grind: "We have not sought in any way the honor and responsibility which the majority of committees contemplate placing upon us, for we have no illusions about the difficulty that we will encounter in discharging this mandate in a proper way. If we are considered better qualified than others to conduct this enterprise, our devotion to the work will force us to respond to the confidence that has been placed in us, but we insist on declaring that we have not in any way solicited it."[80] Did they protest too much? In the next paragraph, they did their best to ensure that Geneva would be chosen: Ascribing "the whole controversy to the hypothetical existence of an international museum in Paris," now a doubtful possibility, they called upon the forthcoming Berlin conference "to decide the museum question before that of the journal."[81] They had, of course, already done their best to counter the ambitions of the Parisians, but just in case their efforts failed, they sought to keep separate and distinct the tasks of the museum and the journal. The journal should not, they noted, be exclusively a museum journal, nor should it carry only news from Paris. Having thus subtly implied that the French might not be capable of producing a truly international journal, the Genevans concluded, "We are not convinced that the simplification which would result from its publication in Paris would compensate for the general advantages that are associated with editing it in Geneva. Besides, at the moment that an international Committee is being instituted, it seems logical to put general services among its prerogatives, in order to permit the national Committees to devote themselves entirely to looking after the interests that are especially entrusted to them."[82]

Once the rival claims of Paris had been disposed of, the Comité International turned to the practical questions of financing and editing the journal. Having estimated the annual cost of producing such a journal at 4,000 francs, the Genevans reported a generally encouraging response from national committees: If those who had already promised to support it did so, and if the others assumed their fair share of subscriptions, then the enterprise could indeed go ahead.[83] Anticipating a favorable outcome, the International Committee asked national committees to provide guarantees of support by sending to Berlin delegates who were authorized to enter into binding financial commitments.

Less controversial was the matter of organizing an international agency to coordinate assistance in wartime, although here again the French committee was opposed to the proposal that had emanated from the Paris conference. Most committees were in favor of the idea that the Comité International should organize such an agency, although several registered their opposition to any suggestion that neutrals should be required to contribute assistance or told how much to contribute. Having assured them that this was not their intention, the Genevans noted that even if such an agency were set up, committees would be free to bypass it if they chose to disregard the greater efficiency that it would bring to the business of distributing help to the belligerents. Naturally, members of the Comité International did not intend to pack up and move all over the continent whenever war was declared; rather, they anticipated organizing a bureau at some convenient location and then monitoring its work from Geneva.[84]

Finally, they turned to the question of the future composition and role of the Comité International itself. Moynier, it will be recalled, had proposed to the Paris conference that each national committee choose one of its most distinguished members as a member of the Comité International; these foreign members would be "more honorific than active"[85] but could be consulted on matters of great importance or urgency. Thirteen of the twenty committees replied positively to this idea, and seven had even proceeded to choose their representative. Four did not provide a response of any kind. The committee in The Hague was unwilling to give its unqualified support, and those in Paris and Brussels opposed the scheme on the grounds that it was impracticable. As they pointed out, these foreign members could scarcely be consulted in advance whenever something had to be decided, nor was it practical to bring them to Geneva all the time.[86]

To be sure, Moynier's proposal had been formulated before the Paris conference had discussed the possible establishment of a journal or the utility of an international agency in wartime. With these new duties on the horizon, members of the Comité International had reconsidered the whole idea of expanding their numbers beyond the group of five in Geneva and had decided that foreign members would be of more use if they stayed at home and from there helped the Genevans to publish the journal and organize neutral aid in wartime. New duties were, however, not the only consideration: Count Bréda's resignation had made them realize that not everyone assumed that they should be the permanent leaders of the movement. Seeking a plausible way to abandon Moynier's earlier scheme, they now claimed—somewhat audaciously—that they were renouncing what they had originally proposed out of deference to the national committees! "The Geneva Committee," they continued, "will preserve its full freedom of action (*conservera sa pleine liberté d'allures*)," while "the prerogatives of our foreign colleagues will be restricted to collaboration with the journal, [and] the sending of assistance from one nation to another in wartime; and their mandate, thus understood and limited, will no longer be exposed to criticism."[87]

At the end of the memorandum, the Comité International announced its intention to submit two draft resolutions to the forthcoming Berlin conference. These resolutions would be considered by a special commission composed of representatives of all national societies; the societies themselves were requested to send delegates to Berlin furnished with voting instructions. Decisions would be taken by majority vote but would be regarded as binding only upon those who voted for them.[88] The first resolution, which was intended to settle the museum issue, read as follows:

> Whereas the proposal made by Count Sérurier to the Paris conference, for the creation in that city of an international museum of sanitary material, does not have the agreement of all national committees; and whereas, in a different light, one can with advantage compensate for this institution by means of collections of the same kind, established in the principal cities through the initiative of local Committees, the Conference passes to the next business.[89]

The second resolution, consisting of five articles, was more complex:

> Acknowledging the existence at Geneva of a Comité International, instituted by the Geneva Conference (1863) and confirmed by the Paris Conference (1867), the Conference resolves that:

Article 1.   The Comité International is charged with publishing a monthly review, in the French language, which will serve in a general way to monitor the work of assistance to wounded soldiers, and as a means of communication among the national Committees.

Article 2.   If the annual cost of this publication exceeds the receipts, the expense will be shared among the national Committees and borne by them in proportion to the size of the population that they represent, but after deducting those sums which they have paid either for subscriptions or as subventions.

Article 3.   In the event of war, the Comité International will organize, in a place chosen for convenience, a bureau of correspondence and information which will in every way facilitate the exchange of communications and the transmission of assistance between the Committees.

Article 4.   Each national Committee will add one of its members to the Comité International, to help it to discharge the mandate which has been conferred upon it by Articles 1 and 3 above.

Article 5.   Apart from the functions which are assigned by the preceding Articles, the Comité International will continue to be charged with taking, in the name of the enterprise, all steps [necessary to promote] the general interest.

A note in parentheses explained that this text followed from the appropriate sections of the memorandum, "with a final article concerning powers of the Comité International which are undisputed, but which have not yet been the subject of any resolution."[90]

With the formulation of these resolutions, the Comité International had taken two significant steps forward. First, it had done its best to prevent further discussion about Paris as a possible site for either the museum or the journal. Second, by appending Article 5, which in effect assigned to itself supreme authority for the development of the movement, the Comité International sought to protect its prerogatives against encroachment by any other body, be it a national committee or an international conference. It is noteworthy that the wording of Article 5 stated explicitly that the Comité International would "continue to be charged" with overall responsibility: This was meant to ensure that no future conference would be able to take away powers that would merely be confirmed, not granted, by the Berlin conference. Taken as a whole, the 1868 *Mémoire* was a shrewd piece of work indeed: In the guise of delivering a report to the national committees about their own opinions, the Genevans had beaten off the French challenge and consolidated their leading role vis-à-vis both the national committees and the international conferences.

One Step Back

The forthcoming Berlin conference was not the only important item on the agenda of the Comité International; while Moynier and his colleagues had been preparing the *Mémoire*, the Swiss Federal Council had been sounding out governments regarding the proposed revision of the Geneva Convention. Here again, France struck a discordant note. Through the Swiss minister in Paris, word reached Geneva that the French government was adamantly opposed to any revision of the Convention that would require it to recognize a role in warfare for volunteer relief workers or oblige it to grant such volunteers specific neutrality.[91] As in the past, it was the war minister, Marshal Randon, who was primarily responsible for France's cautious and uncooperative response. It soon began to dawn on the Genevans that if the 1864 Convention were repealed, and if the signatory states were then unable to agree on an alternative text, the whole enterprise might end in a fiasco. Instead of an improved and unanimously accepted Geneva Convention, there might be a substitute text less widely accepted or, worst of all, no agreement whatever. "Such a result," wrote Moynier in the *Journal de Genève*, "would be disastrous because it is of paramount importance to preserve the unity of this European understanding, so quickly and auspiciously formed, even if it means sacrificing part of the hoped-for reforms."[92] Although Moynier's fears were far from groundless, such a disturbing turn of events had never been contemplated when the delegates to the Paris conference had supported the proposed changes.

Once the Comité International began to question the wisdom of attempting a wholesale revision of the Convention, two courses of action were open to them. On the one hand, they could ask the Swiss Federal Council to postpone any further action until after the Berlin conference had been able to weigh the pros and cons of the whole idea. On the other hand, they could attempt to salvage most of the work done in Paris by securing the agreement of governments not to a reworked Convention but rather to some additional clauses that could be appended to the original agreement and that would come into force only when ratified by all of the signatories to the 1864 Convention. But what would constitute the substance of these additional articles? Not, obviously, the text circulated by the Swiss Federal Council, for it had already provoked the opposition of the French. With the next Geneva conference only weeks away, the Comité International decided to produce a draft of its own and urged delegates to treat this draft, and not the full revision proposed by the Paris conference, as the basis for their discussions. When the delegates arrived in Geneva in early October, they were given a letter urging them *not* to repeal the 1864 Convention and instead to address themselves to a draft, entitled *Enoncé de quelques idées à examiner*; both documents had been written by the Comité International.[93]

Four of the twelve points put forward for discussion addressed issues that had already been raised at the Paris conference: extension of the scope of the Convention to include war at sea; recognition that the personnel of aid societies should enjoy neutrality; belligerents to be held responsible for policing the battlefield; and the adoption of a uniform means of identifying combatants. (Six other items sought to clarify the meaning of clauses in the existing Convention.) The Genevans took the initiative in adding two more proposals that related to the work of the aid societies: One called for tight controls to prevent abuse of the red cross armband; the other, for steps to be taken to ensure that all military personnel were acquainted with the principles of the Convention. Neither was accepted. The delegates rejected tighter controls on the grounds that "no means of repression had presented itself"[94] and decided to leave to individual states the task of familiarizing their armed forces with the terms of the Convention. The same unwillingness to prescribe the conduct of states apparently led them to reject three of the four Paris proposals. Rather than drawing up an additional article that would have granted specific neutrality to aid society personnel, they decided to leave it to individual states to write such a provision into their own military regulations, a solution that, of course, left the French government free to continue ignoring the existence of the national aid society. It soon became apparent that the only significant issue that the delegates were prepared to discuss seriously was that of extending the Convention to cover war at sea.

Several states had appointed senior naval officers as delegates, and they took the lead in drawing up ten additional articles dealing with war at sea. Of these, the most noteworthy was the eighth, which read in part,

> Hospital ships, fitted at the expense of Societies, recognized by governments, signatories of this Convention . . . shall, together with their personnel, be considered as neutral. They shall be respected and protected by the belligerents. They shall make themselves known by hoisting the white flag with the red cross, as well as their national flag. The distinguishing mark of the personnel, in the exercise of their duties, will be an armlet of these same colors; these vessels will be painted white with red battery. They shall carry aid and relief to the wounded and drowning belligerents without regard to nationality. They shall not in any way interrupt the movements of the combatants. During and after an engagement, they shall act at their own risk and peril. Belligerents shall exercise over them the right of control and inspection. They can refuse co-operation, advise them to retire, or detain them if the gravity of circumstances requires it. The wounded and drowning taken on board these vessels cannot be reclaimed by any combatants, and they will be prohibited from serving again during the war.[95]

There is an obvious anomaly here: The very delegates who supported this article, with its clear reference to aid societies recognized by governments, had already refused to consider a similar reference to the role of aid societies in land warfare. Ironically, the precise wording of this article was reported to the conference by one of the French delegates, Rear Admiral Coupvent de Bois, who was apparently unaware that his government had refused to discuss revision of the entire Convention on the grounds that it was unwilling to recognize the existence of aid societies.[96] Devotees of the cause of charity can scarcely have been pleased with a wording that *ordered* them to treat victims impartially, as if they would have done anything else, and reminded them that they did so at their own peril, as if that were not a glorious part of the whole adventure. The delegates obviously felt compelled not only to specify how the aid societies would behave but also to absolve governments of any responsibility for the fate of the volunteers.

All in all, the Geneva conference of 1868 was something less than a resounding endorsement of the aspirations of the aid societies. The Additional Articles upon which it agreed were no more than a token response to the many proposals made in Paris a year earlier; in any case, they would have no legal force until they had been ratified by all those states that were already parties to the 1864 Convention.[97] Four years earlier, the delegates had been treated to garden parties, festivals, and choral performances, as befitted those who were thought to be laying the cornerstone of a new edifice of international morality; in 1868, such hyperbole would have been out of place. It is not that *raison d'état* had suddenly been let loose: State interest had been calculated just as carefully in 1864, but on that occasion the would-be delegates of humanity had chosen not to notice.

The Prussian Example

The successes of Berlin, where the second international conference of aid societies met in 1869, were a welcome change from the difficulties of Paris and the disappointments of Geneva. The city itself was in the first flush of spring as the delegates arrived for the opening of the conference on 22 April. Here in Prussia, the Red Cross idea already seemed to be flourishing. Official recognition and encouragement were apparent on all sides: Literally as well as figuratively, the delegates received a royal welcome; Queen Augusta herself constantly and proudly wore the armband; and Otto von Bismarck, von Roon, and Count von Eulenberg were often to be seen at the conference, sitting in the official box. In addition to the formal sessions, there was a full social program, including theatrical performances, church services, a reception at the royal palace, exhibitions of equipment, and a special display by the Berlin fire department. In all seventeen signatory governments sent official representatives, as did several orders of chivalry; the remainder of the delegates were members of the central committees of the two dozen aid societies already in existence. Among the now customary array of military surgeons, philanthropists, and bureaucrats who made up most of the delegates one name stood out: that of Rudolf Virchow, the German pathologist whose immensely important contributions to medicine were universally acknowledged. Virchow's perceptive intelligence and keen interest in the humanitarian aspects of medicine would make him an interested, not to say controversial, participant in the work of the conference.

With Berlin as the host city, it was inevitable that the activities of the Prussian central committee would exercise considerable influence on the proceedings of the conference. The Prussians had prepared proposals on the two major issues to be discussed—the work of the aid societies in a continental war and their role in peacetime—and these were given pride of place on the agenda; they had also compiled a lengthy history of the Prussian society, by far the longest and fullest of the reports submitted by any national society, which was printed in full in the transactions of the conference.[98] As the victors in Europe's two most recent wars, the Prussians not unnaturally assumed that the other aid societies had a good deal to learn from their experience.

This is not to suggest that success had made the Prussians arrogant or complacent. Far from resting on their laurels, they were continually looking for ways to improve the effectiveness of their total war effort. The 1866 campaign had, in point of fact, interrupted measures that the war ministry was carrying out to reorganize the medical corps and to reform the administration of military hospitals and ambulances. In the spring of 1867, the ministry convened a special conference on the army medical service in order to discover what had been learned in the war against Austria that might usefully be incorporated into further reform measures.[99] Thanks to the influence of Queen Augusta, the special conference had also examined the role of voluntary assistance in the War of 1866. One result of this review was the decision to create a special "sanitary corps" to transport the wounded from the front line to one of the twelve mobile field hospitals attached to every army corps. The army's decision to improve its own services to the wounded meant that there would be no further role on the battlefield for volunteers sent by aid societies. (Significantly, this decision was not published until 29 April, two days after the Berlin conference concluded its deliberations.) The Prussian aid society would now be expected to play a somewhat different role: Instead of sending volunteers onto the battlefield, it would instead arrange for the training of nurses to staff military hospitals and for the creation and equipping of reserve hospitals. The proposals made to the conference by the Prussian central committee reflected these changes, which had already been decided upon by the war ministry.

Before the new business was considered, however, several questions that had been pending since the Paris conference had to be dealt with. Here in Berlin, with such an active national aid society and such strong official support, the pretensions of the French to become the leaders of the international movement seemed almost preposterous. Consequently there was little debate before the delegates approved the motions that had been submitted by the Comité International concerning the location of museums and the establishment of an international journal. It was agreed that the national societies would contribute to defray the costs of producing the journal, but the details of each contribution were left to be settled in subsequent correspondence. There were signs that the Prussians would have liked the conference to formulate precise statutes concerning the mandate and organization of the Comité International, but Moynier, who reported to the conference on its work, came close to ridiculing such ideas: "It is understandable . . . in view of the special nature of its functions, that the Comité International would not know how to be guided . . . by the framework indicated by the Berlin Committee. What, for example, could we say about *statutes* that we have never felt it necessary to give ourselves, or about an *organization* which is so elementary that it is simply a Committee of five members which is answerable to no one and exercises no authority?"[100] Cleverly, Moynier managed to imply that a formal structure was wholly unnecessary, that statutes and organization would have been as out of place for this group as they would have been at a private dinner party. The fact that the Comité International was answerable to no one was undeniable; that it intended to remain so was equally clear. In a revealing admission, he went on to acknowledge that although the Paris conference had given the Comité International no specific authority to seek a revision of the Geneva Convention, "we considered its silence as implying a tacit mandate."[101] Moynier's assertion that it exercised no authority was nonsense: Besides the moral authority that it enjoyed as founder of the movement (and which it had exercised, for example, in ostracizing Dunant), the Comité International not only claimed the right to do everything necessary to advance the cause but insisted that the present conference recognize that it had always enjoyed this prerogative. Seen in this light, Moynier's modesty verged on the disingenuous.

Things did not go so smoothly when the proposed agency for international assistance in wartime was discussed. One of the Russian delegates, General Baumgarten, pointed out the flaws that his compatriots had found in the scheme as proposed:

> If our activity is limited only to [the creation of] the international agency, it will be extremely minimal and insufficient. Our Central Committee proposes that we concentrate the principal activity in wartime not in the creation of an international agency, but in the organization of an International Committee, composed of delegates of all the non-belligerent countries. In our view, all of the assistance—in both materiel and personnel—supplied by the Central Committees of the non-belligerent powers cannot be sent at will to one or the other army, because this would be to abandon neutrality, and there is no doubt that in this form assistance from the non-belligerent powers could not be accepted; it would be quite a different thing, if this assistance were sent to an International Committee charged . . . with sharing the aid, without national distinctions, principally among the sick and wounded of the army in retreat, although it goes without saying that this does not exclude assistance to the sick and wounded of the victorious army.[102]

Divested of its verbosity, the Russian argument was that neutrals, instead of assisting only their friends, should ensure that the assistance available would go first to those most in need. Objections to the Russian proposal ignored the important moral principle that it raised and concentrated instead on its impracticality. How, it was asked, could the committee know in advance of an engagement which side would be victorious? Although the Russians did not regard these objections as insuperable, the delegates decided to approve the agency as proposed by the Comité International and to defer consideration of the Russian position to some future conference. Events would soon demonstrate that this was a lost opportunity to ensure that assistance from neutrals was distributed impartially and on the basis of greatest need.

When the conference eventually considered the wartime role of aid societies, discussion centered on the nine resolutions that had been put forward by the Prussians. These, as Loeffler pointed out, reflected the decisions that had been taken by the central committee in Berlin in the wake of the War of 1866. Loeffler himself had already described these reforms in his book, *Das Preussische Militär-Sanitätswesen und sein reform nach der kriegsfahrung von 1866,*[103] but this work was not yet widely known abroad.[104]

Many of the delegates were therefore amazed when he announced that the Prussian society had decided to leave the organizing of combat ambulances entirely in the hands of the official army medical services. Appreciating the need to justify to this audience such an apparently radical departure, Loeffler explained that reasons of cost and utility had played a big role in this decision.[105] The Berlin committee had balked at the potential outlay on equipment and supplies, and the "nearly insurmountable difficulties" that it would face in obtaining qualified personnel to staff field ambulances in wartime.[106] "And may I also ask you if it would be prudent, if it would be wise to employ the considerable sums which all this organization would require, in order to acquire and

2.4   Chief Prussian delegate to the International Congress of 1864, surgeon Friedrich Loeffler exercised an enormous influence on the development of the Red Cross in Prussia and, after 1871, in the other German states.

maintain materials and supplies which could perhaps remain unused during a long period of peace and which, when the moment comes to put them into service, will perhaps have deteriorated, or have been replaced long since by better and more suitable apparatus?"[107] Cost was not the only factor, however; Loeffler went on to argue that thanks to the 1864 Convention and the Additional Articles, the ambulances of conquered armies could now remain with their wounded without fear of capture, so that there would be less need in future for private charity to put field ambulances onto the battlefield.[108] He also reported that the Order of St. John, which had played such an important role in 1864 and 1866, shared this view and had recently decided that it would no longer directly participate in organizing ambulance services.[109]

Predictably, the Berlin committee's decision did not find much support among the other delegates. In Austria, Baron Mundy reported, the Teutonic Knights and the Knights of Malta had already set aside some 25,000 florins for the construction of reserve ambulances and had pledged their willingness to direct these ambulances in the field in the event of war.[110] One of the Russian delegates claimed that in his country, the national aid society "regards the establishment of voluntary ambulances as one of the finest privileges of private activity";[111] he voiced what was clearly a general feeling among delegates that in this matter the Prussians could do as they pleased, but so would everyone else. The same sentiment dominated reaction to the remainder of the Prussian resolutions, particularly those that stressed the need for societies to act in conformity with the requirements of the military, to organize their war work according to a previously agreed plan, and to operate on the basis of centralized direction.

The Prussians had concentrated on demonstrating what an aid society could do to help the army, but representatives from other countries seemed to be more concerned with discussing what governments could do to help the societies to perform their chosen role. The French, for example, raised the question of the cost of railway transport. It would be most helpful, they argued, if railway companies could be persuaded to provide free transport for the goods and personnel of aid societies. The Italians shared this concern and also proposed that governments ought to provide free lodging and maintenance for volunteers engaged in wartime ambulance work as well as pensions for those severely injured in the course of such work and death benefits for the families of volunteers killed while serving at the front. At this point Rudolf Virchow entered the discussion, pointing out that there was little chance that governments would agree to such proposals, since there was no guarantee that future wars would be over quickly. Prophetically, he continued,

> In some future war it could happen that the number of persons engaged in relief reaches a number so great that existing resources would not suffice to guarantee a pension to all the families of these deceased officials. I can add that even now, in the majority of states on the European continent, the resources available to

invalids are far short of the legitimate claims of this group, and that it would be one of the primary obligations of nations to assist these officials, their families, and in general all persons whose career has perhaps been compromised by the fortunes of war. In my opinion, this task must fall on the aid societies and on other associations formed freely among the populace, as is now the case in our country. Nevertheless, it is no less an important task for the international congress to make the nations aware of their duty to concern themselves with the plight of so many persons who are often forced to risk their lives in services associated with war, and who are frequently rendered as useless to their country as if they had been attached directly to the army.[112]

Virchow was not proposing that pensions for injured noncombatants should be paid for by the state; instead he advocated that they be funded out of voluntary donations. He was, however, already well beyond the imaginative capacities of his fellow delegates, most of whom could not envision warfare on this scale. Nor had they the insight to appreciate that from the state's point of view volunteer relief workers were not a unique group but part of, as Virchow put it, "those who are needed by the military administration, whatever their title, to drive wagons, or for other analogous services, without however being incorporated into the army itself, and who are therefore officially led, or even forced to take part in the movements of armies. Up to now, governments have taken no measures whatever with regard to such persons."[113] To the perceptive Virchow, it was already apparent that the needs of modern warfare would soon require the formation of what later generations would call service or support units and that their functions could easily include providing relief as well as transport. The learned professor was given a polite hearing, but the delegates preferred to continue talking about what made wartime charity unique and admirable and particularly about what made it unique in their own country. Indeed the structure of the conference, with its national delegations, made it inevitable that individual peculiarities would often obscure what were at bottom common problems.

By far the most interesting and revealing sessions at the Berlin conference were those given over to discussing the role of aid societies in peacetime. Once again, the Prussians set the tone of the discussion with a series of resolutions that followed from their conception of the aid societies' role in wartime. According to Dr. Brinkmann, who introduced the resolutions, societies would need to keep prepared for war work and could test themselves in peacetime by working "in circumstances which are analogous to those of war; in the struggle against disease, against misery, against hunger, against the devastating strength of the elements."[114] Yet this did not mean, he argued, that aid societies should try to be all things to all men, and thus lose sight of their principal task:

The real charity of our era can no longer emanate from a vague sentimentality or from vague impulses of the heart; help must not be furnished by chance or without method; the exercise of charity demands precise knowledge, preparation and special study. If we clearly and confidently envisage the task that war imposes on us, we will easily recognize among the miseries which survive in peacetime those which can and should help us to activate, test, and practice our strength. Pure charity and the spirit of devotion can best be practiced where they will not be influenced by the excitements of war, amid the miseries of poverty and disease, and beside the pallets of the neglected; it is amid the terrors caused by pestilential and contagious diseases that the preventive efforts of aid committees will find a sphere of action that is both necessary and likely to produce good results, where they will learn [how to operate a] hospital service, and this activity requires the same resources, the same energy, the same devotion as war itself. It is amid the sudden catastrophes, [which have become] so numerous because of the turbulent unrest of our era, that men of heart and action make themselves known, just like those who, when the moment comes, are called upon to appear as saviors on the battlefield; finally, it is amidst the torments of widespread misery that the firm organization of the committees will be demonstrated by a prompt and thoughtful distribution of assistance.[115]

In practical terms, what the Prussians were proposing was that the national and local committees of the aid societies should undertake the training of nurses to care for the sick poor. The benefits to the poor were, however, scarcely worth mentioning compared with the advantages that this plan would provide for women: "For women we are opening up a field of labor which corresponds perfectly to the aptitudes of their hearts and spirits, and to their strength and their inclinations; we are delivering a great number of them from an existence which lacks joy and satisfaction, and we are introducing them into a sphere of activity which will raise both their spirit and their intelligence."[116] By following this route, Brinkmann claimed, the societies would at one stroke alleviate hardship, prepare trained personnel, and create "a solid foundation among the people upon which they can continue to build." The opinion of the people, he pointed out, was enormously important "because the execution of these laws [for the protection of the sick and wounded] does not depend on Governments alone, and they cannot, with the best will in the world, hold sway unless they are supported by the whole army and population."[117]

Reaction to the Prussian proposals ran the gamut from cautious support to strong disapproval. De Cazenove of France expressed a fear common to many delegates, namely that committees could easily use up all their resources in coping with civil disasters and then be caught short by a sudden outbreak of war. In his opinion, a more limited peacetime role, such as that of assisting the victims of accidents, would keep a society active, keep its work in the public eye, and best of all keep most of its resources available for a future war.[118]

Everyone agreed that coping with peace could be a big problem. A prolonged period of peace, one delegate observed, could "paralyze" the activity of aid societies unless they had already found something useful to do.[119] But which work to choose, and what priority should it have? Another well-thought-out proposal came from the Darmstadt committee (Grand Duchy of Hesse), whose representative, Buchner, spoke first about the danger that would befall the aid societies if they gradually turned into a general association for humanitarianism. If this happened, he predicted, they would surely lose their identity and dissipate their resources. Of course they should undertake some works of practical humanitarianism, he agreed, but in addition they could undertake a much more specific task, the promotion of public hygiene. In Hesse, the aid society had committed itself to spreading knowledge of the theory and practice of hygiene and to promoting hygienic improvements in barracks, hospitals, prisons, and schools. Buchner reminded his fellow delegates of the splendid display by the Berlin fire department that they had witnessed only a few days previously:

> These men are not always occupied in fighting fires; they are therefore engaged in other work, but always in the vicinity of their station, so that they are always ready for their special task, whenever they are needed. I believe that this example can be applied perfectly to our subject. By keeping ourselves on the terrain of hygiene, we remain faithful to the basic purpose, strictly speaking, of our work of assistance; we augment it, and we are consequently ready to pursue it with all our resources.[120]

The strongest opposition to all these proposals for peacetime humanitarian activity came from the Russians. Dr. Hubbenet, speaking for the St. Petersburg central committee, warned that the time was not yet ripe for "such a change, such a complete reversal of the point of view of the Geneva Conference," which could destroy committees that are only just beginning to fulfill their principal task. Warming to his theme, he cautioned delegates not to put aside the focus on wounded soldiers or to transform their association into " a committee to do everything"; if we do that, he warned, "We will relieve few miseries, and we will do irreparable harm to our cause."[121] Donations given to the committees, he reminded his audience, were meant for the relief of sick and wounded soldiers; to do anything else with these funds would be both bad philanthropy and bad political economy and would accomplish little except to alienate actual and potential donors. Concluding that the Prussian proposals, though admirable, were nevertheless impossible to implement, Hubbenet took his seat amid a chorus of "Bravos!" loud enough to find its way into the minutes.[122] Between those who disliked the content of the proposals and those who disliked being told what to do by the various German societies, there was ready support for the Russian position.

Just as a consensus appeared to be developing that individual societies should go their own ways, taking the Prussian proposals merely as possible guidelines for future activity, Virchow once more entered the discussion. In what was certainly the most profound speech given at the conference, Virchow challenged the very essence of the movement by questioning the moral basis of its priorities. He began by acknowledging that the shortages of personnel and supplies which had brought the societies into being were real enough and that the Prussian proposals aimed to fill lacunae that had been obvious in recent wars. But then he shifted his focus to a different question:

> Is there any likelihood . . . of creating, by the methods proposed by the Prussian committee, personnel numerous enough to be able to respond, even approximately, to the demands of a war of great magnitude and of a war that will perhaps last a long time? For I think, gentlemen, that all research in this matter must be based on the supposition that in Europe wars could well break out, that are somewhat longer than those we have seen in recent years. I ask myself, therefore: if at this moment the central direction [of the aid society] were to address this appeal to the country: "Do all these things, organize yourselves, create reserve ambulances, construct barracks, tents for the sick, etc., bring together the necessary personnel and train them," I ask myself, I repeat, if at this moment the population would respond with ardor, with the necessary enthusiasm, to an appeal made on behalf of a war that is perhaps still a long way off? Is this not having recourse to a method that is, at least in part, illusory? Does it not seek forcibly to annex to war a great many activities that belong to civil life, which can find a natural and abundant source of nourishment in the needs of the masses? As if war were the normal state in Europe, and as if peace existed only to prepare for war! Do we never regret during peacetime the absence of a great number of these devoted and trained individuals? Do we not have a sufficiently large charitable task to undertake if we simply cast our glance around us at the ordinary circumstances of life? And if we wish to fulfill this task completely, should we not ask ourselves if it is sufficient to organize these special committees specifically for war? . . . Is it not therefore necessary to establish . . . an organization for peace which should at least parallel them and which, instead of seeming to say, "We are working only towards war," can proudly say, "Positively, definitively and with all our strength, we are working for peace!" . . . If we seriously wanted to make ourselves equal to this task, we would rather try to extend the organization of the committees by founding *a parallel category of committees for peace*, and by saying: We no longer recognize war as the supreme goal, but rather we consider *assistance to the sick and public hygiene* as our general task, as the Hessian committee has already proposed; and it is on this broad foundation that we are organizing, as a special subdivision, a committee for war. This, gentlemen, is the goal that I believe we ought to pursue.[123]

After such a stunning assault on the priorities of the movement, Virchow surprised his audience by endorsing in principle the proposals of the Prussian central committee. He did so, he explained, because he thought it was desirable for the committees "to create examples, models of a sort for the other, grander, more novel evolution that I wish to see accomplished."[124] However, he warned them that they were deluding themselves in thinking that they could ever by this route create sufficient trained personnel for the large wars to come. The value of these measures was, in his opinion, purely exemplary; once they had begun to change attitudes towards helping the sick poor,

I think [Virchow concluded] that the principal task of a future Conference will be to find ways to break out of the narrow circle which now limits our work only to the case of war. For, gentlemen, let us not deceive ourselves: by following the path that has been proposed to us, we will come to believe that assisting the sick in ordinary times is nothing more than a means of education for war, when [in reality] it is itself a goal of such importance that it ought rightfully to claim everyone's full attention.[125]

This was a grand speech, a speech worthy of the Virchow who had been an eloquent advocate of medical and social reform during the Revolutions of 1848 and whose report on the typhus epidemic in Upper Silesia had demonstrated his commitment to improving the health of the common people.[126] For him, charity began not on the battlefield but in the humble dwellings of the poor. Gently but remorselessly, his speech had exposed the selective humanitarianism on which the whole enterprise had been founded. The student of Red Cross history can only marvel at the extraordinary insight that it revealed: In his observations Virchow foreshadowed the very criticisms that pacifists, public health reformers, and philanthropists would in future level at the Red Cross, criticisms that would contribute after World War I to a fundamental rethinking of the priorities of the movement. Half a century was to pass before the Red Cross broke out of the narrow circle of war-related activities that it set for itself in the 1860s.

A grand speech it may have been, but it was largely lost on this audience. Some, undoubtedly, did not grasp what Virchow was driving at; others, trying to reduce his critique to manageable proportions, thought that he was simply arguing for a broader peacetime role than the Hessians had proposed. Finally, Dr. Brinkmann relegated Virchow to the wilderness of idealism by agreeing that "in a distant future" the priorities of the aid societies might be recast, but that "for the moment, we must still limit ourselves [to concentrating on the needs of war]."[127] In the end, the delegates adopted a series of compromises. Almost all of the Prussian proposals were accepted but only as "specially recommended arrangements and measures" from which individual societies could pick and choose as they saw fit. An Austrian amendment considerably watered down the degree of centralized direction that had been part of the original Prussian proposals. Once it had been agreed that the training of nurses—though not the care of the sick poor—was the first priority for peacetime work, the Hessians made one last attempt to persuade the assembly to make public hygiene the official second priority, but it failed to obtain the support of a majority.[128]

Of all the sessions held in Berlin, this one revealed most clearly which societies—and which individuals—had begun to think seriously about the problems associated with establishing permanent societies to deal with needs that were widely perceived to be temporary. Many people had thought Dunant's original suggestion impractical, just because such enthusiasm for wartime charitable work could not be sustained during years of peace. The Prussians were already embarked on a course of action that seemed to them both sensible and defensible; yet they were criticized for trying to do too much. The Hessian alternative was more limited in scope, yet even it had not obtained widespread support. Consequently the delegates left Berlin having discussed what might be done during peacetime without ever committing themselves to do anything in particular beyond preparing for war. However, the temptation to become what the Russians had called "a committee to do everything" had been resisted; Moynier must have been relieved.

Part Two

The Militarization of Charity

The great thing is to get into uniform; then you can start moving yourself around. It's a very exclusive war at present. Once you're in, there's every opportunity.

—Evelyn Waugh, *Men at Arms* (1952)

✚ 3

Trial by Combat

OR ALMOST A DECADE the promoters of aid societies and of the Geneva Convention had enjoyed widespread support and continued success. By 1870 Moynier was sure that they were riding the crest of a great wave of enlightenment and reason that would wash away the remnants of barbarism and create a new and higher stage in the development of civilization. Hardly had he articulated this vision of the future, however, when war broke out between the two most important states in Europe. The Franco-Prussian War of 1870–1871 was to be a watershed in the history of the relationship between war and charity: It provided opportunities for the aid societies of belligerents and neutrals to demonstrate their utility to army medical services and to the wounded themselves, and it gave the Comité International a chance to set up the temporary international charitable agency that had been discussed at the Berlin conference. At the same time, the war was a rigorous trial by combat for both the aid societies and the Geneva Convention. In its wake, there were many who thought that the experience of the war proved that aid societies were a mixed blessing and that the Geneva Convention needed to be rewritten if not rescinded. Thus the postwar years soon became a time of troubles for Moynier and the Comité International, who found themselves having to defend the integrity of their original conception against critics who were more often hostile than friendly. Fearing for the future of the whole enterprise, Moynier beat off successive threats to the Geneva Convention and tried his best to keep national animosities from wrecking what had been achieved so far. In this endeavor he had only very limited success: By the end of the decade, the Genevans' attempt to promote the cause of humanitarianism among nations was at the nadir of its fortunes.

Moynier and the New Law of War

In the spring of 1870, Moynier published his most important work to date, a three hundred-page essay on the Geneva Convention.[1] In it he traced the history of the Convention, provided a lengthy commentary on each of its articles, and described what further measures should be taken to ensure compliance with its provisions. For the historian of the Red Cross, the most interesting section of the essay is the introduction, to which Moynier gave the title, "The New Law of War." Here he revealed with utmost clarity the full moral meaning that he and his Genevan colleagues attached to the enterprise on which they had embarked in 1863, an enterprise that he was modest enough to describe as *"l'oeuvre civilisatrice"*—the task of making the world a more civilized place. If his contribution to *War and Charity* had placed the organization of aid to the wounded in the context of the history of charity, this essay placed both the Geneva Convention and the law of nations it embodied in the context of the history of morality. Expressed in the simplest terms, its message was that states were changing fundamentally the way in which they resolved disputes: War was on the way out, arbitration on the way in. This theme merits close attention because it is another important clue to the direction that the founders of the Red Cross expected their work to take.

The great task of the nineteenth century, in Moynier's view, was the elimination of the last vestiges of barbarism. Of these, "war, which still breaks out so frequently, even in the center of the most advanced civilization, is the most terrible, the most striking expression of this barbarian prejudice."[2] Yet if war itself had not yet been finally eliminated, the last hundred years had, in his view, seen a fundamental transformation in the ways in which Europeans thought about war and about the rights and duties of belligerents. No longer was untrammeled force acceptable; what Moynier believed to be the moral advance of civilization had already condemned pillage and other unnecessary attacks on private property, the breaking of solemn agreements, the poisoning of enemy armies, the assassination of enemy leaders, the massacre of prisoners or of harmless civilians, and countless other practices that had once been considered acceptable means of achieving victory.[3] For this change in attitudes Moynier offered several explanations: The increase in discipline apparent in the standing armies of modern states; the contemporary revival of charity and fraternity; the multiplication of trading and other contacts among the peoples of Europe; and the increased publicity that the popular press gave to the horrors as well as to the heroism of the battlefield.[4] The result of this great transformation, according to Moynier, was the emergence of a new view of war: Reason and humanity now dictated that war should be treated as "an inevitable evil, which must not exceed the limits of strict necessity."[5] It was the task of "the new law of war" to specify these limits as precisely as possible, so as to ensure that wars between states did not obliterate the moral ties that joined the human beings involved in fighting them.

A model of this new kind of war and of the new type of military commander was readily available: During the Sonderbund War of 1847, General Dufour, the commander of the Swiss federal forces, had proved that "a warrior can deserve as many laurels for his clemency as for his [military] exploits."[6] Moynier quoted in full Dufour's celebrated recommendations to his divisional commanders regarding the manner in which the war was to be conducted, including the postscript in which the general expressed his desire that the entire army should behave in such a way that "the whole world will know that this is not a meeting of barbarians."[7] In practice this meant ensuring the safety of defenseless civilians, particularly women, children, the aged, and members of the clergy; scrupulous treatment of hostages; absolute respect for church buildings and property as well as for the property of magistrates and civil officials; compassionate treatment of prisoners and of the wounded; a ban on reprisals in the face of enemy provocation; and a general injunction that all soldiers restrain themselves and spare those that they have conquered on the field of battle.[8] Dufour's clement policy was, arguably, more than a personal moral choice on the part of the federal commander; it was also dictated by the political imperatives of the Sonderbund War, which was fought with as little rancor as possible on the federal side, in order to keep the Swiss Confederation together. Disregarding the special circumstances that prevailed in 1847, Moynier treated the Sonderbund War as a model for the world, expressing his hope that the day would soon come when wars, if fought at all, would be fought with as much prudence and restraint as Dufour and his troops had shown toward the soldiers and inhabitants of the rebellious cantons.

To be sure, this optimistic assessment of the future was based on more than one brief and limited demonstration of civility in the conduct of war. Moynier believed recent history proved that the European powers were united in their desire to reduce the evils of war. Having outlawed privateering in the Treaty of Paris (1856), they had then ratified the Geneva Convention of 1864, negotiated the Additional Articles of 1868, and signed the St. Petersburg Convention of November, 1868, outlawing the use of certain weapons that caused unnecessary suffering. All of the belligerents in the War of 1866—Prussia, Austria, and Italy—had announced to the world their intention to respect (on a reciprocal basis) enemy merchant shipping, and Moynier took these "spontaneous" declarations as evidence of further moral progress.[9] He continued:

> For the moment the path to follow seems quite obvious: it was marked out by the conventions of Paris, Geneva, and St. Petersburg. Evidently this is the direction in which people will strive to erect a barrier against the unleashing of the fury and greed of those in combat; it is necessary that this ditch be dug deeply, in order to ensure that the principle is firmly entrenched that war shall not engender more than the minimum of evils compatible with its existence. By making it stronger at this point today, and at that one tomorrow, we shall eventually have established a continuous line of defense that will bring to the conduct of war as much humanity as possible. To speak more plainly, special treaties which seek to reduce the horrors of war are in all probability going to increase; those which are already in existence will call forth others, some aimed at improving them,

others at filling in gaps, and thus international legislation will ever more accurately reflect contemporary morals. Perhaps the day will come when there will be a general codification of the law of war.[10]

According to Moynier, only one thing could prevent the realization of this program: The suppression of war itself. If arbitration should replace force as the usual method of solving disputes between states, then efforts to humanize warfare would become redundant. Already, in 1856, the powers had evinced some sympathy for the idea of arbitration through the "good offices" of a friendly power; Moynier hoped that there might soon be a disposition to consider the establishment of a permanent international tribunal with the recognized, sovereign power "to render judgments in cases where the law of nations is invoked by one party or the other [and] which would have at its disposal all the bayonets of Europe in order to ensure the execution of its judgments."[11] Public opinion, he expected, would play a very important role in forcing governments to have recourse to arbitration. "Everything indicates that it [opinion] will continue to follow this path, and intervene more and more in quarrels between peoples, imposing its veto on the shedding of blood."[12] Moynier was convinced of the likelihood of this development not only because it was the rational and humane course but because the advocates of peace were becoming more numerous and influential than they had been in the past. "The peace societies are flourishing, especially the International Peace League, whose outstanding leader is the eminent economist, M. Frédéric Passy; they are recruiting adherents by the thousands and their influence, already apparent in the councils of sovereigns, can only extend itself and grow larger and larger. The future belongs to them."[13]

Moynier's *Étude sur la Convention de Genève* ranks alongside *War and Charity* as one of the two most important statements of the ideology of the founders of the Red Cross. (Dunant's *A Memory of Solferino*, although much better known, sheds little light either on the social role of aid societies or on the moral assumptions behind the law of nations.) Had the publication of the *Étude* not been immediately overshadowed by the outbreak of the Franco-Prussian War, Moynier's work might have attracted more attention; after all, he was following in the footsteps of Baron de Montesquieu, Cesare Beccaria, and Emmerich Vattel in desiring to extend to the law of war the same civilizing force that they had applied to civil law, criminal law, and international law.

His confident vision of a less brutal, more rational future was much more than a quaint hangover from the optimism of the eighteenth-century Enlightenment. As Geoffrey Best has shown, there was a strong, widespread movement for peace and international cooperation during the middle decades of the nineteenth century.[14] Moynier was at one with many of his contemporaries in assuming that this was an irreversible trend, the outstanding manifestation in their time of that grand civilizing principle that they believed explained both the last several centuries of European history and the place that Europe had come to occupy in the affairs of the world. It simply did not occur to Moynier that much of the evidence he cited for the moral progress of civilization could have been explained in another way. One of his contemporaries, Karl Marx, could doubtless have provided a less edifying explanation for the outlawing of privateering, pillage, and unauthorized attacks on private property. In 1870, however, there were many more influential people who thought like Moynier than thought like Marx. Not all did, but those who did not share Moynier's belief in the power of law to reflect a higher stage of moral development were likely to endorse Florence Nightingale's common-sense belief that some of the ideas contained in the Geneva Convention were simply impractical. In any case, Moynier's belief in the imminence of arbitration received a considerable setback when, on 19 July, 1870, France declared war on Prussia.

1870: French Disarray

In 1870, the French Society for Aid to Wounded Soldiers (Société de Secours aux Blessés Militaires des Armées de Terre et de Mer; hereafter SSBM or simply the society) was wholly unprepared for a major war. Despite the somewhat pompous speeches that its representatives had given at the Berlin conference, the reality was that the SSBM had little more than a paper existence. True, it had been host of the 1867 conference, but it had been unable to make any significant inroads on the war ministry and hence enjoyed no official status apart from a decree of June 1866, which recognized the "public utility" of its existence. Public indifference was almost as big an obstacle to its development as the hostility of the military.[15] Even the impressive exhibit of ambulance equipment, which it had organized during the Paris Exposition, was also a hollow triumph because by far the greatest number of items displayed came from the Prussian society and from the U.S. Sanitary Commission. In an effort to raise money, the SSBM held several charity balls at the Paris Opera House, but the funds produced were nowhere near what would be needed for a major war. No serious effort had been made to procure supplies, establish relations with the army or the medical profession, or train nurses and ambulance personnel; needless to say, no concerted plan of action had been worked out. For the realities of the battlefield the SSBM was little better prepared than Dunant had been when he found himself amid the carnage of Solferino.

Despite the lack of funds and the absence of a plan, the executive council of the SSBM met as soon as war had been declared and decided that their proper role was to organize, equip, and dispatch to the front as many volunteer ambulances as possible. (By the term *ambulance* they meant not a simply a vehicle for transporting the wounded but a temporary field hospital consisting of physicians and surgeons, male nurses, and all their equipment and transport.) The nation's leading expert in military surgery, Professor Léon Le Fort of the Paris Faculty of Medicine, was selected to organize the volunteer ambulances. This was a somewhat surprising choice because Le Fort was also a vocal critic of voluntary assistance in general and of the French society in particular. His response to *War and Charity* was quoted in the preceding chapter; in the same 1868 essay he had written,

> In France, the aid-societies are directed by Count __, the Marquis __, the Duke of something, excellent gentlemen, full of good intentions, worthy of all eulogy in this respect, much in earnest in their mission too, but who, quite ignorant of military medicine, may very well organize a ball at the opera, an exposition, or a museum; but would be very much puzzled at eight days' notice to set ambulance trains in motion, to assemble a multitude of surgeons, and large hospital supplies; for nothing would be ready.[16]

To his chagrin, Le Fort soon found that the SSBM was in even greater disorder than he had suspected: "When in July 1870 I took on the organization of volunteer ambulances, I was astonished, despite my already unfavorable expectations, to find neither material, nor medical personnel, nor plan of organization, nor money; for it appeared that there were only a few hundred francs in the treasury."[17]

Nevertheless, a medical committee was quickly organized under the presidency of the eminent surgeon Auguste Nélaton. Le Fort himself took charge of one ambulance; his colleague Sée, an anatomist, headed a second, and arrangements were made for two more to be led by other distinguished surgeons. They also selected two of their number to act as liaison between the medical committee in Paris and the ambulances at the front. As far as the physicians were concerned, medical matters were best handled by medical men.

These hastily organized but thoroughly professional arrangements did not, however, sit well with senior members of the SSBM, who felt that they were being left out of all the important work. Count Sérurier, now vice-president, complained bitterly to Nélaton that he now had no significant role to play.[18] The medical men had expected that the council would raise money and, following their advice, purchase and organize whatever supplies were needed. However, the aristocrats who made up the council resented being reduced to collecting subscriptions and organizing storage depots while the surgeons shared in the excitement and glory of the battlefield. No doubt some of them dreamed of playing a role similar to that which the Prussian Knights of St. John had played in the Wars of 1864 and 1866. Whatever the motives, a confrontation between privilege and professionalism soon developed. On 8 August, three days after Le Fort had left Paris with the first ambulance unit, the aristocrats staged a sort of *fronde* against the tyranny of medical expertise. Nélaton was abruptly relieved of his position as surgeon-in-chief, the

111

3.1 The first SSBM ambulance leaves for the front. Caught unprepared by the outbreak of war in 1870, the French Society for Aid to Wounded Soldiers hastily improvised field ambulance units.

medical committee was dissolved, and all ambulances in the field were placed under the direct orders of the president of the SSBM, Count de Flavigny. To lend a veneer of medical legitimacy to their actions, the aristocrats appointed the now elderly Crimean veteran, Dr. Chenu—another erstwhile critic of aid societies—to the new position of inspector and director-general of the medical service of the SSBM.[19] Now free to do as they pleased, the aristocrats set about creating ambulances as quickly as they could. The fact that they were neither medically qualified nor serving military men bothered them not a whit; filled with patriotic enthusiasm, they were determined to demonstrate what a splendid contribution private charity could make on the battlefield.[20] Like Henry Dunant and Louis Appia, they believed that in this field noble motives and sincere devotion were the primary requisites for success.

It soon became apparent, however, that enthusiasm and an air of authority were no substitute for a plan of organization. The aristocrats seemed to think that any medical man of good family and social position could run an ambulance. Some of their choices outraged the professional standards and sensibilities of qualified surgeons such as Le Fort and Nélaton. Ordinary physicians with little or no experience of gunshot wounds, whom the medical committee might have appointed as surgeons' aides, were now put in charge of ambulances.[21] Lacking any sense of proportion, the council assigned far too many personnel to some ambulances and far too few to others. The ratio of doctors to nurses varied from 1:5 in the fifth ambulance to 1:1 in the eighth. The fifth ambulance, with the amazing complement of 164 persons, was assigned only three vehicles to accompany it to its destination. According to William MacCormac, an English surgeon who served with the (neutral) Anglo-American ambulance, "Some of these ambulances [sent out by the SSBM] spent most of their time in marching and counter marching, never reaching, in time to be of use, the actual scene of operations. Their wagons would often stick fast in some country by-road, or in a field, and then they would have to be abandoned."[22] Supplies and equipment were similarly haphazard. Lucas Championnière, surgeon in charge of the absurdly large fifth ambulance, reported to Le Fort that when they opened the equipment boxes, there was

> no presentable amputation saw; only two were found in the boxes, and they were so bad that we sawed femurs with a small handsaw [instead]. There was [only] 1500 grams of chloroform. By way of revenge, they had supplied 18 kilograms of cucumber ointment! Everything was like this. I cannot imagine that we would have seen such things if the direction of the Aid Society had been in the hands of physicians. . . . If our organization had been better at [the decisive battle of] Sédan, we would have been able to look after triple the number of wounded.[23]

To be sure, there is a certain amount of wishful thinking here. Even with its professional expertise, the medical committee could scarcely have overcome the SSBM's basic weaknesses; it might have improvised better, but it would still have been improvising. Indeed, with the Prussians already well into

3.2   The outdoor annex of the Press Ambulance (financed by the newspapers of
Paris) in the rue Ouainot, in 1870. After the war, two of the physicians attached to
this temporary hospital tried to persuade the SSBM to set up a training program for
ambulance personnel, but they failed.

3.3   An improvised ambulance depot at the Porte d'Italie during the Prussian siege
of Paris.

French territory there was no possibility of doing anything else. Still, better improvisation might have been preferable; as MacCormac noted,

> For a moving ambulance, the smaller the quantity of stores taken the better, and these without exception should be carried on horses or mules. The wagons are a serious impediment. . . . What is most needed are a few cases of surgical instruments and appliances, some medicines, chloroform and carbolic acid, one moderate-sized tent, and half a dozen stretchers of the simplest construction, to carry the wounded and to serve as beds. These, and some tins of preserved foods and biscuits, are all that need be carried about. For whatever else may be required, one must trust to the supplies of the place in which one may happen to be.[24]

Unused to improvisation, the aristocrats had outfitted the ambulances as if they were moving from their town houses to their country estates.

The clash of attitudes was particularly obvious in the selection of volunteer male nurses to accompany the ambulances. Experienced surgeons such as Le Fort were furious when the aristocrats decided to accept all volunteers, giving preference to individuals "distinguished by their social position, wealth, and education."[25] These he regarded as nothing more than high-society amateurs, motivated only by transient enthusiasm and curiosity, who had not the slightest idea how to care for the sick and wounded.

> Anyone who knows what is involved in hospital or ambulance service [wrote Le Fort] knows that the services required of a male nurse do not consist of dressing wounds; the nurse must perform a host of manual tasks which the poetry of devotion no longer surrounds with its halo: chopping wood, carrying water, cooking, housecleaning duties, burying the dead, setting up tents, caring for the horses and—no less important in the circumstances—obeying one's superiors and doing everything that the officer has the right to require of the soldier. We had not been *en route* twenty-four hours when a viscount, [who was] a volunteer nurse, had already replied to a surgeon who had asked him to bandage his horse that he had come to bandage the wounded and not horses and, when given the order to fetch wood or water, that he was a nurse and not a domestic servant.[26]

Aristocratic pretension was not the only problem faced by the ambulance surgeons. According to Le Fort, many of the volunteer nurses behaved more like vagabonds than viscounts: "With all too rare exceptions, [they were] the finest collection of idlers and drunks one could ever hope to lead."[27] No doubt some of them *were* idlers and drunks, just as some were unemployed workers and domestic servants; since the council of the society had made no arrangements to train nurses beforehand, they had perforce to take what they could get. Le Fort was horrified to discover that some so-called nurses were more interested in plundering the dead than caring for the living.[28] When Metz surrendered and his ambulance fell under enemy authority, he pleaded with the Prussians to post a guard on the hospital to keep his nurses in line. Worse, the ambulances soon became "the refuge of all the cowards"; Lucas Championnière reported to Le Fort that both in Paris and in the provinces, "men who were frightened or wanting to evade military service" were turning up dressed as volunteer nurses and wearing the red cross armband.[29] Such incidents created great embarrassment for the bona fide surgeons who wore similar uniforms.

On top of all this, the surgeons had to cope with the phenomenon of "bandage dilettantes" (*dilettantes du pansements*), ladies of high social position who decided that it would be great fun to have a hospital of their own and who, as Le Fort commented acerbically, "played doctor with our unfortunate soldiers, like little girls playing mother with their dolls."[30] To be sure, France had no monopoly on "bandage dilettantes"; their counterparts were to be found on the German side and also among the volunteers sent to both sides by the English society. Nor would it be fair to suggest that well-born French ladies were generally useless as nurses. Even the crusty Le Fort paid tribute to those, like one Madame Cahen at Metz, who "did not promenade through the streets of the town with ambulance armbands and crosses; [instead] they were content to earn the recognition of our unfortunate soldiers, just as they deserved all our respect, all our veneration."[31] Indeed, Le Fort came out of the war convinced that society ladies could be very useful to the hospital service, not in changing dressings—the surgeon's task—or in doing menial tasks (a role he believed best filled by trained working-class women) but rather by presiding over the good order, regularity, and tone of the hospital.

The ease with which both ladies of quality and shirkers could obtain red cross armbands is a striking reminder of how little effort had been made by the government to ensure that France complied with the provisions of the Geneva Convention. Not only had the war ministry virtually ignored the existence of the national aid society; it had also done surprisingly little to implement the 1864 Convention, let alone the Additional Articles of 1868. No attempt had been made to familiarize French soldiers with the terms of the Geneva Convention or with the meaning of the Red Cross flag and armband. As the British military attaché wrote from Paris before war broke out, "Nothing has been done here with regard to the Geneva convention. They are also of opinion that it is all very well and pretty in theory, but very difficult if not impossible to carry out in practice. After an action it is about as much as one can do to look after one's own wounded and the neutrality clause might give rise to great inconvenience."[32]

Six years after Intendant de Préval had signed the Convention for France, the military intendance administration had still not succeeded in persuading army surgeons to wear armbands. After the war was over, Le Fort recalled,

> When we arrived at Metz, not one French army doctor, not one male nurse was wearing the armband, not one ambulance vehicle bore the distinctive sign of neutrality; only at the door of some ambulances belonging to the quartermaster-general was there floating a little white pennant with a red woolen Maltese cross in the center, but it was so small that it could scarcely be seen from 200 or 300 meters. Moreover, our army colleagues accepted only with repugnance this

distinctive sign, whose purpose was to protect them, and during the entire campaign the armband was more often to be found in their pocket than on the sleeve of their uniform.[33]

French army surgeons were evidently still wedded to the idea that they were combatants first and physicians second and believed that wearing the badge of neutrality would be seen as a confession of weakness or cowardice.

If the intendance administration permitted French surgeons to conceal their armbands, its policy with regard to the general populace was just the reverse. Armbands were readily available to virtually anyone who wanted one. Le Fort later wrote with feeling about what he called "armband madness" (*la manie du brassard*):

> After [the battles of] Borny and Gravelotte, the military intendance . . . distributed them in profusion. Soldiers performing service tasks, peasants driving requisitioned vehicles but who had nothing in common with the sanitary service, ladies caring for the wounded, all of them wore an armband stamped by the intendance. The abuse soon had serious consequences, of which the least was that it permitted those wretches who follow all armies to go onto the battlefield and pillage the dead, on the pretext of searching for the wounded.[34]

Not surprisingly, the Germans soon began to complain of such behavior and questioned why they should extend the protection of the Convention to an enemy that so flagrantly abused its terms.

Even more notorious was the abuse of Article 5 of the Convention, which relieved civilians who cared for the wounded from the customary obligation of billeting soldiers. The Additional Articles of 1868 had attempted to modify this clause to make it less of a carte blanche, but to no avail; in 1870 the civilian population quickly grasped that claiming to care for a wounded soldier might exempt them from this onerous and universally detested obligation. Flags bearing the red cross symbol quickly appeared on every house and habitation. In those towns and villages where the arrival of Prussian troops was thought to be imminent "houses put out flags as if by magic. The town was filled with ambulances; but if anyone went into one of these improvised hospitals to inquire as to the number of beds available, he most often found that the 'ambulance' contained only one bed, which was that of the owner."[35]

In some cases, the unfortunate soldiers might have been better off had they died in the battle, but one can scarcely blame the peasants for trying to get as much benefit as possible out of the loose wording of Article 5. Needless to say, this behavior was scarcely what Moynier had in mind when he anticipated that the Convention would improve the morality of the common people. Less excusable was the striking ignorance demonstrated by members of the French national aid society and by some volunteer ambulance personnel, who apparently believed that the emblem of neutrality gave them the right to go wherever they wanted or do whatever they pleased, regardless of the exigencies of war. Thus two French volunteer ambulances tried to cross through enemy lines to reach Metz while the city was still besieged.[36] Members of the society became indignant when the Germans sent back captured French ambulances via Belgium or Switzerland, so as to ensure that their personnel did not divulge to the enemy information about troop movements and positions. Their protests, Le Fort observed sadly, "indicate little understanding of the laws and necessities of war, and of the spirit, or even the text, of the Convention."[37] In short, the French record in 1870 was not likely to inspire confidence either in the role of aid societies or in the utility of the Geneva Convention.

1870: German Efficiency

In complete contrast to the shambles on the French side was the careful organization of medical and charitable assistance on the German side. To be sure, the Prussians had reaped the benefit of considerable field experience in wartime conditions. The War of 1866 had been a testing ground for the Prussian aid society, but it had also revealed shortcomings in the organization of the army's field medical services. The embarrassment of Koeniggratz, when army surgeons had found themselves virtually helpless in the face of an inundation of wounded, led to recriminations and calls for a thoroughgoing reform of military medicine.[38] In the spring of 1867, the Prussian ministry of war invited "the most distinguished representatives of science in the civil order, for the most part professors of surgery in the different universities of the country" to attend a conference on the army medical service.[39] Many of these surgeons had been called upon to assist their army colleagues in 1866 and were only too glad to give the ministry the benefit of their experience. The conference met in Berlin for six weeks under the chairmanship of Friedrich Loeffler. Out of its deliberations came a series of measures, implemented in 1868–1869, that entirely reorganized the structure and function of military medical services; these in turn necessitated a corresponding reorganization of the role and work of the aid society.

Centralization, system, and professionalism were the most important features of this reorganization of military medicine. For the first time, the war ministry created, under the command of a surgeon-general (*Generalstabsarzt*), a separate army medical division that was responsible for the provision of all medical services and for the administration of military hospitals. Also for the first time, medical officers were given ranks equivalent to those of regular officers, with which went the right of command; for senior ranks, a system of promotion based on merit and professional competence was introduced.[40] These measures were followed by new instructions—introduced on 29 April, 1869—regarding health and sanitation in the field, the aim of which was to ensure that regimental commanders consulted with medical officers about

3.4   Stretcher-bearers of the Karlsruhe Red Cross, 1870–1871.

everything that pertained to the health of soldiers in the field. At the same time, several important changes were made in the organization of field medical services. The most notable of these innovations was the creation of "sanitation detachments," twelve of which were assigned to every army corps. The role of the sanitation detachment was twofold: Its principal task was to transport the wounded from the front lines to field hospitals in the rear, but it was also equipped and trained to operate a temporary dressing station close to the front for those too seriously wounded to be transported without immediate attention.[41]

The 1869 reorganization also made provision for the creation of a system of evacuation and hospitalization that would ensure proper care for the wounded from the moment they reached a field hospital until they had been sent, by hospital train, back to Germany for convalescence. Every army corps was assigned a distinguished civilian physician or surgeon who would act as a consultant for its medical officers in wartime. Finally, jurisdiction over medical supplies was transferred from general supply officers to officers of the new medical division.[42] Taken as a whole, the reorganization enhanced the authority of medical officers vis-à-vis both line and supply officers; created a well-thought-out system of field medical services, evacuation, and hospitalization; and provided a means by which the army could draw upon civilian medical expertise whenever it was most needed.[43]

These sweeping changes were introduced only five years after Louis Appia had witnessed the Prussians at war with Denmark. What role would civilian

3.5 A branch of the German Red Cross stages a first aid training display.

charity play now that military medical services had been made more professional and more systematic? Already the knights and deacons that Appia had observed during his visit to Schleswig were beginning to appear obsolete; nor was there room in the new Prussian arrangements for "delegates of humanity" who would suddenly arrive on the battlefield. Instead, the Prussians set about making the national aid society into a civilian auxiliary of the military medical service, indeed of the army itself. A leading figure in this transformation was Dunant's great admirer, Queen Augusta.

It was at the queen's instigation that the subject of voluntary assistance had been reviewed by the experts convened by the ministry of war in 1867.[44] They decided that with emergency field medical services and the transport of wounded assigned to the newly created sanitation detachments, the most sensible task for voluntary assistance to perform would be the creation and training of a corps of volunteer nurses. It was known that the various religious foundations, both Protestant and Catholic, could supply no more than nine hundred nurses and perhaps fifty male nurses, a total that fell far short of anticipated needs. As founder and patron of the Women's Patriotic Society, Queen Augusta encouraged local branches to expand their peacetime role to include both the training of nurses who would care for the sick poor and the creation of barrack-hospitals that could be used as reserve hospitals in wartime.

To set an example, she founded the Berlin Society for the Creation and Maintenance of Lazarettos, the principal aim of which was the training of nurses. In April, 1869, the statutes of the national aid society were modified

3.6 Members of the Women's Patriotic Society and their assistants preparing crates of supplies for shipment to the front during the Franco-Prussian War.

to allow local branches to devote some of their resources to caring for the sick poor, training nurses, and building reserve hospitals.[45] Many branches established nursing sisterhoods, in which trainee sisters lived in communities called "motherhouses" (*mutterhausen*), modeled upon religious communities such as the Kaiserwerth Institution.[46] As Catherine Prelinger has pointed out, such communities could expect to draw recruits from "a precarious segment of German womanhood: young single women deprived of a secure existence by the contemporary strains in the traditional economy."[47]

This new approach to voluntary assistance quickly spread beyond Prussia itself to include most of the other German states. Prior to the Paris conference in 1867, the aid societies of the various German states had met together at Wuerzburg, and they met again in Berlin before the opening of the international conference in 1869. At this latter meeting, the Prussians pressed for the formation of a common organization of German aid societies and for the creation of a new central committee in which all of the individual societies would be represented.[48] It need scarcely be added that both the consolidated organization and the reconstituted central committee were devices for extending the influence of the Prussian central committee throughout the German states.

When war with France came in 1870, the German aid societies played the new role assigned to them by the war ministry. There had not yet been time

3.7　Members of a *sanitätskorps* enjoy a well-earned rest period between battles during the Franco-Prussian War.

to train all the nurses that the army required, but volunteers were quickly pressed into service to staff hospitals, quarantine stations, and hospital trains. Once again Queen Augusta set an example for the women of Germany by making bandages to supplement the supplies of the medical division and the aid societies.[49] In keeping with the principle of centralized control articulated in the 1869 regulations, the king appointed Prince Pless to the position of royal commissioner and inspector general of voluntary assistance; from a central office in Berlin, the Prince coordinated all aspects of voluntary assistance and functioned as the sole intermediary between the war ministry and the aid committees.[50] Every aspect of the work of the aid societies came under the supervision of the royal commissioner and his delegates. Volunteers who served on hospital trains found themselves taking orders from these delegates as well as from the military surgeon and escort who accompanied each train. Male and female nurses, supplied by the aid societies to supplement the staff of the army's reserve hospitals, were placed under the authority of the physician in charge of the hospital. Even the hospitals established in the rear by the aid societies themselves were under the control and supervision of delegates of the royal commissioner, as were the dressing and refreshment stations set up in railway stations. All aid society personnel were required to wear armbands, and these were only valid when signed by the prince himself.[51] In short, voluntary assistance was completely subjected to state control, and the aid societies enjoyed no autonomy whatever.

The royal commissioner, Prince Pless, was also grand master of the Order of St. John, and he chose some three hundred knights from this Order and some from the Order of Malta to act as his delegates in dealings with the aid societies. The knights adapted well to this new role, which was essentially that of policing the personnel and work of the aid societies in the interests of the army and the state. Their special status, a mark of aristocratic privilege, had been preserved, albeit at some cost, since they now functioned as servants of the state. Yet the state's reliance upon the social standing and good intentions of the knights ran counter to the thrust of the recent reform of the military medical service because it once again put substantial authority over what were often medical decisions—or decisions about medical personnel—in the hands of those who had no medical training. Among members of the official medical service, there were frequent and virtually unanimous complaints about the interference of zealous but ignorant knight-delegates in matters beyond their competence.[52] Nevertheless, with physicians, hospital attendants, and stretcher-bearers in short supply whenever fighting was heavy, the many contributions of individual members of the Order, some of whom personally defrayed the costs of outfitting bearer corps and field dressing stations, were welcome indeed.[53]

3.8 An improvised field hospital during the Franco-Prussian War; note the sick-bearers carrying in the wounded.

1870: "Wondrous Feats of Charity"

The war between France and Prussia provided the International Committee in Geneva with an opportunity to establish the correspondence and information bureau that had been approved at the Berlin conference. When the committee met on 18 July to discuss the appropriate course of action, Louis Appia, always the activist, tried to persuade his colleagues that they should immediately send whatever help they could to the belligerents and send delegates to the armies who would "testify to the living presence, practical interest, and active sympathy" of the International Committee.[54] No doubt he saw himself being sent as one of the delegates to the Prussian army, where he could relive the exciting moments of the Wars of 1864 and 1866. The others were less enthusiastic: General Dufour cautioned prudence, especially considering that the two powers involved were "the principal supporters of the movement"; Moynier feared that by attempting to do too much, the committee "risked compromising its neutral character and its moral prestige."[55] In the end they decided to establish an information bureau to facilitate communication between national committees and to coordinate the sending of neutral assistance to the belligerents. Basle was chosen as the most appropriate location for the bureau, and a small staff was appointed to run it. The various central committees were informed of these actions in a circular letter (No. 20), dated 18 July, 1870; the bureau operated under the name of the International Agency of Information and Assistance to the Sick and Wounded.[56]

Appia was nevertheless unhappy at such a limited role. Ever the advocate of personal charity on the battlefield itself, he appealed for volunteers, drew up a list of useful articles for them to carry, and urged Moynier (who had gone to Basle to organize the agency) to decide whether the International Committee would encourage volunteers to go on their own—as he had done in the Tiarno—or authorize the formation of an organized corps.[57] On Moynier's return from Basle, Appia informed his colleagues that he had received passports from both the French and the Germans and that he intended to go in person to tend the wounded and to observe the operation of voluntary assistance on both sides. It was a repetition of his 1864 offer to go to Schleswig, but this time the response from his colleagues was markedly less enthusiastic. Indeed, they formally resolved *not* to give him the status of an official delegate "in order to avoid anything that could cast doubt upon the complete neutrality that inspires the International Committee."[58] So Appia set off on his own, traveling via Basle and Karlsruhe to Speyer, where he found his old friend, Loeffler, now senior medical officer of the Prussian Third Army, who gladly provided him with an official authorization and a red cross armband signed by Prince Pless. For the next several months, Appia ran his own show, tending the wounded and helping out in hospitals and dressing stations, all the while keeping Moynier advised of his movements in hastily written letters. When one French newspaper carried a story about a member of the International Committee being at the front, Moynier wrote a formal disclaimer, pointing out that Appia's presence at the front was entirely a personal matter and had no official connection with the International Committee.[59] Not until early December did Appia return to Geneva.

The agency in Basle quickly grew into a four-part operation that eventually required more than thirty people to run it. Several members of the Comité International directed its central office, which was besieged by visiting delegates from various aid societies and by physicians, nurses, and other individuals who desired to help. Such was the degree of ignorance about the provisions of the 1864 Convention that many of these visitors thought there was *one* international aid society that included all countries and expected that it would distribute red cross armbands and flags to anyone who asked for them. Some were annoyed and others disillusioned when they were told that valid armbands could only be obtained from the military authorities of the warring states. The agency borrowed the Basle casino as the site of its information bureau, which handled requests for information about missing soldiers and arranged for the transmission of soldiers' letters to families in France and Germany and for families to send money to relatives who had been taken prisoner. A huge storage depot was established conveniently close to the railway line; "warm clothing, linen, bandage material, foodstuffs, wines, there was everything in this charity warehouse," Moynier wrote enthusiastically after a tour of inspection.[60] In addition to the supplies donated, the agency used a considerable portion of the nearly 300,000 francs it received in donations to purchase additional items requested by the belligerents: more clothing, food and wine, medicines and crutches, cigars, blankets, and so on. Other cash expenditures were made to equip ambulances, to provide surveillance for goods in transit, and to pay for railway transport through Switzerland.[61] Finally, the Basle agency staffed and operated a hospital for wounded French soldiers incapable of further military service—more than 1,500 of them in the course of 1870—who were being repatriated from Germany via Switzerland.

Because aid was sent wherever the need was greatest, the Comité International found itself sending more help to the French than to the German side. With its close rail connection to Lyon, Geneva soon came to be as useful a base as Basle, especially when the scale of the repatriation operation increased with the passage of time. The information bureau set up in Geneva published, with the cooperation of the German military authorities, lists of wounded French soldiers who had been taken prisoner. Geneva established its own supply depot as well as facilities to care for invalids who were being repatriated back to France. Geneva also became the seat of the "special committee for prisoners" that the Comité International decided, with scrupulous legality, to establish as a separate entity with its own emblem—a green cross—because the 1864 Convention had associated the red cross emblem only with sick and wounded soldiers and had been silent about the fate of able-bodied prisoners.[62]

Not all assistance from neutrals came in the form of donations; several national societies decided to provide medical and other relief directly to the armies of the belligerents. Neighboring states were, perhaps not surprisingly, the most active: Both surgeons and supplies were sent by the Belgian, British, Dutch, Italian, Luxembougeois, and Swiss societies. The Russian society also sent delegates, stores, and several military surgeons. Of these foreign operations, the Anglo-American Ambulance has become the best known, thanks to the memoirs of several of its participants, but it would be inaccurate to think of it as an early example of planned cooperation between two national societies.[63] In fact, it was the impromptu creation of several American physicians resident in Paris—none of whom had any connection with the remnants of the Sanitary Commission—assisted by John Furley, a delegate of the British society, whose enthusiastic support for the enterprise was reluctantly confirmed by its cautious president, Colonel Robert Loyd-Lindsay.[64] None of the ambulance units supplied by neutral societies was in any sense under the control of the Comité International or its agency in Basle; this aspect of neutral assistance was entirely uncoordinated, except in so far as each ambulance operating in the war zone had to secure permission from the military authorities in order to carry out its mission.

Paradoxically, the armistice agreement reached in late January, 1871 increased the need for charitable assistance just at a time when donations were already falling behind. General Bourbaki's French Army of the East, excluded from the armistice but incorrectly advised that the war was over, found itself forced to seek refuge in neutral Switzerland, and suddenly the Swiss were confronted with caring for more than 80,000 exhausted and starving French soldiers, at least 5,000 of whom fell into the category of sick and wounded.[65] Moynier, concerned as ever to preserve the legal niceties, quickly established a separate and temporary Central Agency for Assistance to Soldiers Interned in Switzerland.[66] The new agency, working with the Swiss Red Cross, made a special appeal for help, and fresh donations poured in, including 30,000 francs sent by the German Red Cross. Only with the conclusion of peace was the Comité International finally able, in early March, to close down the special services provided by its bureaus in Basle and Geneva; those seeking information about the fate of soldiers still missing were told to direct their inquiries to the Red Cross central committees in Paris and Berlin.[67] In a final report on wartime activities, Moynier calculated that, taking into account gifts in money and in kind, the Comité International had dispensed more than 3 million francs in assistance to the sick and wounded.[68] He concluded on a congratulatory note: In 1863, when the enterprise was begun, "no one could have foreseen the wondrous feats of charity which it would bring forth in 1870."[69]

Lessons from the War

Moynier's satisfaction was to be short-lived. The war may have provided him with a grand demonstration of the power of charity, but others who were equally interested in the relationship between war and charity drew different lessons from it, and these did not always bode well for the future of either the Red Cross or the Geneva Convention. The first of these lessons, not surprisingly, concerned the excellence of the military medical organization of the German army. According to one recent study, knowledgeable contemporaries attributed the evident superiority of German military medicine to its better organization, its rationalized command structure, its emphasis on prevention as well as treatment, and its use of specially trained stretcher-bearers.[70] Vaccination against smallpox and strict attention to hygiene and sanitation in the field meant that German troops remained far healthier throughout the war than had previously been the case: For the first time in the recorded history of warfare in Europe, an army lost fewer men to disease than to enemy action.[71] The Germans also drew praise because their surgeons attempted to reduce infections by using carbolic acid and because their skillful use of railways for evacuating the wounded substantially improved soldiers' chances of recovery. Indeed, so impressive was their overall record that during the next decade every major European state introduced reforms in the organization of military medicine that were inspired by the Prussian example.[72]

Welcome though the Prussian achievements were to those who cared about the plight of sick and wounded soldiers, they nevertheless raised serious questions about the continued need for voluntary aid. When Moynier and Appia were writing *War and Charity*, they had capitalized on the sentimental response to Dunant's book and had presented Europeans with a choice between doing nothing for the sick and wounded and forming aid societies. With the alternatives put so starkly, one scarcely needed to be a philanthropist in order to prefer action to neglect. At that time, only a few informed individuals—Dr. Chenu and Florence Nightingale among them—had questioned whether forming voluntary aid societies was indeed the best way to help the sick and wounded. Now, however, the achievements of the Prussians seemed to indicate that improved military medical organization could dramatically reduce both the incidence and severity of sickness and could substantially improve the care of the wounded. The choice was no longer—if it ever had been—between doing nothing and doing something for the sick and wounded: Now the choice was between Prussian efficiency and French disarray.

The enviable record of the Prussians naturally lent retrospective legitimacy to the decision taken in 1869 to entrust combat ambulance work to the military medical service while severely restricting the role of voluntary assistance. Baldly stated, the Prussians had first removed the would-be "delegates of humanity" from the battlefield to the rear and then demonstrated that these new arrangements left the sick and wounded better off than in any previous war. The lesson was clear to contemporaries: Charles Gordon devoted several pages of his influential *Lessons on Hygiene and Surgery from the Franco-Prussian War* to contrasting the usefulness of the trained Prussian sickbearers with the harm done to the wounded by hastily recruited and untrained French *brancardiers*.[73] "Great care is taken in the selection of men for the corps of krankenträgers, those of known respectability, and they generally married and belonging to the Landwehr, being so employed";[74] the obvious lesson to be drawn was that such men would never shirk their duty and could be relied upon not to pillage or otherwise harm the wounded. In the memoirs of Le Fort and other surgeons who had observed the ambulances organized by the SSBM, Gordon found plenty of evidence that the French stretcher-bearers and male nurses were almost invariably worthless; in the words of one observer, "they were ignorant, dirty, negligent, disobedient, and insolent."[75] At the Berlin conference in 1869, critics of the Prussians had defended the role of the voluntary ambulance; now, they had to reckon with the fact that the French national aid society—admittedly not the best organized—had done little to advance their cause.

In what William H. McNeill has called "the Prussian way of war,"[76] there was really no place on the battlefield for civilian volunteers, especially if they were women. In the words of one experienced medical officer,

> It is rarely that female nurses can with advantage be employed in the field, or even in the second line of assistance. They are unequal to the hardships which are inseparable from field service; and their presence with lazareths [field ambulances] near the scene of operations is seldom advisable, partly from the difficulty of finding them accommodation, supposing that the campaign is made without tents; and the position would entail an amount of danger only justifiable under severe pressure. The employment too in such situations is usually distasteful to the recently wounded, who will often . . . [prefer] the rough aid of those of their own sex. . . . But the positions where their full measure of usefulness could be made available were in the standing and reserve hospitals, near the base of operations and on the lines of communication, and especially in the charge of purely medical cases; in such positions, they carried out the directions of the surgeons with mechanical exactness . . . precise obedience . . . and conscientiousness.[77]

After praising female nurses for their quietness, earnestness, and self-sacrifice, the same writer extolled "their easy adaptability to circumstances [which] is one of their most useful characteristics."[78] This he found manifested in their willingness to scrub floors, make beds, cook meals, and supervise storerooms. (He did not, of course, feel any need to explain why their "easy adaptability" did not extend to serving in field ambulances.) What seemed to recommend women most was not so much their sympathy for suffering but rather their ability to function as obedient servants: efficient, useful, versatile, and, above all, trustworthy. Surprisingly, it was precisely because they were seen to lack some of these qualities that deaconesses were not favored as nurses by German surgeons. In marked contrast to Louis Appia's flattering portrayal of the women from Kaiserwerth and other such institutions, Gordon's evidence indicated that "all medical men agreed . . . that the deaconess sister lacked that implicit obedience to her medical chief which any good nurse would be ready and willing to render" and that they frequently neglected the bodily needs of their patients in preference to their perceived spiritual requirements.[79] The evidence from 1870–1871 seems to indicate, therefore, that the woman who would be most use in wartime possessed qualities more akin to those of a good servant than those of a good Christian.

Not only did the Franco-Prussian War call into question several of the most fundamental assumptions made by the founders of the Red Cross about the need for, and role of, voluntary aid in wartime; it also provided plenty of ammunition for critics of the Geneva Convention, who could now be numbered in the hundreds if not thousands. Virtually everyone involved in the war, belligerent or neutral, knew of instances where the Red Cross flag and armband had been flagrantly abused. Some of these episodes were no doubt apocryphal, but many—far too many—were not. Ominously, the most controversial clauses in the Geneva Convention and the Additional Articles proved to be those that had sought to broaden the humanitarian impulse by encouraging civilians to assist the wounded, by encouraging belligerents to repatriate wounded prisoners judged incapable of further combat, and by providing for the conditional return of captured surgeons and ambulance personnel. There can be no doubt that the war vindicated Nightingale's belief that many of the provisions of the Convention would prove inoperable or unenforceable in practice. Inevitably, therefore, the remainder of the decade was given over to a prolonged debate over whether the Geneva Convention should be rewritten or abolished.[80] At one end of the spectrum were the basically sympathetic souls who blamed its failings primarily on loose wording and human ignorance; at the other, resolute opponents who believed that the whole enterprise had been fundamentally misguided. The longer this debate continued, the more uncertain became the future of both the Geneva Convention and the aid societies themselves.

"A Grave and Delicate Matter"

Understandably, Moynier and his colleagues did not immediately appreciate the extent to which the Franco-Prussian War had thrown into jeopardy what they had thought of as the civilizing mission (*l'oeuvre civilisatrice*) of the Red Cross. In December, 1870, the central committee of the Austrian society, which was to have hosted the next international Red Cross conference in 1871, decided that the conference should be postponed until there had been time for some preliminary discussions about the lessons of the war, the responsibility for which, it was suggested, belonged to the Comité International. Once its wartime agencies had been closed, the Comité turned its attention to the subject, and on 1 June, 1871 it announced a plan to hold a preliminary meeting—an international commission rather than a full conference—in Geneva, perhaps in October or November, to consider the issues and prepare a document that could serve as a basis for discussion at the Vienna conference when it finally did meet.[81] The various central committees were invited to send to Geneva, *before the first day of August,* questions that could be considered by the commission under three principal headings: war relief work of aid societies, relations between the societies of neutral and belligerent states, and revisions to the Geneva Convention. Neutral societies were permitted one delegate each; France and Germany, the belligerents with (presumably) the most to teach the others, were permitted five delegates each. Moynier and his colleagues expressed their hope that in such a gathering the discussions could be "more informal, more intimate" than at a large conference, so that the issues would receive the long and serious study that they deserved.[82] In order to ensure that the atmosphere would be friendly and productive, they decided to "eliminate from the program any sort of inquest into the wrongs which the belligerents might have suffered during the war."[83] In a crucially important note inserted in the next issue of the *Bulletin International,* the Comité revealed its reasons for dropping from the agenda the very subject that many people felt most strongly about:

> The most important consideration that led us to put aside the subject of recriminations on the conduct of the belligerents, is that in so doing the Conference would exceed its rightful sphere of action. The Geneva Convention is a contact between governments, not aid societies; if therefore it has been violated, it could only have been by agents of governments, who are beyond our jurisdiction. If there are grounds for making complaints, this task belongs to whichever of the governments considers itself the injured party, and we have, rightly, seen the French and German authorities protest officially against the conduct of their enemies; they have appealed to public opinion by revealing their complaints to it, finding it to be the proper tribunal to rule on this subject. As for the aid societies, they don't have a say in the matter. Moreover it would be dangerous for them to take sides in the quarrel, for they would antagonize governments who, wearying of such critics, would soon cease to accord them their protection.[84]

It is not difficult to recognize Moynier's legalistic mind at work here. His final point—that governments would be unlikely to cooperate with their critics—was unassailable, but the same cannot be said for the remainder of the argument. His claim that the Convention could only be violated by agents of governments, for example, made little sense when everyone knew that its letter and spirit had sometimes been violated by private citizens and, sometimes, by the aid societies themselves. In circumstances where the personnel of the societies had been granted official authorization, where did the jurisdiction of the societies end and that of governments begin? Was it not possible that the societies would themselves have decided to avoid politically unwise condemnations of individual states, at the same time expressing strongly the need for some sanction beyond that of public opinion? There were several issues here that deserved to be aired and decided by an international conference, yet discussion of them had been effectively precluded by the unilateral action of the Comité International.

Within a few weeks, members of the Comité began to realize that the war's legacy of bitterness would certainly delay, if not defeat, their plans for a conference. Neither the French nor the Germans, they soon discovered, were ready to meet a former enemy around the conference table. Moynier found this new reality particularly hard to accept because he believed that the sort of people who made up the national central committees were motivated as much by humanitarianism as by patriotic sentiment. However, the response to the June circular, even from neutral states, was distinctly lukewarm: Only twelve out of twenty-one central committees even bothered to acknowledge receipt of the circular, and only five sent in responses by the 1 August deadline. With profound regret Moynier and his colleagues were forced to admit that they had misjudged the situation; three weeks later, they sent another circular postponing the preparatory conference for at least a year, making it plain that no firm plans would be made for it unless and until there was obvious pressure in this direction from the various national committees.[85]

Scarcely had this circular gone off in the mail when Moynier had another unpleasant surprise. The principal Swiss army newspaper, published in Basle, carried a story about there being a plot afoot to do away with the Geneva Convention and replace it with uniform provisions added to the military codes of each nation; the implication was that the voluntary aid societies might also be replaced by a militarized sanitary service.[86] The "plotters" were not identified, but since the story was based on a report in the *Wiener Medizinische Wochenschrift*, suspicion pointed toward Austria, a state that had only reluctantly ratified the Convention under pressure of war in 1866.[87] If there was even a grain of truth in such rumors, both the Geneva Convention and the aid societies might find themselves in serious difficulties. Suddenly the atmosphere seemed chillier.

On the eve of the Franco-Prussian War, Moynier had proclaimed the imminence of a "new law of war" befitting a society that was leaving barbarism behind; now, in the wake of the war, he was forced to rethink some of the assumptions on which this optimistic assessment had been based. He realized that he had made a fundamental error in assuming that moral sanction and public opinion would by themselves serve as dependable restraints on the conduct of belligerents. Some sort of penal sanction, he now appreciated, must be built into the law of nations in order to provide a mechanism by which states could seek redress for wrongs suffered at the hands of an enemy that had pledged itself to observe the provisions of the Convention.

Throughout the autumn of 1871, Moynier set his mind to the problem, and when the members of the Comité International assembled for their first meeting of the new year, he read them a paper in which he proposed arbitration as the means by which to settle such disputes.[88] Not only did he freely admit "the inadequacy of a purely moral sanction to check passions once unleashed"; he also now expressed regret that the framers of the Convention had left it to the states themselves to enact the laws necessary to ensure that their nationals would adhere to its provisions.[89] Governments had been careful not to take on these obligations at the time the Convention was drawn up, and most had not felt themselves morally obligated to do so after ratifying it. "Therefore I would like [to propose] a tribunal to which contentious cases could be submitted. This tribunal would conduct an investigation of each case, would hear as required the pleadings of the plaintiff and the accused, and would pronounce upon the guilt or innocence of the defendant; then it would condemn the guilty according to future international law concerning infractions of the Geneva Convention."[90]

To be sure, it was a large assumption that states would be willing and able to negotiate an international agreement that would provide penalties for such infractions, but Moynier, taking heart from the recent success of arbitration in the *Alabama* case, reiterated his claim that as ties between peoples increased states would find themselves more and more pressed to settle disputes by peaceful means.[91] The idea of arbitration would become more appealing to states, he thought, if it was clear that the tribunal was no inquisition: It would act only when a formal complaint had been lodged, only after preliminary investigation by the states involved, and in the full light of publicity.

This proposal for an international judicial institution followed logically from the argument advanced earlier by the Comité International that an international conference of aid societies was not the proper place to hear or judge complaints about violations of the Geneva Convention. Doubtless Moynier hoped to prod the various central committees toward such a realization when he published the text of his paper in the next issue of the *Bulletin International*. (In order to remind them of what had been achieved to date, he had already collected all of the circulars and other official letters of the Geneva committee since 1863 into an impressive volume that was sent to central committees and other interested persons all over Europe.)[92] If this was his intention, it was almost a complete failure. Neither governments nor those in charge of the various aid societies showed interest in the arbitration proposal; indeed, Moynier received a good deal of criticism from knowledgeable legal experts who felt that he had gone too far in proposing that such a tribunal should pass judgments and impose penalties.[93]

By the autumn of 1872, the future of the Geneva Convention was even more problematic than it had been a year earlier. From Paris Moynier received word that members of the French central committee had decided that "the wording of the Convention is illogical and, in practice, untenable. The last war has furnished ample proof of this. The Convention is still incomplete and has fallen into discredit for its impotence by the non-ratification of the Additional Articles. If this *status quo* continues, these gentlemen insist that at some time in the future and before another war, the Powers will declare the Geneva Convention null and void."[94]

Things were little better in Berlin; the president of its central committee advised Moynier that the Convention "has shown itself to be prejudicial to the security of the army" because of the ease with which unauthorized personnel had been able to use and abuse the red cross armband.[95] Finally, in November, Moynier learned that the distressing rumor that had circulated the previous summer was true: Baron Mundy, head of the Austrian national aid society, had visited Paris and London with a proposal that the Geneva Convention be replaced by a set of clauses enacted into the military code of each nation.[96] Six weeks later Mundy himself tried to pressure the Comité International to abandon the Convention, claiming that unless Moynier agreed to the Austrian plan, Mundy would deal directly with the other powers, bypassing Geneva altogether.[97]

Now that the rival plan was out in the open, Moynier and his colleagues had no option but to test informed opinion as best they could. With the utmost discretion, Moynier sent letters to friends of the movement throughout Europe in an effort to find out what they thought about the future of the Convention. His letter to Thomas Longmore was typical:

> We are told that, as a consequence of the abuses and violations to which the last war has borne witness, the Convention today has a goodly number of influential adversaries who would like nothing better than to tear it up. These rumors have alarmed us, even though it seems to be difficult for us to admit that the governments of Europe would wish to reverse their previous decision, but [since] on the other hand we have good reason to fear some sort of more or less disguised plot against the Convention, we think it is our duty to keep watch on it and to undertake an investigation to see what opinion prevails on this subject in the various countries. However, as you will appreciate, this investigation must be of a completely confidential character, in order not to attract the attention of the enemies of the Convention. . . . For the moment we have no firm opinion as to the appropriate course to follow; we have only the impression that, before changing anything that presently exists, we must allow the passions time to cool, and give public opinion time to form itself through reflection. Therefore we dread the premature proposals that will be made to alter the status quo, which we will not be surprised to find pressed upon us from one day to the next. . . . As you see, dear Sir, it is a grave and delicate matter.[98]

Whatever replies Moynier received are presumably preserved in the ICRC archives, from which Boissier has quoted only two: Both the Berlin and St. Petersburg committees assured him that their respective sovereigns did not wish to see the Geneva Convention abrogated.[99] This was at least some reassurance, although as Moynier was soon to learn, the friendship of the tsar's government could not be taken for granted.

The city of Vienna played host to an international exhibition in the summer of 1873, and in other circumstances this would have been an ideal time to hold the conference that had been planned for 1871. Baron Mundy tested the water with the Austrian government, only to be told that any discussion of the Geneva Convention was out of the question because it could revive animosities that were best left alone.[100] Instead, aid societies displayed some of their equipment and the Comité International displayed its publications. In October, Mundy and the Austrian surgeon Theodore Billroth hosted a meeting of medical men at which equipment and ambulance transport were the principal subjects; Louis Appia attended it with his eyes and ears open.[101] He wrote to Moynier that "Geneva must stand firm and keep very closely in touch with what is going on . . . ; some people would have been only too pleased to see us fade away."[102] Appia's warning was timely; it helps to explain Moynier's almost panicky response the following year to a Russian proposal that he feared could sink the Convention once and for all.

In the spring of 1874, Prince Alexander Gorchakov, the Russian foreign minister, sent to the capitals of Europe a draft international convention on the rights and obligations of governments and armies in wartime, with a proposal that it be signed at a congress to be held in Brussels.[103] The draft contained several clauses on the treatment of noncombatants and the wounded, the cumulative effect of which appeared to Moynier to jeopardize what had already been agreed in the 1864 Convention.[104] Fearing that if the subject were opened to debate, the powers might decide to abrogate or annul the Geneva Convention, Moynier quickly mobilized as much support as he could muster. The Comité International sent a circular letter to all central committees, asking them to put pressure on their governments to ensure that whatever agreement was reached in Brussels did no more than confirm the existing Convention in respect to the treatment of the wounded. After a strong lobbying effort, Moynier was relieved when the final text of the Brussels Declaration included just such a confirmation; however the delegates took it upon themselves to appoint a subcommittee that was charged with drawing up a new text to replace the existing Convention.[105] To be sure, that draft would have no more importance than the powers chose to give it, but Moynier was understandably worried that once again the initiative for change seemed to come from outside the circle of the aid societies themselves.

In Defense of Charity

By the summer of 1876, the members of the Comité International had found themselves on the defensive for almost five years. The easy successes that they had enjoyed in 1863 and 1864 were now little more than a memory. Moynier's hope that Europe was ready to develop a new approach to the resolution of disputes now seemed at best premature, at worst far-fetched. When he and Appia had collaborated in writing *War and Charity*, they had

3.9 This horse-drawn ambulance wagon dates from the mid-1870s. In the years that followed the Franco-Prussian War, Europeans became fascinated by the technological challenges of ambulance design.

naturally assumed that the Geneva Convention would have only a beneficent influence upon human conduct; it had never occurred to them that hostile nations might incorporate into their mutual indictments allegations of inhumanity that were fueled by the terms of the Convention itself. Neither had they foreseen the possibility that forming aid societies would not necessarily draw nations closer together. Because they had assumed that enlightened opinion would be on their side and that their only enemies were likely to be incorrigible reactionaries such as Marshal Randon, it was now difficult for them to accept the possibility that there might be less and less place on the European battlefield for the simple Christian charity that had inspired their enterprise since its inception. If the success of Prussia in 1870 was a harbinger of things to come, Moynier and Appia had good reason to fear for the future because in a world dominated by nationalism and militarism, the aid societies and even the Convention itself could come to play roles quite different from those envisioned by humanitarian philanthropists and devotees of the rule of law. Such concerns deserved to be aired, above all at an international conference of aid societies, but both the hostility and indifference that had prevented the convening of a conference at the end of the war were still there at mid-decade.

However, conferences of aid societies were not the only occasions that brought together Europeans interested in the application and development of scientific philanthropy. In October of 1876, Brussels was host to the "Second International Congress of Hygiene, Lifesaving, and Social Economy," the program for which included a discussion of the wartime role of aid societies. The organizers of the conference sought to focus attention on four specific issues: (1) the role to be allocated to civilian help; (2) personnel to be organized and matériel to be prepared; (3) measures to be taken to avoid the abuses that occurred during recent wars; and (4) a federation of the aid committees. It is not clear where the idea of a federation of national committees originated, but when the program arrived in Geneva, Moynier was instantly struck by its possibilities. "Aha, I said to myself, here is a conception of the work of the aid societies which up to the present has scarcely been envisaged. If the spirit of association begets great things, would not an association of associations prove equally fruitful? And in this combining together I glimpsed the germ of great progress."[106]

After persuading Louis Appia to write an essay that would address the first three points, Moynier himself prepared a paper in which he drafted a scheme of federation for the aid societies.[107] For the first time in several years, he was able to think in positive terms; able to do something more than defend the societies and the Convention against their critics and opponents. He seized the opportunity with relish.

The "Federation of the Red Cross" that Moynier envisioned was to be "a union [that would be] as little restrictive as possible"; so that the autonomy of all its members was preserved, any agreement would concern *only* the international relations of the aid societies.[108] Its purpose would be "to transform vague professions of faith into formal promises" by making required what was at the moment still optional: The expectation that the societies would help each other cope with the extraordinary requirements of war. Revealingly, Moynier drew an analogy with "a mutual insurance contract, in which each signatory obtains, in exchange for his commitments, the certainty that if he should need the help of his confederates, they will not leave him bereft of assistance."[109] Not only their generous instincts but also an appreciation of their real interests should lead them in this direction: As he pointed out, they should hasten to make such a pact "before the ever more pronounced isolation in which they are confined by the state of peace creates obstacles to their rapprochement."[110]

This "solemn affirmation of their solidarity in misfortune" would also provide a useful opportunity to tidy up procedures and expectations in the event of war. Instead of the unplanned and uncontrolled response of neutrals to the appeals of the belligerents in 1870, it would be preferable to require that neutral societies offer their assistance to *all* belligerent societies, although the latter would be at liberty to refuse such offers. "Nothing could be more fitting than this rule to prove that the Red Cross intends to remain absolutely outside of the political and other questions which divide peoples; and that in its eyes, as in those of the states signatory to the Geneva Convention, helping a belligerent to care for its wounded is not considered to be taking sides."[111] Moynier also hoped that the pact would spell out appropriate neutral behavior:

> When one society implores fraternal support from another, the latter should not be content with sending it a sum of money more or less drawn out of its treasury. Far more than that is expected of it. What is sought is not merely a subvention, but active cooperation. In such a case, the least that a faithful member of the federation can do is to publicize in its own country the requirements that it has been informed about [by the belligerent], and to put itself at the disposal of charitable persons in order to receive their gifts and offers of service, and transmit them to the appropriate authority.[112]

Finally, to preserve "the excellent principle of centralization in voluntary assistance," Moynier thought that the pact should guarantee to belligerents the right to use as they saw fit whatever personnel or matériel were furnished by neutrals.[113]

It goes without saying that Moynier had no intention of imposing this federation scheme on the national societies. He assumed that they would all see its utility, would all want to join it, and would take steps to do so at some future international conference—hopefully not too far into the future. Since five of the twenty-three had already adopted the name "Red Cross society," he thought this an appropriate name for the federation itself; using this name would also underline the special connection that existed between the aid societies and the army medical services. Naturally there would have to be some sort of central administrative body to look after the common business of the members between periodic international conferences; analogous functions, he pointed out discreetly, were already being exercised by the Comité International in Geneva. If such a federation could be established, he concluded, it would "mark an important and happy stage in the progressive development of the Red Cross."[114]

Presumably Moynier would not have made such a proposal if he had not felt the need to chart more clearly the course that international charity should now take, nor would he have done so unless he thought the idea both possible and desirable. He must, therefore, have been both surprised and disappointed by the response of his audience in Brussels. One after another, delegates took the podium to pour scorn on the very idea of a federation of aid societies. Louis Laussedat, a medical doctor from Paris and a member of the chamber of deputies, was the most vociferous and combative critic of Moynier's "great deception"; he believed that in introducing a particular "doctrine" of charity and a permanent agency to oversee it, the scheme posed a real threat to the autonomy, originality, and vigor of the societies.[115] He was followed by another medical doctor, Heyfelder, from St. Petersburg, who put his finger on the political weakness of the proposal: "We must respect the authority of the Powers. We have no means of forcing a state to recognize a federation which its political interests or its national sentiments force it to repudiate."[116] Even Professor von Held from Wuerzburg, an old friend of Moynier, warned that any such attempt to change the existing situation would be seen as a threat to the liberty of societies and individuals to support the cause of charity as and how they chose. Lest it be thought that the Comité International was strongly behind a proposal that seemed to antagonize delegates from the great power states, Appia hastily intervened to say that Moynier wished it understood that his paper was an entirely personal opinion and should not be treated as representing a collective opinion. In order to spare the author further embarrassment, the presiding officer intervened to summarize the sense of the meeting as "in favor of seeing intimate relations established among the societies, but without centralizing their activity . . . there should be no official tie of federation."[117]

Moynier had advanced his proposal saying that it did not appreciably change the existing state of affairs; that it would simply "provide more certainty by cementing the union of all adherents of the Red Cross."[118] In many ways this was an accurate judgment. Despite what his critics said, this was certainly not an attempt to interfere in the internal affairs of the individual societies; still less was it an attempt to make the Comité International into a supreme executive body. Yet Heyfelder's point was a good one: If governments did not wish to cooperate with such a federation, it would be pointless to set it up. Laussedat had been right but dishonest in his complaint about restrictions on liberty: As things stood at the moment, the aid societies of neutral states could send as much, or as little, help as they liked to the belligerent(s) of their choice. Moynier's proposal would have forced all neutral societies to work actively to provide assistance to any belligerent that called for assistance. Stripping Laussedat's high-flown rhetoric, it is clear that three liberties were threatened by the federation scheme: The right to play favorites among the belligerents, the right to make token gestures, and the right to remain indifferent. This was the reality which Moynier's critics masked behind their emotional pleas on behalf of *"la liberté du coeur."*

In refusing to support the federation plan, Moynier's audience also passed over without remark this opportunity to demonstrate to the world that the Red Cross was, in Moynier's words, "absolutely outside of the political and other questions that divide peoples." It needs to be underlined that the Brussels meeting was simply a gathering of delegates, the majority of whom were individuals important in various philanthropic causes, especially those related to health and hygiene; in no sense was this an international Red Cross conference, nor can it be said for certain that delegates to such a conference would have reacted in the same way. That having been said, however, certain other observations must also be made. The completeness of Moynier's retreat—he even decided not to publish his paper in the *Bulletin International*—suggests that he himself thought that the opinions expressed in Brussels probably were representative of those within the leadership of the aid societies. No doubt word of what had taken place at the Brussels meeting soon became known to many of those who made up the central committees of the national aid societies, yet not one of these individuals or committees publicly expressed support for Moynier's proposal or even called for it to be discussed at an international conference.

It was as if the very idea of a Red Cross federation was so heretical that it had to be suppressed. To be sure, rejection of the federation scheme did not necessarily mean that the corollary was true: Namely, that the Red Cross was *not* above the political and other divisive issues that separated nations; however, as events in the Balkans would soon demonstrate, this was more than a possibility. In the wars between Serbia, the Ottoman Empire, and Russia (1876–1878), the very emblem of neutrality, the Red Cross badge and flag, became a divisive issue.

Cross and Crescent

Moynier was pleasantly surprised when the Ottoman Empire, the only non-Christian state among the great powers, announced its adherence to the Geneva Convention in July, 1865. It is not at all clear why the sultan's government took this decision; in all probability it meant little more than appearing to keep up with the other powers. Certainly the sultan's government gave no sign that it took seriously the implied obligation to encourage the development of a committee or society to aid the wounded. Instead, it appears to have been indifferent if not actually hostile to the idea of a voluntary association becoming involved in anything to do with the army. There is no reason to ascribe this attitude to the natural distrust of an absolute monarchy for public involvement in state affairs. In both tsarist Russia and imperial Japan, it proved remarkably easy to combine a flourishing Red Cross society with an autocratic imperial regime; presumably a similar quasiofficial association of Ottoman bureaucrats could have been formed in Constantinople. However, like the French, the Ottoman government seem to have believed that signing the Geneva Convention committed it to nothing in particular, especially if any change would meet with opposition from the senior levels of the army. This indifference was undoubtedly fortified by the understandable distaste of Ottoman officers for an emblem—a red cross on a white field—that they inevitably associated with Christianity and with the Crusades.

In the circumstances, it is not surprising that most of those interested in promoting the Red Cross idea were either European physicians resident in Constantinople or Ottoman physicians who had trained abroad. The first attempt to establish an aid society in Constantinople was led by the colorful Dr. Abdullah Bey.[119]

A pro-Hungarian liberal who was born Karl Edward Hammerschmidt, he had fled the Habsburg monarchy after the revolutions of 1848, settled in Constantinople, and converted to Islam.[120] The holder of several hospital and

3.10   Abdullah Bey,
founder of the first
Ottoman Society for
Aid to Wounded
Soldiers, which lapsed
after his death.

medical school appointments, Abdullah was promoted to the rank of colonel and chief medical officer of the Imperial Guard for his service during the Crimean War. He was the chief Ottoman delegate to the Paris Exposition of 1867, where he met Moynier and the representatives of many European aid societies. Before leaving Paris, he promised to form an Ottoman society for aid to wounded soldiers. Within a year of his return to Constantinople, he reported success, and in a circular dated August, 1868, the Comité International proudly announced the formation of a provisional Ottoman committee of some twenty-five persons under the patronage of Omer Pasha, the commander-in-chief of the Imperial Guard, and the presidency of Marco Pasha, the inspector-general of the army medical service.[121] This seemed an auspicious beginning, especially when the Ottoman committee sent representatives to the diplomatic conference in Geneva, which considered the Additional Articles, and to the Berlin conference of 1869.[122]

It was, however, one thing to form a society and quite another to secure government recognition and support. By June of 1869, the society claimed to have some sixty-six members, about two-thirds of whom were physicians, including several members of the council of health. Nevertheless, when its newly drafted regulations were presented to the government, approval was flatly denied by the minister of war on the grounds that civilian involvement in military affairs was unacceptable.[123] Apparently as a consolation prize, the sultan offered imperial decorations to both Moynier and Appia.[124] This was the last official communication to pass between Constantinople and Geneva for many years. There was no sign of life from the Ottoman committee during the Franco-Prussian War and no acknowledgment of any of the letters or circulars of the Comité International. Then in 1874 came news of the death of Dr. Abdullah Bey.

Anxious lest the whole scheme should die, Moynier contacted Professor Émile Juillard, a Genevan living in Constantinople, who put him in touch with Dr. Péchédimaldji and the Imperial Medical Society. This body, founded during the Crimean War, was composed largely of European physicians resident in the imperial capital; it received a regular subsidy from the sultan, with which it published the monthly *Gazette Médicale d'Orient.*[125] In the spring of 1876, with the Ottoman army at war with Serbia and the need for supplementary medical assistance already apparent, Péchédimaldji persuaded his colleagues that the Imperial Medical Society should try once again to persuade the government to approve the formation of an aid society. Evidently experienced in dealing with the imperial bureaucracy, he was under no illusions about how difficult it might be to navigate "these inextricable mazes that pass for an administrative network."[126] A delegation of three was chosen to present to the grand vizier a petition that emphasized the potential benefits to the Imperial Army of assistance that would be forthcoming from the societies of other nations.[127] This time the response was more positive: Three days later, with the approval of the council of ministers, Marco Pasha was authorized to convene a special commission to draw up proposed statutes for an aid society.[128]

Once the government began to look seriously at the creation of an aid society, the Red Cross emblem became the central issue. When the commission held its first meeting, Marco Pasha announced that the minister of war had approved the symbol of the crescent instead of the cross for use in the medical services of the Ottoman army. The implication for the aid society was obvious. Realizing how the ground lay, Péchédimaldji wrote urgently to Moynier,

> I beg you, Mr. President, and this information is very necessary to us, to let me know by return if, according to the Geneva Convention or a decision taken sub-

3.11 Dr. Péchédimaldji of the Imperial Ottoman Medical Society often corresponded with Moynier about the difficulties involved in establishing a permanent aid society in the Ottoman Empire.

sequently by the Comité International, any society is obliged to adopt the white flag with the red cross. I believe that this emblem has been one of the main causes for the failure of the first society in Constantinople. Is it permissible for us to modify it, to replace the cross by the crescent, for example? I am really loath to raise such a detail, of no importance in civilized countries, but the Moslem population is so immersed in fanaticism that we fear that this trifle may bring obstacles in the way of the success of our work.[129]

The symbol was hardly a trifle. Ottoman troops, who so far had been told nothing about the Geneva Convention or the symbol of neutrality, had been firing on medical units and mutilating or massacring enemy wounded; the Serbs understandably reacted with outrage, and their protests were supported by other European countries. The many stories of brutality that reached Geneva were enough to convince Moynier that the Red Cross emblem, far from ensuring the safety of the wounded or those tending them, "aroused the savage passions of Mohammed's followers whose immediate instinct is to attack it before all else."[130]

Meanwhile, the Ottoman special commission submitted its draft constitution for the establishment of a Society for Assistance to Sick and Wounded Soldiers; it called for the creation of an executive bureau, a committee of assistance dominated by physicians, and a separate section of ladies charged with receiving membership dues and donations.[131] Finally, early in November, official word was received: The government would approve the society, provided that it was agreed that the ambulances and medical personnel of the army and of the society bore the symbol of the red crescent in place of the cross provided for in the Geneva Convention. Accepting the inevitable, the commission wrote to Moynier to inform him of the situation and asked the Ottoman foreign minister to communicate this decision through the Swiss Federal Council to the other states signatory to the Convention.[132]

In January, 1877, when the specter of war with Russia on the horizon, the Ottoman Red Crescent Society (ORCS) published its first circular, announcing its formation and the adoption of the crescent symbol and issuing a general appeal for assistance. At a meeting held on 16 April, Arif Bey of the Ottoman council of health was chosen president of the executive bureau, and Dr. Péchédimaldji was made head of the relief committee. These appointments were communicated to the Comité International, which in turn circulated the information to all of the national societies.[133] Another ORCS circular was sent out on 9 May, shortly after the war began; it contained a fresh appeal for foreign help and gave details of agents and banks in Europe where contributions could be sent. Yet another, dated 18 July, announced that the sultan had become patron of the ORCS and gave details of the formation of regional committees throughout the empire.[134] A forty-page list of donors was complied and published. Finally, later in the same year, there appeared the first issue of *Le Croissant Rouge*, a new fortnightly journal published by the ORCS, which was edited in Constantinople by a board of local physicians with collaborators in Paris. Its cover listed the following subjects of special interest: "international charity; aid societies for wounded soldiers; medicine; chemistry; hygiene; hospitals; sanitary service; and *varia*."[135] It looked as if the Ottoman society was finally off and running.

The cross-versus-crescent issue was not yet settled, however. The Comité International, having discussed the problem as soon as it learned of the Ottoman action, decided that "a question of external form should not be an insurmountable obstacle to spreading these principles to non-Christian peoples. The adoption of an international sign is indispensable, but agreement on this point would not perhaps be incompatible with tolerance regarding a few variations of detail. . . . One could even admit the modification of the red cross for non-Christian states."[136]

This was all well and good in the abstract, but at the moment war was imminent. What would the Russians do when presented with the red crescent? The Comité International hastily urged the St. Petersburg central committee to persuade its government to recognize the crescent emblem. Meanwhile, the Swiss Federal Council had begun to receive replies from the signatory states. Three of these (Great Britain, Belgium, and Sweden) thought that the substitution would entail a special protocol being added to the Convention;

Italy and Russia both took the position that the Ottoman government should be required to make a special declaration that it would respect the cross emblem. One part of the Russian response is of special interest:

> The choice of the crescent as a sign of neutralization seems unfortunate and likely to excite rather than calm fanaticism. Indeed, the red cross on a white field has been chosen as the unifying symbol not as a Christian emblem, but because it represented the flag of the Swiss confederation, only with the colors reversed. By opposing this to the crescent, one risks giving to the emblems . . . a purely religious character that they did not possess in origin and which it would also be desirable to avoid in the future, with a view to preserving for the Convention the general humanitarian spirit which had served as its basis.[137]

Given what they already knew about how the sultan's soldiers had treated wounded Serbs and Montenegrins, the Russians had every reason, with renewed hostilities imminent, to try to dissuade the Ottoman government from regarding the red cross as a religious symbol. Nevertheless, one has to admire their inventiveness in concocting this pseudo-explanation, for which there is no evidence whatever in the records of the 1863 conference or the 1864 congress. There is no indication that the delegates who chose this distinctive symbol in 1863 did so with the intention of honoring Switzerland or even with the intention of picking a recognized symbol of neutrality.[138] (Indeed we saw in Chapter 2 what the French thought about the fragility of Swiss neutrality.) Although the minutes of the 1863 conference are briefer than one would wish on this point, it is clear that the choice was made in the context of Louis Appia's appeal for a symbol, "the mere sight of which, like the flag for a soldier, could stimulate the *esprit de corps* which would attend this most generous idea, this undertaking common to all civilized mankind."[139] There can be little doubt that in the minds of devout Christians such as Dunant, Moynier, and Appia—not to mention the delegates from the orders of chivalry—the cross was such a symbol. At one and the same time, it could represent both personal Christian charity and the universal aspirations of enlightened humanitarianism. The assumptions behind the choice were probably so obvious to everyone present that no one thought it necessary to explain them in the minutes. However, one can be certain that if it had been the delegates' intention in choosing this symbol to pay special tribute to Switzerland, then this fact would have been explicitly mentioned at the 1864 congress. Indeed, one might plausibly have expected a reference to it at some ceremonial occasion involving the president of the Swiss Federal Council. Nothing of this kind took place. The Russian argument, first advanced in the crisis atmosphere of 1877, was politically ingenious but historically incorrect. The real proof of this is that the members of the Comité International judiciously sidestepped the issue: General Dufour was now dead and Dunant in exile, but Moynier and Appia were perfectly capable of endorsing or rejecting from personal knowledge the truth of the Russian claim. That they did neither suggests a certain shrewdness: After all, there was nothing to be lost in allowing this version of events to gain currency at a time when interest in the movement seemed to be spreading beyond Europe and indeed beyond Christendom.[140]

A less esoteric Russian response came from Alexander II himself on 24 May: The tsar was prepared to recognize the inviolability of enemy medical units bearing the red crescent symbol provided that the sultan gave explicit assurances that his soldiers would respect the red cross symbol when displayed by their enemies. It was not until June, several weeks into the fighting, that mutual assurances were given by the commanders-in-chief on either side.[141] Nevertheless, the newspapers of Europe were soon full of stories of outrageous violations of the Geneva Convention, particularly by the Ottoman soldiers. A number of western correspondents—among them the Crimean veteran Colonel Henry Brackenbury of *The Times*—published a letter in a Constantinople newspaper that was widely reproduced elsewhere: "We expose the following fact to the judgment of the civilised world, an event which occurred the day after the battle [of Chipka] and a few hundred meters from the battlefield: we saw on one side more than fifty wounded Muslims, cared for by Russian army doctors according to the progress of humanity, and on the other side a heap of severed heads which form the horrible trophy of the barbarism of Turkish regular troops."[142]

There were also stories of atrocities committed by Russian Cossack and Bulgarian soldiers against Muslim women and children; whether or not they were true, these could not have been violations of the Convention, which protected only wounded soldiers and medical personnel attending them. However, Moynier was so upset by the stories of outrage that reached him— some of them relayed by Dr. Péchédimaldji—that he presented to the Institute of International Law an *Appeal to the Belligerents and the Press*, which included strong criticism of the needless bloodshed indulged in by Ottoman soldiers.[143] In his mind, the case for an international tribunal to police violations of the Convention was now even stronger.

From Constantinople the ORCS improvised what assistance it could. Some two dozen local committees were organized in Rumelia and Anatolia, but the section of ladies envisioned in the statutes never materialized. Nine field ambulances were sent to the Balkan and Armenian fronts, and a lone sanitary train made five trips to bring wounded soldiers from Rumelia to Constantinople, in the vicinity of which the ORCS operated several temporary barracks hospitals and stationary ambulances. Most of the wounded were, of course, Ottoman soldiers; as the Comité International delicately put it some years later, "the Red Crescent did not often have Russians in its establishments" during the war.[144] A little more than half of the money spent on relief by the ORCS came from foreign sources, most of it from European Red Cross societies but also some from Muslim communities in India and Africa.[145] Its resources were, however, strained beyond the limit in the last stages of the war, when the Russians took Adrianople and, as a consequence, thousands of civilian refugees fled to Constantinople.[146] Again it was necessary to call upon the help of other Red Cross societies.

Yet foreigners who had dealings with the Red Crescent Society were often less than impressed with the behavior of its officers, whether delegates in the field or members of the executive in the capital. One experienced and well-informed observer was Vincent Kennett-Barrington, who spent several months in the Balkans during the Turkish-Serbian and Russo-Turkish Wars

3.12   Wounded soldiers seeking assistance from a Russian ambulance during the Russo-Turkish War.

3.13   An Ottoman field medical unit flying the Red Crescent flag during the Russo-Turkish War.

as commissioner of the British National Aid Society. In March, 1878 he wrote to his wife that "the Red Crescent Society undertook to look after the wounded at Plevna, Kezanlyk and Sofia, but they have done nothing. They sent a special Vice-President down with seven hundred pounds in his pocket and a great flourish of trumpets calling him attaché to the Plenipotentiaries, etc. etc., but he remained eating and drinking with grand dukes and princes at Adrianople, while his wretched fellow-countrymen were starving only a few days journey off."[147] A later letter on the same subject is equally revealing:

> The Red Crescent had a large sanitary train which was got up at great expense, however the Red Crescent do not "hit it off" with the Railway Company, and there is always some difficulty about the train working. The Russians have got so bored with the Red Crescent that they have made an impromptu sanitary train of their own and, putting our surgeon Dr. Neylan in charge, have sent off the 300 Turkish wounded remaining at Philippolis under him. We expect them here in a day or two. I am afraid that the Red Crescent will be very angry indeed. It is

so unfortunate that they cannot do anything well. . . . The real truth is, I fear, that there are too many on the Committee who think of their own selfish ends and vain glory. Another thing is that they do not like parting with their money.[148]

It would be tedious to belabor the point; the reality is simply that the ORCS seemed to be incapable of making a good impression on those familiar with the operation of Red Cross societies elsewhere. In any case, despite the flurry of activity produced by the wars of the 1870s, the ORCS lapsed easily into inactivity once the fighting was finished. The supplies were put into storage, and the surplus funds—£7,000 Ottoman left over at the end of the war—were deposited in the Ottoman Bank, where they remained undisturbed for many years. No representative of the ORCS appeared at either of the international Red Cross conferences held during the 1880s, and the issue of the legal status of the Red Crescent emblem remained undecided.

A Civil Society for Military Medicine?

As if Moynier and his colleagues did not have troubles enough, the summer of 1878 brought yet another cause for anxiety about the future of the Red Cross. As part of the world exposition centered around the newly completed Trocadéro Palace, Paris was playing host to a series of international congresses and conferences. One of these was an "International Congress on Medical Services for Armies in the Field," organized by several leading members of the Paris Academy of Medicine, among them that trenchant critic of voluntary aid societies, Professor Léon Le Fort of the Faculty of Medicine. Attendance was by invitation only, and the organizers made it clear that they wanted only "a small number of completely competent persons" to attend. Four subjects were proposed for discussion during the three-day meeting: assistance to the wounded on the battlefield; whether tent-hospitals near the front could be substituted for evacuation; the use of railway transport for sick and wounded; and "What should be the role of civil societies for aid to the wounded? How can their activity usefully be combined with the functioning of an army medical service?"[149] Several of the greatest names in military medicine and surgery attended this congress, including the aging Baron Larrey, Professor Esmarch from Kiel, and Surgeon-General Longmore from England. The other participants were almost all high-ranking medical officers or professors at schools of military medicine. However, only one of them was an official delegate of a Red Cross society: Dr. Riant of the French SSBM. Three had connections with other aid societies: Louis Appia, who attended not on behalf of the Comité International but rather as a member of the Swiss Red Cross Society; Dr. Gori, a member of the Dutch society; and Dr. Péchédimaldji, in his capacity as president of the Imperial Medical Society of Constantinople. Ten states designated members of the 1878 congress as official delegates; two of these, Longmore and Landa from Spain, had met fifteen years earlier in Geneva.[150] Obviously, this meeting was intended as an opportunity for military medical experts to discuss recent developments in their sphere of interest.

However, both the breadth of the agenda and the selection of invitees caused some concern in Geneva. Although the Comité International had been unable to bring national Red Cross societies together since 1869, the Paris congress was proposing to discuss and arrive at resolutions concerning the aid societies at a meeting where only one of those societies was officially represented, and that one—given its record in 1870—was hardly a role model for the others. States that had not yet ratified the Additional Articles and had resisted attempts to organize a diplomatic congress to rewrite the Geneva Convention were nevertheless able to designate official delegates to the Paris meeting. It must have seemed to Moynier that the senior army medical officers of Europe were meeting to settle the future relationship between war and charity without so much as a by-your-leave to the very philanthropists whose enthusiasm had promoted the growth of voluntary aid societies.

There was certainly reason for Moynier to be apprehensive because Le Fort's experience with the SSBM had convinced him that aid societies, unless severely restricted in their operations, could do more harm than good. Along with other military surgeons, Le Fort had been appalled by a recent decree of the French minister of war that allowed the SSBM a large role in the operation of military hospitals, in the evacuation process, and on the railways; in cases of extreme necessity, it might also be called upon to supplement the field ambulances at the front.[151] Most French military surgeons would have preferred to see their country copy the German system of close regulation of the activities of aid societies and complete subordination to the military medical service.[152] In France, the latitude allowed to the SSBM in the 1878 decree was partially a function of the fact that the army medical service was still subordinated to the Intendance and partially a function of the influence wielded by its socially prominent leaders, including the Duke de Nemours.[153] As far as Le Fort was concerned, the influence of these prominent names was a mixed blessing:

> It is an admirable thing that these honorable names of honorable and honored persons are placed at the head of a benevolent society; but the Aid Society, if it is a benevolent society, should not go beyond this role, it should be content with being a benevolent society. But it wishes to become a civil society for military medicine and, under the protection of these very honorable names, other persons have shown a desire to intervene, indeed have intervened and are still intervening in medical affairs: this is something that I rebel against . . . we cannot permit incompetent people to play at medicine and risk compromising the medical service of the army.[154]

At the end of the discussion, the participants passed a resolution calling for the subordination of all aid society personnel to the authority of the chief physicians of the army and designating as the principal role of aid societies that of supplying the needs of military surgery; the resolution also stipulated that their personnel should only be employed in permanent hospitals, thus effectively excluding them from both the zone of military operations and the *zone d'étapes.* (There is no precise English equivalent of this term; it refers to the staging area between the front and the rear area, commonly known later as the evacuation zone.) Despite some reservations expressed by Riant, this resolution, which had been introduced by Thomas Longmore, passed unanimously.[155]

Inevitably, much of the day's discussion had been a duel between Le Fort and Riant, and it was always Le Fort who made the best thrusts. When Riant attempted to justify the actions of the SSBM on the familiar grounds that urgent wartime necessity explained why Red Cross societies had come into existence, Le Fort scathingly replied,

> But, gentlemen, in the very numerous armies that we have today, we need rifles, cannon, munitions in considerable proportions. If someone came and said to the Government, "Cannon are very expensive and you need a lot of them; we never have enough gunners. Keep only a small number of cannon in your arsenals, and don't spend the resources in your budget to maintain and instruct gunners; I'm going to establish an aid society for the artillery. Rely on me, and when war comes I will furnish you with the quantity of cannon that you lack, and the gunners necessary to operate them." Surely you would regard someone who spoke this way as a madman.[156]

Naturally Le Fort used this splendid illustration to support his point that military medicine was too important to be left to amateurs and deserved to be given adequate funding and proper treatment by the state. However, his example raises a fundamental question that forms a backdrop to the next part of this book: If the great power states regarded it as absurd to have a voluntary aid society for the artillery but sensible—even laudable—to have one for the wounded, what does this reveal about the priorities of these governments and their peoples in the years before the outbreak of World War I?

✚ 4

Humanity & Patriotism

 ETWEEN 1880 AND 1906, the Red Cross was transformed from an institution that owed its first allegiance to the idea of civilization to one that, by its actions as well as its words, wholeheartedly supported the aggressive nationalism and militarism of the period. The international Red Cross conferences of the 1880s made it plain that both the ICRC and the national societies were prepared to live with the cult of the nation. Proposals for a closer federation were suspended, and those who sought a larger international role for the ICRC as a neutral institution of international law found themselves unable to muster support for their position. The leaders of national societies proved themselves adept at prodding organized philanthropy to respond to both the challenges and the likely consequences of the arms race in which the powers were now engaged. Almost everywhere, the relationship between states, armies, and Red Cross societies grew closer. With the real work now being organized at the national level, international Red Cross conferences soon became little more than social occasions at which the participants engaged in high-flown sentiments of mutual admiration.

In order to ensure that these new relationships were not disturbed, a proper distance was assiduously maintained between the Red Cross on the one hand and international movements in favor of peace and disarmament on the other. The fruits of this emphasis on propriety were apparent in 1906, when the 1864 Convention was finally revised to recognize the role of the aid societies as auxiliaries to the military forces. Thus, long before the outbreak of hostilities in 1914, many Red Cross societies had become organizations that, in the minds of governments and peoples alike, existed principally for the purpose of war.

The View from Geneva

The year 1883 was the twentieth anniversary of the Geneva conference of 1863, and Moynier was determined to mark the occasion in some appropriate way. The most fitting event—an international Red Cross conference to bring together delegates from all of the national societies for the first time since 1869—was not something easily organized. In the wake of the Russo-Turkish War, the ICRC had revived the long-postponed plan to hold a conference in Vienna, but the Austrian central committee, after taking informal soundings among the other national societies, reported that it could not detect any widespread enthusiasm for the proposal. Similar efforts by the Russian and Italian central committees yielded similar results.[1] There were widespread fears that an international meeting would reopen wounds between former enemies, revive criticism of the Convention itself, and produce fresh squabbles over whether or not the Red Cross emblem possessed some religious significance. Faced with this situation, Moynier decided to breathe new life into the enterprise by writing a morale-boosting book.

The result was probably his best literary effort on behalf of the cause, a lengthy essay entitled *The Red Cross: Its Past and Future*, which he published in 1882.[2] Although its tone was resolutely optimistic, the troubled decade of the 1870s had clearly left its mark. There is nothing in the essay about war being a lamentable survival of barbarism, about the impending triumph of arbitration, or about the future belonging to the pacifists. He confessed that his "deepest feelings" protested against Helmuth von Moltke's recent claim that war was an element of the divine order; however, the best he could do by way of refutation was to describe war as "an accident . . . a calamity of human origin, from which our race is gradually, though slowly, freeing itself."[3] Instead of predicting the imminent demise of war, Moynier now preferred to point to the proven utility of Red Cross societies: States have come to rely on the Red Cross, he argued, "not as an ephemeral or temporary institution, but as one which responds to necessities of indefinite duration wherever war is waged."[4] Its future was virtually assured, he was now convinced, because the Red Cross was certain to benefit from two contemporary trends that appeared to be unstoppable—the widening of military service obligations and the advance of democracy.

> If . . . people have shown themselves anxious for the soldiers of national armies in modern times . . . may it not be presumed that the more military service is generalized—which is the tendency of the present day—so much the more will the feelings of the masses be deeply involved? Where every family has one or more representatives in the ranks of the defenders of the country, none of its members will resign themselves to a purely passive attitude. Each will do something for the relative or friend that he has seen depart, and whom he knows to be in danger; and the Red Cross, which sympathizes with this desire, will most certainly gain new strength from it.[5]

In Moynier's view, the Red Cross would also benefit from the advance of democracy, whose advocates "bring into greater relief the victims of undeserved suffering, more particularly of that phase of it which is the result of an

imperfect social state"; and since this is also what the Red Cross does, "it has no fear of falling into discredit. It ought, on the contrary, to increase in popularity, and to gain from the change which is being accomplished."[6] Not only would the Red Cross become stronger in what he called "the civilized zone"; as the boundaries of civilization—which he equated with moral progress— expanded, the Red Cross would also spread around the world.[7] Thus, despite

4.1   Members of the ICRC in the 1880s. Of its five original members, only Moynier and Appia now survived; Henry Dunant had been forced to resign in 1867, Dr. Maunoir had died in 1869, and General Dufour in 1875. Louis Micheli de la Rive, a deputy in the Great Council of Geneva, took the place of Dr. Maunoir, and a succession of members of the Favre family took the place of General Dufour. In December, 1870, a young barrister named Gustave Ador—not uncoincidentally the nephew of Gustave Moynier—joined the group to act as Moynier's secretary. In 1874, two additional members were appointed: Édouard Odier, another barrister who had made a successful political career, and Dr. Adolphe d'Espine, professor of medicine at the University of Geneva. In 1884, Louis Appia's nephew, Dr. Frédéric Ferrière, was also invited to join. Missing from this group is Colonel Camille Favre, appointed in 1883. Apart from family relationship and friendship, the usual rule followed by the members of the committee in appointing new members was to assure themselves that they had found someone of similar background and outlook.

---

the events of the last decade, Moynier was able to conclude that there were no black clouds on the horizon and that the Red Cross—"this infusion of new blood in the veins of civilized races"—would continue to flourish as an instrument of moral as well as material progress.[8] Obviously he hoped that this optimistic evaluation of the future would persuade others to look beyond the problems of the 1870s.

Hardly had the members of the ICRC had time to read the essay before he was urging upon them a bold new plan: They should themselves invite representatives of the national societies to Geneva for a Red Cross conference in the late summer of 1884. Some of his colleagues thought this a foolish idea when so many unsuccessful attempts had already been made, but Moynier was adamant that the obstacles facing them were no greater than they had been twenty years earlier. With Appia's support he was able to carry the day, and a circular soon went out inviting national societies and states signatory to the Convention to send delegates to Geneva for a conference to begin on 1 September.[9]

If most of the national societies had ignored or declined this invitation, that would surely have been the end of the international aspirations of the Red Cross, probably the end of the ICRC as well. It was therefore a crucial moment in the history of the enterprise, and the invitation had to be very carefully and attractively worded.

It will be like a hearth [Moynier wrote], the warmth of which will revive the solidarity between those who simultaneously, although in different places, work for the ideas evoked by the Red Cross . . . for there are improvements to be made with regard to international relations that can only be brought about through personal relations between men of all countries who are dedicated to the success of their mutual undertaking. Since 1869, members of aid societies have only been in contact on the battlefields; they should aspire to see each other in a more peaceful setting, one that is more conducive to examining the major interests of the Red Cross.[10]

By making it plain that the proposed conference would focus on the common interests of the national societies rather than on the thorny subject of revision of the Geneva Convention, Moynier's invitation made itself welcome in the national capitals of Europe. Indeed, several central committees had already been sounded out informally by Moynier and had indicated that they could attend a conference held on this basis.

Given the potential for disaster inherent in bringing together the winners and the losers in the three wars for German unification, it was essential to set the right tone from the first moment. No great orator, Moynier sensibly decided not to give the major opening address himself but rather to call upon a figure of great distinction in academic and legal circles: Jules Lacointa, a professor of the law of nations at the Catholic Institute of Paris, who was one of the French delegates to the conference. It seems likely that Moynier and Lacointa discussed what the latter would say; parts of his speech reveal a familiarity with the same themes that Moynier had developed in his recent essay. Much of Lacointa's very long address consisted of what would today be called "stroking" the delegates: Having extolled the cause of aiding the wounded as one "worthy of attracting the most generous and the most courageous,"[11] he described the origins of each national society; he took pains to acknowledge the contribution made by existing charitable societies, religious groups, and the various orders of chivalry; and then he gave a thorough and invariably favorable review of the development of each society. Perhaps as an example of the spirit of fraternity, Lacointa was particularly complimentary about the development of the Red Cross in Germany. He first praised the commercial and customs union and the movement toward unification of the states, which, he claimed, have all advanced the political unity of charitable institutions. Then, pursuing the theme of growing popular support, he noted that "whereas in several other countries, Red Cross work has attracted the support of only the elevated classes, in Germany the people as a whole demonstrate their sympathy for the enterprise."[12] At the same time, he was careful to give each of the smaller German states its due:

Saxony is noteworthy for its hospitals; Hanover, for its sanitary corps; Hesse, for its gymnasts; the Grand Duchy of Baden has successfully formed groups of volunteer bearers; Wurtemberg is distinctive because of its railway cars, its [hospital] trains that have reached perfection. Almost all the German states have set up public courses of lectures on the Convention and on the multiple services that go along with it: Altona and Kiel, we note, possess schools that are justly praised, the Samaritan Schools; in Berlin, Dresden and Leipzig, associations of lady diaconesses are flourishing, as are the Albertine nurses' establishments, which were set up to receive the orphans of war, as well as other benevolent foundations.[13]

In *The Red Cross: Its Past and Future*, Moynier had suggested that—unlike the rather too aristocratic and religious Order of St. John—the Red Cross could become the ideal vehicle through which ordinary families and citizens could provide support to those called up for military service. Now Lacointa seemed to be holding up the German Red Cross, with its unified organization, its popular appeal, and its peacetime program of war-related activities as an especially attractive model for other societies to emulate.

Lacointa went on to tell the delegates exactly what they wanted to hear about Red Cross humanitarianism and its place in the contemporary world. Lest anyone think that charity should be extended to those who rebel against the established order, he praised the "valiant" members of the French society who in 1871 had surmounted the obstacles and dangers placed in their path by the insurgents of the Paris Commune, whom he now accused of "iniquitous confiscation . . . ingratitude and impiety."[14] After this genuflection to the restoration of bourgeois order, he went on to make it clear that *real* fraternity was no threat whatever to a world of nation-states:

> Humanitarian law and all the creations that it engenders are lowering the barriers that separate peoples, but [that process], far from eliminating the individuality of states, puts it into sharp relief. However desirous one is to see brotherhood among nations increase, who would consent to see the sacred notion of the fatherland [*la patrie*] swallowed up in this triumph? . . . If, by a strange error, in order to achieve our international work, it became necessary for us to extinguish in ourselves the flame lit in the hearts of our ancestors and piously tended by so many heroes over the course of each national history, that would be a death sentence for [the cause of] union among states. . . . By uniting the cult of humanity to that of the nation, without subordinating the one to the other, the aid societies are performing a blessed task.[15]

To the Red Cross, in other words, fraternity ought to mean not reducing the barriers that separate nations but rather celebrating the unique achievements of each national society as a contribution to the common enterprise.

But what *was* the common enterprise? One might have thought that it was aid to the wounded, but Lacointa immediately launched into a panegyric to the nobility of arms and armies: "There one encounters love of country, par excellence, as well as valor, self-denial, and contempt for danger; army camps have served as the refuge for the honor of a people, and have prepared, even under the burden of defeat, a national revival."[16] At this point his rhetoric began to take flight and the delegates were treated to exhilarating references to *la grandeur de l'homme* and *l'intensité des souffrances*. Death and pain he described, in a phrase worthy of Joseph de Maistre, as "mysterious wellsprings whence arise the highest virtues."[17] Crudely put, his message to the delegates was that nationalism is fine, war is fine, suffering is fine, and they all encourage the brotherhood of nations! This was a novel conception of the common enterprise of the Red Cross but one that accorded well with, and indeed formed part of, the belligerent nationalism of the late nineteenth century.

If Lacointa's speech suggested that a new phase had begun in the life of the Red Cross, confirmation came when Gustave Ador, speaking for the ICRC, explicitly repudiated Moynier's earlier proposal to create an international Red Cross federation. Few of the delegates knew much about the proposal that Moynier had advanced in Brussels some eight years earlier. By choosing his words with care, Ador managed to suggest that Moynier's plan, though perhaps an appropriate one in 1863, was no longer applicable:

> No longer can the question be dealt with in such simple terms. The [national] Societies do not need to be created: they are already in existence; they all have their own history: they have proved that they are equal to the mission that they have freely accepted, and their past is the best guarantee that they will in the future know how to discharge their international duties courageously. Moreover, a great diversity exists among the Societies from the point of view of their administration; this is explained by the fact that almost all of them consider their national and patriotic action as their principal objective.[18]

After a brief review of differences among the societies in the great power states, he continued: A "rapid glance at their internal organization . . . demonstrates how difficult it would be to conclude an international pact, accepted by a group of Societies that are so independent of one another and all so jealous of working in their own chosen way for the humanitarian cause of the Red Cross."[19] As if to nail down the lid on this coffin, Ador pointed out that without creating any such international structure, the national societies had already zealously carried out plenty of war relief work, whether as neutrals or as belligerents.

Yet this was a travesty of the truth. Moynier's federation proposal was not some ideal blueprint that might have been followed in 1863, when the national societies had yet to be created; on the contrary, it was the fruit of experience, particularly the experience gained during the Franco-Prussian War. Its principal aim was to define clearly the nature of the obligations that neutrals owed to belligerents and to ensure that those obligations would be scrupulously fulfilled. It was, as Moynier so often described it, a mutual insurance policy, in the benefits of which all of the aid societies could share. Nothing in his proposal had sought to diminish the peculiar character of the individual national societies; nor did it force them to adopt some kind of uniform organizational structure. And as for Ador's claim that the record of assistance proved such a structure unnecessary, the reality is that the poor response of the neutral societies during the Russo-Turkish War had been very disappointing.[20]

Why, then, had Ador been so disingenuous? The truth is that most members of the ICRC no longer believed that it was either practical or desirable to prod governments and national societies to advance the civilizing mission by this particular route. They had already learned from the fate of the Additional Articles that there were clear limits to what could be achieved and had decided not to risk further the displeasure of the powers, lest the gains of 1864 be lost in the process.[21] As with the Geneva Convention, so with the Red Cross: The response that Moynier had encountered in Brussels eight years earlier seemed to indicate that Europeans were not yet ready to bind themselves to provide a fund of neutral assistance that would be doled out to the army most in need. Such an arrangement would have made it virtually impossible to subordinate philanthropy to political considerations or national interest, and it was for that reason that Moynier's audience had reacted so strongly against it. Yet his proposal curbed their freedom of action only because it assumed that the principal aim of all Red Cross societies was to provide impartial humanitarian assistance in wartime. Ador could not, of course, admit such unpleasant truths in public, but by caricaturing Moynier's federation proposal, he was able to signal the delegates that the ICRC was ready to live with the political realities of the day. This must have been what Lacointa meant by joining the cult of humanity to the cult of the nation. For Moynier, who believed deeply in the universal moral mission of the Red Cross, this must have been a difficult moment; perhaps that was why the distasteful task was assigned to Gustave Ador.

The Russians Repulsed

There was a stumbling block in the way of this accommodation with reality: One of the larger national societies did not want the improved organization of neutral assistance swept aside. The Russian delegates had come to Geneva intending to persuade the conference that the ICRC should play an even larger role in coordinating assistance from neutral countries and that this role should be confirmed in an amendment to the Geneva Convention. Feodor Oom, who introduced the Russian proposal, argued that the experience gained in recent wars proved that if the Red Cross were to escape criticism, it needed to win the approval and cooperation of the military

This could be done, he suggested ingeniously, by convincing belligerents that leaving the sick and wounded to the Red Cross would permit their commanders to get on with the principal task, that of destroying the enemy.[22] In practice this meant persuading governments to permit the ICRC and its agents to take under their protection all sick and wounded—no matter from which army they came—who could not be cared for by the military medical personnel of the belligerents. He went on to suggest that in any future war, "neutral Europe" (that is, those countries not themselves making war) ought to dedicate itself to diminishing the sufferings of all those involved, and he proposed that the ICRC and its agents should represent the interests of this entity in any future conflict. He envisioned that at the beginning of every

4.2 Feodor Oom, chief Russian delegate to the 1884 conference in Geneva, made an unsuccessful attempt to broaden the powers of the ICRC so as to ensure that violations of the Geneva Convention could be investigated and punished.

conflict the ICRC would establish an international aid center as close as possible to the field of hostilities, there to concentrate all of the assistance furnished by neutral societies. He even suggested that the two opposing armies should postpone their first encounter until this international center was in place and that they should not interfere in any way with its movements, leaving its organizers complete freedom of action to direct aid where and when they chose according to need.

The Russian proposal immediately drew criticism from several delegates. Holleben of Prussia dismissed the whole scheme as unworkable; in war, he said, generals would never accept such a proposition; any aid sent by neutrals—here he was obviously thinking of personnel—would have to be joined to the armies of the combatants and be subject to the military authority of one or the other of them.[23] Louis Micheli of the ICRC also expressed serious doubts about the feasibility of the Russian proposal, which, he noted, went much further than anything done during the Franco-Prussian or Russo-Turkish Wars. He doubted whether the necessary freedom of action would be forthcoming in the middle of hostilities; in any case, he pointed out, the rapidly changing fortunes of armies in battle could mean that assistance would have to be sent quickly first in one direction and then in another; finally, he was unhappy about centralizing all the aid under the ICRC because it might limit the enthusiasm of private charity and because he thought that the national societies of the belligerents should be able to specify what aid was needed and where.[24]

Despite these objections, the Russians were determined to press the point; they introduced a motion calling upon the conference to recognize "the absolute necessity of a completely neutral international institution, the authority of which is recognized by the powers signatory to the Geneva Convention, in order to create a legal and stable connection among the Red Cross Societies. [The Russian central committee] proposes that the Central Committees draw up a proposal for the organization of an institution of this kind, a proposal which should then be submitted for examination by their respective governments."[25]

Faced with a proposal that many governments would likely find unacceptable, the delegates hastened to postpone further debate by referring the matter to the next international conference. Oom's colleague, distinguished Russian jurist Feodor Martens, pleaded with the delegates at least to give the idea approval in principle "because sending it to the next conference is the equivalent of an indefinite adjournment."[26] Nevertheless, the opposition was so strong that the Russians finally had to retreat. The best that Oom could obtain from the conference was an agreement that the Russian proposal would be sent out for study to all central committees; with it would be sent also the conclusions of Ador's report on the role of the ICRC that essentially affirmed maintenance of the status quo.[27] It was agreed that all central committees would study both documents and report their opinions prior to the next international conference, which most delegates expected to be held in Karlsruhe in 1886.

In the rush to dispose of a contentious issue, Moynier's earlier proposal for an international federation of aid societies was altogether lost. Ador had succeeded in making it appear so irrelevant to the matters at hand that it was never sent out for consideration by the national societies. There is no way of knowing how much support it might have garnered, especially in view of the fact that its implementation would not have required an amendment to the Geneva Convention. What is clear is that the more ambitious proposal put forward by the Russians could not have been implemented so easily and that faced only with the choice between the controversial Russian plan and Ador's cautious affirmation of the status quo, the national societies were almost certain to prefer the latter.

The Russians left Geneva annoyed but undaunted. They believed that the delegates would have supported their proposal if only there had been more time for them to study it; instead, the proposal had been misunderstood. The St. Petersburg central committee certainly had no intention of abandoning the proposal, and its members resolved to do everything possible to correct the apparent misunderstandings before the other central committees reported their views to Geneva. The ICRC itself was obviously in no hurry because it did not send out the agreed materials until five months after this latest Geneva conference had adjourned.[28] However, as soon as the papers reached St. Petersburg, the Russians struck a special committee to prepare a new document that would explain more fully what they had in mind.[29]

Two issues in particular needed clarification: The feasibility of a more extensive international aid agency and the role to be played by Red Cross personnel from neutral countries. With regard to the first, the Russians insisted that establishing an international aid center *in the vicinity of the theater of war* was not the same thing as placing it *inside the theater of military operations* and that such an agency, operating on the basis of strict impartiality, was the only way to ensure that the wounded were not left dependent upon "the magnanimity of the conqueror."[30] Regarding the second issue, the Russians made it clear that Red Cross aid from neutral states—both personnel and materiel—would be sent by the international center to the Red Cross society of one of the belligerents, but only on the latter's request and on the condition that it be subsumed into the latter's own organization—and therefore subject to the authority and discipline of that country's army. This, the Russians hoped, would dispel the misunderstandings that had plagued the discussion in Geneva.

> They [delegates of the international Red Cross aid center] are not called upon to play a role that is special or different from that of the Red Cross of the belligerent country; they will not be unfurling a third flag in the theater of war; they will not enter into direct relations with the army commanders; . . . [instead] they will play the role of permanent, although mute, witnesses of the manner in which the obligations . . . of the Geneva Convention . . . in regard to the inviolability of the sick and wounded are fulfilled.[31]

That this was an effort to carry forward the civilizing mission of the Red Cross is apparent from the justification that followed: "The mission of defending this inviolability is precisely a direct obligation of the Red Cross, indeed the very essence of its international character; and the fulfillment of this weighty obligation will depend, everywhere and for a long time to come, on the constant efforts of neutral nations to remind the two belligerent parties that with regard to this inviolability, all nations have incurred the same moral responsibility."[32] The Russians concluded that the grounds for opposing their plan had now been removed: It could no longer be said that they wanted Red Cross personnel to meddle in the dispositions of army commanders, whereas everyone would surely welcome neutrals whose presence would encourage belligerents to observe the provisions of the Geneva Convention.

The surprise in this new Russian document was its conclusion: A bold plan to reorganize the central direction of the international Red Cross in peace and war, complete with a draft statute embodying the proposed changes.[33] Instead of the existing self-appointed and self-perpetuating ICRC, the Russians proposed that a new "International Committee" should be created, composed of members appointed by the central committees of the national societies; the delegate of each country would have one vote on the new International Committee, which would meet once every two years in Geneva. In the interval, its business would be conducted by a bureau of three, chosen from among the members of the new committee. The new bureau would take over the functions that had been exercised by the old Comité International, whose past work the Russians proposed to honor by making Gustave Moynier its president for life. The draft statute specified the duties of the new International Committee; they included working to eliminate misunderstandings about the application of the Geneva Convention and using its moral influence to make the Convention's provisions obligatory. Seven of the draft statute's sixteen articles concerned the role of the new International Committee in coordinating neutral assistance in wartime.

Understandably, the revised Russian plan, sent to Geneva in July, 1885, was scarcely welcomed by the ICRC. Not only did it propose to make the current ICRC—with the exception of Moynier himself—redundant; it went even further than Moynier and his colleagues had ever contemplated in subordinating the overall direction of the international Red Cross—hitherto a jealously guarded mandate—to the authority of the various central committees. Moreover, its provisions for obligatory international assistance, not to mention its ingenious arrangements for neutrals to put moral pressure upon belligerents, threatened to upset the delicate balance between philanthropy and national interest that Moynier had worked so hard to establish at the recent Geneva conference. The Russian proposal flew in the face of the message that Lacointa had given the delegates: Instead of extolling the virtues of nationalism, war and suffering, it sought to extend the principle that the conduct of nations should be subordinated to the interests of humanity.

This awkward Russian proposal could not be wished away, but it could be stalled. Instead of forwarding it immediately to the other central committees, the ICRC simply put it aside until after all the other replies had been received. Several of the central committees were tardy in their responses, and as a result the next conference had to be postponed from 1886 to 1887. Hence it was not until June, 1887, only three months before the Karlsruhe conference, that the ICRC finally circulated the Russian proposal, along with a summary of the replies that had been received in response to the 1885 circular.[34] This delay of almost two years helped to perpetuate the very misunderstandings that the Russians had sought to correct and put their delegates in Karlsruhe at a considerable disadvantage.[35]

Even so, when the subject was raised in Karlsruhe, there was more controversy than the Genevans would have liked. As soon as the Russian delegates arrived, they were told by "everyone else" that their proposals would not be accepted "principally because the representatives of the German committees . . . would never consent to formal recognition of the Comité International."[36] Indeed, the German central committee had already expressed its opinion that the ICRC enjoyed far more authority under the current "tacit recognition" than it would gain from formal recognition in law:

> If the Geneva Committee were to be transformed into an institution of the law of nations, its [current] field of activity would not be enlarged. On the contrary, it would run the risk of finding its freedom of action limited, and of seeing the results of its activity compromised. Its relations with the national Societies would be in any case significantly altered if, instead of dealing with a committee which is their proxy [*mandataire*], they found themselves faced with an international authority which could present them with its wishes or give them orders.[37]

This argument was built around a substantial distortion: It was not the other Red Cross societies but rather the governments themselves who did not wish to create an international authority that might give them orders about how wars were to be waged. In addition, the German position made the highly problematic assumption that the ICRC saw itself as merely the proxy of the national societies. The Germans came closer to the truth in predicting that trying to persuade governments to create a new organ of international law would make a revision of the Geneva Convention not less but far more difficult. Several other national societies—the Austrian, Danish, French, Greek, Hungarian, and Dutch—shared the view that the Russian proposal was undesirable, unnecessary, and impractical; for their part, the Belgians, Italians, and Swedes pronounced it eminently desirable but impossible to achieve at the moment; the recently constituted American society waffled on the issue.[38]

The Genevans came to Karlsruhe expecting difficulties. They were well aware that strong support for the Russians had come from their Balkan client states—Serbia, Bulgaria, and Montenegro; the Portuguese had also given their backing to the Russian proposal.[39] Several other countries remained unknown quantities because their central committees had not replied to the circular, and it was difficult to predict their views. More worrying was the fact that some of those who were opposed to the whole Russian plan—for example, the Austrians—were nevertheless in favor of part of it: the idea of having the members of the ICRC elected by the central committees.[40] If the unique influence of the Genevans was to be preserved, it was essential that reform of the composition of the ICRC *not* be separated from the rest of the Russian proposal, which seemed unpopular enough that its rejection was probable. Thus, when the initial debate became contentious, members of the ICRC encouraged the delegates to entrust further discussion of the issue to a small ad hoc committee in which opponents of the Russian proposal clearly outnumbered its supporters. When the archconservative president of the French Red Cross, the Marquis de Vogüé, was chosen to chair this committee, it was clear that opinion was running strongly against the Russians.

4.3 The quintessential aristocrat: Charles-Jean Melchior, Marquis de Vogüé, member of the Academie Française, president of the French Society for Assistance to Wounded Soldiers, and, later, president of the central committee of the French Red Cross. During the 1880s, his resolute defense of the status quo helped to defeat Russian efforts to find ways to police violations of the Geneva Convention.

Oom and Martens made a last desperate attempt to garner support by withdrawing from their draft two clauses that had seemed to other delegates to imply that the Red Cross might meddle in the affairs of governments, but to no avail.[41] The battle had already been lost.

According to one of the participants, the ad hoc committee rejected the Russian proposal because it did not accord with three recognized "positive facts":

1. First of all, there is in fact a Comité International which, through its own activity, has gained both the position which it presently occupies and the great confidence which it enjoys among all the [central committees].

2. In the various central and national Committees, *the principle of nationality has become more preponderant with every passing year, and today the national Societies are auxiliary institutions of the armies of their countries.*

3. Nevertheless, the enterprise pursues a general goal, which establishes a connection among all the Red Cross Societies, and which is based on

the principles of Christian philanthropy, just as are the provisions of the Geneva Convention.[42]

After taking these facts into account, the committee decided,

It would be most desirable to maintain, as far as possible, the status quo. As a result, it has firmly decided against giving the Geneva Committee precise instructions regarding its mode of activity, or regarding the various goals that it should pursue; it has no desire whatever to regulate the activity of this Committee in the way that the Russian proposal requires; on the contrary, it expresses the wish that the Comité International should continue to perform its philanthropic work, as it has done in the past.[43]

A briefer but perhaps more accurate explanation came from one of the Swiss delegates, who noted that although states might agree to the international regulation of postal and telegraph services and other such matters, when it was a question of war, regulations and sanctions were out of the question.[44]

In vain did the Russians try to swim against the tide. Oom complained that misunderstandings would have been eliminated if only the full Russian proposal had been communicated to the other committees in a timely fashion; Martens delivered a splendid but futile lecture in which he argued that from the point of view of international law the status of the ICRC was bizarre, akin to that of a baptized child whose birth had never been registered; their colleague Iusefovich tried his best to keep the matter of the composition of the ICRC before the Karlsruhe conference.[45] But all this was swept aside by Vogüé, who admitted that the ad hoc committee had deliberately avoided all questions relating to the recruiting and powers of the ICRC, "which we were completely impotent to resolve" and which might have had the effect "of compromising the existence of the Committee, which we are all trying very hard to maintain."[46] The merest hint that fundamental change might produce resignations in Geneva was enough to ensure that the conference rushed to bury the issue.[47] As one of the Prussian delegates candidly admitted, "our Conference has neither the power nor the authority to give the Comité International any other mandate than that which has prevailed up to the present."[48] In the circumstances, it was superfluous for Gustave Ador to remind the delegates that "the Comité has never asked for an extension of its competence; it has never taken the initiative to ask for a more complete definition of its rights."[49]

Despite the protests of Oom and Martens, the Russian proposal was almost certain to be defeated. In fact, it was the Russian plan that Ador might more accurately have described as one suitable for the 1860s. Now, twenty years later, there was widespread agreement that the principle of nationality ought to dictate the limits within which the humanitarian impulse could be permitted to operate. For understandable reasons, the Genevans had adjusted their aspirations accordingly; and without them as allies, this Russian attempt to carry forward the civilizing mission of the Red Cross was bound to fail. Indeed, if there was any movement at all at Karlsruhe, it was in the other direction: Because of the objections of several central committees, the ICRC withdrew its earlier proposal that the national societies pledge themselves "to accept the obligations that follow from the ties of close solidarity which unite them" and substituted an innocuous wording that made no mention whatever of mutual obligations.[50] Here was yet another indication that the further development of the Red Cross was now in the hands of the national societies.

Ingenuity and Involvement

Another reality that had to be faced was the arms race among the great powers; a race that speeded up considerably in the last decades of the nineteenth century. To be sure, the growth of armaments was not a new phenomenon; in 1862 Dunant himself had pointed to the growth of "new and terrible weapons of destruction" as a justification for the formation of aid societies.[51] Moynier and Appia had also taken up this theme in *War and Charity*, arguing that "it would be a disgrace to humanity if its imagination were less fertile for good than for evil" and that the "murderous refinements" of contemporary war should call forth "correlative refinements of mercy."[52] Delegates to the Paris and Berlin conferences in the late 1860s saw exhibited the latest inventions in sanitary and ambulance technology and discussed the utility of establishing museums where such items would be permanently on display. Both Thomas Evans's study of the sanitary aspects of the War of 1866 and Thomas Longmore's influential *Treatise on the Transport of Sick and Wounded Troops* (1869) included illustrations and critical discussions of many of these "refinements of mercy."[53] Several aid societies sent items for display at the world expositions held in Vienna in 1873 and Brussels in 1876.[54] At the Paris Exposition of 1878, the SSBM mounted a huge display of equipment that was described by its organizer, Dr. Riant, as designed for "the rational and rapid transport and hospitalization of the sick and wounded in times of war and epidemic: types of stretchers, railway cars, vehicles, barracks, tents, appliances, etc."[55] Dr. Gruby, another commentator on the 1878 display, observed: "With the science of warfare putting all its energy into finding the best means of destroying the greatest possible number of people in the least possible time, we are all convinced that the *complete* organization of assistance will not be perfected until philanthropy's genius for beneficence has found the means of ensuring that every victim receives the immediate help which his condition requires and which he has the right to expect."[56] It soon became generally accepted that in this era of armament building, the proper task of Red Cross societies was not to protest against these "murderous refinements of war" but rather to complement them through the exercise of "philanthropy's genius for beneficence."

Railways, electricity, and machinery had been seized upon with advantage by the warmakers; they were taken up with equal enthusiasm by the leaders of the aid societies. During the American Civil War, Jonathan Letterman, surgeon-general of the Union army, had demonstrated how to use railways for the efficient evacuation of the wounded.[57] The Prussians gave Europeans a practical lesson on the same subject during their war with France in 1870. One result was the proliferation during the 1870s of designs for hospital railway cars and designs for stretchers that could be placed easily and smoothly inside these cars without disturbing the wounded or interfering with the free passage of medical attendants. All kinds of winches and hoists were employed, both to remove the wounded from ambulance wagons and to put them inside evacuation trains. This emphasis on rapid evacuation was in keeping with the Prussian army's insistence that aid society personnel and ambulances be kept away from the battlefield, but the inventiveness of the age was also directed at providing more efficient assistance on the battlefield itself, thanks to Baron Mundy's promotion of mobile electric searchlights for philanthropic purposes.

As head of the Austrian Red Cross, Mundy had been largely responsible for that society's dedication to maintaining and improving ambulance transport. Mundy himself was fascinated by ambulance technology; along with Evans he had been one of the moving spirits behind the display of ambulance vehicles and equipment at the Paris Exposition in 1867. Evans himself had described some of Mundy's technological innovations in his own book on the 1866 war between Austria and Prussia.[58] It was Mundy who had spoken up so strongly at the Berlin conference in 1869 when the Prussians announced that their aid society would no longer perform ambulance duty at the front. Himself a physician, Mundy was interested in everything to do with field ambulance work: hospital tents, stretchers and other methods of transport, wheeled vehicles, and the design of medical equipment and supplies. Several of his inventions and devices were also displayed at the Paris Exposition of 1878.

By far his most ingenious idea was that of employing a mobile electric searchlight, a huge carbon arc searchlight wired to a dynamo that was itself powered by a steam engine; the whole apparatus was mounted on a vehicle that could be drawn by a team of horses onto a battlefield just as dusk fell, thus enabling the stretcher-bearers and surgeons to find the wounded despite the falling darkness. (This idea doubtless owed something to the memory of Sédan, when darkness had prevented the retrieval of thousands of wounded, many of whom died of exposure during the next few days.) A prototype of the apparatus was built in 1883 by the French firm Sautter Lemonnier, and the first trials were held on the Prater in Vienna. Mundy then took it to Paris, where another demonstration was held on the Champs de Mars in May, 1884. Longmore was so intrigued by the idea that he arranged for Mundy to bring the apparatus to England, where it was demonstrated again in July at

Aldershot; according to the *Daily News*, "a large party of professional experts, including the Director-General of the Army Medical Department, watched the progress of the experiments with great interest."[59]

Such fame had the "mobile electric wagon" achieved that yet another demonstration was arranged for the delegates who attended the international Red Cross conference in Geneva in 1884.

On this occasion the great, flat field of Pleinpalais served—conveniently if rather unsuitably—as a mock battlefield, where members of a local gymnastics club played wounded soldiers as delegates watched them being discovered

4.4   The mobile electric searchlight built by the French firm Sautter Lemonnier and demonstrated on several occasions by Baron Mundy of the Austrian Red Cross.

and retrieved by the men of the Geneva fire department.[60] First the searchers went out into the darkness armed only with lanterns; then they returned to the same field, which was now illuminated by the electric searchlight. The team of experienced physicians and surgeons that watched this demonstration reported that, although the apparatus would obviously be unsuitable for irregular terrain, "the light, which was bright enough to read by, was sufficient to recognize the dead and their identity, to examine the wounded, to be certain about the nature of their wounds, to apply dressings, and place them very easily on stretchers or in vehicles. If necessary, it would have been possible to carry out an emergency surgical procedure, such as a ligature of the arteries in order to stop a serious hemorrhage."[61]

The chief problem with the mobile searchlight, apart from its unreliability—a second demonstration in Geneva had to be called off when the light failed to operate properly—was its impracticality. It required regular terrain on which to move and a completely vanquished army, so as to ensure that the light was not destroyed by enemy rifle fire. As the *Daily News* correspondent at Aldershot noted, such lights, if employed at all, were much more likely to be used to prolong the fighting than to retrieve the dead and wounded.[62] Mundy reported with enthusiasm that the French ministry of war had bought thirty-five of these machines from Sautter Lemonnier and that the German army had acquired its own version from Siemens; he considered the latter inferior because it was less mobile. The 1884 conference formally endorsed this innovative use of electric light and urged the appropriate military authorities to permit its use in future wars.[63] Although a good deal of Red Cross time and effort had been spent on this invention, there is no record of the mobile electric wagon ever having been used in battle to retrieve the wounded. Instead, the usefulness of such mobile searchlights was quickly appreciated by commanders who saw them as a way of continuing armed combat after darkness fell. In this case, therefore, what Dr. Gruby liked to call "philanthropy's genius for benevolence" backfired badly.

The belief that the inventiveness of philanthropy would keep pace with the increasingly lethal weapons of the day was closely related to another proposition that also gained currency in Red Cross circles during the 1880s and 1890s: The argument that because expenditures on weapons of destruction were reaching new heights, Red Cross societies ought to ready themselves for substantially increased expenditures on assistance to the sick and wounded. Florence Nightingale, it will be recalled, believed that states that engaged in military activities had an obligation to look after their troops properly; the new thinking of the 1890s stood that idea on its head by arguing that responsibility for the welfare of the wounded rested not with the government but with the citizenry. Evidence of this new approach can be seen in the work of a conference that met in Paris during yet another international exposition in July, 1889: Its keynote speaker, Dr. Riant of the SSBM, pointedly told his audience, "There is no limit on armaments; how then can

we permit any limit on preparing measures of assistance?"[64] Indeed, the very
title chosen by the organizers of this meeting—the "International Congress
on Measures of Assistance in Wartime"—bespoke a subtle change in priorities: "Charity on the battlefield" and "humanity in warfare" had now been replaced by "measures of assistance" [*oeuvres d'assistance*]. To be sure, like the
congress held in Paris in 1878, this was not an officially recognized international Red Cross conference. Instead, it was largely an opportunity for the
three French Red Cross societies—the SSBM, the Association des Dames
Françaises (ADF), and the Union des Femmes de France (UFF)—to parade
their achievements and aspirations before a distinguished international audience. John Furley and Thomas Evans both attended, and several other participants were official delegates of Red Cross central committees, so the assembly took on the appearance of an official meeting despite the obvious
absence of the ICRC.[65] A further element of continuity was the fact that its
President, the Marquis de Vogüé, had taken such an important part in the
Karlsruhe conference two years earlier. He freely admitted that what happened in Karlsruhe had swept aside the earlier international aspirations of
the Red Cross: "When the aid societies were created, there had been a dream
of creating an international enterprise, but that idea soon had to be re-
nounced, and we ended up with national enterprises. At the Karlsruhe conference it was declared that each society should have a national character, and
should be the auxiliary of its national army."[66] Under his presidency, the 1889
congress went on to deal with issues that lay close to the heart of the Red
Cross enterprise.

Precisely where their national role would lead Red Cross societies was described with characteristic rhetorical flourish by Dr. Riant, who began by
hailing assistance to the war wounded as "the charitable and patriotic crusade
of our era."[67]

> Since the promoters, adherents and collaborators—both male and female—of
> these charitable and patriotic institutions find themselves assembled here, is this
> not an appropriate occasion for sharing so many generous efforts, in order to
> give an even more energetic impulse to the organization of measures of assis-
> tance in wartime? Indeed, since there is no charity without a budget to support
> it, do we not have imposed upon us the necessity of seeking to interest more and
> more in these enterprises, which are daily growing larger and assuming wider
> obligations, that public which is henceforth summoned to active collaboration in
> the work of voluntary assistance to an ever greater degree, whether through per-
> sonal service, or through loans or donations in money or in kind, either immedi-
> ate or deferred? . . . Hence the necessity for preparing, with wisdom and fore-
> thought, the budget—the treasury of charity—a long time ahead, while peace
> provides the leisure for doing so. . . . We must induce the public to consider it as
> a sacred obligation that all shall give unstintingly of themselves, of their gen-
> erosity, and of their devotion. . . . We must ensure that the public is well aware
> that henceforth the budget for charity must be in accord with the budget for
> war.[68]

As states devoted more and more public resources to weaponry and military force, the unique mission of national Red Cross societies was becoming clearer: Their task would be to ensure that all citizens of belligerent states were mobilized for war; that those not risking their lives at the front would willingly accept it as their patriotic duty to volunteer their time and money to help care for the sick and wounded.[69] The debt to be paid in this transaction was no longer a debt to suffering humanity, as symbolized by the wounded soldiers of a defeated enemy, but rather a debt to the nation and its defenders. Hence it was a debt most appropriately paid not by neutrals but by those who belonged to the nation fighting the war; not by an elite of self-appointed delegates of humanity but by an aroused and impassioned citizenry. Thus was patriotism redefining the obligations of humanity.

In magisterial tones Riant described propaganda for the cause as "an inescapable duty for these institutions which are jealous about fulfilling the undertakings that they have made to the army and the country."[70] Yet in most states these "undertakings" had been the result of negotiations between cautious army surgeons and war ministries on the one hand and a small group of enthusiastic partisans of voluntary assistance on the other. If obligations existed, they had been freely entered into by those who had sought to perform this charitable work. Now, however, by a feat of logical sleight of hand, Riant transformed these undertakings into absolute moral obligations owed by citizens to their country and proclaimed it the duty of the aid societies to advise their fellow citizens accordingly. In the name of these same obligations, he argued that charity now must keep pace with the arms race. All this he had the audacity to ascribe to the Geneva Convention, which he termed "this admirable effort of the civilized peoples, which opposes to the evils and the inevitable barbarism of war the thrice-blessed coalition of devotion, charity and science."[71]

In a final rhetorical flourish, Riant invoked the spectacle of dedicated "ladies, from all ranks of society, in France as well as in other countries, who have taken to heart the success of this enterprise . . . [and whose] admirable example and noble sacrifices . . . both for the development of their works of assistance and for the salvation of the country and the army manifests a wondrous zeal which maintains and rekindles itself by being communicated to others."[72] Thus Riant used the active contribution of these "ladies," to whom the values of contemporary society accorded the right to a life of leisure and self-indulgence, not only to encourage his predominantly male and upper-class audience to emulate the enthusiasm of their womenfolk but also to dramatize his message that henceforth no individual or group, no matter what their status, was to be exempt from the work of wartime assistance.

What could aid societies and committed individuals do to promote the cause? Riant was full of suggestions for publicity and propaganda, enough to create a veritable blueprint for the activities of national Red Cross societies for the next twenty-five years. Conferences, speeches, and sermons could be used to spread the word, as could books, journals, tracts, and brochures, "not to mention the incalculable opportunities which the press has at its disposal for introducing the public to the benefits of wartime assistance"; finally, there were special events, such as collection days, auction sales and bazaars, concerts, tableaux, and charity balls.[73] With the money raised from these events, the aid societies could organize ambulance and hospital equipment and materiel for the coming war and thus be ready to provide whatever might be needed, whether it was hospital trains and ships, portable barracks and tents, or surgical dressings from storage depots. In addition, they should offer courses to train both male and female nurses, supplementing the courses with clinical experience gained, ideally, in hospitals established for this purpose by the aid societies. To be sure, Riant's panorama of activities did not come as a surprise to many in his audience; most of the European aid societies were already engaged in similar projects and undertakings or were planning to embark on them in the near future. It was not so much the type of activity as the grand scale of it and the enormous potential for mass involvement in performing it that made Riant's vision of the future so prophetically accurate. Philanthropy's genius for beneficence was likely to be equaled or exceeded by its resourcefulness in mobilizing the citizenry.

Not everyone reacted to the challenges posed by the new weapons with such enthusiasm as did Riant. In 1892, the aging Thomas Longmore—now Surgeon-General Sir Thomas Longmore—tried to assess the likely effect of the new weapons and explosives on the battlefields of the future.[74]

In his view, their enormously increased velocity, greater range, and enhanced penetrative force, alongside the introduction of smokeless powder, made it "obvious that not only the deaths in the field, but also the numbers of wounded, will be very largely increased in future wars, and that these casualties will take place over an extent of battlefield unknown in former experience of warfare. . . . Shells, under the action of [the new chemical] explosives will be broken up into a far larger number of fragments, and that the fragments will be propelled with far greater force than when gunpowder was used as the disruptive agent."[75] Even more interesting than his forecast of the damage that shrapnel wounds would cause was the conclusion that he drew for the work of the aid societies:

> Everything thus tends to show that while the number of sufferers urgently requiring help will be vastly increased in future wars, the means of affording them shelter and surgical attention will be pushed back to a greater distance than has ever before been necessary. If a battle is fought on a very large scale, the number of wounded men most pitifully demanding aid will be so vast that obviously the arrangements made to meet the wants of the probable number of wounded under former circumstances will be quite inadequate to meet future needs. *The question thus arises whether the system of volunteer help to the wounded by neutrals . . . should not be more largely developed in order to meet the necessities of the wounded,* in case, unhappily, hostilities on a large scale should arise again in Europe. The

Sur. Genl Sir Thomas Longmore K.C.B.

4.5 After representing Great Britain at the International Congress in 1864, Thomas (later Surgeon-General Sir Thomas) Longmore valiantly tried to arouse enthusiasm in England for the establishment of a national society to aid the wounded. In the 1890s he tried to alert the Red Cross societies to the carnage that modern weaponry was likely to cause in a war involving the great powers.

question is one which may be very fitly considered at the [forthcoming] International Conference of Red Cross Societies, at Rome.[76]

Longmore's failing health did not permit him to attend the Rome conference in 1892, but his concerns were shared by several others, notably Baron Mundy of Austria and Sir John Furley of the English Order of St. John, both of whom tried to raise the issue in Rome. It is scarcely surprising that these three veterans of the cause, with their shared interest in battlefield charity and ambulance transport, should have regarded the increased potential for destruction not as a reason for mobilizing the citizens of the belligerent states but rather for increasing the extent of neutral philanthropy. This was very much in keeping with the conception of international obligations that Moynier had sought to realize with his earlier proposal for a Red Cross federation. However, no serious consideration of the issue took place in Rome. For procedural reasons, the item was deferred until the seventh and last day of the conference, and by then the delegates had exhausted themselves with an agenda full of less controversial issues.[77] After a brief discussion, the conference resolved that the matter ought to be studied by the various central committees and discussed again at the next conference in five years' time.[78] Clearly there was no great sense of urgency about the increased threat to human life posed by the new weapons; indeed, if most of the delegates in Rome shared Riant's enthusiasm and optimism about the future of philanthropy, this is entirely understandable.

Five years later, when the matter came up again at the Sixth Conference, which was held in Vienna, the response was predictable. Longmore himself had died in 1895, and the British National Aid Society replied with typical aloofness that "having taken no part in earlier Conferences, they did not feel prepared to formulate ideas that could bring new light to the question which occupies the continental societies."[79] The French central committee's reply was no more helpful, stating loftily that its functioning in wartime "is regulated by decrees which it does not think it appropriate to submit to international discussion. In foreseeing the character of future wars, it can only redouble its zeal and augment its resources, in order to perfect its services and put itself in a state to be able to carry out to the best of its ability the role which has been assigned to it."[80]

The message was the same from the Prussian, the Italian, the Austrian, and the Hungarian central committees: work harder, get better organized, raise more money. Apparently none of the big powers was interested in pursuing the issue in the terms posed by Longmore.

Far more typical of the attitude of contemporaries to the new weaponry was the reaction of the Prussian surgeon-general, von Coler:

> With the torrent of troops one country can now pour upon another in the space of a few days, armed with the present highly perfected and terribly destructive weapons, an immense task would be instantaneously set before the Sanitary

4.6   Count Andreas Csekonics, head of the Hungarian Red Cross. In 1867, the
Hapsburg empire became, for administrative purposes, a dual monarchy; this meant
that there were two Red Cross societies, one for the Austrian half and one for the
Hungarian half. The nationalistic *élan* of the Magyars who dominated the latter is
readily apparent in this picture of Count Csekonics, president of the central committee of the Hungarian Red Cross Society.

Corps, and one with which it would be impossible for them to cope, unless
everything were ready beforehand for such a sudden and awful eventuality.
Unity of direction in war, unity of direction in peace, that is what we need. In
the same way as the Army is subdivided in fractions of varied importance subordinated one to the other, so voluntary aid ought to be hierarchically divided,
under one absolute control, whence should issue all orders and decisions.[81]

In the 1860s, technological improvements in communications had forced
states with citizen armies to demonstrate some concern for the plight of the
wounded; now, in the 1890s, technological improvements in weaponry pro-

vided the rationale for the wholesale militarization of Red Cross societies, at least in the great power states.

Recognition and Respectability

The seven international Red Cross conferences held between 1884 and 1912 provided occasions for the national societies to report on their developing relations with governments and military authorities. The basic direction of this evolution was set at the Geneva conference in 1884, when, at the behest of the Italian central committee, two fundamental propositions were discussed and approved: that "the Red Cross owes the military sympathy and deference in peacetime, and absolute obedience in wartime; while the state owes the Red Cross protection, in the form of laws that will assure its special position as an institution recognized by the state."[82] With remarkable candor, Secretary-General Maggiorani of the Italian Red Cross told his audience that "without any doubt, the way to win a good place in the theater of war is to merit it, by giving the army a guarantee of perfect organization, and as little different as possible from military organization."[83] With this goal in mind, the Italian central committee had deliberately transformed itself into a national Red Cross organization and had forged strong links with the military, so that even its peacetime organization was designed to meet the wartime needs of the army. By placing a heavy emphasis on "the unity of the institution," the Italian Red Cross was able to offer itself to the state "as the only [society] qualified to contract with it" and to offer a guarantee of "the most efficacious centralization of the direction, organization, and administration of all its forces."[84]

In Italy, the result of this deliberately sought rapport with the military was the Law of 30 May, 1882, by which the government recognized the Red Cross as an institution different from all other welfare societies and gave it as much prestige and moral authority as possible. It was placed under the surveillance of the ministries of war and marine; awarded a juridical personality; granted the free use in wartime of the railways, the postal service, and the telegraph; and was awarded a monopoly on the use of the emblem of neutrality in civil life. As a mark of its special relationship with the state, the president of the Italian Red Cross Society was henceforth to be appointed by the king on the advice of the ministers of war and marine; with their agreement, the president would choose representatives and delegates to work directly with the army and navy in the event of war. For its part, the Italian Red Cross undertook to maintain the unity and readiness of its organization; to avoid becoming directly involved in peacetime disaster relief (presumably so as not to dissipate its resources); and to provide, in wartime, voluntary personnel and materiel to be assimilated into the army medical service and hospital staff for employment in the rear.[85]

Maggiorani had outlined the essential elements of what would become the common relationship among states, armies, and the Red Cross as it took shape in most countries in the decades prior to the Great War. To be sure, Italy did not create these elements from nothing; several of them had already been pioneered in Prussia. The pace at which this relationship developed would vary from country to country, as would some of its details, particularly with regard to the precise expectations for wartime service. Some national societies—the Russian, Japanese, and American especially—regarded disaster relief as an important part of preparing for war, whereas others—the Italian and Austrian societies, for example—concentrated their work more narrowly. Nevertheless, it is fair to say that greater rapport between national Red Cross societies and the military was an almost universal phenomenon in the period from the 1880s to 1914 and that the dominant feature of this closer relationship was the planned integration of the Red Cross into the wartime military-sanitary arrangements of each country.

The aid societies had once been private philanthropic societies in communication with governments and military authorities for the sole purpose of achieving their own immediate goals for wartime charitable work; now they transformed themselves into true auxiliaries whose tasks, as well as the manner in which they would be performed, were set out well in advance of any future conflict and defined by mutual agreement between the societies themselves and the civil and military authorities. In order to fulfill these tasks, each national Red Cross society came to enjoy a special status vis-à-vis the state and the army. This was no accident: The wartime auxiliary role that was envisioned for it necessarily distinguished it from any other philanthropic or benevolent society in civil life.

States that contemplated going to war or feared being drawn into war naturally had an interest in the size, strength, vitality, and reliability of this auxiliary force. Therefore the arrangements that were negotiated during these years invariably provided ways in which the state's stake in the Red Cross could be protected, often by having a member of the royal or imperial family serve as patron of the national society. Arrangements were devised to ensure that the position of president was occupied by someone in whom the head of state and the government had confidence. In tsarist Russia, for example, Maria Feodorovna, first as empress and then as dowager empress, selected the presidents of the Red Cross society from a list of retiring generals provided by the central committee.[86] Even in republican France, the presidents of the Red Cross included the Duke de Nemours and Marshal MacMahon; from 1904 to 1916, the French society was headed by that venerable aristocrat, the Marquis de Vogüé, whose family motto was, appropriately enough, "Love God, the King, the country, and war."[87] In addition to the presidency, state interests were usually bolstered by the appointment of a certain number of high officials—cabinet ministers and/or high-ranking bureaucrats—and several senior military officers as members of the central committee of each

Red Cross society. Such appointments were inevitably described by the society itself as evidence of the high esteem in which its work was held and as symbols of the seriousness with which states regarded the enterprise.

For their part, states chose to embody in specific laws the special position of the Red Cross society and the Red Cross emblem.[88] National societies were properly incorporated to enable them to raise and invest money, to own property, and to make contracts with government and military departments. An array of advantages not available to any other charitable society was generally accorded to the Red Cross: exemptions from taxes and charges for use of the mails and the telegraph; exemptions from customs duties and, where appropriate, import and export taxes; and exemptions from charges where the railways were state-owned and reductions in charges where they were not. Its special status was also generally recognized by the enactment of laws prohibiting any other civil society or commercial enterprise from using the Red Cross emblem. Such laws served two purposes: They restricted the use of the emblem to the personnel and equipment of the military sanitary service and of the national Red Cross society; and they ensured that the populace would learn to respect the special position of the one civil society that had the right to use this emblem. (In some states, societies other than the Red Cross were officially recognized for wartime relief purposes but usually on the condition that they subordinate themselves to the national Red Cross society for the duration of hostilities.)[89] Some national societies regarded disaster relief or other peacetime work as a useful opportunity to familiarize the populace with the emblem of the organization, so that citizens would come to associate it with works of national benevolence and hence would be likely to support its activities in wartime.

This closer relationship with the military had its corollaries. One was that Red Cross societies were frequently invited to join in the national army's field maneuvers; this practice was begun by the Germans, soon copied in Austria-Hungary and Japan—where field experience became a regular and important part of the training of Red Cross volunteers—and was eventually accepted by all of the great powers with the exception of the Ottoman Empire. Officers in charge of army sanitary corps usually approved of Red Cross participation in maneuvers because it provided an opportunity to disabuse volunteers of any illusions about their likely role in the event of war and to give them at least a taste of military discipline. Another corollary was that Red Cross volunteers began to look more like soldiers than Samaritans. In the Franco-Prussian War, for example, representatives of the British National Aid Society distributed supplies while dressed in civilian clothes; only the Red Cross emblem on their caps and the armband indicated their neutral status.[90] At the society's depot in Saarbrücken, the storekeeper, Mr. Stewart, sported a bowler hat and umbrella. Sir Vincent Kennett-Barrington, who twice acted as field commissioner for the society in the 1880s, was photographed in knee boots and a bowler hat, with his armband on the sleeve of his jacket. After the

4.7 The German Red Cross holding field exercises: Personnel of the volunteer first aid columns demonstrate the loading and unloading of wounded for delegates attending a Red Cross exhibition held in Berlin.

1905 reorganization brought the British Red Cross into a much closer relationship with the war office, all this soon changed. By 1912, members of the London branch on duty at White City Stadium paraded like a military unit, with a wheeled stretcher where an artillery unit might have placed a gun carriage. The uniform worn by male "personnel" during the Great War included a khaki greatcoat and forage cap, almost indistinguishable from the uniform of a private soldier except for the Red Cross badge, which was now sewn over the heart. Members of national Red Cross societies that were preparing themselves for service as belligerents began to dress and speak

accordingly, using military language to describe those "mobilized for active service."

The increasing militarization of charity had complex repercussions for the national Red Cross societies. Instead of regarding themselves as autonomous providers of contingent and supplementary help to the wounded of many nationalities, they began to think of themselves as the auxiliaries of a standing military organization that served the interests of one particular state. Paradoxically, this increasingly national focus made the societies more like one another rather than less so: They began to develop a shared interest in efficiency, which was manifested in the adoption of regularized procedures as well as in the search for better and more functional equipment. On the other hand, closer ties to the state and to the military, coupled with the realities of great power politics, meant that the largest and most influential Red Cross

4.8 Sanitary detachments of the Austrian Red Cross on maneuvers with the Hapsburg army: first aid being provided for the wounded at a Field Ambulance Post. Red Cross detachments in the Habsburg army played a sizable role at the front.

4.9 *The German Red Cross and the Struggle Against Tuberculosis*: The cover of a book-
let (with text in three languages) produced by the German Red Cross for the international Red Cross conference held in Washington, D.C., in 1912. In this fine example
of symbolist art, the dragon being slain by the Red Cross knight represents the
dreaded disease tuberculosis, against which the German Red Cross waged a long and
energetic campaign in the late nineteenth century. Tuberculosis was feared mostly
because of the threat it was believed to pose to the vitality—and hence the fighting
strength—of the nation. The pseudo-medieval imagery of European symbolism must
have caught the imagination of the American Red Cross because the same style, including a less warlike version of the Red Cross knight, was chosen for the stained-
glass windows of the new national headquarters building that opened in Washington
a few years later.

4.10 An "educational workshop" for women recovering from tuberculosis at a sanitarium run by the German Red Cross. Most of these so-called workshops consisted of lectures on personal and household hygiene and of training in the use of sewing machines. Members of the Red Cross believed that by restoring the health of young women they were ensuring the vitality of the next generation of German workers and soldiers.

societies paid great attention to their probable role in a belligerent state and very little to their potential role as neutrals. The humanitarian agenda was thus subtly but inexorably altered: In the 1860s, it had been conceived in universal terms, but by the end of the century, it had been redefined in predominantly national terms.

It is unclear whether members of the ICRC were disconcerted by these developments, which, as Geoffrey Best has observed, cannot have been what the founders of the organization "had expected or desired."[91] Louis Appia, for one, surely cannot have been pleased to see the moral and religious significance of Samaritan charity eroded away by the organizers of efficient auxiliary assistance. As early as 1873, he had confessed to Moynier his fears that the Red Cross could be absorbed "by militarism and official conformity."[92] Five years later, he wrote to Moynier that "the Red Cross should not be regimented; it has a right to a certain freedom [of action]."[93] Moynier may well have shared these concerns, but he was far too discreet to express them in public. Indeed, in shelving his proposal for a federation and designing the 1884 conference as a festival for the achievements of the national societies,

Moynier—certainly inadvertently—helped to create a climate in which the militarization of charity could proceed without serious criticism from the ICRC. There is no doubt that those who attended the 1887 conference left Karlsruhe sharing the Marquis de Vogüé's conviction that nationalism had triumphed over internationalism.

By the mid-1890s, existent realities were even beginning to affect the ICRC's perception of the past, particularly with regard to the international aspirations of the early years. In 1896, Moynier published a pamphlet entitled *Notions essentielles sur la Croix-Rouge*, which was his contribution to contemporary efforts to persuade governments to prohibit misuse of the Red Cross emblem by "lucrative enterprises or even [unqualified] institutions of sanitary philanthropy."[94] The most interesting passage in the essay, however, is his attempt to disabuse readers of the idea that the Red Cross is some sort of ". . .cosmopolitan corporation. Neither at the beginning, nor later, did we spend more than an instant pursuing the chimera of an international Red Cross . . . and it is quite improper that what now exists is sometimes described in that fashion."[95] That the principal author of *La guerre et la charité* could make such a statement nearly thirty years after its publication is evidence of the extent to which Moynier's aspirations had been reshaped by the legacy of the Franco-Prussian War and the buffeting that the Red Cross idea had taken during the 1870s. Now he was entirely realistic when he described the national societies as "having a kind of collective life that could easily be perceived as that of an international association, if one did not know that it emanates from what is only an agglomeration of societies, independent but connected by a community of sentiments and aspirations, united in a brotherly fashion, but not tied to each other by any formal commitment."[96] He even noted, with apparent equanimity, the paradox inherent in the national societies' attitude toward the ICRC: They had been quite happy to assign it the task of deciding when a new society should be recognized, but they had never given it the power to monitor their subsequent performance nor to bring them to heel for shortcomings or irregularities.[97]

Even before the appearance of Moynier's pamphlet, the ICRC had given a clear signal to the national societies that Geneva had no intention of rocking the boat by reviving the altruism of the past. In its report to the Rome conference in 1892, the ICRC disclosed that several years earlier it had been approached by a group of financiers who were prepared to organize a huge lottery on its behalf.[98] (Several national societies—notably those in Greece and Hungary—had already benefited from such fund-raising schemes.) Their intention was to raise an "International Humanitarian Fund" of some 40 million francs to be administered by the ICRC assisted by delegates chosen from the central committees of several countries. Members of the ICRC apparently discussed "this colossal conception" but decided that it presented more problems than advantages and eventually turned down the overtures of the financiers. Their report gave two reasons for this decision. The first was that

4.11   *Above:* Representatives of the British National Aid Society distributing supplies during the Franco-Prussian War. One of the ideals of the founders of the Red Cross was that charitable assistance would be forthcoming in wartime from states that were not themselves belligerents. During the Franco-Prussian War, many neutral societies furnished such aid to both of the warring states.

4.12   *Right:* Mr. Stewart, the British society's storekeeper at Saarbrücken during the Franco-Prussian War. His natty dress and distinctly unmilitary bearing reflect Lord Wantage's view that any assistance that aid societies chose to give to armies was purely supplementary and unofficial.

4.13 *Above:* Members of the British society's London branch on duty at White City Stadium in 1912. The effects of the 1905 reorganization, which drew the Red Cross closer to the War Office and the official army medical services, are readily apparent. No longer civilian "delegates of humanity," these people had become auxiliaries organized on a military basis.

4.14 *Left:* Contrast this uniform worn by British Red Cross personnel on active service during World War I with the civilian dress worn during the Franco-Prussian War. To be sure, in 1870 the society had been neutral, whereas this was obviously not the case after 1914; but that is hardly the whole explanation, because a similar contrast is apparent in the dress worn by representatives of the French SSBM between 1870 and 1914. In all of the major states, Red Cross personnel had by 1914 been transformed into auxiliaries of their armies.

it was unnecessary to raise such a huge treasury in advance because money had never been lacking to succor the wounded in times of need. The second was that the existence of such a fund might "render superfluous any further financial sacrifice on behalf of the Red Cross, yet such [sacrifice] is one of the principal elements of its moral value."[99]

This argument implies that those who bought lottery tickets for such a fund would not be making morally worthy sacrifices, unlike their nobler counterparts who contributed to the Red Cross once a war was actually being fought. The scale by which relative moral worth was measured remains obscure, but apparently what most worried the ICRC was the possibility that once such a fund were in existence "the public might well become disinterested" in the cause "and feel no scruples about doing so."[100] What is clear is that this incident sent the delegates an unstated but unmistakable assurance that the cause of international humanitarianism would not be permitted to undercut the fundraising efforts of the national societies. It is also significant that the ICRC, although charged with organizing an international relief agency in the event of war, saw no need to build up a treasury in advance: Inevitably, this decision meant that fundraising for international humanitarian activity would depend on the response to appeals launched only at the outbreak of hostilities, at the very moment when the citizens of belligerent states would be called upon to augment the revenues of their own national Red Cross societies.

As the definition and direction of the enterprise shifted more and more to the national societies, the international conferences were reduced to social occasions at which ritual and ceremony clearly began to outweigh substance. The best example of this phenomenon is the Seventh Conference, which was held in St. Petersburg in May, 1902. More than a hundred delegates attended this conference, which lasted for a full week. The Russian imperial family entertained the delegates twice at glittering palace receptions, but these were only the high points of what was already a busy social schedule.[101] First the Russian central committee held a reception for delegates at the St. Petersburg House of Nobility. On the following day, a grand opening banquet was held at the Tauride Palace, built by Catherine II for her beloved Prince Potemkin, where the delegates dined amid flowers and exotic plants to music provided by the band of one of the Guards regiments and, more romantically, by a balalaika orchestra. Then came the toasts: First to the emperor and empress, proposed by General de Richter of Russia; then to the dowager empress, proposed by Professor Louis Renault, head of the French delegation; then to all the sovereigns who were represented at the conference, by Bodo von dem Knesebeck, head of the German delegation; then to all the ladies present—*dames*, not *femmes*, according to the minutes—by General de Richter again; then to all the delegates, by the Russian Admiral Kaznakov; and, finally, to the success of the Red Cross, by distinguished Russian jurist Martens, to which Gustave Ador made a formal reply on behalf of the ICRC.

On the following day, the delegates toured the city of St. Petersburg, visited communities of Red Cross Sisters of Mercy, and were given tea at the beautiful Eliagin Palace. The next day was taken up by a reception at Gatchina, given by the dowager empress, followed by a visit to the Imperial Institute of Experimental Medicine, where Professor Ivan Pavlov described the work undertaken in its laboratories. Sunday was given over to visiting the art collections at the Winter Palace. The following day was fully occupied with two receptions, one given by the emperor and empress at the Palace of Tsarskoe Selo and another given by the mayor and members of the municipal Duma (council) of St. Petersburg. Delegates who were not yet completely exhausted were provided with a final excursion to the casino at Sestoretsk, where they could restore themselves by walking on the beach or exploring the pine forests. After the conference closed, most delegates took a special train to Moscow, where, as guests of the local branch, they visited several institutions founded and managed by the Russian Red Cross Society and enjoyed a final lavish banquet at the Mauritania restaurant.

Such full social programs had become typical of international Red Cross conferences by the late nineteenth century. At Karlsruhe in 1887, Rome in 1892, and Vienna in 1897, the host committees had organized banquets, receptions, concerts, and special excursions, and the Russians were simply following in those footsteps when they devised their busy program. The conference naturally provided a unique opportunity for the host society to show itself to advantage before the visitors. On this occasion, for example, the Russians succeeded in making a very favorable impression on the president of the American Red Cross (ARC), Clara Barton, who wrote to her niece—with more enthusiasm than accuracy—that "in Russia everything is Red Cross, all hospital work, all emergency work, nearly all relief work of all kinds, care of children, orphans, foundlings: the women are educated to this work."[102]

Given the rudimentary nature of Red Cross activity in America, where disaster relief had been its exclusive preoccupation for two decades, Barton was understandably impressed by the Russian society's more extensive role; in any case, she was disposed to think well of what she saw after receiving two decorations for her relief work during the Russian famine of 1891–1892.[103] Obviously, international conferences also provided a splendid opportunity for the host nation and society to recognize and reward their friends from abroad.

In St. Petersburg there was little serious discussion of substantive issues affecting the present and future of the Red Cross. The reason for this is simple: Most of the important questions had already been settled by consensus or else put aside in order to avoid conflict. At the Rome conference, for example, delegates had discussed the kind of legislation that was desirable in order to protect the name and emblem of the Red Cross; at Vienna, they had heard reports about relations between national Red Cross societies and the military authorities. At the Karlsruhe meeting in 1887, as already noted, Russian efforts to increase the powers of the ICRC by turning it into an agency that

4.15   Clara Barton, president of the American Red Cross, photographed during the international Red Cross conference held in St. Petersburg in 1902. The American Red Cross had shipped grain to Russia during the severe famine of 1891–1892, and Barton is displaying new Russian decorations awarded in recognition.

could police violations of the Geneva Convention had found no broad support, and so the subject was dropped.[104] A similar fate had befallen those who had attempted to raise the issue of states arming themselves with ever more lethal weapons. There was thus little incentive to raise potentially controversial issues. In any case, it was difficult to maintain a sense of continuity in the business of these conferences, partly because of the five-year interval between them and partly because the composition of the national delegations seldom remained the same from one conference to the next.[105] In these circumstances, many delegates must have found the elaborate, not to say grueling, social program in St. Petersburg and Moscow a welcome and colorful relief after enduring lengthy and predictably fulsome accounts of the work of dozens of national societies.

If such a conference was almost unnecessary from the point of view of work accomplished, it nevertheless served other, less obvious, purposes. For one thing, accepting an invitation to host a conference from the central committee of one of the national societies gave the ICRC a useful means of recognizing and affirming the structure and activity of that society. Paris and Berlin had hosted the first such conferences in the late 1860s, and Rome, Vienna, and St. Petersburg were to enjoy comparable recognition at the turn of the century.[106] All these central committees met the principal criteria that the ICRC used to determine whether a national society was reaching maturity: They functioned as a unified body the authority of which was recognized by local branches throughout the country; and their exclusive right to function as an auxiliary to the military in wartime had been duly recognized by the government. Thus it was not until 1907, two years after the reorganization of the British society, that the ICRC thought it appropriate to hold a conference in London. When the international conference was held in Washington, D.C., in 1912, it was a clear signal that the ICRC approved of the reorganization of the American Red Cross that had taken place in the preceding decade. Had it not been for the outbreak of World War I, the next international conference might well have been held in Tokyo, for only distance had prevented such long overdue recognition of the flourishing Japanese Red Cross Society (JRCS).

In addition to providing an opportunity for the ICRC to put its stamp of approval, as it were, on the work of a particular national society, these Red Cross conferences were enormously important symbolic occasions. As is clear from the list of toasts proposed in St. Petersburg, the conferences provided an occasion for the ceremonial recognition, both individually and collectively, of the sovereigns and ladies upon whose support the Red Cross societies had relied since their inception. Once every five years, and usually in the capital of a great power state, the Red Cross solemnly performed a ritual reaffirmation of its ties to the political and social structure of contemporary Europe. In honoring the sovereigns collectively, the delegates tacitly recognized that without the signatures of their representatives the Geneva Convention could never have come into existence and that without the cooperation of their ministers of war Red Cross societies could not achieve their objectives. In honoring Empress Maria Feodorovna, the delegates acknowledged not only her many real contributions to the development of the society in Russia but also the larger debt owed by the Red Cross to the female crowned heads of Europe, particularly Empress Eugenie of France, an early supporter of Henry Dunant; Empress Augusta of Germany, under whose patronage the Prussian society had flourished and extended its influence throughout the German Empire; and Grand Duchess Louise of Baden, who had founded an association to help the wounded that many regarded as a model for such organizations.

In honoring "the ladies," the delegates acknowledged once again the importance of what General de Richter called "the feminine element" in the work of the Red Cross.[107] By this he meant both the special ability of women to feel and express compassion and the extraordinary zeal that such compassion was thought to arouse in the women who experienced it. Naturally this "feminine element" operated at two levels: The ladies (*dames*) did the directing and fund-raising, and the women (*femmes*) did the menial work of caring for the sick and wounded. In the Russian context, de Richter was able to point to the great ladies who ran various Red Cross committees and communities as well as to the women who were being trained as Sisters of Mercy. Toasts are symbolic acts, and in proposing these toasts, the conference symbolically renewed the special ties of the Red Cross to monarchy, the upper classes, and to women.

Considerably less importance was attached to reaffirming the connections between the Red Cross and international law or those between the Red Cross and medicine. At the St. Petersburg conference, for example, there was no toast to the Geneva Convention or to the rule of law, let alone to the suppression of armed conflict. Instead, Martens, recognized as one of Europe's leading experts in the field of international law, gave a toast to the work of the Red Cross, which he extravagantly compared to the Crusades:

> Between the Crusades and our Red Cross, there are many common features. Just as Peter the Hermit preached the crusade and found an echo in the hearts of all the nations, so we have united to protect our undertaking. We have the same banner: the cross, the red cross on a white field. Under this same banner, the nations have celebrated the exploits and grand deeds with which history is emblazoned . . . and forgotten the animosity, hatreds and political interests which divide nations; in the same way there is no place under our Red Cross banner for national prejudices, nor for the feelings of animosity that one nation may bear towards another. It is the same banner for all: each enemy is a friend, and finds himself under the protection of the same hospitals, the same ambulances, the same institutions that exist for all nations. This, ladies and gentlemen, is the fundamental idea of the Red Cross, this idea which expresses everyone's need to elevate himself above human misery. In the Red Cross one can satisfy that urge which carries our glance towards a sky in which we always imagine that we will see written the words that Constantine the Great saw during the battle: "in hoc signo vinces!"[108]

Remarkably, for a jurist, Martens managed to finish his speech without even mentioning the Geneva Convention.

If international law took a back seat to royalty, feminine compassion, and heroic exploits, so also did medicine. No physician—not even a military surgeon—rose to speak at the opening banquet. Nurses, hospitals, and ambulances were all mentioned but not the name of the most famous Russian military surgeon, Nikolai Pirogov. Ceremonial acknowledgment of the importance of physicians and medicine to the Red Cross was evidently thought unnecessary. True, the delegates were all invited to tour the Imperial Institute of Experimental Medicine with the distinguished Professor Pavlov as their guide, but the tour was optional, and in any case the Institute was as much a testament to the philanthropy of the Romanovs and their cousins, the Oldenburgs, as it was a center of medical innovation. In short, both what was said and what was not said on these ceremonial occasions can serve as useful indicators of the priorities of the Red Cross. None of these priorities, it was already clear, was more important than maintaining its own respectability.

The Resurrection of Dunant

The resurgence of the pacifist movement at the turn of the century created an awkward moment for the Red Cross, especially in 1901, when none other than Henry Dunant was awarded the Nobel Peace Prize, which he shared with pacifist leader Frédéric Passy. The legacy of the Crédit Genevois scandal still hung over the aging Dunant, who dared not travel to Christiania (now Oslo) to receive the award in person lest the prize money be claimed immediately by his creditors. To be sure, Dunant had had nothing to do with the city of Geneva or the ICRC for decades, a circumstance that made his sudden reappearance in the international limelight all the more surprising.

Dunant's resurrection must have amazed Moynier, who had not communicated with him for years. True, he had been very annoyed when Dunant, soon after his resignation in 1867, had founded in Paris the Oeuvre Internationale Universelle d'Humanité en Faveur des Armées de Terre et de Mer (the International and Universal Humanitarian Endeavor on Behalf of Armies and Navies), the letterhead of which bore the Red Cross emblem. Moynier had written to him complaining that this was an abuse of the Geneva Convention; Dunant, equally annoyed, replied that "as the founder of the international enterprise," he had a "perfect right" to use the letterhead, which in any case did not contain the words "Geneva" or "Comité International."[109] However, the offending letterhead was not an issue for long; Dunant was something of a gadfly and, like the Russian anarchist Mikhail Bakunin—whose conspiratorial politics he no doubt abhorred—a compulsive founder of organizations and projects with grandiose titles. Also in 1867, for example, he was planning a new encyclopedia that would bring together all of the great masterpieces of literature and science in one multivolume *International and Universal Library*. Needless to say, not one volume was ever published. In 1870, he founded the Universal Association for the Welfare of Citizens Under Arms, which sought to reduce immorality among soldiers by offering them wholesome opportunities for recreation. During the siege of Paris, he founded a Warm Clothing Committee as an unofficial auxiliary to the SSBM. When peace was restored, Dunant hastily converted the earlier Universal Association into a Universal Alliance for Order and Civilization, which set out to save workers from exploitation by both ruthless employers and socialist agitators. With funds provided by Baroness Léonie Kastner, a sympathetic widow who shared Dunant's Bonapartist loyalties, the Universal Alliance was able to hold a congress, at which it was decided to postpone the struggle for improved working conditions and to embark instead on promoting arbitration as an alternative to conflict. Despite poor health, Dunant visited England and gave lectures on behalf of the Universal Alliance to the Peace Society and to the National Association for the Advancement of Social Science. Soon he became secretary of the Society for the Improvement of the Condition of Prisoners of War, an offshoot of the Universal Alliance. All this bustle and activity, however, took Dunant nowhere; unable to find himself a regular living and pursued by the nightmare of his disgrace, his life was overtaken by poverty, undernourishment, and ill health. For a dozen years, from 1875 to 1887, he lived the life of a vagrant; the brief sensation created by his book about Solferino had long since disappeared, and now he was remembered only in Geneva, with some distaste, by his relatives, creditors, and erstwhile associates.

The strange path that led Dunant to the Nobel Prize began in 1887, when he finally came to rest in the small town of Heiden in eastern Switzerland. Now the recipient of a modest annual stipend from his embarrassed family, he was befriended by Dr. Altherr, the director of the local hospital, where he took up permanent residence. As his health gradually improved, he engaged in some uncharacteristically modest activity: He founded a branch of the Swiss Red Cross in Heiden and began work on his memoirs. He also revived some old friendships, especially with Professor Rudolf Mueller of Stuttgart, whose admiration for the old man had not wavered despite the vagaries of his life.[110] Now a vegetarian, Dunant returned to the Old Testament and pondered the meaning of the apocalyptic prophecies of the Book of Daniel; also a convinced pacifist, he had been profoundly moved by Bertha von Suttner's *Bas les armes* (*Die Waffen nieder*), which he read in 1889.

Word that Dunant was living in obscurity in Heiden gradually spread abroad, and in 1895 he was visited by German journalist Georg Baumberger, who was ever alert to a good story. In September of that year, the illustrated Stuttgart weekly *Ueber Land und Meer* carried a front-page story about "the founder of the Red Cross"; Baumberger's text was accompanied by the now famous photograph of Dunant looking saintly, wise, and at peace with the world. A few months later, Professor Mueller launched a public appeal for funds on his behalf. Meanwhile Dunant, anxious to secure a subsidy to fund publication of the manuscript he had written on the origins of the Red Cross, approached Bertha von Suttner, who visited Heiden in 1896 and received assurances from Dunant that he would join the pacifist movement and write for its publications. Nevertheless, von Suttner, who had known Alfred Nobel for several years before his death, chose to nominate Frédéric Passy for the 1901 Peace Prize. Dunant was nominated by Princess Wiszniewska, president of the Women's International League for General Disarmament. Unable to choose between them, the selection committee decided to split the prize; Dunant protected his award of about 104,000 francs by having a Norwegian friend, Colonel Hans Daae, deposit it in an Oslo bank.

Dunant's rehabilitation and international recognition could not help but cause the ICRC considerable discomfort. Several good friends of the Red Cross could not understand why, after more than thirty years, the events of 1867 could not be forgotten, especially if Dunant's years of poverty were, charitably, regarded as a penance for his sins. Among these was the dowager empress of Russia, Maria Feodorovna, who in 1897 had granted him an annual pension of 4,000 francs. Several other bodies awarded him prizes or stipends, and many individuals contributed to the fund established by Professor Mueller. Yet from the point of view of the members of the ICRC, Dunant the avowed pacifist was, if anything, even more of an embarrassment to the Red Cross than Dunant the discredited bankrupt. For decades, the Red Cross had studiously avoided contact with the pacifists. What would the world make of the fact that "the founder of the Red Cross and promoter of the Geneva Convention" (as Baumberger had called him) was now the darling of the resurgent peace movement while prominent Red Cross figures such as Dr. Riant were doing their best to ready their fellow citizens for war? Who, it might well be asked, had strayed further from the path, Dunant himself, or the Riants of the Red Cross world?

Was it simply a coincidence that the ICRC attempted to formulate a position on the peace movement even before Dunant's prize had been announced? In a short essay entitled "La Croix-Rouge et l'oeuvre de la paix," which appeared in the *Bulletin International* early in 1901, the anonymous author—Moynier or, more likely, Gustave Ador—did his best to rationalize and explain away the gulf that so obviously separated the Red Cross from the pacifists. In this interpretation, both groups were "united by a common sentiment," but because persuading people to renounce war altogether was a task so different from mitigating the suffering of wounded soldiers, "circumstances had dictated a division of roles," and as a result "while accomplishing tasks of different kinds, these [two] associations have not had the occasion to meet one another, or to cooperate in the slightest degree, but this is no reason for not regarding them as two parallel currents of activity striving towards an identical goal."[111] Since parallel lines meet only at infinity, such a formulation not only legitimized the existing gulf but suggested that it would continue well into the future. Indeed, the author took pride in supposing that the Red Cross, "whose program ties it to the present evolution of humanity," would probably move toward the common goal more quickly than the peace movement, "whose societies and congresses have as yet scarcely left the realm of theory and idealistic aspirations."[112] Nevertheless, the author conceded, by drawing attention to the horrors of war, the pacifists were undoubtedly performing a service for the Red Cross; however, the latter could do no more than "indirectly second" the efforts of the former, because "the role of 'good Samaritans,' which [the Red Cross] imposes on its members, and which involves definite and urgent tasks centered on the sick and wounded, does not permit them the leisure to pursue other things. Moreover, they would quickly become suspect among the military, whose confidence in them is indispensable, if they permitted themselves to cast the least disfavor upon the profession of arms."[113]

This was a most ingenious argument. On the one hand, it was faithful to the proposition that Moynier and Appia had put forward in *La guerre et la charité*, that working to reduce the horrors of war does not imply moral approval of armed conflict, and thus it seemed to put the Red Cross in the antiwar camp; on the other, it left the leaders of the national societies—especially in the great power states—free to continue ignoring the peace movement while they persuaded their fellow citizens that preparation for larger, bloodier wars was both normal and desirable. Such an elastic position meant that no one in the Red Cross felt it necessary, in the wake of Dunant's international recognition, to undertake a fundamental reconsideration of its priorities.

"An Official Organization for the Purpose of War"

The ICRC's discomfort over Dunant's prize was only one aspect of a more general malaise that enveloped it at the turn of the century. It was not just that events seemed to be moving too quickly; it was also that several agencies and institutions over which the ICRC had no control were taking an interest in subjects that bore on the relationship between war and organized charity. Even before that awkward announcement from Oslo, there had been disconcerting news from Paris, where the Universal Exposition had provided the French Red Cross with an occasion for holding, in August 1900, yet another "International Congress on Measures of Assistance in Wartime." The moving spirits behind it were (naturally enough) Dr. Riant of the SSBM, Dr. Auguste Duchaussoy of the Association des Dames Françaises, and Dr. Pierre Bouloumié of the Union des Femmes de France; each of the three societies had been recognized by the French government for the purpose of assisting the army's Service de Santé in the event of war, and so, despite a certain amount of friction among them, they together constituted the French Red Cross. To this congress seven foreign governments sent official delegates, two of whom held high office in their national Red Cross society.[114] As in 1889, the French used the occasion to provide the delegates with examples of what governments could and should do to assist national Red Cross societies and of what aid societies could and should do to prepare trained personnel for wartime service.[115] What gave the Genevans greater cause for concern, however, was the fact that the leading French authority on international law, Professor Louis Renault, treated this congress as a sounding board for his own proposed revision of the Geneva Convention.[116] Since Renault was also a member of the executive of the SSBM, he was surely well aware of the ICRC's desire that Red Cross conferences should not run the risk of annoying governments by discussing violations of, or revisions to, the articles of the Convention. True, the 1900 congress was not an official Red Cross conference, but its agenda so clearly reflected the interests and preoccupations of Red Cross societies that this distinction was almost irrelevant.[117] This was now the third occasion on which an ad hoc international gathering in Paris had considered matters that the ICRC deemed to belong within the province of the Red Cross societies.

That was not all: The meeting in Paris came on the heels of the Hague Peace Conference of 1899, which had been called on the initiative of Tsar Nicholas II of Russia, who shared the concerns of many of his contemporaries about the incessant production of ever more lethal weapons. However, instead of opening the new era of peace and disarmament that was trumpeted in the press, the diplomats who attended the Hague Conference speedily set aside the aspirations of the pacifists and drew up a new convention on land warfare and another that finally extended to war at sea the principles of the 1864 Geneva Convention.[118] The great fear of the ICRC was that the delegates at The Hague might, in their enthusiasm for creating new international agreements, override the terms of the existing Geneva Convention, particularly with regard to the use of the Red Cross emblem. In the end these fears proved groundless, but it took considerable skill on the part of the Swiss delegate, Édouard Odier, who was also the secretary of the ICRC, to ensure that the 1864 treaty was simply reaffirmed in the Hague Convention. The delegates at The Hague, who included international jurists with Red Cross connections such as Martens of Russia and Renault of France, were prepared to back away from writing new provisions governing the treatment of the sick and wounded, but they nevertheless called upon the Swiss Federal Council to take early steps to convene a conference specifically devoted to revising the Geneva Convention.[119] Since the calling of the Hague Conference had itself interrupted the Swiss Federal Council's efforts to do just that, this resounding summons to action was in fact superfluous.

These events helped to convince members of the ICRC that the time had come for a full-scale revision of the 1864 Convention, not only in order to placate its many critics but also to revive the flagging prestige and moral authority of the ICRC itself. Moynier himself had already taken the lead, publishing in 1898 an essay, *La revision de la Convention de Genève*, which was in fact a critique of the Swiss government's own revisionist program; moreover, in a paper presented to the Institute of International Law some years earlier, he had once again addressed the question of penal sanctions for violations of the Convention.[120] His own proposal for revision contained two points worthy of attention here: It sought to define as neutral and inviolable persons those "members or agents of civil aid associations, who have subordinated themselves to military authority" and to exempt from confiscation by the enemy "materiel of every kind belonging to civil societies for sanitary assistance."[121] His rationale for this latter proposition was that supplies and equipment belonging to the aid societies should most emphatically not be regarded as part of the public wealth[122] but rather treated as private property, despite the "semi-official character" of those placed in charge of them. Those who drew up the 1864 Convention, he conceded, had been cautious about conferring rights and immunities on

> irresponsible bodies, whose existence was, at that time, still somewhat precarious, but now the Red Cross societies are a known quantity, and their services are universally appreciated; they have proven themselves, in the sphere where they have been permitted to operate, and many governments have publicly taken them under their patronage. It seems therefore that the moment has come to show them the gratitude which is due to them and the confidence which they deserve, by according them the same exemption as has already been given to those whom they aspire to care for. . . . It is true that all of the national societies of which I speak are not equally qualified to claim this privilege, which, I recognize, can only be accorded to associations that offer serious moral and administrative guarantees. It could be said that this is the case with those national Red Cross bodies whose cooperation their respective governments have accepted and whose position in regard to the state has been regularized; but that [situation] does not yet prevail everywhere. On the other hand, the Red Cross does not possess a general organization, nor does it have a central authority which can answer for its conduct in all countries, and consequently the societies which are attached to it cannot claim international recognition *en bloc*, as if they belonged to a unified institution. Nevertheless, diplomacy would not expose itself to any inconvenience if it extended the immunities of the military medical services only to those civil auxiliary societies which function under the direction, or at least with the formal approval, of the authorities of the countries concerned. With this limitation, it would be only just to make a place in the Geneva Convention for the Red Cross, and even for other similar institutions, if there are any.[123]

He went on to point out that this would scarcely be an innovation, since it was already common practice in some states for the military authorities to deliver official armbands, the symbols of neutrality, to those members of the national Red Cross society who accompanied and assisted the medical service. Finally, and with undisguised pragmatism, he argued that such recognition would bring international law into accord with the widespread, inaccurate, but probably ineradicable popular belief that the mere act of displaying a Red Cross flag conferred neutral status on those who did so.[124]

The long-awaited international congress to revise the 1864 Convention finally took place in Geneva in June and July of 1906. Exceptionally hot weather made the plenary sessions an uncomfortable experience for the delegates, often reducing discussion to the bare formalities. The real work was accomplished at meetings of the four committees into which the delegates divided themselves. The proceedings were described by William G. Macpherson, one of the British delegates:

The two influences which predominated most were those represented by the great international jurists who had already taken part in the deliberations of [the Hague Peace Conference of 1899] and, secondly, by the Red Cross Societies, which were especially strongly represented in the delegations of the French, Italian, Russian, and United States Governments. From the military side very little had been expressed to show that the military authorities had any particular desire or interest in revising the Convention of 1864, or in having a Convention at all.[125]

Combatant military officers and naval officers made up only one-quarter of the delegates, whereas military medical officers made up another quarter; the remainder were diplomats, consuls, jurists, and Red Cross leaders from various countries. Renault and Martens played very active roles, and once again the Swiss delegation was led by the secretary of the ICRC, Édouard Odier.

Macpherson later recalled that "the spokesmen of the [Red Cross] societies at the Conference desired that the wishes of the societies to be mentioned in the Convention should be met; such recognition, they said, would encourage and stimulate them to greater effort"; the result was that "two articles have been introduced . . . solely for the purpose of satisfying the demands of the voluntary aid societies."[126] These were Articles 10 and 11, which read as follows:

Article 10.   The personnel of Voluntary Aid Societies, duly recognized and authorized by their Government, who may be employed in the medical units and establishments of the armies, is placed on the same footing as the personnel referred to in the preceding Article,[127] provided always that the first-mentioned personnel shall be subject to military law and regulations.

Each State shall notify to the other, either in time of peace or at the commencement of or during the course of hostilities, but in every case before actually employing them, the names of the Societies which it has authorized, under State responsibility, to render assistance to the regular medical service of its armies.

Article 11.   A recognized Society of a neutral country can only afford the assistance of its medical personnel and units to a belligerent with the previous consent of its own Government and the authorization of the belligerent concerned. A belligerent who accepts such assistance is bound to notify the fact to his adversary before making use of it.[128]

The text of Article 10 can be seen as a somewhat cumbersome realization of Moynier's wish to see the officially recognized societies mentioned in the Convention; it did not mention Red Cross or any other societies by name, and it left enticingly vague the identity of the "other" state that was to be notified before voluntary assistance was employed in the field. In Macpherson's opinion, both these articles were "unnecessary, because such personnel would be protected under Article 9 as being an integral part of the service employed for collecting, transporting, and treating sick and wounded."[129] He was undoubtedly right about Article 10, but Article 11, with its requirement that neutral assistance receive a double authorization, seemed designed to limit rather than encourage participation in wars by the Red Cross societies of neutral countries. This was a very far cry indeed from the mutual humanitarian obligations that Moynier had once hoped the national societies would assume.

By far the most revealing moment at the 1906 conference came when the status of materiel and equipment belonging to the aid societies was discussed. Professor Renault argued strongly that such materiel should be declared private property, so that in war it could not be confiscated by the enemy but only requisitioned (and hence liable to be returned or replaced). Support for this proposal came primarily from the continental European states, whose insistence that it be approved gradually reduced the opposition to a small minority. By far the most eloquent and resolute opponents of this measure were the British delegates, who

> steadily opposed the proposal on the ground that in many countries . . . so-called voluntary aid societies are subsidized by the State for the purposes of war; in others they possess mobilization depôts full of matériel ready to be incorporated in the various echelons of the Military Medical Service when war breaks out, and subject during peace to official military inspection; that in such a condition of affairs these private societies have become an official organization for the purpose of war; and [that] it was neither advisable nor just that they should receive special privileges under the Convention; [and] that it would be an inducement to Governments to make the Voluntary Aid Societies the providers and holders of all matériel for fixed establishments.[130]

In a singularly apt turn of phrase, Macpherson warned that if the conference passed this proposal, "it would make a Convention for the amelioration of the position of the Voluntary Aid Societies rather than for the amelioration of the lot of the sick and wounded."[131]

Macpherson, it appeared, had hit the nail on the head: This was precisely the intention of the continental Red Cross societies, whose representatives rushed to defend the proposal. Renault of France ominously warned that unless the property of the aid societies were exempt from capture "there would be a risk of drying up the sources of generosity on which the societies depended, and the development of the societies would be singularly hampered"; he was seconded by Martens of Russia, who called upon the delegates not to risk ruining the resources and activities of the societies; in the end the proposal was carried by a 20-to-2 vote (Great Britain and Japan), with five abstentions.[132] Neither Renault nor Martens was asked the obvious question: If the societies existed to aid wounded soldiers, no matter what their nationality, then why should donations dry up if the occasional ambulance or storage depot were confiscated by the enemy? Was it likely that such equipment and materiel would be put to any other use than caring for the sick and wounded? Not surprisingly, the underlying issue—that humanitarian endeavor was now being tailored to fit patriotic prejudice—remained unstated, but it was implicit throughout the discussion.

That the British and the Japanese should have been the most resolute opponents of this proposal is entirely understandable. The British National Aid Society had for years resisted on principle any attempt to draw it into closer relations with the War Office, and although the government had promoted a reorganization of the society in 1905, there was still a sizable distance between the development of the Red Cross in Britain and on the continent. This is why Macpherson was able to make his embarrassingly accurate claim that most of the European Red Cross societies had become "official organizations for the purpose of war." His forthrightness naturally won the support of the Japanese, who—as we shall shortly see—had never regarded their Red Cross society in any other light and who, therefore, saw no reason to disguise its official status by resorting to legal niceties. Neither of these delegations was prepared to join European counterparts in supporting a proposition that was, in their opinion, an indefensible piece of subterfuge.

In subtle as well as overt ways, the 1906 Geneva Convention revealed the degree to which the civilizing mission of the Red Cross had been adapted to the requirements of states and armies as well as to the lessons of practical experience gained since the 1860s. The new restrictions on the activity of societies in neutral states were the most obvious example, but another significant change was embodied in the revision of Article 5 of the 1864 Convention, the purpose of which had been to stimulate the charitable impulses of the local population by rewarding them for assisting the wounded. The original intention of the founders of the Red Cross had been to promote the moral elevation of the common people by teaching them to prefer pity to pillage. However, there had been so many instances of the abuse of this provision over the years that many delegates thought the only appropriate course was to eliminate Article 5 altogether. Yet some of the idealism that explained the inclusion of this article in the 1864 Convention was evidently still shared by the Austrians; unhappy about its abolition, they promoted a compromise wording whereby military commanders would be enjoined to appeal to the charitable zeal of the populace. But this was still regarded as too dangerous a proposition, and in the end the conference settled on a new Article 5, which allowed "a competent military authority" to "appeal to the charitable zeal of the inhabitants to collect and take care of, under his direction, the wounded or sick of armies, granting to those who respond to the appeal special protection and certain immunities."[133] In practice, of course, commanders were far more likely to rely on requisitioning the skilled rather than on appeals to charitable zeal, not least because this might enable them to prevent, in Macpherson's words, "indiscriminate handling of wounded on the part of ignorant inhabitants," something that was "likely to make the subsequent fate of the wounded worse instead of better."[134] Requisition would also avoid the ambiguities of the new article's unspecified "certain immunities." What was lost in this revision was the attempt at moral elevation, which had been prompted by the imperatives of charity.

4.16   Members of the ICRC posed for this picture in 1906, when the Geneva Convention of 1864 was finally revised. Of the original "committee of five," only Gustave Moynier survives. Although he is about to go into semiretirement, the committee has now been joined by his son, Adolphe, and nephew, Gustave Ador. *Left to right, standing:* Dr. Frédéric Ferrière; Édouard Naville, the distinguished Egyptologist, appointed 1898; Colonel Camille Favre of the Swiss Federal Army; Alfred Gautier, a barrister and a close colleague of Édouard Odier, appointed 1888. *Left to right, sitting:* Adolphe Moynier, appointed 1898; Adolphe d'Espine; Édouard Odier; Gustave Moynier; Gustave Ador.

The Geneva conference of 1906 was Moynier's last great public occasion. As the last recognized survivor of the committee of five who had organized the International Congress in 1864, he proudly accepted his election as honorary president of the 1906 conference and addressed its opening session in the theater at the University of Geneva. Thereafter he retired to the shadows, leaving Édouard Odier, elected president of the conference, to run its affairs. One of his great ambitions had been achieved when the Hague Convention for the Pacific Settlement of International Disputes established a Permanent Court of Arbitration. He must, however, have been deeply disappointed when the delegates to the 1906 conference refused to support a fresh Russian proposal to insert in the revised Convention a clause binding the parties "to submit all questions which may arise with regard to the interpretation and execution of the Convention to the Permanent Court of the Hague."[135] His great hope—that one day the conduct of war would be subject to a more explicit law—must have seemed almost as far from realization in 1906 as it had been in 1870. Not surprisingly, perhaps, Moynier was ready to leave the affairs of the ICRC more and more in the hands of Gustave Ador and Édouard Odier, but his colleagues refused to let him resign from the presidency. Failing health prevented him from attending the Eighth International Red Cross Conference, held in London in 1907. Apparently, however, his problems did not prevent him from rehearsing for one last time his old grievances against Dunant. Now aged eighty and in semiretirement in the quiet and beautiful district of Champel on the outskirts of Geneva, Moynier produced a short autobiography, which he called *Mes heures de travail;* it includes several pages on the scandalous behavior of Dunant, without ever mentioning him by name.[136] Although Moynier was himself the recipient of numerous awards, decorations, and honorary degrees, it must nevertheless have galled him that Dunant in his old age should have received such dramatic recognition when he had in fact contributed so little to the development of the Red Cross compared to Moynier himself, for whom it had been a life's work. In 1902, when Moynier had been made an associate member of the Institut de France, Academician Léon Auroc had quite properly described him as "the soul of this great work of civilization,"[137] yet the newspaper-reading public would always think of Dunant in this role. The coincidence that had brought the two of them together in 1862 was repeated in 1910, when they died within three months of one another—Moynier on 21 August, Dunant on 30 October. Thus neither of them lived to see how the passions of patriotism would affect Red Cross societies during the Great War.

✚ 5

Organizing for War

As MOYNIER WATCHED the growth of Red Cross societies around the world, he gradually realized how wrong he had been to assume that the Red Cross would easily achieve success in any country acquainted with Christian philanthropic ideas. In this regard, neither the British nor the Americans lived up to his expectations. Despite Britain's long tradition of philanthropy, it took almost as long to form a full-fledged national society in that country as it did in the Ottoman Empire, and even after its formation, squabbles and petty jealousies continued to plague its work. Similarly, despite the impressive philanthropic achievements of the U.S. Sanitary Commission during the Civil War, it took years to persuade the government of the United States to ratify the Geneva Convention and even longer before the American Red Cross Society achieved the kind of official recognition from the military authorities that was already common in Europe. For both countries, the year 1905—more than four decades after the signing of the Geneva Convention—was to be the crucial year for reorganizing the Red Cross on the principle of the militarization of charity.

If Moynier was disappointed by these unexpected delays, he was absolutely astonished by the rapidity with which the Red Cross idea spread to Japan, an Asian country with no tradition whatever of Christian philanthropy. With his complacently Eurocentric definition of civilization, Moynier had expected that it would take perhaps a century for other cultures to appreciate the ethical complexities of Christian humanitarianism. In fact, however, the subordination of organized charity to patriotism and military authority made it easy for the Japanese to adapt the Red Cross idea to their own use, and soon they were giving the Europeans lessons about the usefulness of a carefully organized Red Cross society that serves as a vehicle for rallying the noncombatant population behind the war effort. Foreign observers who witnessed the Japanese triumph over Russia drew the appropriate conclusions, and soon the Japanese Red Cross Society became the model to which other societies looked for guidance, in the same way that the Prussian society had exercised a preponderant influence during the 1870s and 1880s. A measure of the influence of the Japanese model was the alacrity with which the Red Cross societies of the Allies—led by the Americans—promoted "Red Cross patriotism" during the Great War. Had Moynier lived to see it, he would have realized that the delegates of humanity had been replaced by the organizers of war.

The Eastern Approach

The founders of the Red Cross initially conceived of its role in the world in ways that reflected the religious and moral assumptions of the nineteenth-century European bourgeoisie. When they collaborated in writing *La guerre et la charité*, Moynier and Appia had naturally assumed that mercy and compassion were uniquely Christian virtues. The first task for the Red Cross, they believed, was to propagate these virtues more widely within Christendom itself, especially among the common people whose weak moral sense seemed to them to need careful nurture. It did not occur to them to conceive the enterprise more broadly until the Ottoman Empire announced its adherence to the Geneva Convention in July, 1865. Although this decision may have meant little to the sultan or his ministers in Constantinople, it prompted Moynier and his associates to reconsider their conception of the moral role of the Red Cross. If—as it then seemed—Muslims were prepared to accept the obligations imposed by the Convention, there was a distinct possibility that other non-European peoples, whom Moynier naturally thought of as "heathen," might also be attracted to the cause. Instead of conceiving of a civilizing mission that embraced Europe and its former colonies in the New World, he now began to broaden his horizons. One result of this broader outlook was that the Comité International decided to take advantage of an unexpected opportunity to make contact with Japan.

As part of the pro-Western policy of the Meiji reformers, a Japanese embassy toured Europe in the summer of 1873.[1] It was headed by Count Sano, the Japanese minister to the Austrian court, who arranged for its members to see the displays of the aid societies during their visit to the world exposition in Vienna. Later, the embassy visited Switzerland, where there was a meeting in Geneva with members of the Comité International.[2] Moynier later reported that the visitors had "listened sympathetically and accepted some of our publications"; they also discussed the fact that establishing a proper military sanitary service in the Japanese army would be an essential first step on the road to the creation of a Red Cross society.[3]

One result of this meeting was an article that Moynier published in the *Bulletin International* in October, 1873, in which he tried to explain to its readers why such an apparently unusual meeting had taken place. Cautiously, he suggested that the mission of the Convention and the aid societies might become larger than originally thought. To be sure, he was a long way from preaching universalism: It would be "puerile," he stated flatly, to expect "the savages and barbarians, who are still singularly numerous on the face of the globe, to follow this example"; he was, however, ready to admit that there were "races which possess a civilization, albeit one different from ours," and that these peoples had already demonstrated a desire for closer relations with Europeans.[4] In this category he unhesitatingly placed the Japanese, pointing out that increased contacts would present an opportunity to spread the European concept of international law, which "will be useful, not only for day-to-day peaceful contacts, but also in the event of future conflicts, for one knows only too well that this eventuality must be foreseen, even in the midst of the most complete tranquillity."[5] Nevertheless, he made it clear that he was under no illusions about the difficulty of explaining his message to those who were "as yet scarcely familiar with our modern ideas, and little accustomed, thanks to the education they have received, to the practice of benevolence . . . [and to achieve] this progress means a fundamental change in their customs; results of this magnitude are not obtained by the mere stroke of a pen, and a great deal of time is needed to produce them. But precisely because this evolution will take so long, no opportunity to spur it along should be neglected; since the goal is so far away, we must hasten our departure."[6]

As it happened, events moved far more quickly than Moynier anticipated. Count Sano was back in Japan four years later when a bloody civil war known as the Satsuma Rebellion broke out; he quickly took the initiative in forming a benevolent society—*Hakuaisha* in Japanese—to organize relief to sick and wounded soldiers. Thanks to the count's earlier residence in Vienna, the society's statutes were modeled after those of the Austrian Patriotic Society. In a telegram seeking approval from the commander of the loyalist forces, Count Sano noted the huge number of rebel wounded and their terrible plight: "Though the insurgents transgressed against the laws, and fought against the Imperial army, they too are people of the Empire, and retainers of the same lord, and so our hearts cannot bear to be indifferent to them. . . . Civilized nations in Europe and America have institutions, to which people contribute money and goods, to aid the sick and wounded on the battlefields without distinction of nationalities. This is a system which we must learn."[7] Despite Moynier's conviction that it would take the Japanese several decades to adapt to European ideas, the relief society was officially approved and soon received the highest accolade of all: gifts of money and materiel from the emperor and empress. It is worth emphasizing that many of the wounded were declared rebels against imperial authority and that in providing assistance to them the Japanese demonstrated a more inclusive approach to charity than that taken by the French aid society during the uprising of the Paris Commune in 1871, when it assisted only those who fought against the insurgents. This contrast however, was lost on European philanthropists, who continued to believe that the Japanese required lessons from abroad in morality and humanity.

5.1 Count Sano, founder of the *Hakuaisha* (benevolent society), which became the Japanese Red Cross Society.

The *Hakuaisha* was not disbanded after the rebellion was over. When the imperial government announced its adherence to the Geneva Convention in 1886, it became the nucleus around which the Japanese Red Cross Society—*Nippon Sekijuji Sha*—was created.[8] Baron Siebold, secretary of the Japanese legation in Berlin, provided plenty of information about European Red Cross societies and about the procedures for recognition by the ICRC. In 1884, Dr. Hashimoto, of the Japanese army's medical service, and General Oyama, the minister of war, toured Europe in order to study military medical organization, and Moynier invited Hashimoto and Siebold to Geneva for the international conference.[9] On their return to Japan, they drew up a plan outlining the role that the newly reorganized society was expected to play in wartime; an important element in this plan was the creation of a Red Cross hospital, where physicians and other relief personnel could be trained under Hashimoto's supervision. In 1887, delegates of the Japanese society attended the Karlsruhe conference, at which the ICRC officially announced its recognition of the Japanese society. At home a membership drive was immediately undertaken, but its target of 100,000 members was well short of realization when the war with China began in 1894. Nevertheless, this war helped to turn the society into a major operation: At war's end, the society had over 160,000 members and more than 670,000 yen in its treasury.[10] By 1903, its membership was close to 1 million—in other words, one out of every forty-five Japanese now belonged to the Red Cross society. No longer was it a private charitable association: Its position as a public body and auxiliary of the military had been officially recognized in the new Civil Code enacted in 1898.

The Japanese society was highly centralized, hierarchically organized, and very closely tied to the imperial regime. The emperor and empress were both patrons of, and major investors in, the society, and Prince Komatsu was its honorary president.[11] The affairs of the society were managed jointly by the ministers of the imperial household, the army, and the navy. Throughout the empire, provincial governors and mayors were expected to serve as heads of the local branches. The annual meetings of these local branches combined ceremony, business, and entertainment; they were "so arranged as to constitute a great social event of the locality, so that all who belong or wish to belong to good society must partake."[12] Donors of large amounts were especially recognized at these meetings, and provinces with a high percentage of members among the local population could count on the attendance of Prince Komatsu himself at their annual meetings. These usually ended with displays of wrestling and fireworks; this was "an expensive business, but . . . experience has shown that income is much more than the outlay" because so many new members were attracted by these incentives."[13] The society began to publish a monthly magazine in 1890; and to arouse interest among the rural population, Baron Ishiguro, surgeon-general of the army, devised a magic lantern show that could be taken from village to village.

Considering the brief time that it had been in existence, the JRCS performed well during the Sino-Japanese War.[14] Under the direction of the war ministry, the society received all donations from the public and sent them on to the theater of war. It provided both materiel and personnel, the latter in the form of a corps of volunteer assistants who were employed in caring for the wounded. Although the entire operation was under the orders of Baron Ishiguro, who directed the field medical service, the real authority was exercised by Lt.-Col. Shimidzu, the society's delegate-general at army headquarters; in his capacity as intermediary between the JRCS and the field medical service, Shimidzu kept the society informed of how the army was using its assistance and of its continuing needs. He had under him several delegates whose job was to work with the chief medical officer of each army division. The society's main task was to get its trained physicians, pharmacists, and nurses into uniform and ready to work with the army or the navy, either in the *zone d'étapes* or in the rear; needless to say, in either location they were subject to rigorous military discipline. Food, bedding, and transport while on active service were provided by the military authorities, and fixed salaries were paid to all JRCS employees, from the delegate-general himself to the lowliest stretcher-bearer. To demonstrate its gratitude after the war was over, the imperial regime held a special ceremony at which the empress praised the JRCS for its work; Shimidzu was given a medal, and leading members of the society were given titles, distinctions, and other rewards.

After the ceremonial thanks from the regime came a stricter accounting by the Japanese military authorities. From their point of view, the war had revealed some obvious weaknesses in the organization and personnel of the Red Cross society. For an extended campaign on the Asian mainland—the likelihood of which was taken as a given by the JRCS—transport columns, hospital ships, and a chain of supply depots were required as were numerous trained male nurses for service in the *zone d'étapes*. Once more the Japanese turned to the West to see what they could learn. In 1895, Nagao Ariga, a rising star in the field of international law, was sent to Europe to study how Red Cross societies in different states organized their war preparations.[15] On his return, Ariga was charged with drawing up a set of regulations governing wartime service by Red Cross personnel; after two years of work, it was submitted to the war ministry and finally approved in October, 1898.[16] The new regulations committed the society to provide several kinds of assistance in the event of war: Medical aid detachments who would usually be employed in military hospitals; two transport columns for each army division; evacuation ships capable of carrying six hundred sick and wounded; canteens in seaports and railway stations for feeding evacuated soldiers; and supply depots, both temporary and permanent. All Red Cross personnel who had been specially trained for war service were expected to present themselves within twenty-four hours of an appeal being made; as before, they were then subject to military discipline, required to wear a prescribed uniform, and paid a fixed salary. While in the field, they would be under the authority of the society's delegate-general, who was himself subordinate to the director-general of field medical services and the inspector-general of the *zone d'étapes*. In addition, the new regulations stipulated that Red Cross personnel would participate in maneuvers whenever called upon by the military authorities. The purpose of sending them on maneuvers, Ariga frankly admitted, was to ensure that Red Cross personnel had no romantic illusions about their role and to teach them exactly where they were expected to complement the military medical service.

Even among the Japanese, apparently, the idea had spread that Red Cross societies would send their people onto the battlefield to collect the wounded. Ariga pounced on this notion, dismissing it as "not only false, but actually very injurious for the work of the Red Cross"; if people were allowed to retain such illusions, they would certainly be disappointed when they learned the truth.[17] Enthusiasm for Red Cross work would quickly decline, and this would be most unfortunate for the welfare of the army. Ariga claimed that "the advanced state of military science today" had rendered such ideas obsolete, but

Baron Ishiguro was considerably more specific in a set of instructions dated April 1897: Red Cross personnel should be excluded from the combat zone, he stated flatly, because the army could not take responsibility for providing them with food, shelter, and materiel; the state was not prepared to recompense them or their families in the event that they were wounded or killed; and they could not be relied on to accept the strict discipline required in the combat zone. This, he underlined, is why "nothing should be permitted during maneuvers that would give people the idea that the Red Cross Society could play a role in services to the front lines."[18]

Paradoxically, the Japanese, in their efforts to get this message across, often invoked the name of Florence Nightingale, as if *she* had been an advocate of voluntary assistance on the battlefield. One of Ishiguro's subordinates began his defense of the new system with the statement, "Gentlemen, the days of Miss Florence Nightingale are over."[19] Little did he realize that Nightingale would undoubtedly have approved both the improvements made in the army medical service and the limited, clearly subordinate role assigned to the Red Cross. As the next war (with Russia) would soon demonstrate, the Japanese had perfected a system that transformed voluntary assistance into a reliable, disciplined, and effective auxiliary to military organization.

If necessary, the government could also mobilize the JRCS in the event of political disturbances or natural disasters. The term "political disturbance" meant any social disorder short of war, inside or outside the frontiers, in which units of the army or navy were mobilized. Thus Red Cross units were mobilized for service during the "troubles" in Korea in 1894 and in China— the Boxer Rebellion—in 1900.[20] In the case of natural disasters, the JRCS for a long time acted only when requested to do so by the empress and was expected to meet the additional expenses through special donations. War service was always its first priority; for that reason, trained Red Cross personnel were almost never employed in combating epidemic diseases because of the risk of serious illness or death. Even if they were sometimes mobilized in the wake of earthquakes, tidal waves, fires, or floods, the authorities always treated these occasions as opportunities to practice for wartime situations as well as to popularize the society and its work in a particular part of the country. In 1903, local Red Cross sections were allowed to make temporary use of personnel and supplies meant for war service provided there was "no interference with real service in time of war."[21]

Like most European societies, the JRCS had its Committee of Ladies, formally titled the Ladies' Volunteer Nursing Association. For many years Princess Komatsu headed this body, which in Tokyo was composed of the imperial princesses and the wives and daughters of the nobility and ministers of state; at the local level, wives of provincial governors joined the wives and daughters of army officers and civil officials to receive training in the dressing of wounds and the preparation of bandages. Here was perhaps the biggest cultural gulf for the Japanese to cross, because there was no indigenous counterpart to the sisters of charity in Catholic and Orthodox Europe or to the religious communities of Protestant Europe. There were Buddhist nuns in Japan, but they did not engage in nursing. Social convention frowned on the idea of a woman nursing a man who was not of her own family. Consequently,

> only the women of inferior classes could be induced to come into hospital wards and nurse whatever patients chanced to be there. But this was not what the Red Cross Society wanted. What it wanted was a class of refined ladies with intelligence and self-respect, devoting themselves to the work, not for pay, but for patriotism and humanity. Hence in order to bring about [change] artificially . . . it was necessary that the ladies in the highest position should set the example and let the public see that nursing is no mean, mercenary profession, but on the contrary, a very honorable one, nay, almost the only one in which a woman can aspire to be of direct service to the state in time of war. For this purpose, the members of the Committee of Ladies . . . [have] become the moral guides of the professional nurses trained in the hospital of the Society. They take care of their education and supervise their conduct when at home or out in the field of service. . . . Now the nurses of the Red Cross Society are [being] recruit[ed] from among the daughters of well-to-do middle classes, and enjoy the highest reputation in society.[22]

By demonstrating that the imperial family, the military, and the Red Cross society approved of its work, the Committee of Ladies rapidly succeeded in changing Japanese attitudes toward the social acceptability of female nursing. All of the foreign observers who saw Japanese Red Cross nurses in action during the war with Russia reported favorably on their training, ability, and performance. One of the observers, American naval surgeon William Braisted, believed that the subordination of women in traditional Japanese culture was in fact the key to the success of the Red Cross nursing program: "They have been trained to an idea of obedience so absolute that they are peculiarly fitted for work of this kind, especially military work."[23] Here was a case where Japanese tradition, far from being the obstacle that Moynier had feared, actually helped to ensure the success of the Red Cross nursing program.

In fact, Moynier lived just long enough to be aware that the Japanese society was becoming the envy of the Red Cross world, especially in Great Britain and the United States. One wonders if, in old age, he ever reflected on the inaccuracy of his initial assumptions about the length of time required for the Red Cross idea to mature among the Japanese. To be sure, in the mid-1870s, no one could have foreseen the dramatic transformation that the Meiji Revolution would bring to Japan; by the same token, few could have foreseen the degree to which charity would become militarized in the great power states after 1880. It is nevertheless revealing that the Americans, from whom Moynier had expected so much, would find themselves learning from the Japanese, from whom he had expected so little. Beguiled by the record of the

5.2 The victorious General Nogi (*seated third from right*) poses with his staff, the conquerors of Port Arthur; the circled figure is Nagao Ariga, the expert in international law who frequently represented Japan at international Red Cross conferences. Ariga's report on the war against Russia, made to the London conference in 1907, attracted a great deal of attention.

Sanitary Commission during the American Civil War, Moynier had assumed that a disposition toward benevolence would be the principal key to the growth of the Red Cross in any country; the Japanese experience, however, proved that organized patriotism, the subordination of women, and the imminence of war could transform a benevolent society into a flourishing national enterprise dedicated to supporting military aggression and territorial expansion.

Indeed, from the Japanese point of view, benevolence was an inappropriate basis on which to construct war relief work. As Ariga wrote in his report to the Red Cross conference in London in 1907,

> The great principle we follow in the relief work of our society in time of war is the entire separation of obligatory service from benevolent self-sacrifice. We observe that in the Red Cross societies of many lands relief service in time of war is made the immediate object of benevolence, and either the relief organizations are composed entirely of men offering their services gratis for the humane work

of the Society, or else portions of Relief corps are made up of paid members, doing their work as a matter of obligation, while the remaining portions are made up of men and women volunteering their services to the Society from motives of benevolence. That these self-sacrificing men and women are well meaning admits of no doubt, but aptitude for relief work in time of war is not the necessary accompaniment of a kind heart and a benevolent character. Besides, relief service in time of war as part of the Medical Service of the Army and Navy has to be carried on under strict discipline, and there is always hesitation in applying hard disciplinary measures to persons doing their work from benevolence and self-sacrifice. For these reasons, the Japanese Red Cross Society has from the very beginning made the two things entirely separate, assigning to the members of the Society the task of contributing the funds with which to pay and train, in time of peace, persons fit for relief work in time of war, and under obligation to respond to the summons of the Society whenever need occurs, and to render service under such strictness of order and discipline as the nature of the work may require. . . . In the Chinese War [1894–1895], in the Boxer troubles of 1900, and again in the late Russian War, we found out from experience that this is the only right and true principle to be followed in these matters.[24]

The Japanese position amounted to nothing less than a repudiation of the idea of voluntary service in wartime; implicitly, it also repudiated pity, compassion, and self-sacrifice as appropriate motivators for service to the sick and wounded. Instead, a master-servant relationship was created between the Red Cross society and the personnel whom it selected and trained for wartime service; it was deliberately created, so as to give the society complete freedom to accept or reject, promote or dismiss whomever it wished solely on the basis of meritorious performance. In effect, the society functioned as the recruiting and training facility for the auxiliary medical services of the Japanese army and navy. Voluntary activity in wartime was limited to that performed by the Committee of Ladies and, as Ariga candidly admitted, their work—organizing rest stations for evacuees in seaports and railway stations—was "subsidiary, and forms no essential part of the actual relief service of the Society."[25]

Lessons of Manchuria

Under the 1903 Regulations for Relief Service in Time of War, the Japanese Red Cross Society was expected to provide and maintain five different relief corps: relief detachments for the hospital service, transport columns, hospital ships, rest stations, and supply depots.[26] Of these, the transport columns—whose task was vital—proved to be the most difficult to organize, whereas the rest stations—whose role was regarded by the planners as no more than subsidiary—proved to be an unexpected benefit to the society, the troops, and the populace.

5.3   This sketch, entitled "Transport of Patient in a Chinese Boat, with a member of the Japanese Red Cross Society as Escort," appeared in Ariga's *Report Presented to the Eighth International Conference of the Red Cross, London, June 1907.*

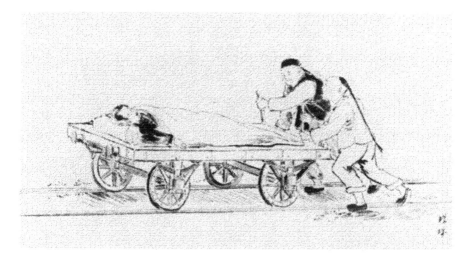

5.4   Another sketch from Ariga's 1907 *Report:* "Patient transported on Hand-Truck propelled by Chinese coolies." Because of the difficult terrain in Manchuria, the Japanese much preferred rail or water transport for the evacuation of wounded.

As the Japanese had already learned in the war against China, the terrain of the Asian mainland made wheeled ambulance transport impossible. To quote Ariga again: "In those parts of the Asiatic continent where the chances of having to use our armies are the greatest, there are no good roads, but only plains and fields, with irregular elevations intersected by sandy depressions which change into rushing torrents in the rainy season, so that we must abandon all idea of having sanitary wagons such as are used by the Red Cross Societies of Europe."[27] Unless a railway or a river ran conveniently through the *zone d'étapes*, wounded soldiers would have to be evacuated by stretcher-bearers, sometimes over considerable distances. Therefore, so that the army would no longer have to rely on coolies, horses, and donkeys requisitioned or hired locally, the Red Cross society offered to organize transport columns of stretcher-bearers.

The society's reserve medical officers and nurses normally used their qualifications to earn their livings between periods of military service. There was, however, little or no demand for trained stretcher-bearers in civilian life, and the society quickly discovered that trainees were not to be found in anything like the numbers required by the army. When the war with Russia began, the society hastily organized a group of veterans into a transport column, but this was only an improvised solution. The military authorities, whose needs were immediate, decided to revert to using Chinese coolie transport wherever possible and to employ the few stretcher-bearers provided by the society as escorts, especially on transport trains for the wounded. This solution, though no doubt the only one possible in the circumstances, did nothing to enhance the society's ability to recruit more stretcher-bearers, because, as Ariga admitted,

> As long as the Army employs Chinese coolies for transport, it is highly injurious to the self-respect of our stretcher-bearers if they are made to do the same sort of work as mean, mercenary coolies, the meanest and dirtiest set of people that can be found in China. The Chinese inhabitants really think that our stretcher-bearers are "Japanese coolies" and call them so. And the depressing effect of this necessarily tells on the quality of the work done, for our stretcher-bearers cannot be induced to do it with satisfaction.[28]

He did, however, concede that the coolies "can walk much faster than our stretcher-bearers, so that their want of sympathy with the patients is more than counter-balanced by the quickness with which the sick and wounded can be carried to the Nursing Stations or Étape Hospitals."[29]

The rest stations, which provided rest and refreshment to wounded evacuees, were left for local branches of the Red Cross to organize, relying on volunteer participation from the local committees of ladies. Establishing and maintaining the rest stations provided an opportunity for enthusiastic volunteers to demonstrate their devotion to the war effort as well as relieving both the military authorities and the central treasury of the society from the expense of operating them. In such a highly centralized and closely regulated system of war relief, the rest stations served as a kind of safety valve, which permitted members of local branches to exercise a rare degree of autonomy, although it was still carefully circumscribed: Both the location of the stations and the kinds of food and drink provided had to be in accordance with the wishes of the military authorities. Only time and money were unrestricted: Volunteers could donate as much of either as they liked.

Since Ariga had already stated that the rest stations were not regarded as essential to the society's program of war relief, it is clear that their importance lay elsewhere. As he reported to the London conference, they were regarded as a great success chiefly because of the opportunity they provided for bringing the army and the people closer together:

> Relief stations are the only places where the soldiers who have done their duty to the country and the benevolent members of the Red Cross Society come face to face with one another, and this direct communication is extremely necessary in order to make the relation between the soldiers and the people, the Army and the Nation, vital and ever-moving in the consciences of both. And it would be a hindrance to this direct communication, if the personnel of rest stations were to do this work by order of some [higher] authority. . . . The soldiers, too, will feel more directly indebted to the people by receiving kindness from the hands and the hearts of the people themselves, than when that kindness comes through the cold impersonality of a society having its controlling organization in Tokio.[30]

By the time evacuees reached the rest stations, which were established only on the Japanese home islands, they had already received most of the medical attention and nursing care that was crucial to their survival. For them, the additional comforts provided by the rest stations were a welcome taste of home and a pleasant introduction to the period of convalescence. Seen from above, however, the rest stations provided another, no less tangible advantage: They served as an avenue through which noncombatants could demonstrate, at their own cost, their support for the imperial government, the army and navy, and the war itself. This was a lesson that would not be lost on the Red Cross societies of Europe and America.

Planning for the exigencies of war was so complete that the Japanese decided in advance to refuse all offers of voluntary aid from abroad, including those from foreign Red Cross societies, unless they were gifts of money or materiel. This decision was not altered by the shortage of stretcher-bearers and only slightly by a temporary shortage of nurses early in the war. At the London conference in 1907, Ariga explained that any widespread use of foreign personnel would have been impossible because of differences in language and customs. Donations of money were received from half a dozen European Red Cross societies; from the ICRC (which sent 1,000 francs to each belligerent); and even from the Russian Red Cross, which sent 2,000 rubles in appreciation for the care given by the Japanese to the wounded sailors from a Russian cruiser, the *Variag*, which was damaged in action. The German Red Cross Society shipped to its Japanese counterpart large quantities of sanitary material, and the Italian society, in a burst of nationalistic ardor, "sent us 250 cases of quinquina [quinine] wine, 75 cases of Marsala wine, 60 cases of Cognac, 80 cases of Verm[o]uth, and 50 cases of macaroni."[31]

Once again, the Japanese relaxed their strictness where lady volunteers were concerned and decided that foreign aid offered in the form of nursing by ladies was "not necessarily unacceptable."[32] This may well have been a decision the Japanese had cause to regret because of the trouble occasioned by the presence of well-meaning foreigners. One of these was the well-known American physician, Dr. Anita Newcomb McGee of Washington, D.C., who immediately offered to bring six hundred female nurses to Japan to help care for the wounded.[33] When the Japanese minister in Washington sent this news to Tokyo, the government and the Red Cross society decided to scale her plan down to manageable proportions and offered to pay the traveling expenses of a party of ten, that is, Dr. McGee and nine selected nurses. They were provided with first-class hotel accommodations in Tokyo, an interpreter, and a distinguished escort in the person of Baron Takagi, retired inspector-general of the navy's medical service and head of the Tokyo Benevolent Hospital. After a month of receptions in the capital and visits to scenic places in the interior of the country, they were sent to work at the Reserve Hospital in Hiroshima.

Their progress aroused considerable comment; back in Washington, Mabel Boardman, the ambitious socialite who was scheming to take over the leadership of the American Red Cross, received this waspish version from a correspondent in Seoul:

> Have you heard of Mrs. McGee and her Red Cross nurses who "volunteered" their services! The Japanese were at their wits ends as to the manner in which they should employ them and have dispatched them to Hiroshima to care for wounded Russians. The expense of their maintenance at "the front" would equal that of an army corps, for foreign food, foreign beds and furniture and English speaking servants would have to be provided. . . . When Mrs. McGee arrived she was met on the pier by Japanese ladies carrying bouquets of fresh flowers, who had waited weary hours in the rain. This enchanted her and was but a prelude to the fetes and entertainments which were given "in her honor" at Tokyo, the purpose being to show appreciation of her kind intentions by stroking her with civility. As she is a lady who likes to be in the public eye, she evinced pleasure under the process.[34]

Once they arrived in Hiroshima, where room and board was provided by their hosts, the Americans were put on the same footing as nurses trained by the Japanese Red Cross Society, with the exception of Dr. McGee herself, who was made a chief nurse. Not much practical nursing could have been done, however, because Dr. McGee soon asked to see many other kinds of institutions, and she and her party spent several weeks visiting other hospitals in Japan and sailing aboard the society's hospital ships to the theater of war, where they visited both an étape hospital and a forward nursing station. The Japanese must have been relieved when the Americans asked to go home in October, 1904, but of course their relief did not show; the Americans were sent on their way with gifts, decorations, and a farewell dinner.

Not all foreign nurses received such lavish treatment. Mrs. T. E. Richardson, a recently widowed English lady, came from London to Japan at her own expense and spent fifteen months working in various institutions run by the Japanese Red Cross Society.[35] Her hosts were impressed by her refusal to go sight-seeing or to attend receptions and by her willingness to work "in company with our Nurses, doing everything like them, and even going to the extent of sweeping and washing the floors with them barefooted."[36] She also made several donations to the society's treasury. Before her departure in July, 1905, she received many tributes from members of the imperial family, the Japanese government, the military authorities, and of course the Red Cross society itself. On her return to England, Mrs. Richardson became an eloquent apologist for Japanese expansion on the Asian mainland; she also foresaw a great role for its Red Cross society, which "is apparently unbounded in its sphere of usefulness, for in future it will . . . bring untold blessings to the shores of Korea and Manchuria. The scheme of [Red Cross] organization which is now being considered will, it is hoped, spread into China as well, and may be the commencement of an era of higher civilization in all these countries."[37]

Even before Mrs. Richardson had arrived in Japan, there had been a more formal visit by two other English ladies, Miss Ethel McCaul and Miss Elaine St. Aubyn. These two were in effect emissaries from Queen Alexandra, who had commissioned them to inspect the work of the Japanese Red Cross Society. This was no casual request: At that very moment, the structure and role of the Red Cross in Britain was under careful review in the wake of a less than exemplary performance during the South African War. Urged on by the king's surgeon, Sir Frederick Treves, Edward VII and Queen Alexandra had both taken a personal interest in the business of improving voluntary aid, and it is not surprising that they should have used this opportunity to avail themselves of first-hand knowledge about the workings of the Japanese Red Cross Society. Ethel McCaul was an obvious choice for the mission: She had been a field hospital nurse with Treves in South Africa, for which she had been awarded the Royal Red Cross decoration, and she had written an article calling for the reform of military nursing in Britain.[38] Her own book about their experiences in Japan, every bit as flattering as that of Mrs. Richardson, bore the odd title *Under the Care of the Japanese War Office*.[39] It may have been suggested by Treves, who also traveled to Japan to see the war for himself and who was promoting closer connections between the War Office and the Red

5.5   Queen Alexandra's emissaries, Miss St. Aubyn and Miss McCaul (R), on a visit of inspection to the Japanese Red Cross Hospital at Feng-Wang-Cheng. Beside Miss St. Aubyn are their escorts, Dr. Tamura and Madame Kuroda of the Japanese Red Cross Society.

Cross in Britain. McCaul lavished praise upon the Japanese Red Cross Society, the success of which she attributed to "the complete union with which the members work together, thus strengthening the hands of the society; and secondly, the society's absolute submission to the War Office."[40]

What impressed McCaul most of all, however, was the extraordinary role that the Japanese Red Cross played in harnessing, for purposes useful to the state, the emotions generated by war:

> The influence of the society's work is felt throughout the country; the very air seems to breathe its name. Surely this society might be described as a national depôt for the generous emotions of the people. In times of great national calamity strong emotional feelings must sweep the entire country, and these far-thinking people have had the wisdom to gather up and utilize to the fullest advantage this inevitable wave of sympathy, by firmly, but kindly, directing it into a right channel, but at the same time closing any other means of outlet, forbidding promiscuous generosity.[41]

As luck would have it, there was another British guest staying at the same hotel in Tokyo as Misses McCaul and St. Aubyn: William G. MacPherson of the Royal Army Medical Corps (RAMC), who had been sent out by the War Office to compile a full report on the medical and sanitary aspects of the Russo-Japanese War.[42] McCaul was suitably impressed by Macpherson's vast knowledge of Red Cross organizations in various countries and notes that they had several discussions about the working of the Japanese society.[43]

Macpherson's knowledge of the European Red Cross societies derived from an already enormous experience: He had attended both the international Red Cross conference in Vienna in 1897 and the second "unofficial" Paris congress of 1900. His report on the Vienna conference had drawn attention to the shortcomings of voluntary aid organization in Britain, and when the South African War had proven many of his fears to be well founded, his views were treated with growing respect both at the War Office and at court. He returned from Japan and Manchuria sharing McCaul's opinion of the role of Red Cross societies in modern warfare and proceeded to popularize it in Britain; as he told his audience in a 1907 lecture at the Royal United Service Institution,

> The outburst of sentiment, which a great national war evokes, somewhat resembles the floods that occasionally pour over a land and wreck the careful work of years. It is a force to be reckoned with. . . . Now the Red Cross Societies are like the barriers which wise men construct to collect and retain the floods, and keep them until they can be utilised at the time, and in the manner, in which they may most materially aid their plans and their labours. The great nations of Europe recognized this *rôle* of Red Cross Societies long ago. The great nation of Japan has recognized it. . . . The United States of America passed an Act of Congress with a similar purpose in 1905; and, in fact, most civilised countries see in Red Cross Societies, organised under state recognition and responsible military guidance, the only method by which popular sentiment can be allowed full play in really useful directions in time of war.[44]

Macpherson was especially enthusiastic about what he, as a military surgeon, understandably regarded as the principal benefit of the existence of Red Cross societies: By furnishing trained personnel to staff the hospitals and other medical establishments in the home territory, Red Cross societies made it possible for most of the surgeons and staff of the military medical service to be sent abroad with the troops.[45] With the increasing possibility of British military involvement on the European continent, the Japanese example began to arouse great interest at the War Office in London.

To be sure, the British were not alone in learning the lessons of Manchuria. Both the U.S. War Department and the U.S. navy sent out medical observers, who compiled extensive reports on the medical and sanitary aspects of the war, including, of course, the role of the Red Cross society in each of the belligerent states.[46] Of these reports, one in particular, written by Major Charles Lynch of the U.S. army medical department, was to have a major influence on future relations between the U.S. army and the American Red Cross. Lynch believed that the Japanese had devised a virtually perfect system of voluntary aid. "The methods by which the energies and money of the people are utilized to advantage in this direction might be safely adopted as a model by any nation," he wrote with conviction.[47] Although not convinced that every country would want to follow the Japanese emphasis on providing personnel rather than materiel, Lynch was nevertheless impressed that "the Japanese Red Cross Society learned from the army what it would need and went systematically to work to furnish this, and not something else which might or might not be useful."[48] From his observations in Japan and Manchuria, he drew up a list of the "primary requirements of a voluntary aid society to render it most efficient in affording aid to sick and wounded in time of war," among which he included the following:

> [It] must be so administered as to gain and retain the confidence of its members and the public generally, or funds will not be forthcoming, and the vast sums required for it will not be on hand; [it] must be imbued with the highest spirit of humanity . . . [so as to avoid] petty jealousies; its patriotism must be such that its efforts will be directed to the assistance of [the army medical] department and not [aspire] to a separate administration . . . ; [it] must have on its board of governors or in another responsible position representation from the army which is empowered authoritatively to indicate the direction which training of personnel should take and what material should be collected; [it] must make arrangements for the training of personnel on lines which will make it effective for army use; an army medical department must know, in the event of war, what aid in the way of personnel and materiel a society is ready to supply; a society must know what will be done with its personnel, in order that it may be instantly dispatched on mobilization; . . . personnel [serving] with an army must fuse with the existing organization of the medical department of that army, or confusion will result; the [society's] personnel, while in the service of the army, must be under military discipline and command.[49]

Lynch returned to Washington full of enthusiasm for transforming the American Red Cross into this ideal vision of what an army medical department would want from a voluntary aid society. Against the backdrop of Japan's impressive victories over Russia, Lynch's observations lent both thrust and direction to the reorganization of the American Red Cross.

American observers who saw the war from the Russian side had a very different story to tell. Raymond Spear reported that among the Russians,

> There was considerable ill feeling existing between the medical department of the army and that of the Red Cross. The army people claimed that the Red Cross were always given the best buildings for their hospitals and conducted their hospitals in such a manner as to tend to the destruction of discipline of both officers and men; also that the daily expense of patients treated was far too much. The Red Cross people, on the other hand, considered that they were, as a class, better than the military medical department and performed better work. The Red Cross doctors received about twice the pay of their corresponding grades in the army medical corps. The Red Cross, too, had innumerable supplies in the form of medicines, instruments, and clothing to distribute. Some of the very best surgeons in Russia were in the service of the Red Cross.[50]

5.6 Convalescent wounded Russian sailors and their Japanese nurses and doctors at the Red Cross's Matsuyama Hospital. The Russians were so grateful to their enemies for rescuing sailors from the sunken cruiser *Variag* that they sent a donation to the Japanese Red Cross Society.

Friction between the Red Cross and the army surgeons was only one of several problems apparent on the Russian side. At the beginning of the war, there were press reports that vast sums of money had gone astray and that the society's funds had been misappropriated. Some of these reports may have been politically inspired: The Russian Red Cross was very closely tied to the tsarist regime, and its liberal and radical opponents delighted in finding scandals that could be used to embarrass the government. To keep a clear distance from the regime and its institutions, the elected local governments (*zemstvos*) of European Russia created their own Zemstvo Red Cross, which operated both hospitals along the railroad lines and rest stations in the *zone d'etapes*. Not to be outdone, the provincial Assemblies of Nobility created a Nobles' Red Cross, and various cities, institutions, and even individuals sponsored Red Cross hospitals and trains of their own creation.[51] The predictable result of all this enthusiasm was a considerable amount of rivalry, overlapping, and confusion. Naturally, Russian Red Cross officials were unhappy about this proliferation of what were, in effect, separate voluntary aid societies only nominally affiliated with the society proper. However, with the urgent needs of the army and navy paramount, it was impossible for them to do anything other than accept the additional aid on the terms set by those proffering it.

5.7 Russian Red Cross nurses leaving St. Petersburg for service at the front during the war with Japan.

In any case, the empress, the dowager empress, and other members of the imperial family had set a pattern of impulsive and ostentatious generosity by paying for beautifully appointed hospital trains, complete with operating rooms supplied with the latest equipment, which were exhibited in St. Petersburg and Moscow prior to being sent to the front.[52] No doubt those who saw them were suitably impressed by the modern facilities, but what the Russian army in Manchuria really needed were line officers who—like the Japanese—took army doctors and military hygiene seriously and encouraged their men to do likewise. Russian soldiers were notoriously careless about the water they drank and disregarded orders from the chief medical inspector to keep infected matter out of their water and to wait until water had been tested before drinking it. By contrast, one observer with the Japanese army reported that "the Japanese soldier is so terrified lest he should chance to miss a fight by going on the sicklist that he listens to & scrupulously observes any regulation which has been made for the regulation of his health. Even if he was half dead with thirst he would deny himself water until it had been boiled & so in all things."[53] Whereas typhoid and all manner of gastroenteric disorders assailed the Russian camps, the Japanese forces were almost entirely free from waterborne or insect-borne diseases (although their soldiers and sailors did fall victim to beri-beri, a thiamin deficiency disease that could have been prevented with better dietary regimen). It was typical of the tsarist

5.8   Russian ladies sewing for the Red Cross. During the war with Japan, titled
Russian ladies met regularly to sew items for Red Cross use. This sewing circle met
at the residence of Grand Duchess Maria Pavlovna; at the nearby Winter Palace both
the empress and the dowager empress presided over sewing circles of their own.

regime's attitude to matters of health that so much attention was lavished on providing care for the wounded, so little given to the prevention of sickness in the army.[54]

Both the failings of the Russians and the achievements of the Japanese led foreign observers, as well as their military and political superiors, to conclude that the lessons of Manchuria could not be ignored. The Russian Red Cross might have appeared impressive when the international conference had met in St. Petersburg, but the war had now demonstrated that there were serious flaws in its organization. At the London conference in 1907, delegates were fascinated by the Japanese delegation's freshly written reports on the war with Russia; as far as Red Cross organization was concerned, the Japanese were now in a position to serve as a model for the western countries. Understandably, their performance attracted the attention of both the British and the Americans, who contrasted it with their own recent experiences during the South African and Spanish-American Wars and who could not but envy the conspicuous success of the Japanese Red Cross Society. To be sure, this was a case of the attraction of opposites: In Japan, the militarization of charity had reached its apogee; in Britain and America the Red Cross had

LES ÉVÉNEMENTS D'EXTRÊME-ORIENT

5.9 This striking drawing—surely be an artist's impression—of Russians transporting their wounded on skis appeared in the Paris newspaper *Le Petit Journal* on 10 April, 1904 (Vol. 15, No. 699).

been until now very much a civilian philanthropy. With the nature and goals of Red Cross organization under review in both countries, it was inevitable that partisans of the Japanese approach would play an important part in the discussions. It was equally inevitable those who sought to "modernize" the Red Cross society in each of these countries would have to wrest control of it from the devotees of a more spontaneous and less bureaucratic approach to charity. In the end, the unique political traditions and differing approaches to voluntary charity in Britain and America ensured that neither country would produce an exact replica of the Japanese model, although the Americans came considerably closer to this goal than did the British.

A Late Bloomer

Between 1900 and 1914, the American Red Cross was transformed from a charitable society preoccupied with disaster relief into a huge national corporation that was closely tied to the government, the armed forces, and the financial establishment centered on Wall Street. The biographers of Clara Barton, whose ouster from the leadership in 1904 was one of many signs that this

5.10   This motley collection of individuals attached to a Russian field ambulance posed for American military observer Captain John Van Rensslaer Hoff, an indefatigable cameraman whose unique collection of photographs of the medical-sanitary aspects of the Russo-Japanese War is preserved in the Prints and Photographs Collection of the History of Medicine Division, National Library of Medicine, Bethesda, Maryland.

5.11 Another photo from the album of Captain John Van Rensslaer Hoff: This Russian ambulance wagon with its mud-encrusted wheels is a striking reminder of the difficulties posed by the harsh Manchurian terrain. It also serves to underline the fact that away from the railway lines transport for the wounded had advanced little since the Crimean War.

transformation was under way, have understandably concentrated on the dramatic personal conflicts associated with these events.[55] The standard history of the American Red Cross—now almost half a century old—attributes these changes primarily to the reform ethos of the Progressive era, which included both the "more effective organization of charity and the general adoption of business methods in philanthropic undertakings" and the maturing of social work, "which was beginning to insist upon scientific methods of relief, professional standards, and trained personnel."[56] In this interpretation, Clara Barton's intensely personal style of leadership was "no longer a practical approach to the general problems of Red Cross disaster relief, to say nothing of possible activities in time of war."[57] Her opponents, on the other hand, were "more in touch with the times"; they reflected "the new trend towards greater efficiency and financial accountability" and believed that "Red Cross leadership should be in the hands of people who would command the support of the wealthy members of the community through their own prominence and social prestige."[58]

Certainly these trends may help to explain the new management style and the new approach to civilian disaster relief that characterized the American Red Cross in the post-Barton era, but neither explains why the reorganization of the society brought it so much closer to the government and the military than it had ever been under Barton's leadership. This is a question that cannot be answered satisfactorily by focusing exclusively on the tensions in Washington society or even on the coming of age of social work in America. The perspective needs to be broadened substantially, to include the medical departments of the American army and navy, the changing relationship between business and the state in early twentieth-century America, the wider world of the Red Cross, and the lessons of Manchuria.

Until 1900 the American Red Cross was no more than a charitable society that had no choice but to engage in civilian disaster relief because it had no other significant role to play. Despite the hopes of Henry Bellows, Charles Bowles, and other former members of the U.S. Sanitary Commission, the government of the United States refused in 1868 to ratify the Geneva Convention. Secretary of State Seward reasoned that America should avoid all such old-world entanglements, but Secretary of War Edwin M. Stanton's strained relationship with the Sanitary Commission during the Civil War made a positive response unlikely in any case.[59] Bellows, as president of the fledgling American Association for the Relief of the Misery of Battlefields, made an attempt to have this decision reversed by a new administration in 1869, but again it failed. After a disastrous attempt to send unmarked and therefore unprotected relief supplies to Europe during the Franco-Prussian War, the members of the association recognized that in a state that had not subscribed to the Geneva Convention further work was futile. In 1872, they decided to disband, and for the next ten years the United States was without a relief society.[60]

When this news reached Geneva, members of the ICRC were dumbfounded. After what Bowles had told them in 1864 about the Sanitary Commission, they had expected that there would be no difficulty whatever in establishing an enterprising and energetic relief society in the United States. Already faced with a mounting chorus of criticism in Europe, they could only lament such a conspicuous failure in the New World; the news added to their growing fears for the future of the whole enterprise. Moynier let five years pass and then wrote to the president of the United States, appealing to him to arrange not only for ratification of the Convention, but also for assurances that the American army would cooperate with an officially recognized relief society to achieve the goal of better treatment for the sick and wounded.[61] If this was to be an uphill battle, Moynier reasoned, the Genevans would have to employ whatever contacts they could, just as they were already doing in Constantinople and Tokyo. The Swiss consul in Washington, John Heitz, could be useful, but he placed the greatest hope in Clara Barton, an American who had come to Europe in 1869 to recuperate after her labors for the wounded (performed quite independently of the Sanitary Commission) during the Civil War. From Louis Appia, whom she happened to meet while visiting Geneva, Barton learned about the 1864 Convention and about the formation of relief societies in Europe. Anxious to participate in wartime relief, she spent some time during the Franco-Prussian War with the Baden Ladies' Relief Society, developing in the process a lifelong friendship with Grand Duchess Louise.[62] She left Europe having promised Moynier and Appia that she would work for the success of the Red Cross idea in America. Moynier therefore chose her to carry his letter to President Rutherford B. Hayes in 1877. Barton was clever enough to realize that one could not sell the Red Cross idea in postbellum America on the basis of its utility in future wars, so she emphasized instead its potential as a humanitarian agency for disaster relief.

In 1882, after a five-year campaign led by Barton with help from Heitz, the White House (now occupied by Chester A. Arthur, who succeeded James A. Garfield after he died as a result of an assassination attempt) finally recommended to the U.S. Congress the ratification of the Geneva Convention; the Swiss Federal Council was notified in June, and America's formal adhesion was proclaimed by President Arthur in July. A year earlier, Barton had taken the first steps to found a relief society, which took the name of the American Association of the Red Cross (AARC); she was expecting it to be recognized by the ICRC as soon as the convention was ratified. It was not to be that easy, however; as Moynier wrote to her, recognition would come once the government had agreed to cooperate with the society, to accept its services in the event of war, and to encourage the centralization under its direction of all wartime aid to the sick and wounded.[63] As Barton soon discovered, the government had no intention of doing any of these things. The secretary of state wrote to the AARC in June, 1882, explaining that the executive branch did not have the authority to delegate such powers as the International Committee demanded, and the secretary of the AARC immediately advised Moynier—presciently, as it transpired—that if action by the U.S. Congress were required, there could be a substantial delay: "It may be the work of a few weeks, but on the other hand it may require years."[64]

This news put the members of the ICRC in something of a quandary. Anxious to put the disappointments of the 1870s behind them, they were at this point still hopeful that an international conference could be arranged in Vienna in 1883, and the prospect of welcoming, at long last, delegates from an officially recognized American society was very enticing. Yet could this happen if the U.S. Congress had not accorded the appropriate standing to the AARC? Moynier had already gathered from Barton that the AARC had been incorporated under the laws of the District of Columbia, and had written to her asking exactly what was the meaning of this status; he also asked whether her appointment as AARC president by then President Garfield was an "officially legal" action or "merely a piece of courtesy on his part."[65] However, after receiving the letter that warned of substantial delay if a congressional charter were required, the ICRC evidently decided to make do with whatever the AARC could obtain by way of recognition. On 22 July, Moynier wrote to its secretary that "if that [official recognition of the centralization of voluntary aid under the AARC] cannot be, one must be contented with less. Lacking the *privilege*, the *permission* will suffice; and if your government is not disposed to accord you more than this minimum, that will be better than nothing: as for ourselves, we will not ask more in order to be satisfied."[66] When Barton replied in August, she advised Moynier that she had received a letter from President Arthur declaring his willingness to serve as president of the advisory board mentioned in the AARC's articles of incorporation and also letters from various members of the cabinet accepting positions on the board of trustees of the AARC. She also told him that Congress had passed a joint resolution authorizing an annual expenditure of $1,000 for the publication of material that would make the American people aware of the existence and work of the Red Cross.[67] At the same time, the State Department forwarded to Geneva copies of all these documents as well as a copy of the articles of incorporation. At this point, the ICRC decided to dispense with further formalities and, apparently, to behave as if a congressional charter had been obtained; its Circular No. 50, sent out to all of the central committees on 20 September, 1882, clearly stated that "the American Association of the Red Cross has been legally constituted by an Act of Congress."[68] This piece of deception may have served its immediate purpose, but it was no more than wishful thinking; as it happened, the "substantial delay" lasted for eighteen years and was only partially removed in 1900.

On this basis, Barton and her fellow delegates from the AARC were enthusiastically welcomed into the world of the Red Cross at the next international conference, which was delayed a year and held in Geneva instead of Vienna. They took little part in the crucial debates about the role of the International Committee but sprang to life when discussion turned to the subject of calamities other than war. In the 1882 circular, Moynier had already acknowledged that "in conformity with a wish expressed by the Berlin Conference [of 1869]" the AARC had decided not to limit its relief program to war alone but to embrace all great disasters that befell their country.[69] In Geneva, discussion centered on a motion from the Greek central committee to annex to the 1864 Convention a resolution enjoining Red Cross societies to provide assistance in times of public calamity. Joseph Sheldon used the occasion to lecture the delegates on the importance which the AARC attached to disaster relief.[70] However, other delegates, especially the Swedes and the Prussians, argued forcefully against requiring participation in disaster relief, on the grounds that this could blur the primary focus on preparation for war. In the end, predictably, this conference avoided any reference to an amendment to the Convention by passing a resolution that, like the one approved in Berlin fifteen years earlier, stated that national societies might engage in disaster relief where they saw it as an appropriate opportunity to exercise the skills that would be needed in wartime.[71] This modest conclusion did not prevent Barton from making exaggerated claims afterwards regarding American influence at the conference.[72]

Back in the United States, Barton tried to correct the somewhat bizarre legal status of the AARC. Between 1887 and 1900, she made no less than eight attempts to secure a federal charter, but all of them encountered congressional opposition to granting special status—legal protection of the Red Cross name and insignia—to what many regarded as just another charity. American companies that already used the emblem as a trademark, among them Johnson and Johnson and Lorillard (tobacco), lobbied against restriction on the grounds that Congress could not impinge upon freedom of contract.[73] Finally, in 1900, Congress passed an act that at last granted the recently renamed American National Red Cross (ANRC)[74] a federal charter, but because of strong opposition in the House of Representatives, its final wording fell far short of granting the organization sole power to control voluntary services to the military in wartime.[75] In Geneva, Moynier was still waiting for evidence that the American Red Cross had achieved the kind of recognition that was typical in most European states, let alone the unique status that it enjoyed in Japan.

The new charter was at best a grudging recognition of the role played by the Red Cross during the Spanish-American War, which has been described as "the distribution of supplies amounting to a total of only a few hundred thousand dollars, a handful of Red Cross workers in hospitals and camps, the recruiting of some seven hundred nurses, and a single mission to the front led by a domineering old lady of seventy-six, perched on a load of hay piled aboard an Army wagon."[76] In the absence of a strong, nationally organized society with a defined relationship to the armed forces, it is difficult to see how Red Cross participation in the war could have been more extensive. As soon as hostilities broke out, the ANRC, which had already mounted a civilian relief operation in Cuba, offered its services to the government but without proposing any specific action. On the other hand, the Cuban Relief Committee in New York, on which the ANRC was represented, promised both money and materiel, an offer that prompted the secretary of state to announce that "this government recognizes, for any appropriate cooperative purposes, the American National Red Cross as the Civil Central American Committee in correspondence with the International Committee for the relief of wounded in war."[77] In the wake of this announcement, both the army and the navy accepted the services of the ANRC for medical and hospital work, but, as Foster Rhea Dulles points out, most of the supplies, camp workers, and nurses were organized and provided by the Red Cross (formerly Cuban) Relief Committee in New York, so that the role of Barton's ANRC was rather small.[78] Indeed, her picturesque ride to the front to assist American wounded at Siboney was an improvised diversion from what was still primarily a civilian relief operation.[79] Given the hostility of Surgeon-General

George Sternberg to the employment of volunteers, Barton was lucky to have even this brief opportunity to play the Samaritan at the front, which Sternberg later had the effrontery to describe as "entirely inadequate to meet the emergency."[80] Like French Marshal Randon, Sternberg regarded the presence of volunteers as a reflection on the army's ability to care for the wounded and absolutely refused to grant special privileges to any voluntary organization. When urged to employ female nurses, he at first refused outright and then, when overruled, turned to Dr. Anita Newcomb McGee and the Daughters of the American Revolution and only later—and grudgingly, at that—to the Red Cross.[81]

When the war was over, Barton's leadership of the ANRC drew more criticism than praise. She was now nearly eighty, and many people hoped that she would choose this moment to retire. Her refusal to do so simply put ammunition in the hands of her critics and opponents, of whom there was now an abundance. The New York Relief Committee, which had sent contributions to her for distribution, strongly criticized her inadequate accounting procedures. Thanks in part to Dr. McGee's influence, the 1900 charter stipulated that detailed annual financial reports be made to Congress and to the State Department, War Department, and the navy, but Barton seemed unwilling to supply them. The governor of New York, Theodore Roosevelt (whose sister was a prominent member of the New York Relief Committee) stated publicly his opinion: "The Red Cross Society should be the right hand of the Medical Department of the Army in peace and war for even the best medical department will always need volunteer aid. . . . The Red Cross should have a federal organization; [and] within every State chapters, which should be in close touch with the National Guard, attending the encampments and forming schools of instruction in military methods."[82] Even some of Barton's close associates, such as George Kennan, recognized that her continuing control of the organization meant that it would not receive support from wealthy and influential people who shared Roosevelt's views.

When, following President William McKinley's assassination in 1901, Teddy Roosevelt became president, it was clear that a complete reorganization of the Red Cross was on the agenda; also sympathetic with this goal were his new secretary of war, William Howard Taft, and Under Secretary John F. Foster at the State Department. Taft was a close friend of Mabel Boardman, the Washington socialite who led the anti-Barton forces within the Red Cross itself, and Foster helped to organize a petition to the president alleging financial irregularities, which provided a pretext for the government to intervene and work toward reorganization. The Army Medical Department also played an important role. Sternberg's successor as surgeon-general of the army, Robert M. O'Reilly, also appreciated the potential importance of a Red Cross auxiliary force, and in November, 1903, he ordered a study of relations between the military and Red Cross societies in other countries, an assignment that was duly carried out by Walter D. McCaw of the Army Medical

Department. McCaw's report, presented in February, 1904, devoted a great deal of favorable attention to the arrangements prevailing in Germany for the regulation of charity in wartime and acknowledged that in matters of Red Cross organization, the United States was behind not only Germany but also France, Russia, Austria, Italy, and Japan.[83] McCaw recommended that the War Department regulate its relations with the ANRC so that the army would know in advance what voluntary aid it could expect in wartime and the Red Cross would know what would be expected of it. This would ensure that voluntary aid did not become "a hindrance to military efficiency" by controlling the offers of help that would be "showered upon the war department when the nation is in arms"; without such organizing in advance, McCaw warned, it might be necessary to refuse offers of help and "to refuse is not only to reject assistance potentially of the greatest value, but also to offend and wound the susceptibilities of our best and most patriotic citizens."[84]

In the end, the reformers had their way. This is not the place to review the sordid squabbles and factional intrigues that occupied almost four years and came close to destroying public respect for the Red Cross in America.[85] Barton may not have displayed great business acumen, but a committee of inquiry that investigated the charges of financial mismanagement and misappropriation brought against her found all of them false and "completely exonerated" her of any wrongdoing.[86] Barton chose this moment (May, 1904) to resign and surprised her closest associates by letting it be known that she too thought it was time for the Red Cross to be reorganized. Given the strength of the forces arrayed against her, she could do little else. President Roosevelt was determined to see reorganization carried through, and even the members of the committee of inquiry recognized that "in the case of a war or a national calamity requiring the cooperation of the government, it would be better to have the Red Cross controlled by leaders in favor with the administration."[87] Barton knew of the recommendations contained in the McCaw report and also of the favorable response they had elicited from the surgeon-general of the army and the War Department. Moreover, the State Department had recently compiled a report on the leadership, financial operations, and fundraising activities of the major European, as well as the Japanese, Red Cross societies. Tabled in the Senate in March, 1904, this study also revealed the relatively primitive state of Red Cross organization in America.[88] Meanwhile, Foster himself had prepared a national plan of reorganization that included closer relations with the government and the War Department. He proposed that the ANRC should be granted special status as the only civilian relief society recognized by the government, that the Red Cross appoint a liaison officer with the War Department, and that its wartime activities be subject to new regulations to be drawn up by the surgeon-general of the army.

Foster's plan formed the basis for the new charter, which Congress approved in late 1904 and which became law early in 1905. Under its terms, the president of the United States was to appoint the chairman of the central

5.12   This cartoon, which originally appeared in the *Washington Star*, was reprinted in the March, 1916 issue of the *American Red Cross Magazine* as part of the society's drive to attract a million members. The caption reads, "UNCLE SAM CONCERNED. Every man, woman, and child in the United States is eligible for membership in the American Red Cross. What will you do to swell this membership? to change the bottom figures?"

committee of the ANRC as well as five other members—one each from the departments of State, War, Treasury, and Justice and the navy. Speaking in support of its passage, Senator William Alden Smith (R-Mich.) of the Committee on Foreign Affairs noted:

> The charter presented in this bill . . . provides for government representation on the central committee, and the auditing of all accounts by the War Department before the [annual] report is presented to Congress. Both are important factors in the plan for building up a well organized Red Cross Society in this country

... under such government supervision as will arouse and maintain public confidence and support ... a reincorporation ... required for its efficiency and more extended usefulness.[89]

The new charter changed the ANRC into a national corporation under government supervision. The first three presidential appointments to the chairmanship of the central committee were all retired high-ranking naval or army officers: Admiral William K. Van Reypen, Robert M. O'Reilly, and General George W. Davis.[90] General Davis, who served from 1906 until 1914, left the day-to-day running of the organization in the hands of the formidable Mabel Boardman. Her friend, Secretary of War Taft, was elected to the largely honorific position of president of the corporation. The central committee included so many prominent Republicans—many from New York City—that it deserved its nickname, the "Republican Red Cross."[91] The victorious reformers happily set out to realize their plans, which included a great increase in membership and funds, the creation of a structure of state and local organizations subordinate to the overall authority of the central committee, and the establishment in Washington of an appropriate national headquarters for the organization. It only remained to complete the transformation by establishing a new relationship between the reorganized Red Cross and the army and the navy.

The 1905 charter contained no specific provision recognizing the ANRC as the sole civilian relief agency to serve with the armed forces. Instead, it stated that the Red Cross was "to act in matters of voluntary relief and in accord with the military and naval authorities as a medium of communication between the people of the United States of America and their Army and Navy." The initiative for specifying precisely what would be communicated lay not with the American people, however, but with the armed forces and especially the Army Medical Department. The task of elaborating its vision of a modern Red Cross society was taken up, naturally enough, by Major Charles Lynch, who had returned from Manchuria just in time to observe the death throes of the Barton regime. In an essay—entitled "What Is the Most Effective Organization of the American National Red Cross for War and What Should Be Its Relations with the Medical Departments of the Army and the Navy?"—Lynch set out a vision of the ANRC transformed into an agency that would work as closely with the armed forces in America as its counterpart did in Japan.[92] To be sure, he recognized that there were substantial differences between the two countries: For example, the United States maintained a considerably smaller army medical corps than did the Japanese and hence would need far more physicians and surgeons in wartime; at the same time, the Americans could always rely on their hospitals and training schools to produce nurses in quantity, whereas the Japanese had to depend for this work upon their Red Cross society. Drawing upon his Manchurian experience, Lynch believed that one obvious duty for ANRC members would be to lobby for the creation of a larger medical service in the American army: "Nothing could be more futile," he wrote, "than to go on year after year with an army organization which makes failure certain in the event of war no matter how strenuous may be the efforts of both army and Red Cross at that time."[93] Lynch was also well aware that in America no voluntary society would operate with such an obvious degree of subservience to authority as did the JRCS.[94]

Perhaps the most striking thing about Lynch's essay, however, was the degree to which it revealed how much he had learned in Japan about providing an outlet for the patriotism of noncombatants.

> It is the right and privilege of the people to provide for their soldiers and sailors and the patriotic impulse to do so could be met in this way with the certainty that all money and gifts would reach their destination. Still it is obvious that [such] gifts . . . may be supplied by the war and Navy Departments as easily as by the people, nor is it probable that money will not be available for this purpose in any war we may have in the future. The worth of such gifts is, therefore, rather in the field which they offer for the display of patriotic sentiment, and for kindling it—those who cannot bear arms should have a part in upholding their country's cause—than in their actual value, though naturally they have a value, saving money in taxation and thus a portion of the burden is put on the willing shoulders of those who presumably can best afford to bear it.[95]

On this basis, he recommended four fields as most suitable for Red Cross activity: rest stations, hospital trains, hospital ships, and transport columns. These activities were best for volunteers, he claimed, because none of them involved much paperwork and none put them in a position where a misplaced humanitarianism might lead them to deplete fighting strength at the front.[96]

Lynch was especially keen on the rest stations, which, following the Japanese model, he divided into a comfort section and a treatment section.

> The comfort section . . . is made up wholly of patriotic men and women of the locality [who] should meet every train or ship to cheer soldiers and sailors on their way and to show interest in them on their return from the front. Water, perhaps lemonade, and the fruits grown in the vicinity, possibly broth or other nourishing food, magazines, the daily papers, etc., may properly be supplied by this section [and] the treatment section, made up of patriotic doctors and nurses, will be expected to give emergency treatment, to readjust dressings and the like.[97]

In Lynch's view, the beauty of the comfort sections was that they gave volunteers useful work while keeping them away from positions in which they might do harm to the sick and wounded. He foresaw a similar role for untrained women in hospitals in the home territory, not as amateur nurses—a prospect that he dreaded—but in "reading to patients, writing letters for them, bringing them flowers and fruit, and in certain selected cases giving them spiritual consolation."[98] However, the more the emphasis was placed on finding things for untrained volunteers to do that did not involve treating the sick and wounded, the more the role of the Red Cross as an organization that existed solely to help them was eroded. It was but a short step from the comfort section envisioned by Lynch to the Red Cross canteens of World War I.

Lynch's essay obviously had considerable influence on the future direction of the army's relationship with the Red Cross. Within a matter of months, the ANRC created a new War Relief Board, headed by O'Reilly, to plan how it would carry out its obligations. No sooner had it been approved than the army presented the ANRC with a statement outlining the responsibilities—personnel, supplies, and transport facilities—that the army expected it to fulfill should the United States find it necessary to raise an army of a quarter of a million men. The Red Cross was to supply at least one hospital ship; three railway surgical operating cars; sufficient materiel for field hospitals; and rest stations in large cities and at railway stations, together with the personnel necessary to run them.[99] All this would take money as well as a high degree of public support, so the ANRC executive had its work cut out for it in trying to raise both.

As the reorganized Red Cross grew closer to the government and the military, it was also becoming increasingly dependent for its funds upon the generosity of wealthy Americans, particularly those living in New York City. In 1910, the Red Cross decided to raise a national endowment fund of $2 million, of which New York was expected to raise at least one quarter. The banking house of J. P. Morgan and Company played a big part; Morgan himself kicked off the campaign with a conditional gift of $100,000, and one of the senior partners, Henry P. Davison, chaired the New York fund-raising committee, which easily reached its half-million dollar target.[100] After initial success, however, the campaign faltered somewhat, and by the end of 1912, only half of the original target of $2 million had been raised, and it was not until 1918 that the endowment fund finally reached its goal.[101] By this time, the United States was in the war, and far more money was needed to sustain Red Cross work at home and abroad. Fortunately for the organization, the New York bankers were still solidly behind its work; as a sign of this support, Davison, with the firm support of the house of Morgan and the concurrence of President Woodrow Wilson, became president of the Red Cross War Council.[102]

Even before the United States was drawn into the conflict in Europe, tensions within North America threatened to boil over into war. As a result, the new role of the ANRC was clarified and extended by a number of what one might call "housekeeping" measures. One of these was a presidential proclamation issued in 1911, when American intervention in the Mexican Revolution was a distinct possibility; it specifically defined Red Cross workers who reported for duty with the military as members of the army sanitary services and hence subject to military laws and regulations.[103] A War Department circular of 10 September, 1912 continued the process by announcing that Red Cross units on active service "constitute a part of the sanitary service of the land forces" and by specifying the supplies and personnel that the society would be expected to provide in the event of war. It also granted the ANRC monopoly status as "the only volunteer society now authorized by this government to render aid to its land and naval forces in time of war," the very recognition that Moynier had sought nearly forty years earlier.[104] A law of 1912 permitted the government to treat mobilized Red Cross workers as "civilian employees" of the military forces, who were to be "transported and subsisted at the cost and charge of the United States."[105] To codify the recent changes, both the army and the navy issued new regulations that described in detail the ways in which Red Cross personnel would cooperate with the forces in the event of war.[106] Finally, both the army nurses corps and the Red Cross National Committee on Nursing were placed under the leadership of Jane Delano, the respected superintendent of nurses at Bellevue Hospital in New York City; no better way could have been found to ensure that in future events the army's need for additional nurses would be met by the Red Cross.[107]

Three tasks remained to ensure that once war came the reorganized Red Cross would be as effective as possible. The first was to appoint an experienced member of the army medical corps to make sure that the Red Cross would be ready to meet its obligations. This was done in February, 1916 when Colonel J. R. Kean, an army surgeon of many years' experience, was authorized by the army surgeon-general to organize Red Cross field and hospital columns as part of President Wilson's "preparedness" campaign.[108] Kean, in turn, wrote a brief but important essay, "The New Role of the American Red Cross," which, in terse military language, made it clear that the old "Fairy Godmother" conception of the Red Cross was a thing of the past and that the army and navy were now telling the Red Cross what to do and how to do it.[109] The publicity that was given to Kean's work in *American Red Cross Magazine* helped to fulfill the second task, which was to ensure that rank-and-file Red Cross volunteers understood the changed circumstances in which they were now working.[110] The final task, of course, was to ensure that the American people responded as they should when asked to contribute money; that need was met, as will be shown below, by the ingenious device of conflating the obligations of American citizenship with membership in the Red Cross.

Fighting to Do Good

At first glance, the history of the Red Cross in Britain and America appears to be remarkably similar, but that similarity is deceptive. Both countries, despite notable philanthropic achievements in the past, took far longer to develop full-fledged aid societies than Moynier had expected. The absence of conscription in either country was clearly one important factor in explaining this delay. Both countries fought major wars at the turn of the century, and neither was satisfied with its arrangements for the care of the wounded. Both countries kept a close eye on the Russo-Japanese conflict, concluded that there were lessons to be learned from it, and in 1905 reorganized their Red Cross societies to achieve a closer integration with the government and the armed forces. In both countries, the Red Cross society began to become a national institution only in the years between 1905 and 1914. Yet here the similarities end. In Britain, neither the Admiralty nor the War Office shared the enthusiasm of the continental powers for creating a strong Red Cross society as an auxiliary to the military and naval authorities. In sharp contrast to the United States, this official indifference was welcomed by the leaders of the British National Aid Society, who wished to keep as much distance as possible between themselves and the War Office. Clara Barton rushed from one disaster to another, dispensing relief to grateful victims of floods and tornadoes, but the British society stirred itself to action only when it learned of wars in Europe, Africa, or Asia or when expeditions were sent to British colonies. In the 1870s, the British society considered and rejected as unnecessary plans for a peacetime organization, and in 1905 it had to be coerced into grudging cooperation with those who thought such work essential. Whereas the Americans took every opportunity to associate with their counterparts at international Red Cross conferences, the leaders of the British society ostentatiously absented themselves, leaving the delegates of the government and the Order of St. John to occupy the seats that might have been theirs. In other words, the differences between these two national societies are at least as important as the similarities.

Florence Nightingale's skepticism about the practicality of the Geneva Convention and her resolute opposition to a civilian-run "voluntary system of purveying and nursing"[111] made it almost inevitable that forming a Red Cross society in Britain would be a difficult task. Her lack of sympathy for the enterprise was compounded by Britain's exceptional position as an imperial power that eschewed conscription and relied chiefly on the Royal Navy to defend its insular situation. Although the British government, as a signatory of the Geneva Convention, ensured that it was always represented at international Red Cross conferences, it took very little interest in the development of a national Red Cross society. Only on the eve of the South African War did official attitudes begin to change, but once they did, the pace of change accelerated dramatically, thanks largely to the "German menace," the accession of a sympathetic monarch, and the painfully obvious contrast between the British performance in South Africa and the Japanese performance in Manchuria. By 1907, when the international conference was finally held in London, it seemed to foreign observers that in Red Cross matters the British had at long last pulled themselves together; however, continued internal bickering before and during World War I proved this judgment premature.

In the wake of the International Congress of 1864, Thomas Longmore had done his best to promote the formation of a national aid society in Britain. At the behest of Dunant and Moynier, he approached notable philanthropists, such as Lord Shaftesbury and Sir Fowell Buxton, but without success; as he reported to Dunant in December, 1865, his countrymen seemed to regard the entire enterprise as "impractical and utopian."[112] In March, 1866, Longmore himself gave a lecture to a distinguished audience at the Royal United Service Institution; its purpose, so he told the Genevans, was to prove to the skeptics that such a scheme was both practical and consistent with British military institutions.[113] When this also failed to arouse support, Longmore despaired; since his official position in the army prevented him from taking further initiatives, he recommended that the Genevans approach the Prince of Wales, who was patron of the Royal United Service Institution.[114] Meanwhile, Nightingale kept up her assault, telling Longmore that "I am more than ever convinced that Governments should be made responsible for their own Sick and Wounded—that they should not decline Volunteer, private, benevolent effort—but that, exactly in the measure that this is *incorporated* in, *not* substituted for Government organizations (for Sick & Wounded) will it be useful. And exactly in the measure that it is not, will it become an evil. I hope you agree with me."[115] Her own lack of enthusiasm was equaled by that of the commander-in-chief (the Duke of Cambridge), who wrote to the War Office that although he had agreed to have the terms of the Geneva Convention promulgated as part of the Articles of War, "he cannot anticipate the possibility of their being carried out with any degree of efficiency."[116]

At this point, several members of the recently revived Order of St. John took up the challenge of creating a national aid society.[117] John Furley attended the Paris conference in 1867 as a delegate of the Order; on learning of the important role played by the Prussian branch of the Order, he convinced his colleagues that they should take the lead in forming a national aid society in England. Another member of the Order, Captain Henry Brackenbury, wrote a series of articles in the *Standard*, in which he made the strongest possible case for voluntary assistance.[118] Early in April, 1869, the Order established a committee to promote the idea; two of its members, Furley and Captain Charles Burgess, left almost immediately to represent the Order at the Red Cross conference in Berlin.[119] In all likelihood, it was during this trip that Furley decided to bring out an English translation of *La guerre et la charité* by Moynier and Appia; scarcely had it appeared when the Franco-Prussian War broke out.[120] Presented with this opportunity to practice what they had been preaching, the St. John committee quickly sought out a potential leader who was well known in both military and government circles. Through his earlier service with the Kent Volunteers, Furley had met one of the heroes of the Crimean War, Colonel Robert Loyd-Lindsay, one of the first recipients of the Victoria Cross, who seemed an obvious choice to head the movement in England. After being approached by Furley, Loyd-Lindsay wrote to *The Times* pleading the case of the war wounded and calling for the formation of a "Society for the Aid of Sick and Wounded in War," to which he was prepared to pledge £1000.[121] The society was duly formed at a meeting held on 4 August; Loyd-Lindsay was made president, and Longmore, Furley, Burgess, and Brackenbury were among its most active members. The Committee of Ladies was headed by Princess Christian; Florence Nightingale agreed to let her name be associated with the Committee of Ladies but played only a modest part in its work.[122] The Comité International in Geneva was notified of these events and—grateful to see signs of life at last—speedily recognized the executive committee of the British National Aid Society as the central committee for Great Britain.

There is no need to review here the hastily improvised but nonetheless extensive and valuable assistance provided to the belligerents by the British society in 1870–1871. Both the work itself and the experiences of those involved in performing it have been described in the society's own publications and in the memoirs of several participants.[123] More to the point here is what happened after the war. Furley, Brackenbury, Burgess, and Longmore wanted the National Aid Society to undertake a peacetime program of preparation and training somewhat akin to those of many continental societies and recommended that it train lifesaving teams, which could provide assistance in peacetime to the victims of road, railway, and industrial accidents and which could also be employed as stretcher-bearers by the army in wartime.[124] However, Loyd-Lindsay was adamant that no such agenda would be followed under his presidency; his view was that leftover cash donations should simply be deposited in the bank and left to gather interest until wanted again in the next war. To follow any other course was, in his opinion, to violate the trust of the donors, who deserved assurance that their gifts would be used by the society solely for the purpose of aiding the sick and wounded in war. Those who took Loyd-Lindsay's side also made the argument that because Britain was unlikely to be engaged in a war with another great power, the country's military preparations were necessarily on a small scale; hence, they claimed, "the public mind . . . was not likely to respond to any elaborate organization or preparation in time of peace."[125] They were also convinced that assembling storehouses of ambulance equipment and materiel was a waste of time and money because much of it might become obsolete by the time it was needed.

It soon become apparent that members of the executive committee were not prepared to oust Loyd-Lindsay over the issue, so in 1873 Furley decided to resign from that body in order "to assist in the formation of another society which should more fully realise the object of my aspirations in respect to the organisation of work for the relief of suffering in time of peace, and which should also be fitted to accomplish the same purpose for our army and navy in time of war."[126] This was not by any means an acrimonious affair;

Furley remained friendly with Loyd-Lindsay and his supporters and in later years twice served as a field commissioner of the National Aid Society. Nevertheless, in this basic difference of opinion lay the origins of the St. John Ambulance Association, established by the Order in 1877 to train several small ambulance corps, the members of which were organized ten years later into the St. John Ambulance Brigade.[127]

To the foreign eye, developments in England soon became bizarre, not to say incomprehensible. Neither the ambulance association nor the ambulance brigade were affiliates of the National Aid Society and so could not properly be described as part of the British Red Cross. Nevertheless, Furley and his activities were well known to the leaders of the continental Red Cross societies; he himself always attended international Red Cross conferences as a delegate of the English branch of the Order of St. John, and his ambulance brigade attracted considerable attention, notably from Baron von Esmarch, who used it as a model for the *Samariterverein* (Lifesaving League) that he established throughout Germany. Loyd-Lindsay, however, made a point of ignoring international Red Cross conferences and never arranged to send a delegate in his place; as a result, the Europeans knew little about the British National Aid Society, which seemed to them to lead something of a phantom existence. Loyd-Lindsay was nonetheless scrupulous in ensuring that the society fulfilled its obligation to aid the sick and wounded whenever there was war: Almost £225,000 was spent during the Franco-Prussian War, more than £10,000 during the Turco-Serbian War of 1876–1877, and more than £30,000 during the Russo-Turkish War of 1877–1878; in addition, the society participated in half a dozen minor British campaigns between 1879 and 1898.[128] Some of the nurses sent out by the society during this period had been trained at Victoria Hospital in Netley; this was Loyd-Lindsay's sole exception to the general ban on the peacetime preparation of personnel and materiel.[129] Well into the 1890s, however, Europeans must have wondered how the British could have managed to create an aid society that seemed intent on ignoring the rest of the Red Cross movement and, alongside it, an ambulance association that did the opposite and yet was not itself part of that movement.

Not until the late 1890s did the British begin, in Furley's words, to "break away from some of our ideas as to insular impregnability and not a few notions as to bureaucratic infallibility, and improve on the example that has been set by some of the Great Continental Powers of Europe."[130] The Jameson Raid, the clash at Fashoda, and what W. L. Langer has called "the new navalism"[131] all contributed to a reconsideration of Britain's security, one that included a reexamination of the adequacy of the Royal Army's medical establishment.[132] In these circumstances, considerable attention was paid by the War Office to the report written by Macpherson, who had represented the British government at the international Red Cross conference held in Vienna in 1897, where there had been a lengthy discussion of the role of Red Cross societies in war and peace.[133] After describing the "special significance" of the continental aid societies, Macpherson pointed out:

> In our country, however, there is no such peace organisation in existence. Voluntary aid, such as would be forthcoming in abundance in the event of our being involved in an international war, would come upon the military authorities in the form of a mass of unorganised and untrained elements, probably so unsuited for the actual requirements of the moment that for a time at any rate, the working and administration of the regular army Medical Service, would be considerably hampered and embarrassed. We have, it is true, organised bearer company units of the Volunteer Medical Staff Corps and, recently, an Army Nursing Sisters reserve, while outside these there are the St. John Ambulance Association, and the National Society for aid to the sick and wounded in war; but these in no way represent what is meant on the continent by the organisation of voluntary aid societies under a National Central Committee of the Red Cross.[134]

In Macpherson's view, the continental arrangements were understandable because, where conscription prevailed, "each home has a direct interest in the welfare of the sick and wounded amongst the troops"; they also yielded important advantages because they freed the regular medical service for work with the army in the field while "saving the national revenue of a considerable proportion of the expense of the medical services of the army."[135] When asked for his comments, Loyd-Lindsay—now Lord Wantage—conceded that although Macpherson's fears might be true in the case of an international war, such an elaborate peacetime organization would have been "both costly and useless" in the relatively minor wars and expeditionary operations of the previous twenty years.[136] He saw no reason to alter the past policy of the National Aid Society or "to undertake operations similar to those which form the daily occupation of many of the Continental Societies."[137]

Lord Wantage's complacent attitude was no longer shared as universally as he believed. Only a few months before the Vienna conference, John Furley had presented a lecture to the Royal United Service Institution entitled "The Convention of Geneva, and the Care of the Sick and Wounded in War."[138] In it he had called upon his countrymen to pay more attention to the provisions of the Convention, to end the abuse of the Red Cross badge by recognizing its official and military character, and to follow the French example by organizing several existing aid societies into one powerful Red Cross organization. The response of his audience was generally positive and Lord Knutsford, who chaired the meeting, concluded it by calling upon those who heard the lecture to formulate some plan that would bring together the various societies that Furley had named.

This was also the view of the War Office, which was now (June 1898) under the direction of Lord Lansdowne. Convinced that the time had come to create a substantial peacetime Red Cross society with branches throughout the British Empire, Lansdowne invited representatives of the National Aid Society, the St. John Ambulance Association, and Princess Christian's recently formed Army Nursing Reserve to attend an informal conference to consider how to bring these bodies into a peacetime working relationship with the Army Medical Department. Although Lord Wantage remained un-enthusiastic about the idea of greater cooperation, he could no longer main-tain a posture of isolation. The result was the formation of a provisional Red Cross committee, which was officially recognized in January, 1899 as the Central British Red Cross Committee (CBRCC).[139]

From the outset the intention of the CBRCC was to plan voluntary aid so as to meet the supplementary requirements of the army medical service; in order to meet this objective, an extensive peacetime organization of local committees was to be formed throughout the empire. These new goals ap-peared likely to transform the Red Cross in Britain into something close to its continental counterparts; when Moynier was informed of the change, he understandably wrote to Lord Wantage asking if this meant that the ICRC should now communicate with the new CBRCC rather than with the Na-tional Aid Society. He must have been puzzled by Lord Wantage's rather stiff reply, which stated that the CBRCC had only one purpose, to centralize vol-untary aid to British troops when the latter were engaged in war; therefore, the National Aid Society would independently continue to aid sick and wounded soldiers (of whatever nationality) under the terms of the Geneva Convention.[140] Since the continental societies had no difficulty in perform-ing both functions, no matter how close their connections with the authori-ties, it must have appeared to the Genevans that the British had only suc-ceeded in adding further confusion to their Red Cross organization. In fact, as subsequent events would make clear, the leaders of the National Aid Soci-ety had little sympathy with the aims of Lansdowne and Macpherson and took every opportunity to block or at least delay the development of an ex-tensive peacetime Red Cross organization.

This underlying hostility was obscured for the moment by the outbreak of the Boer War.[141] The CBRCC saw it as its chief task to prevent overlapping and waste by harmonizing offers of assistance with the actual needs of the army medical service. The National Aid Society was designated to receive donations in money, the St. John Ambulance Association to take charge of donations of materiel. Offers of nursing assistance from women were re-ferred to the Army Nursing Reserve, from men to the St. John Ambulance Brigade. Physicians and surgeons who offered their services were referred to the director-general of the army medical service. Two hospital trains and a hospital ship were fitted out by the CBRCC with funds made available to it by the National Aid Society, and Sir John Furley, already appointed to over-see the equipping of the trains, was sent to South Africa as Red Cross com-missioner. The public response to the CBRCC's appeals for help was over-whelming: Between 1899 and 1901, the National Aid Society received nearly £500,000 in donations and subscriptions, a figure that does not include extensive donations in kind.

Rumors and press reports about the mismanagement of funds donated to help the wounded, coupled with allegations of mistreatment of the sick and wounded in army hospitals, soon led to the establishment of a royal commission. A confident Lord Wantage told its members in March, 1900 that overlapping and wastage had been entirely eliminated due to careful administration of funds by the CBRCC.[142] In any event, no evidence of wrongdoing by the CBRCC or by the National Aid Society was discovered by the royal commission, and the flow of donations was barely interrupted by these proceedings. Nevertheless, at the seat of war, Sir John Furley found his work beset by problems; as he wrote to Lord Wantage in October, 1900, not the least of these was that "no instructions had been issued by the War Office to the military authorities in S[outh] Africa as to the status and objects of the Central British Red Cross Committee."[143]

It needs to be borne in mind that many British officers had been sent to South Africa before the Red Cross committee had been officially recognized, let alone begun its work; yet the War Office made little effort to keep them informed.[144] Instead of individuals and groups whose zeal had been subjected to careful controls before they ever left Britain, Furley found

A scramble [that] . . . only increased the waste and confusion. Men and women, especially the latter, went out to South Africa, all wishing to do something for the soldiers but with no practical idea as to where and how they were to do it. In more than one case, I know that these benevolent persons were assisted forward by military officials simply from a desire to remove them from their own too crowded area of work. Nurses with excellent qualifications were mingled with others who could show no testimonials: and positions were generally assigned to them by officers who professed to know nothing about the Army Nursing Reserve. To use an expression which has become almost classical, every man and woman who thought that they could do something, determined *to run his or her own show*: the result in waste and overlapping was truly appalling, whilst self-advertisement was carried to an extent which was the envy of traders.[145]

As if this were not bad enough, Furley reported that some 4,000 red cross armbands sent by the War Office had never reached his headquarters, although "anyone wishing for such an Armlet had no difficulty in purchasing one either in Cape Town or Durban."[146] The fate of the armbands was linked to the fact that Red Cross supplies had been granted free freight, which was, in his opinion, a costly mistake: "The war in S. Africa has proved that it would have been economy to pay for transport in the ordinary way, as the carriers would then have been responsible for delivery. The loss from non-delivery and irresponsibility has been very great, whilst that from theft on the ship, docks and railway has been incalculable."[147]

Although the official report on voluntary aid in South Africa carefully avoided undermining Lord Wantage's earlier claim that there had been no waste, Furley knew better: Not since 1870 had there been such evident con-

5.13   This artist's impression of Lord Methuen, wounded during the war in the Transvaal, appeared in the Paris newspaper *Le Petit Journal* on 30 March, 1902 (Vol. 13, No. 593). By the end of the century, the Red Cross emblem had become so well known that Europeans grew accustomed to seeing it displayed even in such faraway places as South Africa.

fusion in the Red Cross work of a belligerent state. He returned to England convinced that only a complete reorganization could prevent a repetition of the South African debacle. The death of Lord Wantage (on 10 June, 1901) seemed to remove one huge obstacle to change, especially when his place as chairman of the CBRCC was taken by Furley's friend and associate in the Order of St. John, Viscount Knutsford.[148] However, the National Aid Society named A. K. (Archie) Loyd, a nephew of Lord Wantage and a diehard opponent of change, to replace him as one of its three representatives on the CBRCC. Early in 1903, Furley and Loyd were charged with preparing a scheme to amalgamate the National Aid Society with the CBRCC. This step was certain to fail because Loyd dismissed peacetime organization schemes as "claptrap" and treated any proposed change as treachery to the memory of Lord Wantage. After several frustrating months, Furley wrote to Lord Rothschild (who was now the only member remaining of the original committee of the National Aid Society), seeking his support for a plan to amalgamate both the CBRCC and the National Aid Society "into one Imperial Red Cross Society, the Central Committee continuing to control the whole, as far as concerns the preparation for time of war and its connection with the War Office."[149] In order to ensure that this scheme would bear fruit, Furley recommended that Macpherson be appointed organizing secretary of the new society. "We must have a Secretary [he wrote] who can give the whole of his time to the organisation of Red Cross work throughout the Empire. We have not only Great Britain and Ireland to consider, but India and the Colonies. Each requires a Central Committee working in harmony with the London Committee, and I have no hesitation in recommending Colonel Macpherson as the ideal candidate for such an important post."[150]

Furley was given a fresh chance to promote his ideas when he was appointed to a CBRCC subcommittee that was directed to consider the best means of extending Red Cross organization throughout the country; its other two members were senior military surgeons who shared his views.[151] Their report, completed early in March, 1904, advocated that the CBRCC should become a council representative of the various voluntary aid societies, the War Office, and the Admiralty; that this council should become "the central authority for dealing with Red Cross matters throughout the Empire"; and that district committees, soon to be organized by the council in the counties and the larger towns, be directed to plan what specific supplementary aid they would provide in the event of war and to formulate their plans in such a way as to meet the requirements of the military.[152] All this work was to be under the direction of an organizing secretary; no names were suggested, but everyone knew that Macpherson would be the preferred candidate. The authors of the report were realistic enough to concede that "popular support would not readily be given to Red Cross undertakings if they were carried on under the roof of the War Office,"[153] and they therefore recommended that the new council should share premises with the National Aid Society. At the same time, they proposed that the latter body should abandon its claim to the title "British Red Cross Society," so that it could be assumed by the new council in its dealings with foreign nations and with the ICRC.

There was, however, one very large fly in the ointment. Implementation of these grand plans would cost a considerable amount of money, and the CBRCC had none, or at least none of its own. During the Boer War, it had operated with funds made over to it by the National Aid Society, and the subcommittee proposed that this arrangement should continue in the future. To the outraged Archie Loyd, this meant that the National Aid Society was to be deprived of its position as *the* British Red Cross Society; and that its carefully husbanded treasury of donations was now to be raided by the War Office to pay for a peacetime program with which he and other members of its executive had no sympathy, whereas the St. John Ambulance Association was expected to make no financial contribution but only to supply personnel and materiel in the event of war. Nevertheless, the subcommittee's recommendations were implemented in May, 1904, despite the objections of the representatives of the National Aid Society, who now felt themselves under considerable pressure to cooperate, especially from Lord Knutsford, who let it be known that the king and queen favored the proposed reorganization.

Loyd was nevertheless determined not to give up without a fight. He drew up a lengthy memorandum setting out the society's objections, and in doing so he articulated eight fundamental principles that in his view ought to continue to guide the Red Cross "in this country, which differs in so many ways from the countries in which Red Cross work is a branch of 'Hygiène et Sauvetage' or connected with assistance in street accidents and other charitable work of that kind."[154] These principles are worth quoting in full:

1. The Society must never lose sight of the fact that its main object was relief "in war."
2. There should, therefore, be no outlay on unnecessary display, a simple and clean office at a moderate rent and a working clerk or secretary at a moderate salary, supplemented if necessary and possible by the salary of some other post to which time could partly be devoted particularly in time of peace.
3. No unnecessary expenditure in attending Conferences except where there was something special to communicate requiring personal attendance.
4. No unnecessary organisation about the country. Committees with nothing to do, being a source of trouble and confusion while not wanted, and obtainable on very short notice if wanted.
5. The Society should not become bound, morally or otherwise, to persons in time of peace, to give them employment in time of war, but should select, at the time, the persons qualified up to date.
6. The Society while always in touch with and in harmony with the War Office Authorities should be perfectly independent of them. The natural tendency of a Military Department to assume jurisdiction and claim authority being well recognised and guarded against.
7. On no account should the business of the Society be so conducted as to relieve the War Office of any of its duties in making the provision in time of peace for the proper care of any sick and wounded in time of war; anything like an attempt on the part of the War Office to find out how much of its work it could rely upon getting done by voluntary agencies in the event of war being wholly inadmissible.

8. As in the case of personnel so also with stores and methods of relief there being a liability to become obsolete, the Society should not accumulate materiel in time of peace, but start with the latest materials and methods up to date as each occasion arose, and should supply such extra comforts and such extra attention and care as were beyond the power of the best and most zealous official staff to supply under the pressure of active hostilities.[155]

This is a clear statement of what might be called the "Wantage doctrine," a coherent philosophy of Red Cross work that, by the way, does not in the least conflict with Dunant's original plea for voluntary aid. Loyd's suspicion of the War Office recalls Florence Nightingale's injunction that "no steps should be taken with the public in any country which should lead their War Office to think that its own work . . . will be done for it by anybody else."[156] Indeed his entire memorandum is a declaration of opposition to what he and his associates saw as the pernicious tendencies of the day: rampant militarism, insidious bureaucracy, unseemly display, self-important "busyness," and ill-conceived planning. Furley and his friends in the St. John Ambulance Association might take pride in their uniformed, well-trained, well-organized, and well-equipped detachments, ready at a moment's notice to cooperate with the army medical service, but in Loyd's eyes all this activity was quite unnecessary and served primarily to satisfy the vanity of its promoters. Loyd's position was at bottom a reflection of the values of aristocratic paternalism; as such, it also revealed a distinct lack of sympathy for popular involvement in Red Cross work. His ideal was a self-contained and self-perpetuating body of eminent gentlemen who would act as a board of trustees, spending donated funds wisely whenever necessary and prudently saving them when hostilities came to an end. In his view it was quite unnecessary for the society to make elaborate and costly preparations in peacetime, to train people for the tasks they might be required to perform in the event of war, or to foster popular support for the Red Cross cause by promoting urban ambulance services or by supporting improvements in public hygiene or hospital services. The National Aid Society existed only for its members and for the wounded, who were, as occasion demanded, the objects of the charity; Loyd was determined to resist its being transformed into a permanent, and permanently active, social institution.

Yet Loyd and his chief ally, Lady Wantage, were in no position to fight more than a rearguard action; like Clara Barton they found little support and extraordinarily influential forces arrayed against them. Sir Edward Ward, the permanent undersecretary at the War Office; Macpherson, Keogh, and the senior officers of the RAMC; as well as the leaders of the Order of St. John were all in favor of reconstruction. To these must be added the powerful influence exerted behind the scenes by Sir Frederick Treves, the eminent surgeon who was well known at court for his skill and expertise and better known to the public at large for his relationship with Joseph Merrick, the

Elephant Man.[157] Treves was one of those who had irritated Furley by running his own show in South Africa, and although he had defended the performance of the RAMC while the war was being fought, he was severely critical of it afterwards and offered several suggestions for reform. His influence at court stemmed from the fact that as surgeon to the king he had operated when Edward VII's appendix ruptured in 1902; when the king—who also contracted peritonitis—recovered, Treves was rewarded with many honors and the king's continuing friendship. Early in 1904, when reform of the British Red Cross was already being discussed, the Russo-Japanese War began, and Treves quickly decided to travel to the Far East to observe the war firsthand. While in Japan and Manchuria, Treves was enormously impressed by the well-planned work of the Japanese Red Cross Society; no doubt this enthusiasm for the accomplishments of a highly organized and centralized Red Cross society found its way into conversations with the king and with Queen Alexandra after his return.[158] Treves was not alone in his admiration for the military-medical arrangements of the Japanese: Macpherson, sent out to Manchuria by the War Office, had formed an equally favorable view of the Japanese Red Cross, as had Ethel McCaul, the emissary of Queen Alexandra.[159] Like Furley, Treves was also a close friend of Lord Knutsford, whom he had known from his days at London Hospital, and was happy to explain to the king why the reform that Knutsford was seeking was so important.

In the end, the National Aid Society was forced to concede defeat, but not without causing the reformers considerable difficulty. First the society refused to give the new council any financial support; then it challenged Lord Knutsford and the CBRCC to try to raise money for a peacetime reorganization without the society's endorsement and had the satisfaction of seeing this attempt fail dismally; then, when formally asked to submerge itself in the CBRCC, it refused. In a last attempt to stave off defeat, Lord Rothschild presented the king with a petition, the text of which had been written by Loyd himself and thus was a predictable restatement of the Wantage doctrine.[160] Finally, in a crucial private meeting at Buckingham Palace on 14 March, 1905, the leaders of the society were offered one last chance: It was intimated that if only they would agree to undertake the proposed program of peacetime reorganization, the king was prepared to dismantle the CBRCC and leave the field of Red Cross activity entirely to them. Once again Loyd was adamant in his refusal, reiterating his claims that there was no public support for such a program, that the War Office was behind the whole scheme, and that the supporters of reform merely wished to reduce voluntary assistance in Britain to the submissive position that it occupied in Japan.[161] His intransigence finally convinced the king, who was being advised in these matters by Treves, Viscount Esher, and Sir Edward Ward, that only a royal command would end the society's opposition. Accordingly, in July, 1905—only six months after the reorganization of the American Red Cross—the CBRCC and the National Aid Society were forcibly merged into a new British Red

5.14   The palm-court atmosphere of the international Red Cross conferences held at the turn of the century is nicely captured in this photograph of the opening session of the Eighth Conference, held in London in 1907 to recognize the "coming of age" of the British Red Cross Society.

Cross Society (BRCS), with the king as patron, the queen as president, and Treves as chairman of the executive committee.[162] To salve feelings, Loyd himself, Lady Wantage, and Lord Rothschild were all appointed to the council of the new BRCS, but the real power now lay with Treves and Lord Knutsford. For Sir John Furley, who had been advocating such an organization since the early 1870s, appointment to the BRCS council must have been a sweet, if much belated, triumph.

When the ICRC was informed of the reorganization, it responded by proposing that the 1907 international Red Cross conference be held in London to celebrate the reconstitution of the BRCS. Thus in June of that year, the leaders of the BRCS were briefly required to present a semblance of unity to the assembled delegates, who in any case were far more interested in hearing about the Japanese Red Cross Society's work in the recent war against Russia than they were in hearing about the newly reorganized British society. Hardly had the conference adjourned, however, when a new quarrel erupted between the War Office and the BRCS, soon involving the Order of St. John as well.

If the supporters of the 1905 reform (confirmed by a royal charter in 1908) expected that it would solve the problems associated with organizing voluntary assistance in Britain, they were mistaken. Loyd and his associates, having been dragooned into reluctant compliance, were now determined to ensure that the real sponsors of the reform—in particular the War Office and the Order of St. John—carried out its spirit to the letter. But their definition of its spirit was quite different from that of its supporters, and therein lay the seeds of further conflict. Treves and Knutsford regarded creation of a nationwide peacetime organization as the highest priority, whereas the former National Aid Society leadership believed that the unification of voluntary effort in the event of war was the heart of the matter. Consequently Loyd became outraged once again because the Admiralty and the War Office, when asked to recognize the BRCS as the sole channel through which wartime voluntary aid would be officially received, insisted on exempting from this provision trained personnel supplied by the St. John and (in Scotland) the St. Andrew's Ambulance Associations.[163] Treves was told informally that the Admiralty wished to retain its freedom of action to make contracts and to accept, for example, the offer of a hospital ship from a colonial government should it be forthcoming.[164] It is, however, highly unlikely that the BRCS would have stood in the way of such contracts or offers of assistance; the clear implication of Loyd's account of the affair is that highly placed members of the Order of St. John, especially Lord Knutsford and Sir Alfred Keogh, were working behind the scenes to ensure that the 1905 reform did not prevent making special arrangements between their Order and the military and naval authorities.

As director-general of the Army Medical Department, Sir Alfred Keogh was charged with meeting the needs of both the regular army and the Territorial Force, the latter created in response to the perceived threat of invasion that dominated British military planning at this time.[165] For the regular army, Keogh contracted with the Order of St. John to supply bearer companies that would be formed into a Home Hospitals Reserve. For the Territorial Force, Keogh, borrowing an idea from the Japanese and the Germans, raised with Treves the possibility of having the BRCS organize voluntary aid detachments (VADs), which would be assigned the work of transporting the wounded from field ambulances to the railways and from the railways to the general hospitals.[166] The original plan was that VADs would be organized and controlled at the county level by the local branch of the BRCS; they would be composed of men and women who had received preliminary instruction in first aid and nursing and had received certificates from the St. John Ambulance Association. There was one obvious difficulty with this scheme: The BRCS had not yet created active local branches in every county. The War Office thought that this could be surmounted by permitting "any society organized for the purpose" to administer the VAD scheme in counties that lacked a local branch of the Red Cross, but the BRCS council protested to the secretary of state for war, Richard Haldane, that such a plan would reintroduce the very confusion and overlapping that the 1905 reform had meant to eliminate.[167] Haldane, a close friend of Keogh, quickly reassured them that this was not his intention; to ensure better coordination between the BRCS and the War Office, it was agreed that Keogh himself would become organizing secretary of the BRCS in March, 1910 and would himself take charge of bringing the VAD scheme into operation.[168] However, before Keogh could take up these duties he received a new official appointment and recommended that the BRCS appoint Colonel James Magill of the RAMC as its organizing secretary.

Whether Keogh might have prevented further misunderstandings is mere speculation; what is beyond doubt is that the leaders of the BRCS and the Order of St. John had quite different views about the level of training needed to qualify as a VAD member and about the kind of person at which the training program was directed.[169] The BRCS was soon complaining that the fees charged for its courses by the St. John Ambulance Association put them beyond the reach of many people and constituted a burden on those who held some other first-aid certificate. Such complaints evoked little sympathy from Sir Herbert Perrott, chief secretary of the St. John Ambulance Association, who wrote to one of its members that "some great authorities connected with the Red Cross Society appear to consider it more desireable to have quantity and not quality, and that almost tramps or corner-men are good enough to join Voluntary Aid detachments."[170]

When the Red Cross council decided in 1910 that they would accept as qualifications for VAD service certificates other than those issued by the St. John Ambulance Association, the latter body withdrew from the scheme altogether. This action was regarded as bad faith by most of the BRCS executive, but what really infuriated Loyd and the other former National Aid Society leaders was the sequel to this withdrawal. First, the War Office announced (July, 1910) that it would permit the Territorial Force County Associations *not* to work with the BRCS and gave them the right to "employ any other means of raising the detachments that they think fit."[171] Then, in October, the army council announced that units organized at the county level by the St. John Ambulance Association would be regarded as "the equivalent in every sense" of VADs organized by the BRCS.[172] Once again it seemed that the War Office was prepared to make special arrangements and exceptions for the Order of St. John; in Loyd's words,

> While the St. John Ambulance Association was left in undisturbed (and undisputed) enjoyment of the Home Hospitals Reserve, created for them by Sir Alfred [Keogh] at the same time, they were now permitted and encouraged through the mechanism of the Territorial Associations to undertake and frustrate, as far as the most unremitting efforts could do so, the formation of what the War Office in the original scheme . . . had called . . ."Voluntary Aid Detachments" of the British Red Cross Society.[173]

There is no doubt that many loyal members of the BRCS felt that the War Office had betrayed them over the VAD scheme. At the local level, however, feelings of bitterness and jealousy were more likely to be directed at those connected with the St. John Ambulance Association. The standing of the latter body, it must be said, was not assisted by the behavior of Sir Herbert Perrott, who seems to have gone out of his way to bully and insult the Red Cross. On one occasion, he described his Order (with fearless inaccuracy) as "a body which for nearly 900 years has borne the device of a white eight-pointed cross, and carried on the work for the benefit of the sick and wounded in war, while the device of the Red Cross Society, which represents merely the democratic and socialistic arms of the city of Geneva, was adopted at a Conference held there in the early sixties, and has scarcely the antiquity of half a century."[174] Meanwhile, Archie Loyd was diligently keeping track of every piece of evidence that could be used to demonstrate the bad faith of the War Office and the "mischievous and unjust treatment brought upon us by the claims of the certifying bodies";[175] eventually, he intended have his day in court.

Between 1910 and 1914, the BRCS finally began to take on some of the attributes of the continental Red Cross societies. Local branches were formed everywhere in the country, and many of them were actively involved in raising and training VADs. In March, 1912, it acquired virtually a full-time chairman of the executive committee when Edward A. Ridsdale was appointed to succeed Sir Frederick Treves upon the latter's retirement. A retired Member of Parliament and a financier with worldwide interests, Ridsdale was also a "gentleman of leisure" who could give full attention to the position. Shortly after he took over, the society began to publish the *British Red Cross Journal* on a monthly basis. Soon there was so much activity that the shortage of space at the old central office forced the council to consider moving to new premises. It was agreed that something like £50,000 or £60,000 would have to be raised, but a succession of disasters requiring charitable assistance—among them the sinking of the *Titanic*—led the council to postpone temporarily the proposed fund-raising campaign, and, consequently, the first task of the BRCS after war began in 1914 was to find itself an adequate headquarters. Meanwhile, at the local level sniping between the Red Cross and the St. John Ambulance Association continued unabated, to the point where each central office regularly received complaints that the loyalty, motives, and work of its respective members were being disparaged by persons associated with the rival body. The unfortunate but predictable result of all this backbiting was that by 1914 many people had come to view the BRCS and the St. John Ambulance Association as two separate bodies, which not only did not make common cause with one another but which were open rivals, not only over the VAD scheme but on a broader philanthropic front.

Would the demands imposed by a major war finally put an end to this rivalry, with its lurking potential for overlapping and confusion? The 1905 reform had, of course, been designed for this very purpose, but by 1914 Loyd and Lord Rothschild seemed to be the only ones who cared to remember that fact. Incredibly, in August, 1914 no one at the War Office or the Admiralty claimed to be aware of the arrangements that had been made for official recognition of the BRCS in the wake of the 1905 reorganization, and each of these bodies had to have some recent history explicitly recalled to them by Treves and Loyd before conceding that indeed these earlier agreements were still in force.[176] What was not yet clear was the wartime relationship between the BRCS and the Order of St. John. Keogh and his St. John associates liked to think that the BRCS, like the French Red Cross, was composed of three separate societies, but naturally Loyd took the view that the Order, having fused in 1905 with the National Aid Society and the Army Nursing Reserve, had become a component part of the BRCS. As such, it had no right to engage on its own in matters of assistance to the war wounded apart from its existing contracts with the authorities. This view was not, however, widely shared by the British public, which, partially because of the VAD scheme, had come to think of both bodies as equally involved in wartime voluntary assistance. Nor was it shared, apparently, at the very highest levels: Queen Alexandra herself, already president of the BRCS, muddied the waters considerably when she became president of a Committee of Ladies of Grace of the Order of St. John, which was organized by the Duchess of Bedford to provide assistance to sick and wounded soldiers. In the early days of the war, the St. John Ambulance Brigade was able to mobilize 24,000 trained reserves for immediate service with the British Expeditionary Force, an impressive achievement which the BRCS was as yet in no position to emulate. The plain fact is that many socially influential Britons were simply more comfortable with the upper-class tone and pretensions of the Order than they were with the BRCS, which was perceived, probably erroneously, to be a more democratic organization.

Once the war had begun, the leaders of the BRCS wrote to *The Times* explaining the role that the Red Cross would play in providing assistance to the sick and wounded and appealing for contributions from the public. The management of *The Times* decided to endorse the appeal with a strong editorial in its support; succeeding issues carried reports of the contributions that were flowing in to *The Times*'s Red Cross appeal.[177] On 1 September, the day after the editorial appeared, Lord Plymouth, the new subprior of the Order of St. John, wrote a brief letter in which he admitted,

> There has unfortunately been some friction in various parts of the country between the St. John Ambulance Association and the British Red Cross Society in its local administration. It is felt by both these Societies that in the present circumstances all these past differences should be forgotten and laid aside, so that they should work in complete harmony together, and the fullest use be made of both organizations in the interests of the sick and wounded. It is desired that the County Directors and other officials should cooperate in every possible way to assist the work of both organizations equally.[178]

5.15   Sir John Furley, founder of the St. John Ambulance Brigade, chose this photograph of himself in full regalia as the frontispiece for his autobiography. In all likelihood it was this kind of self-advertisement that provoked Archie Loyd, no great admirer of the Order of St. John, to make an acerbic comment about "the claptrap and
mutual decoration crowd."

He then sent it to Sir Walter Lawrence, who had been appointed several months earlier to head a War Office committee of inquiry into the problems that had arisen over the VAD scheme. With an enviable stroke of boldness, Lawrence, who was well aware of the difficult relations between the two voluntary bodies, took the document to the commander-in-chief, Lord Kitchener, who added these words: "I approve of this and consider it essential.—KITCHENER." He then took it to Ridsdale, the chairman of the BRCS, who agreed to issue a similar letter to the local branches of the Red Cross. In vain did Loyd protest that the Order of St. John had been a part of the BRCS since its foundation in 1905 and hence could not be regarded as an organization equal in status to the BRCS. A few days later, the army council wrote to Lord Rothschild, president of the BRCS, saying that "they are especially glad to learn that you are working in close association with other bodies recognized by Government as forming part of the Red Cross Organization of Great Britain. A great work can be effected by the co-operation of the British Red Cross Society and the Ambulance Department of the Order of St. John of Jerusalem. . . . The Council [feels] sure that your Society and that of the Order of St. John will husband every penny which flows in from the generous people of Great Britain."[179] There was, of course, no such thing as "the Red Cross Organization of Great Britain" but, as Loyd ruefully admitted, "anything like public contradiction or protest in the Press or on a platform was out of the question, and would have recoiled on the parties protesting, as a breach of the 'harmony' which Lord Kitchener 'considered essential.'"[180] The result of these maneuvers was that the BRCS was forced into a partnership with the Order of St. John for the duration of the war. *The Times* removed the words "Red Cross" from the name of its fund and announced that all monies received over and above £200,000 would be shared equally between the BRCS and the Order of St. John; a joint war committee was formed to administer the fund. In vain did Loyd once again protest that from a strictly legal point of view all this was a violation of the constitution of the BRCS: The extraordinary circumstances forced upon them by the war, said his colleagues, justified these special arrangements and made protest unthinkable. Ridsdale, who with Loyd deplored the conduct of the army council, felt that he could no longer deal with the War Office and resigned from the chairmanship. His place was taken by Arthur Stanley, M.P., a brother of Lord Derby and the president of the Royal Automobile Club, who had the unenviable task of guiding the society through World War I. Ironically, Archie Loyd never did get his day in court. In late 1917, he produced a history of the BRCS, which documented in chapter and verse his resentment over the behavior of the War Office and the Order of St. John; both Treves and Ridsdale read it and attested to its accuracy.[181] Accuracy was no longer the principal issue, however: With the war still on, and with plans for postwar cooperation between the two bodies already being discussed, it was scarcely politic to permit copies of it to circulate, and Stanley arranged for it to be quickly and quietly suppressed.

Red Cross Patriotism

The logical conclusion of the militarization of charity was that working for the national Red Cross society became both an outlet for, and a measure of, a citizen's patriotic enthusiasm. In the 1860s, charity on the battlefield had been regarded as an appropriate activity for those who were devoted to the moral elevation of humanity and to the extension of European civilization; but by the early twentieth century, the locus of charity, as well as the purpose of it, had changed substantially. The Germans had been the first to realize that the best place for volunteers was along the evacuation routes and in the hospitals of the rear. From them the Japanese had learned how to create an efficient military medical organization, but they did not merely copy the Germans; they also introduced variations of their own. One of these was the creation of a Red Cross society that unashamedly regarded patriotism rather than humanitarianism as the guiding principle of its activity. In Japan, patriotism equated with devotion to the emperor, but in other countries it was easily equated with the "national destiny," however that was defined. Once devotion to the nation became conflated with devotion to the Red Cross, the patriotism of civilians could be measured by how much work they did for, and how much money they gave to, the national Red Cross society. This was especially true in the United States. Once America entered the war in 1917, contributing money and time to the Red Cross became a kind of patriotic obsession, which brought out the best and the worst in the American genius for publicity and hoopla. In such circumstances, indifference to the war work of the Red Cross verged on disloyalty to the nation. (See the pictorial essay following this chapter for a revealing portrayal of this episode.)

Inevitably, Red Cross patriotism became infused with social tensions and political considerations. The degree to which this happened varied considerably from one country to another. In Great Britain, there may have been a good deal of friction and bad feeling in peacetime, but the exigencies of war forced an end to factional strife. However, where a state was riven by internal social and political divisions, as in Russia, the patriotism of civilians was manifested in the existence of rival Red Cross organizations. The tsarist regime, the nobles, the *zemstvo* liberals, and, in 1917, the urban workers each had their own Red Cross, the structure and aims of which mirrored their conception of Russia itself. Yet the Russian situation—a complex one that deserves separate treatment in another work—was only the extreme example of a phenomenon that is clearly discernible elsewhere. In both France and the United States, for example, groups with their own political agendas endeavored to make Red Cross patriotism serve their own purpose; in each case, support for the Red Cross was seen as an instrument for ridding the nation of "undesirable" influences. In France, a nationalist campaign to train more nurses on the eve of World War I was appropriated by conservative Catholic opponents of urbanization and industrialization, with the result that Red Cross nurses were hailed as a "sacred militia" who would fight to restore the values of another era. On a smaller scale, the same phenomenon is observable in the United States, where self-appointed "loyalists" turned a Red Cross fundraising drive into a heavy-handed attack on those Americans who had the temerity to question the wisdom of their nation's participation in a European war. Each of these episodes merits closer examination in order to achieve a fuller understanding of the possibilities inherent in the concept of Red Cross patriotism.

In France, the shortage of adequately trained nurses surfaced as an issue at the turn of the century. When French troops were dispatched to China at the time of the Boxer Rebellion, the SSBM considered sending some of the nurses (*infirmières*) who had been trained under the auspices of its Committee of Ladies, but instead it decided to rely upon nuns supplied by the Order of St. Vincent-de-Paul. Apparently the members of the central committee of the SSBM, fearing that their own "ladies" might be massacred or tortured by the rebels, were unwilling to expose them to the hazards of such an expedition and convinced themselves that the nuns' religious status would likely ensure them greater respect.[182] This decision led many in France to wonder whether the training programs of the SSBM were of any real use. It also highlighted the friction and rivalries among the French aid societies: In turning to the Sisters of St. Vincent-de-Paul, the SSBM ignored nurses who had been trained in schools run by the other two societies that were also recognized by the government as wartime auxiliaries to the military medical service: the Association des Dames Françaises and the Union des Femmes de France.[183] The former had been founded in 1879 by Dr. Duchaussoy, a breakaway member of the SSBM who, like Sir John Furley, believed that the Franco-Prussian War had proved the need for an active peacetime training program. Where Furley concentrated on training male stretcher-bearers through the ambulance association, Duchaussoy set up a training school for nurses in one of the districts of Paris. However, Duchaussoy was something of an authoritarian figure, unsympathetic to liberalism, let alone feminism, and soon there was a showdown within the ADF that resulted in the secession of a group headed by Emma Koechlin-Schwartz and Dr. Pierre Bouloumié, who formed the UFF in 1881.[184] The French government, seemingly unconcerned by this proliferation of aid societies, recognized all three as "institutions of public utility" that were authorized to assist the armed forces in wartime and made little effort to bring the three groups together until 1907, when a central committee of the French Red Cross was created in which all three societies were represented.[185]

Some of the shortcomings of the situation in which the French found themselves were pointed out in an essay published in 1903 by Dr. Roger

Colomb of Bordeaux.[186] Thoroughly familiar with nursing schools and courses of instruction in other European countries, Colomb found three main problems with the state of military nursing in France. First, because the government was not actively involved, each aid society ran its own courses, and consequently there was no common program or scheme of certification. Second, the students were given courses of instruction "which do not correspond at all to the needs of the Army's *Service de Santé*, and are awarded diplomas which have no value in the eyes of the military authorities"; as a result, France produces "helpers (*secouristes*) rather than true nurses."[187] Third, although Colomb believed that the only proper way to train nurses was to have them in contact with the sick on a regular basis, none of the existing training programs involved a long clinical experience in a civil hospital. Thus, he concluded scathingly, despite the training programs, "at the moment of war, all these ladies with diplomas, so ready to assist the wounded and the sick, cannot render any efficacious service."[188] In his opinion, the only solution was for the three separate French Red Cross societies to pool their resources and create a permanent nursing service on the model of the Army Nursing Reserve in England.[189]

Such a course of action was unlikely to find favor with the leaders of the SSBM, who clung to a more traditional view of the nature and value of women's service. The intensely conservative ideology of its leadership was evident in a semiofficial history of the SSBM, written by Maxime Du Camp, a member both of its executive and of the prestigious Academie Française. According to Du Camp, the obligations of women include devoting part of their time to Red Cross work:

> In those hours of solitude, which are not rare in the course of a day, when the children are taking their lessons, and when the husband is out of the house at work, or in the evening, around the lighted lamp, it is pleasant to work for the unfortunate by taking up bandage-making [*ce travail de lingerie*]. . . . Later, when she takes up the post of nurse [*infirmière*] at the bedsides of the wounded, perhaps she will rediscover with feeling the very bandage that she herself prepared, and this will lead her to recall the pleasant hours spent in preparing the instruments of salvation which her charity is employing. She will have been a worker for nursing before having become a nurse herself, before she engages in correspondence for the poor soldier that she is caring for, and who wishes to hear news of "home." . . . This triple obligation, which is incessant, and which does not diminish in importance in peacetime, is reserved to the women of the Red Cross.[190]

In his view, women—and he is clearly speaking of leisured middle- and upper-class ladies rather than working women—had no real need to be trained as nurses because, as "mistresses of the linen room in peacetime," they would naturally become "mistresses of charity in wartime."[191]

Nor was this all. Du Camp also expected that the housewives of France, in addition to making bandages in their spare time, would collect donations for the Red Cross, asking everyone to give "*pour les pauvres blessés, s'il vous plait.*"

He even advised them always to carry a purse at their belts, "to serve as both a sign and an invitation," and to be sure to "choose propitious moments" such as family birthdays, marriages, births, and anniversaries, "when the spirit is most compassionate, when the heart is most vulnerable" to make their requests; there was, he assured them, no need to fear meeting with refusals or being thought indiscreet, for "let her remember the old saying of French gallantry: what woman wills, God wills."[192] This was indeed a program of peacetime work for women, but it was one firmly based on traditional religious and social assumptions about their proper role.[193] If both nursing and fund-raising could be safely entrusted to the housewives of France, there was no need either for elaborate nurse training programs or for professional managers: The "ladies" would do it all. How regrettable it was, Du Camp concluded, that French womanhood was not completely united under the Red Cross banner. "Certain women have chosen to constitute themselves into isolated groups" because of "such secondary considerations as rank, social situation, position in the world" or, worse, "politics, odious politics"; he warned that such rivalries would have the gravest consequences in wartime.[194]

When a French expeditionary force was sent to Morocco in 1907, the SSBM decided not to risk further criticism and sent several of its lady-nurses, albeit under the care and tutelage of its newly appointed secretary-general, M. de Valence. On their return to France in 1908, an official reception was organized at Nice, at which they were feted by such luminaries as the Count d'Haussonville and the Marquis de Magallon d'Argens. This extraordinary event became a kind of feast of purification, at which the participants did their best to exorcise the pervasive influence of the Dreyfus affair.[195] In honor of the young women, the Marquis had composed verses that offered them extravagant praise for having forsaken "the melodies of the flute for the fury of cannon fire, and the powder of the boudoir for the stink of gunpowder."[196] He was especially enthusiastic about their example of courage and devotion to France, which proved that "our evil dreams about the decline of *la Patrie* are untrue. . . . France is still a flower and a pearl among countries . . . you are our treasures . . . you have brought back to us both honor and hope!"[197] In the wake of the Moroccan expedition, the reputation of the SSBM began to improve, and when severe flooding occurred in the Paris region in 1910, de Valence was quick to deploy nurses, volunteers, and relief equipment in order to demonstrate that the French Red Cross could be of great assistance to the civil population in peacetime.[198]

Naturally the Red Cross became part of the "patriotic revival" that swept France after the second Moroccan crisis in 1911.[199] A harbinger of what was coming was the speech made to an audience of women at Belfort, in eastern France, by Chief Physician Berthier, who frankly admitted that in the coming general European war, the Service de Santé would not be able to cope with the anticipated number of wounded and hence was "counting absolutely on the help of the Nation, on the assistance of the Red Cross Societies."[200] He urged his audience to begin immediately to prepare for the coming conflict:

In a national war. . . you will respond en masse, you will form an army, an army of charity, in which all the women of France, coming to help and encourage the combatants, will be enrolled under the flag of the Red Cross. But, to best fulfill this role, you must begin now to prepare your mobilization—improvisations are harmful—it is necessary to attract new recruits, to whom you will teach what the SSBM is, what it does, and what the *Corps de Santé Militaire* expects of it. The SSBM can use all kinds of activities. It needs propagandists, it needs *ambulancières*, it needs the generosity of the wealthy as much as it needs the offering of the pauper.[201]

A similar note was struck by Lucie Goyal, who, writing in a popular Parisian weekly, assured young women that just as submitting to military discipline had not paralyzed the heroism of men, so service with the Red Cross would provide plenty of opportunities for the heroism of women.[202]

During these years the reading public of France was inundated with books and pamphlets about the wartime role of women. Common to many of them

---

The following series of six drawings (5.16–5.21), intended to demonstrate that throughout history women have played an important role on the battlefield, was part of the campaign waged in France on the eve of World War I to persuade women to train as nurses for the Red Cross. In the final scene (5.21), women (*femmes*) working for the Red Cross have been elevated to the status of ladies (*dames*).

5.16   Women on the battlefield: following the armed bands.

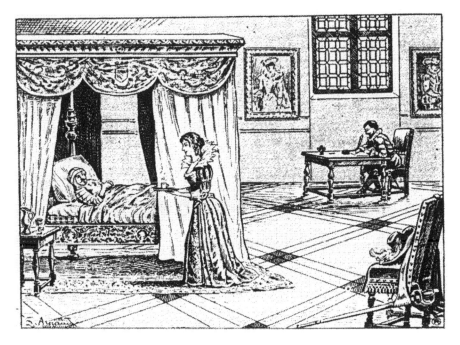

5.17 Women on the battlefield: the châtelaine caring for her wounded knight.

5.18 Women on the battlefield: the regimental canteen woman.

5.19 Women on the battlefield: actresses caring for the wounded in 1870 in the theaters of Paris.

5.20 Women on the battlefield: the Sisters of Charity.

5.21 Women on the battlefield: the ladies of the Red Cross.

was the attempt to provide historical legitimacy for their message. Lucie Goyal, extolling the relationship between charity and discipline, drew parallels between St. Catherine of Siena and the nurses who had gone to Morocco; all of them, she claimed, had demonstrated the same capacity for discipline, precision, rigor, and attention.[203] Others sought to prove that throughout French history women had always accompanied warriors and armies. In *La femme sur le champs de bataille*, for example, the authors presented an illustrated sequence that began in ancient Gaul with women following armed bands and proceeded through the *châtelaine* attending her wounded knight, the regimental canteen woman attending a wounded soldier, the famous actresses who worked in the improvised hospitals of 1870, the Sisters of Charity, and, finally, the ladies of the Red Cross.[204] Another common theme was the need for France to catch up with countries such as Germany, Russia, and Japan, where the national Red Cross societies lacked neither members nor money, or England, where Queen Alexandra's Imperial Military Nursing Service was seen by the French as well in advance of anything that could be mustered across the Channel.[205] A third theme, omnipresent in this literature, was that of paying one's debt to *la patrie* by serving as a nurse for the wounded, who had already paid their debt by serving in the national cause. Quotations from Auguste Comte and Jules Michelet abound as these authors endeavor to prove that women bring to the task of tending the wounded peculiar qualities of sensibility, affection, love, and joy, qualities that make it morally imperative that they, and not men, should perform this task. The theme of service was usually coupled with invocations of the nurse as a reassuring mother figure, a welcome reminder of hearth and home at the bedside of the wounded soldier, and with appeals to "feminine charity . . . this primordial sentiment which is in the heart of every woman, this sentiment of her very nature, which makes the members of her sex rise up and struggle, tenaciously, and with all their energy, against human sickness and pain."[206] Over and over again, the women of France were told what was expected of them, in terms that brooked no dissent: "France, this august and sacred mother, is calling you, women of every age, of every rank, of every condition to help in sustaining her hopes, her strength, and her endurance. . . . I ask you, ladies: who can resist such an appeal?"[207]

One might have thought that all these appeals to history and the special qualities of women would revive the mystique of female nurses as angels of mercy on the battlefield, but not so. De Witt-Guizot, for example, devoted one of his lectures to disabusing his audience of the notion that they might become heroines of the battlefield: This is, he told them, nothing but "a false and romantic fantasy which you must put completely out of your minds."[208] Modern military medicine, he explained, aims to get the casualties out of the zone of action so as not to impair the army's mobility, and so the proper place for nurses was not on or near the battlefield but in evacuation hospitals along the railway lines and in the territorial auxiliary hospitals. In his opinion, Red Cross work offered no room whatever for individualism, fantasy, criticism, or quibbling; instead, it required voluntary submission to the appropriate authorities—in short, "medical obedience, administrative obedience, and military obedience."[209] Given these realities, women should join the Red Cross immediately in anticipation of the coming war and begin learning what their jobs will be and how to do them properly. According to Arnaud and Bonnette, French Red Cross women needed practical hospital training chiefly so that they would become effective aides to physicians by learning how to apply bandages and how to obey without a murmur; in their opinion, such training would encourage humility and prevent nurses from fancying themselves as "*demi-médicins,* with some bookish knowledge of minor surgery and hygiene."[210] State, army, and medical profession: All were combining, with the assistance of the Red Cross, to put women and nurses in their "proper" place.

Yet this does not exhaust the significance of the Red Cross patriotism that flourished in France on the eve of the war. De Witt-Guizot's lectures were sponsored by l'Action Sociale de la Femme, an organization with members who were Catholic in religion, antisocialist and antifeminist in politics, and antimodernist in their cultural outlook. He congratulated his audience for displaying "real feminism" by coming to hear what he had to say and went on to denounce not only the feminist preoccupation with securing the vote, but also the *femmes nouvelles* who, he claimed, were responsible for the loss of respect for women. Like the Marquis de Magallon d'Argens, he believed that Red Cross nurses would restore the old-fashioned respect for women.[211] Reminding his audience of Joseph de Maistre's pronouncement about the divine origins of war, he applauded war as the nationalization of everything, even of human lives; of everything, that is, "except the activity of women, which must be organized voluntarily and practically."[212] "In order for war to be neither ugly nor bestial from the national point of view, it must be victorious; to be victorious, it must be accepted, it must be respected, and it must be organized. This is no chimera, no will o' the wisp; it is a fact, the most real fact that there is in the world."[213] The task of the Red Cross, then, was plain: to organize the wartime activity of women in the national interest. Once organized for social action, women would, he claimed, be in a position to struggle against the three greatest ills of the nation—infant mortality, alcoholism, and tuberculosis—although he was unclear about whether this struggle would be postponed until the end of the war.

Even more explicit in its antifeminism and antimodernism was Andrée d'Alix's *Le rôle patriotique des femmes,* a semiofficial publication of the French Red Cross that appeared in 1914.[214] The widow of a French officer, d'Alix was a fanatical patriot and propagandist on behalf of l'Action Sociale; she was both a frequent contributor to its *Revue du foyer*—where she reminded its readers that "maternity is the patriotism of women"[215]—and an active participant in its Joan of Arc congresses. These congresses, held annually on the eve of the war, purported to discuss ways in which the women of France could be of service to their country, but in fact they were a deliberate attempt by conservative nationalists to undercut the growth of feminism and pacifism—what the right called "antimilitarism"—among young women, especially in urban areas. The principal organizer of the Joan of Arc congresses was the Countess d'Haussonville, who was also president of the Committee of Ladies of the SSBM. She welcomed d'Alix's book, which sought to convince women who may have been flirting with feminism or pacifism that the only rights women enjoy in wartime are "the right to serve and the right to give."[216] The historical figure whose life inspired this definition of the rights of women was, of course, Joan of Arc; in modern times, it was the Red Cross nurses who had gone to Morocco. "When the nation is in danger," wrote d'Alix, "women will say to their men, 'There is you duty, do it! And while you are fighting, I will pray and I will also serve!'"[217] (See the pictorial essay following this chapter.)

The spiritual dimension of Red Cross service was very important to d'Alix. She described Dunant's book about Solferino as an invitation to all women to "join the sacred militia of the Red Cross."[218] Young women who train to become Red Cross nurses will, she claimed, go through "a moral preparation, a novitiate of charity which will exalt and strengthen them through its view of suffering itself. "'The more intense the pain, the more complete the devotion to a more elevated ideal,' that is the motto of the [Red Cross] nurse! It is not reached through calculation or reasoning, but her woman's nature, her character as a Frenchwoman, her Christian spirit will reveal it to her."[219] Such a passage suggests a mystical preoccupation with the realm of the spirit, but in fact d'Alix was very well informed about mundane matters: For example, she was well acquainted with the relative strength, in membership and funds, of other Red Cross societies, and she provided her readers with a glowing description of the work of the Japanese Red Cross Society. She also drew upon popular fiction, including a recent novel by Georges Lechartier, entitled *La confession d'une femme du monde*.[220] Its heroine, Geneviève, disgusted by the falseness of modern life—of which she has had her fill—repents and begins a new life by going to Morocco as a Red Cross nurse; there, while working in the infirmary, she undertakes one of those "voyages of the spirit that were called conversions in the seventeenth century,"[221] from which she derives new courage and new commitment. Geneviève had been recruited for the sacred militia of the Red Cross.

Where were the enemies that these recruits were to fight against? According to d'Alix, there were all around. Both the French countryside and the towns had been corrupted by the press—the anti-Christian, antimoral, antimilitarist press—which had, in her judgment, exposed the young people of France to false and evil influences, the results of which were seen in the growth of alcoholism and immorality, especially among urban factory workers. One lengthy quotation will serve to illustrate the tone and thrust of d'Alix's diatribe against modernity:

It [rural France] is dying every day from growing desertion by its children. They abandon it and move away because they find it dirty, because it appears wearisome, monotonous, capricious, meagre in its gifts, deceptive in its promises. They go to the city to live in a filth much more unhealthy, breathe poisoned air from the factory and the cabaret—or rather the bar, a loftier name, more modern and more American, and above all more dangerous because of its attractiveness. They are dragging material destitution and moral misery along with them, while the pure and invigorating air of the fields no longer serves to give sustenance and growth to the young ones. They suffer, these uprooted ones, they languish, they become corrupt. They live in an intoxication of artificial light, of music halls, and alcohol that bewitches them; but fear of the judgments of others, the appeal of the bar and the cabaret, of an aperitif savored in the radiance of electric light to the noise of the piano or the phonograph, and many other such unhealthy pleasures, all this ensnares them, captivates them, and prevents their return to the countryside. They stay in their black and noxious filth; in their poorly ventilated slum, where their children are the victims of, and provide nourishment for, the three great scourges that are depopulating France and destroying the race: alcoholism, infant mortality, and tuberculosis. Let us keep the peasant in the country, or bring him back to it; let us have him, as he once did, love the healthy life of the fields, and let us search to recreate an atmosphere of simplicity and honesty, working constantly towards his moral and his patriotic education.[222]

Naturally d'Alix saw a huge role for the Red Cross in bringing France back from the abyss. She predicted that young women working as Red Cross volunteers would restore moral fiber to the life of the nation and would play an enormous role in the patriotic education of the countryside. (In practice, this apparently meant helping to persuade peasant women to accept the additional year of military service that had recently been imposed upon their husbands.)[223] In this enterprise they might be assisted, she pointed out, by the recently formed gymnastic and sporting federations, which could be used as a kind of French version of the Boy Scouts in order to promote "patriotic ideas and military tastes among youth."[224] For contemporary efforts at social improvement she had little respect, forecasting with pride, "This peaceful crusade will do more to protect France and the race than all of the research, useful no doubt, to improve the well-being of city-dwellers, and all of the more-or-less observed laws against alcoholism. This will be the best social work."[225] As long as the Red Cross nurse was inspired by the Christian faith and love of the fatherland, d'Alix concluded, she had only to don her white cap and armband in order to become "the apostle of reconciliation and peace."[226] To be sure, this role applied only within France: In no sense was she to become an apostle of reconciliation and peace among nations; on the contrary, her role was to explain war and to make it acceptable; to "present the army as the natural protector of the fatherland, indispensable in order to maintain its dignity in the face of the enemy, and to safeguard its integrity and honor"; and to join "in the fight against antimilitarism, which is a rejection of natural instincts."[227]

By 1914, the French Red Cross had become, in the words of its secretary-general, "a school of patriotism and a social force."[228] Both roles were celebrated on 20 June of that year at ceremonies marking the fiftieth anniversary of the establishment of the Red Cross in France. A special religious service was held at Notre Dame cathedral, presided over by the cardinal-archbishop of Paris and attended by an enormous number of invited guests. Representatives of the government, the civil service, and the army were in attendance, as were the national and regional leaders of the French Red Cross. Beside the Marquis de Vogüé, president of the French Red Cross and of its central committee, sat Gustave Ador, Moynier's successor as president of the ICRC; on one side of Countess d'Haussonville, president of the Committee of Ladies, sat Madame Poincaré, wife of the president of the French Republic, and on the other side sat Madames Pérouse and Carnot, respectively presidents of the UFF and the ADF. The pillars of the choir and nave were hung with French flags alternating with Red Cross flags, and in the transepts sat more than six hundred uniformed nurses, "their place in the arms of this beautiful gothic edifice" chosen to symbolize their role as the strong arms of the society.[229] The liturgy included "Ego sum Resurrectio et Vita" ("I Am the Resurrection and the Life") from the gospel of St. John to pay tribute both to those who had given their lives for France and to "this Red Cross which is ready to give its life to spare the lives of the Nation's soldiers!"[230] In the evening, the dignitaries reassembled in the Amphitheater of the Sorbonne, where the band of the *Garde Républicaine* played the national anthem to herald the arrival of President Poincaré himself, accompanied by representatives of the ministries of war, the marine, and the Service de Santé. It was an occasion for celebrating what the Marquis de Vogüé called "the passions of patriotism."[231] Gustave Ador was very much a part of this occasion: He introduced Poincaré, who presented medals to de Vogüé and to Mademoiselle Génin, whose training school had produced hundreds of Red Cross nurses; he also praised French jurist Louis Renault, for his contribution to the 1906 revision of the Geneva Convention, and the governments who had signed it for recognizing the "essentially national role" of Red Cross societies.[232] Thus it is clear that, far from discouraging the development of Red Cross patriotism, the ICRC actively encouraged it, lending its prestige and moral support to those who sought to promote this version of the Red Cross idea.

*   *   *

In the United States, Red Cross patriotism was slower to develop, but once it emerged—during President Wilson's preparedness campaign of 1916—it soon became a national obsession. With the possibility of war looming larger every day, Wilson and the ARC joined forces to promote the idea that joining and contributing to the Red Cross was the patriotic duty of every American citizen. A poster campaign to encourage Americans to "enroll for national service" in the Red Cross used pictures of the president and quotations from his speeches and featured the Stars and Stripes alongside the Red Cross flag. Similarly undisguised appeals to patriotism soon began appearing on the covers of the *ARC Bulletin,* displacing an earlier icon of Samaritan charity that had been accompanied by the ANRC's motto, "Neutrality and Humanity."

Once the United States entered the war and national fund-raising drives were organized, Red Cross patriotism reached a fever pitch. The rich and famous set a good example: Steel tycoon Andrew Mellon was photographed accepting a Red Cross pin from socialite Virginia Seldon; Mrs. Borden Harriman, a member of one of New York's oldest and wealthiest families, led a group of Red Cross nurses in a parade held in Washington, D.C.

Red Cross publicity began to feature the classic symbols of American patriotism: An imperious Columbia virtually ordered patriots to enroll for national service; George Washington, Uncle Sam, and the Statue of Liberty each adorned the cover of the *ARC Bulletin* during 1918. American citizens responded to these appeals with enthusiasm and ingenuity. All over the country, firefighters spent their idle moments knitting socks and other items for the Red Cross. Schoolgirls in Buffalo, New York, formed a "living Red

5.22 Virginia Seldon and Andrew Mellon. In wartime, the rich and famous took
care to be seen rallying to the Red Cross cause. Here Virginia Seldon, identified as
"a Washington, D.C. society girl, who is becoming a Red Cross member," pins a
badge on the lapel of prominent industrialist and philanthropist Andrew Mellon.

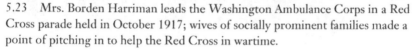

5.23 Mrs. Borden Harriman leads the Washington Ambulance Corps in a Red Cross parade held in October 1917; wives of socially prominent families made a point of pitching in to help the Red Cross in wartime.

Cross" and marched through the streets in this formation. Naturally Hollywood joined in; a poster designed to promote the work of the Red Cross and the Allied Theatrical Motion Picture Team featured a ghostly Red Cross nurse striding across the battlefield to direct stretcher-bearers to the wounded, with the legend, "Not One Shall Be Left Behind!" A poster from the same period was even more direct: It showed a wounded soldier with a Red Cross nurse above him, the nurse crying out, "If You Fail He Dies! He may be your boy—so help him now." The nurses portrayed in these images were always young, demurely pretty, and white-skinned; one would never have known from the publicity that some—perhaps many—of the women who worked for the ARC were none of these things. It is scarcely surprising that the Red Cross mirrored the social divisions of American society (and of the army) by having separate "colored branches" that provided assistance to the "colored" units of the armed forces: Some soldiers—just like some citizens—were evidently more equal than others. Nevertheless, all Americans were enjoined to do their duty for the Red Cross; the logical culmination of this well-orchestrated campaign was a poster that showed the American and Red Cross flags side-by-side above the distinctly unsubtle message, "Loyalty To One Means Loyalty To Both."

5.24 Black workers and soldiers pose outside a canteen operated by the "Colored Branch of the Hamlet [North Carolina] Red Cross." The ARC was virtually forced to establish "colored branches" because of the racial segregation that prevailed in the U.S. Army during World War I.

Indeed it did, as one American public official discovered to his chagrin, when a few unflattering remarks about the ARC resulted in his being convicted under the Espionage Act and sentenced to thirty months in the penitentiary at Leavenworth, Kansas.

This extraordinary case turned on comments made by Louis B. Nagler, assistant secretary of state for Wisconsin, who was approached in November, 1917, to donate money for the war work of the ARC and the YMCA.[233] He refused to do so, and when the canvassers tried to pressure him, he first accused the YMCA and the Red Cross of being "nothing but a bunch of grafters"; then, under further provocation, he shouted, "Who is the government? Who is running this war? A bunch of capitalists composed of the steel trust and munition makers."[234] Three weeks later to his amazement, Nagler found himself hauled before a grand jury, which decided that he ought to be tried under the Espionage Act for having "unlawfully, knowingly, wilfully and feloniously [made false reports and statements about the Red Cross and the YMCA] . . . with the intent of interfering with the success of the military and naval forces of the said United States in its war with the Imperial German

5.25 This poster was part of the drive mounted by the American Red Cross in 1916–17 to raise its membership. The slogan of the drive was, "Be Patriotic! Be Humane! Join the Red Cross!" The message of the poster took on new meaning, however, when a Wisconsin state official who criticized the Red Cross was prosecuted under the federal Espionage Act.

Government, and with the intent . . . of promoting the success of its enemies, to wit, the Imperial Government of Germany."[235] After a three-day trial held in July, 1918, which included testimony by a national Red Cross official about the "leading people" who were working for the Red Cross to "help win the war," the jury returned a guilty verdict, and Nagler received his sentence a month later.[236]

It was Nagler's bad luck that he was of German-American extraction, lived in Wisconsin, and was a great admirer of Senator Robert M. La Follette—so much so that he had the latter's portrait on his office wall. At one level this trial was simply an example—one among many—of wartime hostility to the followers of La Follette, particularly those living in Wisconsin and Minnesota.[237] Only a few weeks earlier, La Follette, an inveterate opponent of American participation in the war, had caused near havoc in the U.S. Senate when he claimed that a majority of Americans actually opposed the war; another senator immediately demanded that La Follette be sent either to jail or to Germany. In the wake of this speech, opinion ran high, especially in La Follette's home state, where Nagler's office decor would have been regarded by some people as indicative of a lack of patriotism. During the trial, much was made of the fact that Nagler himself was of German descent, as if to persuade the jury that this fact alone proved his guilt. The prosecutors sought to cast him as part of an organized group of German-Americans who were using the fund drives as an excuse to criticize the government and the war itself by arguing that the United States had no business fighting what was fundamentally a British war.[238]

It is scarcely surprising that Nagler was indicted under the Espionage Act, which became law on 5 June, 1917. It provided substantial penalties (fines of up to $10,000, and up to twenty years' imprisonment) for anyone found guilty of obstructing military operations in wartime. From the outset, the Espionage Act was used both to persecute Americans of German and Austrian descent and to suppress criticism of the war from any and all quarters. La Follette's voice was by no means the only one raised in opposition; according to David Kennedy, "The socialists charged that the war was a capitalists' quarrel, and that America was now fixing bayonets not to make the world safe for democracy, but to redeem the loans made to the Allies by Wall Street bankers."[239] The attorney general of the United States, Thomas W. Gregory, encouraged abuse of the Espionage Act by exhorting judges to suppress dissent and by chastising those who, in his opinion, were not sufficiently vigorous in its use. Gregory welcomed, perhaps even encouraged, the questionable investigative activities of such self-appointed guardians of democracy as the American Protective League.[240] Nagler's outburst that "a bunch of capitalists" were running the war effort may well have been true—especially of the war council of the ARC—but truth was no defense against the superpatriots of the American Protective League. The Department of Justice file on the case is curiously silent about who first reported the incident to the authorities.

The most interesting part of the case, however, has to do with the judge's perception of the relationship between the Red Cross and the U.S. government. Nagler's lawyer moved to quash the indictment handed up by the grand jury on the grounds that "the Red Cross and the YMCA are no part of the military or naval forces of the United States" and hence could not be covered by the terms of the Espionage Act. However, the prosecution countered that the Red Cross was "a national corporation" and "an agency of the government" and that at the time Nagler's words were uttered, units of the Red Cross had already been mobilized and thus constituted "a part of the sanitary service of the land and naval forces of the United States."[241] After hearing both sides, the trial judge denied the defendant's motion to quash, giving three reasons for his refusal.[242] The first was, "In a republican form of government, like ours, with war conducted as it is today, there can and should be no refined or limited definition of the term 'military and naval forces.'" With a candor that was all too rare during the war, he observed that doctors and surgeons were engaged in "repair" work that was not that different from the maintenance work done on air force bombers, despite the fact that medical personnel belonged to the sanitary department rather than to a combat unit. Second, he found nothing in the Geneva Convention of 1906 that would prevent recognizing members of the American Red Cross as part of the military and naval forces of the country. Third, he held that interference with the fund-raising efforts of the Red Cross was the same as interfering with its field work, because without funds it could not carry on this work. The judge's ruling virtually ensured that Nagler, who had already admitted to having made the statements in question, would be convicted.

The *ARC Bulletin*, issued by the Red Cross national headquarters in Washington, D.C., reported the Nagler trial on its front page under the headline "Slanderer Is Convicted."[243] The story quoted at length from the judge's ruling denying the motion to quash. A later issue of the *ARC Bulletin* reported the sentence, especially the fact that the judge had noted Nagler was an educated man in a position of public trust and that the judge had stated, "If men high in places of trust make remarks of this character, and are not punished, it would not be fair."[244] Meanwhile, the attorney general of the United States received a report from the U.S. attorney in Wisconsin assuring him that "his [Nagler's] conviction will have the effect of rooting out disloyal activities in this State. I also feel that his conviction will have a tendency to put an end to the propaganda that has been carried on in this part of the country against any work of organizations such as the Red Cross, the Y.M.C.A., the Y.W.C.A., and kindred organizations."[245] Nagler's appeal to the U.S. Supreme Court had not yet been heard when the war ended in November, 1918. The Department of Justice was apparently in no hurry for a decision from the Court. Eventually, in July, 1920, the solicitor general was advised by his staff that since the jury had obviously been animated by "patriotic fervor" the Department of Justice ought to confess error because "this case is of such a weak character on the facts that it would probably result in the [Supreme] Court, with propriety, reversing the judgement of the District Court."[246] The case was quietly dropped.

The significance of the Nagler case goes beyond the obvious dimensions of war hysteria and superpatriotism. Because his offense had been to criticize the Red Cross, the case also reflected the enormous transformation that had taken place in recent years in the relationship between the government of the United States and the American Red Cross Society. Such an episode would have been inconceivable during the Spanish-American War—even if an Espionage Act had then been in place—for the very good reason that in 1898 there were no significant connections between the American government and the Red Cross society. The crucial developments that laid the groundwork for a case such as this took place during the years from 1904 to 1912, developments that decisively altered the relationship between the American Red Cross, on the one hand, and the War Department and the army on the other. The result, as Louis Nagler learned the hard way, was that citizens could no longer treat the Red Cross as an ordinary charitable organization that engaged in periodic fund-raising drives. The reorganized American Red Cross had become a national corporation, behind which stood the power, prestige, and authority of the U.S. government; as the poster proclaimed, "Loyalty To One Means Loyalty To Both."

*　　*　　*

During the four years of carnage that began in 1914, the Red Cross societies of the great powers proved how well they had organized to fulfill what Gustave Ador had called "their essentially national role." The societies and their leaders have produced copious reports and memoirs that record what they did for the sick and wounded, and there is no need here to recapitulate information that is already available in published form.[247] This chapter has instead endeavored to explain how they came to be in a position to act as officially recognized auxiliaries to the military medical services and to serve both as outlets for the patriotism of noncombatants and as vehicles for the collection of voluntary taxes in aid of the war effort. Florence Nightingale, had she lived long enough, would doubtless have been appalled to see how much of the burden of war governments gladly transferred to the willing shoulders of Red Cross societies and how readily their citizens provided the funds that made such a transfer possible.

Voices of protest at what the Red Cross societies were doing were, however, few and far between, almost nonexistent in the belligerent states. Thanks to Lavinia Dock, one small but eloquent voice found its way into the pages of the *American Journal of Nursing*. It was the voice of Jeanne van Lanschot Hubrecht, the former president of the Dutch National Association of Nurses:

For more than two years [she wrote in 1916] we have been witnesses of all the horrors of this war, we have heard about the great cruelty and non-civilization of these times, we hear about millions of men killed, or maimed for life, and we should do everything to make war impossible. We ought to show another kind of courage, of love for our country. We should have the great moral force to refuse every kind of work that would promote war. It would be a deed of sublime courage for it would mean sitting still in a time when men would expect us to show our love for them and our country by doing their work. . . . I know many women are of the same opinion, that a general refusal to take part in a movement for preparedness would be the best way of averting war. Even nurses should strike, or nurse the soldiers only on the condition that every man who regained his health should be allowed to go back to his work, and not to the front. To nurse a man back to health and then send him once again to the battlefield, is something monstrous. The nurses should say, "These men belong to us and we want them to return to their useful peace-work." He who is opposed to war must also be opposed to every measure that promotes war, and an efficient nursing service certainly does, when under military control.[248]

In this passage there are echoes of Article 6 of the 1864 Geneva Convention, which provided that enemy wounded might be returned to their own side "on condition of not again bearing arms during the continuance of the war." However, Hubrecht was a voice crying in the wilderness; she was not speaking for the Dutch Red Cross nor, indeed, for Red Cross nurses in general. In the great power states, certainly, Red Cross societies had long since ceased discussing ways to avert war, or to make it less barbaric, or to make it more difficult for states to undertake. Gripped by the passions of patriotism, they undertook to perform whatever repair work the armies required of them.

Pictorial Essay

JEHANNE D'ARC

PATRONNE DES INFIRMIÈRES DE LA CROIX ROUGE FRANÇAISE

INTER ARMA ✚ CARITAS

1   During the battle of Patay in 1429, Joan of Arc, seeing a wounded English soldier, dismounts and helps the dying man. It was probably inevitable that the French
Red Cross would adopt Joan of Arc as the "patroness" of their nurses, but the
choice takes on added significance when it is recalled that in the prewar years the
right-wing antifeminist organization l'Action Sociale de la Femme had organized
"Joan of Arc Congresses" under the leadership of Countess d'Haussonville, president of the Committee of Ladies of the SSBM.

2   "Le Brassard" (The Armband)—a French postcard from World War I. During
the war, the Red Cross nurse, flag, and armband generated a great deal of
appallingly bad poetry, most of it little more than doggerel verse. French aristocrats, by contrast, were particularly given to romantic effusions such as the poem
that appeared on this postcard by Viscount de Borrelli. A rough translation would
read:

Long ago, to tend with her slim and gentle fingers
A wounded man who lay motionless in the bare countryside,
The goddess Pity descended among us.——
She was going to fly away as she had come
When the little soldier, humble cannon-fodder that he was,
Wished to know at least the name of the stranger;
And then the goddess, in order to let him know her name,
Picked up a clean white cloth and, with a smile,
After dipping her finger in the wounded man's blood,
Made a cross on it——not knowing how to write——
And now the women of France have put it on their arms!

3   An auxiliary hospital of the French Red Cross. The patriotic outpourings of
polite society—Joan of Arc, the goddess Pity, and so on—bore little relationship to
the day-to-day work of the French Red Cross. In reality, much of it consisted of
running auxiliary hospitals such as the one pictured here.

Le sang qui coule à flots dans leurs si larges veines
Près des frères blessés fait oublier nos peines !

4   This French postcard, sent to Britain in June, 1917, cleverly linked blood and
sacrifice in its praise for those who nursed the soldiers of *la patrie*. The couplet may
be loosely translated as follows: "Being near our wounded brothers makes us forget
our pains/ When we see the blood that gushes so generously in their veins."

5 Although there is no evidence that this postcard was officially approved by the French Red Cross, its unmistakable message undoubtedly reflected the feelings of most Allied soldiers. In reality "sanitary dogs" or "ambulance dogs"—whether patriotic or not—were used most extensively by the German army. In Belgium and Italy, dogs were used both as a form of transport and to locate wounded men after dark. In the French army, the high command first tolerated, then abolished, then reestablished the use of "sanitary dogs."

HEAVEN'S LIGHT OUR GUIDE

QUEEN MOTHER OF A MIGHTY NATION,
QUEEN IN THOUGHT AS WELL AS STATION,
WHO DOST NOBLY TAKE THY STAND
WITH THE GALLANT RED CROSS BAND.

W & D. Downey.   61, Ebury St., London.

6 This postcard, with its jumble of images and fulsome rhyme, was sold to raise money for the British Red Cross during World War I. The flags are those of Great Britain and its Allies. Queen Alexandra, who had founded the Imperial Military Nursing Service in 1902, believed strongly in the development (by which she meant militarization and popularization) of the British Red Cross. Thus the invocation of Florence Nightingale was not entirely out of place here despite the latter's earlier opposition to unregulated civilian volunteers dispensing charity on the battlefield. Note that the Lady's famous Lamp now radiates "Heaven's Light." After the death of King Edward VII, his widow became Queen Mother; hence, "Queen Mother of a Mighty Nation."

The Gentlewoman

The Illustrated Weekly Journal—Gentlewomen

No. 1276.—Vol. XLIX.   Saturday, December 19th, 1914   Price 6d. By post, 6½d.

THE CHILDREN'S PART.

7   The cover illustration of *The Gentlewoman* ("The Illustrated Weekly Journal for Gentlewomen," 19 December, 1914. The caption reads, "The Children's Part. Miss Christine Powis collecting from a small boy in St. James's Park in aid of the funds of the Red Cross Society, for which she is working, dressed as a Red Cross nurse." Pictures such as these, in a magazine read by virtually every governess in England, helped to spread the message that even the children of the privileged classes were doing their part for the Red Cross cause. By the end of the war, plans were being made to make the Junior Red Cross into a permanent institution.

8

Little is known about this poster, the color original of which is strikingly beautiful, but it was obviously produced after the United States entered World War I. It is preserved in the Prints and Photographs Collection of the History of Medicine Division, National Library of Medicine.

OFFICIALLY DESIGNATED BY
AMERICAN RED CROSS
AS A MEMBER OF THE
ALLIED THEATRICAL
AND MOTION PICTURE TEAM
FOR THE SECOND AMERICAN RED CROSS WAR FUND

"NOT ONE SHALL BE LEFT BEHIND!"

THIS THEATRE IS RENDERING A PATRIOTIC SERVICE, IN SENDING
A MESSAGE OF MERCY AND AID TO THE AMERICAN HEROES WHO ARE
FIGHTING FOR US ON THE BATTLEFIELDS OF FRANCE.

9   This theater poster, used to raise money for the ANRC War Fund, was drawn by James Montgomery Flagg; it shows a ghostly Red Cross nurse bravely directing stretcher-bearers through the mud of the Western Front. As anyone who had served at the front knew only too well, many wounded were left behind, only to die agonizing deaths in the stinking mud of the trenches.

10 This postcard was typical of the less-than-subtle propaganda used to raise money for the ANRC during World War I. In reality, whether a wounded soldier lived or died had often been determined before he came under the care of nurses supplied by the Red Cross.

The GREATEST MOTHER in the WORLD

11   The noted American graphic artist A. E. Foringer created this famous poster for the ANRC's 1918 fund-raising campaign. Its design, reminiscent of Michelangelo's *Pietà*, portrayed the Red Cross nurse as an enormous enveloping mother, cradling in her arms the wounded and bandaged body of an almost childlike soldier. Besides its dramatic impact, the poster also conveyed the implicit message that parents need not fear for their sons' lives so long as the Red Cross had sufficient money to do its job.

12 In Buffalo, New York, enthusiastic schoolgirls formed themselves into a "Living Red Cross" for this parade, held during the war to help promote contributions to the ANRC War Fund.

13 An American Red Cross Canteen in Bordeaux, France, 1917–1918. Canteens such as this one, with a clientele who look extraordinarily healthy, reveal that the ANRC had now abandoned the practice of confining its work to the sick and wounded; instead, it functioned as a service organization for all combatants. Not only the smiles but also the careful intermingling of sailors, doughboys, a French officer, and a black American (unthinkable on the Home Front) suggest that this picture was staged for Red Cross publicity purposes.

THE SPIRIT OF AMERICA

JOIN

14 Anxious lest its vastly increased membership decline with the coming of peace, the American Red Cross requested the well-known war artist Howard Chandler Christy to design a poster for its 1919 membership drive. This demure, virginal nurse, literally wrapping herself in the flag to embody "the Spirit of America," may be somewhat less sexy than most of the so-called Christy Girls, but her diaphanous bodice no doubt caught the attention of many passing males.

15 Americans promoted Red Cross patriotism with as much ingenuity as enthusiasm. In this poster by Edwin Howland Blashfield, an imperious Columbia and equally imperious Red Cross nurse virtually command all loyal citizens of the Republic to contribute to the annual fund-raising drive.

16 In this Harrison Fisher poster from 1918, the Red Cross nurse once again wraps herself in the flag and President's Wilson's injunction is symbolically fortified by the authority of Congress. With a Bolshevik government already installed in Russia, this must surely have been the last occasion on which an American president spoke approvingly of 'comradeship.'

VOL. IV.   JULY. 1909   No. 3.

AMERICAN
RED ✚ CROSS
BULLETIN

NATIONAL HEADQUARTERS
WASHINGTON D C

17 July 1909: Protector in War and Peace

In 1909, the cover illustration of the American Red Cross Bulletin contrived to represent the Red Cross as a sort of fertility goddess who protected soldiers in wartime and victims of natural disasters in peacetime.

18 March 1916: Neutrality and Humanity

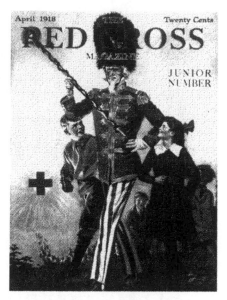

19 April 1918: Uncle Sam Leads the Junior Red Cross

20 September 1918: The Red Cross as Protecting Angel

By 1916, the new cover of the renamed *Magazine* reflected America's status as a neutral: The medallion shows a military Good Samaritan below the legend, "Neutrality and Humanity." By 1918, after a year of war, the covers have begun to emphasize patriotism at the expense of humanity; on the April, 1918 cover, for example, a uniformed Uncle Sam leads a parade of children for the Junior Red Cross. The September, 1918 cover returned to the theme of protection: An enormous guardian angel shields both soldiers and civilians from the fury of war as a Red Cross nurse leads women and children to safety under the angel's billowing robes. The October 1918 cover was a masterpiece of patriotic symbolism: On the ground, an American doughboy, a British Tommy, and a French *poilu* advance toward the enemy with fixed

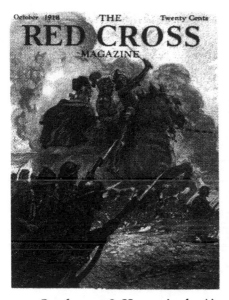

21　October 1918: Heroes in the Air
and on the Ground

22　November 1918: Do What the
Statue of Liberty Expects

bayonets, and in the sky overhead
George Washington, Joan of Arc, and
St. George urge them forward. With no
inkling of the impending Armistice that
would halt the fighting, the November,
1918 cover encouraged women to
become nursing recruits for the Red
Cross, under the stern but no doubt
approving eye of the Statue of Liberty.
By January, 1919, the realization has
dawned that the war is really over, and
the battle-scarred but victorious combatants—soldier, sailor, and Red Cross
nurse—deserve the gratitude of their
fellow-citizens. The earlier Red Cross
emphasis on humanity and protection
for the wounded was quickly abandoned
along with neutrality once America
became a belligerent.

23　January 1919: Battle-scarred but
Victorious

March 1919 · THE · RED CROSS · MAGAZINE · Twenty Cents

24 March 1919: The Triumphant Allies

Two months later, the cover portrayed Britain and France—the Allies who fought for Belgium when it was attacked in 1914—with barely enough strength left to cheer the victory. Their flags hang at rest, but a miraculous wind—summoned, no doubt, by the Statue of Liberty—manages to ensure that only the Stars and Stripes still flies bravely. With such a vision of the future, Harry Davison went to Paris to help Woodrow Wilson and Colonel House organize the peace.

Part Three

The Pains of Rebirth

And so, unavoidably, came peace, putting an end to organized war as we'd come to know it.

—*Beyond the Fringe* (1960)

✚ 6

Victory
& Virtue

T HE END OF WORLD WAR I sparked several efforts to reorganize the Red Cross at the international level. Whereas some of these sought to consolidate and extend the traditional role of the ICRC and the national societies, others asserted the need to create an entirely new kind of Red Cross for the anticipated new era of peace and international cooperation. Support for the idea of a limited reorganization came primarily from the ICRC and from the national societies of the smaller European states; proposals for a much more ambitious reform came from the newest of the great powers, America and Japan, as well as from Soviet Russia, where the Bolsheviks were sweeping away all vestiges of the old state order. The founders of the Red Cross had always sought to extend the reach of the organization beyond the European heartland; in 1919 it seemed that the American and Asian offshoots of the movement might rejuvenate the soil from which they had sprung. Yet the point must not be pressed too far; the Japanese quickly fell in with the Americans, who also found support for their plans among the British, the French, and the Italians. With Russia for the moment beyond the pale of civilization, the Soviet proposals could safely be ignored; so what rapidly took shape was a power struggle between the Red Cross societies of the victorious Allies, led by the Americans, and the ICRC, which understandably feared for its own survival if the reformers were to triumph.

At the heart of this conflict lay a fundamental disagreement over what role the Red Cross ought to play in modern society. Broadly speaking, the advocates of sweeping change sought to shift the focus of the movement from war and wounds to illness and misfortune, from assisting the military medical services in wartime to assisting the public health services in peacetime; they also believed that a new international Red Cross organization was called for, one specifically designed to direct and coordinate this new emphasis on improving health and relieving misery. On both counts, they soon found that they would receive only limited cooperation from the ICRC, which had its own, rather less ambitious, plans for the future and which was intent on preserving as much as possible of the traditional role of the Red Cross, the rationale for which seemed to the ICRC to be as strong in the 1920s as it had been in the 1860s. The ICRC's determination to survive was not always appreciated by would-be reformers; one impatient American critic described its members as behaving like "custodians of the sacred fire."[1]

The ICRC and the War

Part of the explanation for this postwar struggle lies in the fact that the wartime experience of the members of the ICRC was very different from that of the leaders of the ARC. Whereas the belatedly belligerent Americans were trumpeting their Red Cross patriotism and spending huge sums of money through the ARC to provide assistance to their armed forces and bolster the flagging morale of their allies, the members of the ICRC had spent the war— all four years of it—running various ad hoc international agencies and endeavoring to remind belligerents of their obligations under the Geneva Convention.

In this war the ICRC played the role of neutral intermediary, but it was a role vastly different from that which had been envisioned in the 1870s and 1880s by those who believed that the conduct of belligerents should be subject to the moral authority of "neutral Europe," as represented by the ICRC. The unwillingness of the national societies to accept binding moral obligations toward each other, and their willing support for the militarization of charity, substantially altered the possible roles that the ICRC could hope to

------

6.1   The Red Cross "Family Tree," produced by the ICRC for the Swiss National Exhibition in Berne in 1914. Its imagery faithfully reflects the ICRC's perception of the first half-century of the movement's history. The tree with three trunks is rooted in the city of Geneva, and it is surely no accident that the tree appears to gain strength as it passes the small island upon which sits the statue of Jean-Jacques Rousseau. The flags on the left-hand trunk are those of the governments that ratified the Convention between 1864 and 1913. (At 1906 a large branch represents the revision of the Convention.) The flags on the right-hand trunk are those of the states in which societies to aid the wounded were formed between 1863 and 1913. (The flag of the United States appears twice because the first society disbanded in 1872 and a new one had to be formed ten years later.) The middle trunk represents the work of the ICRC itself, beginning with the Schleswig mission in 1864 and ending with the Balkan mission in 1913; the disks are the gold medals awarded to the ICRC by the world expositions of 1867, 1878, and 1900. By 1919, the ICRC's diverse wartime activities could be added to the central trunk, but there is no room in this vision of the growth of the Red Cross for the new international organization that was advocated by Harry Davison and his colleagues from the Allied Red Cross societies.

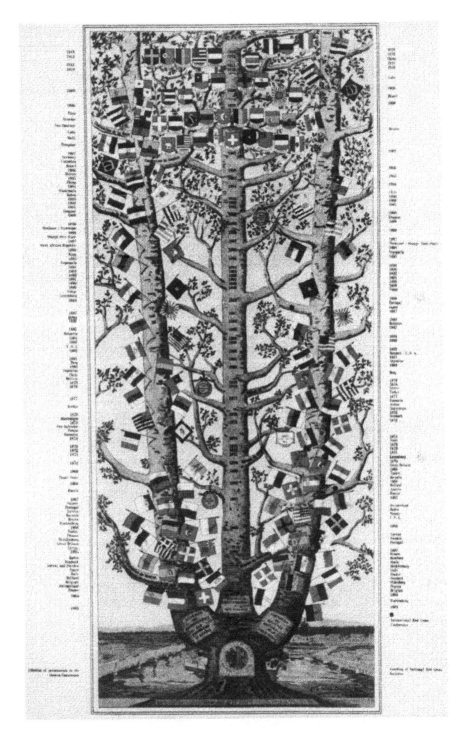

play in a major war. At one time, Moynier and others had hoped that the national societies of belligerent states would monitor the conduct of their own governments or armies to ensure that the principles enshrined in the Convention were observed; instead, the national societies shamelessly and enthusiastically endorsed the claims of their own governments and military leaders that these principles had been violated only by the enemy. With each national society dutifully functioning according to prearranged plans as an organized auxiliary to the medical services of its armed forces, there was now little need for an international agency to coordinate the sending of neutral assistance to the medical services of the belligerents. The original purpose of the international conference called in 1863—to permit volunteers to go onto battlefields to remedy the insufficiency of army medical services—had largely been met in another way, thanks to the reforms carried out in the medical services of most of the belligerent states, reforms that included the militarization of their Red Cross societies. In these changed circumstances, any international agency established by the ICRC would inevitably play a different role from those that it had organized in the 1870s.

Instead of coordinating neutral medical relief to the sick and wounded, the ICRC's wartime role became that of a clearinghouse for gifts, correspondence, and information about not only the wounded but also prisoners of war (POWs), whose fate had yet to be regulated by the Geneva Convention. Even before World War I began, the new priorities that the ICRC was adopting were visible in the work of the agency that it established in Belgrade during the Balkan Wars (1912–1913). Its duties included gathering and sending gifts in cash or kind to the wounded of all belligerent armies; sending on correspondence addressed to the wounded and forwarding letters or news to the families of sick or wounded soldiers; collecting and forwarding correspondence and gifts for prisoners of war; and serving as an intermediary for the exchange of information between prisoners and their families.[2] This extension of Red Cross activity to include POWs who were neither wounded nor sick had been discussed and approved at the international conference held in Washington, D.C., earlier in the year.[3] In many ways the tasks of the Belgrade agency prefigured those that would be assumed by the new International Prisoner of War Agency established in Geneva on the outbreak of World War I.

In its new role, the international POW agency was operating largely as a wartime extension of the national societies, whose ability to function as reassuring intermediaries between civilian families and their relatives in the armed forces was interrupted, obviously, if the latter were captured or hospitalized by the enemy. Since governments had come to appreciate the value of allowing national Red Cross societies to play this role, they made little objection when the circumstances of war forced an improvised solution to the problem, despite the fact that such an extension of Red Cross activity had not been authorized in the 1906 revisions to the Geneva Convention. Much the same could be said about the ICRC's decision, in the early weeks of the war, to open a civilian section of the agency. Thus the POW agency and its various sections soon became a kind of gigantic orderly room, which endeavored to locate those soldiers, sailors, and civilians whose families, armies, and governments had, for the moment, lost track of them. From the point of view of the belligerent governments, a neutral agency fully occupied with shipping parcels, delivering letters, maintaining files, and answering inquiries about the fate of individuals was infinitely preferable to one that actively sought to impose moral limits upon the conduct of war; moreover, its existence was useful, in that it gave anxious citizens an opportunity to transcend the limits that warfare imposed on communication.

In its first circular after the outbreak of war in 1914, the ICRC noted: "From now on, the Red Cross movement will have to commit itself to a degree of activity unprecedented in its intensity."[4] Although this prediction applied to almost all of the national societies, particularly to those in the belligerent states, it was especially true of the ICRC itself. Lacking any paid staff, its members largely put aside both their personal and professional lives to devote themselves to humanitarian activities for the duration of hostilities. In addition to running the agency—which by 1918 had sent nearly 2 million parcels and amassed a card file on almost 5 million individuals—the members of the ICRC had to deal with repeated difficulties concerning the repatriation of captured medical personnel and of the severely wounded, doing what they could to secure uniform and humane treatment of POWs. At the beginning of the war, the ICRC had "respectfully" reminded belligerents of their obligations under the 1906 Revised Convention, and when complaints about violations were received, it sent the information on those deemed serious to the governments involved with the expectation that they would investigate and deal with the incidents in question. Not surprisingly, it found that governments were far more enthusiastic about charging their enemies with violations of the Convention than they were about investigating complaints concerning the behavior of their own troops.

As the war dragged on and the carnage showed no sign of abating, the voice of the ICRC became louder. In mid-1916, it issued an appeal to belligerent and neutral states in which it condemned reprisals on prisoners as "a relapse into barbarity, unworthy of nations which have given the Red Cross the high position it holds in their armies."[5] A year later, it explicitly condemned the Germans for torpedoing appropriately marked hospital ships, and in 1918 it condemned chemical warfare as "a barbarous innovation which science is in the course of perfecting, that is, making it more murderous and more refined in its cruelty."[6] To be sure, chlorine, phosgene, and mustard gas had made their dreadful appearances much earlier, but the members of the ICRC did not at first see it as appropriate for them to speak out against weapons prohibited by the Hague Convention rather than the Geneva Convention. However, in 1918, fearing that the belligerents were about to extend chemical warfare via long-range artillery and aircraft bombing, they decided to dispense with legal proprieties and make their revulsion unmistakably clear. In the 1880s, Red Cross enthusiasts had claimed that advances in weapons technology would stimulate "philanthropy's genius for beneficence"; but now the ICRC admitted that "scientific progress in aeronautics, ballistics and chemistry have merely aggravated the suffering and, above all, extended it to the whole population, so that war from now on will be nothing but a ruthless work of destruction."[7] Dr. Frédéric Ferrière, who headed the civilian section of the international POW agency, was even more forthright in his condemnation: "In the name of the humanitarian principles of the Red Cross, we should proclaim aloud that war conducted in this way is inhuman, immoral, contrary to the law of nations and revolting to every decent human conscience."[8] By war's end, members of the ICRC had already begun to formulate an agenda for the postwar years, which included as high priorities the drafting of new international agreements concerning the treatment of both civilians and POWs and the search for means by which to ensure that in the future belligerent governments would observe the Hague regulations concerning the conduct of warfare. If the law of nations were not to be dismissed as a mockery, there was a great deal of work to be done to reestablish its credibility.

The Red Cross, too, had to adjust to the postwar world. Literally within days of the signing of the Armistice, the ICRC sent a circular letter concerning the postwar activity of the Red Cross; it was sent to all of the national societies and to the governments of the erstwhile belligerents.[9] Its tone and contents are revealing: After expressing "joy and gratitude" at the ending of "this butchery," the circular went on to note that the major focus of ICRC activity during the war—the care and treatment of POWs—would soon end; now was the moment to consider in what other ways the sufferings of war could be diminished. The pressing duty of the Red Cross, it asserted, was to "do something on behalf of the unfortunate victims of this terrible scourge": Employment of some sort for wounded soldiers—the mutilated, the invalids, the helpless, those suffering from tuberculosis—and support for the widows, orphans, and aged parents of those soldiers who had died during the war. The circular noted that efforts to assist these needy groups were already under way in some countries and were being sponsored either by the state or by private societies. However, the ICRC suggested that a greater degree of cooperation might ensue if governments and national Red Cross societies were to exchange information about their intentions at a conference to be held for this purpose.[10] The circular concluded by asking recipients to respond to these suggestions.

No one familiar with the prewar history of the ICRC would have found any surprises in this document. From its earliest days, the ICRC had always taken the view that the most important peacetime tasks of the national societies included caring for the victims of the last war while preparing improved ambulance services for the next. To be sure, the colossal scale of the war just ended meant that immediate needs far exceeded all previous endeavors on behalf of the wounded and other victims of war. In these circumstances, an exchange of information and intentions among governments and national societies was therefore especially appropriate. Nor was there anything especially novel in the ICRC's expressed concern for the ravages of tuberculosis; as the ICRC was well aware, the French and especially the German national societies had for decades been heavily involved in campaigns to reduce the incidence of tuberculosis among their civilian populations, particularly among men of military age and among young women who might bear the next generation of soldiers. The same was true of its proposal for an international conference: In the past the ICRC had frequently nudged the national societies toward what it regarded as a desirable course of action by proposing an international conference. The November circular makes it clear that, although recipients of this letter were at liberty to suggest whatever they pleased, the ICRC for its part had no intention of proposing a substantial reordering of the priorities of the Red Cross movement. If new initiatives were needed, they lay principally in the area of international law.

Davison's Dream

During these very weeks an entirely different vision of the future of an international Red Cross was taking shape in the mind of Henry P. Davison, chairman of the war council of the American Red Cross. Four days after the Armistice took effect, Davison, full of enthusiasm and satisfaction after completing a tour of ARC operations in Europe, sailed from Bordeaux to New York. En route, he studied the figures and realized that the ARC would finish the war with a surplus of close to $75 million in its treasury. Immediately, he put forward an idea that he claimed would be both "a great service to mankind and a creditable finish to our Red Cross movement." In a letter written aboard ship to friend Harvey Gibson, the ARC commissioner in France, Davison sketched out his vision of the immediate future. If he could secure the approval of Woodrow Wilson and the adherence of the British, French, and Italian Red Cross Societies, he planned to

> go to Geneva and suggest to the International Red Cross that they immediately invite . . . delegates from the various Red Cross organizations throughout the world for a conference at a date which would give the most remote plenty of time to arrive. I would there organize a real International Red Cross with the idea that much good could come from such an organization. . . . I have a feeling that if there is anything whatever in the question of the League of Nations, there is common ground in the Red Cross which would bring together all the nations, leading to a better understanding, and that . . . there could be cooperation at least along humanitarian lines. For instance, I can see a medical force organized which would formally adopt a regime for fighting tuberculosis and that there

would be a world-wide fight against the plague. There would also be adopted a recognized formula for treating with other plagues incident to certain localities, such as yellow fever, typhus, etc. It is not beyond reason to believe that there might develop a plan of cooperation for treating with the destitute where they are in masses resulting from the war. In fact, I can think of many moves which might be made, but which would evolve from a getting together and exchange of views. The adoption of a system of reports relative to health conditions, disasters, etc., which would be cleared through the International Red Cross.[11]

This passage reveals the full extent of Davison's bold vision for the future: The need to create a "real" International Red Cross that would take the lead in such humanitarian enterprises as the struggle against epidemic disease and the organization of relief for those made destitute by war. Almost certainly, his vision of the future was influenced by observing the work of Gibson's ARC commission in Europe, which was already involved in efforts to improve the level of popular health in France.[12] He was also aware of the work of the Rockefeller Foundation's International Health Board and of its joint sponsorship of the ARC's mission to Serbia in 1915 to control an ominous outbreak of typhus.[13] Also implicit in this vision is Davison's somewhat naive belief that international cooperation for humanitarian purposes would be relatively easy to achieve because nations would be likely to separate humanitarian matters from those areas where their political and economic interests were directly involved.

It must also be said that the tone of this letter reveals Davison's almost complete ignorance of the character and history of the Red Cross movement outside America and indeed prior to his own relatively recent involvement with the ARC. About the ICRC and the European Red Cross societies, he understood only the little that he had been able to pick up during the war, and that little had not impressed him very much. Understandably proud of what the ARC had been able to achieve in a very few years, Davison believed that the rest of the Red Cross world needed to be rejuvenated by an infusion of American enthusiasm and American money. Not only that, but he also had a deep sense of urgency about achieving his objective: "My thought is that if anything is going to be done along this line, it must be done immediately, because minds are now more or less groping and pliable, whereas in a few months they will become cold and it will be difficult. Of course, at the outset, the Red Cross organizations of the Central Powers would not be invited, but as soon as peace is declared they should be invited."[14] Although conceding that at the moment his plan was little more than a daydream, Davison went on to alert Gibson to the possibility that at short notice he might require a villa on the Riviera, several top-ranking legal and medical advisers, and a secretarial staff, not to mention "a first-class car and the best chauffeur in France." A senior partner at the house of J. P. Morgan, Davison was used to thinking big and acting decisively; at this stage, it never occurred to him that he would encounter difficulties in reordering the Red Cross world to suit his vision.

6.2   President Wilson and the war council of the American National Red Cross.
The war council, an ad hoc body for which there was no provision in the organization's charter, was established as soon as the United States entered the war in order
to reassure potential donors—and especially Wall Street—that the American Red
Cross was being run by hardheaded businessmen experienced in finance and administration. Mabel Boardman, who had effectively run the ARC since its reorganization
in 1905, was rudely pushed aside for the duration of the war. *Left to right, front row:*
Robert W. DeForest (vice-president of the ARC); President Wilson (president of
the ARC); William Howard Taft (chairman of the executive committee); Eliot
Wadsworth (vice-chairman of the executive committee). *Rear row:* Henry P. Davison
(chairman of the war council); Grayson M.P. Murphy; Charles D. Norton; Edward
N. Hurley. Absent: Cornelius Bliss, Jr. (Neither Wilson nor DeForest were members
of the war council.)

Only a week after returning to America, Davison had an interview with
President Wilson at the White House, at which he outlined his plan for creating a "virile effective international Red Cross."[15] Wilson's reaction was extremely positive: He liked the idea of the Red Cross societies of the world
being reorganized "under the not too obtrusive leadership of the American
Red Cross" and hoped that such an enterprise "would react back upon the
American people with something of the same sort of stimulation that they
received from the work which they did for actual war"; he urged Davison to

travel to Geneva as quickly as possible and to confer with members of the ICRC, or as Wilson put it, the "rather amiable gentlemen" who made up "the present international committee."[16] At Davison's request, Wilson provided him with a letter asking him "to come to France at an early date for the purpose of conferring with me and others there as to the international relations and cooperations of the Red Cross."[17]

Encouraged by the president's support, Davison spent considerable time explaining his plan to William E. Rappard of the Swiss legation in Washington; Rappard, a recently appointed member of the ICRC, had arrived in Washington in June of 1917 carrying a letter of introduction from Gustave Ador to President Wilson.[18] Rappard apparently greeted the proposal with enthusiasm and, somewhat rashly perhaps, assured Davison of the cooperation of the ICRC in Geneva.[19] Convinced of the need to move quickly, Davison threw himself into activity. After securing the approval of the war council of the ARC and the agreement of his associates at the Morgan house, he made his second Atlantic crossing in a month; scarcely had he disembarked before he was explaining his idea to Sir Arthur Stanley of the British Red Cross.[20] Stanley was personally sympathetic and was, in any case, grateful to Davison for the handsome donation that the BRCS had received from the war council of the ARC earlier in the year. However, his freedom of action had been somewhat circumscribed by the decision taken in March, 1919 to maintain and promote postwar cooperation between the BRCS and the Order of St. John. The expanded peacetime activity that Davison contemplated, he explained, would require an amendment to the charter of the BRCS.

Meanwhile, President Wilson, now in Paris himself to attend the peace conference, began to wax eloquent about the future of the Red Cross and its place in the new international order that he expected to create:

> As the Geneva Convention . . . was born of war and for service in time of war [he wrote to Davison], what is more fitting than that at this time there should be a re-birth of that convention born of peace and for service in time of peace? . . . Nothing could be more appropriate than that at the earliest possible moment there should be held a meeting of the Red Cross organizations of the world—excepting those of the Central Powers, who could be given an opportunity to participate after peace shall have been declared—to consider, develop and adopt plans which should result in relieving the suffering and promoting the betterment of the peoples of the earth. . . . The experience of the American Red Cross has clearly demonstrated during the war that incalculable good could be accomplished by organized voluntary endeavor not alone in war but in peace. I feel with you that it is not only our opportunity but our obligation to place our experience and the results of our efforts at the disposal of the other Red Cross organizations of the world. . . . I am sure, therefore, that our friends, the distinguished gentlemen having responsibility for the conduct of the International Red Cross, will avail of the opportunity themselves which your plan affords, to

summon a conclave which should prove inspiring and result in benefits to the world.[21]

Wilson's purple prose reveals that he appears to have been under the impression—as perhaps Davison was, too—that the projected world conference of Red Cross societies would be competent to produce a new or revised Geneva Convention; in fact, it could have produced no more than a draft because such an agreement would have required a full diplomatic congress composed of representatives of the states party to the 1906 Convention. This went well beyond the sort of postwar Red Cross conference that the ICRC had suggested in its circular.

Over the next few weeks, more pieces of the plan fell into place: With Wilson's approval, Colonel Edward House approached Lloyd George and the other Allied leaders while Davison spoke to the leaders of the Allied Red Cross societies.[22] Keeping to his original intention, Davison went to Cannes to develop his plans; the necessary money for this enterprise was readily available thanks to a special appropriation of $2.5 million granted him by the ARC war council.[23] On 25 January, Colonel House wrote from Paris that the Allied governments were lining up behind the plan and that he (House) would be discussing this "splendid" idea with Gustave Ador, who was to see him the following day.[24] On 1 February, Davison formed a "Committee of Red Cross Societies," representing the United States, Britain, France, Italy, and Japan; its stated purpose was to prepare and present "to the Red Cross Societies of the whole world an enlarged program of action in the general interest of humanity."[25] The time had come for direct talks with the ICRC, and Davison telegraphed to arrange a meeting of the "Cannes committee" with the ICRC in Geneva on 12 and 13 February.[26]

Members of the ICRC were understandably concerned about both the scope of Davison's proposal and the seemingly breakneck speed with which he expected it to be implemented. This was by no means the first time in the history of the Red Cross that someone had proposed transforming it into an international welfare society, and the ICRC had always refused to endorse such a change on the grounds that the original and special purpose of the Red Cross—assistance to sick and wounded soldiers—would easily become lost amid the potentially countless rival claims for support. Davison's dream of a peacetime Red Cross that would provide relief in cases of disaster, pestilence, or famine *and* work for the prevention and eradication of disease was far more sweeping in its scope than the modest expansions of Red Cross activity that had been proposed—and usually rejected—in the past; indeed, it resembled nothing so much as Rudolf Virchow's searching critique of the priorities of the movement at the Berlin conference in 1869.

Moreover, the manner in which Davison was proceeding smacked too much of steamroller tactics. Without denigrating the considerable achievements of the ARC during the recent war, it was entirely possible not to share

Davison's blithe assumption that this record gave him the right to reorganize the work of Red Cross societies throughout the world. The ICRC knew better than to regard the Committee of Red Cross Societies as anything other than an American operation in disguise: Davison was its heart and soul as well as its banker. He seemed to expect that "the amiable gentlemen of Geneva" would welcome his plans, endorse in advance whatever proposals the Cannes committee chose to elaborate, and call upon the Red Cross societies of the world—excluding, for the moment, those of the Central Powers—to endorse them at a conference that the ICRC would call solely for that purpose. Such arrogance could not be permitted to carry the day.

Nevertheless, President Wilson's open and enthusiastic support for Davison's scheme put the members of the ICRC in a quandary: Despite their reservations, they could scarcely appear to be uncooperative without appearing to set themselves against the tide of postwar optimism. In any case, Rappard had already led the Americans to believe that there would be no difficulties in Geneva, and the ICRC itself had already hailed President Wilson "as the indefatigable defender, on the world stage, of the principles of humanity and justice which it [the ICRC] itself labours to make prevail."[27] Moreover, it was impossible to ignore Davison's argument about the need to move quickly in order to take advantage of the atmosphere of cooperation generated by the end of the war; the ICRC had said very nearly the same thing in its circular letter. Thus if members of the ICRC were inclined to reject Davison's plan as hasty and ill-conceived, prudence dictated that they do so with the greatest tact and restraint.

When Davison and his associates arrived in Geneva on 12 February, they were received by members of the ICRC not at their cramped wartime office but at the Athénée, a site that was chosen, no doubt, because of the opportunity it provided to give the brash Mr. Davison a much needed history lesson.[28] Members of the ICRC wished to make it clear that they were no temporary wartime creation, invented only so that belligerents could communicate with one another through a neutral intermediary; rather they were the trustees of the Red Cross movement, the direct heirs of its founders, who had collectively accumulated nearly sixty years of activity and experience on its behalf. They were not about to be cast aside merely because some influential Americans had recently discovered the potential of Red Cross organizations. For this occasion Gustave Ador, conscious of his position as Moynier's nephew and successor as president of the ICRC, returned from his official duties in Berne.

The meeting, though cordial, did not go well. The only thing that all could agree on was that a reconsideration of the role of Red Cross societies was both timely and necessary. Beyond that, agreement stopped. Davison wanted the members of the ICRC to endorse the proposals of his Committee of Red Cross Societies; this they refused to do, on the grounds that such an endorsement would preempt the invitation that had already been sent to all national societies asking them to make suggestions for the future work of the Red Cross. True, Davison's proposals enjoyed the apparent support of five national societies, but from the Genevans' point of view, they should be taken no more—or less—seriously than proposals advanced by any five national societies. Davison wanted the ICRC to call an international conference immediately, without including the national societies of the Central Powers; this the ICRC refused to do on the grounds that the universalism of the Red Cross precluded the very idea of exclusion, temporary or otherwise. Davison stated that his committee intended to submit its proposals to a conference of experts to be held at Cannes as soon as practicable; the ICRC replied that, although the five associated societies could seek whatever expert advice they chose, the ICRC would continue to withhold its endorsement and would leave it to the five to persuade other national societies to support the Cannes proposals at the international conference.[29] Faced with this unexpectedly intransigent response, Davison and his associates then formally withdrew all of the proposals that they had put to the ICRC and asked the latter to refrain from mentioning the formation of the Committee of Red Cross Societies in any forthcoming communications to the national societies.[30] As a gesture of goodwill after all its refusals, the ICRC did agree that it would take steps to convene an international Red Cross conference within thirty days of the signing of the peace treaty. Davison's group retired, not without some disappointment, to Paris to further plans for convening the conference of public health experts in Cannes.

On 13 February, while the Allied Red Cross representatives were still in Geneva, the ICRC issued an appeal concerning the conference.[31] One of the most carefully worded documents ever issued by the ICRC, the appeal contrived to suggest that Davison and his associates were simply responding with enthusiasm to the idea of an enlarged, peacetime Red Cross, for which the ICRC now credited its own circular of 27 November, 1918. The visit to Geneva by representatives of the five Red Cross societies was described as an opportunity "to explore, with the International Committee, the best means of attaining the immediate goal. In this visit, where a complete agreement was noted between the International Committee and the Red Crosses, the questions which will be taken up at the Conference were examined."[32] The ICRC stated, correctly, that the five Red Cross societies had their own agenda for peacetime health work: The struggle against tuberculosis and malaria and the promotion of child health, hygiene, and public health. True to its own principles, however, it followed up by pointing out that other national societies might be especially interested in the plight of victims of war or in the formation of nurses corps and that all were welcome to send their suggestions. As if to emphasize its distance from the Davison proposals, the ICRC noted that "there is no question of providing ready-made solutions which will be imposed by a vote" and announced unambiguously that the task of leading the way to this "Red Cross of Peace" would become part of its own work, which it was beginning by calling the conference. Thus the appeal underlined the primacy of the ICRC while studiously avoiding the real differences that had surfaced at the Geneva meeting, thus giving the rest of the Red Cross world a quite misleading impression of harmony.

It is not that members of the ICRC were against all change; it is rather that they—understandably—mistrusted any innovations over which they might lose control. Even Marguerite Cramer, who, like Rappard, was not unsympathetic to a broader peacetime program, warned that the Red Cross could never hope to become a panacea for all of the woes of humanity.[33] Yet Davison himself was so full of his own desire to create a "real" and "virile" Red Cross that he was unable to appreciate the legitimate apprehension that his proposals caused. Seen from the Genevan perspective, they threatened to relegate the ICRC to the limited and occasional role of wartime neutral intermediary; they threatened to replace the ICRC's moral leadership of the international movement with some as yet undefined but probably representative body; they threatened to alter drastically the traditional focus of the Red Cross on soldiers and victims of war; and, most ominous of all, perhaps, they implied that what had been for more than half a century a successful voluntary organization of dedicated amateurs now needed the leadership and guidance of technical and professional experts in public health. Indeed, one could say that Davison's disappointment with his reception in Geneva is a measure of how little he understood the role that the ICRC had played in history of the Red Cross movement.

For the moment, of course, he kept his disappointment to himself; publicly, he remained as optimistic as ever. Immediately upon his return to Paris, Davison invited the international press corps, as well as members of the political, diplomatic, and cultural elite, to a dinner at the Palais d'Orsay Hotel on 21 February, at which he announced the formation of the Committee of Red Cross Societies and described the plan for a broader peacetime organization of an international Red Cross.[34] Naturally he gave no hint that the response to his plan in Geneva had been anything other than cordial and explained that the purpose of the conference soon to be held in Cannes was to formulate an extended program of Red Cross activity that would be submitted to the forthcoming Geneva conference. Davison went on to outline his hope of presenting to this conference "a program formulated by the recognized talent of the world as the last word" for combating infectious diseases and improving hygiene, sanitation, and nursing. He envisioned the establishment at Geneva of a permanent international agency to serve as a medium of communication among the Red Cross societies of the world and also the formation of "a bureau devoting itself not to the actual study of human disease but to the coordination of the results of such studies."[35] Had such a bureau been in operation in 1918, Davison pointed out, it might have been possible to plan a campaign against the current influenza epidemic and hence to have saved many lives. Thus, he concluded, the press should not only help to promote public support for the scheme but realize that the plan needed to be "put into immediate and practical execution. . . . We will submit a proposal which should cause this plan to function within six months."[36] To lend further support and credibility to the enterprise, Davison had (with the assistance of Colonel House) secured from President Wilson a telegram that he proceeded to read aloud; the message stated that Wilson was "heartily in accord with the steps now being taken" and expressed his hope that Davison's plans "may have the support and active assistance of all governments and of all peoples before whom they may be brought."[37] Those attending the dinner also received a three-page memorandum outlining Davison's plans, copies of which, he announced, had been sent to all of the Allied and most of the neutral Red Cross societies.[38]

This was a completely new approach to Red Cross leadership: The ICRC did not believe in such contrived exercises in public relations. With his grand plans, his backing from Wilson, his conference of experts, and his pointed comments on the influenza epidemic, Davison was deliberately creating high expectations about what the Red Cross might achieve in the future, expectations that depended for their success not only upon the as yet undeclared support of other Red Cross societies but also upon the speedy convening of the next Geneva conference. Having raised such grand expectations, Davison was unlikely to let obstacles stand in his way. Doubtless a full report on these events was sent back to Geneva by Rappard and Alfred Gautier, whom Gustave Ador had prudently sent to Paris to keep the ICRC informed about the actions of this determined and unpredictable American.[39]

Seizing the Golden Moment

With plans for the Cannes conference well under way—it was to convene at the Çercle Nautique (Yacht Club) on 1 April—Davison began to reconsider his course of action. When he had first conceived the idea of an expanded peacetime Red Cross, he had assumed that its realization would necessitate the drafting of a new Geneva Convention.[40] This assumption had since been fortified by a legal opinion from J. B. Moore, an eminent American authority on international law.[41] However, the ICRC's insistence that all national societies without exception be invited meant that such a conference could not be convened until after the peace treaty had been signed. Moreover, in late February, an additional problem emerged: Because of the strength of anti-German feeling in Britain, it now appeared that the desired conference in Geneva might be delayed not weeks or months but perhaps years.

On 24 February, Davison received a letter marked "Private and Confidential" from Sir Arthur Lawley of the British Red Cross, the contents of which must have caused him some foreboding:

The Red Cross Council met today to discuss the proposals made in the Statement which you presented on Friday night in Paris, & while—generally speaking—your conception of the part which in future the Red Cross is to play in the world commends itself to that august body, discussion for the moment centres round the invitation issued by the International Committee & particularly the question of the inclusion of the Central Powers as participants in the Conference. Some of our people take the line that it is impossible for them to meet the Germans even after the peace is signed, seeing that they have grossly violated the Geneva Convention & are "beyond the pale." Whatever decision may be come to concerning that particular matter it is pretty certain that our Red Cross Society will raise the point in whatever answer they may send to the International Committee at Geneva. I feel pretty confident that the Geneva Committee will stick resolutely to their attitude of strict neutrality, so there may be some lengthy parlaying before even the Conference is assembled or at all events before the British Red Cross Soc[iet]y decides to accept the invitation. Our people will I think fall into line with you all right on the general question of extending the scope of Red Cross activities during peace time & will be glad to see our Charter amended to that end. We may find them a bit sticky concerning the assembling of experts at Cannes in the near future. [Sir Arthur] Stanley is taking steps to sound some of our friends quietly before there is any question of an official invitation being issued. . . . Both he & I are a bit anxious lest our Council should feel they are being "rushed" (this I have already told you) though they know they are not committed to any definite policy or to any cut & dried scheme. They are *all* of them anxious to get our Charter amended so as to enable us to undertake peacetime activities. The rest will follow![42]

Lawley's timely warning was yet another large spoke in Davison's wheel. With considerable restraint, he replied that he was "a bit disappointed" and that "if the world is ever to become normal we must accept a peace, when signed, as a peace in fact and not a peace in theory"; he also reiterated his belief that his plan "must be done now if it is going to be done at all."[43] Privately, he must have wondered what would become of his grand scheme if the French Red Cross were to take the same attitude as the British about postwar meetings with the Germans.

Just at this moment, when the universalism of the Red Cross seemed to be both a blessing and a curse, Davison was reminded that there was no firmer friend of his cause than Woodrow Wilson, to whom he had written at length about his plans. Replying on 26 February, the President once again expressed his fervent support for Davison's plan: "Nothing could be more appropriate. . . . I know of nothing more in harmony with the spirit of the time and more important to the future than unification in common effort for the welfare of all mankind. . . . In your undertaking I wish you would feel that . . . if there is anything I can do to assist I shall regard it as a privilege."[44] Of course there was something that Wilson could do. If Davison was right that his scheme had to be realized immediately or not at all, then the president could be immensely useful. Wilson had, after all, persuaded the other Allied leaders to express their support individually for an enlarged peacetime Red Cross; what if he were—at Davison's request—to persuade them to go further and lend the official backing of the League of Nations to the scheme? The Covenant of the League of Nations, Davison knew, was being negotiated at that very moment as part of the agenda of the peace conference: Perhaps a way could be found to tie the new international Red Cross organization to the League of Nations by recognizing its existence in the covenant itself. What made this course of action particularly attractive was that Davison could then launch his scheme immediately, without waiting for the emotions of the Allies to cool down sufficiently for them to be able to meet their former enemies at the Geneva conference.

Davison had many times in the past spoken of his rejuvenated international Red Cross as a sort of humanitarian counterpart to the League of Nations. However, he had always assumed that it would derive its authority from a renegotiated Geneva Convention; not until this moment did he conceive of the possibility of an organic connection between the League of Nations and an international Red Cross.[45] Nevertheless, if Wilson would play his part, the golden moment could still be seized and Davison would still be able to create his "real" International Red Cross.

In a lengthy and carefully worded letter to Wilson, Davison explained the situation in which he found himself. He began by noting that "your various statements relative to the League of Nations might have been taken as a presentation of the purposes of our Red Cross program. It harmonizes in every particular and can be made an immediate demonstration of the spirit of your conception and purposes."[46] He then proceeded to explain the problems that had recently emerged regarding the holding of a Red Cross conference in Geneva, in particular the unwillingness of the British and French to meet the Germans, whom he understood were not to be admitted to the League of Nations for some time after the peace accord was signed. In this situation, Davison continued, there were only two alternatives: Either postpone the Geneva conference indefinitely, which would be tantamount to abandoning his plan for a reorganized international Red Cross; or, as he delicately put it, "to proceed in some relation to the League of Nations."[47] Without actually saying so, Davison made it clear that he had really given up on the ICRC and now saw Wilson's League of Nations as his only hope:

> We are largely committed to the [ICRC], assuming of course that they will play their part and assume the responsibility. For your information, I have been much disappointed in them. I find the organization very weak and without imagination or courage. . . . [Because of recent events] we are fairly well along in our plan with the [ICRC]. But if conditions are to be different than I anticipated, I feel the responsibility of reconsidering this fundamental point in our plan. As our endeavors and purposes are exactly those of the League of Nations, it is most natural that we should be allied to the League [of Nations], to effect which would not necessarily conflict with the [ICRC] as it now exists. It could function

as heretofore in case of war, but it would amount to little in times of peace, which however has been the case heretofore. There is one important consideration, however, and that is that the Red Cross was born in Geneva and for sentimental reasons it would be quite too bad to have a development which would rob Geneva or Switzerland of its prestige in this particular. On the other hand, as a new world is being formed and precedents count for little, the question is forced upon us, would it be better to organize a League of Red Cross Societies to be composed of the Red Cross societies of the nations constituting the League of Nations, to be domiciled at the home of the League of Nations [which was itself yet to be decided—JFH], its organization to be modeled after the League of Nations?[48]

This letter Davison sent to Colonel House, along with a covering note that asked House, should he approve of the idea, to put it to Wilson for a decision. "In the letter I have endeavored to make clear the one question which must be decided. . . . I shall need an authoritative word from him to use with my Committee, if we are to change our program. While there would be some embarrassment in making a change, of course there would be no doubt about its being done. While it is not essential that this point be settled immediately, we should make our decision within the next two or three weeks."[49] Needless to say, Davison did not say anything publicly about the possibility of an alliance with the League of Nations; nor did he, so far as one can tell, discuss the idea formally with the Committee of Red Cross Societies. The ICRC was purposely left completely in the dark. With the Cannes conference scheduled to meet from 1 to 10 April, Davison was obviously hoping for a positive response from Wilson before the conference had finished its business. His personal timetable still called for returning to New York in late May, as he reaffirmed in a letter to J. P. Morgan.[50]

A favorable response from Wilson was almost a certainty, although the president was not yet in a position to commit the other Allied leaders. What seems clear, however, is that the program of Davison's organization and its future role in the world of the Red Cross were far less important to the peacemakers in Paris than its immediate impact as a practical demonstration of the new spirit of cooperation on which Wilson's advisers had staked their hopes. One of them, Professor Charles Seymour, wrote to Davison in mid-March about the response of his colleagues to the plan for an international Red Cross organization:

> Perhaps the chief germ of trouble in the past has been not so much the lack of a mechanical international organization, but the lack of this international spirit. From this point of view, it seems incontestable that your conception is the most important step as yet taken towards the elimination of international conflicts, and that your plan trebles the chance of success offered by the League of Nations. . . . Everyone whom I have seen here, whether at the [Hotel] Crillon, or the Quai d'Orsay has felt the grandeur and importance of your conception, and is thoroughly enthusiastic about it.[51]

Wilson himself, anxious to capitalize on such a concrete demonstration of the benefits of internationalism, quickly sent Davison a positive response, in which he proposed that they "tie the Red Cross up in some proper way with the League of Nations and arrange for the admission of other nations to the Red Cross International Organization when they are admitted to the League of Nations."[52] Meanwhile, Davison had the Cannes committee's lawyer, Chandler Anderson, prepare alternative drafts of an article concerning the Red Cross that could be included in the Covenant of the League of Nations; these he sent on to Colonel House.[53] Both drafts cited the improvement of public health as the chief, though not the only, goal of the Red Cross; one referred to "the principle of international cooperation through the action of national Red Cross organizations" while the other specifically mentioned an "International Red Cross League."[54] Presumably the contents of these draft articles were discussed by House and Davison when they met on 27 March, just before Davison left Paris for the conference in Cannes.[55]

On 28 March, Rappard, who had learned from House what was now being contemplated, reported on these developments to the ICRC, and it was at this point that the alarm bells started to ring in Geneva. After their initial meetings with Davison, the members of the ICRC had expected him to pause and consider whether his plan might need to be rethought. Indeed, they had already received from the council of the British Red Cross Society a lengthy memorandum that expressed reservations about the scope, speed, and propriety of the Davison plan.[56] If the Red Cross societies of the other Allied powers reacted in the same way as the British, the ICRC might reasonably have expected the Davison initiative to grind to a halt. What they had not reckoned on was Davison's audacity, which combined well with Wilson's desire for a practical demonstration of idealism. Members of the ICRC were well aware of President Wilson's favorable attitude toward Davison's scheme, but it had never occurred to them that these two Americans would devise a plan to reorganize the Red Cross under the aegis of the League of Nations without the participation of the ICRC or the approval of an international Red Cross conference.

The immediate issue was the timing of the Geneva conference, which Davison's committee had asked the ICRC to call on 5 May, provided that the peace treaty had been signed by then. The ICRC had assumed that the Allies would ensure that the peace treaty contained a clause requiring Germany to repudiate its wartime violations of the Red Cross and, once the treaty had been signed, that a fully international Red Cross conference could be held.[57] However, when Rappard asked Colonel House about the American government's attitude, the latter replied that "in view of the mood that he had noted on the part of some of the Allies, though deploring it himself, he thought it better in any case to convene two successive and separate conferences for the Societies of the Allies and neutral countries on the one hand and for the Societies of the Central Powers on the other."[58] Not without some irritation, the

ICRC wired Davison in Cannes: "Your Committee has just asked us to convene this conference for May 5, and we accepted. Now we are told that even if the peace treaty had been signed by then, the conference could not be a universal one. Will you please indicate very clearly to us what the committee of which you are chairman wishes us to do at this time?"[59] Davison, unwilling to show his hand until he had received further assurances from Wilson about the League of Nations covenant, replied cagily: "Owing to a recent and important development, I am unable for the moment to reply more fully to your telegram, much as I regret this"; however he invited the ICRC to send delegates to Cannes in order to keep it abreast of developments.[60]

Meanwhile, Davison was moving ahead by leaps and bounds. Before leaving Paris, he sent a confidential telegram to colleague Thomas Cochran at the Morgan house asking him to bring together several of Davison's closest associates from the war council and the ARC commission in Europe in order to "give them picture situation here."[61] Its content reveals that the rationale for a new Red Cross organization, as well as its basic structure and direction, had already taken clear shape in his mind before the conference of experts convened in Cannes.

> The movement [for a new international Red Cross organization] has assumed serious and large importance and the more clearly the project is understood, the more its importance is realized, particularly in view of the daily increasing distress in Europe. On every hand one hears words of grave concern regarding the destitution and increasing unrest throughout all Eastern Europe. In fact, many are fearful it may be too late to make peace even though terms shall be written and signed. Aside from the action of Governments in supplying food, the proposed agency is the only one in the world to even contribute to the alleviation of distress, and is recognized by those familiar with the conditions as the most potent agency with which to fight the flames. . . . Plan of organization now proposed will be similar to that of organization of League of Nations, but there must be a Director General located at Geneva, who would have responsibility similar to that of [ARC] Commissioner of France. There would be under him two general departments: the Scientific and the Relief. . . . You will appreciate the importance of securing the right man for Director General. His essential qualities must be character and executive ability, in addition, desirable he should be diplomatic, have good presence and able to speak French, latter not absolutely essential. Confidentially, I personally would give this man any part of fifty thousand dollars a year for two or three years, if such a man can be found in America to undertake the work for that period. . . . There must be just the man for the job. Please find him and cable me.[62]

This was as close as Davison ever came to providing a political rationale for his humanitarianism. Not a word was said about Bolshevism or the Russian Revolution, but in March, 1919, those at the Morgan house knew exactly what conclusions to draw from Davison's fears about the spreading flames of unrest in eastern Europe. Russia itself was already in the grip of revolution, but if an organization such as he proposed could help to keep the lands of the former

German and Austro-Hungarian Empires from the same fate, then the sooner it was created the better. In New York, the search began to find the right man to undertake the direction of the new agency.

Davison amazed the slow-moving Red Cross world by assembling his conference of experts in Cannes for ten days at the beginning of April. When the ICRC representatives arrived in the lavish surroundings of the Çercle Nautique, they found themselves surrounded by the world's leading authorities in public health, epidemiology, sanitary science, hygiene, and nursing. Davison had invited more than fifty of the most illustrious medical and scientific names of the day, among them Aldo Castellani from Italy; Émile Roux and Albert Calmette from France; and Sir Arthur Newsholme, Sir Ronald Ross, and Henry Kenwood from Great Britain. The American delegation was a veritable who's who of medicine, public health, and philanthropy, including Hermann Biggs, Hugh Cumming, Emmett Holt, Wycliffe Rose, Frederick Russell, Richard Pearson Strong, and William H. Welch. In a separate nursing section of the conference, social reformer Lilian Wald from America joined seven recognized leaders of military nursing from Britain, France, and Italy.

Davison's invitation (and the promise of all expenses paid) had brought together virtually all those who were recognized as having been at the forefront of the bacteriological revolution, the new public health, modern medical education, and scientific philanthropy.[63]

The Cannes conference did exactly what Davison wanted: It put the scientific stamp of approval on his vision of the future. Its participants—none of whom had much familiarity with the workings of Red Cross societies—implicitly shared his belief that the recent war had proved the Red Cross could be "an agency for good of unparalleled force and power" and were certain that "for the prevention of disease and the betterment of the health and the general welfare of the people in all countries . . . the potential usefulness of the Red Cross . . . is unlimited. . . . No other organization is so well prepared to undertake these great responsibilities at the present time."[64] Accordingly, the conference endorsed the idea that an association or league of national Red Cross societies should be organized and that an international bureau of hygiene and public health should be attached to it. Strong and Castellani, well known for their work in containing the typhus epidemic in Serbia in 1915, were the foremost advocates of the formation of this bureau, but they were largely preaching to the converted. An emergency campaign against typhus and the rapid development of child welfare work were singled out as the two highest priorities for the new bureau to undertake; in addition, the conference drew up a series of resolutions and memoranda relating to preventive medicine, tuberculosis, malaria, venereal diseases, and nursing to indicate "some of the lines of activity which the new organization may wisely follow."[65] Once the bureau was established, it would be expected to formulate programs in other fields, such as mental hygiene, industrial hygiene, foods, and nutrition. Further resolutions called upon Red Cross societies everywhere to encourage "wise Public Health Legislation and efficient Public

6.3 The Cannes Conference, April 1919. Highlighted are: *Foreground:* Henry P. Davison. *Seated, left to right:* Hans Morgenthau, Richard Pearson Strong, Emmett Holt, Émile Roux, William H. Welch, Sir Arthur Newsholme (partially obscured), Sir Ronald Ross, Hermann Biggs (partially obscured). *Standing, left to right:* Alicia Lloyd-Still, Julia Stimson, A. W. Gill (all delegates to the Nursing Section); Frederick Russell, Wycliffe Rose, Hugh Cumming, Henry Kenwood, Aldo Castellani.

Health Administration"; to prepare suitable plans and designs for "proper housing for workingmen"; and to erect as war memorials buildings that could be used as health and community centers.[66] Seemingly, no aspect of health and hygiene, whether personal or public, was to be left unattended.

While the program was still being formulated by the experts, Davison moved closer to organizing his "real" International Red Cross. He evidently disregarded a message that reached him on 3 April, indicating that the ICRC was now willing to fall in with House's suggestion and hold two successive Red Cross conferences, for the Allies and the Central Powers respectively.[67] Four days later, Davison announced to the assembled experts that news had been received from Paris that—at Wilson's urging—the Covenant of the League of Nations would contain the following article (number 25): "The members of the League agree to encourage and promote the establishment and co-operation of duly authorized voluntary national Red Cross associations having as purposes the improvement of health, the prevention of disease and the mitigation of suffering throughout the world."[68] On the initiative of Biggs and Welch, delegates replied with a telegram to the Allied leaders, setting out graphically the threat posed by the typhus epidemic already raging in central Europe and offering the services of Davison's Committee of Red Cross Societies to fight the epidemic and provide relief to those stricken by famine.[69]

As soon as he learned the news from Paris, Davison decided to present the ICRC with a fait accompli. He told Edouard Naville, who had come to Cannes, that he had decided to proceed immediately to transform his committee into a "League of Red Cross Societies" without waiting for the proposed Red Cross conference in Geneva.[70] His associates in New York had already found "the right man" for the job of heading the new League: Frederick Lane, then Wilson's secretary of interior. On 9 April, Davison sent a long cable to Lane, in which he described his plans for the League and offered him the position of director-general; he mentioned the original plan for a Red Cross conference in Geneva after the peace but noted that "recent developments made it advisable to proceed with organization irrespective any such conference."[71] The outline that he gave Lane indicated how far his plans had taken shape: The organization would likely be based in Geneva; it would be open by invitation to Allied and neutral Red Cross societies; its board of governors would be composed of representatives of the five founding members, "which would probably control indefinitely but in any event for five years"; its staff would be divided into medical, relief, and publicity departments, the last aimed at encouraging the development of Red Cross societies around the world; its expenses for the first three years would be underwritten by the $2.5-million appropriation from the ARC, although member societies would be invited to contribute their fair share.[72] A few days later, he wrote to Wilson in Paris, telling him, "We are to adopt the name of 'The League of Red Cross Societies,' and our organization will be formulated

along the lines of the organization of the League of Nations."[73] He also informed the president that he and his associates believed Secretary of Interior
Lane to be the person best qualified for the position of director-general of
the new League and asked for Wilson's reaction.

So far Davison had largely had his own way, but

> on April 16th the British surprised us by demanding in a highly proper way the
> position of Director-General, saying that they would insist on my being Chair-
> man of the Board but they felt the next job should go to them. . . . This pleased
> me very much from one point of view as it places an increased responsibility
> upon them, but from the other point of view it is not quite as satisfactory be-
> cause the success of the endeavor depends largely upon the type of man who
> takes the job. The other members [of the Cannes committee of Red Cross soci-
> eties] were not at all in sympathy with the British but I stood with them and shall
> continue to do so up to May 5th, when they are to produce or we will then find
> the man. This accounts for the delay in connection with Lane.[74]

Davison was also forced to explain this awkward situation to President
Wilson, who had already indicated that, if necessary, he was prepared to release Lane from his cabinet position.[75] Concerning the motives of the
British, Sir Arthur Stanley later wrote that "we—the representatives of the
other four countries concerned in the matter—were unanimous in the opinion that the personnel of the League should be distributed among as many
countries as possible,"[76] but this was simply a retrospective justification; at
the time, he was afraid that the council of the British society, already extremely wary of Davison's plans, would decide that it was being stampeded by
the Americans and might refuse to endorse the creation of the League. The
prospect of appointing a British candidate to this important staff position
would ease these fears as well as reassure the leaders of the BRCS that the
new League would not attempt too much too soon. Within days, Stanley
proposed General Sir David Henderson, who had been a leading figure in
the Royal Air Force at the outbreak of the war and had subsequently directed
aircraft production.[77] Davison's confidential inquiries in the City of London
produced favorable references: Henderson was described in one letter as
"distinctly diplomatic and has vision . . . pushful in the best sense . . . the
most charming of men in appearance and manner, and I believe he would get
on well, not only with people of his own country but with foreigners."[78]
Without further ado, Davison told Stanley that Henderson was acceptable
and would be formally appointed after the committee's meeting on 5 May, at
which the formation of the League was to be officially announced.[79]

In the last days of April, the ICRC made a concerted attempt to dissuade
Davison and his associates from going ahead with their plans. On its behalf
Gustave Ador sent two letters, in which he raised numerous objections to the
immediate creation of the proposed League; to reinforce their effect he and
two other members of the ICRC traveled to Paris in order to meet with the

members of the Cannes committee. The ICRC's case consisted of four main points. First, the Red Cross movement had always been universal in scope, whereas membership in the proposed League was to be by invitation only; consequently, national societies that were duly recognized by the ICRC—such as the German Red Cross Society—could be excluded from the League. Second, whereas at international Red Cross conferences all national societies were equal, the proposed structure of the League's board of governors would make the societies of the wartime Allies far more influential than those of other states. Third, the future shape of the international Red Cross ought, according to the ICRC, to be decided at an international conference called for that purpose, not by the independent action of five societies, no matter how large their membership or how powerful their governments. Finally—and this was a very sore point—the ICRC feared that "they [the Red Cross societies] will ask if the creation of a new league destined to supplant the former International Red Cross is intended; or rather a separation of the duties of the Red Cross, reserving for the new Association charitable action in time of peace, and to the old charitable action in time of war."[80] Their greatest fear was that if the ICRC were relegated to the sidelines during periods of peace, then the future of the international Red Cross would be shaped by the League's board of governors, which was tilted heavily in favor of the Allies. American money, coupled with American ignorance of the history of the Red Cross elsewhere, were likely to force upon the movement a completely new shape and direction that might not be welcomed by some of the other national societies, let alone by the ICRC.

At the same time, the members of the ICRC were forced to concede that Davison was right about capturing "the golden moment"; recapitulating their interview, Davison wrote:

> President Ador and his confreres saw, without necessity of our arguments, the need for prompt action before the Red Cross momentum, accelerated by the experiences of war, shall have slackened, the ardor cooled, and the lessons learned from experience be forgotten. He and they fully appreciated our earnest desire to utilize what has been learned in the tragedy of war to mitigate the tragedies of disease and calamity. . . . It is our idea that now is a propitious moment to pursue this object . . . [through] the enlistment in the constructive measures of peace of the same degree of public devotion and sacrifice which mankind has hitherto devoted to the problems of war.[81]

Because they recognized the validity of Davison's argument about capitalizing on this unique period of postwar optimism, it was impossible for the ICRC, no matter how much it disliked the committee's plans, to dismiss them as unworthy or wrongheaded. Who knew for certain how much time might have to elapse before the peace treaty was signed and before the Red Cross societies of the Allies declared themselves willing to sit down with their former enemies or what chances there might be then for approving an extended program of peacetime activity? Besides, although the members of the ICRC insisted that such a major change ought to be decided on at an international conference, they had no legal power to force the five national societies to postpone action. As Davison's legal adviser, Chandler Anderson, correctly pointed out, the ICRC exercised those powers that had been bestowed on it from time to time at international conferences by the national societies themselves; and if the latter were competent to do that they were also competent to create and empower some other body.[82] The ICRC, which had always opposed any formal, constitutional definition of its relationship to the national societies or to the international conferences, now found itself hoist on its own petard.

Despite these last-minute efforts, Davison forged ahead. On 5 May, the members of the Committee of Red Cross Societies, meeting in Paris, signed the "Articles of Association" that created the League of Red Cross Societies, composed initially of the five Allied Red Cross societies; other societies could join with the approval of the League's board of governors, which Davison himself would chair.[83] The articles of association set out the purposes of the League as follows:

1. To encourage and promote in every country in the world the establishment and development of a duly authorized voluntary national Red Cross organization, having as purposes the improvement of health, the prevention of disease, and the mitigation of suffering throughout the world, and to secure the co-operation of such organizations for these purposes.
2. To promote the welfare of mankind by furnishing a medium for bringing within the reach of all the peoples the benefits to be derived from present known facts and new contributions to science and medical knowledge and their application.
3. To furnish a medium for co-ordinating relief work in case of great national or international calamities.[84]

In a press release announcing the League's formation, Davison harkened back to the assumptions underlying the intention of its founders

to devise an agency which could adequately cope with the world's problems of disease and disaster. From the outset it was clear to us all that there was no institution in the World so well adapted to this task as the Red Cross, because of the peculiar hold which it has upon the hearts of all peoples . . . ; because of the amazing development of its powers in the recent war; because of the anxiety of its membership not to lose the opportunity for service when war service is no longer needed; because, in short, of the consensus of opinion medical and lay that the health problems of the world can never be solved by Doctors alone nor by Governments alone but must enlist the hearty volunteer cooperation of the peoples themselves, and that no organisation can mobilise peoples of divergent views as can the Red Cross.[85]

As a statement of the beliefs and aspirations of the founders of the League, this cannot be bettered: Because peoples and governments had rallied round national Red Cross societies during the war, the Red Cross was therefore ideally suited to become a universal agency for coping with the problems of disaster and disease. The logic of this argument seemed to Davison and his associates to be unshakable, and none of the medical experts summoned to Cannes—many of whom were aware of the various Red Cross efforts already under way to control disease in eastern Europe—thought of questioning its premise. In reality, however, the unprecedented growth of Red Cross work in the belligerent states owed far more to popular patriotism and militarism than to any sense of universal obligation to suffering humanity. For the founders of the League to assume that governments and Red Cross societies—especially those of the victorious Allies—could or would mobilize their citizens to conquer disease and disaster throughout the world with as much enthusiasm as they had shown for conquering their enemies on the battlefield was a non sequitur of truly gigantic proportions.

And what of the ICRC? Article 1 of the new League's articles of association recognized the ICRC for having stimulated and promoted "for so many years" relief work in time of war and continued:

> It is contemplated that this League will work in complete accord and co-operation with the International Committee, that by supplementing the war-time activity of the International Committee with an intelligent peace-time program it will prove a natural complement to the International Committee, that this co-operation will in due time lead to an organic union with the International Committee, whose continuing functions are essential to the world, and that as a result of this combined effort the best traditions of the Red Cross will be maintained and made of ever-widening usefulness to the peoples of the world.[86]

This statement was obviously meant to reassure the ICRC that there was still to be a place for them in the Red Cross world. In an unusual display of tact, Davison even ensured that the published version of the articles of association bore on its cover the words "Geneva, Switzerland. May, 1919." However, there was another reason why the reference to an organic union was necessary; as President Wilson had already reminded Davison, his new organization "has no formal affiliation with the League of Nations."[87] Article 25 of the Covenant of the League of Nations neither recognized nor mentioned the League of Red Cross Societies; in fact it merely encouraged the cooperation of national societies along new lines. Reading between the lines of Wilson's letter, the message was that Davison's new organization would be forced to seek its legitimacy from the Red Cross world and not from the League of Nations.

The likelihood that a union between the new League and the ICRC would be easy to achieve was questionable because more was now at issue than the unwillingness of the Allies to meet their former enemies. Davison had deliberately disregarded the arguments put to him by the ICRC and, using his contacts with Wilson and House, had forged ahead according to his own timetable. Inevitably, such behavior would cause resentment in Geneva. Moreover, it was not difficult for anyone to see that in Davison's conception of an organic union the LRCS would become *the* international Red Cross in peacetime, with the ICRC limited to the role of wartime neutral intermediary. In any future negotiations about a union, the LRCS would expect to take over what the ICRC regarded as three of its most important peacetime functions—serving as the principal channel of communication among the central committees of the national societies, calling international conferences, and publishing the *Bulletin International*. Conceivably, even the composition of the ICRC and its role in certifying the status and credentials of national societies might also be opened up for discussion and revision. Potentially, there was a great deal at stake and, from the point of view of the ICRC, much that had to be protected.

The first step in warding off the challenge was to respond appropriately to Davison's audacious and well-publicized announcement of the formation of the League. Members of the ICRC may have deplored his action, but they could scarcely say so in public; after all, five important national societies had founded the LRCS, and there was no telling how many others might join it in the near future. Therefore it was vital that the ICRC speedily communicate with the other national societies in order to make it clear that its own existence had not been compromised by the creation of the League and to prevent any possible confusion about its own future. On 20 May, therefore, the ICRC issued a circular letter in which it described and responded to what had happened since its February meeting with the Committee of Red Cross Societies. Applauding the eagerness of Davison and his associates to begin their expanded program of peacetime activity, the ICRC was careful neither to welcome the formation of the League nor to approve the manner of its creation. Instead, the circular reaffirmed that the ICRC "remains the medium of all the Red Cross Societies, which it has always been by virtue of the successive decisions of the [international] Conferences. The organization now created should in no way supplant it, but rather spread and extend its activities."[88] Shrewdly, the ICRC quoted liberally from the conciliatory letter that Davison had sent to Geneva just before announcing the formation of the League; in it he had described it as "a plan of action whose way must be considered as purely transitory" and had affirmed that "the League is not a secession nor even a separation, but a convenient plan of operation for the immediate utilization of the spirit and resources of [the] Red Cross as developed during the war."[89] He also conceded that the League should become a universal body as soon as circumstances permitted. Having thus made their point, the members of the ICRC did not explicitly promise to cooperate with the League; rather they claimed to be studying what kind of support and collaboration they might be able to give it without compromising their principles of impartiality, balance, and neutrality. The circular concluded by reemphasizing the urgency of convening the proposed international conference as soon as the peace treaty had been signed and ratified.

Once again, the ICRC had composed a circular that skillfully combined reportage with editorial comment; as a perceptive senior member of the ARC commented after reading the circular, "the Committee is trying to be very careful to see that the Red Cross societies do not take the League too seriously."[90] Less temperate was the response of Stockton Axson, whom Davison had persuaded to serve as acting secretary-general of the LRCS; he counseled the new head of the ARC to "ignore it as it would not be possible to frame a reply which would be at one and the same time polite and truthful. This communication is wrong in purpose and false in its representations—some of the quotations from Mr. Davison's letter are wilful distortions."[91] Axson may well have been right about the distortions, but he overlooked the fact that Davison himself had been less than honest in his dealings with the ICRC. From the fulsome rhetoric of Davison's letters and speeches, one would never have discerned his underlying contempt for what he regarded as the feebleness of the ICRC or his compulsion to create a "real" and "virile" Red Cross. In Geneva, the golden moment no longer held much attraction; it had been displaced by Gustave Ador's growing conviction—never publicly stated—that the LRCS was an unwelcome and illegitimate child, foisted upon the Red Cross world by the urgency and determination of Harry Davison.

False Start

If Davison's beacon of hope was to shine forth for all to see, then the newly created LRCS had to do something big—and do it quickly—while it was still in the glare of publicity. Only a week after the formation of the LRCS had been announced, an opportunity seemed to land in its lap: The Allies, through their Supreme Economic Council (SEC), wrote to Sir David Henderson, asking to what extent the LRCS "would be prepared, as regards finance, supplies and personnel, to co-operate with them" to combat distress and prevent disease in eastern and southern Europe.[92] Davison, always keen on grand schemes and immediate action, instantly formulated a plan whereby the LRCS would "assume at once full control over and responsibility for all war emergency relief in Europe."[93] The plan had several components: First, the Allied armies would immediately donate all of their suitable surplus supplies to the Red Cross—either to the LRCS or the national societies; second, the ARC commission in Europe would close down, turning over all of its supplies and most of its personnel to the LRCS; third, the ARC was to give the LRCS close to $8 million, roughly the sum that its European commission might have expended on relief over the next year or so; finally, all member societies of the LRCS would be invited to contribute to this relief effort. With one bold stroke, Davison's plan would, as he saw it, meet the postwar emergency, launch the LRCS on the international scene, and enable the ARC to make a timely and graceful withdrawal from its extensive European responsibilities.

The day before he sailed for New York, Davison met with senior officials of the ARC European commission; one of those present noted in his diary that Davison "made the rather astonishing proposition that it [the LRCS] should take over the entire work of the American Red Cross in Europe, personnel, money, supplies, everything. This came as a great surprise to our commission which had been planning to go on with the work as long as such great need continues."[94] Davison left Europe hoping that with this plan he had ensured the success of the LRCS. Over the next few days, Henderson worked out with the Supreme Economic Council the details of implementation: The SEC would put at the disposal of the LRCS surplus medical and hospital equipment from the British and American armies; the LRCS, having obtained authorization from the governments of the affected countries, would send into the field medical and sanitary personnel to undertake a program of preventive measures to stop the spread of epidemic disease and would coordinate this work with that of the SEC's own relief committee.[95] Provided that the American and British governments and Red Cross societies would play their parts, Henderson wrote, the LRCS would be able to take advantage of this "extraordinary opportunity to manifest its value in the coordination of Red Cross relief where and when it was most needed."[96]

For this plan to work, the LRCS needed the cooperation of the governments, armies, and Red Cross societies of the Allies, but most of all it needed the approval and support of the ARC. The new head of the ARC, Livingston Farrand—former president of the University of Colorado—had been selected by Davison, who knew that he was sympathetic with Davison's grand plans for the LRCS. However, now that the ARC was back on a peacetime footing, its president did not possess the absolute powers exercised by the ARC war council; the ARC executive committee, rather than Farrand personally, would decide whether to accede to Davison's wishes and close down the European commission and transfer its supplies, personnel, and budget to the LRCS. Even before Davison arrived back from Paris, Farrand had received from Robert Olds, the ARC commissioner for Europe, a lengthy and carefully argued letter in which Olds questioned whether Davison's hastily devised plan was in the best interests of the ARC, other national Red Cross societies, and even, in the long run, of the LRCS itself.[97]

On 20 May, an impromptu meeting took place in Paris to consider the bombshell that Davison had dropped before his departure. It was attended by the three senior members of the European commission (Olds, George Rockwell, and Frank Persons); Stockton Axson as acting secretary-general of the LRCS; and Otis Cutler, Davison's close friend and troubleshooter, who had agreed to stay and "cover" for Davison until Henderson could get the various departments of the LRCS organized and running properly. The question that they addressed, Persons wrote afterwards, was this: "Shall the Red Cross Societies be asked to merge their resources and activities, or to participate in a co-operative enterprise under the auspices of the League?"[98] The latter was the strong preference of Olds and Persons, who convinced the others that this was indeed the best way for the LRCS to operate. This meeting had three important consequences. First, the ARC executive committee felt itself obliged to pay as much attention to the advice of Olds and his associates as to the wishes of Davison.[99] Second, the discussion stimulated Persons to draft a document that outlined, clearly and systematically, the ideal future relationship between the LRCS and its member societies; a document that in the absence of any rival or comparable blueprint from Davison was to become one of the cornerstones of LRCS policy.[100] Third, the forceful arguments of Olds and Persons convinced Axson that their perception of the situation was correct, and he summoned up the courage to write to Davison explaining his reasons for supporting them.[101]

Unlike Olds or Persons, Axson cannot be accused of having a vested interest in the survival of the European commission, and therefore his analysis of the situation merits special attention:

> To us [Olds, Persons, and Axson himself] the fundamental question as to whether the League is to be conceived of as primarily a co-ordinating or an operating agency, is in no way altered by the two present emergencies, namely (1) the desirability of getting A. R. C., as an independent concern, out of Europe as quickly as possible, and (2) the necessity of making the most effective possible provisions for handling the government supplies allocated to the League from the Supreme Economic Council. . . . We are convinced that, as the League can never be stronger than its constituent members, it would be dangerous to take steps, or make announcements, that would leave the American people to suppose that the A. R. C. has been "assimilated." . . . One of the things that most appealed to me in Mr. Persons' analysis, is the constant stress laid on the work of the League in promoting strong R. C. societies everywhere [and] . . . it would be unfortunate for its first activity to leave . . . the impression that this particular national society, to which the League owes its very existence, was being diminished and rendered anaemic by its alliance with the League.[102]

After noting Olds's fear that "the spirit and power" of the ARC would begin to wane if its work were taken over by the League, Axson observed that Olds's position

> may be taken to represent the views of many thoughtful and influential Americans who have been serving A. R. C. during the war. These people have a loyalty to the A. R. C. second only to their loyalty to their country. To many of them A. R. C. is a religion, to some the only religion they admit. They would, I believe, all be willing to have their A. R. C. join hands with other Red Cross societies in a world-embracing undertaking, but would not view complacently a plan which seemed to them to sap the independent life out of the A. R. C. . . . I am anxious that nothing shall be done that does not carry conviction, as well as elicit assent with the best of the A. R. C. constituency. Then there is the great rank and file of A. R. C. membership which I fear cannot follow if we run too fast.[103]

Axson, of course, was right about patriotic loyalty having infused the ARC; indeed, the war council's leadership of the ARC had unashamedly sought to capitalize on this loyalty. What Davison had not appreciated, however, was that since the Armistice the work of the European commission had come to embody what Olds called the "spirit and power" of the ARC. It was as if the Americans in Europe, in their enthusiasm for helping the civilian population of their wartime allies, had forgotten that the ARC had a peacetime role to play in the United States; they reacted as if Davison had proposed dismantling the ARC itself rather than recycling the personnel and supplies of its European commission. Part of the explanation for this strong reaction must lie in the fact that many of the leading figures in the European commission in 1919 had little memory of the prewar work of the ARC, and the rank and file who had volunteered for the ARC during the war—and who would be expected to contribute to future fund-raising drives—had none at all.

In the end, the ARC executive decided to approve Davison's plan for the distribution of relief through the LRCS but with several conditions attached, the most important being that this approval was subject to the LRCS receiving substantial donations of army supplies from the governments of both the United States and its allies. Although it agreed to set aside a fund of $8 million for subsequent appropriations to the LRCS, none of this money was to be made available until detailed information about the relief program was forthcoming and until it was clear how much financial support the LRCS would receive from the other member societies.[104] Farrand cabled Olds that these were the conditions under which ARC relief operations in Europe would be turned over to the LRCS as soon as possible.[105] Olds's lengthy reply to Farrand noted that Henderson and Strong—the latter soon to become medical director of the LRCS—had also subscribed to the view that any LRCS relief work should be carried on indirectly, "in all cases through Commissioners of National Societies serving virtually as mandatories of the League and with its advice and material assistance whenever necessary."[106] He reiterated Persons's argument that the "vital permanent object of League is promotion and development of native societies. Consequently, League should not be put in position of withdrawing when emergency work is ended. . . . [Instead it] should depend upon a commission of a national society for emergency relief which should be the first step in the whole program leading through development of native society to final assumption of all responsibility by native society. All this program should be under the general direction of League."[107] Since most of the relief work was expected to be undertaken in Poland and Czechoslovakia—new states that lacked national Red Cross societies—the Olds-Persons position made some sense. However, it also served as a useful screen for keeping the ARC's European presence alive, a matter of considerable importance to Olds.

There was no good reason why the LRCS itself could not have become directly involved in relief work, provided it had the funds and personnel, and certainly no reason for it to withdraw completely when the emergency had passed, because its objectives included the prevention of disease and the improvement of health as well as the coordination of relief and the creation of new Red Cross societies. The truth is that Olds was deeply suspicious of any intrusion upon the unique position of trust that he believed the ARC had come to enjoy in Europe because of its relief work. He was willing to cooperate with Herbert Hoover's American Relief Administration (ARA), which posed no threat to the autonomy of the ARC, but he was not about to abandon the field of Red Cross endeavor to a fledgling international agency such as the LRCS. As he wrote to Farrand, Europeans had come to trust the ARC:

> That deep feeling is universal and sincere. . . . The simple and easily understandable idea of a rich, powerful and obviously disinterested people coming to the help of those in distress everywhere has caught the imaginations of all classes of society. . . . They trust us because we do not represent any government and because they know we are absolutely disinterested. . . . If we take the American Red Cross as such, out of the field, something will be gone which cannot be replaced. The American Red Cross is concrete. It is understood, and it is trusted. I cannot believe it is possible for an International League ever to have the same place in the minds and hearts of the common people of all nations. Surely not right away.[108]

At bottom, Olds believed that the creation of the LRCS was unnecessary and even dangerous; in his mind the ARC in Europe already embodied the true spirit of disinterested humanitarianism, and he did his best to defend its uniqueness. It was Davison himself who had first decided to rush the creation of the LRCS and then suggested that it should replace the ARC in Europe; the result of his precipitate behavior was that within a few weeks he had managed to alienate not only the ICRC but also the leaders of the ARC in Europe. Henderson and his embryonic organization would pay the price for Davison's haste.

It soon became apparent that the conditions imposed by the executive of the ARC might not be met. Olds sent Farrand some discouraging news about the army supplies:

> Have encountered unmistakable disposition on part sub-committee of Economic Council to promote the sale of those supplies on favorable terms to the various governments within whose jurisdictions they may be needed, on understanding that such governments would make supplies available for relief work to be conducted under auspices of League. We should consider this outcome most unfortunate because it would unquestionably make Red Cross effort subservient to governmental and political influences.[109]

Meanwhile, Henderson was fearful that the future of the LRCS could be jeopardized by the ARC's insistence that all the governments and Red Cross societies of the Allies contribute both supplies and funds for the relief program and cabled Davison to request that he persuade the ARC to reconsider. Only the British had any resources at the moment, he pointed out, and the others were best "educated by degrees" rather than dictated to.[110] Davison did not reply directly to this request. Instead, he sent Henderson a lengthy cable in which he explained how his own position on the relief issue had been "perhaps somewhat revised after considering [the] matter here with officials [of the] American Red Cross"; he also asked Henderson to consider "whether the time may not come when you would like very much to have Colonel Olds associated with you in the League," a clear indication that he had been forced to abandon his earlier plan.[111] At the same time, Farrand sent Henderson a message that the ARC "simply desires that support beyond its own be given League" and that its position should be understood to be "both elastic and liberal"; however, for immediate purposes he authorized Henderson to spend only $175,000, which was the sum remaining in the war council's previous allocation to Davison for organizing the Cannes conference and establishing the LRCS.[112] Clearly, access to even a part of the $8 million supposedly set aside for the LRCS was not yet permitted.

If the leaders of the ARC in Washington were cautiously optimistic about the future of the LRCS, the leaders of the British Red Cross Society were distinctly lukewarm. Sir Arthur Stanley was partially responsible for this state of affairs because—under pressure from Davison—he had reneged on his promise to the council of the BRCS that no appointment would be made to the director-generalship of the LRCS without its prior consent. When the BRCS council met on 13 May, several of its members were clearly irritated at being asked, after the fact, to approve the decision of the League's board of governors to appoint Sir David Henderson. Stanley did his best to portray Henderson—who, as the others were aware, had neither medical qualifications nor previous Red Cross experience—as the best man for the job; he also reported that the appointment had found favor with the British representatives at the Paris Peace Conference, including Arthur Balfour, Lord Robert Cecil, and Sir Eric Drummond, the newly appointed secretary-general of the League of Nations.[113] Nevertheless, the BRCS council refused to confirm Henderson's appointment, noting that "in the circumstances . . . [it] should be made without their intervention" because Davison's plea about the "urgent necessity for beginning the work" had not allowed them "the time which would be required to consider so important a matter as fully as they would desire."[114]

Money was also an issue. At the same meeting, members wanted to know how much membership in the LRCS was going to cost. Once again Stanley found himself in difficulty, for he had assured an earlier meeting that a society joining the LRCS incurred no financial liabilities; now he had to explain that each member of the LRCS would be given the opportunity to contribute to its expenses and that "in his opinion it would put the British Red Cross Society in a very awkward position if it were decided that it was intended to find no part of the money."[115] In July, after the issue had been considered by a committee, Stanley was forced to tell the disappointed Henderson that the BRCS council had determined that none of its general funds could be used for LRCS purposes and that in its judgment this was not the moment for launching a huge public appeal for funds to support the work of the LRCS.

Instead, British contributions to the LRCS would be decided on an annual basis, "with reference to the actual work taken in hand."[116] Finally, in October, the British government and the BRCS each gave £30,000 to the LRCS but with the stipulation that two-thirds of each donation be spent on relief work in Czechoslovakia.[117] Since the leaders of the LRCS had planned a more extensive operation in Poland than in Czechoslovakia, the condition imposed by the British—which probably reflected the kind of political influences that Olds had feared—was an unexpected limitation on their plans. Understandably, Henderson had found that dealing with the BRCS was exasperating; he wrote to Davison that its leaders were "very efficient in finding objections to any course of action which is proposed."[118] To add to Henderson's disappointment, the French Red Cross reported that it had no funds available for LRCS relief work and the Italian and Japanese societies sent no replies whatever. Without substantial assistance from either governments or national Red Cross societies, the LRCS could play no more than a minor role in postwar relief in Europe.

Davison failed to appreciate that he did the LRCS no service by trying to thrust it so quickly into the field of relief. After all the publicity that had surrounded the Cannes conference and the establishment of the LRCS, those close to the situation expected the new body to begin the struggle against disease that had been planned by the experts in public health and child welfare and wondered why the LRCS was becoming involved in short-term emergency measures when the Cannes program had emphasized long-term preventive and educational measures. Axson gave Davison a broad hint that chasing after the elusive army supplies had been a mistake.[119] That was not the only problem, however. As Davison soon discovered, it was one thing to get the experts together for a conference lasting a few days; it was quite another to get one of them to devote several years to building up the medical department of the LRCS. During the Cannes conference, he had tried to persuade Wycliffe Rose, head of the Rockefeller Foundation's International Health Board, to accept the directorship of the LRCS medical department, and Rose evidently promised to give the proposal serious consideration.[120] Not until after his return to New York did Davison learn that Rose had decided to decline the position, whereupon he immediately contacted "our leading specialists, Dr. Welch, Dr. Flexner, Dr. Biggs, Dr. Rose and Dr. Farrand, and put to them very clearly the responsibility of finding a competent, qualified man for the position."[121] Their unanimous recommendation was Richard Pearson Strong, who first agreed to take the position and then refused it, saying that he would have to return to his teaching and research duties at Harvard Medical School.[122] Davison, Farrand, and Axson then decided to approach Surgeon-General Merritte W. Ireland for his advice but changed their minds when they learned that in response to pressure from the ARC, President A. Lawrence Lowell of Harvard had reluctantly agreed to give Strong a one-year leave of absence.[123] The LRCS finally had a credible general medical director, even if a fresh search for Strong's successor had to begin immediately. This solution must have caused Davison as much pain as pleasure because he found himself with less and less time to give these matters.

April in Paris and Cannes had been an exhilarating time, and Davison's hopes for the LRCS had soared, but the summer months in New York proved considerably less encouraging. After returning to the Morgan house, he had found himself, as he wrote to Henderson, "catapulted into a position of great stress because of responsibilities of my firm in connection with European and American finance, so that I have been driven harder, perhaps, than ever before in my life."[124] Although he tried to fuel Henderson's enthusiasm with assurances that Farrand was a strong friend of the LRCS and that nothing would stop the eventual carrying out of its program, Davison soon realized that the political tide in the United States was turning against further foreign involvement.[125] By August, he was railing against the Republicans in the Senate for opposing the Treaty of Versailles and the League of Nations; against the high cost of living, which was helping to provoke resentment from organized labor; and against unnamed "forces working within our country to stir up feelings against everything foreign."[126] Nevertheless, he concluded that "all of this leads me to be more hopeful than ever for our League. I believe that if our organization is effected satisfactorily and within reasonable time, we will be in a position to make ourselves felt by doing constructive work of incalculable benefit."[127] This was not simply whistling in the dark: Davison believed that all these disturbances portended a coming day of reckoning, when society would be set on a truer course by those who were capable of exercising moral leadership. When this time came, institutions such as the LRCS would, he hoped, be ideally placed to point the way.

The New Crusade

Henderson may not have become the overlord of European relief programs, but with the funds provided by the ARC he was able to set up shop in Geneva on a scale that must have surprised the ICRC, whose members had never had the luxury of a patron to pay all their bills. In June, the LRCS established headquarters at 9, Cour St. Pierre, in the very shadow of the cathedral where Calvin had introduced the reformed religion. It must have been hard for Gustave Ador and his colleagues to accept the fact that another Red Cross flag was now flying in the heart of the old city thanks to the presence of this parvenu organization, the creation of which they had tried to prevent. Nevertheless, in what was seen as a brave show of cordiality, a member of the ICRC, William Rappard, offered himself for appointment as secretary-general of the LRCS; Henderson gladly agreed, and the two of them moved into the building in Cour St. Pierre. Almost certainly, there was more to this maneuver than met the eye. Several national societies had already responded positively to Davison's invitation to join the LRCS, and the ICRC had encountered some criticism for the unfriendly tone of its May circular about the founding of the LRCS. In the circumstances, it was prudent some gesture be made that implied that collaboration between the two bodies would not, after all, be so difficult to arrange.[128] If a member of the ICRC was seen to take a prominent position with the LRCS, the national societies would be reassured and unlikely to insist, at least for the moment, on any more formal evidence of recognition. Rappard, who had encouraged Davison from their first meeting in Washington, was the obvious choice; indeed, he was arguably responsible for the difficulties in which the ICRC now found itself, so it was fitting that he should be made to deal with the consequences. At the same time, as secretary-general of the LRCS he was ideally placed to monitor its activities and to keep the ICRC apprised of both its plans and its difficulties. The ICRC remained convinced that the future development of the Red Cross should be settled at a full international conference and not by the impetuous and increasingly questionable judgment of Harry Davison.

As membership in the LRCS expanded, the calling of that Red Cross conference, which was to have been held in Geneva thirty days after the signing of the peace treaty, became problematic. The original agreement, that the five members of the Committee of Red Cross Societies would propose an extended peacetime program that would be considered alongside other plans for postwar reorganization, had now been rendered pointless by the creation of the LRCS. At least in theory, the other Red Cross societies that had joined it—more than twenty by late summer—had in doing so accepted its definition of a peacetime program.[129] "Will the League's Articles of Association now be ratified by a future international Red Cross conference?" the Swedish Red Cross Society inquired of Henderson at the time of its adherence. His reply was negative: The League's constitution had been drawn up by the founders and had been accepted by societies that had already joined; though no society was or had been forced to join against its will, only members had the right to pass judgment on the constitution.[130]

Henderson may well have thought it likely that such conferences would eventually be replaced by meetings of the general council of LRCS, but he realized that the ICRC was still determined to go ahead with this conference. As he wrote to Davison,

> I do not think that the International Committee will now let it be abandoned, whatever we say. They seem to have the idea that the League does not want this conference and in spite of all the effusive politeness they show us, they are making a good many little attacks on the League. I am not at all afraid of the International Committee, and I think everything will turn out all right. They are naturally a little jealous at the League getting into what they considered their own field.[131]

When Davison replied, he asked Henderson to inform the ICRC that in view of the changed conditions since the original request in February there was, at least from the League's point of view, no longer any reason for calling such a conference; but that if the ICRC chose to call such a conference, then the League would cooperate in every possible way. He also admitted to Henderson that "in view of all which has transpired, it would be inopportune to carry on a large program as was previously contemplated," suggesting instead that, rather than urge Red Cross societies to adopt the program elaborated at the Cannes conference, the League should simply explain what it was doing and planned to do and seek their cooperation and support. For the first time, a note of caution is apparent: Perhaps Davison was beginning to realize that running the ARC war council had given him an exaggerated view of what could be achieved by Red Cross societies in peacetime.

For its part, the ICRC would have liked nothing better than to convene the first postwar international conference of Red Cross societies, but it was hamstrung by the delays that plagued the negotiation and ratification of the Treaty of Versailles. Instead of being held as planned in May, 1919, the conference was postponed until September, 1920, primarily to please the British and the French; as that deadline approached, the ICRC was asked to postpone it again, this time by the Americans joined by the British and French, for an additional six months.[132] The ICRC agreed to these postponements only with great reluctance. In its view, there were several other important issues to be addressed besides the future development of the Red Cross, and only its desire to have former enemies eventually meet one another in Geneva could justify the delays. The awkward fact was, however, that the longer such a conference was postponed, the more time the LRCS was given to establish its own distinctive identity and the more difficult it would become to undo this creation of the victorious Allies.

During the next few months, the various offices that made up LRCS headquarters began to take shape in Geneva. As director of the general medical department, Strong, working from the agenda laid out at the Cannes conference, rapidly created no less than ten subdepartments: Medical Information, Child Welfare, Tuberculosis, Communicable Diseases, Nursing, Sanitation, Vital Statistics, Social Hygiene, Malaria, and Industrial Hygiene. In all but the last two cases, a chief and assistant chief were immediately appointed, as was a librarian; two additional physicians were needed to run the Public Health Laboratory, yet another to run the Museum of Hygiene. By March, 1920, Strong had under him a paid staff of seventeen experts in public health, epidemiology, sanitary engineering, and nursing plus clerical and secretarial staff. The Department of Publicity and Publication, headed by William G. Hereford and divided into four language sections and three functional bureaus, employed at least another dozen individuals. Frank Persons became the tirelessly energetic director of the Department of Organization, which employed yet more staff to implement his plans for the growth of Red Cross societies on a worldwide basis. Henderson liked keeping the senior officers separate from the junior ones, so the technical experts who ran the departments and bureaus were housed not at Cour St. Pierre but elsewhere, most of them in the former Hôtel du Parc. In practice this meant that Henderson and Rappard concentrated on what might be called the diplomatic aspects of establishing the LRCS—relations with governments, the League of Nations, the ICRC, and so on—whereas the technical experts dealt primarily with each other and with the national societies, including both those already established and those in the process of formation. In these circumstances, a peculiar ethos soon grew up among the technical experts, one that quickly came to distinguish the LRCS from the other elements of the Red Cross world and, especially, from the ICRC.

Many of the experts hired by the LRCS saw themselves not as mere employees or bureaucrats but rather as crusaders in the service of humanity. According to Georges Milsom, head of the French section of the publicity and publication department, the LRCS had been founded at a crucial moment during the age-old struggle between Good and Evil. With the world in such great distress, Evil appeared to have the upper hand: Misery, disease, epidemics, and suffering were everywhere. However, Good was striking back: With a fervor reminiscent of the Geneva conference of 1863, Milsom proclaimed that the Red Cross societies of the world were organizing "a supreme effort against the powers of suffering and death" by mounting "this peaceful offensive, this new crusade . . ." against all forms of suffering.[133] This crusade was all the more important because of the widespread sense of disillusionment that so quickly followed the Armistice:

> Fifteen months since the Armistice, and Europe has not yet come out of its stupor. More than a year, and the immensity of the disaster is only beginning to be apparent. More than 10 million men killed in the flower of life; three times more mutilated and incurable; the devastation and destruction of millions of square kilometers of countryside that was once prosperous, peaceful, and happy; war debts exceeding the hundreds of billions; the economic and social life of all peoples disrupted, and threatened by famine and poverty! . . . After more than a year, the general feeling is that a huge deception has taken place. Surely this cannot be the peace that was so ardently desired, so wonderfully dreamt about, throughout the long night [of war].[134]

According to Milsom, there was only one way to remedy this disillusionment, and that was to follow the path indicated by the Cannes conference, "to make the light of science and the warmth of human sympathy penetrate into every corner of the world."[135] A new science, appropriate for a new world of peace, would point the way: "After the science of war which kills, comes the science which strives to save life and encourage it; after science in the service of Death, we have science in the service of Life."[136]

Public health was the obvious "science in the service of life," but the structure of the LRCS also allotted an important place to two other, more recent "sciences": organization and publicity. Its organization department was staffed by experts who were ready to advise national Red Cross societies on their own organizational structure and on methods for increasing their membership and for obtaining the funds with which to undertake an expanded sphere of operations. Naturally, these experts drew on the wartime experience of the Allied Red Cross societies (especially that of the Americans), which had raised unprecedented sums by various means from a vast number of donors. Their colleagues in the publicity department were even more explicit in acknowledging their debt to wartime experience:

> The war brought to nearly every intelligent person in the world a realization . . . of the tremendous force and power of publicity or propaganda. The very mistakes that were made, the blunders and the bungling, made it apparent that here was a comparatively new force with great potentiality for good or harm, which could not safely be left in the hands of inexperienced amateurs, however laudable their zeal, however praiseworthy their intentions. It now becomes the opportunity of the Red Cross to make the best use of this modern science in order to push forward its peace-time programme for the welfare of humanity through co-ordinated effort to relieve suffering and combat disease.[137]

All three departments stood ready to advise the member societies of the LRCS on how to establish their own departments of organization and publicity and their own bureaus of experts in public health, so that they would be ready to participate to the full in this new crusade against disease and suffering. As the catalyst in this new social movement, the LRCS would undertake

> a great work of synthesis, the creation of a network grouping the strengths of the Red Cross, information, methods, experiments, statistics, research, publications, experience; each Red Cross doing its share for the greater benefit of all, the most experienced helping the neophytes; each Red Cross always preserving complete freedom of action as regards its own organization and activity; each Red Cross equally able to make its voice heard, the League not being a closed and autocratic circle, but the true federation of Red Cross societies.[138]

In this view, the experts in Geneva who stood at the center of this network would become the very heart and lifeblood of the whole organism, in marked contrast to the "closed and autocratic" ICRC.

A grand opportunity for the experts to explain their hopes for the LRCS came when the first meeting of the general council of the organization was fixed for March, 1920. The articles of association had left the calling of this meeting to the chairman of the board of governors, and in December, 1919, Davison made the decision to call it. He may well have been prompted to take this action on receiving a legal opinion in which Chandler Anderson pointed out the flimsy legal situation of the LRCS in the event—which now seemed likely—that the United States refused to join the League of Nations.[139] For LRCS personnel, however, the legal situation was of far less interest than the fact that delegates of all the member societies would be assembling in Geneva, where they could be fired with enthusiasm for the tasks at hand. Milsom, whose faith in the LRCS verged on religious devotion, readied himself to preach the new crusade in a speech that concluded,

> There can be no doubt that the League will strengthen the feeling of fraternity, of solidarity among peoples, without which the League of Nations can be only a precarious enterprise. Only an active and energetic human solidarity, such as that conceived by the Red Cross, and particularly by the League, can get us out of the chaos in which the world has found itself once the upheaval [of war] came to an end. No organization is better placed to serve the cause of genuine internationalism than the Red Cross. Its emblem signifies not only human sympathy, but also neutrality among nations, races, religions, and classes. . . . [For it is also] capable of diminishing class hatred, by transforming the environment in which the poor live, and by struggling against misery and suffering. It is undeniable that the Red Cross, with its popularity, and its complete anonymity, seems to be the one force for good which is most capable of bringing about a just and peaceful solution of the great social problem that is gripping the world, so long as it can accomplish the formidable task which the League's vast program entails.[140]

In other words, the LRCS would save the world. This was not the first time that such hopes had been vested in the Red Cross by those who saw their world thrown into disarray, nor was it the first time that an international Red Cross federation had been conceived as exemplifying a new standard of morality and a new form of moral leadership for humanity. What was really new about this crusade was its faith in expertise: With American money and "know-how" scientific and technical experts sitting in Geneva would put right the ills of the world. Just as Marguerite Cramer had feared, the LRCS was deliberately turning the Red Cross into a panacea for all the sufferings of humanity. This was a course fraught with risks, but the newly appointed staff of the LRCS, full of enthusiasm for remaking the world, happily disregarded such warnings.

✚ 7

New Wine
& Old Bottles

THE RED CROSS WORLD took several years to recover from the disruption created by Harry Davison and Woodrow Wilson. The ICRC, which had no intention of abrogating its historic place as the leader and conscience of the international Red Cross movement, was spurred by these events to undertake a sweeping reconsideration of its role. Meanwhile, the enthusiastic young men and women who staffed the LRCS were keen to replace what they regarded as the staid and antiquated approach of the ICRC with a dynamic and contemporary focus upon the improvement of public health. Understandably, each of these bodies assumed that it would soon devour the other; and their separate plans for creating an "organic union" initially reflected this assumption. However, it soon became apparent that neither body could count on the support of all the national societies if its goal were to eliminate its rival; once that lesson was learned, the leaders of the ICRC and the LRCS were forced, in some cases reluctantly, to find a way to live with one another. Even so, the search for this modus vivendi took years; only in 1928 was final agreement reached on a new structure for what officially became an entity called the "International Red Cross," a structure that—with minor modifications—has survived until the present day.[1] By this agreement, a much truncated version of the LRCS became one of the three elements that were deemed to make up the International Red Cross, the other two being the ICRC and the national societies.

The LRCS was never able to become the "real" or "virile" International Red Cross that Harry Davison had envisioned. In this failure the ICRC was to play a definite but not a decisive part; of much greater importance was the fact that the very conception of the peacetime health program of the LRCS had been flawed from the outset. The grand program outlined at the Cannes conference rested on two large and unproved assumptions: first, that governments would be as determined to improve public health in peacetime as they had been to defeat their enemies in wartime; and second, that national Red Cross societies could be transformed into appropriate vehicles for assisting governments to achieve this goal. The leaders of the LRCS soon realized that neither the political will nor the extensive funds required to implement the Cannes program would be forthcoming, not even from the founding societies of the LRCS. Although, thanks to Davison, the ARC had set aside a large fund on which the LRCS could draw, American support for the LRCS was never as strong as it had been for the extensive European operations of the ARC. In any case, that support was to be drastically reduced in the course of the decade as the tide of isolationism reached its flood. Despite the fact that their British and French allies believed that the new emphasis on public health work reflected American influence, the reality is that the Cannes program—though largely the work of American experts—had never been approved by the ARC itself; and when its new president, Farrand, tried to climb aboard the public health bandwagon, he met strong opposition from within the ARC as well as from other organizations such as the American Medical Association. Not even the Rockefeller Foundation, arguably the midwife of the program adopted at Cannes, was prepared to come to the rescue of the medical department of the LRCS. Thus Davison's vaunted new international Red Cross body was soon confining its work to popular hygiene instruction, the encouragement of public health nursing, and the Junior Red Cross, this last functioning as an agency for propaganda among children of school age. In this form, the LRCS was no threat either to the continued existence of the ICRC or to the priorities of the national societies, who could take as much or as little as they chose from what the LRCS had to offer. Even if the LRCS failed to meet Davison's expectations, however, its creation had an undeniable impact on both the ICRC and the national Red Cross societies, old bottles that sought ways to accommodate at least some of the new wine of internationalism and social improvement.

"Immense Labors Are Before Us"

Hopefulness about the future of the LRCS was never greater than in March, 1920, when its first General Council was held in Geneva. In anticipation of this meeting, the various departments and bureaus of the League's secretariat prepared brochures outlining their objectives, and Henderson, Strong, Persons, and Brown prepared reports that were submitted to the delegates for discussion. In all these efforts there was a conscious feeling that a new era was beginning in the history of the Red Cross, described in one of the brochures as "an era characterized by efforts to prevent disease and suffering as well as to relieve them."[2] According to Harry Davison, whose opening address set the tone for the meeting, the task that lay before the LRCS was nothing less than the salvation of civilization itself:

> Who is there living today with anything like a sympathetic interest who is not burdened with the consciousness of the unspeakable destitution, disease, sickness,

The Visiting Nurse
drives away diseases
and brings health.

7.1   Illustration from a pamphlet on popular health education, entitled *Elements of Hygiene*, produced in 1921 by the League of Red Cross Societies. Its emphasis was on promoting maternal and infant health by instructing readers about the dangers of tuberculosis, alcoholism, flies, and impure drinking water. (There is no copy of this pamphlet in the archives of the League of Red Cross Societies in Geneva, but one is preserved in the papers of C.-E. A. Winslow, housed in the Sterling Library at Yale.)

7.2   Greek members of the Junior Red Cross learning about vaccination technique. This class, typical of the health education programs organized for members of the junior Red Cross in the 1920s, took place at a Teachers' Training School in Athens.

and physical and moral degradation resulting from the scourges and ravages of war? How far reaching and terrible are their effects, and what force is there today with which to meet them? Who is there amongst us who is not asking himself whether civilization is to break, whether madness is to dethrone sanity and whether or not the war with all its horror may after all have been but the beginning of something worse to follow?

Do you realize that today there is in the world no humanitarian force which can be called upon in this great crisis to serve all men, everywhere, whatever their race, creed or color save that enrolled under the banner of the Red Cross? Surely through our joint effort we should be able to marshal efficient forces to combat and avert this new and terrible force of hopeless abandon to the end that civilization may be saved, that peoples will acquire or will again have confidence in each other and that their minds may be brought to the belief that there is yet in the world something for which to live.[3]

Ironically, many of these would-be saviors of civilization were almost prevented from reaching the Geneva meeting by a nationwide strike on the French railways. The American delegation traveled from Paris in cars driven by Red Cross chauffeurs, but their vehicles had to be hauled by horses through heavy snow in the Jura Mountains.[4] The British, Canadian, and Australian delegations, also delayed by the strike, arrived two days late; the Japanese delegates, including Dr. Arata Ninagawa, a member of the League's board of governors, reached Geneva just in time to attend the closing session. Despite these difficulties, the atmosphere was cordial, even jubilant, especially at the news that the American Red Cross had authorized $500,000 for LRCS expenditures "to be utilized in carrying out preliminary investigation and study of the conditions prevailing in any country for which Red Cross assistance is desired." Resolutions were passed thanking the ARC for its "enlightened generosity" and Davison himself for his "wholehearted enthusiasm."[5] On the final evening of the meeting, Davison gave a closing banquet in the foyer of the Grand Theater; this was the culmination of a social program that included a dinner at the newly rebuilt Hôtel Les Bergues hosted by the Rappards, a reception at Parc de la Grange hosted by the cantonal and municipal authorities, and a reception at ICRC headquarters in the Promenade du Pin. With its opening session held in the Hôtel de Ville and other sessions at the Athénée, this first LRCS meeting of the new era also established symbolic ties with the founders of the Red Cross and the originators of the Geneva Convention.

Naturally there was a great deal of interest in how the ICRC would respond on this occasion. Its members had been invited to attend as guests of the LRCS: Gustave Ador, Vice-President Adolphe d'Espine, and Secretary-General Paul Desgouttes (filling a newly created position), sat in on most of its sessions, but Rappard was of course a central figure.[6] The governors of the LRCS would have been delighted to offer the presidency of the General Council to Gustave Ador, but he made it clear in advance that he would refuse, so it was offered instead to Rappard, who cleverly used his acceptance speech to remind the delegates that "as President of the International Committee and the representative of the entire International Red Cross throughout the world," Ador would necessarily have been forced to refuse "the presidency of our General Council from which certain National Red Cross societies remain excluded for the moment."[7] After this swipe at the pretensions of the LRCS, Rappard yielded the floor to Ador himself, who, in the most cordial terms, made the position of the ICRC crystal clear.

Reminding the delegates that the ICRC had helped to establish most of the societies they were in Geneva to represent, Ador pointed out that the ICRC's role as founder of the Red Cross had been recognized at the nine international conferences that had been held since 1864 because the national societies have acknowledged "the need for a central, neutral, independent organ that is able to exercise a moral influence and to maintain the unity of the Red Cross."[8] After praising its "scrupulous impartiality during the recent war"—a claim almost unique among this gathering—he moved to his main point:

The International Committee has worked hard to maintain international conventions and to safeguard the principles of humanity. Its sole strength derives from its absolute independence, free from any official or political influence. No statute can restrain its liberty of action. Any codification of its competence would be a hindrance. In defending justice and charity, it must incarnate the universal conscience, above and beyond national rivalries. Was the constitution of the League of Red Cross Societies in the spring of 1919 an attack on the rights and competence of the International Committee? I think not. It will be in the future—with the consent of the national societies—what it has been in the past, what it is at present. It remains the defender of the ideals and of the principles of universality of the Red Cross, seeking to realize a unity of action. Through its enquiries, its missions abroad, its *Revue* and its *Bulletin*, it will be an organ of information and mediation, ready whenever the Red Cross societies so signify to cede this task to those more competent than it is. Between the League and ourselves, on the field of charity, there can be neither jealousy or rivalry.[9]

He went on to claim that the ICRC had actually urged several national societies to join the LRCS and pointed to Rappard's position with the LRCS as evidence of a desire for cordial and close relations. Nevertheless, he stated clearly that the League "lacks the character of universality that is at the base of the Red Cross," noting that the ICRC had "since the beginning made express reservations in this regard"; however, he professed himself certain that "the founders of the League do not intend to maintain for long this abnormal situation, which only the sorrowful events of the war can justify."[10] Somewhat surprisingly, he observed that in seeking to improve public health and to prevent illness, the League was pursuing practical goals; and that by coordinated effort, practical solutions would be forthcoming. He concluded with this backhanded assurance: "The League is destined to become a veritable executive organ without substituting for the International Committee which will remain the necessary link among all the Red Cross Societies."[11]

Embodied in Ador's speech were the main elements of the ICRC's position vis-à-vis the LRCS, a position that he was prepared to defend to the death. Despite the fact that a majority of the national societies had already joined the LRCS, the ICRC took the position that its own powers had been confirmed repeatedly by international conferences and could only be altered at the behest of some future conference to which delegates of all national societies had been invited by the ICRC. Would the delegates to such a conference be certain that they could find or create a body that they could trust to do a better job of defending the ideals and principles of the Red Cross than the ICRC had done for six decades? The answer to that question was almost certainly no, which is likely why he posed the issue in this way. In short, Ador was telling the delegates that unless and until all of the national societies decided otherwise, the ICRC would do as it saw fit; and that the LRCS should stick to its "practical" health work and not even think of challenging the ICRC's established role as the medium of communication between the national societies, let alone its desire to "incarnate the universal conscience."

Ador's speech was by far the most important event of this General Council meeting, most of which was devoted to familiarizing the delegates with the Cannes program and the necessary steps that would have to be taken by the LRCS secretariat and by the national societies for its fulfillment. Yet another reminder of the Cannes conference was the arrival of a carefully timed message about the relationship between the LRCS and the League of Nations. Davison announced to the assembly that he had received a letter from the president of the council of the League of Nations, Arthur Balfour, in which the latter drew attention to the "ravages inflicted by disease upon the war-worn and underfed populations of Central Europe . . . [which] have reached appalling proportions" and called upon the LRCS "to organize an effort worthy of its unique position for dealing with a calamity which, following hard on war, seems almost worse than war itself."[12] Balfour made it clear, however, that he was writing without having consulted the other members of the council, and it soon became apparent that he had been urged to write this letter by (unnamed) "Red Cross officials."[13] If Davison (for it must have been him) thought that such a maneuver would bring the LRCS and the League of Nations closer together, he was wrong. The delegates responded to Balfour's letter with a polite "après vous, Alphonse": If the governments represented in the League of Nations would first agree to supply food, clothing, and transportation to the population of the stricken regions, then the LRCS would organize a worldwide appeal for medical personnel and supplies.[14] When Balfour learned what had transpired, he was annoyed and told Sir Eric Drummond that he did not appreciate his letter having been used to "force the hand" of the League of Nations.[15] Once again Davison had tried to direct events from behind the scenes and once again it had backfired: This incident did nothing to endear the LRCS to the political leadership of the League of Nations.

Before the General Council adjourned, the delegates passed a final resolution commending themselves for

the spirit of this conference, which strives for nothing less than the improvement of the health and physical welfare of mankind. Immense labors are before us, but our path is now clearly defined. We have found here a true unity of purpose. We have been thinking and feeling in larger terms than those of national egoism. . . . We have also seen more clearly than ever before that the health of one people is related to the health of all; that as the germ recognizes no frontiers neither should the prevention and the cure. In the name of the League we therefore devote ourselves to the duties that we have assumed for the benefit of humanity.[16]

Fine words, to be sure, but once the delegates had departed to their home countries, it was hard to find much evidence at LRCS headquarters that the new crusade was really under way. In contrast to the "clearly defined path" allegedly discerned by the delegates, the prevailing feeling among LRCS staff seems to have been one of confusion coupled with worry about the future.

Some of their anxiety stemmed from sudden and serious concern over Henderson's health and its possible effect on his ability to lead the organization. According to Rappard, "The General had obviously been very ill during the conference and had struggled on without letting people know of it."[17] Once the General Council meeting had ended, Henderson abruptly left Geneva for an Alpine holiday "to try to get rid of some bronchial trouble."[18] In his absence, Rappard tried to keep up morale, but this was difficult because Henderson's poor health had evidently prevented him from drawing up a firm operating budget for the next year's work; consequently neither the total amount available nor the various departmental allocations were known. Richard Strong, whose year as general medical director was already coming to an end, felt this uncertainty keenly. He had been invited to a meeting in London on 20 April, called by the council of the League of Nations to discuss matters relating to health and disease, and he needed to know for certain what the LRCS would be able to undertake and which activities could appropriately be left to other international agencies.[19] Rappard professed sympathy; he had already been told by one of the staff that "the members of the Medical Department were being paid too much by the League to do nothing, and too little for what they could do, and that they must have a definite budget."[20] Both Strong and Persons made it clear that they wanted immediate decisions, but Rappard could only reply that he simply did not know what allocations Henderson was likely to set. He agreed that quick action was "a matter of life and death" and frankly stated his opinion that "the League will live if it is very active now, but, if allowed to drift on now, will become purely ornamental, and for this latter purpose, the [ICRC], which costs much less, has many advantages."[21] Rather ominously, the only firm decision taken in Henderson's absence was to produce a heavily illustrated volume of minutes of the General Council's deliberations as a souvenir to send to the delegates.

After a rest, Henderson was able to resume his duties, but poor health continued to plague him over the next several months, which were, in any case, not an auspicious time for the LRCS. Although Persons drew up detailed plans for an extensive Red Cross relief program in central Europe, there was increasing evidence that the organization, with its grand plans for fighting disease and promoting health, was not being taken very seriously by those on whose support it depended. For example, despite the fact that there had been almost a year in which to find a permanent replacement for Strong, no figure of eminence in the field of public health was prepared to take the position. Rappard was clearly unhappy; as he wrote to Davison, "We will all have to work very hard if we are to keep even a part of the promises which we have made to the world. I have never felt that more strongly than now, and I am extremely impatient to see the League, and particularly the Medical Department, allowed to enter upon the effective execution of its programme."[22]

To spare Davison the embarrassment of failure, one distinguished member of his American advisory group, Hermann Biggs, of the New York City Health Department, agreed to go to Geneva for five months as acting medical director, but this was simply another, and not very successful, stopgap measure. Public health experts, it seems, were more ready to applaud the idea of a Red Cross health program than they were to accept responsibility for implementing it. Meanwhile, the ARC commission in Europe continued its work under the direction of Robert Olds; no representative of the LRCS was invited to an important conference of its staff held in Venice in June, 1920, to plan the next stage of its postwar relief programs; indeed the existence of the LRCS was scarcely acknowledged during its proceedings.[23]

Already it was becoming apparent that, whatever they may have urged in Geneva, the Red Cross societies of the Allies were not about to conduct appeals to raise funds for LRCS relief work, let alone for extensive medical programs. From London, Sir Arthur Stanley wrote to Davison explaining that heavy taxation and fears for the future "have, for the moment, dried up all the sources from which we have been accustomed during the last five years to obtain our funds. At the same time, every hospital in the country is in debt and has accumulated repairs and renewals, to deal with which demand a very large sum of money. We—the Red Cross—have offered our help which has been gratefully accepted and now it is up to us to make good."[24] With this campaign for the hospitals and another for the Imperial Relief Fund already under way, it was clearly out of the question for the British Red Cross Society to launch another campaign on behalf of the LRCS. The French were more sympathetic, but only up to a point; like the British, they had no intention of conducting a fund-raising appeal at this time to support the work of the LRCS. Of the French attitude Rappard wrote to Davison, "They are interested, full of good will, and sincerely hopeful for the future. However, there is a tone of reserve [in an accompanying article] that will not escape your attention."[25] Worst of all was the news from Washington. The ARC, it seemed, was now contemplating a special appeal to support an extensive child welfare program in Europe to be run by its own commission in cooperation with the ARA; in view of this, Farrand told the central committee that in his opinion "it would be unwise to conduct a special appeal for the League [LRCS] at this time."[26] No wonder the General Council in Geneva had turned Balfour's request back upon the politicians: This was a convenient way of disguising the unwillingness of the national societies to undertake a major fund-raising program on behalf of the LRCS.

Part of the reason why the ARC was ready to support its European commission more strongly than the LRCS was that a groundswell of opposition to Davison and all his works had formed around Mabel Boardman and other veterans of the prewar era. In Boardman's case, the hostility was personal as well as ideological: She would never forgive Eliot Wadsworth and Davison for pushing her aside during the war, and she was determined to have her revenge. Moreover, she and her allies on the central committee resented Davison for having imposed Farrand upon them as their postwar leader; staunch Republicans, they did not believe that the ARC should undertake a health program in the United States, and they distrusted Farrand's sympathy for public health work at both the national and international levels. In April, 1920, Boardman, whose memory for constitutional impropriety rivaled that of Archie Loyd, launched an assault by correspondence, badgering Farrand with letters and memoranda questioning the legality of the formation of the war council, the legality of its appropriations to Davison as head of the international commission, and the propriety of Davison's expenditures while occupying this position.[27] When, she wanted to know, had the ARC's executive committee authorized all these actions, and when had it specifically approved ARC membership in the LRCS? These were all excellent questions, for Davison, in his overbearing way, had taken much for granted, and Farrand had to scramble to provide replies that would keep Boardman at bay.[28] Embarrassingly, it came to light that the executive committee had never ratified the actions of the American delegates who had signed the League's Articles of Association in Paris on 5 May, 1919. As it had done once before in the case of the war council, the executive committee was forced to record its retrospective approval of the action. At the same time, one of Boardman's allies, John Skelton Williams, who was treasurer of the ARC, launched a full-scale investigation of the financial records of the international commission. When Davison realized what was afoot, he wrote to Farrand that it was vital to keep this controversy quiet and not let any details leak out to the public. He tried to fend Williams off with bluster, writing, "If he [Williams] made an issue and it became public . . . the result might be measured by the suffering and perhaps death of no less than a million children in Europe and that I did not believe that he or any other individual would want to assume such a responsibility even if there were foundation for his charges: that whatever the facts were they could be dealt with inside the family and should be so confined."[29] There is no doubt that this campaign, and the larger ideological hostility from which it sprang, contributed to Farrand's growing frustration with the ARC. Davison's glowing assurances about the future had not come to pass, and Farrand began to wonder why he should remain with an organization that was neither unanimous nor enthusiastic about improving public health and fighting poverty.

Davison himself was not unmoved by the campaigns of Boardman and Williams, particularly by their suggestions that he had recklessly committed ARC money to support a dubious international agency in Geneva that other Red Cross societies now appeared unwilling to support. The first year of LRCS operations had cost the ARC $500,000, most of which had been spent on salaries and travel expenses for members of the secretariat. At its March meeting, the board of governors had approved an operating budget of $700,000 for 1920–1921.[30] After returning to Washington and consulting with Farrand, Davison decided that LRCS operations had to be scaled down considerably and so reported to the executive committee of the ARC. Taking the line that the League's medical program ought to be postponed until more Red Cross societies were ready to take advantage of it, Davison proposed to slash the 1920–1921 budget of the LRCS from $700,000 to $400,000; the lower figure, he rationalized, would ensure that the ARC's original allocation could be used to support the LRCS for five years, if necessary.[31] This drastic step took some of the wind out of Boardman's sails and also provided Farrand with useful ammunition against the critics of costly health programs. It would be inappropriate, however, to portray this decision as one taken solely to placate the opposition within the ARC; Davison almost certainly realized while he was in Geneva that there was a huge discrepancy between what the Cannes conference had recommended and what Red Cross societies were able and willing to undertake.[32] The British, for their part, were pleased to learn that ARC support for the LRCS was assured for an additional year, albeit on a reduced scale.[33] At best lukewarm in their support for the LRCS, they approved any measure that postponed the day when they would have to pay a proper share of its expenses.

Henderson might have wished to protest, but the reality was that the ARC was paying the piper and therefore called the tune. He had no choice but to accept the revised budget, but with unusual candor he let Davison know that he disagreed strongly with this shift in priorities:

> I cannot help thinking that . . . this view is based on European rather than American experience. . . . I think that pure missionary work among the Red Cross Societies, unless backed by a medical programme of some kind, will be completely sterile. I believe that we and the Red Cross Societies could go on talking in circles for four or five years without any serious effect whatever. . . . People can . . . understand the advantage of the collection and dissemination by a central body of information concerning those diseases which seriously affect the health and efficiency of nations, and the existence of a body prepared to do this I have found to be perhaps the greatest incentive to Red Cross Societies to develop themselves in order to take advantage of what is offered. I do not therefore believe that we shall attain any great success in a purely organizational campaign if medical work is to be entirely postponed.[34]

The effect of such a large budget cut on the morale of the technical staff was predictable. The first to resign was Dr. Leonard Finley, who had headed the child welfare department. Then Walter Clarke's social hygiene department— "social hygiene" being a euphemism for venereal diseases, a subject that many Red Cross members found distasteful—was shut down by Henderson in the first of a series of cuts. Others who saw the writing on the wall began to look for positions elsewhere.

The difficulties in which the LRCS soon found itself had not, of course, been caused solely by the ARC's decision to reduce its operating budget. The chief of the tuberculosis department, Dr. Edouard Rist, had already complained to Davison that there was too great a gulf between the heads of departments and bureaus, on the one hand, and "the powers" at Cour St. Pierre on the other.[35] When Dr. Biggs arrived in early September, his first impression of the LRCS was anything but flattering. "I am deeply impressed [he wrote to Davison] with the resemblance of this organization to that of a huge machine in which the force and power generated are expended in its own operation and in which the useful production is disproportionately small. The relation of cost to production seems to have played no part in the calculations, and in fact no one seems to have known or been interested in the cost of any activity."[36] Henderson, for his part, found Biggs unsympathetic to the problems that inevitably arose in dealing with voluntary societies rather than governments and too narrowly American in his view of the world.[37] Their difficulty in working together was only one more piece of evidence that the universal crusade against disease that had been so eloquently preached only a few months earlier was in danger of turning into a spectacular flop.

Sparring Partners

No doubt Rappard kept the ICRC well informed of the many travails that the LRCS was experiencing. Whatever their past feelings about Davison's overbearing behavior and dubious judgment, Gustave Ador and his colleagues can have derived little satisfaction from the current situation. If there was to be a universal federation of Red Cross societies—and the growing membership of the LRCS suggested that the idea was a popular one—it surely deserved to be more thoughtfully and realistically planned, more broadly funded, and far better administered than the pathetic creation housed at Cour St. Pierre. With Henderson's leadership faltering, the medical program at risk, and the date of the long-awaited international conference now finally fixed for March, 1921, the ICRC began to gather the strength to reassert its moral authority within the Red Cross movement. Still well enough to be aware of the changed mood in Geneva, Henderson wrote to Davison that the ICRC had now embarked on "a campaign of bitter propaganda among the Red Cross societies" and that he expected the ICRC to challenge the pretensions of the LRCS in the field of peacetime Red Cross work.[38] Ador had already made the attitude of the ICRC plain, and if its members decided to adopt an aggressive posture, the LRCS was now hardly in a position to respond effectively.

This news could not have come at a worse time for Davison, who had been told by his doctors to take an extended holiday to recover from the strain of overwork. He followed their advice but could not escape a feeling of responsibility for having allowed the LRCS to become the absurd machine that Hermann Biggs had so aptly described. "When I went West for my holiday," he wrote Farrand in September, "the only burden I carried was that of the League. It was on my mind constantly and annoyed me considerably because I realized I could do nothing and yet I could not dismiss it."[39] The only way out of this dilemma, since he could not personally go to Geneva and take an active role as chairman of the board, was to find a substitute. Davison evidently wanted an individual with managerial skills and a strong business background, because his choice fell upon William G. Pearce, the former general manager of the Northern Pacific Railroad. Davison and Otis Cutler had persuaded Pearce to go to Geneva for as long as necessary to exercise all the powers of the chairman in Davison's absence. On 27 October, Davison cabled Henderson to this effect, suggesting that Pearce might become vice-chairman of the board.[40]

This news hit Geneva like a bombshell. For members of the ICRC, it was the final proof—if further proof were needed—that Harry Davison still believed that all the international Red Cross needed was the firm managerial hand of an experienced American businessman. Moreover, it virtually broadcast what Davison already knew: Like Henderson, he too was seriously ill and would likely never be able to take an active role as chairman of the board of the LRCS. One did not have to be a pessimist to regard this as the last nail in the coffin of the LRCS. For Rappard, who had plenty of other options, there was no longer any useful purpose to be served by remaining as its secretary-general; as soon as the news about Pearce reached Geneva he resigned and was immediately appointed director of the mandate section of the League of Nations secretariat.[41] Lacking Rappard's mobility, Henderson reacted more cautiously: In order not to undermine his own position as director-general, he refused to deal with Pearce except on an unofficial basis but assured Davison that he would welcome informal advice and assistance.[42]

In fact, Henderson's own situation was precarious: Only days later, he cabled Davison that he had been advised by his physician not to spend the winter months in Geneva and proposed several alternative courses of action, one of which was resignation.[43] Davison was again on leave of absence from the Morgan house; his reply to Henderson was "the third letter I've written in five months" because of "neuritis in the head" (which soon proved to be a brain tumor).[44] In this extraordinarily frank letter, Davison confessed that throughout his life he had "never been able to accept failure or indeed moderate success" and that he was intensely concerned about the fate of the LRCS because of being "largely responsible for its organization, and, therefore, for the many and exceedingly difficult problems inherent in it . . . [that] have been passed on to you."[45] While in Geneva, he had observed that Henderson was "overtaxed and under great strain" and attributed this to the fact that the latter "either did not have sufficient or the right kind of assistance at the top"; hence his decision to send Pearce, whom he described as "a gentleman of qualifications which the League peculiarly needs."[46] He envisioned that, with Pearce's help, Henderson would no longer be overtaxed and that he—Davison—would have the terrible burden of the League's fortunes lifted from his shoulders. Perhaps already suspecting that his "neuritis in the head" might prove fatal, Davison had chosen this way of absolving himself from further anxiety about the affairs of the LRCS.

Henderson was right in predicting that the ICRC was preparing to challenge the League's belief that the coordination of peacetime Red Cross work, especially the struggle against disease, was its exclusive field of activity. At the March General Council meeting, a resolution had been passed, which stated that pending the establishment of an organic union the two bodies would cooperate "to work for the development of the Red Cross in the largest conception of the idea and to work without rivalry in their respective fields for the relief of suffering humanity."[47] Henderson and his staff assumed that this meant that the ICRC would regard war work as its proper field and would recognize peace work as the proper field of the League. This assumption proved to be both naive and incorrect. The ICRC defined its field—as Ador plainly stated—as guarding the fundamental principles of the Red Cross without any limitation on the terrain where those principles might be applied; therefore it saw no reason why it should not promote and coordinate peacetime programs that would help to extend what the resolution had called "the largest conception of the idea" of the Red Cross. In a significant break with prewar tradition—prompted, one suspects, by the founding of the League—it had already established close ties with the Save the Children Fund International Union, and it was becoming increasingly concerned with organizing relief efforts on behalf of refugees from the civil war in Russia.[48] National Red Cross societies soon found themselves receiving appeals from both the LRCS and the ICRC, sometimes with regard to similar projects. When the Assembly of the League of Nations convened for the first time in Geneva in December, 1920, the ICRC, which had learned a thing or two from Harry Davison, issued a press release in which it defined its peacetime duties to include work on behalf of victims of war, sickness, and civil calamities; moreover, it noted the part that the ICRC was playing in the struggle against the spread of typhus. At LRCS headquarters, these developments were interpreted as part of an attempt by the ICRC to prove to the world that a separate organization such as the League was quite unnecessary.

This was too much for Henderson, who, despite his poor health, decided that such a thinly disguised challenge had to be fended off, so he wrote a short article on relations between the LRCS and the ICRC that appeared in the December issue of the *Bulletin of the League of Red Cross Societies.*[49] Its purpose, he stated forthrightly, was to persuade the national societies, in advance of the forthcoming international conference, "that the [ICRC] and the League are both necessary; that indeed their duties are complementary; that there is no reason, and that there ought to be no occasion for rivalry or even for overlapping of functions."[50] He had nothing but praise for the ICRC's "general direction of all matters connected with the amelioration of the conditions of warfare, with the interpretation of the Geneva or other conventions, and with the relations between national Red Cross Societies in time of war," and he observed that both its composition and its location had enabled it to perform these demanding tasks: "No body of international composition could have hoped to preserve the attitude of impartiality which is almost natural to these selected citizens of Geneva, the most resolutely neutral of all the Cantons of neutral Switzerland."[51] After the compliments, however, came the forceful central argument of the piece:

> It is evident, however, that a body organised as is the *Comité International* for the purpose of ensuring impartiality in time of war, and of considering . . . juridical questions which may arise between different countries or different Red Cross Societies, would be a quite unsuitable agency for the practical administration of a peace programme of the united Red Cross Societies. In the first place, it is in no way representative; its continuity is preserved by nomination by the committee itself, and its members are not removable. No Red Cross Society has any voice in its composition or any weight in its deliberations. It could not be expected that the Societies would entrust their joint business in peace time to a body which was entirely outside and above their control. Nor would it be a satisfactory solution if the *Comité International* were reorganized on a representative basis, and made responsible, for such a change would certainly impair, if it did not destroy, its value as the impartial referee between belligerents. The truth is that, although a national Red Cross Society may very well combine its war and peace functions, the same international body cannot properly combine the duties of a central agency for the societies both in war and peace. . . . [For these wartime functions] a neutral, extra-national body is required, in fact exactly such a body as the *Comité International*.[52]

After drawing this clear line between wartime and peacetime activity, Henderson concluded with two final points that were sure to draw a reaction from the ICRC: He dismissed the League's lack of universality as "a temporary difficulty" that was "not of much importance," and he stated flatly that "the claim of the *Comité International* to organise and coordinate the peace work of the Red Cross Societies dates from the hour when these societies organised another body to fulfill these very duties."[53]

In essence, Henderson was asking the ICRC to accept the formation of the LRCS as an accomplished fact and to accept the jurisdictional line that he believed had been drawn between international Red Cross work in war and peace. Such a simple solution might well have appealed to some national societies, not to mention the leaders of other international agencies who were by now perplexed by the existence of two seemingly rival Red Cross bodies, both with international pretensions. Yet it was precisely this simple solution that the ICRC was determined to fight because—assuming the peace was durable—its members feared that this division of roles would relegate them to no more than an auxiliary role within the international Red Cross movement. Henderson's plea for acceptance backfired: It helped to convince members of the ICRC that the time had come for them to seize the initiative. With the international conference now only a few months away, the ICRC adopted a complex flanking strategy that involved undermining the credibility of the LRCS while publicly appearing to cooperate with it and attempting to persuade the national societies that they would be far better served by endorsing the ICRC as the guardian of the Red Cross idea in both war and peace.

Obviously, Henderson's effrontery in challenging the suitability of the ICRC for promoting peacetime work could not be ignored. The ICRC's unsigned reply, which appeared in the February issue of the *Bulletin International*, claimed merely to correct certain errors of fact in Henderson's account, but in fact it went a good deal further than this, casting the ICRC as "the recognized center of the international activity of the Red Cross societies . . . [which has] sought to promote all kinds of assistance among peoples, without regard to the causes of the suffering that required help: conflicts among nations, disasters, diseases, epidemics, famine, etc."[54] To be sure, all of the practical work that could be cited as evidence of the ICRC's broader involvement was of recent date, but there is no doubt that since the Armistice the ICRC had done much more than ever before to organize and promote relief for civilian populations, especially in Czechoslovakia and Poland. In response to a request from the Supreme Economic Council of the Allies, it had also organized disinfection stations on the Polish, Ukrainian, Finnish, and Baltic borders in order to prevent the spread of typhus to central and western Europe.[55] In short, the ICRC could claim to have been as involved in relief and public health work as had the LRCS and for a somewhat longer period of time; several of its peacetime undertakings had begun even before the founding of the LRCS in May, 1919. As it had done when Davison first came to Geneva, the ICRC once again took credit for having first encouraged the national societies to consider extending their field of activity in its circular of November, 1918. All this evidence was meant to dispose of Henderson's claim that the ICRC only became interested in peacetime activity *after* the LRCS had been organized.

As to Henderson's allegation that the unrepresentative character of the ICRC prevented it from becoming the coordinator of peacetime activity, the ICRC haughtily replied that if the national societies had felt the need for such a central representative organ "it would not have been necessary for that purpose to create a new alliance of Red Cross societies separate from that which has existed for 50 years."[56] What particularly annoyed the ICRC, apparently, was that the question of its composition and recruitment had not been raised by Davison and his associates at their initial interview, and hence it seemed inappropriate for Henderson to suggest that this had been a major reason for the founding of the LRCS as a separate entity. Predictably, the ICRC reminded Henderson that its composition and recruitment had been discussed by several international conferences and that on these occasions the will of the delegates had been that no changes be made in the status quo—a claim that was strictly true yet disguised considerably more than it revealed about those past deliberations. Nevertheless, given the national societies' conspicuous lack of interest in the history of these questions, the ICRC's claim was likely to go unchallenged.

The ICRC's reply also claimed that at the February, 1919 interview with Davison and his associates, Edouard Naville had spontaneously broached the question of "the representation of the Red Cross societies at the central organ of the universal Alliance of Red Cross societies." However, the published record of that meeting shows only that Naville suggested the ICRC might "very probably ask for some help from abroad, and make a place in its midst for collaborators who would be capable of carrying the new work through to a successful conclusion," which is not necessarily the same thing.[57] Some verbal sleight of hand was obviously at work here: A "universal Alliance of Red Cross societies" had suddenly been invented to stand in reproachful contrast to the less-than-universal LRCS and, by implication, apparently, the ICRC had become the central organ of that "universal Alliance." It might well be asked whether Gustave Moynier would have recognized in the periodic conferences of the national societies something called a "universal Alliance" with the ICRC as its acknowledged center. He and others who had longed to see a genuine federation of Red Cross societies created would surely never have mistaken the loose association of the prewar years for a "universal Alliance." Indeed, Moynier himself had always been disappointed by the national societies' consistent refusal to undertake any common program or indeed to accept binding obligations toward one another. For the ICRC now to claim that a "universal Alliance" was already in existence distorted the historical record, but the distortion helped to give credence to the notion that the LRCS was an unnecessary organization. There was, however, nothing inaccurate in the ICRC's description of itself as "a private institution which leads an autonomous and independent existence";[58] unlike the LRCS, the ICRC could not be said to exist solely by the will of the national societies, because its founding antedated their formation.

Even before this stiff reply to Henderson appeared in print, the ICRC set about persuading some of the national societies that the LRCS could be replaced by a more suitable body. In January, 1921, for example, ICRC delegates who were visiting Rome, Athens, and Sofia promoted the idea of forming an International Red Cross Union "under the direction of the Comité International, with the assistance and advice, and perhaps cooperation, of a committee of delegates from the various national Red Cross societies."[59] The LRCS discovered what was afoot when one of its staff members, T. B. Kittredge, was told about the scheme by the president of the Bulgarian Red Cross, Ivan Gueschoff. This plan envisioned the establishment in Geneva of "an office that would coordinate and reinforce the efforts of the national societies in their struggle against physical and moral destitution, and would administer an international fund meant to support activities undertaken for the benefit of the victims of such misery. This fund should be sustained by subventions from the national Red Cross societies."[60] The present LRCS, Kittredge also reported, had been described as "pronouncedly Anglo-Saxon in membership, ideas, and its direction. It is suspected of being a form of propaganda machinery for Anglo-Saxon and particularly for American ideas and influence."[61] As a result of this campaign, the Bulgarian Red Cross had come to believe that "a genuine union must be accomplished under a leadership and direction, whose real neutrality, and whose genuine international character cannot be doubted, that is, under the Comité International."[62] Sensibly, Kittredge concluded "that the Red Cross Societies of the world will never contribute from their funds to support two international organizations. If the Union International de la Croix Rouge is established, and maintained by contributions of member societies, the fate of the [LRCS] is clear."[63]

The idea of forming an "International Red Cross Union" was not, as Kittredge believed, simply a devious attempt to put the LRCS out of business; it was rather the first clear indication of the searching reassessment in which the ICRC had been engaged in an attempt to come to grips with the enthusiasms and aspirations of the postwar world. A much fuller picture of the ICRC's new thinking soon emerged, on the eve of the Tenth International Conference, in an important article entitled "International Activity in Peacetime." Here the ICRC sought to define, for the guidance of delegates from the national societies, both the nature of future peacetime activity and its own role in it. Lest any would-be delegates be inclined toward Henderson's simple solution, the ICRC announced that it had no intention of functioning as an institution exclusively concerned with charity in wartime; that in the postwar era such a role was no longer inappropriate and would be unacceptable to its members, who had no wish "to remain the sole international institution whose unique raison d'être derived from the possibility of further wars."[64] In a major departure from prewar tradition, the ICRC stated flatly that it would no longer make charitable activity in wartime its principal peacetime objective; instead, it intended to play a more complex role, one that would meet the "continuing need" of the national societies

> for an organ which plays the role of a moral agency, the guardian of the fundamental principles of the institution and the propagator of its principles in the world, charged with ensuring that they are maintained and soundly applied; in particular at this time when new Red Cross societies are being founded. Besides all that must be done to ameliorate the physical and sanitary conditions of men's lives, it will always be necessary to keep alive in their minds and hearts the feelings which have inspired, and which should inspire in future, all practical activity, and also to seek and propose positive solutions.[65]

The ICRC's day was far from done: Not only would it continue to speak out on behalf of "*Caritas*, this general law of humanity which is the motto of the

Red Cross"; it also envisioned "for many years yet a vast field of work for the apostle and spiritual depository of the central idea of the Red Cross, which will be at one and the same time both the moral and juridical counsellor of the institution and its pioneer of the avant-garde."[66] The message to the delegates was unmistakably clear: If they wished to keep the authentic Red Cross idea alive, they must not only reject any attempt to confine the ICRC to an exclusively wartime role but also welcome and support its revised and expanded peacetime mission.

As if that were not enough, the ICRC also drew a direct connection between its moral authority, on the one hand, and its composition and established mode of operation on the other. Aware that the propriety of its exclusively Swiss membership might be questioned, the ICRC pointed out something that Henderson had already noted: Thinking and acting independently and internationally was "unquestionably easier" for citizens of a neutral country such as Switzerland. Moreover, though conceding that "very serious objections" could be raised against its procedure of recruitment through co-optation, the ICRC nevertheless affirmed that the community of views that resulted was "an essential advantage" for the pursuit of a common goal, one likely to be lost if any kind of electoral system was substituted for co-optation.[67] To complete the picture, the ICRC reiterated its determination to remain financially independent of any government or association that was outside the Red Cross movement and reminded the national societies that they would all be expected to contribute something to enable the ICRC to meet its more extensive responsibilities. With the argument couched in these terms, it was very difficult indeed for any delegate to challenge either the composition or the operating procedures of the ICRC without appearing to jeopardize both the independence and the internationalism of the Red Cross, attributes that the ICRC had succeeded in identifying with its own corporate, and historically autonomous, existence.

What, then, did the ICRC conceive to be the work of the Red Cross in peacetime? "We must first of all repair, as far as possible, the ruins of all kinds left behind by the war."[68] In practical terms, this meant that the national societies of the belligerent states would naturally be engaged, along with their governments, in repairing the human and material damage caused by the war; in those regions, such as eastern Europe, where the task was beyond the resources of any one country, foreign Red Cross societies would be expected to provide assistance. Once these obligations were undertaken, national societies could begin to organize their peacetime work, which would be divided between disaster relief and "a general mobilization of Red Cross societies against diseases in general."[69] The former would involve preparing relief measures to deal with disasters such as earthquakes, volcanic eruptions, tidal waves, cyclones, epidemics, and floods. The latter, according to the ICRC, would necessitate an unremitting, organized, constant, and generalized struggle against the evils which attack humanity from the very cradle of the infant, harming the development of the human being and destroying public health. It will entail prophylactic measures of all kinds against the diseases of childhood, against the scourges of society, [but it must be] a program that is always open to modification, transforming itself according to the needs of each region and each epoch, and which will require all the activity and all the vigilance of the Red Cross societies for a long time to come.[70]

Almost two years after the Cannes conference had proclaimed the struggle against disease to be the obvious goal of peacetime Red Cross work, the ICRC had finally accepted this program, albeit in a form that ensured that its pursuit would not be permitted to push aside other desirable peacetime activities.

Nevertheless—and this point is crucial the ICRC was far from suggesting that the forthcoming conference should simply ratify either the purposes for which the LRCS had been created or the structure and role specified for that organization by its articles of association. Instead, in a deliberate effort to occupy the moral high ground, the ICRC proclaimed three principles to be essential for guiding this peacetime work: (1) universal charity, implying both political and religious neutrality; (2) complete independence from governments and all their agencies; and (3) the systematic organization and coordination of efforts on an international scale.[71] If these principles were accepted by the national societies, then the ICRC, with its traditions of universalism, neutrality, and independence, would naturally play an important role in developing and overseeing the peacetime work of the Red Cross movement. Measured against the test of these principles, the LRCS would inevitably be found wanting, for it was neither universal in its membership, neutral in its politics, nor independent in its finances. These deficiencies would therefore impair—or so the ICRC assumed—the ability of the LRCS to function on its own as an international coordinating agency. Thus, graciously but relentlessly, the ICRC's argument reached its logical conclusion: The forthcoming Tenth Conference should invite the secretariat of the LRCS, already established in Geneva, "to function in future, in close collaboration with the [ICRC], as a permanent bureau of inquiry and consultation for the practical activity of Red Cross societies in peacetime."[72] And, lest any question be raised about the powers of the international conference (for example, vis-à-vis those of the board of governors of the LRCS), the ICRC affirmed that international conferences "remain the highest deliberative bodies [*les assises suprêmes*] of the Red Cross."[73]

If the information that Kittredge had received in the Balkans is put alongside the article just described, the overall strategy of the ICRC becomes clear: The LRCS was to vanish from the scene, along with its board of governors and General Council; in their place was to arise a new International Red Cross Union, composed of all the national societies and directed by the existing ICRC, its membership possibly augmented on occasion by an undetermined number of representatives from the national societies. In Geneva there would be a permanent Red Cross secretariat, which would be charged with organizing investigations and temporary missions and with publishing the *Revue* and the *Bulletin International.* The secretariat would function as the organ of both the ICRC and the national societies, and the latter could turn for advice and assistance in their peacetime work to one part of the secretariat, a bureau specializing in public health matters; this bureau, presumably employing some of the technical experts then working for the LRCS, would be the only surviving vestige of that body.

Far from acceding to Henderson's plea for mutual tolerance and cooperation, the ICRC was evidently determined to banish the existing LRCS from the international scene. In its view, the LRCS was too American in outlook; too close to the governments of the Allies; and too much dominated by trained experts in public health and social work. And though these experts were no doubt well intentioned, in the opinion of the ICRC they simply did not understand the fundamental bases upon which the Red Cross had been founded. In the ICRC's unflattering picture of the LRCS there were, to be sure, elements of both personal jealousy and institutional rivalry, but there was also some substance. Symptomatic of the overwhelmingly American outlook of the LRCS is the fact that the Fourth of July was an unquestioned holiday for its staff. A small matter, perhaps; but in larger matters, American dominance was even more obvious. As Chapter 6 made clear, the LRCS was far more the creation of the Allied governments, and especially of President Wilson and Colonel House, than it was the creation of Red Cross societies; several of the so-called founding societies had reservations about the scope and direction of LRCS activities. The huge American subsidy that had been set aside for the LRCS was the work—as Mabel Boardman never tired of pointing out—not of the peacetime ARC but of the outgoing war council, a body that derived its legitimacy not from the constitution or membership of the ARC but from Wilson's proclamation and the support of the Wall Street financial establishment. The LRCS secretariat may have been located in Geneva, but its staff operated on the basis of assumptions derived from the advent of social work and the new public health in American universities, assumptions that were not necessarily shared by the postwar membership of the ARC, let alone by the members of other national Red Cross societies. Whatever the gulf that may have separated the immediate concerns of these societies from the lofty moral stance of the ICRC, an arguably greater one separated them from the LRCS secretariat, whose staff seemed not to appreciate that *of course* the first concern of all national societies would be to repair the damage caused by the war. Thus the British Red Cross, for example, which was forced to devote shrinking revenues to the rebuilding of Britain's local hospitals, felt chided by the LRCS for lack of commitment to the international cause but praised by the ICRC for fulfilling such a pressing postwar obligation. Where the ICRC had scrupulously avoided telling national societies how to organize themselves, the experts employed by the LRCS were already urging both old and new Red Cross societies to replicate at the national level the departmental structure of the LRCS secretariat. The truth is that after sixty of years of experience, the ICRC knew how to handle the national societies; the LRCS still had a great deal to learn. In such circumstances, Henderson's plea for tolerance and cooperation was simply naive.

If the strategy of the ICRC was to eliminate the LRCS, its tactical maneuvers, at least in public, were subtle enough to conceal this goal. Its master stroke—carried out at the same moment when its delegates in the Balkans were doing their best to undermine the LRCS—was to propose and eventually sign a one-year working agreement with the LRCS, under which a Joint Relief Commission, composed of members of both bodies, was established.[74] Under its terms, both bodies agreed to coordinate their relief efforts through the medium of the new commission. Although at first glance this action might seem to contradict its overall strategy, the ICRC in fact secured several important advantages by signing such an agreement on the very eve of the Tenth Conference. For one thing, it was now able to reassure outsiders that the two Red Cross bodies were indeed cooperating; moreover, if it were accused of working to undermine the LRCS, it could point to the working agreement as evidence of its good intentions. Even more important was the fact that this agreement to cooperate in organizing peacetime relief was tantamount to an admission by the LRCS that the role of the ICRC was far broader than that of wartime neutral intermediary. Finally, the agreement's one-year term effectively removed the question of ICRC-LRCS relations from the agenda of the Tenth Conference, leaving the ICRC with a perfect opportunity to secure from the conference further recognition of its special role and broader sphere of action within the Red Cross movement. Although Henderson took the agreement as a sign that even closer cooperation was likely in the future, the truth is that the ICRC obtained far more from it than did the LRCS; on learning of its terms, Robert Olds commented shrewdly: "It struck me as exactly the sort of agreement I should want if I were in the place of the Comité International and intended eventually to put the [LRCS] out of business."[75] To make assurance doubly sure, an unpublicized side agreement stipulated that the chairman of the joint relief commission would be named by the ICRC; not surprisingly, Gustave Ador himself assumed this position. Henderson and the LRCS had been finessed.

With this advantageous agreement in hand, the ICRC was able to obtain from the Tenth Conference resolutions that not only confirmed but extended its role. Because the LRCS representatives were confined to the role of "guests"—a status they shared with delegates of the League of Nations—they were in no position to challenge the ICRC's skillful orchestration of the occasion. Admittedly, not everything went as the ICRC might have hoped: Both the French and Belgian societies refused to attend on the grounds that the German Red Cross Society had yet to admit or express regret for Germany's wartime violations of the Geneva Convention. Thus, despite the ICRC's best efforts, the Tenth Conference was not a fully universal occasion.[76] The agenda was easier to manage: Many of the resolutions passed by the conference had been drafted in preliminary form by the ICRC itself, and those that concerned the future role of the ICRC naturally reflected the views that it had already expressed in the *Revue*. The passage of Resolution 16 was a particular triumph for the ICRC: Not only did the conference confirm both the existing organization and all of the previous mandates of the ICRC, but it added a crucial clause that effectively sabotaged the international aspirations of the LRCS: "The Conference approves the activity of the International Committee in peacetime. It recognizes the Committee as the guardian and propagator of the fundamental, moral and legal principles of the organization and appoints it to watch over their dissemination and application throughout the world."[77]

Many of those who voted for this resolution belonged to national societies that were themselves members of the LRCS. This is not surprising: The delegates were as full of good intentions as they were ignorant of the underlying issues. They undoubtedly believed that in approving this resolution they were simply expressing their appreciation for the role played in the past by the ICRC and welcoming its wider philanthropic role in the present and future. Most of them believed that there was, or certainly ought to be, a place for both the ICRC and the LRCS; few of them realized that this resolution would be used by the ICRC as ammunition in its continuing struggle with the LRCS over the future shape and direction of the Red Cross.

Gustave Ador's announcement of the formation of the joint relief commission had encouraged the delegates to believe that the ICRC and the LRCS were now prepared to cooperate with one another in promoting Red Cross ventures. Accordingly, the Tenth Conference entrusted both bodies with a joint mandate: To urge the peoples of the world, nations and individuals alike, to renounce the spirit of war. The result of this commission was the publication, on 19 July, 1921, of an "Appeal for Peace," signed by both the ICRC and the LRCS. Brimming with pieties about the evils of war and the need for an international outlook, the appeal conceded that the achievement of "genuine internationalism" would require "close and sincere collaboration from governments, parliaments, independent associations, the press, ministers of all religions and, especially, the Red Cross Societies."[78] Nevertheless, it emphasized that "all these forces need, in addition, the overriding motive of *personal conviction*. Everyone, whatever his or her possibilities, must help to create the peaceful conditions needed. Nobody should judge others from the standpoint of personal egoism, anger, fears or emotions, but in a spirit of harmony and mutual aid."[79]

Other than urging people to change their attitudes—or, better, to repudiate the less admirable characteristics of human nature—the appeal made no concrete proposals for the reduction of war-mindedness. Apparently Edouard Naville had tried to convince his ICRC colleagues to recommend to the Tenth Conference that Red Cross societies make a concerted attempt to persuade the states of the world that both conscription and aerial warfare should be abolished, but he had been unsuccessful.[80] Mindful of the fact that the conference would also be attended by delegates of many of the states that were signatories to the 1906 Revised Geneva Convention, his colleagues cautioned against alienating the very governments whose support would be essential for any revision or extension of the terms of the Convention. Given that the ICRC had already discussed the pressing need to secure international agreements covering prisoners of war and civilian refugees, the argument for caution appeared to be insurmountable.

The authors of the appeal were at pains to reassure the world that the Red Cross was not abandoning its neutrality by working "not only in time of peace but also *for peace*."[81] However, the difficulty with placing such great emphasis on personal conviction was its implication that war had no other cause than human willfulness: If only individuals would always act in a spirit of harmony and mutual aid, the appeal seemed to suggest, then war would be avoided. True, social institutions were invoked, but again the implication was that if only politicians, public figures, the press, and the clergy helped to create peaceful conditions, then war would disappear. Yet unless the Red Cross gave some explicit direction as to how these peaceful conditions could be created in a postwar Europe rent by political, economic, and social tensions, the appeal was as likely to produce real change as a parental plea to squabbling children to cooperate and be nice to one another.

Moreover, the justification offered for this change of course—that the destructiveness and totality of the Great War had forced the Red Cross to rethink its attitude toward war and peace—was implausible if not downright dishonest. The horror of the Great War was no more than the fulfillment of predictions made in the 1880s and 1890s about the changing nature of war and the increasing scale and destructiveness of the weaponry employed. Individuals of high prestige and considerable experience, such as Sir Thomas Longmore and Baron Mundy, as well as the military medical planners of several states, had repeatedly warned members of the Red Cross at both national and international meetings of the ghastly prospect that awaited Europe if a major war broke out. Yet neither the national societies, which were scrambling among themselves to organize for maximum wartime efficiency, nor the international conferences, which provided a forum where they could brag about their efforts to prepare for the coming war, were seriously interested in questioning where all this activity might lead. On the contrary, they had treated these ominous warnings as fresh challenges to the genius of philanthropy. Besides, in the decades prior to 1914, the ICRC and the national societies had been careful to distance themselves from both the advocates of disarmament and the apostles of pacifism, salving their consciences, if necessary, by resorting to Moynier's rationalization that the Red Cross was simply following a different route to the same goal. Thus it is fair to say that not only had the Red Cross not been exempt from the war-mindedness of the prewar era: It had contributed positively to its growth, popularity, and pervasiveness. Had those who framed the 1921 appeal looked more closely at the history of the Red Cross itself, they might have appreciated the difficulty inherent in transforming an institution that had worked for war as well as during war into one that could work for peace as well as during peace. They might also have pondered how it was that those who professed to act out of concern for the welfare of suffering humanity—the sincerity of whose personal convictions is not in question here—had managed to play an essential role in assisting states to fight larger and bloodier wars.

*　　*　　*

The Tenth Conference was a turning point in the history of the Red Cross. The ICRC's bold decision to endorse the expansion of peacetime Red Cross activity—and to put itself at the head of this enterprise—signaled that its members were ready to participate—albeit on their terms—in reshaping the Red Cross movement to match the new concerns of the postwar world. This almost revolutionary step, which demonstrated how far the ICRC had come since its November, 1918 circular, was to lay the basis for the enormous expansion of ICRC activity during the rest of the twentieth century. Its immediate effect was to ensure that the desire of the LRCS to remake the Red Cross, not to mention the postwar world, would remain no more than an unfulfilled aspiration. Now that the era of militarized charity appeared to have ended, the national societies were also seeking new roles for themselves and looking for sources of inspiration and direction. Hence they were unwilling to see either of the two international Red Cross bodies eliminated; both, they believed, could serve useful purposes provided neither attempted to supplant the other. The 1921 "Appeal for Peace" was a tentative first step, not only toward a new role for Red Cross societies but also toward encouraging the ICRC and the LRCS to cooperate more fully with one another.

Red Cross efforts to promote internationalism during the 1920s were so extensive and complex that they would merit treatment in a separate volume. Here one need only say, by way of an epilogue, that it proved impossible to create any organic union between the ICRC and the LRCS and that it took until 1928 to find a structure for an International Red Cross with which both bodies, as well as the national societies, could live comfortably. The negotiations that were undertaken to this end were so protracted and, at times, acrimonious that they exhausted and discouraged many of the participants. Readers who wish to follow them in detail may do so elsewhere.[82] Here it suffices to say that in the first stage both the ICRC and the LRCS tried to eliminate each other; when that failed, their negotiators tried to create a completely new body, but despite ingenious efforts they found it impossible to please everyone; then the national societies, convinced that the partisan interests of the negotiators were blocking cooperation, decided to take it upon themselves to resolve the problem, but they proved no better at it than had their predecessors. In the end, all that could be done was to admit defeat and recognize that since amalgamation was out of the question, only a statutory association of the ICRC, the LRCS, and the national societies could provide a way out of the dilemma in which the Red Cross found itself. That association, in which the ICRC managed to preserve both its autonomy and its right of initiative, was finally approved in 1928. This agreement has often been hailed as a great step forward in the development of the Red Cross, but it seems more accurate to regard it as a sedative that those involved gladly swallowed to relieve the pains of rebirth.

✚ Conclusion: Champions of Charity

Iɴ ᴛʜᴇ ᴄᴏᴜʀꜱᴇ ᴏꜰ ꜱɪx ᴅᴇᴄᴀᴅᴇꜱ, the Red Cross had spread throughout Europe and around the world. The conference in Geneva in 1863 had brought together no more than a handful of interested individuals from a score of European states; by contrast, the Tenth Conference in 1921 was attended by hundreds of delegates from Red Cross societies spread over six continents. Nowadays, members of the Red Cross movement like to think of this earlier period as a time when the seed planted by Henry Dunant took root and began to flourish in country after country, the activity of each national society signifying the continuous growth and development of a healthy plant. Implicit in this picture of Red Cross history is an unquestioning belief that what was created and carried out in the name of the Red Cross faithfully reflected the charitable aspirations of its founders. Implicit also is an assumption that the seed Dunant planted was indeed the seed of humanitarianism and that the growth of the Red Cross since 1863 is, before all else, evidence of a continuing and deepening commitment to humanitarian principles on the part of those countries that have signed the Geneva Conventions and officially recognized their national Red Cross (or Red Crescent) society.

In 1965, what are now called the seven fundamental principles of the Red Cross were proclaimed in Vienna by the Twentieth Conference: Humanity, Impartiality, Neutrality, Independence, Voluntary Service, Unity, and Universality. Elaborated for the guidance of Red Cross members in the second half of the twentieth century, these principles were claimed to have a historical basis; as if they had been both the inspiration for, and the goal of, all noteworthy Red Cross activity during the first hundred years of the movement's existence. The first question to be asked, therefore, is whether the broad outlines of this picture of Red Cross history are confirmed by the evidence that has been presented here. The short answer is, "On the whole, no."

In 1863, the Genevan founders of the Red Cross believed, like Evelyn Waugh's memorable Brigadier, that "there's nothing wrong with war except the fighting." Consequently they set out not to abolish war but to make it less barbaric by improving the lot of sick and wounded soldiers through the formation

346

of voluntary aid societies. These self-appointed champions of charity in wartime sought to achieve four related objectives. The first was to send onto the battlefields of Europe bands of volunteers, inspired by the purest motives of Christian charity, who would be able to supplement the presumed insufficiency of army medical organization. The second was to stimulate among the common people—whether they were soldiers or civilians—feelings of respect for those killed and wounded in battle, no matter what uniform they were wearing, so as to ensure that the ideals of a civilized society were extended to warfare itself. In order to encourage and protect the observance of standards of decent behavior in wartime, the Genevans promoted a third objective: The signing of an international convention that would grant special protection to the wounded and to those caring for them, whether the latter were army surgeons or civilian volunteers recognized for this purpose by commanders in the field. Soon a fourth objective also appeared desirable: The creation of a vast charitable army composed of neutral volunteers who, through the good offices of an international committee or federation of aid societies, would put themselves at the disposal of belligerents.

Three of these four objectives were swept aside almost immediately by the objections of contemporaries. The first—volunteers on the battlefield—was strenuously opposed by army commanders who did not relish the prospect of these self-styled delegates of humanity invading the zone of hostilities and threatening to undermine military discipline; the commanders' opposition was bolstered by that of army surgeons, who feared that civilian meddling might compromise the recognition that military medicine had only recently won because of its increased visibility and capability. The second objective—that of civilizing the common people—was steadily overshadowed and eventually rendered irrelevant by technological innovations that had the effect of barbarizing warfare anew: What moral purpose was served by teaching peasants not to pillage or mutilate wounded soldiers when allegedly civilized states were prepared to resort to aerial and submarine warfare, the bombardment of civilians, and even the use of poison gas? The fourth objective—the creation of a neutral charitable army upon which belligerents could draw in time of need—failed to gain the support of the great powers, whose leaders balked at the notion of a neutral Europe dictating standards of humane conduct to would-be belligerents and who were, understandably, far more ready to harness the charitable energies of their citizens for predominantly national purposes; hence the support and recognition that they gave to national Red Cross societies. Thus, of the four original objectives of the founders, only the third—the signing of an international convention regarding the treatment of the sick and wounded in war—was attained during the period covered by this book. To recognize this fact is not to diminish their achievement but rather to appreciate that the signing of the Geneva Convention was a part—and *only* a part—of a much broader humanitarian agenda, the rest of which remains to this day largely unfulfilled. Viewing the enterprise in this light surely raises a question about the degree to which humanitarianism, rather than self-interest, motivated the states that drew up and ratified the 1864 Convention. What Longmore called "the altered circumstances of our times" made signing the Convention a plausible course of action for European states in the mid-1860s; what needs to be understood, however, is that the same circumstances militated against achieving the other three objectives on the philanthropists' agenda, at least in the form in which they were originally envisioned.

National Red Cross societies, though not mentioned in the 1864 Convention, were formed to meet its stated goal, "the amelioration of the condition of the sick and wounded in war." As is well known, the condition of the sick and wounded improved substantially between the Crimean War and World War I, and the casual observer might be tempted to assume that this improvement was due principally to the work of the newly formed Red Cross societies. Yet was it? In 1863, the delegates had presumed that the resources of military medical formations would always be inadequate to cope with the numbers of wounded resulting from great battles and that bolstering the numbers of those caring for the wounded would in itself reduce mortality from wounds. This presumption was shared by Moynier and Appia, who anticipated that volunteers would be able to bring immediate comfort to the wounded on the battlefield itself: water, a dressing, perhaps some wine or tobacco, words of companionship, and a prayer for the souls of the seriously wounded. In the long run, however, most states and armies preferred not to encourage the presence of volunteers on the battlefield, and thus it was not this kind of immediate comfort that the aid societies were permitted to provide. As the great powers organized for war in the decades before 1914, the role of the Red Cross was deliberately chosen to place it not in the zone of hostilities but in the *zone d'étapes* and in the rear. Thus, instead of volunteers tending the wounded in the heat of battle, as Appia had witnessed in Schleswig, Red Cross units now found themselves assigned to railway stations, evacuation depots, hospital trains or ships, and convalescent hospitals. In these new roles they assuredly provided a great deal of welcome comfort for the wounded but at a point when comfort rarely made the difference between death and survival. Additional comfort and attention may have speeded the recovery of the wounded and almost certainly improved their morale, which is why this role was thought to be an appropriate one for the Red Cross rather than the army. Armies, after all, are not in the business of making life more comfortable and pleasant.

In these circumstances, credit for reducing morbidity and mortality must be given to the principal military and medical innovations of the late nineteenth and early twentieth centuries. Medical understanding of typhus, typhoid fever, malaria, yellow fever, and the gastrointestinal and venereal diseases that incapacitated armies was greatly increased by the germ theory and by knowledge of the vector transmission of disease. As the Japanese army was to demonstrate during the war with Russia, attention to such a seemingly simple matter as the purity of drinking water could have a dramatic effect on the incidence of disease in armies in the field. Once line commanders saw clear evidence that water purification, immunization, and vector control all helped to make armies healthier, they realized that preventive medicine was an investment that could pay huge dividends. Healthier soldiers were nevertheless still liable to be wounded in battle, and they benefited from better surgical procedures, thanks to the introduction of antiseptic and, later, aseptic surgery and of anesthesia. However, there is more to better wound care than improved surgical procedures. Better management of the sick and wounded also depended on the systematic development of procedures and technology for the controlled evacuation of casualties. Armies that gave their medical officers control over evacuation, hospital management, and medical supplies found that their wounded recovered more quickly and completely than those—like the French and the Russians in World War I—that gave no such autonomy to medical officers.

To these important innovations, the voluntary aid societies were little more than witnesses, and not always welcome ones at that. The line commanders, military surgeons, and veterinarians who applied these innovations in the field were usually, and often justifiably, suspicious of well-meaning volunteers. Nevertheless, to the extent that Red Cross personnel were acquainted with these medical innovations during their training and supervised in the field by those who understood their significance, they may be said to have functioned as useful supernumeraries of the bacteriological revolution. However, the reverse may also be true: It would be as foolish to assume that the ministrations of Red Cross personnel invariably assisted the recovery of the wounded as it would be to repeat those blanket condemnations of well-meaning but incompetent volunteers that are often found in military medical memoirs. Whatever the charitable motivations of Red Cross volunteers, it is indisputable that the innovations just described played a far more important role in reducing morbidity and mortality in the field than did comfort.

If the existence of Red Cross societies made little difference to the health of armies or to the improved care of the wounded, why then did the aid societies not only survive but flourish during these years? Here it is useful to recall Léon Le Fort's pointed comment at the Paris medical congress in 1878, which may be paraphrased as follows: "If the principal argument for the Red Cross is that we never have enough doctors and nurses in wartime, then why don't we have a charitable society for the artillery, because we never have enough cannon and gunners, either, do we? But if I suggested forming one for that purpose, you'd all think me mad." His point, of course, was that governments and armies ought to take military medicine and surgery every bit as seriously as cannon and gunners; in 1878 few of them did. However, his question becomes even more interesting if it is turned around: Why did states that would never have dared to rely on private charity to supplement the artillery find it appropriate to grant official recognition to voluntary aid societies that sought to supplement the army medical administration?

The answer to *that* question was already hinted at by Florence Nightingale, who, it will be recalled, had replied to Dunant's first overture in 1864 that "such a society would take upon itself duties which ought to be performed by the government of each country and so would relieve them of responsibilities which really belong to them and which they can properly discharge and being relieved of which would render war more easy." In other words, cannon and gunners were too important to be left to contingent charity, but governments were happy to permit Red Cross societies and personnel to assume much of the work and expense associated with caring for the sick and wounded. In the name of humanitarianism, state after state smoothed the way for the Red Cross, granting it exemptions from taxes and duties, free use of the post and telegraph, and free or reduced charges on the railways. However, governments also heeded Nightingale's warning that voluntary charitable effort would be an evil unless it were completely incorporated into the official military medical structure. Therefore, the condition that they attached to these privileges was an unreserved and prior agreement by the aid societies that in the event of war they would put themselves entirely under military control and subordinate their personnel to military discipline.

So Nightingale was correct in her prediction that the existence of Red Cross societies would "render war more easy." Like Dunant and Moynier, she died in 1910, and by then she had been proven even more correct. To be sure, in 1864 she could scarcely have foreseen the era of mass-participation warfare that Europe, Japan, and the United States were to enter even before her death. However, with the advent of the new warfare, the great powers themselves became champions of charity toward the sick and wounded as they began to understand what a useful role these societies could play as mediators of the values of militarism and as promoters of what might be called a "discourse of sacrifice" that drew the entire civilian population into voluntary support for war. This deliberate militarization of charity provoked little opposition from within the Red Cross. There were a few exceptions—Lord Wantage and Sir William MacCormac come to mind—who remained stalwart champions of an earlier and far more limited conception of charity in wartime, but on the whole the Red Cross societies—not surprisingly in an era of unbridled nationalism and militarism—aided and abetted the militarization of charity. The leaders of most national societies enthusiastically prepared for whatever war service the army and the government wished them to perform, greeting the need for more money and personnel as a fresh challenge to the genius of philanthropy.

By the 1890s, it was evident to old hands such as Sir Thomas Longmore and Baron Mundy that increasingly lethal weapons and more efficient explosives would make future wars an unimaginable horror for army medical services. Faced with this prospect, Dunant, the oldest hand of all, embraced pacifism, an implicit admission that he had abandoned the assumption that spreading the Red Cross idea would make war more civilized. However, the leaders of the national societies responded to the threat of bloodier wars by proclaiming that it was now their duty to ensure that budgets for charity kept pace with the ever-increasing expenditures on weaponry; a proposition that masked an essential distinction, charity being funded not by tax revenue but by voluntary contributions. No longer was concern about preparedness for war confined to governments, armies, and the aid societies. Now Red Cross societies—and of course they were not alone in this—began to teach and preach that war and preparation for war had become, in Michael Mann's phrase, "a normal and desirable social activity" in which it was everyone's patriotic duty to participate.[1] No longer did their volunteers wear civilian clothing in wartime, as they had done in 1870; by 1914, Red Cross "personnel" were "mobilized for active service" in uniforms that looked increasingly like those worn by the troops. The uniforms served certain purposes: They reminded the wearer and reassured army commanders that the Red Cross was indeed under military control; and they demonstrated to the civilian population that the work of nurses and of ambulance personnel was regarded as valued service to the nation.

What of the ICRC itself? Despite the alarms raised by Longmore and Mundy, it had little to say about the dangers of total war, or about the need to combat war-mindedness, until after the devastation of the Great War had become apparent. In the wake of the 1870s, that troubling decade when it seemed that even their one success—the Geneva Convention—might be overturned, the Genevans dared not risk alienating the very great powers upon whose support the entire enterprise turned. And of these, only the Russians seemed prepared to pursue further the original philanthropic agenda, and their support was insufficient to offset the unwillingness of the other powers to do the same. The inevitable result of this strategic retreat was that the ICRC, instead of leading the way (as Moynier had hoped) toward the peaceful resolution of conflict, found itself acting principally as a service agency for the conscript armies of the belligerents. The sending of presents and letters; the information provided about the missing to anxious families; the effort to reduce the chaos created by floods of civilian refugees: These were not the personal acts of compassion and devotion that had been envisioned by Moynier and Appia in *La guerre et la charité*, but at least they made the inconveniences of war more acceptable, its hardships more tolerable, and its disruption more manageable.

As the recognized auxiliaries of the military medical administration, national Red Cross societies helped to promote the culture of militarism, with its emphasis on centralized and hierarchical authority, and on discipline, planning, and timing. Stretcher-bearers, ambulance units, nurses, and hospital workers all were now trained in military fashion; in Japan, Germany, and Austria-Hungary, Red Cross personnel went on field maneuvers with the military. Preparation for war also involved organizing supplies of materiel and equipment; in making choices about what to use and what to discard, the emphasis was on what Dr. Riant had called "the rational and the rapid." Ambulances were systematically improved long before they were motorized; temporary hospitals were created in railway cars and on ships, at railway stations and in seaports. Most national Red Cross societies distributed to their local branches approved patterns for everything from bandages to bed sheets to barracks hospitals. This growing emphasis on speed, simplicity, and uniformity in design accompanied the adoption of uniforms for Red Cross personnel.

Most important of all, Red Cross societies proved themselves adept at employing the concepts of service and sacrifice both to popularize and to justify the additional labor obligations that men and women—*especially women*—were expected to accept if they were living in a belligerent state. Pictures, postcards, and posters incessantly drove home the message that since the wellborn and privileged, who presumably were entitled to lives of self-indulgence, were all making sacrifices, everyone else must do likewise. This was aimed especially at women, whose very nature, it was said, made them caring, compassionate, and devoted. Paradoxically, the very countries that had previously claimed that women were so weak as to require special protection from the law urged upon women war work that required a great deal of strength and stamina.[2] A favorite theme in Red Cross propaganda was that of service to the nation: Since men were risking life and limb at the front, women were urged to match that selfless example of devotion to the national cause. Not surprisingly, leading Red Cross women in Britain and the United States were also antisuffragists; their male associates made speeches in which they repeated the claim that voluntary work in wartime was a display of the strength of what they called "real feminism," as if all other kinds were fraudulent. In this manner, Red Cross societies became the recruiting agents for a charitable army composed largely of women volunteers, funded through what amounted to voluntary taxation.

In 1883, Gustave Moynier had predicted that the Red Cross could only benefit from the spread of conscription and the advance of democracy and that its universal success would be ensured by the advance of "moral progress." Its subsequent development proved him right, but largely—and perhaps not surprisingly—for the wrong reasons. He believed that the spread of conscription, by forcing citizen-soldiers to act in accordance with the terms of the Geneva Convention, would promote the growth of humanitarian attitudes; and that conscription, by increasing civilian concern for family members who had been called up, would ensure that citizen-volunteers would help the aid societies to flourish in peacetime, the better to perform their designated role in war. What he did not foresee was that the cost of training, clothing, feeding, arming, and transporting the huge armies obtained through conscription would place unimagined burdens upon national budgets and that in those circumstances states could not resist the temptation to pass on to their citizens the one aspect of war for which civilians proudly donated their money and labor: the care of the sick and wounded. Here again, Nightingale saw the future more clearly than Moynier.

The advance of democracy, so Moynier believed, would be accompanied by the moral edification of the common people. In his opinion, Red Cross societies could be both the agents and the beneficiaries of this process: Although founded by members of the social elite, aid societies could help to teach civic duty and moral responsibility; as the circle of the enlightened widened, societies would naturally broaden their membership to the point where they would become enormous national undertakings. Part of this task of enlightenment was, of course, to promote the rule of law in international affairs and to persuade people to abandon the use of force to settle disputes between nations. Moynier had expected the democratic age to reduce enthusiasm for war and curb its violence; he never forced himself to confront the possibility that democratic societies—although not inclined to fight one another—might nevertheless prove to be just as warlike as their predecessors.

The French revolutionaries had justified conscription as a duty that citizens ought to perform as one of their obligations to the republic that had brought them greater freedom. However, conscription was by no means confined to republics; as Peter Paret has observed, "autocratic systems did not find it difficult to substitute deference and apolitical patriotism for a freer political life as a justification for compulsory military service."[3] As military service became a normal part of the duty of the citizen or the subject in most European states, Red Cross societies sprang up, initially as a way of demonstrating that governments and social elites were not indifferent to the fate of those who had accepted their duty and had paid a price for doing so. By the late nineteenth century, states were increasingly drawing upon working classes and peasants to meet fresh demands for manpower, and it soon became apparent that national Red Cross societies were useful vehicles for shaping the feelings of ordinary people, not only about military service itself but also about the duties of noncombatants to do everything possible to support the national military effort. Michael Mann has pointed out that with the emergence of mass mobilization warfare "citizens did more than wave banners. Men fought in the front line, and men and women accepted additional labour burdens in the 'rear.'"[4] Red Cross societies helped to impart a sense of obligation to the state and the army to all those who had not been directly called up for service: women, men past service age, and even children. Not surprisingly, they did so in ways that preserved existing social inequities. For example, the conservative rationale of deference and patriotism was typically employed to justify and control women's service as auxiliaries to the military medical establishment even where—as in France—the conscription of men was explained as an obligation of republican citizenship. In kingdoms and empires—from Great Britain to Russia to Japan—the existence of Red Cross societies gave members of the ruling families countless opportunities to demonstrate to their subjects, high and low, that accepting the additional obligations of wartime and performing them in a disciplined manner was the very essence of loyalty and patriotism. Royal patronage and encouragement of the Red Cross and well-publicized war work for it also helped to popularize the institution of monarchy. Finally, by reassuring the anxious that charity budgets would keep pace with swelling military budgets, the aid societies also helped to make less unpalatable the arms race in which the great powers were engaged in the years between 1880 and 1914. Thus it seems fair to say that at least until the Armistice in 1918 national Red Cross societies played an important role in helping to legitimize what Paret has called "the totality of modern war, in which civilians may have to be as heroic as the men in uniform."[5]

The states that had championed militarized charity did not know what would happen to their Red Cross societies when the Great War ended. If they were no longer needed to ensure that noncombatants did their part for the war effort, and if a fresh outbreak of war was too horrible to contemplate, then logically the societies would become moribund. Yet to admit this would have meant exposing a reality that had been successfully cloaked in the rhetoric of patriotism and the discourse of sacrifice. Far better in these circumstances to encourage those who protested against "disbanding the charity army" and claimed to have found a new peacetime role for the Red Cross in leading a crusade against human suffering in all its forms. Besides, in 1919 it was politically expedient for the Allied leaders to hold out the hope of a better world to come. This helps to explain why Woodrow Wilson championed the idea of a rejuvenated and redirected Red Cross when it was put to him by Harry Davison. The public health experts whom Davison assembled in Cannes never thought to ask whether it was feasible for national Red Cross societies to undertake the sort of health program that they thought desirable. Unthinkingly but understandably, they assumed that the Red Cross societies had grown in numbers and resources during the war solely because they had been engaged in a struggle against suffering and that this struggle had only to be transposed from the military to the civilian population. Yet the new Red Cross League, despite the best efforts of its staff, failed to become the leader of a new crusade against misery and disease. Even the American Red Cross, whose surplus war funds had provided the money to operate the new body, was reluctant to champion the more extensive approach to charity that was explicitly recognized in the Articles of Association of the LRCS.

It was no easy task to convert societies that had been auxiliaries of the military medical establishments into agencies for social improvement and public health reform. The universal goals that the LRCS set for itself in 1919 were a dramatic change from the more selective humanitarianism that had been at the heart of the Red Cross enterprise since the beginning. In his book about Solferino, Dunant wrote that the Italian women who had helped to care for the French and Austrian wounded had spurred each other on with the cry, *"tutti fratelli"* (all are brothers). However, at least until 1919, those who joined Red Cross societies learned by observation that the fraternal treatment of wounded enemy soldiers was a temporary charitable imperative: It lasted only until they were returned to their own army, after which they suddenly ceased to be brothers. Only such a carefully constructed, not to say constricted, definition of humanitarianism made it possible for the Red Cross movement to ignore Virchow's appeal for a reconsideration of its priorities, Nightingale's warnings about the dangers of making it easier for states to make war, and Dunant's eventual espousal of pacifism.

Notes

Introduction

1. These issues are discussed in my *Politics and Public Health in Revolutionary Russia, 1890–1918* (Baltimore: Johns Hopkins University Press, 1990).

2. An honorable exception is Geoffrey Best, whose *Humanity in Warfare: The Modern History of the International Law of Armed Conflicts* (London: Weidenfeld and Nicolson, 1980), contains brief but suggestive comments about the Red Cross (pp. 141–150).

3. In these cases I have relied on versions of documents provided by the few individuals who have had access to the ICRC archives, especially Pierre Boissier, whose *From Solferino to Tsushima*, originally published in 1978, is the first of a two-volume *History of the International Committee of the Red Cross*, published by the Henry Dunant Institute in Geneva.

4. See, for example, Max Huber, *La pensée et l'action de la Croix Rouge* (Geneva: ICRC, 1954).

5. Two of the best known are Martin Gumpert, *Dunant: The Story of the Red Cross* (London: Eyre and Spottiswoode, 1939), and Fernand Gigon, *The Epic of the Red Cross or, The Knight-Errant of Charity*, trans. Gerald Griffen (London: Jarrolds, n.d. [1946?]).

6. Gustave Moynier, *The Red Cross: Its Past and Future*, trans. John Furley (London: Cassell, Petter, and Galpin, 1883), p. 47.

7. A broader field was examined by Geoffrey Best (see above, n. 2). The older works are C. Lueder, *La Convention de Genève au point de vue historique, critique, et dogmatique* (Erlangen, Germany: Édouard Besold, 1876); Louis Gillot, *La revision de la Convention de Genève au point de vue historique et dogmatique* (Paris: Rousseau, 1902).

8. Michael Mann, *States, War, and Capitalism: Studies in Political Sociology* (Oxford: Basil Blackwell, 1988), p. 124. For other approaches to the subject of militarism, see Alfred Vagts, *A History of Militarism* (New York: W. W. Norton, 1937), and Quincy Wright, *A Study of War*, 2d ed. (Chicago: University of Chicago Press, 1965).

Chapter 1

1. Henry Dunant, *A Memory of Solférino* (English version), Geneva: International Committee of the Red Cross, 1986, p. 73, n. 1. All quotations are from this English version, the original of which was published by the American National Red Cross in 1939. An earlier English translation, "by Mrs. David H. Wright of the Philadelphia chapter of the American Red Cross," appeared under the title *The Origins of the Red Cross: "Un Souvenir de Solférino," by Henri Dunant* (Philadelphia: John C. Winston, 1911). The first French edition was entitled *Un Souvenir de Solférino par J. Henry Dunant* (Geneva: Fick, 1862); the title page also bore the words, "Ne se vend pas" (not for sale). Note that Dunant spelled his name Henry, not Henri.

2. *Help for Sick and Wounded, Being a Translation of "La guerre et la charité," by MM. Moynier and Appia,* trans. John Furley (London: John Camden Hotten, 1870), p. 32.

3. For details concerning Dunant's early life and charitable work, see Christian-Friedrich Haje and Jules-Marie Simon, *Les origines de la Croix-Rouge* (Stuttgart: A. Lindheimer; Amsterdam: Delsman and Nolthenius, 1900), pp. 3–5.

4. Quoted in Pierre Boissier, *From Solferino to Tsushima: History of the International Committee of the Red Cross* (Geneva: Henry Dunant Institute, 1985), p. 37.

5. On Dunant's business interests in Algeria, see Marc Descombes, *Henry Dunant* (Geneva: Editions Rene Coeckelberghs, 1988), pp. 23–33.

6. These two pamphlets were called, respectively, *Memorandum au sujet de la Société des Moulins de Mons-Djémila, au capital de 1 million, par Jean-Henry Dunant,* and *L'empire de Charlemagne rétabli: Le Saint Empire romain reconstitué par sa Majesté l'Empereur Napoleon III;* for further details of their contents, see Descombes, *Dunant,* pp. 32–33.

7. Dunant, *Solférino,* pp. 27–28.

8. Ibid., pp. 21, 32, 78.

9. Ibid., pp. 30–31.

10. Ibid., pp. 31, 51.

11. Ibid., p. 45.

12. Ibid., p. 52.

13. Ibid., p. 121.

14. Ibid., pp. 108–109.

15. Although he praised the French NCOs, it was for their "unusual" eagerness and bravery. Ibid., p. 34. For the amputation scene, see ibid., pp. 89–92.

16. Ibid., p. 70.

17. Ibid., pp. 114–115.

18. Ibid., p. 123.

19. Ibid., p. 53.

20. Ibid., p. 93.

21. Ibid., p. 77.

22. Ibid., p. 71.

23. Ibid., p. 88.

24 . Ibid., p. 110n.

25. Ibid., p. 75.

26. Ibid., pp. 54, 62.

27. Ibid., p. 64. Tobacco could serve as a tranquilizer of sorts in the absence of anything better; cigar smoke was useful in covering up the stench of gangrene.

28. Ibid., p. 65.

29. Ibid., pp. 86–87, 96.

30. Ibid., pp. 110–111.

31. Ibid., p. 72.

32. Ibid., pp. 121–122.

33. Ibid., p. 102

34. Ibid., pp. 115, 117.

35. Ibid., p. 116

36. Ibid., p. 52n.

37. Ibid., pp. 117–118. Emphasis added.

38. Ibid., p. 118.

39. Ibid., pp. 119–120; Dunant also cited John Howard, apparently because he was under the impression that Howard had brought sanitary reforms to all the prisons and hospitals he visited during his travels in Europe.

40. Ibid., pp. 124–125.

41. Ibid., p. 125.

42. Ibid., p. 126.

43. Ibid., pp. 126–127.

44. See the examples cited by Boissier, *From Solferino*, pp. 40–41.

45. Ibid., p. 47.

46. On the SGUP's work, see Bernard Lescaze, *La Société Genevoise d'Utilité Publique en son temps, 1828–1978: contribution a l'histoire économique et sociale de Genève* (Geneva: SGUP, 1978).

47. For these deliberations, see "Documents inédits sur la fondation de la Croix-Rouge: Procès-verbaux du 'Comité des Cinq,'" *Revue Internationale de la Croix-Rouge* 69 (1948):861–879 (hereafter "Documents inédits").

48. On Dufour's military career, see Joachim Remak, *A Very Civil War: The Swiss Sonderbund War of 1847* (Boulder: Westview Press, 1993).

49. Maunoir had spent some time in London as a medical student; moreover, his second wife was an American from Boston. Roger Durand, "Théodore Maunoir est aussi un fondateur de la Croix-Rouge," *Gesnerus* 34 (1977):139–155.

50. Appia was eight years older than Moynier and had completed his student days in Heidelberg and Paris just before Moynier began his.

51. There is an English translation of the textbook: P. L. Appia, M.D., *The Ambulance Surgeon or Practical Observations on Gunshot Wounds*, ed. T. W. Nunn and A. M. Edwards (Edinburgh: Adam and Charles Black, 1862).

52. Lescaze, *La Société Genevoise d'Utilité Publique*, p. 79.

53. In June of 1864, however, the same group was to claim that this decision was not taken until after the Geneva conference of 1863, but this was untrue. See the minutes of the meeting of 17 February, 1863 in "Documents inédits," p. 865. Contrast this with the statement in *Secours aux blessés: Communication du Comité International faisant suite au compte rendu de la Conférence Internationale de Genève* (Geneva: Fick, 1864), p. 8.

54. "Documents inédits," pp. 864–879.

55. "Documents inédits," pp. 866–867.

56. "Documents inédits," pp. 867–870.

57. "Documents inédits," pp. 871–872.

58. *Comité international de secours aux militaires blessés. Actes. Recueil annoté de toutes les pièces importantes du Comité International depuis son origine en 1863* (Geneva: Soullier and Wirth, 1871), pp. 1–4.

59. Boissier, *From Solferino*, pp. 145–147.

60. According to E. Evrard, an exception to this practice occurred in 1677; see his "La première neutralisation par acte juridique d'un hôpital militaire de campagne: L'Hôpital Militaire Français de Marchienne-au-Pont (1677)," in *Revue Internationale des Services de Santé des Armées de Terre, de Mer, et de l'Air*, special number (1967). I am indebted for this reference to Professor Robert J.T. Joy.

61. Boissier, *From Solferino*, pp. 129–130, 147.

62. John Pringle, *Observations on the Diseases of the Army* (London, 1753), p. viii.

63. See Louis Duncan, "Medical Men in the American Revolution," *Army Medical Bulletin*, no. 25 (1931), pp. 72–73, 81.

64. A full discussion of the historical antecedents of the Geneva Convention is beyond the scope of this book. Readers who wish to explore the subject in more detail should consult Geoffrey Best, *Humanity in Warfare: The Modern History of the International Law of Armed Conflicts* (London: Weidenfeld and Nicolson, 1980), as well as C. G. Fenwick, *International Law* (London: Allen and Unwin, 1924); W. E. Darby, *International Tribunals* (London: Dent, 1904); M. O. Hudson, *International Tribunals* (Washington, D.C., 1944).

65. Cited in the document entitled "Historical Precedents," attached to the file, "The Geneva Convention of 1864—Its Proceedings," U.S. National Archives, Record Group 200: Records of the American National Red Cross, 1881–1916 (First Series), Box 6, folder 041, "2nd International Red Cross Congress," p. 42. Hereafter cited as "Historical Precedents."

66. [Augustin] Cabanès, *Chirurgiens et blessés à travers l'histoire. Des origines a la Croix-Rouge* (Paris: Albin Michel, 1918), pp. 609–610; Boissier, *From Solferino*, pp. 150–151.

67. Quoted in Boissier, *From Solferino*, p. 150.

68. *Help for Sick and Wounded*, pp. 189–190.

69. "Historical Precedents," pp. 43–44. The text of Percy's draft was reprinted in *Secours aux blessés*, pp. 31–32.

70. Basic works on the sanitary reform movement are R. A. Lewis, *Edwin Chadwick and the Public Health Movement* (London: Longmans, Green, 1952); J. M. Eyler, *Victorian Social Medicine: The Ideas and Methods of William Farr* (Baltimore: Johns Hopkins University Press, 1979); William L. Coleman, *Death Is a Social Disease: Public Health and Political Economy in Early Industrial France* (Madison: University of Wisconsin Press, 1982); and Ann F. LaBerge, *Mission and Method: The Early-Nineteenth-Century French Public Health Movement* (New York: Cambridge University Press, 1992).

71. This phrase appeared in a lecture delivered by Longmore on 16 March, 1866, and was published by Furley in *Help for Sick and Wounded*, p. 365.

72. For the Russian side, see J. S. Curtiss, "Russian Sisters of Mercy in the Crimea, 1854–1855," *Slavic Review* 25 (1966):84–100. On Nightingale's role in the Crimean conflict, see Sue M. Goldie (ed.), *"I Have Done My Duty": Florence Nightingale in the Crimean War, 1854–1856* (Iowa City: University of Iowa Press, 1987).

73. J.-C. Chenu, *Rapport au conseil de santé des armées sur les résultats du service médico-chirurgical aux ambulances de Crimée et aux hopitaux militaires francais en Turquie, pendant la campagne d'Orient, en 1854, 1855, et 1856* (Paris: Masson, 1856).

74. For Nightingale's interest in nursing in military hospitals, see Monica E. Baly, *Florence Nightingale and the Nursing Legacy* (London: Croom Helm, 1986), pp. 103–122; see also F. B. Smith, *Florence Nightingale: Reputation and Power* (London: Croom Helm, 1982), pp. 72–113.

75. J. L. H. Keep, *Soldiers of the Tsar: Army and Society in Russia, 1462–1874* (Oxford: Clarendon Press, 1985), pp. 373–374.

76. Boissier, *From Solferino*, p. 160; Giorgio Del Vecchio, "On the History of the Red Cross," trans. R. Parsons, *Journal of the History of Ideas* 24 (1962):578.

77. Luigi Appia, *Aforismi sul transporto de' feriti* (Naples: Stamperia della Regia Universita, 1862); see also Roger Boppe, *L'homme et la guerre: Le docteur Louis Appia et les débuts de la Croix-Rouge* (Geneva: Muhlethaler, 1959), p. 39.

78. *Help for Sick and Wounded*, pp. 365–366.

79. Ibid., pp. 366–367.

80. Ibid., p. 366.

81. On Russell, see Olive Anderson, *A Liberal State of War: English Politics and Economics During the Crimean War* (London: Macmillan, 1967), pp. 71–76.

82. *La guerre et la charité; traite théoretique et pratique de philanthropie appliquée aux armées en campagne, par G. Moynier et L. Appia* (Geneva: Cherbuliez, 1867). The English translation by John Furley appeared in 1870; see n.2 above.

83. *Help for Sick and Wounded*, p. 32.

84. Ibid., p. 32.

85. Ibid., pp. 50–51.

86. Ibid., p. 51.

87. Ibid., p. 55.

88. Dunant's tour of the German capitals is described in detail in Boissier, *From Solferino*, pp. 64–67.

89. Florence Nightingale had set an example for the compilation of this kind of data with her *Notes on Matters Affecting the Health, Efficiency, and Hospital Administration of the British Army* (London: Harrison and Sons, 1858).

90. Quoted in Boissier, *From Solferino*, p. 63.

91. Ibid., p. 68.

92. By "volunteer nurses" the authors meant both males and females; as the following Article 8 makes clear, their expectation was that male nurses (*infirmiers*) would serve either at the front or in hospitals, whereas, for reasons of propriety, female nurses (*infirmières*) would always be assigned to hospital duty.

93. *Compte rendu de la Conférence Internationale réunie à Genève les 26, 27, 28, et 29 Octobre 1863 pour étudier les moyens de pourvoir à l'insuffisance du service sanitaire dans les armées en campagne* (Geneva: Fick, 1863), pp. 14–16. This draft also appears, in slightly different versions, in *Help for Sick and Wounded*, pp. 103–105, and Boissier, *From Solferino*, pp. 58–59.

94. *Compte rendu de la Conférence Internationale réunie a Genève les 26, 27, 28, et 29 Octobre 1863 pour étudier les moyens de pourvoir à l'insuffisance du service sanitaire dans les armées en campagne*. Geneva: Fick, 1863, p. 33 (hereafter *Geneva 1863: Compte rendu*).

95. Ibid., p. 35.

96. Ibid., p. 37

97. Ibid., p. 49

98. Ibid., p. 57.

99. In their introduction to *Secours aux blessés*, written in June 1864, members of the Geneva committee acknowledged the British achievement but argued that "at least for the moment" they could not expect such a solution from continental countries with different administrative traditions. *Secours aux blessés*, p. 11.

100. *Geneva 1863: Compte rendu*, p. 50.

101. Ibid., p. 54.

102. Ibid., p. 55.

103. Ibid., p. 63.

104. Ibid., pp. 68–70.

105. Ibid., pp. 75–76.

106. Ibid., p. 79.

107. Ibid., p. 90

108. Ibid., p. 84.
109. Ibid., p. 88.
110. Ibid., p. 93.
111. Ibid., p. 98.
112. Ibid., p. 109.
113. Ibid., p. 118
114. Ibid., pp. 117–119.
115. Ibid., p. 119.

116. The source of the claim that it was General Dufour who suggested the Red Cross emblem was Dunant himself; the accuracy of his *Memoirs* may be questioned because they were composed many years after the event. See "Le Brassard de la Croix-Rouge: Extrait des Memoires d'Henri Dunant," Dunant Papers (Bibliothèque Publique et Universitaire de Genève), Ms. fr. 2101.f.9.

117. However, it is perhaps revealing that in the introduction to *Secours aux blessés*, p. 16, the Geneva committee, noting that the Geneva conference of 1863 had adopted the red cross emblem, described their work as "a crusade on behalf of the unfortunate wounded." This was the first articulation of an image that was to recur frequently in Red Cross history.

118. During the Sonderbund War of 1847, Swiss federal troops wore a red armband with a white cross, derived from the Swiss flag (which was in turn derived from the coat of arms of the Canton of Schwyz).

119. No less an authority than Pierre Boissier has expressed strong reservations about the "tribute to Switzerland" argument, citing as evidence the fact that the Swiss Federal Council tried to persuade the Geneva committee to employ a St. Andrew's cross in order to avoid confusion with the Swiss federal colors. They would, he rightly observes, hardly have taken such a step if they had believed that they were repudiating a compliment to their country. Boissier, *From Solferino*, p. 77. So long as the archives of the ICRC remain closed to independent researchers, it will be impossible to settle this matter once and for all.

120. *Geneva 1863: Compte rendu*, p. 113.
121. Ibid., p. 114.
122. Ibid., pp. 134–135.
123. Ibid., pp. 133–134.
124. Ibid., pp. 130–131.
125. Ibid., p. 144.

126. Ibid., pp. 147–149; the translation, with slight modifications, is from Boissier, *From Solferino*, pp. 80–81; another version appears in *Help for Sick and Wounded*, pp. 105–106. The most accessible version of the text is in D. Schindler and J. Toman, eds., *The Laws of Armed Conflicts* (Geneva: Henry Dunant Institute, 1981), pp. 209–212.

127. "Documents inédits," pp. 876–878.

128. *Secours aux blessés*, p. 28. Moynier drew a careful distinction between volunteers recruited by an aid committee and local civilian helpers who—like Dunant at Solferino—spontaneously came to the aid of the wounded.

129. Organized by volunteers in the early days of the Civil War, the U.S. Sanitary Commission sought authorization from the government to act as the civilian agency for assistance to the Army Medical Bureau. Although initially faced with hostility from the army and from individuals within the government, the Commission received

official recognition from the War Department in June, 1861, and it soon became the main vehicle for civilian aid to the war effort. The Sanitary Commission is discussed in more detail below.

130. Boissier, *From Solferino*, p. 88.

131. *Secours aux blessés*, p. 18. The Geneva committee referred particularly to "the chivalrous spirit of the Spanish," who assisted the cause in that country.

132. Ibid., p. 20.

133. Boissier, *From Solferino*, p. 88.

134. Miliutin's reply is summarized in *Secours aux blessés*, p. 23; see also Boissier, *From Solferino*, p. 90.

135. For the relationship between the Polish uprising and Russian internal policy, see Daniel T. Orlovsky, *The Limits of Reform: The Ministry of Internal Affairs in Imperial Russia, 1802–1881* (Cambridge, Mass.: Harvard University Press, 1981), pp. 76, 124, 165.

136. Boissier, *From Solferino*, p. 89. Managing the British response from behind the scenes, Florence Nightingale had written to Longmore that it was necessary "to draw up such a statement of our present arrangements as will satisfy the Geneva folk that every precaution has been taken & can be taken & make it as long & as complete as possible—then return it to me. I will send it to the W[ar] O[ffice]—& they will make an authoritative document out of it." Wellcome Tropical Institute, Royal Army Medical Corps Collection No. 1139, Longmore Papers 54/7, Nightingale to Longmore, 23 July, 1864.

137. Quoted in Boissier, *From Solferino*, p. 42.

138. Longmore Papers 54/7, Nightingale to Longmore, 23 July, 1864.

139. Longmore Papers 54/13, Nightingale to Longmore, 28 February, 1867.

140. Longmore Papers 54/5, 16 May, 1869.

141. J.-C. Chenu, *Observations sur l'insuffisance du Service de Santé en campagne* [Paris] [1864]. This pamphlet, a copy of which is in the ICRC Library, bears pagination that suggests that it was a hastily composed addition to his magnum opus on the Crimean War (see n.73 above).

142. Chenu, *Observations*, pp. 710–711.

143. Ibid., pp. 726–737.

144. Ibid., p. 721.

145. Elisée Reclus, "La Commission sanitaire de la guerre aux Etats-Unis," *Revue des Deux Mondes* 51 (1 May, 1864):155–172.

146. Chenu, *Observations*, p. 744.

147. It is interesting to note that in the introduction to *Secours aux blessés*, p. 13, the Geneva committee attempted to minimize objections to their proposals, claiming that its critics were concerned only with secondary issues, such as how the volunteers would be maintained or whether they should be allowed on the battlefield. In the case of Nightingale and Chenu, this claim does not stand up to scrutiny.

148. Chenu, *Observations*, p. 747.

149. The French were not alone on this issue; the Danish government also refused to sanction the presence of volunteers on the battlefield itself. See *Secours aux blessés*, p. 17.

150. The text of this letter, from the emperor's aide-de-camp, Colonel Favé, to Dunant, appears in *Secours aux blessés*, pp. 18–19.

151. Boissier, *From Solferino*, p. 105.

152. Ibid., pp. 103

153. Ibid., pp. 105–106.

154. Quoted in ibid., p. 106.

155. These negotiations are described in detail in ibid., pp. 108–109.

156. *Secours aux blessés*, p. 30.

157. Ibid., p. 29.

158. Quoted in Boissier, *From Solferino*, p. 112.

159. President Abraham Lincoln's refusal to send an official U.S. delegate reflected not only that country's policy of avoiding "foreign entanglements" but also his determination to avoid giving foreign governments—particularly those of Great Britain and France—any excuse for meddling in the American Civil War.

160. Moynier admitted this in his opening statement. See "Proceedings of the International Congress, Geneva, 1864," NARA RG 200 (Records of the American National Red Cross), Box 6, Folder 041, "2d International Red Cross Congress," p. 12. (Hereafter cited as "Proceedings.")

161. Ibid., pp. 8–9.

162. Ibid., pp. 9–10.

163. Ibid., p. 12. Members of the Geneva committee had already pointed out how "singular" it was that immediate assistance to the wounded on the battlefield itself, once "the point of departure for the whole enterprise," was quickly being relegated to an accessory position. *Secours aux blessés*, p. 13.

164. "Proceedings," p. 13.

165. Ibid., p. 19.

166. William Q. Maxwell, *Lincoln's Fifth Wheel: The Political History of the United States Sanitary Commission* (New York: Longmans, Green, 1956), p. 274.

167. "Proceedings," p. 19.

168. Ibid., p. 39.

169. Ibid., pp. 36–37.

170. "Report to the Executive Committee of the European Branch of the United States Sanitary Commission," NA 200/ANRC, Box 1, Folder 004, Charles S. P. Bowles, p. 15. (Hereafter cited as Bowles Report.)

171. For the final text, see Schindler and Toman, *The Laws of Armed Conflicts*, pp. 213–216.

172. Bowles Report, p. 17.

173. Ibid., p. 17.

174. Ibid., pp. 17–18.

175. Boissier, *From Solferino*, pp. 119–120.

176. Article 7 of the Convention specified: "An armband (brassard) shall . . . be allowed for individuals neutralised, but the delivery thereof shall be left to military authority," whereas Article 8 entrusted to commanders-in-chief of the belligerent armies the details of the execution of the Convention.

177. A proposal that would have committed all signatories to encourage, patronize, and protect a national society was omitted from the draft convention submitted for discussion in 1864 because it became clear to the organizers that many states wished to retain complete discretion in this matter: NARA RG 200, Records of the American National Red Cross, Box 6, Folder 041, "2nd International Red Cross Congress," p. 14.

178. Maxwell, *Lincoln's Fifth Wheel*, pp. 275–276.

179. Ibid., p. 276.

180. See above, n.163

181. Edmund C. Fisher, *The English Branch of the United States Sanitary Commission. The Motive of Its Establishment, and the Result of Its Work* (London, 1865), pp. 4, 8. I am indebted for this reference to James H. Cassedy.

182. The records of the 1864 meetings show that Bowles made little contribution to the diplomatic congress that, meeting at Town Hall, drew up the Geneva Convention; his speeches about the Sanitary Commission were made at the informal and poorly attended meetings of representatives of central committees of national aid societies, held at the Athénée. See "Une Conférence Oubliée de la Croix-Rouge à Genève en 1864," *Bulletin International de la Croix-Rouge* 15 (1884):126–135.

183. On "Lieber's Code" and Union Army General Order 100, to which it gave rise, see Richard S. Hartigan, *Lieber's Code and the Law of War* (Chicago: Precedent, 1983), and Albert G. Love, "The Geneva Red Cross Movement: European and American Influence on its Development," *Army Medical Bulletin* (Carlisle, Pa., 1942). For an earlier agreement concerning the treatment of captive medical officers, see James O. Breeden, "The Winchester Accord: The Confederacy and the Humane Treatment of Captive Medical Officers," *Military Medicine* 158 (1993):689–692.

184. These included the *United States Sanitary Commission: A Sketch of Its Purpose and Its Work, Compiled from Documents and Private Papers* (Boston: Little, Brown, 1863); *The Sanitary Commission of the United States Army: A Succinct Narrative of Its Work and Purposes* (New York: Sanitary Commission, 1864; reprint edition, New York: Arno Press and New York Times, 1972); and Georgeanna M. Bacon, *Three Weeks at Gettysburg* (New York: A. D. F. Randolph, 1863).

185. Bowles Report, p. 9.

186. *Secours aux blessés*, pp. 179–187.

187. Durand, "Théodore Maunoir," p. 146, quotes the doctor's wish to "get up an agitation" on behalf of the cause of help for the wounded as well as his belief that the peoples of Europe needed to be made aware of the issues involved.

188. Boissier, *From Solferino*, p. 61.

189. On the desire of the French national society to make Paris the center of the Red Cross movement, see *Conférence Internationale des Sociétés de la Croix-Rouge: Compte rendu*, vol. 2 (Paris: 1867), pp. 151–153.

190. William H. McNeill, *The Pursuit of Power: Technology, Armed Force, and Society Since A.D. 1000* (Chicago: University of Chicago Press, 1982), p. 242.

191. *Help for Sick and Wounded*, p. 32.

Chapter 2

1. *Secours aux blessés. Communication de Comité International faisant suite au compte rendu de la Conférence Internationale de Genève* (Geneva: Fick, 1864), pp. 45–144. Presumably the thirty-eight letters that he claims (p. 46) to have sent back to Geneva are in the archives of the ICRC.

2. Ibid., p. 58.

3. Ibid., p. 55.

4. On the origins and early history of the Kaiserwerth Institution, see Catherine M. Prelinger, *Charity, Challenge, and Change: Religious Dimensions of the Mid-Nineteenth-Century Womens' Movement in Germany* (Westport, Conn.: Greenwood Press, 1987), pp. 18–23.

5. *Secours aux blessés,* p. 62.

6. Ibid., p. 62.

7. Ibid., pp. 118–119.

8. Ibid., p. 109.

9. Ibid., p. 115.

10. Ibid., pp. 76–77.

11. Ibid., pp. 111–113.

12. Ibid., p. 144.

13. *Help for Sick and Wounded, Being a Translation of "La guerre et la charité" by MM. Moynier and Appia,* trans. John Furley (London: John Camden Hotten, 1870), pp. 31–32.

14. Ibid., p. 33.

15. Ibid., pp. 33–34.

16. Ibid., p. 34.

17. This paragraph summarizes the argument advanced by Moynier in ibid., pp. 34–40.

18. Ibid., p. 40.

19. *Gazette Médicale de Lyon* (1 September, 1865), as quoted in *Help for Sick and Wounded,* p. 117.

20. *Help for Sick and Wounded,* p. 118.

21. Ibid., p. 119; *Compte rendu de la Conférence Internationale réunie a Genève les 26, 27, 28, et 29 Octobre 1863 pour étudier les moyens de pourvoir à l'insuffisance du service sanitaire dans les armées en campagne* (Geneva: Fick, 1863), p. 8.

22. A similar argument was put forward by the Belgian Dr. Feigneaux: "En abritant sous le drapeau de charité, contre les horribles et inévitables désastres que la guerre entraine, des hommes différents par leur nationalité, par leur langue, par leurs coutumes, l'institution des *secoureurs volontaires* à faire aimer et bénir la paix." *Des secours volontaires en temps de guerre* (extrait des *Annales de l'Association Internationale pour le Progrès des Sciences Sociales*) (Brussels: Henri Manceaux, 1866), pp. 20–21.

23. *Gazette Médicale de Lyon* (1 October, 1865), as quoted in *Help for Sick and Wounded,* p. 118.

24. *Help for Sick and Wounded,* pp. 42–44.

25. Léon Le Fort, *Guerres de Crimée et d'Amérique. Examen comparatif de la mortalité* (Paris: E. Martinet, 1868) (reprinted from *Gazette Hebdomadaire de Médicine,* 1868); an abridged English translation, preserved in the Longmore Papers as LP 26/41, appeared in *The Medical Record* [1868], pp. 572–578.

26. Quoted in Pierre Boissier, *From Solferino to Tsushima: History of the International Committee of the Red Cross* (Geneva: Henry Dunant Institute, 1985), p. 173.

27. Paul Kennedy, *The Rise and Fall of the Great Powers* (New York: Random House, 1988), p. 185.

28. *Compte rendu des travaux de la Conférence Internationale tenue à Berlin du 22 au 27 Avril 1869, par les délégués des gouvernments signitaires de la Convention de Genève et des Sociétés et Associations de Secours aux Militaires Blessés et Malades* (Berlin: J. F. Starcke, 1869), p. 389 (hereafter *Berlin 1869: Compte rendu*); Thomas W. Evans, *Sanitary Institutions During the Austro-Prussian-Italian Conflict . . . ,* 3d ed. (Paris: Simon Raçon, 1868), pp. 32–35.

29. Evans, *Sanitary Institutions,* pp. 56–57.

30. *Berlin 1869: Compte rendu*, p. 389.

31. Evans, *Sanitary Institutions*, p. 40; *Berlin 1869: Compte rendu*, pp. 340, 398ff.

32. Evans, *Sanitary Institutions*, p. 40.

33. Ibid., pp. 57–58.

34. Ibid., pp. 76–77.

35. Ibid., p. 78.

36. Brian Bond, *War and Society in Europe, 1870–1970* (London: Fontana Press, 1984), p. 15.

37. Evans, *Sanitary Institutions*, p. 80.

38. Ibid., pp. 84–85.

39. Ibid., pp. 87–88.

40. Boissier, *From Solferino*, pp. 177–178.

41. As quoted in ibid., p. 179.

42. For more details, see ibid., pp. 182–184.

43. This account is based on those of Roger Boppe, *L'homme et la guerre: Le docteur Louis Appia et les débuts de la Croix-Rouge* (Geneva: J. Muhlethaler, 1959), pp. 97–103, and Boissier, *From Solferino*, pp. 186–190.

44. Boppe, *L'homme et la guerre*, p. 97.

45. Boissier, *From Solferino*, pp. 204–205.

46. As quoted in ibid., pp. 203–204.

47. *Help for Sick and Wounded*, p. 131.

48. Boissier, *From Solferino*, p. 206.

49. Quoted in ibid., p. 206.

50. Ibid., pp. 206–208.

51. Boissier himself raises some questions about it; see *From Solferino*, pp. 204–205.

52. See, for example, Martin Gumpert, *Dunant: The Story of the Red Cross* (London: Eyre and Spottiswoode, 1939); the theme is prominent in all of the more recent biographies of Dunant.

53. Gustave Moynier, *Les Conférences Internationales des Sociétés de la Croix-Rouge* (Geneva: CICR, 1901), p. 10.

54. According to the published proceedings of the conference, the three Americans were delegates of the U.S. Sanitary Commisssion, but that body had ceased to exist in December, 1865. It is curious that they did not list themselves as members of the American Association for the Relief of Misery on the Battlefield, which had been founded in January, 1866, by many of the same people who had been involved in the Sanitary Commission. For the official list of delegates, see *Conférence Internationale des Sociétés de la Croix-Rouge. Compte rendu*, vol. 2 (Paris: 1867), pp. 6–14. (This two-volume work will be hereafter *Paris 1867: Compte rendu*.)

55. For this text, as well as Moynier's comments on it, see Gustave Moynier, *Étude sur la convention de Genève pour l'amélioration du sort des militaires blessés dans l'armées en campagne (1864 et 1868); droit de gens* (Paris: Cherbuliez, 1870), pp. 72–73, 109–111 (hereafter *Étude*).

56. See "Propositions de la Conférence de Wurzbourg, 22 août 1867," in ibid., pp. 112–115.

57. See "Texte proposé par la Conférence de Paris, 29 août 1867," in ibid., pp. 116–121.

58. For a brief summary of the proceedings of the Paris conference, see Boissier, *From Solferino,* pp. 209–211; the debates may be followed in detail in *Paris 1867: Compte rendu.*

59. *Paris 1867: Compte rendu,* vol. 1, part 1, p. 36.

60. Ibid., vol. 1, part 2, pp. 23–24.

61. Ibid., vol. 1, part 2, p. 25.

62. Boissier, *From Solferino,* p. 211.

63. *Projet d'organisation d'hospitaliers militaires, par le Comte F[élix] de B[réda]* (Paris: E. Dentu, 1863).

64. Quoted in Boissier, *From Solferino,* p. 212.

65. For the text of his report, see *Paris 1867: Compte rendu,* vol. 2, pp. 151–153.

66. Ibid., vol. 2, pp. 184–185.

67. Ibid., vol. 2, pp. 185–186.

68. Ibid., vol. 2, pp. 245–246.

69. Boissier, *From Solferino,* p. 219.

70. *Paris 1867: Compte rendu,* vol. 2, p. 250ff.

71. Boissier, *From Solferino,* p. 216.

72. *Memoire adressé par le Comité International de secours pour les militaires blessés à Mm. les présidents et les membres des comités centraux dans les divers pays* (Geneva: Soullier, Landskron , and Wirth, 1868), pp. 5–7.

73. Ibid., p. 9.

74. Ibid., p. 8.

75. Ibid., p. 10.

76. Ibid., p. 11.

77. Ibid., p. 11. The titles of these periodicals were, respectively, *Bulletin de la Société de Secours aux Blessés Militaires, La Charité sur les Champs de Bataille,* and *Kriegerheil.*

78. Ibid., pp. 11–12.

79. Ibid., p. 12.

80. Ibid., p. 13.

81. Ibid., p. 13.

82. Ibid., p. 14.

83. Ibid., pp. 15–16.

84. Ibid., pp. 18–19.

85. Ibid., p. 20.

86. Ibid., p. 22.

87. Ibid., p. 22.

88. Ibid., p. 24.

89. Ibid., p. 25.

90. Ibid., p. 25.

91. For Boissier's treatment of this issue, see *From Solferino,* pp. 219–220.

92. "La Convention Internationale du 22 août 1864 et le Congrès de Genève du 5 Octobre 1868," extrait du *Journal de Genève* du 17 Septembre, 1868, copy in Longmore Papers 23/15. No doubt in the hope of reaching a wider audience, Moynier also sent a letter and a copy of his article to *La Charité sur les Champs de Bataille* in Brussels (where they appeared in vol. 3, no. 4 [October 1868], p. 1).

93. Moynier, *Étude,* pp. 75–76, 122; Boissier, *From Solferino,* pp. 219–220.

94. *Protocole de la Conférence Internationale réunie à Genève en Octobre 1868. Projet d'Articles Additionels* (Geneva: Fick, 1868), p. 18 (hereafter *Protocole . . .1868*). Regrettably, the compilers of this slim volume paid far more attention to the formalities of procedure than to the substance of the debates.

95. The text of this draft article may be found in the appendix to Gustave Moynier, *The Red Cross: Its Past and Future*, trans. John Furley (London: Cassell, Petter, and Galpin, 1883), pp. 183–184.

96. On this point, see Boissier, *From Solferino*, p. 224.

97. For the text of the Additional Articles, see "Projet d'Articles Additionels à la Convention du 22 Août 1864," appended to *Protocole . . .1868*; see also Moynier, *Étude*, pp. 76–92, 123–131. For ready reference to the text in English, see D. Schindler and J. Toman, *The Laws of Armed Conflicts* (Geneva: Henry Dunant Institute, 1981), pp. 217–220.

98. The proceedings were published in both a German and a French edition; reference is made here only to the French edition.

99. *Berlin 1869: Compte rendu*, p. 418; see also W. B. McAllister, "Fighting the Good Fight: German Military Medicine, 1860–1914" (unpublished M.A. thesis, University of Virginia, 1990), pp. 7–16.

100. *Berlin 1869: Compte rendu*, pp. 263–264.

101. Ibid., p. 265.

102. Ibid., p. 227.

103. Published in Berlin, 1868.

104. Although it had already been reviewed in *La Charité sur les Champs de Bataille* 3(12) (April, 1868):49.

105. As part of their effort to convince the delegates that Prussia was taking the right path, the organizers of the conference included an afternoon demonstration by the stretcher-bearers of the Prussian army; in addition to witnessing the efficient removal of "wounded" from a simulated battlefield, the delegates were invited to lie down themselves on the stretchers, which were then placed aboard specially constructed ambulance railway cars. The scene is described in a report in *Militärische Wochenblatt* (Berlin), no. 35 (28 April, 1869).

106. *Berlin 1869: Compte rendu*, p. 64.

107. Ibid., p. 64.

108. Ibid., pp. 64–65.

109. Ibid., p. 65. One would like to know more about the circumstances that led to this decision—was the Order pressured by the war ministry?—but the sources are too sparse to permit anything more than speculation.

110. Ibid., p. 67.

111. Ibid., p. 68. This claim was more than a little misleading; in 1868 the Russian society had not even begun to establish voluntary ambulances and would not do so in any serious fashion until after its reorganization in 1876.

112. Ibid., p. 89.

113. Ibid., p. 90.

114. Ibid., p. 154.

115. Ibid., pp. 155–156.

116. Ibid., p. 157.

117. Ibid., pp. 156–158.

118. Ibid., pp. 159–160. Léonce de Cazenove was one of the movement's strongest supporters in France. His *La guerre et l'humanité au XIXe siècle* (Paris: A. de Vresse, 1869), helped to broaden knowledge in France about the work of aid societies in other European countries.

119. *Berlin 1869: Compte rendu*, p. 161.

120. Ibid., pp. 162–163.

121. Ibid., p. 180.

122. Ibid., p. 181.

123. Ibid., pp. 185–186.

124. Ibid., p. 187.

125. Ibid., p. 187.

126. Richard H. Shryock, *The Development of Modern Medicine: An Interpretation of the Social and Scientific Factors Involved* (Madison: University of Wisconsin Press, 1979), p. 211.

127. *Berlin 1869: Compte rendu*, pp. 190–191.

128. Ibid., pp. 191–207.

Chapter 3

1. Gustave Moynier, *Étude sur la convention de Genève pour l'amelioration du sort des militaires blessés dans l'armées en campagne (1864 et 1868); droit de gens.* (Paris: Cherbuliez, 1870).

2. Ibid., p. 3.

3. Ibid., p. 7.

4. Ibid., pp. 8–12.

5. Ibid., pp. 14–15.

6. Ibid., p. 18.

7. Quoted in ibid., pp. 19–20. For a thorough discussion of Dufour's role during the Sonderbund War, see Joachim Remak, *A Very Civil War: The Swiss Sonderbund War of 1847* (Boulder: Westview Press, 1993), pp. 75–161.

8. For the text of Dufour's "humane and generous" Order of the Day of 5 November, 1847—a specific general order to his troops—see Remak, *A Very Civil War*, pp. 94–96.

9. Moynier, *Étude*, pp. 23–28.

10. Ibid., pp. 30–31.

11. Ibid., p. 33.

12. Ibid., p. 34.

13. Ibid., pp. 34–35.

14. Geoffrey Best, *Humanity in Warfare: The Modern History of the International Law of Armed Conflicts* (London: Weidenfeld and Nicolson, 1980), pp. 128–147.

15. Marie-Thérèse Laureilhe, typescript, "Les Débuts de la Croix Rouge en France jusqu'à la fin de l'Année Terrible, 1863–1871," (Paris: SSBM, 1989), p. 3.

16. Wellcome Tropical Institute, Royal Army Medical Corps Collection No. 1139, Longmore Papers 26/41, *The Medical Record* [1868], pp. 577–578.

17. Léon Le Fort, *La chirurgie militaire et les sociétés de secours en France et à l'étranger* (Paris: Germer Baillière, 1872), p. 234.

18. Ibid., p. 235.

19. Ibid., p. 235.

20. The same set of assumptions has evidently pervaded the French Red Cross Society's view of its own role during the war; see Laureilhe, "Les Débuts," pp. 5–13.

21. Ibid., p. 236.

22. William MacCormac, *Notes and Recollections of an Ambulance Surgeon, Being an Account of Work Done Under the Red Cross During the Campaign of 1870* (London: Churchill, 1871), p. 26.

23. As quoted in Le Fort, *La chirurgie militaire*, p. 237.

24. MacCormac, *Notes and Recollections*, p. 27.

25. Le Fort, *La chirurgie militaire*, p. 226.

26. Ibid., p. 227.

27. Ibid., p. 228.

28. Ibid., p. 228; this is confirmed in Charles H. Boyland, *Six Months Under the Red Cross, with the French Army* (Cincinnati, Ohio: Robert Clarke, 1873), p. 26.

29. Le Fort, *La chirurgie militaire*, p. 229.

30. Ibid., p. 230.

31. Ibid., p. 230.

32. Col. Claremont, British Military Attaché in Paris to War Office, undated, in Longmore Papers LP 27/13.

33. Léon Le Fort, "Le Service de Santé dans les armées nouvelles," *Revue des Deux Mondes* 86 (November, 1871):124–125.

34. Ibid., p. 125.

35. Ibid., p. 126; Dr. Boyland made essentially the same observation in *Six Months*, p. 28.

36. Le Fort, "Le Service de Santé," p. 126.

37. Ibid., p. 126.

38. W. B. McAllister, "Fighting the Good Fight: German Military Medicine, 1860–1914" (unpublished M.A. thesis, University of Virginia, 1990), pp. 8–9.

39. *Compte rendu des travaux de la Conférence tenue à Berlin du 22 au 27 Avril 1869 par les délégués des gouvernements signataires de la Convention de Genève et des Sociétés et Associations de Secours aux Militaires Blessés et Malades* (Berlin: J. F. Starcke, 1869), p. 418 (hereafter *Berlin 1869: Compte rendu*).

40. McAllister, "Fighting the Good Fight," pp. 9–10.

41. Pierre Boissier points out that the increasing range of artillery made it necessary to move most field medical facilities well back from the front lines. Pierre Boissier, *From Solferino to Tsushima: History of the International Committee of the Red Cross* (Geneva: Henry Dunant Institute, 1985), p. 242.

42. McAllister, "Fighting the Good Fight," pp. 14–15.

43. For other evaluations of these reforms, see Charles A. Gordon, "Notes on the Service of Armies During War," *British and Foreign Medico-Chirurgical Review* 53 (1874):477–501; John Shaw Billings, "Notes on Military Medicine in Europe," *Journal of the Military Service Institution of the United States* 3 (1882):234–247; Charles L. Heizmann, "The French and German Sanitary Corps on the Battlefield," *Journal of the United States Military Service Institution* 6 (1885):333–335.

44. *Berlin 1869: Compte rendu*, p. 418.

45. Ibid., pp. 419–420. The Women's Patriotic Society had since 1866 subordinated itself to the central committee of the Prussian national aid society.

46. On the "motherhouse" system, see Herbert Grundhewer, "Von der freiwilligen Kriegskrankenpflege bis zur Einbindung des Roten Kreuzes in das Heeressan-

itätswesen," in Johanna Bleker and Heinz-Peter Schmiedebach (eds.), *Medizin und Krieg: Vom Dilemma der Heilberufe 1865 bis 1965* (Frankfurt-am-Main: Fischer Taschenbuch Verlag, 1987), p. 37 and *idem*, "Die Kriegskrankenpflege und das Bild der Krankenschwester im 19. und frühen 20. Jahrhundert," in ibid., pp. 140–141.

47. Catherine M. Prelinger, *Charity, Challenge, and Change: Religious Dimensions of the Mid-Nineteenth-Century Womens' Movement in Germany* (Westport, Conn.: Greenwood Press, 1987), p. 21.

48. *Berlin 1869: Compte rendu*, p. 423.

49. McAllister, "Fighting the Good Fight," p. 16; for an overview, see Grundhewer, "Von der freiwilligen Kriegskrankenpflege," pp. 37–38.

50. Le Fort, *La chirurgie militaire*, p. 260; Boissier, *From Solferino*, p. 242.

51. This rule was in place even before the outbreak of war; the British military attaché in Berlin wrote to the War Office that "every possible restriction is laid on the undue assumption of the badge of neutrality. I am informed that the warrants under which civilians as hospital assistants and attendants, and which those who wear the armlet are bound to have in their possession, are only valid when signed by the Director of the Volunteer establishment. . . . The badge is so easily obtained, so simple in its nature, that too great care can hardly be taken to ensure its being worn only be authorized persons." Memorandum of Col. Beauchamp Walker, 11 March, 1870, in Longmore Papers LP 27/10.

52. Le Fort, *La chirurgie militaire*, p. 262. These complaints about interfering "Johanniter" (as the Knights of St. John were called) were repeated by several surgeons and other personnel of the British National Aid Society who participated as neutrals in medical and other relief efforts during the Prussian occupation of northern France; see *Questions on the Operations of the British National Society for Aid to the Sick and Wounded in War, and Replies Thereto, by Various Members of the Society's Staff and Others: Being the Results of Their Experiences in the Franco-German War, 1870–1871* (London: Harrison and Sons, [1872]), pp. 39–41.

53. For a summary account of the work of the Order of St. John in this war, see E. E. Hume, *Medical Work of the Knights Hospitallers of St. John of Jerusalem* (Baltimore: Johns Hopkins University Press, 1940), pp. 305–307.

54. Roger Boppe, *L'homme et la guerre: Le docteur Louis Appia et les débuts de la Croix-Rouge* (Geneva: Muhlethaler,1959), p. 125.

55. Quoted in ibid., pp. 125–126.

56. Boissier, *From Solferino*, p. 263. For the text of the circular, see *Comité international de secours aux militaires blessés. Actes. Recueil annoté de toutes les pièces importantes du Comité international depuis son origine en 1863)* (Geneva: Soullier and Wirth, 1871), pp. 171–173.

57. Boppe, *L'homme et la guerre*, pp. 127–129.

58. Minutes of the meeting of 27 July, 1870, as quoted in ibid., p. 130.

59. Ibid., pp. 130–131.

60. *Actes*, p. 215.

61. The agency used nearly a dozen auxiliary personnel to ensure that its shipments of supplies reached their intended destination without mishap. Initially, the Swiss railways provided free transport for agency shipments, but this privilege was withdrawn on 15 November, 1870. Ibid., p. 215.

62. Ibid., pp. 221–222.

63. On the origins and work of the Anglo-American Ambulance, see MacCormac, *Notes and Recollections*, pp. 19–20, 29; Charles E. Ryan, *With an Ambulance During the Franco-German War: Personal Experiences and Adventures with Both Armies, 1870–1871*

(New York: Charles Scribner's Sons, 1896); Henry Rundle, *With the Red Cross in the Franco-German War, A.D. 1870–1871* (London: Werner Laurie, [1909]).

64. For Furley's version of events and his difficulties with Loyd-Lindsay, see *Questions on the Operations*, pp. 112–113.

65. For the circumstances that accounted for Bourbaki's plight, see Michael Howard, *The Franco-Prussian War* (London: Collins, 1967), pp. 425–431.

66. *Actes*, pp. 228–230, 239–241; see also Boissier, *From Solferino*, pp. 254–255.

67. *Actes*, p. 231.

68. Ibid., p. 246.

69. Ibid., p. 247.

70. McAllister, "Fighting the Good Fight," p. 18. The outstanding contemporary work on the subject is Charles A. Gordon, *Lessons on Hygiene and Surgery from the Franco-Prussian War* (London: Baillière, Tindall, and Cox, 1873).

71. McAllister, "Fighting the Good Fight," pp. 19–20. "This was, therefore, the first war of magnitude in which the mortality from battle casualties (among the Germans) exceeded that from disease"; Fielding H. Garrison, *Notes on the History of Military Medicine* (Washington: Association of Military Surgeons, 1922), p. 179.

72. McAllister notes that both the Austrians and the Italians had reorganized along Prussian lines by 1872; Britain followed suit in 1873, as did Weurtemburg, Saxony, and Bavaria in 1874; the French "made some improvements" in the mid-1870s, as did the Russians in 1876; see "Fighting the Good Fight," p. 20.

73. Gordon, *Lessons*, pp. 29–32.

74. Ibid., p. 32.

75. Quoted in ibid., p. 34.

76. William H. McNeill, *The Pursuit of Power: Technology, Armed Force, and Society Since A.D. 1000* (Chicago: University of Chicago Press, 1982), p. 242.

77. As quoted in Gordon, *Lessons*, p. 36.

78. Ibid., p. 36.

79. As quoted in ibid., p. 37.

80. For a thorough analysis of the legal and moral debates that followed the Franco-Prussian War, see Best, *Humanity in Warfare*, chap. 3; for the criticisms of the Convention, see Boissier, *From Solferino*, pp. 247–254, 279–280; for more detailed treatment, see C. Lueder, *La Convention de Genève au point de vue historique, critique et dogmatique*, (Erlangen, Germany: Edouard Besold, 1876), pp. 224–252.

81. For the text of this announcement, see *Actes*, pp. 232–234.

82. Ibid., p. 234.

83. Ibid., p. 235.

84. Ibid., p. 236.

85. Circular No. 27, 25 August, 1871, in *Actes*, pp. 250–251.

86. *Allgemeine Schweizerische Militärzeitung*, no. 33 (27 August, 1871):272.

87. Lueder, *La Convention de Genève*, p. 197; Boppe, *L'homme et la guerre*, p. 156, calls the episode "a grave affair."

88. Gustave Moynier, *Note sur la création d'une Institution Judiciaire Internationale propre à prévenir et à réprimer les infractions à la Convention de Genève* (Geneva: Soullier and Wirth, 1872).

89. Ibid., pp. 2, 7.

90. Ibid., p. 7.

91. The *Alabama* was a British-built ship used for raiding by the Confederate states during the Civil War; it inflicted serious damage on the merchant shipping of the

Union. The U.S government's claim for recompense from the British was settled in 1872 when both parties agreed to accept the verdict of an international tribunal (which met, incidentally, in the same room of the Hôtel de Ville in Geneva where the 1864 Convention had been signed). Given the spectacle of two powerful states settling their differences by arbitration, pacifists began to believe that Europe was entering a new era.

92. This was the *Actes du Comité International de Secours aux Militaires Blessés*, published in Geneva by Soullier and Wirth in September, 1871.

93. Boissier, *From Solferino*, pp. 283–285. However, the idea was taken up by members of the Institute of International Law—Moynier was one—which was founded in Ghent in 1873.

94. Quoted in ibid., p. 280.

95. Also quoted in ibid., p. 280.

96. Huber-Saladin to Moynier, 3 November, 1872, as quoted in ibid., p. 280.

97. Ibid., p. 281.

98. Longmore Papers, Moynier to Longmore, 28 December, 1872.

99. Boissier, *From Solferino*, p. 281.

100. Ibid., pp. 275–276.

101. On the origins of this meeting, see Lueder, *La Convention de Genève*, p. 196.

102. Quoted in Boissier, *From Solferino*, p. 277.

103. For a full discussion, see Lueder, *La Convention de Genève*, pp. 198–217.

104. The wording of the Russian draft is reproduced in ibid., pp. 203–204. For Boissier's treatment of the issue, see *From Solferino*, pp. 289–293.

105. For the text of the Brussels declaration (which was never ratified by all of the governments whose representatives signed the protocol), see D. Schindler and J. Toman, eds., *The Laws of Armed Conflicts* (Geneva: Henry Dunant Institute, 1981), pp. 25–34.

106. *2e Congrès International d'Hygiène, de Sauvetage, et d'Economie Sociale. Bruxelles, 1876. Compte rendu*, vol. 2 (Paris: 1877), p. 383.

107. "Fédération des Comités de secours aux militaires blessés," ibid., pp. 383–394.

108. Ibid., p. 386.

109. Ibid., p. 386.

110. Ibid., p. 394.

111. Ibid., pp. 387–388.

112. Ibid., p. 388.

113. Ibid., p. 388.

114. Ibid., p. 394.

115. Ibid., pp. 395–396.

116. Ibid., pp. 396–397.

117. Ibid., p. 397.

118. Ibid., p. 394.

119. This summary is based on two principal souces, both of them somewhat unfamiliar. The first is a dossier entitled "Circulaires et documents divers de la Société Ottomane de Secours aux Blessés Militaires et du Croissant Rouge," in the possession of the ICRC Library in Geneva, Ancien Fond No. 693 (hereafter "Circulaires et documents"); the second is Zuhal Özaydin, "Osmanli Hilâl-i Ahmer Cemiyeti Sâlnâmesi ("Yearbook of the Ottoman Red Crescent Association") (unpublished M.A. thesis, Is-

tanbul University, 1987), hereafter "Ottoman Yearbook." For the latter reference I am indebted to Professor Dr. Nil Sari of Istanbul University and Dr. Inci Bowman of the University of Texas Medical Branch at Galveston.

120. His place of birth is uncertain: One modern source gives Vienna, but Moynier believed that he was a Bavarian by origin. Perhaps his parents were Bavarian residents of Vienna.

121. Circular No. 30, 8 August, 1868, in *Actes*, pp. 110–111. The date of foundation was given as 20 June, 1868; Abdullah Bey was its secretary-general.

122. These were, respectively, Husny Effendi, the military attaché at the Ottoman Embassy in Paris, and Aristarchi Bey, the Ottoman ambassador to Prussia.

123. "Ottoman Yearbook," pp. 3–4.

124. "La Croix-Rouge en Turquie" (a memorandum in Moynier's own hand, dated 15 December, 1875), in "Circulaires et documents," p. 2.

125. "Ottoman Yearbook," p. 4.

126. "L'oeuvre de la «Croix Rouge» et la Turquie," *Gazette Médicale d'Orient* 20(4) (July, 1876):51.

127. For the text, see ibid., p. 52. According to a fragmentary clipping in "Circulaires et documents," this meeting took place on 21 July, 1876.

128. See the letter from Marco Pasha to Dr. Nouridjan, 24 July, 1876, in ibid., p. 52. For the membership of the commission, see *Revue de Médicine et de Pharmacie de l'Empire Ottoman* 2(3) (15 January, 1877):34.

129. Péchédimaldji to Moynier, 12 August, 1876, as quoted in Boissier, *From Solferino*, p. 304.

130. As quoted in ibid., p. 305.

131. The full text appears in *Revue de Médicine et de Pharmacie de l'Empire Ottoman* 2(3) (15 January, 1877):36–37.

132. *Revue de Médicine et de Pharmacie de l'Empire Ottoman* 2(3) (15 January, 1877):38; see also Boissier, *From Solferino*, p. 305.

133. *Mémoriale des vingt-cinq premières années de la Croix-Rouge, 1863–1888* (Geneva: CICR, 1888), p. 276.

134. For the text of all these announcements, see "Circulaires et documents."

135. *Le Croissant Rouge* 1(1) (1877), no more published. A copy of this, the sole issue, is preserved in the ICRC Library, Ancien Fond No. 3133.

136. Procès-verbaux of the Comité International meeting of 9 December, 1876, as quoted in Boissier, *From Solferino*, p. 306.

137. *Gazette de Lausanne*, no. 21 (21 April, 1877):1, copy in "Circulaires et documents."

138. For the first discussion of this matter, see Chapter 1.

139. *Compte rendu de la Conférence Internationale réunie à Genève les 26, 27, 28, et 29 Octobre 1863 pour étudier les moyens de pourvoir à l'insuffisance du service sanitaire dans les armées en campagne* (Geneva: Fick, 1863), pp. 93–94.

140. Faced in later years with the prospect of an uncontrollable proliferation of symbols, and always anxious to maintain as far as possible the unity of the distinctive sign, the ICRC and several international Red Cross conferences have come to treat the "tribute to Switzerland" idea as part of the movement's doctrine. It is stated explicitly in Article 38 of the 1949 Geneva Convention. For a discussion of the emblem issue from the contemporary point of view of the ICRC, see François Bugnion, *The Emblem of the Red Cross: A Brief History* (Geneva: ICRC, 1977).

141. Grand Duke Nicholas's assurance on this point was reported to a meeting of the ORCS held on 18 August; see the clipping from the newspaper *Turquie*, 24 August, 1877; ICRC Library, Ancien Fond No. 4299, "Correspondance du Comité du Croissant Rouge du Constantinople. Articles de Journaux. 1877. Dossier."

142. Originally published in the German-language newspaper *Ansblatt* in Constantinople, this letter was republished in *Allgemeine Schweizer Zeitung* on 9 August, 1877 (clipping in ICRC Library, Ancien Fond No. 4299); Boissier, *From Solferino*, p. 308, prints an even more graphic account of a similar incident.

143. On the *Appeal to the Belligerents and the Press*, see Boissier, *From Solferino*, pp. 308–309.

144. *Mémoriale*, p. 277.

145. "Ottoman Yearbook," p. 6.

146. For the experiences of an Australian surgeon who served with the Ottoman army medical service throughout the war, see Charles S. Ryan, *Under the Red Crescent* (London: John Murray, 1897).

147. Peter Morris, ed., *First Aid to the Battlefront: Life and Letters of Sir Vincent Kennett-Barrington (1844–1903)* (Stroud, England: Allen Sutton, 1992), p. 153.

148. Ibid., p. 154.

149. *Congrès International sur le Service Médical des Armées en Campagne, tenu à Paris les 12, 13 et 14 août 1878* (Paris: Imprimerie Nationale, 1879), pp. 2–3 (hereafter *Congrès 1878: Compte rendu*).

150. A complete list of members and official delegates appears in ibid., pp. 3–5. The official delegates represented England, Austria, Bavaria, Belgium, Spain, France, the Netherlands, Portugal, Russia, and the Kingdom of Saxony. Prussia was not represented; whether Loeffler was invited is unknown.

151. *Décret du 2 mars 1878, portant règlement pour le fonctionnement de la Société de Secours aux Blessés Militaires* (Paris, J. Dumaine, 1878); copy in ICRC Library, Ancien Fond No. 1872.

152. For the larger context, see Allan Mitchell, "'A Situation of Inferiority': French Military Reorganization After the Defeat of 1870," *American Historical Review* 86 (1981):49–67.

153. The struggle of the medical service to liberate itself from the Intendance has been examined in William B. McAllister, "Fighting Reformers: The Debate Over the Reorganization of the French Military Medical Service, 1870–1889," in *Essays in History* (Charlottesville, Va.: Corcoran Department of History, 1993).

154. *Congrès 1878: Compte rendu*, p. 121.

155. Ibid., pp. 133–134.

156. Ibid., p. 112.

Chapter 4

1. Pierre Boissier, *From Solferino to Tsushima: History of the International Committee of the Red Cross* (Geneva: Henry Dunant Institute, 1985), pp. 333–334.

2. Gustave Moynier, *La Croix-Rouge, son passé et son avenir* (Paris: Sandoz et Thullier, 1882). John Furley's translation, entitled *The Red Cross: Its Past and Future*, was published in 1883 (London: Cassell, Petter, and Galpin).

3. Furley, *The Red Cross: Its Past and Future*, pp. 149–150. In a letter to Bluntschli, the distinguished expert in international law, von Moltke had written (11 December, 1880) that "war is an element in the order of the world established by God Himself." Quoted in ibid., p. 149.

4. Ibid., p. 149.

5. Ibid., p. 151.

6. Ibid., p. 152.

7. Ibid., pp. 154–155.

8. Ibid., p. 172.

9. Meeting of 23 January, 1884, summarized in Boissier, *From Solferino*, p. 334; the invitation was sent as Circular No. 53, dated 10 March, 1884.

10. ICRC Circular No. 53, 10 March, 1884, p. 2. (There is a copy of the circular in the Clara Barton Papers, microfilm reel 67, frames 271–272.)

11. Jules Lacointa, *Discours prononcé le 2 Septembre 1884 sur la Convention de Genève et les Sociétés de la Croix-Rouge* (Paris: Jules Gervais, 1884), p.16.

12. Ibid., p. 17.

13. Ibid., pp. 17–18.

14. Ibid., pp. 25–26. When the uprising broke out in Paris, leading members of the SSBM moved their seat of operations to Versailles. The Communards thereupon treated the SSBM as a politically hostile organization and confiscated some of its supplies. Medical units under the direction of the SSBM at Versailles treated only soldiers loyal to the French Republic. The whole affair is discussed, though without much objectivity, in Laureilhe, "Les Debuts de la Croix-Rouge en France," pp. 14–18. In *The Red Cross: Its Past and Future*, Moynier admitted that in situations of civil war, "the Red Cross has not always been well inspired" and that sometimes "political considerations have exercised much more influence on it then they ought to have done" (p. 115). He may well have had the SSBM in mind when he wrote these lines, but he never ventured to make this oblique criticism more explicit.

15. Lacointa, *Discours*, pp. 27–28.

16. Ibid., p. 29.

17. Ibid., p. 29.

18. *Troisième Conférence Internationale des sociétés de la Croix-Rouge tenue à Genève du 1er au 6 Septembre 1884. Compte rendu* (Geneva: ICRC, 1885), p. 77 (hereafter *Geneva 1884: Compte rendu*).

19. Ibid., p. 79.

20. On Moynier's disappointment with the response to the appeals of the international agency established by the Comité International in Trieste during the war, see Boissier, *From Solferino*, pp. 310–311.

21. In *The Red Cross: Its Past and Future*, Moynier had admitted that "since this unsuccessful attempt [the Geneva conference of 1868], the Societies, in order not to annoy the Governments, have abstained from meddling with questions which do not come within their province" (p. 51). He had already spent several paragraphs explaining that "the Convention of Geneva and the Aid Societies are not, then, one and the same thing" (p.47).

22. What follows summarizes his speech; for the text, see *Geneva 1884: Compte rendu*, pp. 63–66.

23. Ibid., p. 68.

24. Ibid., pp. 67–68.

25. Ibid., pp. 84–85.

26. Ibid., p. 85.

27. Ador's report had concluded that the *Bulletin International* should continue to be published with the collaboration of the national societies; that periodic international conferences should continue to be held; that the national societies should affirm the ties of solidarity that would exist among them in wartime and should accept the [unspecified] obligations which would follow from this affirmation; that it was in the general interests of the Red Cross to retain a Comité International; and that in wartime this committee or its agency would ensure communication among the aid societies. Ibid., p. 83.

28. Circular No. 58, 16 February, 1885; copy in ICRC Library, Ancien Fond No. 2822.

29. This committee was composed of Oom and three other members of the executive of the Russian Red Cross Society and (by invitation) Professor Martens. *Note sur le rôle du Comité International et sur les relations des comités centraux de la Croix-Rouge* (St. Petersburg: Trenké et Fusnot, [1885]), p. 1; copy in ICRC Library, Ancien Fond No. 2677.

30. Ibid., p. 7.

31. Ibid., p. 9.

32. Ibid., pp. 9–10.

33. Ibid., pp. 11–15.

34. Attachment to Circular No. 66, 22 June, 1887. In the text of this circular, the ICRC explained that it had been unable to do anything further with the Russian *Note* when it had received it in 1885 because the Russians had sent only ten copies of the text. This is no more than an excuse: It is obvious that if the ICRC had wanted to circulate it to all of the central committees in a timely fashion it could have arranged to have it printed or requested more copies from St. Petersburg. There is reason to think that the Genevans had no plans to circulate the *Note* prior to the next conference and intended simply to summarize its contents in their report; only when the Russians insisted on publication of the *Note* did the ICRC comply. See *Du rôle du Comité International et des rélations des comités centraux de la Croix-Rouge. Rapport présenté par le Comité International à la Conférence Internationale des sociétés de la Croix-Rouge à Carlsruhe, en 1887* (Geneva: B. Soullier, 1887), p. 9, n.1 (hereafter cited as *Rapport 1887*).

35. At the Karlsruhe conference in 1887, Oom expressed regret that the Russian *Note* had taken so long to reach the other central committees but disclaimed responsibility for the delay. After the conference was over, he wrote, "It is beyond doubt that if, instead of being sent out in the month of June 1887, our project had been circulated to Central Committees in 1885, many misunderstandings and fears could have been eliminated in time, and we could have counted on the success of our project." *Journal de St. Pétersbourg* 17/29, no. 277 (October, 1887); copy in ICRC Library, Ancien Fond No. 4256.

36. Ibid.

37. *Rapport 1887*, p. 3.

38. The arguments made by the central committees are summarized in *Rapport 1887*, pp. 4–9.

39. *Journal de St. Pétersbourg*, 17/29, no. 277 (October, 1887).

40. Ibid.

41. These were clauses (c) and (e) of Article 7; for the text, see appendix 1. *Quatrième Conférence Internationale des Sociétés de la Croix-Rouge tenue à Carlsruhe du 22 au 27 Septembre 1887. Compte rendu.* (Berlin: [Central Committee of German Red Cross Societies], 1887), p. 88 (hereafter cited as *Carlsruhe 1887: Compte rendu*).

42. The participant quoted here (with emphasis added) is the Saxon delegate Criegern-Thumitz. *Carlsruhe 1887: Compte rendu*, p. 92.

43. Ibid.

44. Ibid., p. 99.

45. Ibid., pp. 93, 95, 97.

46. Ibid., p. 98.

47. In my opinion, Boissier's treatment of the Karlsruhe conference (*From Solferino*, pp. 339ff) obscures many of the issues that were at work. According to him, the crucial issues were only those related to turning the ICRC into a legally recognized body and preserving the liberty of the national societies. In fact, there were several other important questions, such as whether the ICRC should have a stipulated mandate; whether its recruiting of members should follow fixed rules; whether the national societies would recognize any mutual obligations in wartime; and whether they would accept the very substantial reorganization of neutral assistance in the field proposed by the Russians. I will pass over his argument (*From Solferino*, p. 343) that there was no need to reform the central body of the Red Cross because mortality rates from infected wounds were on the decline.

48. *Carlsruhe 1887: Compte rendu*, p. 98.

49. Ibid., p. 94. In reality, as we saw in Chapter 2, the Comité International engaged in some judicious maneuvering prior to the Berlin conference in 1869 in order to secure its position against a further challenge from the French.

50. For the objections, see ibid., pp. 18–19. The substitute wording, as approved: "The national Societies of the Red Cross, while remaining absolutely independent as regards their internal organization, recognize that the end which they pursue in common makes it a duty for them to consider themselves united by a tie of close solidarity." Ibid., p. 23.

51. See above, Chapter 1, n. 35.

52. See above, Chapter 1, n. 85.

53. Thomas W. Evans, *Sanitary Institutions During the Austro-Prussian-Italian Conflict . . .* , 3d ed. (Paris: Simon Racon, 1868); Thomas Longmore, *Treatise on the Transport of Sick and Wounded Troops* (London: H.M.S.O., 1869).

54. The authoritative work on this subject is by "M. le Docteur" Gruby: *Sociétés et matériel de secours pour les blessés militaires (exposition de 1878).* 2 vols. (Paris: Eugène Lacroix, 1884). Despite its title, Gruby's book in fact covers all of the expositions held prior to 1884.

55. A. Riant, *Le matériel de secours de la société à l'exposition de 1878. Manuel pratique . . .* (Paris: Imprimerie Nationale, 1878), title page.

56. Gruby, *Sociétés et matériel*, vol. 1, p. xiii.

57. Jonathan Letterman, *Medical Recollections of the Army of the Potomac* (New York: D. Appleton, 1866); for a country-by-country survey, see Paul Redard, *Transport par chemins de fer des blessés et malades militaires* (Paris: Doin, 1889).

58. Evans, *Sanitary Institutions, passim.* It is therefore surprising to find no reference to Mundy in a recent history of ambulance technology: John S. Haller Jr., *Farmcarts to*

Fords: A History of the Military Ambulance, 1790–1925 (Carbondale: Southern Illinois University Press, 1992). See "An Essay on Ambulance Wagons," in *Sanitary Institutions*.

59. "Electricity in Military and Ambulance Work," *Daily News* (London), 26 July, 1884.

60. A copy of the program for this event is preserved in the ICRC Library, Ancien Fond No. 353: *Note sur l'appareil d'éclairage électrique ayant servi aux expériences pour l'évacuation des blessés et l'enterrement des morts pendant la nuit après une bataille*, (Paris: Imprimerie Chaix, 1884).

61. *Troisième Conférence Internationale des Sociétés de la Croix-Rouge tenue à Genève du 1er au 6 Septembre 1884. Compte rendu.* (Geneva: CICR, 1885), p. 412 (hereafter *Geneva 1884: Compte rendu*).

62. *Daily News*, 26 July, 1884.

63. *Geneva 1884: Compte rendu*, pp. 58, 73.

64. *Congrès International des Oeuvres d'Assistance en Temps de Guerre, tenu à Paris les 17, 18, 19 et 20 Juillet 1889* [Compte Rendu] (Paris: L. Baudoin and Cie, J.-B. Baillière and Fils, 1890), p. 22 (hereafter *Oeuvres d'assistance en temps de guerre*).

65. Besides the French, the central committees of five Red Cross societies (Belgium, Denmark, Spain, the Congo, and Greece) were represented by official delegates; ibid., p. 11.

66. Ibid., p. 30.

67. Ibid., p. 19.

68. Ibid., pp. 20, 22.

69. In the twentieth century, a variant of this mission has become part of the culture of the Swiss *haute bourgeoisie*, whose young people, themselves shielded from war by Swiss neutrality, are expected to assist the ICRC and the national Red Cross society in their efforts to mitigate the effects of wars fought elsewhere.

70. *Oeuvres d'assistance en temps de guerre*, p. 24.

71. Ibid., p. 23.

72. Ibid., p. 23.

73. Ibid., p. 23.

74. Sir Thomas Longmore, C.B., "The New Military Weapons and Explosives," *British Medical Journal* (5 March, 1892):521–522; reprint in ICRC Library, Ancien Fond No. 2005. In the British army, surgeon-general was a rank and did not signify that the holder was head of the medical department, which had its own director-general.

75. Ibid., p. 521.

76. Ibid., p. 522 (emphasis added). Longmore noted that neutral assistance had been accepted by both belligerents in the Franco-Prussian War and was now "admitted under certain restrictions in the official regulations of most countries."

77. Conference agendas were formulated by incorporating items submitted by national central committees, but the British National Aid Society, led by the idiosyncratic Lord Wantage, made it a point to ignore international Red Cross conferences. Longmore had always attended them as a delegate of the British government. In Rome his communication was relegated to "Any Other Business," the last item on the agenda.

78. *Cinquième Conférence Internationale des Sociétés de la Croix-Rouge tenue à Rome du 21 au 27 Avril 1892. Compte rendu.* (Rome: Forzani, 1892), pp. 400–401, 419 (hereafter *Rome 1892: Compte rendu*).

79. *VIme [Sixième] Conférence Internationale des Sociétés de la Croix-Rouge. Vienne 1897.* (Vienna: Reisser and Werthner, 1898), p. 23 (hereafter *Vienna 1897: Compte rendu*). For the peculiar position of the English society in the world of the Red Cross, see Chapter 5.

80. *Vienna 1897: Compte rendu*, p. 204.

81. Von Coler's speech, delivered to an assembly of delegates of the German Red Cross societies, was quoted at length by Sir John Furley in a lecture given at the Royal United Service Institution in April, 1896, entitled, "The Convention of Geneva, and the Care of the Sick and Wounded in War," p. 12; copy in Furley Papers, British Red Cross Archives.

82. *Geneva 1884: Compte rendu*, pp. 139–140.

83. Ibid., p. 140.

84. Ibid., p. 141.

85. Ibid., pp. 142–143.

86. On the Russian Society of the Red Cross, see *La Société Russe de la Croix Rouge. Aperçu hisorique de son activité* (St. Petersburg: Trenké and Fusnot, 1902). This book, specially prepared for the 1902 conference, was an updated and abridged version of *Istoricheskii Ocherk deiatel'nosti Russkogo Obshchestva Krasnogo Kresta*, sost. pod red. M. M. Fedorova, V. F. Botsianovskim (St. Petersburg, 1896).

87. See his obituary, by Édouard Trogan, in *Le Correspondent* 25 (25 Novembei, 1916):577–587.

88. The following states had done so by 1907: Argentina (1903), Austria (1903), Belgium (1891), Bulgaria (1904), Denmark (1894), Germany (1902–1903), Hungary (1889, 1898), Italy (1882, 1884), Japan (1898), Norway (1902), Portugal (1896), Rumania (1895), Serbia (1906), Spain (1899, 1902), and the United States of America (1905); in Russia it was unnecessary to pass a law forbidding use of the emblem because the administration of the Red Cross society was a branch of the Ministry of the Interior, and use of the emblem was therefore a government monopoly.

89. After 1905, the British War Office insisted on making special arrangements with the St. John and St. Andrew's ambulance associations despite its general agreement with the British Red Cross Society; one result was a great deal of friction and even hostility among the various societies. For a revealing account of this situation, see A. K. Loyd, *An Outline of the History of the British Red Cross Society from Its Foundation in 1870 to the Outbreak of the War in 1914* (London: British Red Cross Society, 1917).

90. Until 1905, the English society was reluctant to call itself "the British Red Cross"; for an explanation, see Chapter 5.

91. Geoffrey Best, *Humanity in Warfare: The Modern History of the International Law of Armed Conflicts* (London: Weidenfeld and Nicolson, 1980), p. 142.

92. Quoted in Roger Boppe, *L'homme et la guerre: Le docteur Louis Appia et les débuts de la Croix-Rouge* (Geneva: Muhlethaler, 1959), p. 170.

93. Appia to Moynier, 20 May, 1878, as quoted in ibid., p. 192.

94. Gustave Moynier, *Notions essentielles sur la Croix-Rouge* (Geneva: Georg, 1896), p. 13.

95. Ibid., p. 27.

96. Ibid., p. 30.

97. Ibid., pp. 33–42.

98. *Le Comité International de la Croix-Rouge de 1884 à 1892* (Geneva: CICR, 1892), p. 23. The approach evidently took place in 1885, and so the matter could have been referred to the Karlsruhe conference for discussion, had the ICRC chosen to do so.

99. Ibid., p. 23.

100. Ibid., p. 23.

101. The information in this paragraph is based on the "Conference Chronicle" in *Septième Conférence Internationale de la Croix-Rouge tenue à St-Pétérsbourg du 16 au 22 Mai 1902. Compte rendu.* (St. Petersburg: Trenké and Fusnot, 1903), pp. 357–364 (hereafter *St. Petersburg 1902: Compte rendu*).

102. Clara Barton to Ida Barton Riccius, 18 June, 1902; Clara Barton Papers, microfilm reel 68, frame 458.

103. While in St. Petersburg, Barton received Russia's highest civilian decoration, the Silver Cross, from the tsar himself and the Order of the Red Cross of Russia from the dowager empress. See "Diary May 30–31 1902," in Clara Barton Papers, microfilm reel 68, frame 484.

104. Boissier, *From Solferino*, pp. 341–342. For a more general review of their proceedings, see Gustave Moynier, *Les conférences internationales des sociétés de la Croix-Rouge* (Geneva: Comité International de la Croix-Rouge, 1901).

105. At the London conference in 1907, one of the British organizers noted that final arrangements had been complicated by the fact that other societies sent in at the last minute both items for the agenda and changes in the composition of their delegations. *Huitième Conférence Internationale de la Croix-Rouge, tenue à Londres du 10 au 15 Juin 1907. Compte rendu* (London: British Red Cross Society, 1908), p. 285.

106. After 1884, the only conference not held in the capital of a great power state was the 1887 meeting, for which the International Committee selected Karlsruhe in Baden—where the Red Cross had an excellent friend in Grand Duchess Louise—because it was unwilling to risk difficulties with any of the great powers that had been involved in the squabbles that followed the Franco-Prussian War. Since Prussia had already been recognized in 1869, the choice of Baden was also a way of recognizing the important role played in the German Red Cross by the lesser states.

107. *St. Petersburg 1902: Compte rendu*, p. 359.

108. Ibid., p. 361. It should be noted that no delegation from the ORCS attended the St. Petersburg conference, although the Ottoman ambassador to Russia, Husny Pasha, was listed as an official delegate. Whether he heard Martens's extraordinary speech is not known.

109. Dunant to Moynier, 29 April, 1869; reproduced in Marc Descombes, *Henry Dunant* (Geneva: Editions René Coeckelberghs, 1988). For this summary of Dunant's life between 1867 and 1901, I have drawn heavily on Descombes's work, supplemented by Boissier, *From Solferino*, pp. 286–288, 353–355.

110. In 1896, Professor Mueller delivered an adulatory lecture entitled, "Henry Dunant, Founder of the Red Cross and of the Geneva Convention"; the text may be found in his *Entstehungsgeschichte des Roten Kreuzes und der Genser Konvention* (Stuttgart: [n.p.], 1896).

111. *Bulletin International de la Croix-Rouge* 32(125) (1901):74.

112. Ibid., pp. 74–75.

113. Ibid., p. 77.

114. The most influential figure among them was the British delegate, William G. Macpherson of the Royal Army Medical Corps. North America was well represented because Canada, the United States, and Mexico all sent delegates; the best known of these was Clara Barton, president of the American National Red Cross Society.

115. The proceedings may be followed in *Congrès international des oeuvres d'assistance en temps de guerre* (hereafter *Congrès 1900*), vol. 1: *Procès verbaux sommaires* (Paris: Imprimerie Nationale, 1901); and vol. 2: *Rapports et comptes rendus des séances* (Paris: Imprimerie Générale Lahure, 1901).

116. *Congrès 1900*, vol. 2, pp. 40–43.

117. *Congrès 1900*, vol. 2, pp. 2–3.

118. On the cynicism that dominated the Hague Conference's discussion of troop size, war budgets, and weaponry, see Boissier, *From Solferino*, pp. 368–369.

119. Ibid., pp. 371–373.

120. Gustave Moynier, *La revision de la Convention de Genève. Étude historique et critique* (Geneva: CICR, 1898), especially pp. 47–52; idem, *Considérations sur la sanction pénale à donner à la Convention de Genève* (Lausanne: Imprimerie F. Regamey, 1893).

121. Moynier, *La revision*, pp. 47, 49.

122. Ibid., p. 27. The French text is "puisque ces choses ne font nullement partie de la fortune publique."

123. Ibid., pp. 33–34; it seems likely that the phrase "other similar institutions" referred to such bodies as the Knights of Malta and the Order of St. John, which, in some countries, were recognized by governments for wartime auxiliary service.

124. Ibid., p. 34.

125. W. G. Macpherson, "The Geneva Convention," *Journal of the Royal Army Medical Corps* 15 (November, 1910):613.

126. Ibid., p. 620.

127. The preceding Article 9 extended "respect and protection" to "personnel engaged exclusively in the collection, transport, and treatment of the wounded and the sick, as well as in the administration of medical units and establishments, and the chaplains attached to armies."

128. Quoted from the English translation (p. 17), in *Papers Relating to the Geneva Convention, 1906, Presented to Both Houses of Parliament by Command of His Majesty* (London: H.M.S.O., 1908) [Cd. 3933]. The most accessible modern version of the 1906 text appears in D. Schindler and J. Toman, eds., *The Laws of Armed Conflicts* (Geneva: Henry Dunant Institute, 1981), pp. 233–244.

129. Macpherson, "The Geneva Convention," p. 620.

130. *Papers Relating to the Geneva Convention*, p. 25.

131. Ibid., p. 42.

132. Ibid., p. 42.

133. Ibid., p. 16.

134. Macpherson, "The Convention of Geneva," p. 617.

135. *Papers Relating to the Geneva Convention*, p. 45.

136. Gustave Moynier, *Mes heures de travail [imprimé comme manuscrit]* [Geneva] [1907], pp. 53–63. There is a copy of this scarce work in the Documentation Center of the French Red Cross in Paris.

137. "Gustave Moynier, 1826–1910," *Bulletin International de la Croix-Rouge* (October, 1910):28.

Chapter 5

1. Readers may wish to compare the account given here of the origins of the Japanese Red Cross Society with that provided by Olive Checkland in part 1 of her recently published *Humanitarianism and the Emperor's Japan, 1877–1977* (London: St. Martin's Press, 1994). Checkland is more interested in the treatment of prisoners of war than the care of the sick and wounded; in that sense her work complements my own, although I do not share her somewhat naive approach to the subject of humanitarianism. For the early period, at least, her research seems patchy: She does not, for example, make use of the two most important sources on the rise of the society, both written by Nagao Ariga (see below, notes 2 and 14).

2. Nagao Ariga, *La Croix-Rouge en Extrême-Orient. Exposé de l'organisation et du fonctionnment de la Société de la Croix-Rouge du Japon* (Paris: A. Pedone, 1900), p. 10 (hereafter *CREO*).

3. Ibid., p. 13.

4. "L'ambassade japonaise," *Bulletin International des Sociétés de Secours aux Militaires Blessés* 5(17) (October, 1873):11–12.

5. Ibid., p. 12.

6. Ibid., p. 12.

7. Keiichi Kawamata, *The History of the Red Cross Society of Japan* [Tokyo] [1922], p. 34. I have taken the liberty of correcting some of the most egregious errors in the author's English.

8. The summary that follows is based on Nagao Ariga, *The Red Cross Society of Japan: Its Organization and Activity in Time of Peace and War*, Presented to the Universal Exposition of St. Louis, U.S.A: [n.p.], 1904), pp. 5–6.

9. *Mémorial des vingt-cinq premières années de la Croix-Rouge, 1863–1888* (Geneva: CICR, 1888), p. 178.

10. Ariga, *CREO*, p. 76.

11. The emperor provided the society with a capital endowment of 100,000 yen, from which it derived an annual income of 5,000 yen; the empress provided the society's hospital with an annual allowance of 5,000 yen. By 1903, the society's annual income from all sources was nearly 3 million yen. Ibid., pp. 6, 8.

12. Ibid., p. 9.

13. Ibid., p. 9.

14. The subject is exhaustively treated in *Le service de secours de la Société de La Croix-Rouge du Japon pendant la guerre de la 27e–28e de Meiji (1894–1895)* (Paris: A. Pedone, 1897), from which the information in this paragraph is drawn.

15. Ariga acknowledges considerable assistance from the ICRC and from the French, Italian, and Bavarian societies: *CREO*, pp. 76–77.

16. For a French translation of the text, see "Règlement concernant le service de secours en temps de guerre. (Ratifié par le Ministre de la guerre, le 28 Octobre 1898)," in *CREO*, pp. 81–87.

17. *CREO*, pp. 127–128.

18. *CREO*, p. 129.

19. *CREO*, p. 133.

20. Ariga, *The Red Cross Society of Japan*, p. 28.

21. Ibid., p. 31.

22. Ibid., p. 14.

23. Surgeon W. C. Braisted, USN, "The Japanese Red Cross Nurse," *American Red Cross Bulletin* 3(2) (April, 1908):13.

24. *The Japanese Red Cross Society and the Russo-Japanese War. A Report Presented to the Eighth International Conference of Red Cross Societies Held in London, June, 1907.* Compiled by Dr. Nagao Ariga. (London: Bradbury, Agnew, 1907), pp. 35–36.

25. Ibid., p. 36.

26. For the complete text, see ibid., appendix III, pp. 268–280.

27. Ibid., p. 40.

28. Ibid., pp. 182–183.

29. Ibid., p. 183.

30. Ibid., p. 227.

31. Ibid., pp. 242–243.

32. Ibid., p. 244.

33. This account draws heavily on Ariga's version of the visit, in ibid., pp. 244–245. McGee summarized her experience in Japan in "Work at the Army Reserve Hospital of Hiroshima," *Trained Nurse* 33 (1904):304–309, and in "How the Japanese Save Lives," *Century Magazine* 70 (1905):133–143.

34. Mabel T. Boardman Papers. General Correspondence, 1894–1945, Box 4, Edwin Morgan to Mabel Boardman, 8 June, 1904.

35. Her experiences are recorded in Mrs. [T. E.] Richardson, *In Japanese Hospitals During War-Time. Fifteen months with the Red Cross Society of Japan (April 1904 to July 1905)* (Edinburgh: Blackwood, 1905).

36. Ariga, *The Japanese Red Cross Society and the Russo-Japanese War*, p. 246.

37. Richardson, *In Japanese Hospitals*, p. ix.

38. The Royal Red Cross was created in 1883 by Queen Victoria for nursing sisters who had displayed special devotion and competence in field hospitals, or in naval or military hospitals in Britain. On its history, see Anne Summers, *Angels and Citizens: British Women as Military Nurses, 1854–1914* (London: Routledge and Kegan Paul, 1988), pp. 175–181, and, on McCaul, pp. 212–217. See also E. McCaul, "Some Suggestions for Army Reform," *Nineteenth Century* 50 (April, 1901):58–87.

39. Ethel McCaul, *Under the Care of the Japanese War Office* (London: Cassell, 1905).

40. McCaul, *Under the Care*, p. 210.

41. Ibid., p. 211.

42. See *The Russo-Japanese War. Medical and Sanitary Reports from Officers Attached to the Japanese and Russian Forces in the Field. (Principally by W. G. Macpherson)* (London: H.M.S.O., 1908). Macpherson specifically acknowledges his debt to McCaul for information about the sanitary regulations in force at Japanese First Army Headquarters, which she had visited but he had not. Ibid., pp. 359–360. Macpherson summarized his findings in "The Medical Organization of the Japanese Army," *Journal of the Royal Army Medical Corps* 6 (1906):219–250, and "The Organization and Resources of the Red Cross Society of Japan," ibid., pp. 467–478.

43. McCaul, *Under the Care*, pp. 43–44.

44. W. G. Macpherson, *The Role of the Red Cross Societies in Peace and War* (London: J. J. Keliher, 1907), p. 5. The text of this important lecture was also published in *Journal of the Royal United Service Institution* 51 (1907):1345–1363.

45. Ibid., p. 4. He made a similar point in a report, "The Reserve Hospitals in Japan": "As the war progressed, the relief sections of the Red Cross Society were gradually brought into the reserve hospitals to replace the civil nursing orderlies [employed by the army], as these were pushed up to the line of communication hospitals, and also take over the beds in the sections of the reserve hospitals as they expanded." Macpherson, *The Russo-Japanese War*, p. 333.

46. See Raymond Spear, *Report on the Russian Medical and Sanitary Features of the Russo-Japanese War to the Surgeon-General, U.S. Navy* (Washington: Government Printing Office, 1906); William C. Braisted, *Report on the Japanese Naval Medical and Sanitary Features of the Russo-Japanese War to the Surgeon-General, U.S. Navy* (Washington: Government Printing Office, 1906); "Report of Col. Valery Havard, Assistant Surgeon-General, U.S.A., Observer with the Russian Forces in Manchuria," in *Reports of Military Observers Attached to the Armies in Manchuria During the Russo-Japanese War*, part 2 (Washington: Government Printing Office, 1906); "Report of Maj. Charles Lynch, Medical Department, General Staff, U.S. Army, Observer with the Japanese Forces in Manchuria," in ibid., part 4 (Washington: Government Printing Office, 1907).

47. "Report of Maj. Charles Lynch," p. 49.

48. Ibid., p. 61.

49. Ibid., pp. 62–63.

50. Spear, *Russian Medical and Sanitary Features*, p. 15. For a revealing discussion of the lowly position of doctors in the imperial Russian army, see Nancy Mandelker Frieden, *Russian Physicians in an Era of Reform and Revolution, 1856–1905* (Princeton, N.J.: Princeton University Press, 1981), pp. 263–282.

51. Spear, *Russian Medical and Sanitary Features*, pp. 12–14.

52. For a description, see ibid., pp. 39–41.

53. Wellcome Tropical Institute. Royal Army Medical Corps Collection. Reports of Medical Services, Collected by Sir Charles Burchell. No. 446/2: Sir Ian Hamilton's Report on the Medical Service in the Russo-Japanese War, p. 31.

54. For a general survey of the tsarist regime's priorities in matters of health, see chapter 1 of John F. Hutchinson, *Politics and Public Health in Revolutionary Russia, 1890–1918* (Baltimore: Johns Hopkins University Press, 1990).

55. For the most recent, see Elizabeth Brown Pryor, *Clara Barton, Professional Angel* (Philadelphia: University of Pennsylvania Press, 1987), pp. 296–364. Earlier biographies include Corra Bacon-Foster, *Clara Barton, Humanitarian* (Washington, D.C.: Columbia Historical Society, 1918); William E. Barton, *The Life of Clara Barton*, 2 vols. (Boston: Houghton Mifflin, 1922); Blanche Colton Williams, *Clara Barton, Daughter of Destiny* (Philadelphia: J. B. Lippincott, 1941).

56. Foster Rhea Dulles, *The American Red Cross: A History* (New York: Harper and Bros., 1950), p. 64.

57. Ibid., p. 66.

58. Ibid., p. 68.

59. Gustave R. Gaeddert, "The Barton Influence, 1866–1905," vol. 2 of "The History of the American National Red Cross" (unpublished typescript, Washington, D.C., 1950), pp. 4–6. On Stanton's relationship with the Sanitary Commission, see William Q. Maxwell, *Lincoln's Fifth Wheel: The Political History of the United States Sanitary Commission* (New York: Longmans, Green, 1956), *passim*; also Charles Stillé,

History of the U. S. Sanitary Commission (Philadelphia: J. B. Lippincott, 1866) pp. 109–127.

60. This tale of refusal and failure is ignored by those who, like William Q. Maxwell, hold to the view that the United States was in some way the midwife of the Red Cross in Europe.

61. Moynier to the president of the United States, 19 August, 1877, published in Clara Barton, *The Red Cross in Peace and War* (Washington, D.C.: American Historical Press, 1899), pp. 36–41.

62. For details regarding this experience, see Pryor, *Clara Barton*, pp. 162–167.

63. Gustave Moynier to Clara Barton, 24 March, 1882; Clara Barton Papers, microfilm reel 68, frame 545. She published an abridged version of this letter in her *The Red Cross: A History of This Remarkable International Movement* (Washington, D.C.: American National Red Cross, 1898), pp. 81–82.

64. Walter P. Phillips to Gustave Moynier, 6 July, 1882; Clara Barton Papers, microfilm reel 13, frames 28–30.

65. Gustave Moynier to Clara Barton, 24 March, 1882; Clara Barton Papers, microfilm reel 68, frame 545. The AARC's articles of incorporation, dated 1 October, 1881, listed as aims the American ratification of the Geneva Convention, official recognition by the government, and the organization of a national system for the relief of suffering caused by war or other calamities. This document was not an act of Congress but merely a certificate of incorporation in the District of Columbia, signed by the District's commissioner; as such, it established the Red Cross in the District of Columbia but not elsewhere in the United States. For more details, see Gaeddert, "The Barton Influence," pp. 22–25.

66. Gustave Moynier to Walter P. Phillips, 22 July, 1882, p. 4; Clara Barton Papers, microfilm reel 68, frames 547–548.

67. Gaeddert, "The Barton Influence," p. 30. Gaeddert must have seen these letters, dated 11 and 14 August, 1882, in the American Red Cross archives during the 1950s, before the records were transferred to the National Archives. I have been unable to find them, either in the Clara Barton Papers at the Library of Congress or in the records of the ANRC at the National Archives and Records Administration (NARA).

68. ICRC Circular No. 50, 20 September, 1882, p. 2 (copy in Clara Barton Papers, microfilm reel 67, frames 269–270).

69. Ibid., p. 3.

70. *Troisième Conférence Internationale des Sociétés de la Croix-Rouge tenue à Genève du 1er au 6 Septembre 1884. Compte rendu* (Geneva: ICRC, 1885), pp. 179–183.

71. Ibid., p. 431.

72. It was apparently on the basis of Sheldon's role in this debate that Barton later repeatedly told American audiences that peacetime disaster relief was an "American amendment" to the Geneva Convention. This piece of hyperbole has now become part of the mythology of the American Red Cross. It is repeated by Barton's most recent biographer (Pryor, *Clara Barton*, p. 239), who compounds the absurdity by claiming, "In a lasting tribute to Clara Barton, this addition to the Treaty of Geneva [that is, the Geneva Convention] was entitled the 'American Amendment.'" The official historian of the Barton era, Gustave Gaeddert, was much more cautious in his treatment of her claim (see "The Barton Influence," pp. 53–54); Gaeddert concluded

that peacetime disaster relief was something that "she [Barton] loved to think of as 'the American Amendment' to the Treaty of Geneva" (p. 254). To put Barton's inflated notion in perspective, one need only cite the record of the Russian Red Cross, which, in the 1870s alone, responded to an earthquake, several great fires in urban and rural areas, a flood, a diphtheria epidemic, and an outbreak of plague. For details, see *La Société Russe de la Croix-Rouge. Aperçu historique de son activité* (St. Petersburg: Trenké and Fusnot, 1902), pp. 46–50. By the time Barton visited St. Petersburg in 1902, the Russian Red Cross had been involved in peacetime disaster relief for more than thirty years.

73. Gaeddert, "The Barton Influence," pp. 33–34.

74. Although the word "National" formed part of the official title of the organization until after World War II, in practice it was usually dropped in favor of the simpler "American Red Cross." Here the acronym ARC will be used unless specific reference is made to the ANRC (as, for example, in citations to the "Records of the ANRC" held by the National Archives and Records Administration).

75. Gaeddert, "The Barton Influence," pp. 35–40.

76. Dulles, *The American Red Cross,* p. 61. This colorful summary perhaps underestimates the usefulness of the nurses, particularly in the recruit camps, where typhoid was rampant.

77. Secretary of State to the Secretary of War, 24 May, 1898, published in Barton, *The Red Cross in Peace and War,* p. 379. For more details, see Gaeddert, "The Barton Influence," pp. 141–144.

78. Dulles, *The American Red Cross,* pp. 45–59. See Barton, *The Red Cross in Peace and War,* p. 395, for the letters of acceptance from the secretaries of the war and navy departments.

79. The surgeon of the base hospital at Siboney wrote of his gratitude for the help provided by the Red Cross, "coming [as it did] from people in no way connected with the military service." See "Report of the Surgeon-General," in *Annual Report of the War Department* (Washington: Government Printing Office, 1898), p. 801.

80. Ibid., p. 724.

81. Barton understandably resented Sternberg's behavior, not least because she had been assured by the secretary of war that the Red Cross could be asked to supply personnel for medical and hospital work as auxiliary to the hospital service of the army of the United States. For Sternberg's position, see ibid., pp. 723–724; also Barton, *The Red Cross in Peace and War,* pp. 494–495.

82. Roosevelt's gubernatorial address of 2 January, 1899, quoted in Clyde Buckingham's "Memorandum on the Reorganization of the ANRC," NARA RG200 (Records of the ANRC), Box 8, File 051.

83. "Major Walter McCaw's Study on Relationship That Should Exist Between Army and Charitable Organizations, 1904," in NARA RG 200 (Records of the ANRC), Box 8, File 052.3.

84. Ibid., p. 1. For Gaeddert's treatment of the McCaw Report, see "The Barton Influence," pp. 259–262.

85. The entire story, in all its squalid detail, is told by Gaeddert in "The Barton Influence," pp. 183–245.

86. For details of the charges and of the work of investigating committee, see ibid., pp. 221–228. In fact the investigating committee aborted its hearings when credible

witnesses could not be produced. It never reported back to Congress; instead its members joined in the work of reorganization.

87. Ibid., p. 252.

88. U.S. Senate, *Red Cross Society in Foreign Countries,* 58th Cong., 2d sess., S. Doc. 178. For a summary of its contents, see Gaeddert, "The Barton Influence," pp. 263–268.

89. As quoted in Gaeddert, "The Barton Influence," p. 271.

90. Admiral Van Reypen had been a member of the American delegation to the St. Petersburg conference in 1902; his candidacy had been promoted by the anti-Barton faction.

91. On the political complexion of the Red Cross leadership after 1905, see Gustave R. Gaeddert, "The Boardman Influence, 1905–1917," vol. 3 of "The History of the American National Red Cross" (Washington, D.C., 1950, typescript), pp. 5–6. Taft retained his position with the ANRC after being elected president of the United States and urged his successor, Woodrow Wilson, to continue the tradition.

92. NARA/RG200 (Records of the ANRC) Box 36, File 494.2. The essay was recognized by the National Association of Military Surgeons, which awarded Lynch the Enno Sander Prize and reprinted it in *Military Surgeon* 21 (1907):397–426. It was also published in volume 3 of the *American Red Cross Bulletin* (January, 1908).

93. NARA/RG200 (Records of the ANRC) Box 36, File 494.2, p. 8.

94. Ibid., p. 7.

95. Ibid., p. 12.

96. Ibid., p. 24.

97. Ibid., pp. 24–25.

98. Ibid., p. 20.

99. Gaeddert, "The Boardman Influence," pp. 44–45.

100. Ibid., pp. 97–98.

101. Dulles, *The American Red Cross,* pp. 91–92.

102. For Davison's account of the circumstances that led to his appointment as head of the war council, see the thirteen-page "Memorandum Regarding My Connection with the American Red Cross" (undated, but probably written in April, 1917), contained in the Davison Papers, American Red Cross Headquarters.

103. Gaeddert, "The Boardman Influence," pp. 46–47.

104. NARA/RG200 (Records of the ANRC), Box 36, item 11; see also Gaeddert, "The Boardman Influence," p. 47.

105. Ibid., p. 50.

106. Ibid., pp. 51–52.

107. Ibid., p. 54. Chief nurse of the army from 1909 to 1912, Delano went on to play an important role in the mobilizing of Red Cross nurses during World War I. For more on her career, see Mary E. Gladwin, *The Red Cross and Jane Arminda Delano* (Philadelphia: W. B. Saunders, 1931), and Mary A. Clarke, *Memories of Jane Delano* (New York: Lakeside, 1934). For the general subject of Red Cross nursing in the United States, see Portia B. Kernodle, *The Red Cross Nurse in Action, 1882–1948* (New York: Harper and Bros., 1949), and Lavinia Dock et al., *History of American Red Cross Nursing* (New York: Macmillan, 1922).

108. *American Red Cross Magazine* 11 (1916):82–84. For a more detailed discussion of relations between the Army Medical Department and the American Red Cross in this period, see *The Medical Department of the United States Army in the World War,*

vol. 1 of *The Surgeon-General's Office* (Washington: Government Printing Office, 1923), pp. 92–105, 543–556).

109. *Military Surgeon* 38 (1916):539–544.

110. See, for example, vol. 11 (1916), pp. 111–113.

111. Wellcome Tropical Institute. RAMC Collection. Longmore Papers 54/7: Nightingale to Longmore, 23 July, 1864.

112. See the extensive correspondence between Longmore and the Comité International from January through December, 1865, in Longmore Papers 23/2 to 23/7 inclusive.

113. His intentions are revealed in a letter to Dunant dated 1 December, 1865, in Longmore Papers 23/7. The text of the lecture was printed as an appendix to the English translation of *La guerre et la charité*: see *Help for Sick and Wounded, Being a Translation of "La guerre et la charité" by MM. Moynier and Appia*, trans. John Furley (London: John Camden Hotten, 1870), pp. 361–400. For the significance of its content, see John F. Hutchinson, "Rethinking the Origins of the Red Cross," *Bulletin of the History of Medicine* 63 (1989):571.

114. Longmore to Dunant, 4 June, 1866, in Dunant Papers Ms. fr. 2115n/236 (Bibliothèque Publique et Universitaire de Genève). There is no record of an approach being made to the Prince of Wales at this time.

115. Nightingale to Longmore, 14 February, 1867, in Longmore Papers 54/12.

116. Field Marshal the Duke of Cambridge to the War Office, 21 February, 1870, in Longmore Papers 27/9.

117. On the revival of the Order in England, see Nigel Corbet Fletcher, *Annals of the Ambulance Department. Being the History of the St. John's Ambulance Association and Brigade.* (London: St. John Ambulance Association, 1949), and Joan Clifford, *For the Service of Mankind: Furley, Lechmere, and Duncan, St. John Ambulance Founders* (London: Robert Hale, 1971).

118. S. H. Best, *The Story of the British Red Cross* (London: Cassell, 1938), p. 32.

119. Corbet Fletcher, *Annals*, pp. 10–11.

120. Burgess later complained that he did the largest part of the work of translating and publishing *Help for Sick and Wounded* (which appeared in 1870) and implied that Furley took all the credit for himself. See the extraordinary *Memorial of John Charles Burgess to the Committee of the National Society, London, June, 1878*, copy in ICRC Library, Ancien Fond No. 4065.

121. *The Times*, 22 July, 1870, p. 7. Only four days earlier, Burgess had written a letter to the same newspaper proposing the formation of a national aid society. Whether he and Furley were collaborating in these efforts is not clear; as Anne Summers has commented, the Loyd-Lindsay letter "rather upstaged Burgess's" because of his eminent social position. (Loyd-Lindsay's father-in-law was the governor of the Bank of England, Lord Overstone.) See her *Angels and Citizens: British Women as Military Nurses, 1854–1914* (London: Routledge and Kegan Paul, 1988), p. 136.

122. These events are described in Corbet Fletcher, *Annals*, p. 11; Best, *Story*, pp. 26–27; and A. K. Loyd, *An Outline of the History of the British Red Cross Society From Its Foundation in 1870 to the Outbreak of War in 1914* (London, BRCS 1917), pp. 6–7. Col. Loyd-Lindsay had received the Victoria Cross for placing the British colors on the heights of Alma as they were taken from the Russians. The 4 August meeting was presided over by the Duke of Manchester, who was Lord Prior of the Order of St.

John in England. Sir Harry Verney, Member of Parliament, brother-in-law of Florence Nightingale, and a good friend of Thomas Longmore, was elected to the executive committee of the society.

123. See *Questions on the Operations of the British National Society for Aid to the Sick and Wounded in War . . . in the Franco-German War, 1870–1871* (London: Harrison and Sons, [n.d.]), *passim; Red Cross Operations in the North of France, 1870–1872* (London, Spottiswoode, 1872); John Furley, *Struggles and Experiences of a Neutral Volunteer,* 2 vols. (London: Chapman, 1872); William MacCormac, *Notes and Recollections of an Ambulance Surgeon* (London: J. and A. Churchill, 1871); Henry Rundle, *With the Red Cross in the Franco-German War, A.D. 1870–1871* (London: Werner Laurie, [1909]); Mrs. H. Templer, *A Labour of Love Under the Red Cross During the Late War* (Guernsey: Le Lievre, 1872).

124. Best, *Story,* pp. 48–49; John Furley, "Ambulance Work and Matériel in Peace and War," *Journal of the Royal United Service Institution* 36 (1892):841.

125. Loyd, *Outline,* p. 10. Among Loyd-Lindsay's supporters on this issue was influential surgeon William (later Sir William) MacCormac.

126. Sir John Furley, *In Peace and War: Autobiographical Sketches* (London: Smith, Elder, 1905), p. 384.

127. The best account of these developments is to be found in Summers, *Angels and Citizens,* pp. 166–171.

128. For a summary of these expenditures, see Loyd, *Outline,* pp. 7–9. On several occasions during these years, the commissioner entrusted with representing the British National Aid Society was Vincent (later Sir Vincent) Kennett-Barrington, whose letters to his wife provide a faithful and at times grim picture of what real Red Cross work was like between the Franco-Prussian War and World War I: Peter Morris, ed., *First Aid to the Battlefront: Life and Letters of Sir Vincent Kennett-Barrington (1844–1903)* (Stroud, N.H.: Allen Sutton, 1992). See especially pp. 190–200 for his comments on friction between Lord Wantage and the army medical service during the Egyptian campaign in 1885.

129. On the fate of this training scheme, which was initially criticized by Florence Nightingale and later abruptly canceled by the War Office, see Summers, *Angels and Citizens,* pp. 158–159.

130. Furley, "Ambulance Work," p. 844.

131. W. L. Langer, *The Diplomacy of Imperialism, 1890–1902* (New York: Knopf, 1951), ch. 13.

132. One result of this reconsideration was the founding of the Royal Army Medical Corps in 1898. Another was the creation of the Army Nursing Reserve in 1897; see Summers, *Angels and Citizens,* pp. 191–192.

133. *Report on the Sixth International Conference of Red Cross Societies* (London: Harrison and Sons, 1898); there is a copy in the Wantage Papers, catalogued as D/WAN/14/1/1.

134. Ibid., pp. 4–5.

135. Ibid., p. 5.

136. "Comments" by Lord Wantage on Major Macpherson's report of 1898, copy in the Wantage Papers D/WAN/14/1/2a, p. 2.

137. Ibid., p. 3.

138. The text of this lecture is to be found in the Furley Papers (item L22), preserved at the British Red Cross Library and Archives.

139. The CBRCC consisted of two representatives from the Army Nursing Reserve (Princess Christian and Miss Wedgwood); three from the British National Aid Society (Lords Wantage and Rothschild and Sir William MacCormac); two from the St. John Ambulance Association (Lord Knutsford and Sir John Furley); and from the War Office came the deputy director-general and the assistant director of the Army Medical Service and the officer in charge of Mobilisation Services. Lansdowne appointed Wantage chairman of the committee and Major Macpherson its secretary. See the extract from *United Services Gazette* (as well as other correspondence on this subject) in the Wantage Papers D/WAN/1/11/1.

140. Lord Wantage to Gustave Moynier, 23 October, 1899, in Wantage Papers D/WAN/14/1/15.

141. This paragraph summarizes information from Best, *The British Red Cross*, pp. 63–94; Furley, *In Peace and War: Autobiographical Sketches*, pp. 389ff; and the official *Report by the Central British Red Cross Committee on Voluntary Organisations in Aid of the Sick and Wounded during the South African War* (London: H.M.S.O., 1902). An excellent analysis of this war's important place in the politics of nursing reform is given in Summers, *Angels and Citizens*, pp. 193–231. For more general accounts of the war that include a good deal of information on its medical aspects, see Thomas Pakenham, *The Boer War* (New York: Random House, 1979), and Byron Farwell, *The Great Anglo-Boer War* (New York, Harper and Row, 1976).

142. For Lord Wantage's testimony, see "Minutes of Evidence before Lord Justice Collins regarding the Central British Red Cross Committee, 30 March, 1900," copy in Wantage Papers D/WAN/15/2/105, pp. 109–118.

143. Sir John Furley to Lord Wantage, 29 October, 1900, in Wantage Papers D/WAN/15/2/119, p. 3.

144. The War Office was not the only body that left its people in ignorance. Furley's assistant, Gerard Bonham Carter, wrote to his mother from Cape Town on 11 February, 1900, "Strange to say we have not in our office a single copy of the Red Cross Rules & Regulations which is rather awkward at the present moment." Wantage Papers D/WAN/ 15/2/119, p. 2.

145. Furley to Wantage, 29 October, 1900, pp. 3–4.

146. Ibid., p. 4. Members of a German Red Cross ambulance with the Boers reported, "When the capture of Jacobsdal by the British was considered imminent, the inhabitants of the town prepared Red Cross brassards in bulk; and, in fact, one scarcely met an individual without a Red Cross brassard. Moreover, amongst all these ambulance men and hospital attendants . . . there was quite a large number of individuals who, the evening before, were in the firing line and had fired on the British, and who did not hesitate to take up their rifles again when the enemy evacuated the place." Quoted in W. G. Macpherson, "The Geneva Convention," *Journal of the Royal Army Medical Corps* 15 (November, 1910):616.

147. Furley to Wantage, 29 October, 1900, p. 5.

148. Before he became the second Viscount Knutsford, Sidney Holland had been chairman of the London Hospital, in which capacity he had raised an enormous amount of money for its work. He was also a resolute foe of the registration of nurses, whether military or civil. On the latter issue, see Summers, *Angels and Citizens*, pp. 223, 238–240.

149. Sir John Furley to Lord Rothschild, 30 June, 1903, in Wantage Papers D/WAN/16/1/1, p. 3.

150. Sir John Furley to Lord Rothschild, 30 June, 1903; Wantage Papers D/WAN/16/1/1, pp. 3–4.

151. The other members were Lt.-Col. Alfred Keogh, deputy director-general of army medical services, and his assistant, Major T. McCulloch. There is a copy of the confidential report of this subcommittee in the Wantage Papers D/WAN/16/1/2.

152. Among the "supplementary aids" suggested were hospital ships and trains, means of transport, auxiliary hospitals, and convalescent homes. Ibid., p. 6.

153. Ibid., p. 6.

154. See his memorandum entitled, "The Central British Red Cross Council," dated 9 September, 1904 in the Wantage Papers D/WAN/ 16/1/1.

155. Ibid., pp. 5–6.

156. Longmore Papers 54/13, Nightingale to Longmore, 28 February, 1867.

157. There is a recent, chatty biography: Stephen Trombley, *Sir Frederick Treves: The Extra-Ordinary Edwardian* (London: Routledge, 1989).

158. Loyd, *Outline*, pp. 16–17; Trombley, *Treves*, p. 151. For a sample of his findings, see Frederick Treves, "Medical Aspects of the Russo-Japanese War," *British Medical Journal*, no. 1 (1904):1395–1396.

159. See W. G. Macpherson, *The Russo-Japanese War: Medical and Sanitary Reports from Officers Attached to the Japanese and Russian Forces in the Field.* (London: War Office, Department of the General Staff, 1908), especially pp. 330–346.

160. These maneuvers may be followed in the extensive collection of documents and letters on the subject preserved in the Wantage Papers, covering the period from September, 1904 to July, 1905: D/WAN/16/1/6 to 16/1/22.

161. A. K. Loyd to Lady Wantage, 14 March, 1905, in Wantage Papers D/WAN/16/1/21, p. 2.

162. There is a heavily laundered but still tendentious version of these events in Loyd, *Outline*, pp. 18–21.

163. As Loyd noted, "During the Boer War . . . a *paid* staff of hospital attendants had been engaged by the War Office under contract with the St. John Ambulance Association, and the St. Andrew's Ambulance Association, to assist the Army Medical Service of the regular Army in time of war. Similar contracts had been made by the Admiralty." Loyd, *Outline*, p. 24. It was the right (not the obligation) to make similar contracts in future that the authorities wished to retain. This conflict may be followed in the documents printed in Loyd, *Outline*, pp. 20–25.

164. Ibid., p. 23.

165. On Keogh's efforts to prepare the medical service for a major war, see James Murray, "Sir Alfred Keogh: Doctor and General," *Irish Medical Journal* 80 (1987):429.

166. On the origins of the VAD scheme, see Loyd, *Outline*, pp. 27–37.

167. Treves to Haldane, 16 July, 1909, printed in ibid., pp. 29–30.

168. Haldane to Treves, 20 July, 1909, printed in ibid., p. 31.

169. The feud between the two organizations over the VAD certificate issue can be followed in exquisite detail in Loyd, *Outline*, pp. 37–49, and from the St. John side in Nigel Corbet Fletcher, *The St. John Ambulance Association: Its History and Its Part in the Ambulance Movement* (London: St. John Ambulance Association, 1930).

170. As quoted in Loyd, *Outline*, p. 39.

171. War Office circular, 29 July, 1910, as quoted in Loyd, *Outline*, p. 46.

172. Sir Edward Ward to the Secretaries of the Territorial Force County Associations, 8 October, 1910, quoted in Loyd, *Outline*, p. 47.

173. Ibid., p. 49.

174. As quoted in ibid., p. 40.

175. Ibid., p. 49.

176. For the details of this amazing episode, see Loyd, *Outline*, pp. 59–60.

177. Both the letter and the editorial are reproduced in ibid., pp. 65–66.

178. The text is printed in ibid., p. 67.

179. The full text appears in ibid., p. 69.

180. Ibid., p. 70.

181. Treves wrote that it was "clear, concise, fearless and accurate to the smallest point," and Ridsdale noted, "It sets out what happened, and the monstrous behaviour of the W[ar] O[ffice] very thoroughly." Treves to Loyd, 13 January, 1918; Ridsdale to Loyd, 4 January, 1918; extracts from both letters were inserted by Loyd into the few copies of his *Outline* that escaped Stanley's notice.

182. *La Société de Secours aux Blessés Militaires des Armées de Terre et de Mer en Chine, 1900–1901. (Croix-Rouge Française)* (Paris: Siège Central, 1901), p. ii.

183. On the founding of the ADF, see *Extrait des écrits du Docteur Duchaussoy sur l'Association des Dames Françaises dont il est le fondateur* (Abbeville, France: C. Paillart, 1897); on the history of the UFF, see *Union des Femmes de France: Cinquantenaire, 1881–1931* (Paris: UFF, 1931).

184. Some of the personal animosity generated by these events may be savored, undiminished after thirty years, in *Refutation du discours de M. Bouloumié sur l'évolution de la Croix-Rouge en France* (Amiens, France: Imprimerie Grau, 1911).

185. The relevant official documents may be found in *Recueil des décrets, status, règlements et instructions concernant le Société de Secours aux Blessés Militaires. Croix Rouge Française* (Paris: Croix Rouge Française, 1936).

186. Roger Colomb, *Rôle de la femme dans l'assistance aux blessés militaires* (Bordeaux, France: Imprimerie Y. Cadoret, 1903).

187. Ibid., p. 96.

188. Ibid., p. 99.

189. Ibid., pp. 102–109.

190. Maxime Du Camp, *La Croix-Rouge en France. Société de secours aux blessés militaires de terre et de mer* (Paris: Hachette, 1889), pp. 256–257. An abridged version—180 pages instead of 342—was published three years later by the SSBM: Maxime Du Camp, *La Croix Rouge de France* (Paris: Siège central de la SSBM, 1892).

191. Ibid., p. 258.

192. Ibid., p. 260.

193. Compare Du Camp's assumptions about women and charity with those of the author of the first French work on the subject, which was published by the Paris Society for Religious Tracts: Mme William Monod, *La mission des femmes en temps de guerre* (Paris: Nouvelle Bibliothèque des Familles, 1870), to which Louis Appia lent a certain unofficial standing by contributing a laudatory preface.

194. Du Camp, *La Croix-Rouge en France*, pp. 261–262.

195. Between 1897 and 1899 France was rocked by a scandal that erupted over the conviction for treason, in 1894, of a Jewish officer, Captain Alfred Dreyfus. Accused of having convicted Dreyfus on the basis of secret and forged evidence, army leaders tried to defend themselves by appealing to tradition, the Church, and the honor of the army; meanwhile, supporters of Dreyfus hotly defended the principle of individual freedom. In the wake of the Dreyfus affair, the French Right espoused what Eugen Weber calls "a new nationalism [that] played a great part during the prewar years in

persuading France that a conflict was inevitable." Weber, *A Modern History of Europe* (New York: Norton, 1971), p. 806.

196. *Aux jeunes filles de la Croix-Rouge revenant de Maroc. Strophes dites dans la réunion de la Croix-Rouge tenue à Nice . . . le 30 Mars, 1908. Par le Marquis de Magallon d'Argens*, p. 1.

197. Ibid., p. 1.

198. For a full report on these relief measures, see *La Société Française de Secours aux Blessés Militaires et les inondations de 1910* (Paris: SSBM, [1911]).

199. On the significance of the patriotic revival, see Paul Kennedy, *The Rise and Fall of the Great Powers* (New York: Randon House, 1987), pp. 223–224.

200. *Les devoirs de la femme en vue de guerre. Discours par M. le médicin-principal Berthier, médicin-chef de la place de Belfort . . . le 25 Juin, 1910* (Belfort: Comité de la Croix-Rouge, 1910), p. 3.

201. Ibid., p. 33.

202. "Croix-Rouge Française. La Société de Secours aux Militaires Blessés," *Revue Hebdomadaire*, no. 30 (27 July, 1912):480.

203. Ibid., p. 479.

204. L. Arnaud and P. Bonnette, *La femme sur le champs de bataille* (Paris: Henri Charles-Lavauzelle, [1912]), pp. 19, 29, 51, 65, 75, 97.

205. Ibid., pp. 97–99; F. de Witt-Guizot, *La femme et la guerre. Comment une femme peut-elle servir la France en temps de guerre?* (Paris, SSBM, 1913), pp. 21–23. On the development of the military nursing service in England, see Summers, *Angels and Citizens*, pp. 221–231.

206. Arnaud and Bonnette, *La femme sur le champs de bataille*, p. 110.

207. De Witt-Guizot, *La femme et la guerre*, p. 48.

208. Ibid., p. 29.

209. Ibid., p. 31.

210. Arnaud and Bonnette, *La femme sur le champs de bataille*, p. 99.

211. De Witt-Guizot, *La femme et la guerre*, pp. 7, 38.

212. Ibid., p. 26; see also pp. 11–12, 48.

213. Ibid., p. 48.

214. Andrée d'Alix, *Le rôle patriotique des femmes* (Paris: Perrin et Cie., 1914). Although this book was not published by the SSBM, its cover bore the words "La Croix-Rouge Française" and the badge of the Geneva cross; author d'Alix also thanks the SSBM for putting its library and archives at her disposal while she was writing the book (p. xxv).

215. Ibid., p. xxiii.

216. Ibid., preface (unpaged).

217. Ibid., p. 132.

218. Ibid., p. 16.

219. Ibid., p. 336.

220. Paris: Plon, [1911].

221. D'Alix, *Le rôle patriotique*, p. xix.

222. Ibid., pp. 92–93.

223. Ibid., p. 97.

224. Ibid., p. 101.

225. Ibid., p. 92.

226. Ibid., p. 337.

227. Ibid., p. 97.

228. "Rapport de M. de Valence," in *Le cinquantenaire de la fondation de la Croix-Rouge en France* (Paris: SSBM, 1914), p. 298 (copy in ICRC Library, AF 1581).

229. Ibid., p. 256.

230. Ibid., p. 257.

231. Ibid., p. 262.

232. Ibid., p. 267.

233. For a detailed analysis, see John F. Hutchinson, "The Nagler Case: A Revealing Moment in Red Cross History," *Canadian Bulletin of Medical History* 9 (1992):177–190.

234. NARA/RG 267 (Department of Justice), No. 26864, *United States v. Louis B. Nagler*, p. 12 .

235. Ibid., p. 13.

236. Ibid., pp. 23, 44–45.

237. On La Follette's opposition to the war and attempts to suppress his views, see David P. Thelen, *Robert M. La Follette and the Insurgent Spirit* (Boston: Little, Brown, 1976), pp. 140–145.

238. The fate of German-Americans during the war is discussed in John Higham, *Strangers in the Land: Patterns of American Nativism, 1860–1925* (New Brunswick, N.J.: Rutgers University Press, 1955), pp. 194–222; see also David M. Kennedy, *Over Here: The First World War and American Society* (New York: Oxford University Press, 1980), pp. 66–69. A more recent study of the "home front" is Ronald Schaffer, *America in the Great War: The Rise of the War Welfare State* (New York: Oxford University Press, 1991).

239. Kennedy, *Over Here*, p. 70.

240. Ibid., p. 78; see also Higham, *Strangers in the Land*, pp. 210–212.

241. *United States v. Louis B. Nagler*, pp. 146–148.

242. Ibid., pp. 149–151.

243. *The Red Cross Bulletin* 2(33) (12 August, 1918):1.

244. *The Red Cross Bulletin* 2(36) (2 September, 1918):1.

245. NARA/RG 267 (Department of Justice), No. 9–19–763, Albert C. Wolfe, U.S. Attorney, Western District of Wisconsin, to the Attorney-General, Washington, D.C., 29 August, 1918, p. 1.

246. NARA/RG 267 (Department of Justice) No. 9–19–763, Memorandum from R. C. Stewart, Assistant Attorney-General, to the Solicitor-General.

247. See, for example, Henry P. Davison, *The American Red Cross in the Great War* (New York: MacMillan, 1919); *Reports by the Joint War Committee . . . of the British Red Cross Society and the Order of St. John of Jerusalem in England on Voluntary Aid Rendered to the Sick and Wounded at Home and Abroad and to British Prisoners of War, 1914–1919*, with appendices (London: H.M.S.O., 1921); Geoffrey de Grandmaison, *La Croix-Rouge Française: La Société de Secours aux Militaires Blessés Pendant la Guerre* (Paris: Bloud and Say, 1922).

248. Jeanne C. van Lanschot Hubrecht, "A Letter from Holland," *American Journal of Nursing* 17 (1916):230.

Chapter 6

1. Henry P. Davison Papers, American Red Cross Headquarters. Robert E. Olds to Otis Cutler, 31 August, 1921.

2. ICRC Circular No. 144, 16 November, 1912; as quoted in André Durand, *From Sarajevo to Hiroshima: History of the International Committee of the Red Cross* (Geneva: Henry Dunant Institute, 1984), p. 23. To be sure, the Belgrade agency also served as an intermediary for at least some of the relief supplied by neutrals; for a list of national societies that sent assistance, see ibid., p. 25.

3. For the text of the relevant resolution, see Durand, *From Sarajevo,* p. 21.

4. As quoted in ibid., p. 32.

5. As quoted in ibid., p. 80.

6. Ibid., p. 89; on the hospital ships, see p. 64.

7. Ibid., p. 89.

8. Quoted in ibid., pp. 88–89.

9. ICRC Circular No. 174, 27 November, 1918; NARA/RG 200 (Records of the ANRC), Box 52, Folder 041. International Red Cross Committee.

10. Ibid., p. 3.

11. Davison Papers. Davison to Harvey D. Gibson, 22 November, 1918, pp. 2–3.

12. For a summary of ARC relief work in Europe, see Foster Rhea Dulles, *The American Red Cross: A History* (New York: Harper and Bros., 1950) pp. 173–194.

13. On the Serbian mission, see Gustave R. Gaeddert, "The Boardman Influence, 1905–1917," vol. 3 of "The History of the American National Red Cross" (unpublished typescript, Washington, D.C., 1950), pp. 306–310. For a more detailed treatment, see Richard P. Strong et al., *Typhus Fever with Particular Reference to the Serbian Epidemic* (Cambridge, Mass.: American Red Cross at Harvard University Press, 1920).

14. Ibid., p. 3.

15. Davison used these words himself in his cable #10580, to Harvey D. Gibson, 10 December, 1918; quoted in Clyde E. Buckingham, *For Humanity's Sake: The Story of the Early Development of the League of Red Cross Societies* (Washington, D.C.: Public Affairs Press, 1964), pp. 31–32.

16. For an approximation of what took place at the White House meeting, see Davison Papers, "Memorandum of Interview between President Wilson, and Mr. Davison and Mr. Axson (ARC National Secretary and Wilson's brother-in-law)—December 2, 1918."

17. Davison Papers. Wilson to Davison, 3 December, 1918.

18. Woodrow Wilson Papers. Ador to Wilson, 23 June, 1917.

19. ARC cable # 10580, Davison to Gibson 10 December, 1918, quoted in Buckingham, *For Humanity's Sake,* p. 32

20. Sir Arthur Stanley, "Recollections of the Early Days of the League," *Red Cross Courier* 8(9) (1 May, 1929):5.

21. Woodrow Wilson Papers. Wilson to Davison, 7 January, 1919.

22. House to Lloyd George, 14 January, 1919, in Charles Seymour (ed.), *The Intimate Papers of Colonel House* (Boston: Houghton, Mifflin, 1928), vol. 4, pp. 257–259; also quoted in Buckingham, *For Humanity's Sake,* pp. 36–37

23. War council minutes, 15 January, 1919, as quoted in Buckingham, *For Humanity's Sake,* p. 40. However, this sum was only half of the $5 million that Davison had requested; Eliot Wadsworth evidently thought it prudent to withhold some of the funds until more was known about how Davison's plans were developing. Davison Papers, Davison to Wadsworth, date incomplete [January, 1919], cable #17267.

24. Woodrow Wilson Papers. House to Davison, 25 January, 1919.

25. Georges Milsom, "The History of the Red Cross," *World's Health* 3(1) (January, 1922):20.

26. According to André Durand, *From Sarajevo,* p. 149, the ICRC received telegrams from Davison on 4 and 6 February. Copies of these telegrams have not been preserved in the Davison Papers.

27. Woodrow Wilson Papers. Edouard Naville, interim president of the ICRC, to Wilson, 9 December, 1918. Naville was serving as interim President during the absence in Berne of Gustave Ador, who had been serving on the Swiss Federal Council, and was elected president of the confederation for 1919.

28. For Durand's version of these events, see *From Sarajevo,* pp. 148–153. Wishing his readers to believe that the ICRC was already in the forefront of change, Durand resorts to some quite ingenious stretching of tenuous evidence.

29. For the minutes of these meetings, as recorded by the ICRC, see *Bulletin International de la Croix-Rouge* (15 March, 1919):334–351. Davison's memorandum appears in *Revue Internationale de la Croix-Rouge* 1(4) (15 April, 1919):393–402. See also Durand, *From Sarajevo,* pp. 148–153; Buckingham, *For Humanity's Sake,* pp. 45–46; Davison Papers, Robert E. Olds to Otis Cutler, 31 August, 1921.

30. Durand, *From Sarajevo,* p. 153.

31. Davison Papers. "Appel du Comité International de la Croix-Rouge a Genève" (13 February, 1919).

32. Ibid., p. 1.

33. See Renée-Marguerite Cramer, "La tâche de la prochaine conférence internationale de la Croix-Rouge," *Revue Internationale de la Croix-Rouge* 1(4) (15 April, 1919):403–411.

34. A copy of his address on this subject is preserved in NARA/RG 200, Box 55, Folder 041. LRCS Origins 1919.

35. Ibid., pp. 7–9.

36. Ibid., p. 12.

37. Davison Papers. House to Wilson, 16 February, 1919; Wilson to House, 17 February, 1919.

38. Davison Papers. "Memorandum submitted by Henry P. Davison, Chairman, Committee of Red Cross Societies . . . Paris, February 21, 1919."

39. Durand, *From Sarajevo,* p. 153.

40. This idea is clearly stated in a letter to President Wilson written in January, 1919: Davison to Wilson, 2 January, 1919, NARA/RG 200, Box 55, Folder 041. LRCS Origins 1919.

41. Davison Papers. J. B. Moore to Davison, 21 January, 1919; Buckingham, *For Humanity's Sake,* p. 44.

42. Davison Papers. Sir Arthur Lawley to Davison, 24 February, 1919.

43. Davison Papers. Davison to Sir Arthur Lawley, 3 March, 1919.

44. Wilson to Davison, 26 February, 1919. NARA/RG200. Box 55, Folder 041. LRCS Origins 1919.

45. In my opinion, André Durand muddies the waters considerably by implying (*From Sarajevo,* pp. 147, 151, 155) that Davison sought from the outset to establish close ties between the League and the international Red Cross. It is certainly true that Davison thought that an international humanitarian organization would be a fine expression of the ideals behind the League. He may even have thought that its eventual structure could resemble that of the League, but not until after his talks with the

ICRC did he begin to contemplate the idea of tying his new organization to the League itself. This is scarcely surprising, since it was only during his visit to Geneva that he began to realize how difficult it might be to arrange the conference that would, he hoped, renegotiate the Geneva Convention. Durand speculates (p. 155) that Davison's main concern was to keep his "international relief body" from being absorbed by other agencies that were already operating in postwar Europe, but the evidence I have seen points squarely to his disillusionment with the ICRC as the primary reason why he turned to the League of Nations.

46. Davison Papers. Davison to Wilson, 9 March, 1919, p. 1.

47. Ibid., p. 2.

48. Ibid., p. 2.

49. Davison Papers. Davison to Edward House, 9 March, 1919.

50. Davison Papers. Davison to J. P. Morgan, 15 March, 1919.

51. Woodrow Wilson Papers. Davison to Wilson, 15 March, 1919, enclosing note received from C. H. Seymour, an advisory member of the Peace Commission.

52. Davison Papers. Wilson to Davison, 26 March, 1919.

53. House Papers. Davison to Edward House, 30 March, 1919. Buckingham, *For Humanity's Sake*, pp. 63–64, is incorrect in stating that House himself wrote the proposed articles.

54. For the text of these draft articles, see David Hunter Miller, *The Drafting of the Covenant* (New York: Putnam, 1928), vol. 1, p. 400.

55. Woodrow Wilson Papers. Davison to Wilson, 27 March, 1919: "This afternoon I have had an opportunity to go over the whole subject with Colonel House, who says he will speak to you about it, so I will not take up your time by writing."

56. British Red Cross Archives. Memorandum from Lord Lansdowne to the secretary of the ICRC, 7 March, 1919.

57. British Red Cross Archives. Edouard Naville to the president, British Red Cross Society, 25 March, 1919.

58. Rappard's report is quoted in Durand, *From Sarajevo*, p. 156.

59. A copy of this telegram has not been found in the Davison Papers, but it is quoted, presumably from the ICRC archives, in ibid., p. 156.

60. Ibid., p. 156.

61. Davison Papers. Cable, Davison to J. P. Morgan, marked "Confidential. For Thomas Cochran," 27 March, 1919.

62. Ibid., pp. 1–2.

63. Sir William Osler's name had been on the original list, but he declined. NARA RG/200 Box 56, Folder 041. LRCS Medical Conference at Cannes. The list of invitees, together with Davison's proposed agenda, appeared in *Military Surgeon* 44 (1919):643–645.

64. *Proceedings of the Medical Conference Held at the Invitation of the Committee of Red Cross Societies, Cannes, France, April 1 to 11, 1919* (Geneva: League of Red Cross Societies, 1919), p. 12.

65. Ibid., p. 13.

66. Ibid., pp. 13–14.

67. Hoover Institution Archives. LRCS Box 1, Folder 8, Cannes Conference. Cable from Otis Cutler (ARC Headquarters in Washington) to Davison, 3 April, 1919.

68. Davison read the text of the article to the seventh session of the conference on 7 April, 1919: *Proceedings of the Medical Conference*, p. 82.

69. The text of this telegram is reproduced in ibid., pp. 162–164.

70. Durand, *From Sarajevo*, p. 157.

71. Davison Papers. Telegram, Davison to Franklin K. Lane, 9 April, 1919, p. 1.

72. Ibid., pp. 3–4.

73. Davison Papers. Davison to Woodrow Wilson, 13 April, 1919.

74. Davison Papers. Davison to Thomas Cochran, 23 April, 1919.

75. Woodrow Wilson Papers. Davison to Wilson, 23 April, 1919.

76. Arthur Stanley, "Recollections of the Early Days of the League," *Red Cross Courier* 8 (1 May, 1929):6.

77. On Henderson's wartime career, see John H. Morrow, *The Great War in the Air: Military Aviation from 1909 to 1921* (Washington, D.C.: Smithsonian Institution Press, 1993).

78. Davison Papers. E. C. Grenfell to Davison, 26 April, 1919, marked "Confidential."

79. Buckingham, *For Humanity's Sake*, p. 79.

80. Davison Papers. Davison to ICRC, 3 May, 1919, p. 4. (Here Davison quotes this passage from the letter sent to him by the ICRC, dated 23 April, 1919.) In a separate meeting with Dr. Ninagawa of the Japanese society, the same argument was made by Miss Cramer: Arata Ninagawa, *The Facts About the Formation of the League of Red Cross Societies* (Tokyo: [n.p.], 1926), p. 8. In this extraordinary pamphlet, Dr. Ninagawa tries to take credit for being the originator of the peacetime program of the League; the degree of his interest in its affairs is perhaps better measured by his regular absence from meetings of its board of governors during the 1920s.

81. Davison Papers. Davison to ICRC, 3 May, 1919, p. 2.

82. Buckingham, *For Humanity's Sake*, p. 83.

83. A copy of the articles of association is preserved in NARA/RG 200, Box 55, Folder 041. LRCS Origins 1919.

84. Ibid., pp. 3–4.

85. "Press Release, 7 May, 1919," in NARA RG/200, Box 55, Folder 041. LRCS Origins 1919, p. 4.

86. "Articles of Association," p. 3.

87. Woodrow Wilson Papers. Wilson to Davison, 5 May, 1919.

88. ICRC Circular No. 182, in NARA/RG 200, Box 55, Folder 041. LRCS Origins 1919, p. 2.

89. Ibid., p. 2; Davison to ICRC, 3 May, 1919, in NARA/RG 200, Box 55, Folder 041. LRCS Origins 1919.

90. George Murnane to Livingston Farrand, 11 July, 1919, in NARA/RG 200, Box 55, Folder 041. LRCS Origins 1919.

91. Stockton Axson to Livingston Farrand (undated) in NARA RG/200, Box 55, Folder 041. LRCS Origins 1919.

92. Quoted in Henderson to Farrand, 23 May, 1919, NARA RG/200, Box 55, Folder 041. LRCS Origins 1919.

93. Davison Papers. Olds to Farrand, 13 May, 1919. Davison must have known about the invitation in advance and broached his plan to Olds a day or two before the letter was received by Henderson.

94. Ernest P. Bicknell, *With the Red Cross in Europe, 1917–1922* (Washington, D.C.: American National Red Cross, 1938), p. 262.

95. Henderson to Farrand, 23 May, 1919, p. 2, in NARA RG/200, Box 55, Folder 041. LRCS Origins 1919.

96. Ibid., p. 3.

97. Davison Papers. Olds to Farrand, 13 May, 1919; for an extensive paraphrase of its contents, see Buckingham, *For Humanity's Sake,* pp. 89–93,

98. W. Frank Persons to Otis Cutler, 21 May, 1919, p. 9, in NARA RG/200 Box 55, Folder 041. LRCS Origins 1919.

99. The crucial discussion on this subject is summarized in Buckingham, *For Humanity's Sake,* pp. 99–101.

100. Persons to Cutler, 21 May, 1919 in NARA RG/200 Box 55, Folder 041. LRCS Origins 1919.

101. Axson to Davison, 27 May, 1919 in NARA RG/200 Box 55, Folder 041. LRCS Origins 1919.

102. Ibid., p. 2.

103. Ibid., pp. 3–4.

104. Buckingham, *For Humanity's Sake,* p. 101.

105. Farrand to Olds, 12 June, 1919. Hoover Archives. LRCS Box 1, Folder 10, "Conference Minutes." See also Buckingham, *For Humanity's Sake,* pp. 100–101.

106. Olds to Farrand, 14 June, 1919; Hoover Archives, LRCS Box 1, Folder 10 "Conference Minutes."

107. Ibid.

108. Davison Papers. Olds to Farrand, 13 May, 1919.

109. Olds to Farrand, 14 June, 1919, pp. 2–3. Hoover Archives. LRCS Box 1, Folder 10 "Conference Minutes."

110. Henderson to Davison, 14 June, 1919. Hoover Archives, LRCS Box 1, Folder 2, "ARC Headquarters, Washington, D.C."

111. Davison to Henderson, 30 June, 1919, in NARA RG/200, Box 55, Folder 041. LRCS Origins 1919.

112. Farrand to Henderson, 16 and 30 June, 1919, in ibid.; Davison Papers, Davison to Farrand, 8 May, 1919.

113. British Red Cross Archives. "Minutes of an Extraordinary Meeting of the Council," 13 May, 1919, pp. 2–3.

114. Ibid., p. 3.

115. Ibid., p. 2.

116. Davison Papers. Secretary, BRCS to Sir Arthur Stanley, 22 July, 1919.

117. Statement by Ernest Bicknell, 27 October, 1919 in Hoover Archives. LRCS Box 1, Folder 10, "Conference Minutes—ARC and LORCS."

118. Davison Papers. Henderson to Davison, 8 July, 1919.

119. Davison Papers. Axson to Davison, 15 July, 1919.

120. In his cable to Lane from Cannes, Davison boasted, "The man recognized as best in any country has been here and is so impressed with opportunity he has consented to take head medical department for one year provided can secure leave." Davison Papers, Davison to Franklin K. Lane, 9 April, 1919.

121. Davison to Henderson, 17 July, 1919, p. 1, NARA RG/200, Box 55, Folder 041. LRCS—International Commission of the ARC, 1918—22.

122. Ibid., p. 2.

123. The pressure was evidently applied in person by Eliot Wadsworth: ibid., p. 2; Welch and Biggs may also have intervened.

124. Ibid., p. 4.

125. "I am fully conscious, Sir David, of the fact that the delays may have caused you to be somewhat discouraged. . . ." Ibid., p. 4.

126. Davison Papers. Davison to Henderson, 7 August, 1919.

127. Ibid.

128. Rappard admitted the criticism in a letter to Davison: Davison Papers, Rappard to Davison, 3 July, 1919.

129. By the end of May, 1919, the founding members had been joined by Belgium, China, Norway, and Portugal; in June, by Brazil, Peru, Australia, Canada, Argentina, Greece, Sweden, and the Union of South Africa; in July, by New Zealand, Denmark, Rumania, Venezuela, and Cuba; in August, by India, Netherlands, Serbia, and Spain.

130. Davison Papers. Henderson to Prince Carl of Sweden (president of the Swedish Red Cross Society), 8 July, 1919.

131. Davison Papers. Henderson to Davison, 18 July, 1919.

132. Durand, *From Sarajevo*, p. 169.

133. *Réunion du Conseil Général de la Ligue des Sociétés de la Croix-Rouge. Session de Mars, 1920. Compte rendu.* (Geneva: LRCS, 1920), p. 343. Hereafter *LRCS Geneva 1920: Compte rendu.*

134. Ibid., p. 344.

135. Ibid., p. 345.

136. Ibid., p. 347.

137. League Archives, Geneva. Box 1, "Origins." Collection of departmental brochures, March, 1920. Department of Publicity and Publication, p. 4.

138. *LRCS Geneva 1920: Compte Rendu,* p. 346.

139. Davison Papers. Chandler P. Anderson to Davison, 29 November, 1919.

140. *LRCS Geneva 1920: Compte Rendu,* p. 348.

Chapter 7

1. For the detailed negotiations that led up to this agreement, see André Durand, *From Sarajevo to Hiroshima: The History of the International Committee of the Red Cross* (Geneva: Henry Dunant Institute, 1984), pp. 174–194; on the current structure of the international Red Cross and the role of the ICRC, see David P. Forsythe, *Humanitarian Politics: The International Committee of the Red Cross* (Baltimore: Johns Hopkins University Press, 1977), and Geoffrey Best, *War and Law Since 1945* (Oxford: Clarendon Press, 1994).

2. League Archives, Geneva. Box 1, "Origins," Departmental Brochures (March, 1920). Program of the Department of Sanitation, p. 1.

3. *Réunion du Conseil Général de la Ligue des Sociétés de la Croix-Rouge. Session de Mars, 1920. Compte rendu* (Geneva: LRCS, 1920), p. 23. (Hereafter *LRCS Geneva 1920: Compte rendu.*)

4. NARA RG/200 Box 58, Folder 041. League Meetings-General Council. "Report of the Delegates Appointed From the American Red Cross to Attend the First General Council of the League of Red Cross Societies," p. 3.

5. Ibid., p. 25.

6. The secretariat of the League of Nations was also invited; Sir Eric Drummond did not attend but sent a letter of good wishes with his representatives, Dr. I. Nitobe and Rachel Crowdy. *LRCS Geneva 1920: Compte rendu,* p. 7.

7. Ibid., p. 25.

8. Ibid., p. 26.

9. Ibid., p. 26.

10. Ibid., p. 26.

11. Ibid., p. 27.

12. Ibid., p. 255.

13. Henry P. Davison Papers. Sir Arthur Stanley to Sir David Henderson, 10 March, 1920.

14. *LRCS Geneva 1920: Compte rendu*, p. 350.

15. Davison Papers. Stanley to Henderson, 10 March, 1920. For speculative comments about Davison's motives, see Clyde E. Buckingham, *For Humanity's Sake: The Story of the Early Development of the League of Red Cross Societies* (Washington, D.C.: Public Affairs Press, 1964), p. 131.

16. *LRCS Geneva 1920: Compte Rendu*, pp. 355–356.

17. NARA RG/200, Box 58, Folder 041. League Meetings-General Council. Minutes of Meeting of Heads of Departments (of LRCS secretariat), 16 March, 1920, p. 2.

18. Ibid., p. 1.

19. For the League of Nations perspective on these developments, see Martin Dubin, "The League of Nations Health Organisation and the Development of the Public Health Profession," in Paul Weindling (ed.), *International Health Organisations and Movements, 1918–1939* (Cambridge: Cambridge University Press, 1995).

20. This was the opinion of Dr. Octave Monod, associate chief of the department of tuberculosis: NARA RG/200, Box 58, Folder 041. League Meetings-General Council. Minutes of Meeting of Heads of Departments (of LRCS secretariat), 16 March, 1920, p. 1.

21. Ibid., p. 2.

22. Davison Papers. William Rappard to Davison, 17 May, 1920.

23. For more details on the work of this conference, see Buckingham, *For Humanity's Sake*, pp. 147–149.

24. Davison Papers. Sir Arthur Stanley to Davison, 16 June, 1920.

25. Davison Papers. Rappard to Davison, 13 September, 1920.

26. Davison Papers. Farrand to central committee members, 23 September, 1920.

27. See the extensive correspondence on this subject in NARA RG/200, Box 55, Folder 041. International Commission of the ARC, 1918–1922.

28. Davison Papers. Farrand to Boardman, 26 April, 1920, replying to Boardman to Farrand, 17 April, 1920.

29. Davison Papers. Davison to Farrand, 21 September, 1920.

30. Buckingham, *For Humanity's Sake*, p. 158. That Henderson had left Geneva without informing Rappard and other staff members of this decision is an indication of how seriously his poor health had affected his work.

31. NARA/RG 200, Box 94, Volume 8. Minutes of the Executive Committee, 28 April, 1920.

32. In a letter that he wrote to Farrand six months after the Geneva meeting, Davison admitted that he had foreseen difficulties ahead and had left Geneva with "grave concern" for the League's future. Davison Papers, Davison to Farrand, 21 September, 1920.

33. Davison Papers. Sir Arthur Stanley to Davison, 16 June, 1920.

34. Davison Papers. Henderson to Davison, 11 June, 1920.

35. Davison Papers. Davison to Henderson, 26 March, 1920.

36. Davison Papers. Biggs to Davison, 10 September, 1920.
37. Buckingham, *For Humanity's Sake*, p. 167.
38. Davison Papers. Henderson to Davison, 6 September, 1920.
39. Davison Papers. Davison to Farrand, 21 September, 1920.
40. Davison Papers. Davison to Henderson, 27 October, 1920.
41. Davison Papers. Rappard to Davison, 28 October, 1920.
42. Davison Papers. Henderson to Davison, 6 November, 1920.
43. Davison Papers. Henderson to Davison, 11 November, 1920.
44. Davison Papers. Davison to Henderson, 20 November, 1920, p. 1.
45. Ibid., p. 2.
46. Ibid., p. 3.
47. *LRCS Geneva 1920: Compte rendu*, p. 354.
48. On the ICRC's relationship with the Save the Children Fund, see Durand, *From Sarajevo*, pp. 162–166.
49. David Henderson, "The International Red Cross Committee and the League of Red Cross Societies," *Bulletin of the League of Red Cross Societies* 2(3) (December, 1920):105–110.
50. Ibid., p. 105.
51. Ibid., p. 108.
52. Ibid., pp. 108–109.
53. Ibid., p. 110.
54. "La Ligue et le Comité International de la Croix-Rouge," *Bulletin International des Sociétés de la Croix-Rouge* 52(222) (15 February, 1921):174.
55. For details, see ibid., pp. 174–175. American efforts to fight typhus in Poland are described in A. E. Cornebise, *Typhus and Doughboys* (Wilmington: University of Delaware Press, 1982).
56. "La Ligue et le Comité," p. 172.
57. Compare the version of what Naville said in ibid., p. 172 with the published text of his speech, which appeared in *Bulletin International* 50(199) (15 March, 1919):339.
58. "La Ligue et le Comité," p. 176.
59. See the memorandum from T. B. Kittredge in Sofia to LRCS headquarters in Geneva dated 21 March, 1921; Hoover Archives, LRCS Box 1, Folder 7, Bulgarian Red Cross, p. 1
60. Ibid., p. 2.
61. Ibid., p. 1.
62. Ibid., p. 1.
63. Ibid., p. 3.
64. "Activité internationale de la Croix-Rouge en temps de paix," *Revue Internationale de la Croix-Rouge* 3(26) (15 February, 1921):97. Two years earlier, Edouard Naville had told Davison and his associates that "the Red Cross is an institution of war." *Bulletin International des Sociétés de la Croix-Rouge* 50(199) (15 March, 1919):337.
65. "Activité internationale," p. 97.
66. Ibid., p. 98.
67. Ibid., pp. 98–99.
68. Ibid., p. 92.
69. Ibid., p. 93.
70. Ibid., p. 93.

71. Ibid., pp. 93–94.
72. Ibid., p. 95.
73. Ibid., p. 99.
74. Durand, *From Sarajevo*, p. 168; see also Buckingham, *For Humanity's Sake*, pp. 179–180.
75. Davison Papers. Robert E. Olds to Otis Cutler, 31 August, 1921; quoted in Buckingham, *For Humanity's Sake*, p. 180.
76. The Soviet Red Cross also declined to attend the Tenth Conference, understandably, on the grounds that it had not been officially invited. When the Bolsheviks reorganized the Russian Red Cross in January, 1918, the ICRC refused to treat this event as comparable to the reorganizations carried out in Britain or the United States in 1905; instead it took the position that a wholly new society had been created and that it must seek recognition de novo from the ICRC. Meanwhile, elements of the tsarist Russian Red Cross, forced into emigration by the Russian Civil War, reorganized as best they could in Geneva, Sofia, Helsinki, and Constantinople. Despite the fact that these ad hoc emigré organizations no longer operated on Russian territory, the ICRC had no difficulty in recognizing them and dealing with them. When the Tenth Conference was called, the ICRC decided on its own initiative to invite, in a personal capacity only, both representatives of the Russian Red Cross in Exile—as the emigres called themselves—and Z. P. Soloviev, the deputy commissar of health protection and president of the Soviet Red Cross. The former accepted the invitation; the latter declined. Not until August of 1921 was the Soviet Red Cross recognized by the ICRC. And despite the fuss that the ICRC made about the LRCS not having included the German or Austrian Red Cross societies from its inception, the LRCS did not admit the Soviet Red Cross until 1934; there are no documents in the archives of the LRCS that would suggest the ICRC ever put pressure on the LRCS to admit the Soviet Red Cross. For an explanation of the ICRC's behavior with regard to Soviet Russia, see Durand, *From Sarajevo*, pp. 106–107; on the Bolshevik reorganization of the Russian Red Cross, see John F. Hutchinson, *Politics and Public Health in Revolutionary Russia, 1890–1918* (Baltimore: Johns Hopkins University Press, 1990), pp. 174–181.
77. Quoted in Durand, *From Sarajevo*, p. 171.
78. Quoted in ibid., p. 196.
79. Ibid., p. 196.
80. Durand, *From Sarajevo*, p. 197, provides no source citation for his treatment of this matter, but it seems clear that the issue was discussed at a meeting of the ICRC held in late 1920 or early 1921.
81. Quoted in ibid., p. 197.
82. There is a useful summary of the four stages through which they passed in Durand, *From Sarajevo*, pp. 174–194; many of the relevant documents can be found in *Les éléments du problème de la réorganisation de la Croix-Rouge Internationale: Rapport* (Paris: Ligue des Sociétés de la Croix-Rouge, 1923).

Conclusion

1. Michael Mann, *States, War, and Capitalism: Studies in Political Sociology* (Oxford: Basil Blackwell, 1988), p. 124.

2. On female protective legislation in France and the United States, see Mary Lynn Stewart, *Women, Work, and the French State: Labour Protection and Social Patriarchy, 1879–1919* (Montreal: McGill-Queen's University Press, 1989), and Susan Lehrer, *The Origins of Protective Labor Legislation for Women, 1905–1925* (Albany: SUNY at Albany Press, 1987).

3. Peter Paret, *Understanding War: Essays on Clausewitz and the History of Military Power* (Princeton, N.J. : Princeton University Press, 1992), p. 18.

4. Mann, *States, War, and Capitalism*, p. 151.

5. Paret, *Understanding War*, p. 52.

Selected Bibliography

An Explanatory Note

Two imperatives have shaped the organization of this bibliography. The first is my obligation as a historian to identify the principal sources upon which the book is based. The second is my desire to help in mapping an area that has hitherto been something of a bibliographic wasteland. Accordingly, though I have followed the traditional structure in listing first the manuscript collections and public documents that I have consulted (see the first two major sections below), I have chosen not to lump together in one section all of the published works that I have used. Instead, I have tried to group them in ways that I hope will prove useful to future researchers in the field. The third section ("The International Red Cross") contains selected official publications of the institutions that compose the International Red Cross: the ICRC; the International Conferences; the LRCS (now the International Federation); and the historical publications of the Henry Dunant Institute, which is the research arm of the International Red Cross. The national Red Cross societies also form part of the International Red Cross, but this book has concentrated on the history of only a few of them—specificially, those in the great power states; therefore the fourth section ("National Red Cross Societies") lists by country the most important works written about or published by the national societies of the United States, Great Britain, France, Germany, Japan, the Ottoman Empire, and Russia. As president of the ICRC for almost half a century, Gustave Moynier's literary output on behalf of the cause was prodigous: In the section entitled "The Red Cross Works of Gustave Moynier," I have listed all of his published works concerning the Red Cross, in order of their appearance. The last four sections of this bibliography contain "unofficial" publications that bear in some way on the history of the Red Cross. Because this book ends in 1921, I have treated books and articles published before that date as primary sources; they are listed in the sixth and seventh sections. Secondary sources—books and articles published after 1921—are cited in the eighth and ninth sections. Works by the same author within a section are arranged chronologically in order of appearance. Publishing information that cannot be confirmed from the original source has been placed inside brackets.

Manuscript Collections

SWITZERLAND

Geneva

Bibliothèque Publique et Universitaire. Salle de Manuscrits
- The [Henry] Dunant Papers

Library of the International Committee of the Red Cross
- L'Ancien Fond du CICR

Documentation Center of the International Federation of Red Cross and Red Crescent Societies

* Archives of the League of Red Cross Societies

UNITED KINGDOM

London

Imperial War Museum

* Womens' War Work: British Red Cross Society and Hospitals
* The Papers of Dame Katharine Furse

Museum and Archives of the Most Venerable Order of the Hospital of St. John of Jerusalem

* Sir John Furley's Letterbooks and Scrapbooks

Wellcome Institute for the History of Medicine

* Royal Army Medical Corps Collection, No. 1139: The Longmore Papers

Barnett Hill, Wonersh, Guildford, Surrey

British Red Cross Society Library and Archives

* The Wantage Papers
* Minute-Books of the Council of the British Red Cross Society

UNITED STATES OF AMERICA

Washington, D.C.

The Library of Congress, Division of Manuscripts

* The Clara Barton Papers
* The Mabel T. Boardman Papers
* The William Howard Taft Papers
* The Woodrow Wilson Papers

American National Red Cross: Headquarters Library

* The Henry P. Davison Papers.
* The History of the American National Red Cross (unpublished typescript; for individual volumes, see below).

Bethesda, Maryland

National Library of Medicine. History of Medicine Division

* Autobiography and Papers of Jefferson Randolph Kean, 1904–1950

Landrum, South Carolina

* "Memoirs of Admiral [William Knickerbocker] Van Reypen," unpublished manuscript, n.d., in the possession of his granddaughter, Mrs. Arthur Farwell.

New Haven, Connecticut

Yale University Manuscripts and Archives, Sterling Memorial Library

- The Charles-Edward Amory Winslow Papers.
- The Edward M. House Papers

Palo Alto, California

The Hoover Institution Archives

- Papers: The League of Red Cross Societies

Public Documents

GREAT BRITAIN

"Report upon the Military Medical Exhibits in the Exhibition at Paris, 1879." In *Report of the Army Medical Department for 1888.*
Sick and Wounded in War. Papers Relating to the Geneva Convention, 1906. London: H.M.S.O., 1908.

UNITED STATES OF AMERICA

Washington, D.C.

National Archives and Records Administration

- Record Group 200: Records of the American National Red Cross, 1881–1916 (First Series); 1917–1934 (Second Series).
- Record Group 267: Department of Justice, Case Files. *United States of America v. Louis B. Nagler*

The International Red Cross

PUBLICATIONS OF THE COMITÉ INTERNATIONAL/ICRC

Periodicals

The Comité International/ICRC has published the *Bulletin International des Sociétés de la Croix-Rouge* (Geneva) continuously since 1869 and the *Revue Internationale de le Croix-Rouge* since 1919 (volume 50 of the *Bulletin* was combined with volume 1 of the *Revue*; the two have been published together—but with a separate numbering system—since then). Between 1869 and 1885, the *Bulletin* was called the *Bulletin International des Sociétés de Secours aux Militaires Blessés.*

Books and Pamphlets

Compte rendu de la Conférence Internationale réunie à Genève les 26, 27, 28 et 29 Octobre 1863 pour étudier les moyens de pourvoir à l'insuffisance du service sanitaire dans les armées en campagne. Geneva: Fick, 1863.

Secours aux blessés. Communication du Comité International faisant suite au compte rendu de la Conférence Internationale de Genève. Geneva: Fick, 1864.

Mémoire adressé par le Comité International de secours pour les militaires blessés à Mm. les présidents et les membres des comités centraux dans les divers pays. Geneva: Soullier, Landskron, and Wirth, 1868.

Protocole de la Conférence Internationale réunie à Genève en Octobre 1868. Projet d'Articles Additionels. Geneva: Fick, 1868.

Comité International de Secours aux Militaires Blessés. Actes. Recueil annoté de toutes les pièces importantes du Comité International depuis son origine en 1863). Geneva: Soullier and Wirth, 1871.

Le Comité International de la Croix-Rouge de 1863 à 1884. Geneva: B. Soullier, 1884.

Du rôle du Comité International et des rélations des comités centraux de la Croix-Rouge. Rapport presenté par le Comité International à la Conférence Internationale des sociétés de la Croix-Rouge tenue à Carlsruhe, en 1887. Geneva: B. Soullier, 1887.

Mémorial des vingt-cinq premières années de la Croix-Rouge, 1863–1888. Geneva: CICR, 1888.

Organisation générale et programme de la Croix-Rouge. Geneva: B. Soullier, 1889.

Célébration du 25me anniversaire de la fondation de la Croix-Rouge. Extrait du «Bulletin International». Geneva: CICR, 1889.

Le Comité International de la Croix-Rouge de 1884 à 1892. Geneva: CICR, 1892.

Le Comité International de la Croix-Rouge de 1892 à 1902. Geneva: CICR, 1902.

The International Red Cross Committee in Geneva, 1863–1943. Geneva: ICRC, 1943.

Huber, Max. *La pensée et l'action de la Croix-Rouge.* Geneva: CICR, 1954.

INTERNATIONAL RED CROSS CONFERENCES

[1st: Paris, 1867] *Conférence Internationale des Sociétés de la Croix-Rouge. Compte rendu.* 2 Vols. Paris: La Commission générale des délègués, 1867.

[2nd: Berlin, 1869–also published in German] *Compte rendu des travaux de la Conférence Internationale tenue à Berlin du 22 au 27 Avril 1869, par les délégués des gouvernements signataires de la Convention de Genève et des Sociétés et Associations de Secours aux Militaires Blessés et Malades.* Berlin: J. F. Starcke, 1869.

[3rd: Geneva, 1884] *Troisième Conférence Internationale des sociétés de la Croix-Rouge tenue à Genève du 1er au 6 Septembre 1884. Compte rendu.* Geneva: CICR, 1885.

[4th: Karlsruhe, 1887–also published in German] *Quatrième Conférence Internationale des sociétés de la Croix-Rouge tenue à Carlsruhe du 22 au 27 Septembre 1887. Compte rendu.* Geneva: CICR, 1887.

[5th: Rome, 1892–also published in Italian] *Cinquième Conférence Internationale des sociétés de la Croix-Rouge tenue à Rome du 21 au 27 Avril 1892. Compte rendu.* Rome: Forzani, 1892.

[6th: Vienna, 1897–also published in German] *VIme Conférence Internationale des sociétés de la Croix-Rouge. Vienne, 1897.* Vienna: Ch. Reisser and M. Werthner, 1898.

[7th: St. Petersburg, 1902–also published in Russian] *Septième Conférence Internationale de la Croix-Rouge tenue à St. Pétersbourg du 16 au 22 Mai 1902. Compte rendu.* St. Petersburg: Trenke and Fusnot, 1903.

[8th: London, 1907–also published in English] *Huitième Conférence Internationale de la Croix-Rouge, tenue à Londres du 10 au 15 Juin 1907. Compte rendu.* London: British Red Cross Society, 1908.

[9th: Washington, 1912–also published in English] *Neuvième Conférence Internationale de la Croix-Rouge tenue à Washington du 7 au 12 Mai 1912. Compte rendu.* Washington: American National Red Cross, 1912.

[10th: Geneva, 1921] *Dixième Conférence Internationale de la Croix-Rouge tenue à Genève du 30 Mars au 7 Avril 1921. Compte rendu.* Geneva: CICR, 1921.

SELECTED INTERNATIONAL CONGRESSES

2e Congrès International d'Hygiène, de Sauvetage, et d'Économie Sociale, tenu à Bruxelles, 1876. Compte rendu. 2 Vols. (Paris: 1877).

Congrès International sur le Service Médical des Armées en Campagne, tenu à Paris les 12, 13, et 14 Août 1878. Paris: Imprimerie Nationale, 1879.

Congrès International des Oeuvres d'Assistance en Temps de Guerre, tenu à Paris les 17, 18, 19 et 20 Juillet 1889. Paris: Baudon-Baillière, 1890.

Congrès International des Oeuvres d'Assistance en Temps de Guerre tenu à Paris, du 20 au 24 Août 1900. Procès-verbaux sommaires. Paris: Imprimerie Nationale, 1901.

Congrès International des Oeuvres d'Assistance en Temps de Guerre tenu à Paris, du 20 au 24 Août 1900. Rapports et comptes rendus des séances. Paris: Lahure, 1901.

PUBLICATIONS OF THE LEAGUE OF RED CROSS SOCIETIES (LRCS)

Periodicals

During the period covered by this book, the LRCS produced two serial publications: the *Bulletin of the League of Red Cross Societies* (vols. 1–2, 1919–1921) and the *International Journal of Pubic Health* (volumes 1–2, 1920–1921). In 1922, the *Bulletin of the League of Red Cross Societies* was renamed *World's Health;* under this title volumes 3–11 appeared between 1922 and 1930. Later LRCS publications are not relevant to our story.

Bulletin of the League of Red Cross Societies. Geneva, vol. 1 (1919–1920), vol. 2 (1920–1921). Beginning with volume 3 (1922), the title changed to *World's Health.*

Books and Pamphlets

The League of Red Cross Societies. Paris: Secretariat of the League, 1925.

The League of Red Cross Societies, 1919–1929. Paris: LRCS, 1929.

Les éléments du problème de la réorganisation de la Croix-Rouge Internationale: Rapport. Paris: LRCS, 1923.

Proceedings of the Medical Conference Held at the Invitation of the Committee of Red Cross Societies, Cannes, France, April 1 to 11, 1919. Geneva: LRCS, 1919.

Réunion du conseil général de la Ligue des Sociétés de la Croix-Rouge. Session de Mars 1920. Compte rendu. Geneva: LRCS, 1920.

Dunning, H. W. *Eléments pour l'histoire de la Ligue des Sociétés de la Croix-Rouge.* English edition: *Elements for the History of the League of Red Cross Societies.* Geneva: LRCS, 1969.

PUBLICATIONS OF THE HENRY DUNANT INSTITUTE

Boissier, P. *Histoire du Comité International de la Croix-Rouge de Solférino à Tsoushima.* Paris: Librairie Plon, 1963. English edition: *From Solferino to Tsushima: History of the International Committee of the Red Cross.* Geneva: Henry Dunant Institute, 1985.

Durand, André. *Histoire du Comité International de la Croix-Rouge de Sarajevo à Hiroshima*. Geneva: Henry Dunant Institute, 1978. English edition: *From Sarajevo to Hiroshima: History of the International Committee of the Red Cross*. Geneva: Henry Dunant Institute, 1984.

Perruchoud, Richard. *Les resolutions des conferences internationales de la Croix-Rouge*. Geneva: Institut Henry-Dunant, 1979.

Schindler, Dietrich, and Jiri Toman, eds., *The Laws of Armed Conflicts: A Collection of Conventions, Resolutions, and Other Documents*. 2d ed. Geneva: Henry Dunant Institute, 1981.

National Red Cross Societies

(This section includes works that are principally about national Red Cross societies as well as works published by the societies themselves.)

THE AMERICAN RED CROSS

Beginning in 1906, the ARC began to publish the *American National Red Cross Bulletin*, but the word "National" was dropped from the title after the first year. With volume 9, number 4 (October, 1914), the title was changed to *American Red Cross Magazine*, and this journal continued publication until August, 1920, when it folded. Meanwhile, in 1917 (to confuse matters even further) one department within ARC national headquarters—the Department of Chapters, which was run by the prewar leader of the ARC, Mabel Boardman—began to publish a journal called the *Red Cross Bulletin*. Five volumes of this journal appeared between March, 1917, and December, 1921, when it was superseded by the *Red Cross Courier*.

The American Association for the Relief of the Misery of Battle Fields. Letter of Rev. Henry W. Bellows, D.D., to M. J. Henri Dunant, Secretaire du "Comité Internationale de Secours aux Militaires Blessés." New York: [The Association], 1866.

American Red Cross Child Health Program, 1921–1922. Medical Conference at Paris Headquarters February 2–3, 1922. Paris: Medical Department of the American Red Cross, 1922.

Ames, Fisher Jr. *American Red Cross Work Among the French People*. New York: Macmillan, 1921.

Barton, Clara. *The Red Cross: A History of This Remarkable International Movement*. Washington, D.C.: American National Red Cross, 1898.

———. *The Red Cross in Peace and War*. Washington, D.C.: American Historical Press, 1899.

———. *A Story of the Red Cross: Glimpses of Field Work*. New York: D. Appleton, 1913.

Bicknell, Ernest P. *Pioneering with the Red Cross: Recollections of an Old Red Crosser*. New York: Macmillan, 1935.

———. *With the Red Cross in Europe, 1917–1922*. Washington, D. C.: American National Red Cross, 1938.

Boardman, Mabel T. *Under the Red Cross Flag at Home and Abroad*. Philadelphia: J. B. Lippincott, 1915.

Davison, H. P. *The American Red Cross in the Great War*. New York: MacMillan, 1919.

Dulles, Foster Rhea. *The American Red Cross: A History.* New York: Harper, 1950.

Gilbo, Patrick F. *The American Red Cross: The First Century.* New York: Harper and Row, 1981.

"The History of the American National Red Cross" (unpublished typescript prepared by the Historical Division). Washington, D.C.: American National Red Cross, 1950.

- Vol. I, "The European and American Background," by Gustave R. Gaeddert.
- Vol. II, "The Barton Influence, 1866–1905," by Gustave R. Gaeddert.
- Vol. III, "The Boardman Influence, 1905–1917," by Gustave R. Gaeddert.
- Vol. IV, "The American National Red Cross in World War I, 1917–1918," by Gustave R. Gaeddert.
- Vol. V, "The American Red Cross in Peace, 1919–1939," by Marian B. Clausen.
- Vol. XXVIII, "Liquidation Activities of the American National Red Cross in the Post-Armistice Period, World War I," by Joseph Bykovsky.

History of the Red Cross; the Treaty of Geneva, and Its Adoption by the United States. Washington: American Association of the Red Cross, 1883.

Kernodle, Portia B. *The Red Cross Nurse in Action, 1882–1948.* New York: Harper and Bros., 1949.

THE BRITISH RED CROSS

Annals of the Ambulance Department: Being the History of the St. John Ambulance Association and Brigade. Compiled by Nigel Corbet Fletcher. London: St. John Ambulance Association, 1949.

Barker, Granville. *The Red Cross in France.* London: Hodder and Stoughton, 1916.

Best, S. H. *The Story of the British Red Cross.* London: Cassell, 1938.

Fletcher, Nigel Corbet. *The St. John Ambulance Association: Its History and Its Part in the Ambulance Movement.* London: St. John Ambulance Association, 1930.

Loyd, A. K. *An Outline of the History of the British Red Cross Society from Its Foundation in 1870 to the Outbreak of the War in 1914.* London: [The Society], 1917.

Magill, [Colonel Sir] James. *The Red Cross. The Idea and its Development. A Sketch.* London: Cassell, 1926.

Morrah, Dermot. *The British Red Cross.* London: Collins, 1944.

Macpherson, W. G. *Report on Voluntary Organizations in Aid of the Sick and Wounded During the South African War.* London: Central British Red Cross Committee, 1902.

Questions on the Operations of the British National Society for Aid to the Sick and Wounded in War, and Replies Thereto, by Various Members of the Society's Staff and Others: Being the Results of Their Experiences in the Franco-German War, 1870–1871. London: Harrison and Sons, [n.d].

Red Cross Operations in the North of France, 1870–1872. [Final Report of the Boulogne Branch of the British National Society for Aid to the Sick and Wounded.] London: Spottiswoode, 1872.

Report by the Central British Red Cross Committee on Voluntary Organizations in Aid of the Sick and Wounded During the South African War. London: H.M.S.O., 1902.

Reports by the Joint War Committee and the Joint War Finance Committee of the British Red Cross Society and The Order of St. John of Jerusalem in England on Voluntary Aid

*Rendered to the Sick and Wounded at Home and Abroad and to British Prisoners of War,
1914–1919.* London: H.M.S.O., 1921.

THE FRENCH RED CROSS

L'Association des Dames Françaises. Paris: [n.p.], 1929.
Cent ans de Croix-Rouge Française au service d'humanité. Paris: Hachette, 1963.
Le cinquantenaire de la Croix-Rouge en France. Paris: Société Française de Secours aux
    Blessés Militaires, [1914].
D'Alix, Andrée. *La Croix-Rouge Française. Le rôle patriotique des femmes.* Paris: Perrin,
    1914.
De Boissac, E. *La Société Française de Secours aux Blessés Militaires pendant la paix.* Paris,
    J. Dumaine, 1875.
Du Camp, Maxime. *La Croix Rouge en France. Société de secours aux blessés militaires de
    terre et de mer.* Paris: Hachette, 1889.
———. *La Croix Rouge de France.* Paris: Siège Central, 1892.
De Witt-Guizot, F. *La femme et la guerre.* 2d ed. Paris: Société de Secours aux Blessés
    Militaires, 1913.
Foucault, Albert. *Croix-Rouge Française: La Société de Secours aux Blessés Militaires,
    1864–1934.* Paris: Spes, 1936.
Grandmaison, Geoffroy de. *La Croix-Rouge Française: La Société de Secours aux Blessés
    Militaires Pendant la Guerre.* Paris: Bloud and Say, 1922.
Laureilhe, Marie-Thérèse. "Les debuts de la Croix-Rouge en France jusqu'à la fin de
    l'Année Terrible, 1863–1871." [Typescript] Paris: Société de Secours aux Blessés
    Militaires, 1989.
*La Société de Secours aux Blessés Militaires des Armées de Terre et de Mer en Chine,
    1900–1901. (Croix-Rouge Française).* Paris: Siège Central, 1901.
La Société de Secours aux Blessés Militaires et les inondations de 1910. Paris: SSBM, [1911].
Recueil des décrets. Status, règlements, et instructions concernant la société. Paris: SSBM
    Siège Central, [n.d.].
Société de Secours aux Blessés Militaires des Armées de Terre et de Mer. Paris: Siège de la
    Société, 1867.
Union des Femmes de France: Cinquantenaire 1881–1931. Paris: Siège Social, [1931].

THE GERMAN RED CROSS

Grossheim, [Generalarzt] von. *Die Deutsche Vereinsorganisation vom Roten Kreuz und
    der Rettungsdienst.* Berlin: Central-Comite der Deutschen Vereine vom Roten
    Kreuz, 1912.
Gruneisen, F. *Das Deutsche Rote Kreuz in Vergangenheit und Gegenwart.* Potsdam:
    Deutsches Rotes Kreuz Präsidium, 1939.
Kimmle, Ludwig. *Das sanitätskolonnenwesen vom Roten Kreuz in Deutschland.* Berlin:
    Heymann, 1908.
———. *Das Deutsche Rote Kreuz; Entstehung, Entwicklung, und Leistungen der Verein-
    sorganisation seit Abschluss der Genfer Convention f. J. 1864.* 3 vols. Berlin: Boll and
    Pickardt, 1910.
Knesebeck, Bodo von dem, ed. *Das Deutsche Rote Kreuz und die Tuberkulose-bekämp-
    fung.* Berlin-Charlottenburg: Central-Comite der Deutschen Vereine vom Roten
    Kreuz, 1912.

THE JAPANESE RED CROSS

Ariga, Nagao. *La Croix-Rouge en Extrême-Orient. Exposé de l'organisation et du fonctionnement de la Société de la Croix-Rouge du Japon.* Paris: A. Pedone, 1900.

———. *The Red Cross Society of Japan: Its Organization and Activity in Time of Peace and War*, Presented to the Universal Exposition of St. Louis, U.S.A.: [n.p.], 1904.

———. *The Japanese Red Cross Society and the Russo-Japanese War. A Report Presented to the Eighth International Conference of Red Cross Societies Held in London, June, 1907.* London: Bradbury, Agnew, 1907.

Kawamata, Keiichi. *The History of the Red Cross Society of Japan.* [Tokyo, 1922].

Materials Relating to the History of Relief Work in Japan. [Tokyo]: Japanese Red Cross Society, 1934.

Le service de secours de la Société de la Croix-Rouge du Japon pendant la guerre de la 27e-28e année de Meiji (1894–1895). Paris: A. Pedone, 1897.

THE OTTOMAN RED CRESCENT SOCIETY

Özaydin, Zuhal. "Osmanli hilâl-i ahmer cemiyeti sâlnâmesi" ("The Almanac of the Ottoman Red Crescent Society"). Unpublished M.A. thesis, University of Istanbul, 1987.

THE RUSSIAN RED CROSS SOCIETY

Bagotzky, Serge. *La réorganisation de la Croix-Rouge internationale.* Berne: The [former tsarist] Russian Red Cross Society, 1924.

Fedorov, M. M. and Botsianovskii, V. F., eds. *Istoricheskii ocherk deiatel'nosti Rossiiskogo Obshchestva Krasnogo Kresta [A Historical Outline of the Activity of the Russian Red Cross Society].* St. Petersburg: Gosudarstvennaia Tipografiia, 1896.

La Société Russe de la Croix-Rouge. Aperçu historique de son activité. St. Petersburg: Trenke and Fusnot, 1902.

Note sur le rôle du Comité International et sur les relations des comités centraux de la Croix-Rouge. St. Petersburg: Trenké et Fusnot, [1885].

The Red Cross Works of Gustave Moynier
(Listed in order of appearance.)

Gustave Moynier, *La guerre et la charité; traité théoretique et pratique de philanthropie appliquées aux armées en campagne, par G. Moynier et L. Appia.* Geneva: Cherbuliez, 1867.

———. *La neutralité des militaires blessés, et du service de santé des armées.* Paris: [no publisher listed] 1867.

———. *Étude sur la convention de Genève pour l'amelioration du sort des militaires blessés dans l'armées en campagne (1864 et 1868); droit de gens.* Paris: Cherbuliez, 1870).

Help for Sick and Wounded, Being a translation of La Guerre et la Charité by Gustave Moynier and Louis Appia. Translated by John Furley. London: John Camden Hotten, 1870.

———. *Note sur la création d'une Institution Judiciare Internationale propre à prévenir et à réprimer les infractions à la Convention de Genéve.* Geneva: Soullier and Wirth, 1872.

———. *Les dix premières années de la Croix-Rouge.* Geneva: Fick, 1873. AF 2815.

———. *Ce que c'est la Croix-Rouge.* Geneva: B. Soullier, 1874.

———. "Fédération des Comités de secours aux militaires blessés," *2ème Congrès International d'Hygiène, de Sauvetage, et d'Economie Sociale, Bruxelles, 1876. Compte rendu.* Paris, 1877, Vol. 2, pp. 383–402.

———. *La Croix-Rouge, son passé et son avenir.* Paris: Sandoz et Thuiller, 1882.

———. *The Red Cross, Its Past and Its Future.* Translated by John Furley. London: Cassell, Petter, and Galpin, 1883.

———. "De quelques faits récents relatifs à la Convention de Genève," Extrait de la *Revue de droit international et de législation comparée,* 1886.

———. "Les causes du succès de la Croix-Rouge," a paper read to the Academy of Moral and Political Sciences of the Institut de France, 21 April, 1888; also appeared as the preface to the *Mémorial* published by the ICRC in the same year. AF 680.

———. *Conférence sur la Convention de Genève.* Geneva, Soullier, 1891.

———. *Considérations sur la sanction pénale à donner à la Convention de Genève. Présentées à l'Institut de Droit International.* Lausanne: F. Regamey, 1893.

———. *Notions essentielles sur la Croix-Rouge.* Geneva: Georg and Cie., 1896.

———. *La revision de la Convention de Genève. Étude historique et critique.* Geneva: CICR, 1898.

———. *Les conférences internationales des sociétés de la Croix-Rouge [1 sér.]* Geneva: CICR, 1901.

———. *La fondation de la Croix-Rouge. Mémoire présenté au Comité International par G. M., président.* Geneva, 1903.

———. *Rappel succinct de l'activité déployée par le Comité International de la Croix-Rouge . . . 1863–1904.* Geneva: CICR, 1905.

———. *Mes heures de travail.* Geneva: [1907].

Books Published Before 1921

Appia, P. L., M.D. *The Ambulance Surgeon or Practical Observations on Gunshot Wounds.* Edited by T. W. Nunn and A. M. Edwards. Edinburgh: Adam and Charles Black, 1862.

Appia, Louis. *Noël à l'ambulance, épisode de la Guerre Russo-Turque. Récits authentiques.* Paris: [n.d.] (English translation 1881).

Arnaud, L., and P. Bonnette. *La femme sur le champ de bataille.* Paris: Charles Lavauzelle, [n.d.].

Bayol, [Lieutenant]. *Esperanto et Croix-Rouge.* Paris: Presa Esperantista Societo, 1906.

Beaufort, [le Comte de]. *Questions philanthropiques.* Paris: Imprimerie Nationale, 1875.

Billroth, T., and J. von Mundy. *Über den Transport der im Felde Verwundeten und Kranken.* Vienna: C. Gerold, 1874.

Bogaevskii, P. *Krasnyi krest' v razvitii mezhdunarodnogo prava [The Red Cross in the Development of International Law].* 2 vols. Moscow: A.A. Levenson, 1906, 1913.

Bouloumié, P. *L'effort antituberculeux de l'Union des Femmes de France. Son programme, ses réalisations.* Paris: Vigot, 1919.

Boyland, George H. *Six Months Under the Red Cross, with the French Army.* Cincinnati: Robert Clarke, 1873.

Braisted, William C. *Report on the Japanese Naval Medical and Sanitary Features of the*

Russo-Japanese War to the Surgeon-General, U. S. Navy. Washington, D.C.: Government Printing Office, 1906.

Cabanès, [Augustin] *Chirurgiens et blessés à travers l'histoire. Des origines a la Croix-Rouge* (Paris: Albin Michel, 1918), pp. 609–610;

Cacheux, Emile. *Le sauvetage en France et à l'étranger. Ce qu'il est, ce qu'il devrait être.* Paris: Paul Baudry, 1896.

[Chenu, J.-C.] *Observations sur l'insuffisance du service de santé en campagne.* [Paris] [1864].

Deacon, J. B. *Disasters and the American Red Cross in Disaster Relief.* New York: Macmillan, 1918.

[Dunant, Henry]. *Un Souvenir de Solférino par J. Henry Dunant.* Geneva: Fick, 1862.

———. *Fraternité et charité internationales en temps de guerre.* 7th ed. Paris: Hachette, 1866.

Eastlake, F. W., and Y. Yoshi-Aki. *Heroic Japan: A History of the War Between China and Japan.* Yokohama: Kelly and Walsh, [1896].

Edmonds, J. E., ed. *Organisation of Voluntary Medical Aid in War in Austria, France, and Germany.* London: H.M.S.O., 1901.

Evans, Thomas W. *History of the American Ambulance Established in Paris During the Siege of 1870–1871.* London: Sampson Low, 1873.

Evans, Thomas W., M.D. *Sanitary Institutions During the Austro-Prussian-Italian Conflict. . . .* 3rd ed. Paris: Simon Raçon, 1868.

Evatt, Surgeon-Major G. J. H. *Suggestions for the Organization of the Volunteer Medical Service and for the Utilization of Volunteer Medical Aid in War.* Woolwich, England: F. J. Cattermole, 1885.

Extrait des ecrits du Docteur Duchaussoy sur l'Association des Dames Françaises dont il est le fondateur. Abbeville, France: Paillart, 1897.

Fauntleroy, Archibald. *Report on the Medico-Military Aspects of the European War.* Washington, D.C.: Government Printing Office, 1915.

Feigneaux, [Dr.]. *Des secours volontaires en temps de guerre* (extrait des *Annales de l'Association Internationale pour le Progrès des Sciences Sociales*). Brussels: Henri Manceaux, 1866.

Fisher, Edmund Crisp. *Military Discipline and Volunteer Philanthropy.* 2nd ed. London, 1864.

———. *The English Branch of the United States Sanitary Commission. The Motive of Its Establishment, and the Result of Its Work.* London: W. Ridgway, 1865.

François, Alexis. *Le berceau de la Croix Rouge.* Geneva: A Jullien; Paris: E. Champion, 1918.

Furley, John. *Struggles and Experiences of a Neutral Volunteer.* 2 vols. London: Chapman, 1872.

———. *Among the Carlists.* London: Tinsley, 1876.

———. *On the Carriage of Sick and Injured Persons.* London: Spottiswoode, 1883.

———. *The Convention of Geneva, and the Care of the Sick and Wounded in War.* [London: Royal United Service Institution], 1896.

———. *In Peace and War: Autobiographical Sketches.* Smith, Elder, 1905.

———. *The Origin and Development of the St. John Ambulance Association.* London: St. John Ambulance Association, 1909.

Gillot, Louis. *La revision de la Convention de Genève au point de vue historique et dogmatique.* Paris: Rousseau, 1902.

Gordon, Charles Alexander. *Lessons on Hygiene and Surgery from the Franco-Prussian War.* London: Baillière, Tindall, and Cox, 1873.

Gruby, [M. le Docteur]. *Sociétés et matériel de secours pour les blessés militaires (exposition de 1878).* 2 vols. Paris: Eugène Lacroix, 1884.

Grunberg, J. *De l'organisation des secours aux blessés dans les grandes villes. (Les ambulances urbaines de l'Hôpital Saint-Louis).* Paris: Société d'Éditions Scientifiques, 1897.

Haje, Ch.-F., and J.-M. Simon. *Les origines de la Croix-Rouge.* Stuttgart: A Lindheimer; Amsterdam: Delsman and Nothenius, 1900.

Hare, James H., ed. *A Photographic Record of the Russo-Japanese War.* New York: P. F. Collier and Son, 1905.

Kingsley, Rose G. *The Order of St. John of Jerusalem (Past and Present).* London: Skeffington, [1918].

Lacointa, Jules. *Discours prononcé le 2 septembre 1884 sur la Convention de Genève et les Sociétés de la Croix-Rouge.* Paris: Jules Gervais, 1884.

Le Fort, Léon. *La chirurgie militaire et les sociétés de secours en France et à l'étranger.* Paris: Germer Baillière, 1872.

Longmore, [Surgeon-General] Thomas. *The Sanitary Contrasts of the British and French Armies During the Crimean War.* London: Charles Griffin and Co., 1883.

———. *Introductory Address to the Surgeons on Probation.* . . . Glasgow: Bell and Bain, 1884.

———. *A Manual of Ambulance Transport.* 2d ed. Edited by [Surgeon-Captain] William A. Morris. London: H.M.S.O., 1893.

Longmore, Thomas. *Treatise on the Transport of Sick and Wounded Troops.* London: H.M.S.O. [1869].

Lueder, C. *La Convention de Genève au point de vue historique, critique, et dogmatique.* Erlangen, Germany: Édouard Besold; Paris: C. Reinwald; Brussels: C. Muquardt; 1876.

[Lynch, Maj. Charles.] *Report of Major Charles Lynch, Medical Department, General Staff.* Part 4 in *Report of Military Observers Attached to the Armies in Manchuria During the Russo-Japanese War.* Washington, D.C.: Goverment Printing Office, 1907.

MacCormac, [Sir] William. *Notes and Recollections of an Ambulance Surgeon, Being and Account of Work Done Under the Red Cross During the Campaign of 1870.* London: Churchill, 1871.

McCaul, E. *Under the Care of the Japanese War Office.* London: Cassell, 1905.

Macpherson, W. G. *Report on the 6th International Conference of Red Cross Societies, Vienna, 1897.* London: H.M.S.O., 1898.

———. *The Russo-Japanese War. Medical and Sanitary Reports from Officers Attached to the Japanese and Russian Forces in the Field.* London: H.M.S.O., 1908.

Marcks, Friedrich. *Das Rote Kreuz: Ein Überblick über seine Entstehung und Entwicklung und seine Bethätigung in Deutschland.* Gütersloh: Bertelsmann, 1900.

Mauriac, E. *L'organisation des secours publics en cas d'accidents en Allemagne et en Autriche-Hongrie.* Bordeaux: Feret et Fils, 1890.

[Munthe, Axel] "A Doctor in France," *Red Cross and Iron Cross.* London: John Murray, 1916.

Pearson, E. M., and L. E. McLaughlin. *Service in Servia under the Red Cross.* London: Tinsley Bros., 1877.

Proceedings of the 5th Annual Meeting of the Association of Military Surgeons of the United States. Cincinnati: Earhart and Richardson, 1896.

Redard, Paul. *Transport par chemins de fer des blessés et malades militaires.* Paris: Doin, 1889.

Refutation du discours de M. Bouloumié sur l'evlution de la Croix-Rouge en France, par Dr. Duchaussoy, fondateur de l'Association des Dames Françaises. Amiens, France: Imprimerie Grau, 1911.

Riant, A. *Le matériel de secours de la société à l'exposition de 1878. Manuel pratique.* Paris: Imprimerie Nationale, 1878.

Riencourt, [le Comte de.] *Manuel des blessés et malades de la guerre.* Paris: Librairie Militaire de J. Dumaine, 1876.

Richardson, [Mrs. T. E.] *In Japanese Hospitals During War-Time. Fifteen Months with the Red Cross Society of Japan (April 1904 to July 1905).* Edinburgh: Blackwood, 1905.

Rundle, Henry. *With the Red Cross in the Franco-German War, A.D. 1870–1871.* London: Werner Laurie, [1909].

Ryan, Charles E. *With an Ambulance During the Franco-German War. Personal Experiences and Adventures with Both Armies.* New York: Charles Scribner's Sons, 1896.

Spear, Raymond. *Report on the Russian Medical and Sanitary Features of the Russo-Japanese War to the Surgeon-General, U. S. Navy.* Washington, D.C.: Government Printing Office, 1906.

Strong, Richard P. et al. *Typhus Fever with Particular Reference to the Serbian Epidemic.* Cambridge, Mass.: American Red Cross at Harvard University Press, 1920.

Templer, [Mrs.] H. *A Labour of Love Under the Red Cross, During the Late War.* Guernsey, U.K.: Le Lievre, 1872.

Treves, [Sir] Frederick. *The Tale of a Field Hospital.* London: Cassell, 1900.

United States Sanitary Commission, European Branch. *Report of Charles S. P. Bowles* . . . . London, 1864.

Vivian, E. C., and J. E. H. Williams. *The Way of the Red Cross.* London: Hodder and Stoughton, 1915.

Wienand, Adam. *Der Johanniter-Orden der Malteser Orden, der ritterliche Orden des hl. Johannes vom Spital zu Jerusalem.* Hrsg. von A. W. 2nd ed. Cologne: Wienand Verlag, 1977.

Wilson, Woodrow. *The Papers of Woodrow Wilson.* Vol. 53, Nov. 9, 1918–Jan. 11, 1919. Edited by David W. Hirst et al. Princeton, 1985.

Articles Published Before 1921

Billings, F. "The Work of the American Red Cross Mission to Russia." *Journal of the American Medical Association* 59 (1917):1687–1694.

Billings, John Shaw. "Notes on Military Medicine in Europe." *Journal of the Military Service Institution of the United States* 3 (1882):234–247.

Burgess, Charles J. "The Red Cross: Its Origin and Work. By One Who Has Served under the Flag." Parts 1, 2. *Colburn's United Service Magazine,* no. 647 (October, 1882):168–183; and no. 648 (November, 1882):319–336.

Duchaussoy, [Auguste] "Notice historique sur l'Association des Dames Françaises." *Bulletin de l'Association des Dames Françaises* 29(12) (1913):3–7.

Felix-Faure Goyal, Lucie. "Croix-Rouge Française. La Société de Secours aux Militaires Blessés." *La Revue Hebdomadaire,* no. 30 (27 July, 1912):465–480.

Furley, John. "Ambulance Work and Material in Peace and War." (Lecture at R.U.S.I., 10 June 1892.) *Journal of the Royal United Service Institution* 36 (1892):827–857.

Gordon, Charles A. "Notes on the Service of Armies During War," *British and Foreign Medico-Chirurgical Review* 53 (1874):477–501.

Havard, V. "Notes on the Russian Red Cross Society." *Military Surgeon* 20 (1907):1–15.

Heizmann, Charles L. "The French and German Sanitary Corps on the Battlefield," *Journal of the United States Military Service Institution* 6 (1885):333–335.

Kean, Colonel J. R. "The New Role of the American Red Cross." *Military Surgeon* 38 (1916):539–544.

Langermersch, A. Van. "Histoire de la Croix-Rouge." *International Congress History of Medicine* 1st (Antwerp) (1920):257–267.

Le Fort, Léon. "Le Service de Santé dans les armées nouvelles." *Revue des Deux Mondes* 86 (November, 1871):88–133.

Longmore, [Sir] Thomas, C. B. "The New Military Weapons and Explosives." Reprinted from *British Medical Journal* (5 March, 1892).

Macpherson, W. G. "Report on the International Congress of *Oeuvres d'assistance en temps de guerre* held in Paris, 20 to 24 August 1900; on the organization and resources of voluntary aid in France, and on the Russian army medical service exhibits at the Paris Exhibition." *Army Medical Department Reports* 41 (1901): 390–426.

———. "The German Regulations for Utilizing Voluntary Aid in War." *Journal of the Royal Army Medical Corps* 1 (1903):459–486.

———. "The Organization and Resources of the Red Cross Society of Japan." *Journal of the Royal Army Medical Corps* 6 (1906):467–478.

———. "The Role of Red Cross Societies in Peace and War." *Journal of the Royal United Service Institution* 1 (1907):1345–1363; this was also published in his *The Role of the Red Cross Societies in Peace and War.* London: J. J. Keliher, 1907.

———. "The Organization of Different Armies For the Removal of Wounded From the Battlefield." *Journal of the Royal Army Medical Corps* 19 (1912):479–490.

Zannerawkin, K. S. "Organization of First Aid at Dressing Stations and Transport of Wounded to Hospitals—Equipment for that Purpose in the German and French Armies and the Role of the Red Cross in Such Activity." *Military Surgeon* 33 (1913):163–167 and 274–277.

Books Published Since 1921

Acheson, Roy M. *Wycliffe Rose of the Rockefeller Foundation, 1862–1914: The Formative Years.* Cambridge: Killycarn Press, 1992.

Anderson, Benedict. *Imagined Communities: Reflections on the Origins and Spread of Nationalism.* London: Verso, 1991.

Baly, Monica E. *Florence Nightingale and the Nursing Legacy.* London: Croom Helm, 1986.

Bane, Suda Lorena and Ralph H. Lutz. *Organization of American Relief in Europe, 1918–1919.* Stanford, Calif.: Stanford University Press, 1943.

Barton, William E. *The Life of Clara Barton, Founder of the American Red Cross.* 2 vols. Boston: Houghton Mifflin, 1922.

Best, Geoffrey. *Humanity in Warfare: The Modern History of the International Law of Armed Conflicts.* London: Weidenfeld and Nicolson, 1980.

———. *War and Law Since 1945.* Oxford: Clarendon Press, 1994.

Bleker, Johanna, and Heinz-Peter Schmiedebach, eds. *Medizin und Krieg: Vom Dilemma der Heilberufe 1865 bis 1985.* Frankfurt am Main: Fischer Taschenbuch Verlag, 1987.

Bond, Brian. *War and Society in Europe, 1870–1970.* London: Fontana Press, 1984.

Boppe, Roger. *L'homme et la guerre: Le docteur Louis Appia et les débuts de la Croix-Rouge.* Geneva: J. Muhlethaler, 1959.

Brittain, Vera. *Testament of Youth.* London: Victor Gollancz, 1933.

Buckingham, Clyde E. *Red Cross Disaster Relief: Its Origin and Development.* Washington, D. C.: Public Affairs Press, 1956.

———. *For Humanity's Sake: The Story of the Early Development of the League of Red Cross Societies.* Washington, D. C.: Public Affairs Press, 1964.

Buhler-Wilkerson, Karen. *False Dawn: The Rise and Decline of Public Health Nursing, 1900–1930.* New York: Garland, 1989.

Checkland, Olive. *Humanitarianism and the Emperor's Japan, 1877–1977.* London: St. Martin's Press, 1994.

Clifford, Joan. *For the Service of Mankind: Furley, Lechmere, and Duncan, St. John Ambulance Founders.* London: Robert Hale, 1971.

[D'Abernon, Helen] *Red Cross and Berlin Embassy, 1915–1926: Extracts from the Diaries of Vicountess D'Abernon.* London: John Murray, 1946.

Deák, István. *Beyond Nationalism: A Social and Political History of the Habsburg Officer Corps, 1848–1918.* New York: Oxford University Press, 1992.

Descombes, Marc. *Henry Dunant.* Geneva: Editions René Coeckelberghs, 1988.

Dubin, Martin. "The League of Nations Health Organisation and the Development of the Public Health Profession." In *International Health Organisations and Movements, 1918–1939,* ed. Paul Weindling. Cambridge: Cambridge University Press, 1995.

Dock, Lavinia L. et al. *History of American Red Cross Nursing.* New York: Macmillan, 1922.

Duncan, L. C. *The Medical Department of the U.S. Army in the Civil War.* Gaithersburg, Md.: Butternut Press, 1985.

Dunn, J. C. *The War the Infantry Knew, 1914–1919: A Chronicle of Service in France and Belgium.* London: Jane's, 1988.

Durand, Roger, and Jacques Meurant, eds. *Préludes et pionniers. Les précurseurs de la Croix-Rouge, 1840–1860.* Geneva: Société Henry Dunant, 1991.

Evans, R. J. W., and Hartmut Pogge von Strandmann, eds. *The Coming of the First World War.* Oxford: Clarendon Press, 1988.

Farmborough, Florence. *Russian Album, 1908–1918.* Edited by J. Jolliffe. Salisbury, England: Michael Russell, 1979.

Forsythe, David. *Humanitarian Politics: The International Committee of the Red Cross.* Baltimore: Johns Hopkins University Press, 1977.

Fredrickson, George M. *The Inner Civil War: Northern Intellectuals and the Crisis of the Union.* New York: Harper and Row, 1965.

Gagnebin, Bernard and Marc Gazay. *A la rencontre de Henry-Dunant.* Geneva: Georg, 1963.

Garrison, Fielding H. *Notes on the History of Military Medicine.* Washington, D. C.: Association of Military Surgeons, 1922.

Gignon, Fernand. *The Epic of the Red Cross or, The Knight-Errant of Charity*, trans. Gerald Griffen. London: Jarrolds, [1946].

Goldman, Nancy Loring, ed. *Female Soldiers—Combatants or Noncombatants: Historical and Contemporary Perspectives.* Westport, Conn., Greenwood Press, 1982.

Goodman, N. M. *International Health Organizations and Their Work.* 2nd ed. Edinburgh: Churchill Livingstone, 1971.

Gumpert, M. *Dunant: The Story of the Red Cross.* Two editions: New York: Oxford University Press, 1938; and London: Eyre and Spottiswoode, 1939.

Haller Jr., John S. *Farmcarts to Fords. A History of the Military Ambulance, 1790–1925.* Carbondale: Southern Illinois University Press, 1992.

Hart, Ellen. *Man Born to Live: Life and Work of Henry Dunant, Founder of the Red Cross.* London: Gollancz, 1953.

Hartigan, Richard S. *Lieber's Code and the Law of War.* Chicago: Precedent, 1983.

Headrick, Daniel R. *The Tools of Empire: Technology and European Imperialism in the Nineteenth Century.* New York: Oxford University Press, 1981.

———. *The Tentacles of Progress: Technology Transfer in the Age of Imperialism, 1850–1940.* New York: Oxford University Press, 1988.

Heudtlass, W. *J. Henry Dunant, Gründer des Roten Kreuzes.* Stuttgart: W. Kohlhammer, 1985.

Hoover, Herbert. *Years of Adventure.* New York: Macmillan, 1951.

———. *An American Epic.* Chicago: Henry Regnery, 1960.

House, [Colonel.] *The Intimate Papers of Colonel House.* Edited by Charles Seymour. Boston: Houghton Mifflin, 1928.

Howard, Michael. *The Franco-Prussian War.* London: Collins, 1967.

Howard, Michael, ed. *Restraints on War. Studies in the Limitation of Armed Conflict.* Oxford: Oxford University Press, 1979.

Howard-Jones, Norman. *Les bases scientifiques des conférences sanitaires internationales, 1851–1938.* Geneva: World Health Organization, 1975. English edition: *The Scientific Background of the International Sanitary Conferences 1851–1938.* Geneva: World Health Organization, 1975.

Hume, Edgar Erskine. *Medical Work of the Knights Hospitallers of Saint John of Jerusalem.* Baltimore: Johns Hopkins University Press, 1940.

Joyce, James. *Red Cross International and the Strategy of Peace.* New York: Oceana Pub., 1959.

Keegan, John. *The Face of Battle.* New York: Viking Press, 1976.

Kennedy, David M. *Over Here: The First World War and American Society.* Oxford: Oxford University Press, 1980.

Lacaisse, René. *L'hygiène internationale et la Société des Nations.* Paris: Editions du "Mouvement Sanitaire," 1926.

Lamont, Thomas W. *Henry P. Davison: The Record of a Useful Life.* New York: Harper, 1933.

Langer, W. L. *The Diplomacy of Imperialism, 1890–1902.* New York: Knopf, 1951.

Lescaze, Bernard. *La Société Genevoise d'Utilité Publique en son temps: 1828–1978.* Geneva: Société Genevoise d'Utilité Publique, 1978.

Love, Albert G. *The Geneva Red Cross Movement: European and American Influence on its Development.* Carlisle, Pa.: Association of Military Surgeons of the United States, 1942.

Macdonald, Lyn. *The Roses of No Man's Land.* London: Macmillan, 1980.

Maxwell, William Q. *Lincoln's Fifth Wheel: The Political History of the United States Sanitary Commission.* New York: Longmans, Green, 1956.

McAllister, W. B. "Fighting the Good Fight: German Military Medicine, 1860–1914." Unpublished M.A. thesis, University of Virginia, 1990.

McNeill, William H. *The Pursuit of Power: Technology, Armed Force, and Society Since A.D. 1000.* Chicago: University of Chicago Press, 1982.

Miller, David Hunter. *The Drafting of the Covenant.* New York: G. P. Putnam, 1928.

Morley, Felix. *The Society of Nations.* Washington, D. C.: Brookings Institution, 1932.

Morris, Peter, ed. *First Aid to the Battlefront: Life and Letters of Sir Vincent Kennett-Barrington (1844–1903).* Stroud, England: Alan Sutton, 1992.

Ninagawa, Arata. *The Facts About the Formation of the League of Red Cross Societies.* Tokyo, 1926.

Noailly, Frédérique. *La Croix-Rouge au point de vue national et international, son histoire, son organisation.* Paris: Librairie Générale de Droit et Jurisprudence, 1935.

[Olmstead, F. L.] *Defending the Union: The Civil War and the U. S. Sanitary Commission 1861–1863.* Vol. 4 of *Papers of F. L. Olmstead.* Edited by J. Turner Censer. Baltimore, Md.: Johns Hopkins University Press, 1986.

Paret, Peter. *Understanding War: Essays on Clausewitz and the History of Military Power.* Princeton, N.J.: Princeton University Press, 1992.

Peacey, B. *The Story of the Red Cross.* London: Muller, 1969.

Prelinger, Catherine M. *Charity, Challenge, and Change: Religious Dimensions of the Mid-Nineteenth-Century Women's Movement in Germany.* Westport, Conn.: Greenwood Press, 1987.

Pryor, Elizabeth B. *Clara Barton, Professional Angel.* Philadelphia: University of Pennsylvania Press, 1987.

Ralston, David B. *Importing the European Army: The Introduction of European Military Techniques and Institutions into the Extra-European World, 1600–1914.* Chicago: University of Chicago Press, 1990.

Remak, Joachim. *A Very Civil War: The Swiss Sonderbund War of 1847.* Boulder: Westview Press, 1993.

Renwick, E. D. *A Short History of the Order of St. John.* 6th ed., rev. and continued by I. M. Williams. London: Order of St. John, 1971.

Rohrer, Margarete von. *Im Krieg gegen Wunden und Krankheit.* Brünn: Rohrer, 1943.

Sand, René. *The Advance to Social Medicine.* London: Staples Press, 1952.

Shryock, Richard H. *The Development of Modern Medicine: An Interpretation of the Social and Scientific Factors Involved.* Madison: University of Wisconsin Press, 1979.

Smith, F. B. *Florence Nightingale: Reputation and Power.* London: Croom Helm, 1982.

Spender, J. A. *Sir Robert Hudson, A Memoir.* London:: Cassell, 1930.

Stone, Norman. *Europe Transformed, 1878–1919.* Cambridge, Mass.: Harvard University Press, 1984.

Summers, Anne. *Angels and Citizens: British Women as Military Nurses, 1854–1914.* London: Routledge and Kegan Paul, 1988.

Surface, Frank M., and Raymond L. Bland. *American Food in the World War and Reconstruction Period.* Stanford: Stanford University Press, 1931.

Tatham, Meaburn, and James E. Miles, eds. *The Friends' Ambulance Unit 1914–1919: A Record.* London: Swartmore Press, [n.d.]

Trombley, Stephen. *Sir Frederick Treves: The Extra-Ordinary Edwardian*. London: Routledge, 1989.

U.S. Army Medical Department. *The Medical Department of the United States Army in the World War*. Vol. 1: *The Surgeon General's Office*. Washington, D.C.: Government Printing Office, 1923.

Articles Published Since 1921

Armeny, Susan. "Organized Nurses, Women Philanthropists, and the Intellectual Bases for Cooperation among Women, 1898–1920." *Nursing History: New Perspectives, New Possibilities*, ed. Ellen Condliffe Lagemann. New York and London: Teachers' College Press, 1983.

Bogacz, Ted. "War Neurosis and Cultural Change in England, 1914–1922: The Work of the War Office Committee of Inquiry into `Shellshock.'" *Journal of Contemporary History* 24(3) (April 1989):227–256.

Brown, E. R. "Public Health in Imperialism: Early Rockefeller Programs at Home and Abroad." *American Journal of Public Health* 66(9) (September 1976):897–903.

Brown, Joan G. "Sir John Furley and the St. John's Ambulance Movement." *Bygone Kent* 6 (1985):739–743.

Buhler-Wilkerson, Karen. "False Dawn: The Rise and Decline of Public Health Nursing in America, 1900–1930." *Nursing History: New Perspectives, New Possibilities*, ed. Ellen Condliffe Lagemann. New York and London: Teachers' College Press, 1983.

Chernin, Eli. "Richard Pearson Strong and the Manchurian Epidemic of Pneumonic Plague, 1910–1911." *Journal of History of Medicine and Allied Sciences* 44 (1989):296–319.

Des Gouttes, Paul. "L'abus du nom et du signe de la Croix-Rouge." *Revue Internationale de la Croix-Rouge* (Geneva), no. 3 (1921):977–998.

Egorysheva, I. V. "Novye dannye iz istorii Krasnogo Kresta v dorevoliutsionnoi Rossii." [New data on the history of the Red Cross in prerevolutionary Russia] *Sovetskoe zdravookhranenie*, no. 2 (1981):57–60.

Enomoto, Juji. "La naissance des idées humanitaires au Japon. IV. 6. Les origines de l'activité de la Croix-Rouge au Japon." *Revue Internationale de la Croix-Rouge* (Geneva), no. 456 (1956):687–694.

Evrard, E. "La première neutralisation par acte juridique d'un hôpital militaire de campagne: L'Hôpital Militaire Français de Marchienne-au-Pont (1677)." *Revue Internationale des Services de Santé des Armées de Terre, de Mer, et de l'Air*, special number (1967).

Gagnebin, Bernard. "Les archives Henri Dunant." *Revue Internationale de la Croix-Rouge* (Geneva) 38(449) (May, 1956):255–260.

Haddad, Farid Sami. "Docteur Cassim Izzeddine (1854–1928) inspecteur de l'administration sanitaire de l'Empire Ottoman." *Annual Report of the Orient Hospital* (Beirut, Lebanon) 23 (1970):21–36.

Kohler, Robert E. "Science and Philanthropy: Wickliffe Rose and the International Education Board." *Minerva* 23 (1985):75–95.

McAllister, William B. "Fighting Reformers: The Debate Over the Reorganization of the French Military Medical Service, 1870–1889." *Essays in History*. Charlottesville, Va.: Corcoran Department of History, 1993.

Mitchell, Allan. "'A Situation of Inferiority': French Military Reorganization After the Defeat of 1870." *American Historical Review* 86 (1981):49–67.

———. "Obsessive Questions and Faint Answers: The French Response to Tuberculosis in the Belle Epoque." *Bulletin of the History of Medicine* 62 (1988):215–235.

More, Ellen. "'A Certain Restless Ambition': Women Physicians and World War I." *American Quarterly* 41(4) (1989):636–660.

Morgenstern, S. "Henri Dunant and the Red Cross." Parts 1–2. *Bulletin of the New York Academy of Medicine* 55 (1979):949–56; and 57 (1981):311–326.

Paulsen, George E. "Helping Hand or Intervention? Red Cross Relief in Mexico, 1915." *Pacific Historical Review* 57 (August, 1988):305–326.

Prelinger, Catherine M. "The Nineteenth-Century Deaconessate in Germany: The Efficacy of a Family Model." In *German Women in the Eighteenth and Nineteenth Centuries: A Social and Literary History*, ed. Ruth-Ellen B. Toeres and Mary Jo Maynes, 215–229. Bloomington: Indiana University Press, 1986.

Scott, Joan W. "Women and War: A Focus For Rewriting History." *Women's Studies Quarterly* 12(2) (Summer 1984).

———. "Reconceptualizing Two World Wars." *Behind The Lines: Gender and the Two World Wars*, ed. Margaret Randolph Higonnet et al. New Haven: Yale University Press, 1987.

Tovbin, M. M. "Obshchestvo krasnogo kresta v SSSR (pervoe desiatiletie)." ["The Red Cross Society in the USSR (first decade)"]. *Voprosy istorii*, no. 4 (1978):204–210.

Vecchio, Giorgio del. "On the History of the Red Cross" (translated from Italian by R. Parsons). *Journal of the History of Ideas* 24 (1962):577–583.

Winslow, C.-E. A. "Suggestions for a Red Cross Health Programme." *International Journal of Public Health* (Geneva) 1921:488–508.

About the Book and Author

A character in an Evelyn Waugh novel once remarked, "There's nothing wrong with war—except the fighting." In *Champions of Charity*, John Hutchinson argues that while they set out with a vision to make war more humane, the world's Red Cross organizations soon became enthusiastic promoters of militarism and sacrifice in time of war.

The mass armies of the nineteenth century were stalked by disease and slaughtered by ever more destructive weaponry, arousing the indignation and humanitarian concern of self-appointed battlefield Samaritans, who envisioned a neutral corps of volunteer nurses who would aid and comfort wounded soldiers, regardless of nationality. But the champions of charity soon became champions of war.

Florence Nightingale was among the few at the time to recognize the dangers lurking in the Red Cross vision. She refused to join and warned its founders that the governments of the world would cooperate with the Red Cross because "it would render war more easy." She was right; starting in the late nineteenth century, armies simply used the Red Cross to efficiently recycle wounded men back into the front lines.

In World War I, national Red Cross societies became enthusiastic wartime propagandists. This was true in every combatant nation, and it is a transformation well portrayed by the fascinating selection of art in this book. Soon Red Cross personnel were even sporting military-style uniforms, and in the United States, the Red Cross became so identified with the war effort that an American citizen was convicted of treason for criticizing the Red Cross in time of war!

The Red Cross played an especially important role in encouraging the mass involvement of women in the "home front" for the first time. It did this through magazines, postcards, posters, bandage-rolling parties, and speeches that blended romantic images of humanitarianism and war into a unique brand of maternal militarism. A true pioneer in mass propaganda, the Red Cross taught millions that preparation for war was not just a patriotic duty but a normal and desirable social activity.

The Red Cross societies had proven their usefulness in mobilizing civilians in wartime, and most of their functions were taken over by government agencies by the time of World War II. Gradually the Red Cross became better known for its work in public health, disaster relief, and lifesaving classes. But the legacy of a darker past still lingers: the red cross on a white background found on army ambulances, or the unsubtle subtext of sacrifice and heroism in Red Cross television advertising.

It is a legacy the Red Cross itself has preferred not to acknowledge in its own self-congratulatory literature. For not only was the humanitarian impulse that inspired the creation of the Red Cross easily distorted, but this urge to militarize came from within its own ranks. This startling and provocative history of the Red Cross reminds us of the hidden dangers that sometimes come cloaked in the best of intentions.

John F. Hutchinson is professor of history at Simon Fraser University and is author of *Politics and Public Health in Revolutionary Russia, 1890–1918*.

Index